How to Fix *just about* Everything

How To Fix *just about* Every-thing

Bill Marken

More Than 550 Step-by-Step Instructions for Everything From Fixing a Faucet to Removing Mystery Stains to Curing a Hangover

THE FREE PRESS

New York · London · Toronto · Sydney · Singapore

THE FREE PRESS
A Division of Simon & Schuster, Inc.
1230 Avenue of the Americas
New York, NY 10020

●com|press

Designed and produced by .com press
.com press is a division of Weldon Owen Inc.,
814 Montgomery Street, San Francisco, CA 94133

Printed in the United States by Phoenix Color
10 9 8 7 6 5 4 3 2 1

Library of Congress Cataloging-in-Publication Data

Marken, Bill.
   How to fix (just about) everything : more than 550
   step-by-step instructions for everything from fixing
   a faucet to removing mystery stains to curing a
   hangover / Bill Marken.
      p. cm.
   1. Repairing—Amateurs' manuals.   2. Dwellings—
   Maintenance and repair—Amateurs' manuals.
   I. Title.
TT151 .M37 2002
640'.41—dc21   2002021451

ISBN 0-7432-3468-5

CEO: John Owen
President: Terry Newell
COO: Larry Partington
VP, International Sales: Stuart Laurence
VP, Publisher: Roger Shaw
Creative Director: Gaye Allen
Production Manager: Chris Hemesath
Series Manager: Brynn Breuner
Art Editor: Colin Wheatland
Design Assistant: Amber Reed

Managing Editor: Laurie Wertz
Art Director: Diane Dempsey Murray
Production & Layout: Joan Olson
Illustrators: Ron Carboni, William Laird

Copy Editors: Jacqueline Aaron,
   Gail Nelson-Bonebrake, Elissa Rabellino,
   Cynthia Rubin
Proofreaders: Lisa Bornstein, Arin Hailey
Indexer: Ken DellaPenta

For information regarding special discounts for bulk purchases, please contact Simon & Schuster
Special Sales at 1-800-456-6798 or business@simonandschuster.com

CONTENTS

FOREWORD

A NOTE TO READERS

EVERYDAY ANNOYANCES

OCCASIONAL DISASTERS

CLOTHING

HOME REPAIR

PLUMBING & ELECTRICAL

APPLIANCES

COMPUTERS & HOME ELECTRONICS

FURNITURE & HOUSEWARES

CLEANING

COOKING

SPORTS & RECREATION

INDEX

CONTRIBUTOR CREDITS

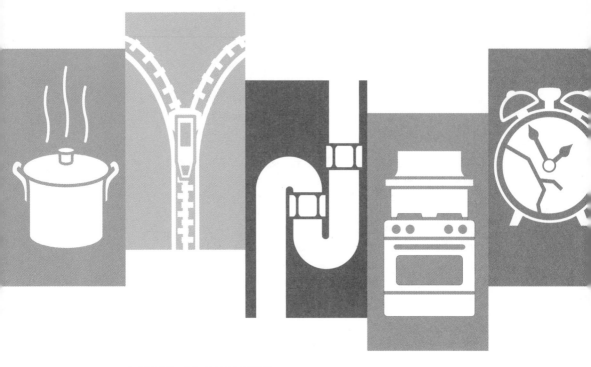

A NOTE TO READERS

When attempting any of the steps in this book, please note the following:

Risky activities: Certain activities described in this book are inherently dangerous or risky. Before attempting any new activity, you should always know your own limitations and consider all applicable risks (whether listed or not).

Professional advice: While we strive to provide complete and accurate information, it is not intended as a substitute for professional advice. You should always consult a professional whenever appropriate, or if you have any questions or concerns regarding medical, legal or financial advice.

Physical or health-related activities: Be sure to consult a physician before attempting any health- or diet-related activity, or any activity involving physical exertion, particularly if you have any condition that could impair or limit your ability to engage in such an activity.

Adult supervision: The activities described in this book are intended for adults only, and they should not be performed by children without responsible adult supervision.

Violations of law: The information provided in this book should not be used to violate any applicable law or regulation.

Foreword

In these pages you'll find out how to fix a drippy faucet, how to deal with chronic printer jams and how to mend Barbie's broken arm. Kind of like life itself, don't you think? You never know what's going to break next around the house—or fall apart, crack, leak, freeze up or otherwise let you down.

Turn to this book when the inevitable annoyances-to-disasters happen around your home or in your daily life. As you'll see, we have ventured well beyond the toilet-to-roof-gutter territory of most fix-it books to also include solutions for less tangible problems in need of repair, such as family feuds, broken hearts and bad credit.

Each of the 551 topics is presented in clear and concise step-by-step fashion to make solving your problems as quick and easy as possible. Make sure you also read the tips and warnings for additional helpful advice. (How else will you know that you can smooth a sticky zipper by rubbing it with candle wax?) Look for the handy icons on every topic to determine the degree of difficulty. And if it turns out that our essential steps don't provide all the details for your specific problem, you'll find suggestions for where to get further help.

I could not have done this book without the help of many others. Shoot, in this case, I couldn't have done one page myself, with the possible exception of Fix Your Basketball Free Throw and Fix a Stopped-Up Toilet, both of which subjects have occupied way too much time over my life. I relied on expert men and women who not only possess the enviable hands-on skills such as sewing and nailing but who can write clearly and accurately to lead all the rest of us by the hand through the necessary steps. In my 30-plus years working on how-to magazines and books, I may not have learned how to fix everything, but I have certainly learned to know whom to trust to write about it. You'll find the names of the talented and skilled contributing writers on the contributors page in the back of the book.

Let's also acknowledge Courtney Rosen, who saw the need for presenting how-to information in clear and concise fashion when she had the vision to launch eHow.com, which provided the content for the best-selling *How to Do (Just About) Everything.* Special thanks to Sharon Beaulaurier, who made a major contribution to this book as a writer and all-around idea generator. And thanks, too, to Laurie Wertz, the book's managing editor, whose editing and organizational skills—and patience—were put to the test by the diversity and details of the wide-ranging subject matter.

May you never have 551 things break down in your everyday life. But if you do, we sincerely hope you will use this book to help fix them.

Bill Marken

Bill Marken

OOKED PICTURE • UNPLUG A STUCK AEROSOL CAN • GIVE BARBIE A MAKEOVER • DEAL WITH A STUCK WINE CORK • REPAIR A BOOK • RE
ORING • FIX BAD HABITS • REPAIR A BROKEN EYEGLASS FRAME • REPOSITION A SLIPPED CONTACT LENS • FIX A RUN IN STOCKINGS • JOC
EAKOUT • REPAIR A TORN FINGERNAIL • FIX CHIPPED NAIL POLISH • FIX A STUCK ZIPPER • FIND A LOST CONTACT LENS • ELIMINATE BAD I
Y THAT STICKS • STOP TELEMARKETERS AND JUNK MAIL • GET SUPERGLUE OFF YOUR SKIN • EXTRACT A SPLINTER • SOOTHE A SUNBURN
HANGOVER • STOP HICCUPS • MEND A BROKEN HEART • MEND A FAMILY FEUD • TREAT A SMALL CUT OR SCRAPE • FIX HAIR DISASTERS • T
TTER SEATS • FIX A BILLING MISTAKE • FIX A BAD GRADE • FIX BAD CREDIT • RECOVER FROM JET LAG • RESUSCITATE AN UNCONSCIOUS F
F PRONOUNS • FIX A RUN-ON SENTENCE • FIX MISUSE OF THE WORD GOOD • FIX YOUR DOG OR CAT • CORRECT BAD BEHAVIOR IN DOGS •
SSING BUTTON • REMOVE LINT FROM CLOTHING • FIX A DRAWSTRING ON SWEATPANTS • REPAIR A HEM • REPAIR LEATHER GOODS • MEND
UNDER YOUR CASHMERE • FIX A SWEATER THAT HAS SHRUNK • FIX A SWEATER THAT HAS STRETCHED • FIX A HOLE IN A POCKET • FIX A H
LLING FROM CLOTHING • FIX A FRAYED BUTTONHOLE • REMOVE DARK SCUFFS FROM SHOES • TREAT STAINS ON LEATHER • PROTECT SUEI
JIET SQUEAKY HINGES • TROUBLESHOOT LOCK PROBLEMS • TIGHTEN A LOOSE DOORKNOB • TIGHTEN A LOOSE DOOR HINGE • FIX A BIND
PLACE CRACKED TILE • TROUBLESHOOT MOLD ON INTERIOR WALLS • REPLACE CRACKED TILE GROUT IN A TUB OR SHOWER • FIX A DRAF
INDS • TROUBLESHOOT WINDOW SHADE PROBLEMS • FIX BROKEN GLASS IN A WINDOW • REPAIR A WINDOW SCREEN • REPAIR ALUMINUM
AMAGED PLASTER • REPAIR WALL COVERINGS • TOUCH UP PAINTED WALLS • TROUBLESHOOT INTERIOR-PAINT PROBLEMS • SOLVE A LEAD-
ARDWOOD FLOOR • RESTORE A DULL, WORN WOOD FLOOR • TOUCH UP WOOD-FLOOR FINISHES • REPAIR DAMAGED SHEET-VINYL FLOORII
OUSE • CHILDPROOF YOUR HOME • PREVENT ICE DAMS • CURE A FAULTY FIREPLACE DRAW • START A FIRE IN A COLD CHIMNEY • FIX A WO
AL A GARAGE FLOOR • REFINISH A GARAGE OR BASEMENT FLOOR • CONTROL ROOF LEAKS • REDIRECT RAINWATER FROM A DOWNSPOU
AMAGED ASPHALT SHINGLE • PATCH A FLAT OR LOW-PITCHED ROOF • REPAIR ROOF FLASHING • TROUBLESHOOT EXTERIOR-PAINT PROBLE
W WATER PRESSURE • FIX LEAKING PIPES • STOP A TOILET FROM RUNNING • FIX A LEAKY TOILET TANK • FIX A STOPPED-UP TOILET • STOP
OGGED SINK OR TUB • REPAIR A TUB-AND-SHOWER VALVE • REPAIR CHIPPED FIXTURES • QUIET NOISY PIPES • DEFROST YOUR PIPES • DIA
ONSUMPTION • REPLACE A RECEPTACLE • FIX AN ELECTRICAL PLUG • REPLACE A LIGHT FIXTURE • INSTALL A NEW DIMMER • FIX A LAMP •
OORBELL • FIX A WOBBLY OVERHEAD FAN • ADJUST WATER-HEATER TEMPERATURE • RELIGHT A WATER-HEATER PILOT LIGHT • TROUBLESH
E MAKER • GET RID OF MICROWAVE SMELLS • FIX A REFRIGERATOR THAT COOLS POORLY • FIX A GAS OVEN THAT HEATS POORLY • CLEAN
SHWASHER PROBLEMS • CORRECT AN OVERFLOWING DISHWASHER • FIX A LEAKY DISHWASHER • FIX A DISHWASHER THAT FILLS SLOWLY
WASHING MACHINE THAT FILLS SLOWLY • FIX A WASHING MACHINE THAT "WALKS" ACROSS THE FLOOR • FIX A CLOTHES DRYER THAT DRIE
K YOUR VACUUM CLEANER • REPLACE VACUUM CLEANER BRUSHES • TROUBLESHOOT A PORTABLE AIR CONDITIONER • FIX A WINDOW AIR
OCESSOR • FIX A TOASTER • DIAGNOSE MICROWAVE OVEN PROBLEMS • TROUBLESHOOT A GAS GRILL • FIX A TRASH COMPACTOR • REPA
ART • TROUBLESHOOT A CRASHING COMPUTER • CLEAN UP LAPTOP SPILLS • FIX BAD SECTORS ON A HARD DISK • QUIT A FROZEN PC AP
FECTED COMPUTER • IMPROVE YOUR COMPUTER'S MEMORY • GET RID OF E-MAIL SPAM • CHANGE A LASER PRINTER CARTRIDGE • FIX A P
GURE OUT WHY A PRINTER WON'T PRINT • FIX SPELLING AND GRAMMAR ERRORS • RECALL AN E-MAIL IN MICROSOFT OUTLOOK • DIAGNO
LES • TROUBLESHOOT A PALM OS PDA • RESET A PALM OS PDA • REMOVE FINGERPRINTS FROM A CAMERA LENS • TROUBLESHOOT A CD-I
LVAGE A VIDEOCASSETTE • TROUBLESHOOT A DVD PLAYER • STRENGTHEN FM RADIO RECEPTION • STRENGTHEN AM RADIO RECEPTION •
JAMMED SLIDE PROJECTOR • GET BETTER SPEAKER SOUND • TROUBLESHOOT A DIGITAL CAMCORDER • TROUBLESHOOT A DIGITAL CAME
GHTBULB • FIX A BROKEN WINEGLASS STEM • FIX BLEMISHED WOOD FURNITURE • REPAIR GOUGES IN FURNITURE • RESTORE FURNITURE
AMOUFLAGE A DOG-SCRATCHED DOOR • REPAIR A SPLIT CARPET SEAM • RID CARPETS OF PET ODORS • REINFORCE A SAGGING SHELF • I
DINTS OF CHAIRS AND TABLES • REUPHOLSTER A DROP-IN CHAIR SEAT • REVIVE A CANE SEAT • REINFORCE A WEAK BED FRAME • FIX UP A
OTTERY • REPAIR CHIPPED OR CRACKED CHINA • UNCLUTTER YOUR HOME • CLEAN CRAYON FROM A WALL • GET WAX OFF A TABLECLOTH
AINS • REMOVE CHEWING GUM FROM CARPETING • REMOVE BLEACH SPOTS FROM CARPETING • REMOVE PET STAINS • ELIMINATE WINE S
AINS FROM TILE GROUT • REMOVE MILDEW FROM WALLS AND CEILINGS • DISINFECT A TOILET BOWL • REMOVE FIREPLACE GRIME • GET F
LEAN OIL SPOTS FROM A GARAGE OR DRIVEWAY • REMOVE STAINS FROM BRICK • WASH AN OUTDOOR GRILL • FIX A FALLEN SOUFFLÉ • RE
SCUE OVERPROOFED YEAST DOUGH • FIX YOUR KID LUNCH • GET RID OF TAP-WATER MINERAL DEPOSITS • CALIBRATE A MEAT THERMOM
AUCE • RESCUE A BROKEN SAUCE • REMOVE FAT FROM SOUPS AND SAUCES • FIX LUMPY GRAVY • SUBSTITUTE MISSING INGREDIENTS • R
JRNED RICE • REMOVE COOKING ODORS • FINISH UNDERCOOKED MEAT • SALVAGE AN UNDERCOOKED TURKEY • FIX AN OVERSEASONED
ALE BREAD • SMOOTH SEIZED CHOCOLATE • SOFTEN HARDENED SUGARS OR COOKIES • FIX BREAKFAST FOR YOUR SWEETHEART • MEND
GGING TOOLS • RESTORE A BROKEN FLOWERPOT • SHARPEN PRUNING CLIPPERS • REMOVE RUST FROM TOOLS • REVIVE WILTING CUT FL
ET RID OF RAMPANT BRAMBLES • TROUBLESHOOT BROWN SPOTS ON A LAWN • CONTROL MAJOR GARDEN PESTS • RID YOUR GARDEN OF
ONPERFORMING COMPOST PILE • FIX BAD SOIL • SHORE UP A RAISED GARDEN BED • REMOVE A DEAD OR DISEASED TREE LIMB • TROUBL
RAINAGE • TROUBLESHOOT ROSE DISEASES • IDENTIFY AND CORRECT SOIL DEFICIENCIES IN ROSES • TROUBLESHOOT ROSE PESTS • OVE
AMAGED DECK BOARDS • REPAIR DECK RAILINGS • STRENGTHEN DECK JOISTS • FIX A RUSTY IRON RAILING • REPAIR A GATE • REPAIR A F
RACKED OR DAMAGED CONCRETE • IMPROVE THE LOOK OF REPAIRED CONCRETE • REPAIR AN ASPHALT DRIVEWAY • REVIVE WOODEN OU
ARDEN PONDS • CLEAN SWIMMING POOL WATER • TROUBLESHOOT HOT TUBS AND SPAS • REPLACE BRICKS IN WALKWAYS AND PATIOS • S
AR WITH JUMPER CABLES • SHUT OFF A CAR ALARM THAT WON'T QUIT • FREE A CAR STUCK ON ICE OR SNOW • DE-ICE YOUR WINDSHIELE
JRN-SIGNAL COVER • FIX A CAR FUSE • FIX DASHBOARD LIGHTS THAT WON'T LIGHT • REMOVE CAR SMELLS • CHECK TIRE PRESSURE • INF
PROPERLY INSTALLED CHILD CAR SEAT • TROUBLESHOOT LEAKING OIL • CHECK AND ADD POWER-STEERING FLUID • CHECK AND ADD CC
ROKEN EXHAUST PIPE • CHECK AND ADD ENGINE OIL • CHECK AND ADD BRAKE FLUID • CHECK AND ADD FLUID TO YOUR AUTOMATIC TRA

OUR GUITAR • GET RID OF RED-EYE IN PHOTOGRAPHS • REDUCE PUFFINESS AROUND YOUR EYES • REMOVE A SPECK FROM YOUR EYE • S
EMORY • FIX AN ELECTRIC CAN OPENER THAT DROPS THE CAN • TROUBLESHOOT A CELL PHONE • KEEP MIRRORS FROM FOGGING • ZAP A
KEEP A SHAVING NICK FROM BLEEDING • GET RID OF SPLIT ENDS • UNTANGLE HAIR SNARLS • FIX FRIZZY HAIR • FIX BLEEDING LIPSTICK •
ICKY SOCIAL SITUATION • FIX A BAD REPUTATION • CLEAN LIPSTICK FROM A COLLAR • FIX A BAD RELATIONSHIP • SALVAGE A BAD DATE •
LEEDING NOSE • BEAT THE MONDAY MORNING BLUES • GET OUT OF A FIX • EXTRACT A BROKEN KEY • RETRIEVE KEYS LOCKED INSIDE A C
STOP SOMEONE FROM CHOKING • STOP AN ANT INVASION • STABILIZE A CHRISTMAS TREE • RESCUE AN ITEM FROM THE DRAIN • FIX IMPE
SKUNK ODOR FROM YOUR DOG • GET A CAT OUT OF A TREE • CORRECT BAD BEHAVIOR IN CATS • TREAT A CAT FOR MATTED FUR • REPLA
EAM • TREAT MILDEW DAMAGE • GET STATIC OUT OF YOUR LAUNDRY • DEAL WITH A CLOTHES-MOTH INFESTATION • FIX A SEPARATED ZIP
UR SOCK • TREAT MIXED-WASH ACCIDENTS • TAKE WRINKLES OUT OF CLOTHING • FIX A HOLE IN JEANS • REPAIR A SNAG IN A SWEATER •
TAINS • WASH SNEAKERS • PICK UP A DROPPED STITCH IN KNITTING • RESTRING BEADS • FRESHEN SMELLY SHOES • FIX A SAGGING CLO
R • FIX A RUBBING DOOR • FIX A DRAFTY DOOR • TUNE UP SLIDING DOORS • FIX A SHOWER DOOR • SEAL WALL JOINTS AROUND A TUB O
W • REPAIR A FAULTY WINDOW CRANK • REPAIR VERTICAL BLINDS • REPAIR VENETIAN BLINDS OR MINIBLINDS • REPAIR WOOD OR PLASTIC
REEN WINDOWS • INSTALL NEW SASH CORDS IN WINDOWS • FIX A TIGHT OR LOOSE WINDOW SASH • REPAIR MINOR DRYWALL DAMAGE •
OBLEM • REPLACE A DAMAGED CEILING TILE • REPLACE A WOOD FLOORBOARD • QUIET SQUEAKING FLOORS • REPAIR A WATER-DAMAGE
R A VINYL-TILE FLOOR • SILENCE SQUEAKY   STER • REPLACE CAULKING ON THE OUTSIDE OF
NG STOVE • REPAIR AND PREVENT WOOD RO   TCH A GUTTER LEAK • TROUBLESHOOT A WET BAS
AGGING GUTTER • UNCLOG GUTTERS AND D   • REPAIR A CRACKED OR SPLIT WOOD SHINGLE •
ARAGE-DOOR TENSION • TROUBLESHOOT A   TES • LOOSEN A RUSTY NUT OR BOLT • TROUBLE
NK SWEATING • FIX FLUSHING PROBLEMS •   FAUCET • FIX A STOPPER THAT DOESN'T SEAL • C
UMP PUMP PROBLEMS • TROUBLESHOOT ELE   USE • SWAP A FAULTY LIGHT SWITCH • REDUCE E
HOOT FLUORESCENT LIGHTING • FIX A LOW   E THERMOSTAT • TROUBLESHOOT HOLIDAY LIGHT
TING SYSTEM • REFRESH A SMELLY REFRIGE   MS • FIX A LEAKING REFRIGERATOR • REPAIR A C

CTIONING GAS BURNER • REPAIR A RANGE H   FIX AN ELECTRIC OVEN THAT HEATS POORLY • DIA
P YOUR APPLIANCES • CONTROL GARBAGE   E DISPOSAL • DIAGNOSE WASHING MACHINE PRO
• FIX A HAIR DRYER • TROUBLESHOOT A CLO   AT SPUTTERS • FIX AN IRON THAT LEAVES SPOTS C
NER • FIX A DEHUMIDIFIER • REPAIR A CONS   DER • HANDLE A MIXER THAT OVERHEATS • REPAIR
G MACHINE • TROUBLESHOOT SMOKE ALAR   OARD SPILLS • TROUBLESHOOT A COMPUTER THA
• REMOVE A WINDOWS PROGRAM • SPEED U   OUSE • REPLACE YOUR PC'S BATTERY • CLEAN A
AT FAILS ITS SELF-TEST • CORRECT MONITOR   PAPER JAM • TROUBLESHOOT A RECURRING PRIN
ONE MODEM PROBLEMS • TROUBLESHOOT A   REEN GLARE • GET TOP-NOTCH SCANS • RECOVE
ESTORE A CD • REPAIR A WARPED CD • CLE   • EXTRACT A JAMMED VIDEOTAPE • ADJUST VCR
OTE CONTROL • FIX AUDIOCASSETTES • FIX   OT A CASSETTE DECK • REPLACE BROKEN RABBI
BLESHOOT A CD PLAYER • REPLACE A HEAD   RASS • SHINE SILVER SAFELY • REMOVE A BROKEI
PLACE A BROKEN TOWEL ROD • REMOVE ST   E FOR NATURAL DISASTERS • FIX A FRAYED CARPE

Everyday Annoyances

BORING BATHROOM • REPLACE A SHOWER   NACE FILTER • REPAIR A BROKEN SLIDING DRAWE
DD CHAIR • FIX A WOBBLY WOOD CHAIR • SH   OR CRACKED PORCELAIN • REPAIR CHIPPED OR CI
WAX FROM CARPETING • GET RID OF CEILIN   MOVE MYSTERY STAINS FROM CLOTHING • REMOV
A RUG OR TABLECLOTH • REMOVE BURN M   NITURE • STRIP WAX BUILDUP FROM FLOORS • RE
DORANT STAINS • ELIMINATE CIGARETTE ODOR • RESTORE SHINE TO YOUR JEWELRY • WASH DIRTY WINDOWS • REMOVE GRIME FROM MI
UMBLED CAKE • FIX A PERFECT CUP OF TEA • PATCH A TORN PIE CRUST • KEEP A PIE CRUST FROM GETTING SOGGY • FIX DOUGH THAT V
A DULL KNIFE • REMOVE RUST FROM A CAST-IRON PAN • REPAIR LAMINATE COUNTERTOPS • REMOVE STAINS FROM A STONE COUNTERTO
R CHOLESTEROL • TREAT BURNED POTS AND PANS • RESCUE A BURNED CAKE OR PIE • PUT OUT A KITCHEN FIRE • REMOVE THE BITTERN
AN UNDERSEASONED DISH • REMOVE OVEN SPILLS • CLEAN UP OIL SPILLS • FIX A DRINK FOR ANY OCCASION • DISENTANGLE PASTA • RE
N CUTTING BOARD • KEEP A MIXING BOWL STEADY • FIX GARDEN TOOL HANDLES • REPAIR A LEAKY HOSE NOZZLE • MEND A LEAKY HOSI
HARPEN A POWER MOWER BLADE • SHARPEN PUSH MOWER BLADES • REPAIR BALD SPOTS ON GRASS • RID YOUR GRASS OF DOG URINE
OUBLESHOOT HERBS • TROUBLESHOOT HOUSEPLANTS • OVERCOME SHADE PROBLEMS • RID SOIL OF PESTS AND DISEASES • REVIVE A
EES AND SHRUBS • REPAIR A LEAKING IRRIGATION SYSTEM • UNCLOG A SPRINKLER SYSTEM • CLEAN A CLOGGED DRIP SYSTEM • FIX PO
NGUS DISEASES IN ROSES • REPAIR DECK STEPS • RENOVATE A WEATHERED DECK • TIGHTEN LOOSE DECKING • REMOVE DECK STAINS •
E • LEVEL AND SMOOTH A GRAVEL PATH • FIX A POTHOLE IN A DIRT OR GRAVEL DRIVEWAY • REPLACE PATIO STONES, TILES AND PAVERS
NITURE • RESTORE WEATHERED METAL FURNITURE • REPAIR CHAIR STRAPS AND WEBBING • REVIVE RUSTED IRON FURNITURE • TROUBLE
LLED CAR • SHUT OFF A JAMMED HORN • CHANGE YOUR CAR'S BATTERY • TROUBLESHOOT A CAR THAT WON'T START • FIX A FLAT TIRE •
RNED-OUT SIGNAL BULB • FIX A BURNED-OUT HEADLIGHT • ADJUST HEADLIGHTS • FIX A STUCK BRAKE LIGHT • REPLACE A BROKEN TAIL
TIRES • FIX A STUCK CONVERTIBLE TOP • DIAGNOSE A LEAK INSIDE YOUR CAR • REPLACE YOUR AIR FILTER • HANDLE A FAULTY REPAIR •
OOL AN OVERHEATED ENGINE • REPLACE A LEAKING RADIATOR HOSE • CHANGE YOUR WIPER BLADES • ADD WINDSHIELD-WASHER FLUIE
• TROUBLESHOOT YOUR BRAKES • ADD BRAKE FLUID TO THE CLUTCH MASTER CYLINDER • TROUBLESHOOT DASHBOARD WARNING LIGI

1 Remove a Ring That's Stuck on a Finger

Maybe that ring's been on your finger for a mighty long time. Or perhaps the hot weather has caused your fingers to swell. Here's how to ease a ring off.

Steps

1 Soak your hand in ice-cold water if it is swollen. Wait 5 to 10 minutes for the swelling to recede.

2 Apply lubricant around the ring and up the length of your finger. Hand lotion, dishwashing liquid or olive oil will do the trick.

3 Twist the ring as you slowly work it up and over the knuckle. You may need to apply some force to get it over the first knuckle. Make sure to twist, not tug.

4 If the ring still won't budge, visit a doctor to have it removed.

What You'll Need

- Hand lotion, dishwashing liquid or olive oil

Warning

If you're experiencing swelling from an injury, it is important to remove any rings before the swelling worsens, because the rings might cut off the finger's blood supply.

2 Fix a Drawer That Sticks

If you are tired of wrestling with your bureau every time you need a pair of socks, it's time to fix that sticking drawer.

Steps

1 Examine the bureau. Is it off center or crooked? Reposition the bureau if necessary. Drawers may stick in an off-center bureau.

2 Swap the sticking drawer with another same-size drawer in the bureau. Often this will solve the problem.

3 If this doesn't help, look in the bureau opening where the drawer slides in. Is there an obstruction, like a nail or a lost sock? If a nail is poking out, hammer it into the wood. If a sock is causing the problem, remove it.

4 If you don't find any obstructions, lightly sand the runners of a wood drawer, then rub them with paraffin, beeswax or bar soap. If the drawer is metal, wipe the runners with a dry rag and apply a small amount of lubricating oil.

5 If the bottom of the drawer sags, causing it to drag, slip out the bottom of the drawer (if possible). Then flip it over and reinsert it into the drawer.

6 If one of the corners or sides is loose, glue it into place with wood glue. Hold the sides together with a corner clamp while the glue dries.

7 Consider the following option as a last resort, since it alters the drawer permanently. Sand down a side of the drawer so it fits smoothly into the bureau.

What You'll Need

- Hammer
- Sandpaper
- Paraffin, beeswax or bar soap
- Rag
- Lubricating oil
- Wood glue
- Corner clamp

Tips

Excess moisture due to rain or humidity makes wood swell and often causes the drawers to stick. Application of wax, such as beeswax or paraffin, seals the wood and helps prevent moisture-induced swelling.

See also 319 Repair a Broken Sliding Drawer.

3 Fix a Wobbly Table

A wobbly table is one of life's little annoyances. It's an easy fix that requires only the simplest of tools. See 325 Fix a Wobbly Wood Chair for more ideas.

Steps

1 Place the table on a hard, level surface so you can examine the source of the wobble.

2 Look at the leg that is causing the wobble. Some table legs have a glide, a round metal or plastic knob on their foot to protect floors against scratches. If the glide is missing, buy a replacement at a hardware store. This will fix the wobble.

3 If a loose joint is causing the problem, tighten any screws in the joint and secure it with wood glue. Hold the joint in place with a corner clamp while the glue dries. Or, if you don't have a clamp, wrap a length of rope tightly around the joint and another leg of the table.

4 If one leg is slightly shorter than the others, lengthen it. Use a tape measure to determine the length of the short leg and of one of the other legs. The difference between these two measurements is the figure you need to repair the wobble (see steps 5 through 10).

5 Use a sharp butcher knife to slice a wine cork so that the height of the cork is the same as the difference between the legs. If the difference is very slight, a thin piece of cardboard will do the trick (see Tips).

6 Remove any dirt or buildup from the shorter table leg with a rag or stiff brush.

7 Place the cork underneath the short leg to make sure it removes the wobble. Adjust the cork's length if necessary.

8 Use wood glue to adhere the cork onto the leg. Wipe away any residual glue with a damp rag.

9 Allow the glue to dry completely before moving the table.

10 If an extension leaf of the table is wobbly, insert a small wedge of wood between the tabletop and the extension support (the arm that holds up the leaf).

What You'll Need

- Glide
- Screwdriver
- Wood glue
- Corner clamp or rope
- Tape measure
- Sharp butcher knife
- Wine cork
- Cardboard
- Rag or stiff brush
- Small wedge of wood

Tips

For a very slight wobble, glue a thin piece of cardboard underneath the short leg instead of a cork.

If you are seated at a wobbly table in a restaurant, wedge a book of matches under the short leg to reduce the wobble temporarily.

4 Repair a Torn Photo

If a photograph is extremely old, rare or of archival quality, it's best not to repair tears; consult a photography professional. However, if the value of the photograph is primarily sentimental, follow these steps.

Steps

1 Gather the pieces of the torn photograph on a flat, dust-free surface. Make sure your hands are clean and dry.

2 Fit together the torn pieces on a piece of cardboard.

3 Place another piece of cardboard on top of the photograph and gently flip over both pieces of cardboard with the photograph in the middle.

4 Remove the top piece of cardboard.

5 Apply acid-free archival tape to the back of the photograph. Acid-free tape, available at photography and framing shops, will not cause any yellowing or staining over the years.

6 Use acid-free tape on the front of a photo only if the tape is designed for this purpose. If you do so, smooth out the tape carefully to avoid creating any air bubbles.

What You'll Need

- Cardboard
- Acid-free tape

Tips

You can scan a damaged photograph onto a computer and use image-editing software to remove flaws, tears or signs of aging.

If you want to display a delicate or an old photograph, it's best to use a copy.

5 Untangle a Phone Cord

Phone cords that are routinely stretched, twisted or twiddled tend to tangle over time. It's easy to undo the wildest of tangles using the following approach.

Steps

1 Unplug the cord from the handset and let the cord drop. Sometimes the cord will simply unravel into its proper shape.

2 If the cord is still tangled, start at the end that's plugged into the phone and work out the tangles with your fingers. Avoid any unnecessary stretching or twisting.

3 After you work out all the tangles, start again at the phone end and run your fingers along the cord's length, resetting coils that are twisted in the wrong direction to prevent future tangles.

4 Allow the cord to fall into its natural coils and plug the cord back into the handset.

Tips

Avoid twisting the cord in the wrong direction when you pick up and hang up the handset. These minitwists uncoil the cord and cause tangles.

Buy a swivel jack for the handset to prevent tangles.

6 Open a Stuck Jar Lid

Since timing is everything in the kitchen, you'll want to open a jar quickly and get back to your sauté or soufflé. Try these tricks.

Steps

1 If the jar is new, use a triangular-tipped bottle opener to apply pressure and break the vacuum seal. Do this by placing the triangular tip underneath the lid and pulling the lid away from the jar until you pop the seal.

2 If this doesn't work and you suspect that food is stuck in the lid, tap the lid with a wooden spoon to knock away the food.

3 Wrap the lid in a dish towel to give your hands traction as you twist. Or put rubber bands around the lid to get a good grip. The rubber bands that hold together bunches of vegetables are ideal.

4 If the lid still won't budge, run the lid (not the jar) under hot water for a minute. This will cause the metal lid to expand so it comes off easily.

What You'll Need

- Bottle opener
- Wooden spoon
- Dish towel
- Rubber bands

Tip

If you don't have a bottle opener with a triangular tip, break the vacuum seal by tapping the lid against a countertop.

7 Peel Off a Bumper Sticker

Sometimes a bumper sticker's adhesiveness far outlasts the power of its message. Here's how to banish that outdated statement from your vehicle's bumper or window.

Steps

1 If the sticker is located on a window, scrape it off the glass with a razor blade.

2 If the sticker is on a bumper, first try to peel it off. On rubber bumpers, some stickers might peel away easily.

3 If that doesn't work, fill a basin with boiling-hot water. Wear rubber gloves to protect your hands.

4 Dip a rag or sponge in the hot water and then press it against the bumper sticker.

5 Hold the rag or sponge over the sticker for 10 minutes. If possible, hold it in place with a string or wire.

6 Remove the rag. Use a plastic spatula or plastic putty knife to peel away the sticker. Work slowly to avoid scratching or chipping the paint.

7 If bits of sticker remain, soak them with hot water for another 5 to 10 minutes, then scrape them away. Repeat until you've removed all remnants.

8 After removing the sticker, wash the bumper with hot, soapy water and buff it with a dry, lint-free cloth.

What You'll Need

- Razor blade
- Basin
- Rubber gloves
- Rag or sponge
- String or wire
- Plastic spatula or plastic putty knife
- Soap
- Lint-free cloth

Tip

Paint thinner can help remove stickers on chrome bumpers. Do not use paint thinner on plastic, rubber or painted surfaces.

8 Remedy Sleep Problems

Restful sleep is as important as a healthy diet and exercise, and yet many people toss and turn the night away. Use this chart to find out about some common sleep disorders. If you want to find a doctor who specializes in sleep disorders, visit the Web site for the American Academy of Sleep Medicine at www.asda.org.

PROBLEM	SYMPTOMS	POSSIBLE CAUSES	SOLUTIONS
Bruxism	Clenching or grinding jaws while asleep; painful or stiff jaw, headaches and aching teeth in morning	Stress; prominent or strong jaw; improper pillow support	Physical therapy; mouthpiece to protect teeth; surgery to repair the jaw joint (TMJ) in severe cases
Fibromyalgia	Pain in muscles, ligaments and tendons; chronic fatigue; fitful sleep and insomnia	Unknown	Exercise and relaxation techniques; prescription medication (sometimes helpful)
Gastroesophageal reflux	Heartburn (worse when lying down); coughing or choking disrupts sleep	Stomach acid rises into the esophagus and disturbs sleep. Difficult to diagnose.	Avoid large meal and/or spicy foods before bedtime. Raise head of bed. Heartburn medication.
Insomnia	Inability to fall asleep or stay asleep; daytime drowsiness	Stress; schedule change; swing shift; altitude; traumatic event; psychiatric disorder; medication; caffeine; alcohol	Remove cause if possible. Healthy sleep habits; regular exercise; treatment by sleep specialist; prescription sleeping pills (short-term only)
Narcolepsy	Sudden onset of deep sleep; paralyzing hallucinations; constant drowsiness	Unknown, possibly neurological. Relatively rare.	Prescription stimulants to counter drowsiness
Night leg cramps	Painful tightening of leg muscles awakens sleeper	Muscle tightness or tension; potassium shortage	Massage area or apply heating pad. Flex foot until cramping stops. Eat bananas or other potassium-rich food.
Night sweats	Extreme sweating during sleep	Fever; hereditary	Keep sleeping area cool. Wear light pajamas.

PROBLEM	SYMPTOMS	POSSIBLE CAUSES	SOLUTIONS
Night terrors	Common in young children; child screams in terror while asleep	Fever; medication; hereditary	More distressing for parent to watch; child is asleep and will not remember it. Usually outgrown by age 7.
Nightmares	Terrifying dreams, often accompanied by intense fear or feeling of being overwhelmed	Fever; stress; traumatic event; depression; medication	Avoid violent TV, movies or news prior to sleep. Peaceful sleep environment; psychotherapy; anti-anxiety medication
Periodic limb-movement disorder	Twitching of limbs; fitful sleep; daytime drowsiness; insomnia	Unknown	Prescription muscle relaxants and sleeping pills in severe cases
REM sleep behavior disorder	Kicking, hitting or other violent acts while asleep	Muscles are not paralyzed during sleep, so sleeper acts out dream. Typically affects males. Worsens with age. Relatively rare.	Remove sharp objects and hazards from bedroom. Prescription sedatives or other drug therapy in severe cases
Restless leg syndrome	Strong urge to twitch or move legs; insomnia; daytime drowsiness	Unknown. Increases with age and use of diuretics.	Hot bath or leg massage; exercise; treatment of underlying disorder or cessation of diuretic; diuretic; prescription meds in severe cases
Sleep apnea	Loud snoring with difficult breathing; morning headache; daytime drowsiness; high blood pressure and heart irregularities	Obstructed airways. Becomes more extreme with age and/or weight gain.	C-PAP (Continuous Positive Airway Pressure) sleep mask; surgery; radio-frequency treatment; weight loss
Somnambulism	Sleeper walks and carries out simple tasks	Sleep deprivation; hereditary; medication; excessive caffeine	Healthy sleep habits; prescription medication in severe cases

9 Unstick a Stamp From an Envelope

Did you just stick a $2 stamp on the wrong envelope? Or is that a rare Tahitian stamp you want to remove? This process works for both self-adhesive stamps and the lick-and-stick variety.

Steps

1 Remove the envelope's contents. Place them in a new envelope.

2 If the envelope is of a neutral color, fill a sink or basin with an inch (2.5 cm) of warm water and submerge the envelope.

3 Soak the envelope for 10 to 15 minutes. If the envelope is brightly colored, do not soak it—the color might run and ruin the stamp. Instead, hold it over a steaming kettle.

4 Pull the paper away from the stamp with your fingers. Remember, you want to preserve the stamp, not the paper.

5 Blot the stamp with paper towels.

6 Allow the stamp to air-dry for an hour, then use glue to affix it to the new envelope.

7 Or, if you plan to add it to your stamp collection, place the stamp between two pieces of cardboard and press it under a heavy book. If the stamp's back is still sticky, place the sticky side on a sheet of plastic. Allow the stamp to dry overnight.

What You'll Need

- New envelope
- Basin
- Paper towels
- Glue
- Cardboard
- Heavy book
- Sheet of plastic

Tips

If stamps become stuck to each other, briefly steam them, then carefully separate. You can also preserve the envelope by steaming instead of soaking.

Some antique stamps are more valuable with the original envelope and postmark intact. Consult a philatelic expert if in doubt.

10 Straighten a Crooked Picture

The easiest way to confirm that a picture is hung straight is to place a carpenter's level on top of the frame. Here's how to achieve perfection without the aid of a level.

Steps

1 Use a tape measure to measure the distance between both bottom corners of the picture frame and the floor.

2 Adjust the frame until the corners are equidistant from the floor. For example, if one corner measures 37 inches (94 cm) above the floor and the other corner is 37¼ inches (94.6 cm) above the floor, adjust the frame until both corners are 37⅛ inches (94.3 cm) from the floor.

3 Use a pencil to lightly mark where the frame corners should be. Make sure the marks are not visible at eye level.

4 Use these pencil lines for guidance in the future when you need to restraighten the frame.

What You'll Need

- Tape measure
- Pencil

Tip

If the picture is chronically crooked, the hook in the wall or the picture hanger might be off center. Measure and adjust it accordingly.

11 Unplug a Stuck Aerosol Can

Aerosol cans containing spray paint, insecticides, hairspray or cooking oil occasionally get plugged up or stuck in the off position. Often you can fix the problem with a little quick maintenance work.

Steps

1 Check to see if there are cleaning instructions on the can. If so, follow those instructions.

2 If the material inside the can is toxic, don protective goggles, a breathing mask and gloves. Work outside to ensure proper ventilation. Always keep the tip pointed away from your body.

3 Run warm water over the aerosol tip for a minute to loosen any materials that are stuck to it. Do not immerse the can in water, because it might explode. (If the can contains oil-based paint, wipe the tip with mineral spirits, not water.)

4 Use a rag to wipe away built-up grime. Dry off the can's tip before you test it.

5 If it still does not work, carefully pull off the tip.

6 Soak the tip in water (or mineral spirits for oil-based paint) and scrub away grime with a stiff brush.

7 Dry off the tip before you replace it.

8 If it still doesn't work, look for a customer-service number on the can and call it. Some manufacturers will send you a coupon for replacing your can.

9 To prevent future clogs in cans of spray paint, turn the can upside down after you use it and spray for 5 seconds until clear air comes out. This cleans out the aerosol tip and tube.

What You'll Need

- Goggles
- Breathing mask
- Gloves
- Rags
- Mineral spirits
- Stiff brush

Warning

Use extreme caution with aerosol cans because the contents are under pressure. Keep the can away from heat or flame, and do not puncture or immerse it.

12 Give Barbie a Makeover

Avoid restoring a Barbie if you think it might be a collectible; they're most valuable in their original condition. Barbie models vary from year to year, so some of these instructions might not apply to your doll.

Steps

Hair

1 Wash the hair with gentle shampoo and rinse it thoroughly in warm water.

2 Apply a mild conditioner. If the hair is stuck together, leave the conditioner in for 10 minutes.

3 With the conditioner still in the hair, comb out snarls with a small comb. (It's best to use the comb that came with the Barbie doll.) Start at the bottom of the hair and work your way toward the scalp.

4 Rinse out the conditioner. This may take several rinses.

5 While the hair is still wet, set it in curlers. Use bobby pins for tight curls and small foam curlers for larger curls. Use a tiny orthodontic rubber band for a ponytail holder.

6 Dip the hair in hot water to set the curls.

7 Let the curls dry overnight. Remove the curlers and style the hair.

Face and body

1 If your doll is especially grimy, soak the Barbie in mild dishwashing liquid and warm water for 15 minutes.

2 Wipe away dirt with a soft, damp cloth. Use a cotton swab to clean crevices.

3 Tackle any ink or grease stains with a cotton swab soaked in rubbing alcohol.

4 For really tough ink stains, apply acne cream with a "vanishing formula," such as Oxy 10 or Clearasil. Place the Barbie in the sun for a day and then scrape away the cream. Repeat several times if necessary.

5 Repaint any chipped or missing facial features, such as brows or lips, with a fine brush and acrylic hobby paints.

6 If the head is torn at the neck area, fix it with glue designed for plastic, such as Permatex.

7 If you want to replace a broken limb with a good one taken from another Barbie, plunge the torso and limb in boiling water for 30 seconds. This will soften up the vinyl and make it easier to pry off the old limb and pop in the new one.

What You'll Need

- Shampoo
- Conditioner
- Small comb
- Bobby pins
- Small foam curlers
- Orthodontic rubber bands
- Dishwashing liquid
- Cloth
- Cotton swabs
- Rubbing alcohol
- Acne cream
- Fine brush
- Acrylic paints
- Glue for plastic

Tips

If you have an old or rare Barbie, hire a professional doll doctor to clean her.

"Green ear," caused by corrosion of the metallic posts in a Barbie's earrings, is very difficult to get rid of. It's best to camouflage this with a hat or a curl of hair. Use hydrogen peroxide to arrest green ear; it sometimes spreads even after you've removed the earrings.

To keep a Barbie doll in tip-top shape, store it in a cool, dry place out of direct sun.

Warning

Some products may bleach or stain vinyl. If in doubt, test on a small, less visible area.

Do not blow-dry Barbie's hair. The heat will damage its delicate fibers.

13 Deal With a Stuck Wine Cork

Old or dried-out corks sometimes crumble or slip into the bottle. The bits of cork can pollute the wine and its flavor. But you can salvage that vintage for your dining pleasure.

Steps

1 Slowly pour the wine into a pitcher or wine decanter. If the cork is the first thing to pop out and you don't see any floating debris, your problem is solved.

2 If the cork has crumbled, remove cork debris by placing a fine-mesh strainer over the pitcher or decanter before you pour the wine into it. Taste-test the wine before serving it to make sure it isn't spoiled.

3 If appropriate, serve the wine directly from the pitcher or decanter. If you prefer to use the original bottle, proceed to step 4.

4 Form a narrow noose on one end of a 15-inch (38-cm) piece of medium-gauge wire, then bend the noose so it looks like a soup ladle. Bend a tiny hook on the other end to prevent the wire from slipping into the bottle.

5 Slip the noose end of the wire into the empty bottle.

6 Turn the bottle upside down so the cork falls to the neck of the bottle.

7 Pull the noose up to the neck and make sure it catches the cork.

8 Gently tug the wire out of the bottle. It will drag the cork with it.

9 Pour a tiny bit of wine back into the bottle and swill it around to capture any remaining bits of cork. Pour this wine out.

10 Place a funnel in the bottle and pour the wine back into the bottle. Pour slowly at a horizontal angle to minimize disturbance to the wine.

What You'll Need

- Pitcher or decanter
- Fine-mesh strainer
- Medium-gauge wire
- Funnel

Tip

If you open a lot of old bottles of wine, buy a cork hook designed to remove corks from bottles. Also, a butler's friend—a twin-bladed cork puller—lifts the cork from the sides, easing the removal of disintegrating corks.

14 Repair a Book

The repair of antique, historical or rare books requires special knowledge and should be left in the hands of professionals. There are some basic repairs, however, that you can perform on most books.

Steps

Tears and holes in pages

1 Open the book to the page you are going to repair. Place waxed paper underneath the page to protect the underlying pages.

2 Snip out a patch of rice paper that is at least ⅛ inch (3 mm) larger than the tear or hole. If you are repairing a tear, snip out a patch that is large enough to be folded over the page edge to cover both sides of the tear. Crease the rice paper patch where it will bend over the page edge.

3 Apply acid-free glue sparingly to the rice paper and then use tweezers to smooth the rice paper over the tear or hole. Smooth out any air bubbles under the rice paper with the tweezers or your finger.

4 Place waxed paper over the rice paper to protect the preceding pages. If you are fixing a hole, place a second rice paper patch on the other side of the page. If repairing a tear, simply fold the rice paper patch over the tear.

5 Close the book and place it under heavy books (phone books are good), covered bricks or a book press to weigh it down while the glue dries. Allow the glue to dry overnight, then carefully open the book and remove the waxed paper. Repeat with a second layer of rice paper if necessary. The text will still be legible through the transparent rice paper.

Dirt, stains or markings

1 Brush away any debris with a soft brush before you attempt other repairs. Carefully scrape away caked-on stains, such as wax drippings, with a dull paring knife.

2 Remove pencil markings and dirt smudges with a white plastic eraser. Erase gently, working from the spine outward to the page's edge. If the paper is colored, test on an inconspicuous spot to make sure the eraser doesn't remove the coloring. Use a soft brush or a vacuum to remove eraser dust.

3 If an eraser doesn't remove a marking (such as ink), try to rub it away with very fine, well-worn sandpaper. Be gentle as you use the sandpaper—discontinue immediately if the paper deteriorates or becomes thin. Don't use sandpaper near printed text as it will remove the ink. Brush or vacuum away dust.

4 Cover crayon markings or grease stains with a generous amount of rubber cement. Allow the rubber cement to dry and then rub it off in little balls. It will remove much of the stain with it. Repeat

What You'll Need

- Waxed paper
- Scissors
- Rice paper
- Acid-free glue
- Tweezers
- Heavy books, covered bricks or a book press
- Soft brush
- Dull paring knife
- White plastic eraser
- Vacuum
- Very fine, worn sandpaper
- Rubber cement
- Pencil eraser
- Blotting paper or paper towels
- Hair dryer
- Hydrogen peroxide or denatured alcohol
- Lint-free cloth
- Peroxide bleach or lemon juice
- Knitting needle or skewer
- Ace bandage

Tips

Buy high-quality rice paper and acid-free glue appropriate for paper at an art supply store.

Test your repair techniques on a book that you don't care about before you perform repairs on your cherished books. Never perform a repair that might cause irreversible damage to a book. If in doubt, consult a professional.

Inquire at a used or antique bookstore to find a qualified book restorer.

if necessary and then remove any residual stain with a pencil eraser or fine sandpaper. Don't use rubber cement on printed text as it will strip away the ink.

Dampness and mildew

1 Place blotting paper or paper towels between each page of the book and then place it underneath heavy books, covered bricks or a book press to press out moisture. Replace the blotting paper or paper towels every half hour until the book is completely dry. This may take several days.

2 Or stand the book upright and ajar so that the pages are separated. Hold a hair dryer at least 6 inches (15 cm) away from the pages and blow-dry the book. Reduce warping by pressing the book under heavy books, covered bricks or a book press. Some warping will be inevitable.

3 To remove mildew from a book, dust away any loose mildew with a fine brush. If the book is damp, dry it completely. Then apply hydrogen peroxide or denatured alcohol to the book with a lint-free cloth to kill the mildew. Blot away excess liquid and dry the book thoroughly.

4 Remove dark mildew stains with diluted peroxide bleach or lemon juice. Apply sparingly and dry thoroughly afterward. Dry the book in the sun if you use lemon juice.

Broken spine or hinge

1 Insert waxed paper between the cover and first and last pages, between the cover and the hinge, or between any pages that might come into contact with glue.

2 Apply acid-free glue sparingly to the separated hinge or spine. Use a knitting needle or barbecue skewer to insert the glue along the length of the spine between the cover and the binding. An acid-free glue stick works especially well for repairing paperback spines and covers. Blot away any excess glue from the cover, hinges, spine and pages.

3 Wrap the entire book in waxed paper and then wrap the book firmly in an Ace bandage to hold it in place while the glue dries. Make sure the spine and hinges are properly aligned. Weight the book under heavy books, covered bricks or in a book press overnight.

4 The next day, carefully remove the bandage and waxed paper.

5 Use cloth tape to reinforce a book spine only if the book is for utility or educational purposes. It ruins the collector value.

6 If the spine of the book needs replacing, consult a professional book restorer.

Use a lambswool duster to remove dust from a book, or vacuum it using a brush attachment every six months. Wipe leather book covers with leather cleaner. Never use detergent or water to wash a book.

Store books in an area where they will be protected from moisture or excessive dryness, sunlight, extreme temperatures, insects and mice. Shoving too many books onto a shelf will damage book spines, as will tilting or leaning books.

Ensure that the area where you are storing the books is dry. Purchase a dehumidifier if necessary to remove moisture from the air. A bit of lavender oil rubbed into the bookshelves can help prevent mildew.

15 Restring Your Guitar

If a string snaps during your guitar solo, you'll want to fix it quickly and return to playing. Here's how to restring an acoustic (steel-stringed) folk guitar.

Steps

1 Remove the broken string by popping out the pin on the bridge and unwinding it from the head. Discard the string.

2 Thread the ball end of a new string through the bridge and secure it with the pin.

3 Stretch the new string up the neck, into the nut and through the eye of the tuning machine on the head of the guitar.

4 Sharply bend the string to help hold it in place on the peg.

5 Turn the tuning peg counterclockwise to tighten the string. Turn it at least one rotation. Make sure you don't turn it too tight.

6 While you turn the tuning peg, apply light pressure to the pin to keep it from popping out as tension develops.

7 Pull the string with your thumb and index finger to stretch the new string, then turn the tuning peg a bit to retighten it.

8 Use wire cutters to snip off the excess string, leaving about 1 or 2 inches (2.5 to 5 cm).

9 Tune the new string to the other strings or to a guitar tuner.

What You'll Need

- New guitar string
- Wire cutters

Tips

To keep the sound of your guitar crisp and bright, change the strings every three months, more often if you play it a lot. Pros change their strings once a week.

Most electric guitars require that you thread the string through a hole in the back side of the body to the bridge. Thread the string through the tuning peg as you would on an acoustic guitar.

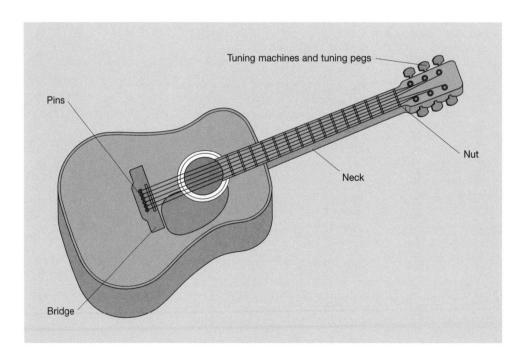

Tuning machines and tuning pegs

Pins

Nut

Neck

Bridge

16 Get Rid of Red-Eye in Photographs

Red-eye occurs when the camera flash reflects the blood vessels of the retina into the lens. Here are some ways to prevent and remove this devilish effect.

Steps

Fixing red-eye

1 Purchase a special pen that reduces red-eye from a photography shop. Draw over the red-eye on your photographic prints to reduce the red-eye effect.

2 Or scan the picture into your computer and use image-editing software to fix the red-eye. Most such programs have a feature especially designed for this purpose. You can remove the spinach caught in your subject's teeth while you're at it.

3 Bring the photograph to a photo-editing shop if you do not have a scanner and image-editing software.

Preventing red-eye

1 Try to put distance between the camera's lens and flash to reduce red-eye. If possible, hold the flash an arm's length from the camera or point the flash toward a white surface, such as a wall, so the flash does not flood the subject's eyes.

2 If the flash is immobile, reduce the size of the subject's pupils by turning on bright lights or by shining a bright light briefly in the person's eyes prior to taking the picture.

3 Use the red-eye reduction feature available on many cameras. This feature constricts the pupils with a series of low-level flashes prior to taking the picture.

4 Put tissue paper or a white filter over the flash to diffuse its brightness. The tissue paper shouldn't come into direct contact with the hot flashbulb. Some camera shops sell flash diffusers.

What You'll Need

- Anti–red-eye pen
- Scanner
- Image-editing software
- Tissue paper or a white filter
- Flash diffuser

Tips

Pictures taken indoors or at sunset are more susceptible to red-eye because pupils dilate to adjust to the low-light conditions.

For more photography tips, see 551 Improve Your Photography Techniques.

Warning

The multiple flashes of red-eye reduction cause a brief delay in the taking of the picture and may increase the chances that your subject will blink.

17 Reduce Puffiness Around Your Eyes

As you sleep at night, fluids sometimes accumulate around your eyes, giving you that tired appearance. Here are some steps you can take to reduce the puffiness.

Steps

1 Gently tap the swollen area with your fingertips to encourage fluids to flow elsewhere.

2 Apply a cool, soothing substance to your eyes for 5 minutes to reduce fluid retention. Try cucumber slices; a refrigerated gel mask; damp, chilled tea bags; or a damp, cold cloth.

3 Drink plenty of water. Water retention, which causes bloating, occurs when the body has too much salt and not enough fluids to flush it out.

What You'll Need

- Cucumber slices, gel mask, chilled tea bags or cloth

Warning

Visit a doctor if you have sudden, severe swelling in the eye area; it may indicate sinusitis or an allergy.

18 Remove a Speck From Your Eye

If an object is floating on your eye or inside the lid, follow these steps to get relief. Always seek medical help immediately if you're dealing with an object that's stuck or embedded in an eye.

Steps

1 Wash your hands with soap and water before you touch any part of the eye. Resist rubbing it, no matter how much it may itch.

2 Grab your upper lashes and gently pull your upper lid down over your lower lid. This will cause tears to form, which may flush the object out.

3 Tilt your head to the side over a sink and use a medicine dropper or small pitcher to pour a tiny stream of warm water into your eye to flush out the speck.

4 If the particle is not flushed out, go to a well-lit mirror and pull down the lower lid with your finger. If you spot the offending object, gently remove it with a clean tissue or swab.

5 If the object is under your upper lid, elicit the help of a friend. Look down while your friend lifts up the upper lid by the lashes. Place a cotton swab behind the lid and flip the lid backward over the swab. Hold the swab in place while your friend carefully removes the object with a clean tissue or swab.

What You'll Need

- Soap
- Medicine dropper or small pitcher
- Mirror
- Tissue
- Cotton swab

Tip

If your removal efforts irritate the eye, give it a rest. Often your eye will work the speck out on its own.

Warning

If the eye is very irritated or you are unable to remove the object, seek medical help.

19 Stop Snoring

Snoring is not just a nuisance for your bedmate (or, in extreme cases, for your neighbor). It can be a sign of a serious medical disorder called sleep apnea. The first issue to address regarding chronic snoring is whether this is a symptom of sleep apnea.

Steps

1 Are you overweight? Do you constantly feel drowsy? Do you struggle to breathe while asleep? Do you have high blood pressure? If so, consult a doctor who specializes in sleep disorders. These are all telltale signs of sleep apnea.

2 Use a single low pillow. Sleeping on too many pillows can stretch and narrow the nasal passage. If, however, you are congested, elevate the head by placing books under the mattress to encourage better drainage.

3 Try to sleep on your stomach, since snoring is less likely to occur in this position. You can buy anti-snoring pillows designed to keep snorers on their side while asleep.

4 Adopt a healthy lifestyle. Extra weight, smoking, alcohol and drugs all exacerbate snoring.

5 Review your meds. Sleeping pills, antihistamines and other medications increase snoring.

6 Consult your doctor if you suspect that allergies and nasal congestion may be causing the problem. Make sure your allergy medication is antihistamine free.

7 Try an over-the-counter nasal strip. These strips may widen the nasal passages and decrease congestion to reduce snoring.

8 Ask your dentist about using an oral appliance designed to reduce snoring.

9 Discuss the treatments for sleep apnea with a sleep-disorder specialist. These include surgery, radio-frequency treatment and a sleeping mask that aids breathing.

What You'll Need

- Low pillow or anti-snoring pillow
- Nasal strips
- Oral appliance

Tips

If you are the bedmate of a snorer, use earplugs. The loud noise may prevent you from getting restful sleep and lead to sleep deprivation.

See also 8 Remedy Sleep Problems.

Warning

Severe sleep apnea is potentially fatal if left untreated. An obstruction in the respiratory passage interferes with a person's ability to breathe while sleeping. In severe cases, the sleeper may stop breathing for a minute or even longer.

20 Fix Bad Habits

Some bad habits are such a part of our daily lives that it's easy to forget we have them. This chart will remind you of your bad habits and help you get rid of them.

HABIT	GENERAL COMMENTS	REMEDIES
Smoking	Causes cancer, gum disease and bad breath	- Nicotine patch, gum - Join support group. - Consult doctor.
Cursing	Inappropriate in certain settings, especially in presence of kids; might signal anger-management problems	- Substitute with words that sound similar to curses. - Ask spouse or child to charge dollar for every curse. - Consider anger-management classes.
Gossiping	Sign of insecurity or boredom with one's own life; might hurt feelings or welfare of others	- Take up new hobby to keep your mind off other people's business.
Whining	Sign of immaturity; annoys others	- Focus on the positive. - Before you speak, think about what kind of impression you'll make.
Chewing with mouth open	Sign of bad manners or possibly just a stuffed nose; makes poor impression at business lunches	- Take nasal decongestant. - Breathe through nose when eating.
Spitting	Considered rude; illegal in some countries; spreads germs	- Swallow, don't spit. - Chew gum instead of tobacco.
Nail biting	Sign of nervousness; destroys nails; unhygienic	- Paint nails with foul-tasting polish. - Wear gloves.
Caffeine addiction	Provides extra alertness and energy but might cause anxiety and health complications	- Wean yourself off it with lower doses of caffeine. - Get good night's sleep to feel more alert naturally.

HABIT	GENERAL COMMENTS	REMEDIES
Procrastinating	Stems from fear of failure or adverse feelings toward particular activity; results in late fees, missed opportunities, stress, insomnia, daytime drowsiness	• Use daily calendar and to-do list to monitor tasks. • Provide personal incentives for completing things.
Fidgeting	Caused by nervousness or excess energy; can be distracting to others	• Practice meditation and deep breathing to relax mind and muscles. • Exercise regularly to burn excess energy. • Reduce caffeine intake.
Exaggerating	Stems from desire to improve truth; may lead others to distrust you; borders on lying in extreme cases	• Use a disclaimer so listeners realize you are exaggerating, as in "I'm exaggerating a little bit, but ..."
Name dropping	Sign of insecurity at social gatherings; usually backfires, alienating more than it impresses	• Resist urge to mention specific names. • Work on confidence building. • Realize people will like you for being genuine.
Interrupting	Sign of poor listening skills; frustrates people talking to you	• Meditate to improve your focus and ability to listen to others.
Flaking out	Reflects fear of commitment and disregard for others; causes others not to depend on you; may change relationships	• Only say yes to social engagements that truly interest you. • Force yourself to carry out plan once you make it.
Kissing and telling	Displays lack of concern for others; considered tacky and petty	• Count to 10 before blurting out what's on your mind. • Put yourself in your subject's shoes.
Bragging	Can be sign of insecurity or pride; may cause jealousy in others	• Realize the only person you need to impress is yourself.

21 Repair a Broken Eyeglass Frame

With the help of an inexpensive eyeglass repair kit, you can perform minor repairs on eyeglass frames. The kits are sold at drugstores and hardware stores.

Steps

1 Examine the cause of the problem with a magnifying glass. Is the hinge stretched out? Is the screw loose or missing? Did the hinge break off?

2 If the hinge is stretched out, cover the tips of a pair of pliers with masking or duct tape to avoid scratching the frames and then use the pliers to bend the hinge gently back into place. Or slide an orthodontic rubber band (available from dentists) or a small rubber ring (an eyeglass repair kit may include this) over the loose hinge to hold it in place.

3 If the screw is loose, tighten it with a tiny screwdriver from the eyeglass repair kit. The tip of a paring knife will serve as a screwdriver in a pinch.

4 If the screw is lost, replace it with one of the screws from the kit, or slip a miniature safety pin into the screw hole and close it. If the repair kit's screw does not fit into the hole, do not force it, as that might strip the threads inside the frame.

5 Dab a tiny bit of clear nail polish on the hinge screw once you've tightened it to hold the screw in place. Let dry.

6 If the metal hinge has broken off the frame, wash both surfaces and scrape away any paint or old glue. Then use a toothpick to dab fast-bonding glue to the break. Hold the pieces in place for 60 seconds to allow the glue to dry.

7 If the earpiece keeps slipping off the frame or has broken off, re-adhere it with fast-bonding glue. If you get the glue on your skin, wipe it off with acetone-based nail-polish remover.

What You'll Need

- Magnifying glass
- Pliers with tape on tips
- Orthodontic rubber bands
- Eyeglass repair kit and/or miniature safety pin
- Clear nail polish
- Toothpick
- Fast-bonding glue

Tip

Ask your optometrist about making regular eyeglass adjustments to prevent breakage from wear and tear. In this process, the optometrist disassembles, cleans and tightens the glasses.

Warning

Do not use fast-bonding glue to hold your lenses in place. It will make it impossible to remove them in the future.

If fast-bonding glue gets into your eyes or mouth, seek medical attention at once.

22 Reposition a Slipped Contact Lens

If your contact lens slips out of place, fear not. It's nearly impossible for it to disappear behind your eyeball.

Steps

1 Wash your hands thoroughly before touching any part of the eye.

2 Pull up your upper lid while you look down at a mirror to search for the lens. Pull down your lower lid to search for the lens in the lower part of your eye.

3 If you are still unable to locate the lens, put saline solution in your eye and move your eye up, down and side to side. This might dislodge the lens.

4 If you are still unable to find it, take a breather. The lens might work its way out if you rest your eye. Add more saline solution if your eye is feeling irritated.

5 Once you've located the lens, close your eye and use your finger to move it gently back into place. It might help to roll your eye toward the lens.

6 If the lens has curled up like a taco shell, move it to the outer corner of your eye and remove it.

7 If you are unable to locate the lens or if you are suffering from extreme pain, contact your eye doctor.

What You'll Need

- Mirror
- Saline solution

Tip

A lens can curl up and lodge itself deep in the upper lid. Search carefully for it.

Warning

If a contact lens repeatedly slips out of place, visit your eye doctor for a refitting. An improper fit can lead to a corneal abrasion, an ulcer or an infection.

23 Fix a Run in Stockings

The expense of replacing ruined stockings adds up quickly. Here is how to fix a tiny run or hole with clear nail polish before the damage becomes irreparable.

Steps

1 Act immediately. Holes and tiny runs quickly tear apart the weave of the stocking.

2 If you are wearing the stockings, insert a tiny piece of paper or tissue behind the hole or run to protect your skin.

3 Remove excess nail polish from the brush and then dab the polish around the hole or at both ends of the run.

4 Remove excess polish from the stockings with nail-polish remover on a cotton swab. The polish will be visible after it dries, especially on dark-colored stockings.

5 Check to make sure the polish is not adhering to the paper or tissue, and then allow the polish to dry for 3 to 5 minutes.

What You'll Need

- Paper or tissue
- Clear nail polish
- Nail-polish remover
- Cotton swab

Tip

Catch runs before they start. Inspect the toes and waist-line of stockings after each wearing. Apply clear polish to weak spots or small holes.

24 Jog Your Memory

The busier life becomes, the easier it is to forget names, numbers and important dates. These mnemonic tricks can help you out.

Steps

People's names

1 Repeat the name when you first hear it: "Nice to meet you, Harold."

2 Think of a relative or friend who has the same name: "This fellow has the same name as Uncle Harry."

3 Make a mental joke about this person's name: "This fellow is quite bald to be named Harry." Keep the joke to yourself, though.

4 Find a melody or rhyme in the name, as both aid memory: "Anne Maureen plays the tambourine."

5 Ask the person to spell the name, if it is unique, to etch it into your memory.

Phone numbers

1 Look for a connection between the numbers and your life (ages, birth dates, number of siblings) to anchor it to your memory. Also see if the numbers resemble a historical date, such as 1492.

2 Find a formula that fits the number. For example, 347-8643 could be "3 plus 4 equals 7, and ½ of 8 and 6 are 4 and 3."

3 If you have a phone nearby, examine the keys to see if the phone number spells anything memorable.

4 Sing the number to a familiar tune until you've memorized it.

Birthdays and anniversaries

1 Fill in all important dates on a calendar at the beginning of every year. Hang the calendar in a prominent position and check it on a weekly basis.

2 Set up the reminders available on many e-mail systems so you receive an e-mail message to prompt you on an especially important day.

3 To remember the general time frame of a birthday, imagine the person in a costume appropriate to the birthday month. For example, imagine him or her in a pilgrim outfit if the birthday is in November or in leprechaun attire for a March baby.

4 Use your sense of smell to remember your wedding anniversary. If you got married in May, perhaps the scent of lilacs will remind you of that special day.

Tips

Employ as many senses as possible to fix an item in your memory. Sight and smell are especially effective at anchoring memories.

Regular exercise, a balanced diet and adequate sleep increase your overall alertness and make it easier to remember things.

Warning

The use of alcohol, drugs or medications can decrease memory performance.

25 Fix an Electric Can Opener That Drops the Can

If your electric can opener drops the can, it means there is too much space between the cutter and the feed gear (the gear that guides the can). To fix this problem, insert washers behind the feed gear to close the gap; this process is called shimming.

Steps

1 Unplug the can opener.

2 Remove the cutter arm from the machine. It usually has a release lever or button that allows you to do this.

3 Scrub away buildup on the feed gear with dishwashing liquid, hot water and a stiff brush. Dry thoroughly.

4 Unscrew and remove the back of the can opener's case. You'll see a large gear on the same shaft as the feed gear; this is the spur gear.

5 Put masking or duct tape on the tips of a pair of pliers to protect the feed gear.

6 Hold the spur gear in place with a rag (or a screwdriver if the spur gear has a hole) as you twist off the feed gear with pliers (see A).

7 Buy washers the same size as the feed gear; you'll find these at a hardware store. Place one or more of these washers onto the feed gear's shaft (see B).

8 Replace the feed gear and cutter arm. There should be about $\frac{1}{32}$-inch (1-mm) gap between the parts. Add or remove washers, if necessary, until you reach the desired spacing.

9 Reassemble the machine and plug it in. If the machine continues to drop cans, add another washer.

What You'll Need

- Dishwashing liquid
- Stiff brush
- Screwdriver
- Pliers with tape on tips
- Rag
- Washers

Tips

If the feed gear's teeth are worn out, buy a new gear from the manufacturer or from a parts supplier (look under "Appliances" in the yellow pages).

Clean the cutter arm and the feed gear regularly with dishwashing liquid, hot water and a stiff brush.

Warning

Never immerse an electric can opener in water.

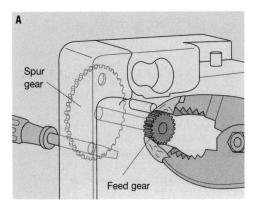

A

Spur gear

Feed gear

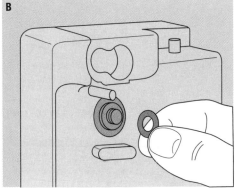

B

26 Troubleshoot a Cell Phone

Cellular phones don't always function as perfectly as you might wish. This chart offers some solutions for common problems with these devices. If you don't find an answer here, bring your phone to an authorized cell-phone center. Avoid taking apart the phone, because this will void most warranties.

PROBLEM	SOLUTIONS
Phone won't turn on	• Make sure battery is charged and fully plugged into phone. • Remove battery from phone and use rag to brush away dirt that may interfere with connection. Reconnect and try again. • If using cigarette-lighter adapter, make sure it's properly plugged in. • Make sure charger is properly plugged into outlet and into battery.
Battery won't charge	• Plug lamp or other electrical device into outlet to verify that outlet works. • Borrow friend's charger to see if charger or battery is problem. Replace charger or battery if necessary.
Heavy static	• Make sure antenna is up. • Check to see if battery is low. • If indoors, move toward window or go outside to get better reception. • Remember that tunnels, basements and elevators interfere with cell-phone reception. • In case of storm, wait for it to subside. • Contact your service provider if you have chronic static; phone may be defective.
Can't make calls	• Try again. Network may be full. • Change locations to get better signal. • If display says "No SVC" or "No Service," you are in area with no service. Wait until you enter area with service. • Check to see if battery is low. • If you are outside service area, contact customer service (try 611 on cell phone). Some service areas require PIN numbers to protect against fraud.
Keys won't work	• Look for display of symbol that looks like lock. Keypad may be locked. Display often tells you how to unlock it. If not, check owner's manual.
Can't hear other person	• Make sure volume is not turned down entirely.
Phone squeaks	• Turn down volume.

PROBLEM	SOLUTIONS
Can't receive calls	• Confirm that neither call forwarding nor automatic voice-mail pickup is activated. • Make sure ringer volume is turned up. • Confirm that ringer is on (not in silent mode). • Change locations for better reception. • If display says "No SVC" or "No Service," you are in area with no service. Wait until you enter area with service. • Call customer service. You may have restrictions on incoming calls.
Interference from another call	• Check that antenna is up. • Change locations for better reception. • Switch to digital phone.
Calls drop off	• Check battery. It may be low. • If you constantly lose calls, consider switching to provider with better coverage and/or to digital phone. Providers that offer digital service combined with analog tend to have better coverage.
Can't make long-distance calls	• Call your service provider (try 611 on cell phone). You may be out of calling range and/or may need PIN number to dial long-distance numbers.
Phone got wet	• Remove battery from phone and allow both to dry thoroughly. • If rust or corrosion develops, wipe off with a stiff brush. • If phone still does not work, replace it.
Display not working	• Extremely cold conditions may affect display function. Keep phone at room temperature.

Complaints about service provider	• Call customer service to register complaint (try 611 on cell phone).
	• If that does not resolve problem, contact:
	    FCC Consumer Information Bureau
	    Customer Services Network Division
	    445 12th St. SW
	    Washington, DC 20554

27 Keep Mirrors From Fogging

Think of the time you can save by preventing fogged-up mirrors. Here is a trick to earn yourself an extra five minutes of snooze time.

Steps

1 Apply a thin layer of shaving cream or liquid soap to the mirror with a lint-free cloth. The cream or soap will form a thin film that will prevent fogging.

2 Buff in the cream or liquid soap until it is evenly and thinly applied. A slight film will be visible, but it should dissipate after a few hot showers.

3 Leave the cream or soap on the mirror—do not wash it off with water. You'll find that your mirror no longer fogs up after a hot shower.

4 Reapply the shaving cream or liquid soap after a week or two when the mirror begins to fog up again. Wash the mirror with glass cleaner between applications to avoid a buildup of film.

What You'll Need

- Shaving cream or liquid soap
- Lint-free cloth
- Glass cleaner

Tip

Because a small film is left on the mirror, you might want to try this method only on the portion of the mirror that you use to shave or apply makeup.

28 Zap an Acne Breakout

If you awake on the morning of a special day to discover a red pimple on the tip of your nose, all hope is not lost. Here's how to remedy an unwelcome pimple.

Steps

1 Tempting as it is, don't try to pop the pimple by squeezing, pinching, or picking at it. This will just inflame the pore and spread the oils that caused the pimple.

2 Apply ice to the area for 2 minutes every half hour. This will help shrink the pimple and possibly reduce it to an invisible size.

3 Apply a flesh-tinted acne medication that contains benzoyl peroxide, salicylic acid or sulfur. Since these medications dry out the skin, apply only to the pimple area.

4 If you'd like, use an oil-free powder to cover up the medicated area and reduce any shine.

5 If the pimple is already coming to a head and it's too late to use the ice treatment, use heat. Wash the area with soap and water. Apply a hot, damp compress to the pimple for 60 seconds. This increases circulation and helps bring the pimple to a head. Remove the compress and apply gentle pressure to drain the pimple; do not squeeze. If the pimple does not drain, reapply heat and try again. Do not force the pimple to drain. Wash the area with soap and water after pimple drains.

What You'll Need

- Ice
- Acne medication
- Oil-free powder
- Soap
- Hot compress

Tip

If you wear makeup and facial moisturizers, choose products that are noncomedogenic (won't cause pore buildup) and nonacnegenic (won't cause acne). Remove all makeup nightly.

29 Repair a Torn Fingernail

To avoid nail breakage, moisturize your nails and use gloves when you're washing dishes or gardening. Here's how you can fix those unavoidable nail snafus.

Steps

1 Remove any polish from the nail. Start with clean, dry nails.

2 Cut a patch from a tea bag, coffee filter or swatch of silk. The patch should be large enough to cover the tear.

3 Put a drop of fast-bonding glue on a toothpick and apply it to the tear. Use nail glue or a household glue containing cyanoacrylate. If you get any glue on your skin, wipe it off with acetone-based nail-polish remover.

4 Hold the nail in place with the toothpick for 30 seconds. If the tear is small, this alone will fix it—no need for a patch.

5 Dab the glue on the patch, then pick up the patch with tweezers.

6 Use the toothpick or a manicure stick to smooth the patch onto the tear. Act quickly because the glue dries fast.

7 Allow the glue to dry thoroughly for 1 minute. Then smooth out any rough edges with an emery board and a nail buffer. File nails in a square instead of an oval shape to prevent breakage.

8 Apply colored nail polish to camouflage the patch.

What You'll Need

- Nail-polish remover
- Tea bag, coffee filter or silk swatch
- Nail glue or fast-bonding glue
- Toothpick
- Tweezers
- Manicure stick
- Emery board
- Nail buffer
- Colored nail polish

Warning

If glue gets in your eyes or mouth, seek medical attention immediately.

Do not use glue containing cyanoacrylate to attach artificial nails.

30 Fix Chipped Nail Polish

If your manicure is more than a week old when it chips, it's probably time for a new one. Otherwise you can easily remedy chips that occur between manicure sessions.

Steps

1 Moisten your index fingertip with nail-polish remover on the hand that doesn't have the chipped nail.

2 Rub this finger on the chipped area to smooth away any globs or rough edges.

3 Let it dry and then brush a small amount of nail polish on the chipped area.

4 After the polish has dried, apply a clear coat of nail polish or polish sealant to prevent future chipping.

5 Wipe the polish residue off your fingertip with a cotton ball and nail-polish remover.

6 Avoid fast-drying polishes, which tend to chip more easily.

What You'll Need

- Nail-polish remover
- Nail polish
- Clear nail polish or polish sealant
- Cotton ball

Tips

Use toothpaste to remove ink stains from polish.

Acetone-based nail-polish removers dry out nails, which can cause them to split or break.

31 Fix a Stuck Zipper

You've probably run into this jam before: You're zipping up a jacket, and the lining suddenly gets caught in the zipper's teeth. Here's how to get out of it.

Steps

1 Stop zipping as soon as you feel something is caught.

2 Examine the zipper to locate the problem. The inner lining may be caught, so check the inside of the garment or sleeping bag.

3 Gently pull the lining away from the zipper. Tug lightly if necessary. Pull at the lining, not at the zipper. Pulling the zipper tab up or down will worsen the problem.

4 If any teeth became separated as you removed the lining, push them back into place.

5 Run your fingers along the length of the zipper and push the lining away from the zipper to prevent future snags.

6 Use a little force to pull the zipper to the bottom. Then rezip, making sure to avoid the lining as you go.

Tips

If a missing tooth causes the zipper to get stuck, run the zipper quickly over the area of the missing tooth. The momentum will help the zipper stay on track.

If the zipper is sticking because it's worn or old, rub a No. 2 pencil along the teeth. The graphite will smooth out the rough spots.

See 532 Unjam a Sleeping-Bag Zipper for more tips.

32 Find a Lost Contact Lens

It's unfortunate that contact lenses are too small to have beepers for these moments of panic.

Steps

1 If you have dropped a lens into the sink, plug the drain immediately and turn off the water. Gently pat the sink and surrounding area with your fingertips to find the lens. (If it went down the drain, see 69 Rescue an Item From the Sink.)

2 Check your clothing carefully to see if the lens fell into a sleeve or got caught in a hem or pocket.

3 Ask everyone who is searching for the lens to remove their shoes. Someone might discover it by stepping on it.

4 Turn off the lights and search the vicinity with a flashlight or bright lamp. Get down so you're at eye level with the floor and look for any glint from the lens.

5 Place a nylon over the end of a vacuum hose and secure it with a rubber band. Keep the nozzle about 1 inch (2.5 cm) above the floor. Turn on the vacuum. The nylon will catch the lens.

6 Clean, rinse and disinfect the lens before you place it in your eye.

What You'll Need

- Flashlight or bright lamp
- Vacuum with hose attachment
- Nylons
- Rubber band

Tips

When you are removing contact lenses, place a dark towel on the table or counter to make it easier to spot a dropped lens.

If you have a child who tends to lose contact lenses, consider tinted ones. They're easier to spot, and some types don't affect eye color.

33 Eliminate Bad Breath

Nothing zaps the romance from a smooch quicker than bad breath. Here are some tips for keeping your breath nice and fresh.

Steps

1 Practice good oral hygiene to kill the bacteria that cause bad breath: Brush twice a day and floss once a day. Use an oral rinse. See the dentist twice a year. Breath mints, sprays, mouthwash and gum mask bad breath but don't resolve it.

2 Use a plastic spoon to scrape off white residue on your tongue—this is often the culprit. Or buy a tongue scraper at a drugstore.

3 Brush after eating foods such as milk, cheese and fish. The breakdown of protein in the mouth contributes to bad breath.

4 Avoid dry mouth—it's an environment that promotes bad breath. Breathe through your nose, drink plenty of water and steer clear of alcohol.

5 Clean dentures in an antiseptic solution nightly.

6 See your dentist if the problem continues. Bad breath can be a sign of gum disease, faulty dental work or some other medical problem. Certain medications, the onset of menstruation, drinking coffee, smoking and fasting can also cause bad breath.

What You'll Need

- Toothbrush and tooth-paste
- Dental floss
- Oral rinse
- Spoon or tongue scraper
- Antiseptic solution

Tip

You may have bad breath even if you can't smell it. Ask someone you trust for an honest opinion.

Warning

Beware pill remedies that promise to solve bad breath caused by gastrointestinal problems. This type of bad breath is quite rare.

34 Keep a Shaving Nick From Bleeding

Few things are more unsightly than a bloody nick on a freshly shaved face—except for a bloody nick with tissue clumped over it. Here's how to remedy shaving mishaps sans tissue.

Steps

1 Wipe away blood with cool water and a cotton swab or tissue.

2 Wet the tip of a styptic pencil. Made with paste containing aluminum sulfate, a styptic pencil stops bleeding quickly. You'll find styptic pencils in the shaving-supplies section of drugstores.

3 Dab the pencil over the nick and the surrounding area. This will cause some temporary stinging.

4 Rinse the pencil with water after each use and allow it to dry thoroughly.

5 Avoid future nicks by shaving with a sharp blade and applying moisturizer to your freshly shaved skin.

What You'll Need

- Cotton swab or tissue
- Styptic pencil
- Moisturizer

Warning

Do not use styptic pencils around the eyes or in other sensitive areas.

35 Get Rid of Split Ends

When hair becomes dry or damaged, the hair shaft splits at the end. Here's how you can keep those unsightly splits from spoiling the looks of your locks.

Steps

1 Keep brushing to a minimum since it promotes breakage. Brushing wet hair is a definite no-no; use a wide-toothed comb when hair is wet.

2 Strive for low-maintenance hair. Hair dryers, curling irons, perms and hair colors all damage hair. If you must blow-dry, use a cool setting and keep the dryer 6 inches (15 cm) from your hair.

3 Protect your hair from extreme weather. Wear a hat on sunny days and keep hair well moisturized in the dry winter months.

4 Apply a leave-in conditioner or pomade to the ends of your hair daily to keep them strong.

5 Snip away any split ends you spot. Cut at least 1 inch (2.5 cm) above the split. A split end will split the hair all the way up to the scalp, so snip it as soon as you spot it.

6 Schedule a trim with your hairstylist if you start seeing a lot of split ends.

What You'll Need

- Wide-toothed comb
- Hat
- Leave-in conditioner or pomade
- Scissors

Tip

Ask your stylist to recommend thermal protection products.

Warning

Be wary of promises from the makers of products for split ends. These bind the hair shaft temporarily. The only real cure is a haircut.

36 Untangle Hair Snarls

Snarls or tangles often indicate damaged hair, so handle this problem with the greatest degree of delicacy.

Steps

1 Apply hair conditioner or hand lotion to the fingers of one hand.

2 Hold the tangle in the hand that does not have lotion on it. You will use the other hand to work out the snarl gently.

3 Comb your fingers through the snarl. Begin at the bottom of the snarl and work toward the scalp.

4 For really bad snarls, wet the hair and apply conditioner. Leave the conditioner in the hair while you finger-brush it.

5 Gently comb out the hair with a wide-toothed comb to prevent more snarls from developing.

What You'll Need

- Conditioner or hand lotion
- Wide-toothed comb

Tip

Holding the tangle in one hand while you finger-brush protects the scalp and hair roots from tugging.

37 Fix Frizzy Hair

Curly hair by its very nature is delicate. When it becomes damaged or dry, the curls frizz out. Here are some tricks to keep frizziness at bay.

Steps

1 Learn to like your curls. Straightening efforts and hair relaxants damage hair.

2 Keep shampooing to a minimum since shampoo tends to dry out hair. If you do wash your hair daily, dilute shampoo with an equal amount of water.

3 Use a daily conditioner to keep hair moisturized. Finger-brush your hair while the conditioner is in it. Then rinse.

4 Apply a leave-in conditioner or anti-frizz serum to your damp hair.

5 Deep-condition your hair once a week.

6 To touch up your hair in the afternoon, moisten your fingers with water and a small amount of conditioner. Run your fingers through your hair and smooth out the frizz.

What You'll Need

- Daily conditioner
- Leave-in conditioner or anti-frizz serum
- Deep conditioner

Tips

Find a hairstylist who specializes in curly hair to get suitable style and product recommendations.

Humidity can make straight hair frizzy. Use leave-in conditioner or anti-frizz serum.

38 Fix Bleeding Lipstick

Make sure he notices the fireworks of your good-night kiss, not your messy lipstick. Bleeding means that you've applied your lipstick improperly. Here's how to get it right.

Steps

1 Apply foundation to your lips and allow it to dry for a minute. The foundation fills in the tiny creases around your lips where the lipstick will likely seep.

2 Follow up with a light application of translucent face powder.

3 Line your lips with a lip liner. This not only outlines the shape of your lips but creates a border to keep the color right on your lips, where it should be.

4 Fill in the outline with the lipstick color, either using a makeup brush or directly applying the lipstick.

5 Allow the color to set for a few moments and then lightly powder your lips to seal in the color.

6 Touch up your lips with lip liner and lipstick throughout the day. If the lipstick bleeds, remove it with a moistened cotton swab and reapply the foundation, powder, liner and lipstick.

What You'll Need

- Foundation
- Translucent face powder
- Lip liner
- Makeup brush
- Lipstick
- Cotton swab

Tip

Matte (nonglossy) lipsticks are less likely to run than glossy or shiny ones.

39 Fix a Piano Key That Sticks

Humidity causes wooden piano parts to warp or swell and is often the culprit behind sticking keys. Start by evaluating the problematic key. These are general guidelines for uprights, not grand pianos.

Steps

White keys sticking (warped key slip)

1 If several white keys stick, the key slip may be warped and rubbing against the keys. Unscrew the key slip to loosen it a bit.

2 Insert cardboard shims between the key slip and the key block (see A). A business card folded in two will also do the trick.

3 If the keys continue to stick, remove the key slip to insert more shims along the length of the key bed. Keep the shims shorter than ¾ inch (2 cm) so they don't interfere with key movement.

Key or keys sluggish (swollen keys)

1 If the key slip is not the problem, the key or keys may be swollen. Consider this possibility if it's humid or damp outside.

2 If a white key is sluggish, press down the key and one of its adjacent keys all the way with your index and middle fingers.

3 Keep the keys depressed while you insert a screwdriver between them with your other hand (see B). Insert it midway along the wide part of the keys. Make sure the screwdriver's tip is at least ¼ inch (6 mm) wide and slim enough to fit between the keys.

4 Twist the screwdriver slightly to nudge the keys apart.

5 Release the keys. Repeat one more time if necessary.

6 If a black key is sluggish, press down the black key and an adjacent white key.

7 Insert the screwdriver about ¼ inch (6 mm) above the end of the black key's front slope.

What You'll Need

- Screwdriver
- Cardboard or business card
- Paring knife
- Pen and paper

Tips

Call a piano technician if none of these solutions fixes the sticking key. Dozens of possible problems can cause keys to stick.

You can use the paring knife and screwdriver tricks on both upright and grand pianos.

Keep the piano in an environment that's free of humidity to avoid warping and swelling of piano parts. Contact a piano professional about buying a dehumidifier if humidity is unavoidable.

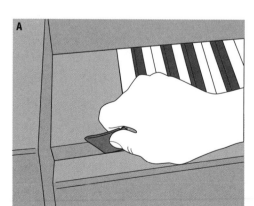

8 Turn the screwdriver *very gently* to create space between the keys. Keep in mind that the black keys are delicate.

Key or several keys sticking (foreign object)

1 If one or more keys stick, a foreign object (a coin or a paper clip) might be interfering. A paring knife may dislodge the object.

2 Firmly hold the handle of the paring knife perpendicular to the key bed and insert the blade between two adjacent keys. It will look as if you are stabbing the keys.

3 Keep the paring knife vertical (perpendicular to the keys) and pull it toward you to clear the space. This often dislodges the object.

4 If the key continues to stick, you'll need to look inside the piano. Consult your owner's manual to find out how to remove the lid, music shelf, fallboard and fallstrip using a screwdriver. Label the screws as you remove the parts.

5 Once you've removed the parts, examine the problematic key or keys. If a foreign object is obstructing the key or keys, remove it.

6 If not, the object may lie underneath the key. Put your finger on the rear of the key to keep it from slipping out as you use your other hand to lift its front about ½ inch (12 mm).

7 While you have the key pulled up, shake it a little to dislodge anything underneath, and then let the key drop back into place.

8 Reassemble the piano in the following order: first the fallstrip, then the fallboard, then the music shelf, and finally the lid.

Warning

These instructions are intended as general guidelines and may not apply to your model. If in doubt, leave it to a pro.

Do not attempt to disassemble your piano if it's a grand; call a piano technician.

Do not remove the keys; it may be difficult to put them back into place.

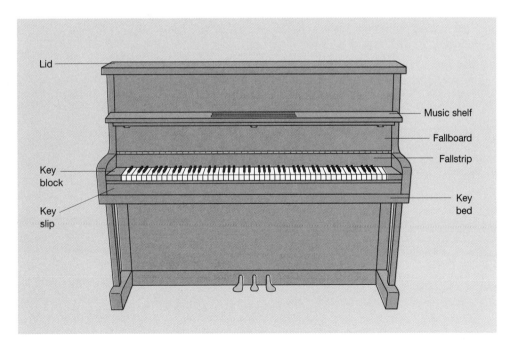

40 Stop Telemarketers and Junk Mail

Your home phone number and address are a hotly traded commodity for retailers, telemarketers, credit card companies and direct-mail companies. Guard your private information carefully to help prevent it from getting into their hands. Here are some tips to put an end to unsolicited annoyances.

Steps

Telemarketers

1 Try not to give out your phone number to businesses. Read waivers carefully; some waivers are written deliberately to confuse the consumer. Financial institutions need your permission to sell your personal information.

2 Never give your phone number when filling out survey, contest, warranty or sweepstakes forms. These are specifically designed to gather phone numbers and addresses.

3 Keep your home number unlisted to make it more difficult for telemarketers to track you down. Consider getting a new, unlisted phone number if telemarketing calls are out of control.

4 Buy a phone that has a caller ID display so you can screen incoming calls. Allow voice mail to pick up if the incoming call number is blocked or unfamiliar. A phone with caller ID helps you skirt the extra fees phone companies charge for their call-blocking services.

5 If you do receive a sales call, ask the caller to "place this number on your Do Not Call list." Under federal law, a company cannot call you again for 10 years once you make this request. If you have multiple phone lines, ask the caller to put those numbers on the company's Do Not Call list, too.

6 If you want to document your request so that you can sue the company if it doesn't follow through, ask for the person's name and the company's name and phone number or address. You are entitled to this information under law.

7 Keep a log by your phone to document the companies you have told to put you on their Do Not Call list and the date and time of these calls. If they call you again, you have a right to sue them for up to $500 per call.

8 If you want to make telemarketers jump through extra hoops, request a written copy of their Do Not Call policy. They are required to mail this document to you if you request it, and you can sue them for $500 if they fail to do so.

Tips

Tax-exempt charities and opinion polls are not covered under the FCC's telemarketing laws.

Under federal law, telemarketers must inform you that they are trying to sell you goods or services. If they mislead you about the purpose of their call, you can report them to the FCC and they may be fined up to $10,000.

It is illegal for a company to use an artificial or prerecorded voice in an attempt to sell you something. The company can be fined if you report it to the FCC.

Junk mail

1 Protect your address just like you protect your phone number. Do not give it out to businesses unless necessary. Ask the phone company to omit your address from your listing if you list your phone number at all.

2 If you must share your address with a company, request in person or in writing that the company not sell, share or rent your information.

3 When you move, do not fill out a change-of-address form at the post office. The post office sells this information. Use a temporary mail-forwarding form, which is not sold, to redirect your mail while you contact relevant people and businesses individually.

4 Do not use supermarket club cards, which are used to track your spending habits for marketing purposes. Shop at stores that do not offer club cards, or register as a "John Doe" if you can't avoid club cards.

5 Avoid sending in product warranty cards if you can. Read the fine print to make sure it is absolutely necessary before you do so. These cards are designed to collect people's private information. If you do send one in, be sure to write "Do not sell, share or rent my information" on it.

6 When you donate money to a charity or nonprofit, request that they do not sell, share or rent your information to other parties.

7 Write to Direct Marketing Association Mail Preference Service, P.O. Box 9008, Farmingdale, NY 11735. Your name will be added to a database of addresses that do not want unsolicited mail; many national direct mailers will respect this request for five years.

8 Call 1-888-5OPT-OUT to bar credit rating agencies from sharing your information for two years. You'll need to provide your social security number when you call. Financial institutions are some of the worst junk-mail offenders.

9 Conduct a search online for "stop junk mail" to find various services that will do the legwork for you—for a fee.

See also 262 Get Rid of E-mail Spam.

IORING • FIX BAD HABITS • REPAIR A BROKEN EYEGLASS FRAME • REPOSITION A SLIPPED CONTACT LENS • FIX A RUN IN STOCKINGS • JO
EAKOUT • REPAIR A TORN FINGERNAIL • FIX CHIPPED NAIL POLISH • FIX A STUCK ZIPPER • FIND A LOST CONTACT LENS • ELIMINATE BAD
Y THAT STICKS • STOP TELEMARKETERS AND JUNK MAIL • GET SUPERGLUE OFF YOUR SKIN • EXTRACT A SPLINTER • SOOTHE A SUNBUR
HANGOVER • STOP HICCUPS • MEND A BROKEN HEART • MEND A FAMILY FEUD • TREAT A SMALL CUT OR SCRAPE • FIX HAIR DISASTERS •
TTER SEATS • FIX A BILLING MISTAKE • FIX A BAD GRADE • FIX BAD CREDIT • RECOVER FROM JET LAG • RESUSCITATE AN UNCONSCIOUS
F PRONOUNS • FIX A RUN-ON SENTENCE • FIX MISUSE OF THE WORD GOOD • FIX YOUR DOG OR CAT • CORRECT BAD BEHAVIOR IN DOGS
SSING BUTTON • REMOVE LINT FROM CLOTHING • FIX A DRAWSTRING ON SWEATPANTS • REPAIR A HEM • REPAIR LEATHER GOODS • MEN
UNDER YOUR CASHMERE • FIX A SWEATER THAT HAS SHRUNK • FIX A SWEATER THAT HAS STRETCHED • FIX A HOLE IN A POCKET • FIX A
LING FROM CLOTHING • FIX A FRAYED BUTTONHOLE • REMOVE DARK SCUFFS FROM SHOES • TREAT STAINS ON LEATHER • PROTECT SUE
JIET SQUEAKY HINGES • TROUBLESHOOT LOCK PROBLEMS • TIGHTEN A LOOSE DOORKNOB • TIGHTEN A LOOSE DOOR HINGE • FIX A BIN
PLACE CRACKED TILE • TROUBLESHOOT MOLD ON INTERIOR WALLS • REPLACE CRACKED TILE GROUT IN A TUB OR SHOWER • FIX A DRA
INDS • TROUBLESHOOT WINDOW SHADE PROBLEMS • FIX BROKEN GLASS IN A WINDOW • REPAIR A WINDOW SCREEN • REPAIR ALUMINU
AMAGED PLASTER • REPAIR WALL COVERINGS • TOUCH UP PAINTED WALLS • TROUBLESHOOT INTERIOR-PAINT PROBLEMS • SOLVE A LEAL
RDWOOD FLOOR • RESTORE A DULL, WORN WOOD FLOOR • TOUCH UP WOOD-FLOOR FINISHES • REPAIR DAMAGED SHEET-VINYL FLOOR
JUSE • CHILDPROOF YOUR HOME • PREVENT ICE DAMS • CURE A FAULTY FIREPLACE DRAW • START A FIRE IN A COLD CHIMNEY • FIX A W
AL A GARAGE FLOOR • REFINISH A GARAGE OR BASEMENT FLOOR • CONTROL ROOF LEAKS • REDIRECT RAINWATER FROM A DOWNSPOL
AMGED ASPHALT SHINGLE • PATCH A FLAT OR LOW-PITCHED ROOF • REPAIR ROOF FLASHING • TROUBLESHOOT EXTERIOR-PAINT PROBL
W WATER PRESSURE • FIX LEAKING PIPES • STOP A TOILET FROM RUNNING • FIX A LEAKY TOILET TANK • FIX A STOPPED-UP TOILET • STC
OGGED SINK OR TUB • REPAIR A TUB-AND-SHOWER VALVE • REPAIR CHIPPED FIXTURES • QUIET NOISY PIPES • DEFROST YOUR PIPES • D
ONSUMPTION • REPLACE A RECEPTACLE • FIX AN ELECTRICAL PLUG • REPLACE A LIGHT FIXTURE • INSTALL A NEW DIMMER • FIX A LAMP
OORBELL • FIX A WOBBLY OVERHEAD FAN • ADJUST WATER-HEATER TEMPERATURE • RELIGHT A WATER-HEATER PILOT LIGHT • TROUBLESH
E MAKER • GET RID OF MICROWAVE SMELLS • FIX A REFRIGERATOR THAT COOLS POORLY • FIX A GAS OVEN THAT HEATS POORLY • CLEAN
SHWASHER PROBLEMS • CORRECT AN OVERFLOWING DISHWASHER • FIX A LEAKY DISHWASHER • FIX A DISHWASHER THAT FILLS SLOWLY
WASHING MACHINE THAT FILLS SLOWLY • FIX A WASHING MACHINE THAT "WALKS" ACROSS THE FLOOR • FIX A CLOTHES DRYER THAT DRI
C YOUR VACUUM CLEANER • REPLACE VACUUM CLEANER BRUSHES • TROUBLESHOOT A PORTABLE AIR CONDITIONER • FIX A WINDOW AI
OCESSOR • FIX A TOASTER • DIAGNOSE MICROWAVE OVEN PROBLEMS • TROUBLESHOOT A GAS GRILL • FIX A TRASH COMPACTOR • REF
ART • TROUBLESHOOT A CRASHING COMPUTER • CLEAN UP LAPTOP SPILLS • FIX BAD SECTORS ON A HARD DISK • QUIT A FROZEN PC A
FECTED COMPUTER • IMPROVE YOUR COMPUTER'S MEMORY • GET RID OF E-MAIL SPAM • CHANGE A LASER PRINTER CARTRIDGE • FIX A
GURE OUT WHY A PRINTER WON'T PRINT • FIX SPELLING AND GRAMMAR ERRORS • RECALL AN E-MAIL IN MICROSOFT OUTLOOK • DIAGN(
LES • TROUBLESHOOT A PALM OS PDA • RESET A PALM OS PDA • REMOVE FINGERPRINTS FROM A CAMERA LENS • TROUBLESHOOT A CD
LVAGE A VIDEOCASSETTE • TROUBLESHOOT A DVD PLAYER • STRENGTHEN FM RADIO RECEPTION • STRENGTHEN AM RADIO RECEPTION
JAMMED SLIDE PROJECTOR • GET BETTER SPEAKER SOUND • TROUBLESHOOT A DIGITAL CAMCORDER • TROUBLESHOOT A DIGITAL CAM
GHTBULB • FIX A BROKEN WINEGLASS STEM • FIX BLEMISHED WOOD FURNITURE • REPAIR GOUGES IN FURNITURE • RESTORE FURNITURE
MOUFLAGE A DOG-SCRATCHED DOOR • REPAIR A SPLIT CARPET SEAM • RID CARPETS OF PET ODORS • REINFORCE A SAGGING SHELF •
INTS OF CHAIRS AND TABLES • REUPHOLSTER A DROP-IN CHAIR SEAT • REVIVE A CANE SEAT • REINFORCE A WEAK BED FRAME • FIX UP
TTERY • REPAIR CHIPPED OR CRACKED CHINA • UNCLUTTER YOUR HOME • CLEAN CRAYON FROM A WALL • GET WAX OFF A TABLECLOT
AINS • REMOVE CHEWING GUM FROM CARPETING • REMOVE BLEACH SPOTS FROM CARPETING • REMOVE PET STAINS • ELIMINATE WINE
AINS FROM TILE GROUT • REMOVE MILDEW FROM WALLS AND CEILINGS • DISINFECT A TOILET BOWL • REMOVE FIREPLACE GRIME • GET
EAN OIL SPOTS FROM A GARAGE OR DRIVEWAY • REMOVE STAINS FROM BRICK • WASH AN OUTDOOR GRILL • FIX A FALLEN SOUFFLÉ • F
SCUE OVERPROOFED YEAST DOUGH • FIX YOUR KID LUNCH • GET RID OF TAP-WATER MINERAL DEPOSITS • CALIBRATE A MEAT THERMON
UCE • RESCUE A BROKEN SAUCE • REMOVE FAT FROM SOUPS AND SAUCES • FIX LUMPY GRAVY • SUBSTITUTE MISSING INGREDIENTS • F
JRNED RICE • REMOVE COOKING ODORS • FINISH UNDERCOOKED MEAT • SALVAGE AN UNDERCOOKED TURKEY • FIX AN OVERSEASONEI
ALE BREAD • SMOOTH SEIZED CHOCOLATE • SOFTEN HARDENED SUGARS OR COOKIES • FIX BREAKFAST FOR YOUR SWEETHEART • MEN
GGING TOOLS • RESTORE A BROKEN FLOWERPOT • SHARPEN PRUNING CLIPPERS • REMOVE RUST FROM TOOLS • REVIVE WILTING CUT F
ET RID OF RAMPANT BRAMBLES • TROUBLESHOOT BROWN SPOTS ON A LAWN • CONTROL MAJOR GARDEN PESTS • RID YOUR GARDEN O
ONPERFORMING COMPOST PILE • FIX BAD SOIL • SHORE UP A RAISED GARDEN BED • REMOVE A DEAD OR DISEASED TREE LIMB • TROUB
RAINAGE • TROUBLESHOOT ROSE DISEASES • IDENTIFY AND CORRECT SOIL DEFICIENCIES IN ROSES • TROUBLESHOOT ROSE PESTS • OV
AMAGED DECK BOARDS • REPAIR DECK RAILINGS • STRENGTHEN DECK JOISTS • FIX A RUSTY IRON RAILING • REPAIR A GATE • REPAIR A
RACKED OR DAMAGED CONCRETE • IMPROVE THE LOOK OF REPAIRED CONCRETE • REPAIR AN ASPHALT DRIVEWAY • REVIVE WOODEN O
ARDEN PONDS • CLEAN SWIMMING POOL WATER • TROUBLESHOOT HOT TUBS AND SPAS • REPLACE BRICKS IN WALKWAYS AND PATIOS •
R WITH JUMPER CABLES • SHUT OFF A CAR ALARM THAT WON'T QUIT • FREE A CAR STUCK ON ICE OR SNOW • DE-ICE YOUR WINDSHIEL
RN-SIGNAL COVER • FIX A CAR FUSE • FIX DASHBOARD LIGHTS THAT WON'T LIGHT • REMOVE CAR SMELLS • CHECK TIRE PRESSURE • IN
PROPERLY INSTALLED CHILD CAR SEAT • TROUBLESHOOT LEAKING OIL • CHECK AND ADD POWER-STEERING FLUID • CHECK AND ADD C
ROKEN EXHAUST PIPE • CHECK AND ADD ENGINE OIL • CHECK AND ADD BRAKE FLUID • CHECK AND ADD FLUID TO YOUR AUTOMATIC TF
OUBLESHOOT A WINDSHIELD-WASHER PUMP • REPAIR MINOR DENTS • CHANGE A HUBCAP • FIX AN IGNITION KEY THAT WON'T TURN •

EMORY • FIX AN ELECTRIC CAN OPENER THAT DROPS THE CAN • TROUBLESHOOT A CELL PHONE • KEEP MIRRORS FROM FOGGING • ZAP
KEEP A SHAVING NICK FROM BLEEDING • GET RID OF SPLIT ENDS • UNTANGLE HAIR SNARLS • FIX FRIZZY HAIR • FIX BLEEDING LIPSTICK •
ICKY SOCIAL SITUATION • FIX A BAD REPUTATION • CLEAN LIPSTICK FROM A COLLAR • FIX A BAD RELATIONSHIP • SALVAGE A BAD DATE •
LEEDING NOSE • BEAT THE MONDAY MORNING BLUES • GET OUT OF A FIX • EXTRACT A BROKEN KEY • RETRIEVE KEYS LOCKED INSIDE A
STOP SOMEONE FROM CHOKING • STOP AN ANT INVASION • STABILIZE A CHRISTMAS TREE • RESCUE AN ITEM FROM THE DRAIN • FIX IMP
SKUNK ODOR FROM YOUR DOG • GET A CAT OUT OF A TREE • CORRECT BAD BEHAVIOR IN CATS • TREAT A CAT FOR MATTED FUR • REPLA
EAM • TREAT MILDEW DAMAGE • GET STATIC OUT OF YOUR LAUNDRY • DEAL WITH A CLOTHES-MOTH INFESTATION • FIX A SEPARATED ZIP
UR SOCK • TREAT MIXED-WASH ACCIDENTS • TAKE WRINKLES OUT OF CLOTHING • FIX A HOLE IN JEANS • REPAIR A SNAG IN A SWEATER
TAINS • WASH SNEAKERS • PICK UP A DROPPED STITCH IN KNITTING • RESTRING BEADS • FRESHEN SMELLY SHOES • FIX A SAGGING CLO
R • FIX A RUBBING DOOR • FIX A DRAFTY DOOR • TUNE UP SLIDING DOORS • FIX A SHOWER DOOR • SEAL WALL JOINTS AROUND A TUB C
W • REPAIR A FAULTY WINDOW CRANK • REPAIR VERTICAL BLINDS • REPAIR VENETIAN BLINDS OR MINIBLINDS • REPAIR WOOD OR PLASTI
CREEN WINDOWS • INSTALL NEW SASH CORDS IN WINDOWS • FIX A TIGHT OR LOOSE WINDOW SASH • REPAIR MINOR DRYWALL DAMAGE
OBLEM • REPLACE A DAMAGED CEILING TILE • REPLACE A WOOD FLOORBOARD • QUIET SQUEAKING FLOORS • REPAIR A WATER-DAMAGE
R A VINYL-TILE FLOOR • SILENCE SQUEAKY STER • REPLACE CAULKING ON THE OUTSIDE OF
NG STOVE • REPAIR AND PREVENT WOOD RO TCH A GUTTER LEAK • TROUBLESHOOT A WET BA
AGGING GUTTER • UNCLOG GUTTERS AND D REPAIR A CRACKED OR SPLIT WOOD SHINGLE
ARAGE-DOOR TENSION • TROUBLESHOOT A ITES • LOOSEN A RUSTY NUT OR BOLT • TROUBL
NK SWEATING • FIX FLUSHING PROBLEMS • FAUCET • FIX A STOPPER THAT DOESN'T SEAL • C
UMP PUMP PROBLEMS • TROUBLESHOOT ELE USE • SWAP A FAULTY LIGHT SWITCH • REDUCE F
HOOT FLUORESCENT LIGHTING • FIX A LOW E THERMOSTAT • TROUBLESHOOT HOLIDAY LIGH
TING SYSTEM • REFRESH A SMELLY REFRIGE MS • FIX A LEAKING REFRIGERATOR • REPAIR A C
CTIONING GAS BURNER • REPAIR A RANGE H FIX AN ELECTRIC OVEN THAT HEATS POORLY • D
P YOUR APPLIANCES • CONTROL GARBAGE E DISPOSAL • DIAGNOSE WASHING MACHINE PRO
• FIX A HAIR DRYER • TROUBLESHOOT A CLO AT SPUTTERS • FIX AN IRON THAT LEAVES SPOTS •
NER • FIX A DEHUMIDIFIER • REPAIR A CONS DER • HANDLE A MIXER THAT OVERHEATS • REPAI
NG MACHINE • TROUBLESHOOT SMOKE ALAR DARD SPILLS • TROUBLESHOOT A COMPUTER THA
• REMOVE A WINDOWS PROGRAM • SPEED U OUSE • REPLACE YOUR PC'S BATTERY • CLEAN A
AT FAILS ITS SELF-TEST • CORRECT MONITOR PAPER JAM • TROUBLESHOOT A RECURRING PRIN
ONE MODEM PROBLEMS • TROUBLESHOOT A REEN GLARE • GET TOP-NOTCH SCANS • RECOVE
ESTORE A CD • REPAIR A WARPED CD • CLE • EXTRACT A JAMMED VIDEOTAPE • ADJUST VCF
OTE CONTROL • FIX AUDIOCASSETTES • FIX OT A CASSETTE DECK • REPLACE BROKEN RABBI
BLESHOOT A CD PLAYER • REPLACE A HEAD RASS • SHINE SILVER SAFELY • REMOVE A BROKE
PLACE A BROKEN TOWEL ROD • REMOVE ST FOR NATURAL DISASTERS • FIX A FRAYED CARPI
BORING BATHROOM • REPLACE A SHOWER NACE FILTER • REPAIR A BROKEN SLIDING DRAWE
OD CHAIR • FIX A WOBBLY WOOD CHAIR • SR OR CRACKED PORCELAIN • REPAIR CHIPPED OR C

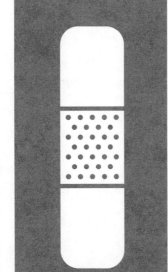

**Occasional
Disasters**

WAX FROM CARPETING • GET RID OF CEILIN MOVE MYSTERY STAINS FROM CLOTHING • REMO
M A RUG OR TABLECLOTH • REMOVE BURN N NITURE • STRIP WAX BUILDUP FROM FLOORS • R
DORANT STAINS • ELIMINATE CIGARETTE ODOR • RESTORE SHINE TO YOUR JEWELRY • WASH DIRTY WINDOWS • REMOVE GRIME FROM M
UMBLED CAKE • FIX A PERFECT CUP OF TEA • PATCH A TORN PIE CRUST • KEEP A PIE CRUST FROM GETTING SOGGY • FIX DOUGH THAT
A DULL KNIFE • REMOVE RUST FROM A CAST-IRON PAN • REPAIR LAMINATE COUNTERTOPS • REMOVE STAINS FROM A STONE COUNTERTO
R CHOLESTEROL • TREAT BURNED POTS AND PANS • RESCUE A BURNED CAKE OR PIE • PUT OUT A KITCHEN FIRE • REMOVE THE BITTER
AN UNDERSEASONED DISH • REMOVE OVEN SPILLS • CLEAN UP OIL SPILLS • FIX A DRINK FOR ANY OCCASION • DISENTANGLE PASTA • R
N CUTTING BOARD • KEEP A MIXING BOWL STEADY • FIX GARDEN TOOL HANDLES • REPAIR A LEAKY HOSE NOZZLE • MEND A LEAKY HOS
HARPEN A POWER MOWER BLADE • SHARPEN PUSH MOWER BLADES • REPAIR BALD SPOTS ON GRASS • RID YOUR GRASS OF DOG URINE
OUBLESHOOT HERBS • TROUBLESHOOT HOUSEPLANTS • OVERCOME SHADE PROBLEMS • RID SOIL OF PESTS AND DISEASES • REVIVE A
EES AND SHRUBS • REPAIR A LEAKING IRRIGATION SYSTEM • UNCLOG A SPRINKLER SYSTEM • CLEAN A CLOGGED DRIP SYSTEM • FIX PO
NGUS DISEASES IN ROSES • REPAIR DECK STEPS • RENOVATE A WEATHERED DECK • TIGHTEN LOOSE DECKING • REMOVE DECK STAINS •
E • LEVEL AND SMOOTH A GRAVEL PATH • FIX A POTHOLE IN A DIRT OR GRAVEL DRIVEWAY • REPLACE PATIO STONES, TILES AND PAVERS
NITURE • RESTORE WEATHERED METAL FURNITURE • REPAIR CHAIR STRAPS AND WEBBING • REVIVE RUSTED IRON FURNITURE • TROUBL
LED CAR • SHUT OFF A JAMMED HORN • CHANGE YOUR CAR'S BATTERY • TROUBLESHOOT A CAR THAT WON'T START • FIX A FLAT TIRE
RNED-OUT SIGNAL BULB • FIX A BURNED-OUT HEADLIGHT • ADJUST HEADLIGHTS • FIX A STUCK BRAKE LIGHT • REPLACE A BROKEN TAIL
TIRES • FIX A STUCK CONVERTIBLE TOP • DIAGNOSE A LEAK INSIDE YOUR CAR • REPLACE YOUR AIR FILTER • HANDLE A FAULTY REPAIR
OOL AN OVERHEATED ENGINE • REPLACE A LEAKING RADIATOR HOSE • CHANGE YOUR WIPER BLADES • ADD WINDSHIELD-WASHER FLUI
• TROUBLESHOOT YOUR BRAKES • ADD BRAKE FLUID TO THE CLUTCH MASTER CYLINDER • TROUBLESHOOT DASHBOARD WARNING LIG
R SPARK PLUG WIRES • DIAGNOSE CAR SMELLS • CLEAN THE OUTSIDE OF YOUR CAR • RESTORE YOUR CAR'S SHINE • WASH THE INTERIO

41 Get Superglue Off Your Skin

While superglue is ideal for fixing things, it's downright scary when the glue bonds to your skin. Most fast-bonding glues, including nail glue and plastic-bonding glue, contain cyanoacrylate and require careful handling. Here's how you can extract yourself from a sticky situation.

Steps

1 Do not attempt to tear or force apart the glue. This could tear your skin.

2 Apply acetone-based nail-polish remover to the area. The acetone breaks down the bond.

3 If there's a lot of glue on your skin, soak the skin in nail-polish remover to dissolve the bond.

4 Clean the area with soap and water after removing the glue.

5 If you don't have nail-polish remover, soak the affected skin in warm, soapy water.

6 Slowly roll the skin to work apart the bond as the warm water soaks through. Continue doing this until the skin is free of glue.

What You'll Need

- Nail-polish remover
- Soap

Warning

If you get superglue in your eye or mouth, keep the eye or mouth open while you rinse it with water for 15 minutes. Seek medical attention immediately.

42 Extract a Splinter

It's amazing how much a tiny sliver of wood, glass or fiberglass can hurt when it lodges in your skin. Remove a splinter promptly to reduce discomfort and the chance of infection.

Steps

1 Wash your hands and the splinter area with soap and water.

2 Sterilize a pair of fine-tip tweezers by boiling them in water for 5 minutes, or by holding them over a flame until they are red-hot. Let cool.

3 Gently pinch the area around the splinter to make it poke up.

4 If the splinter is under the skin, use a sterilized needle, manicure scissors or nail clippers to cut a tiny opening in the skin.

5 Grasp the tip of the splinter with the tweezers. Slowly pull it out.

6 Squeeze the area to encourage blood, which helps to wash out any germs.

7 Wash the area with soap and water.

8 If you develop redness, inflammation, a fever or nausea, visit your doctor. A remnant of the splinter may be causing infection.

What You'll Need

- Soap
- Fine-tip tweezers
- Needle, manicure scissors or nail clippers

Tips

If it's difficult to see the splinter, ask a friend to hold a magnifying glass over the area while you work.

To protect yourself from splinters, wear work gloves when doing landscaping, construction or rough work.

43 Soothe a Sunburn

Ouch! You fell asleep on the beach and now you're in some serious pain. The sun bakes your skin just as a fire does, and when you expose your skin for too long, it will burn. Here's how to soothe those lobster-red body parts.

Steps

1 Bathe or shower in cool water to bring down your overall body temperature. Soak for 10 to 15 minutes.

2 Peel the skin from an aloe vera leaf and gently lay on the burn. Or, apply 100 percent aloe vera gel to soothe the pain and promote healing.

3 Aspirin, ibuprofen or acetaminophen can ease the stinging and swelling somewhat (see Warning).

4 If your legs or arms are sunburned, keep them elevated.

5 If your eyelids are burned, place chilled, damp tea bags over them to soothe them.

6 Sleep in loose-fitting pajamas or nothing to reduce pain.

7 Stay out of the sun for several days while your skin heals, or at least keep sunburned body parts covered up with a hat and protective clothing.

8 If you experience blistering, fever, chills or weakness as a result of your sunburn, contact your doctor. Do not pop the blisters or apply lotions or gels to them.

9 In the future, follow the "slip, slop, slap" rule: Slip on a long-sleeved shirt, slop on some broad-spectrum sunscreen (15 SPF or higher), and slap on a hat and sunglasses whenever you're going outside, especially between 10 a.m. and 4 p.m., when the sun's strongest. Use 25 SPF or higher if you'll be exposed for an extended period or are fair-skinned. Reapply sunscreen liberally every 1 to 2 hours (more frequently if you are swimming or sweating).

What You'll Need

- Aloe vera plant or gel
- Aspirin, ibuprofen or acetaminophen
- Tea bags
- Loose-fitting pajamas
- Hat and protective clothing

Tip

Be sparing in the application of lotions, gels or oils on a sunburn. They can seal the heat into the skin and prevent it from cooling. Never put butter on a burn.

Warning

Never give aspirin to children.

Visit a dermatologist if you develop any odd skin conditions after spending time in the sun. It might be an early sign of skin cancer.

Avoid sunburn sprays containing benzocaine, which irritates some skin types.

44 Fix a Sticky Social Situation

Awkward social situations are an excruciating yet inevitable part of our human existence.
Here's how to make them as painless as possible.

PROBLEM	SOLUTIONS
You receive an invitation you don't want to accept	• Decline with a vague yet believable excuse: "Paul and I regretfully decline your kind invitation. We have a family obligation that evening."
You forget someone's name	• Try to distract him or her by asking a friendly question: "Hi there! How's the new truck?" • If you cannot hide the fact that you've forgotten, apologize and ask. It happens to the best of us.
Someone calls you by the wrong name	• Correct him or her politely and make light of it: "It's actually Sharon, but people call me Shannon so often that I respond to both."
You mistakenly think someone is pregnant	• There is no way you can undo this insult. Never, ever ask a woman if she is pregnant. If you suspect it, ask her a leading question such as: "Is there any exciting news in your life?"
You put your foot in your mouth	• Apologize sincerely, then drop the subject. If you attempt to explain yourself, you risk creating further insult. If you are lucky, others will forgive and forget.
You're under- or overdressed	• Improvise if possible. Borrow a blazer to dress up your attire; wear a sweater to hide your fancy dress. • If improvisation is out of the question, wear your outfit with aplomb. There is no greater accoutrement than self-confidence.
You're asked to guess someone's age	• Reply with a vague yet witty response: "Oh, the last time I guessed someone's age, I had a martini poured in my face!" • If you can't evade the question, subtract five years from your best estimate.
You're asked your own age	• This is a rude question, and you needn't answer it. Some suggestions: "Old enough to know better." "Young enough to get that question." "Ageless, and you?"
You run into an ex with your spouse	• Greet your ex politely, introduce that person to your spouse and ask about his or her well-being. Then excuse yourself promptly. Out of sensitivity to your spouse, do not ask about your ex's love life or compliment his or her appearance.

PROBLEM	SOLUTIONS
You're invited to more than one party	• Accept the invitation that you received first unless the other invitation involves a major event for a family member or close friend.
	• If invitations are received within the same time frame, accept the one that is most appealing. Respond to both invitations promptly.
You encounter someone you dislike at a party	• Greet him or her politely, then gracefully excuse yourself from further conversation. A party is not the place to settle old scores.
You leave a party early	• Thank the host and give an excuse for your departure. Be discreet to avoid sending out a signal that the party is over.
You can't get a gabber off the phone	• Apologize and give an excuse that has the undertone of urgency: "I'm sorry. I need to pull the roast from the oven before it burns."
A friend asks for an honest opinion	• Assess the situation. If your opinion might help the friend through troubled waters, share it in private.
	• If it will hurt the friend's feelings, a white lie is appropriate. Keep it general: "You look lovely."
A co-worker has a crush on you	• Drop references to a "special someone" in your life, whether real or not.
	• If asked on a date, be polite yet firm in your refusal, unless, of course, you are interested.
You have a crush on a co-worker	• If the person reports to you, do not pursue it. You risk facing sexual-harassment charges.
	• Otherwise, drop subtle hints to ascertain whether your interest is reciprocated. If the vibes say yes, ask him or her out, but be prepared to accept rejection.
A colleague has an odor problem	• Ask a close friend of the co-worker or a manager to address the problem. Some thoughtful tips from a friend or manager might help.
Colleagues expect you to join in scuttlebutt	• Decline to participate; use humor to keep the mood light. Eventually colleagues will stop turning to you for a scoop if you never provide any.

45 Fix a Bad Reputation

Perhaps the phrase conjures up visions of dueling at dawn, but the fact remains that a bad reputation is not to be taken lightly. At work, it can cost you business opportunities, job promotions and customer loyalty. It can hurt your private life as well. Here's how to mend a damaged reputation.

Steps

In your professional life

1 Assess the substance of the bad reputation. Is there any truth to it? Or are you the victim of jealousy or whiners?

2 Seek a second or third opinion from trusted colleagues to determine if there is any validity to your bad reputation.

3 Reconsider your managerial style if you are in a position of leadership. Could you make subtle changes? Are you a good communicator and listener? Do you give clear instructions? Are raises overdue?

4 If you determine that you need to improve a personal attribute, make a commitment to yourself to change your ways.

5 Apologize to employees, clients or customers if you realize that your behavior or words have hurt your professional relationship, and let them know you will work hard to improve the situation.

6 Tell those around you that you're trying to improve. Others will be impressed if you can admit to your own flaws, and they might have some good pointers.

7 Perform one act every single day that counteracts your bad reputation.

8 If the bad reputation is not your fault, find out where it originates. Mention the rumors in a direct but nonconfrontational way: "Burt, I heard that some folks think I am having an affair with Helen in graphics. I'm sure you know there's no truth to the matter." Most gossipmongers will clam up if confronted.

In your private life

1 Examine the way you treat others. Is there any truth to the bad reputation?

2 Seek a second opinion from your spouse, a trusted friend or a therapist. Ask if they have recommendations and listen carefully to their answers.

Tips

Some personal attributes that might give you a bad reputation include greediness, selfishness, cruelty, thoughtlessness, flakiness, unfaithfulness, poor hygiene, sloppiness and laziness.

Some qualities to aspire to are excellent listening skills, the ability to laugh at your flaws, kindness, good manners, cleanliness, discipline, loyalty and honesty.

Take a genuine approach to your pursuit of self-improvement. Mend your ways because it's the right thing to do, not because you are obsessed with your image.

3 If you determine that you need to improve a personal attribute, make a commitment to yourself to change your ways.

4 Apologize to loved ones whom you have hurt and let them know you will work hard to improve the relationship.

5 Tell others that you're trying to improve. They can hold you to your commitment even when you lapse.

6 Perform one act every single day that counteracts your bad reputation.

7 If you are the victim of malicious gossip, address its source. Be firm yet nonconfrontational. The gossiper is probably jealous, and if you respond with anger or emotion, it will delight him or her no end.

46 Clean Lipstick From a Collar

Get that smear of lipstick off your collar before you end up singing the Connie Francis blues. These tricks will help you erase lipstick reminders.

Steps

1 Treat stains as soon as possible. If you can't launder the garment right away, blot the stain with water to keep it from setting.

2 Consult the cleaning instructions on the clothing care label. If the item is dry-clean only, bring it to a professional dry cleaner.

3 If the item is washable, cover the stain with baking soda and moisten it with a damp sponge or brush. Let it sit for 5 minutes.

4 Next, apply prewash stain remover to the lipstick and allow it to soak according to the instructions. If the stain is set in or heavy, allow the stain remover to soak in overnight.

5 Wash the item according to the label's instructions. Repeat if the stain remains.

6 Air-dry the item. Do not put it in the dryer if a remnant of the stain remains, because heat will set the stain.

7 Bring the garment to a professional dry cleaner if you can't remove the stain.

What You'll Need

- Baking soda
- Sponge or brush
- Prewash stain remover
- Laundry detergent

Tip

If you don't have baking soda in your cupboard, apply denatured alcohol or ammonia to the stain, or use a nongel toothpaste containing baking soda.

47 Fix a Bad Relationship

Poor communication often derails the most important relationships in a person's life. The ability to listen is the best tool you can bring to any reconciliation efforts. This checklist of other pointers can help you patch things up with the parties indicated.

Steps

Spouse

1 Remember that love is a verb. Choose to love your spouse for better or for worse.

2 Communicate even if it results in an argument. Choose a private place and a time when you won't be interrupted.

3 Outlaw any name calling, references to past history, and cheap shots during the argument. Stick to the issue at hand.

4 Listen to your spouse attentively without interruption. Pay attention to the emotions that lie behind the words and body language. Do not try to change those feelings or offer solutions; just validate them by listening.

5 Don't go to bed angry at each other. Call a truce before bedtime. Most things look better in the morning.

6 Take action. Do something every day that shows your love for your spouse even if you don't feel love. Love has a funny way of creeping back into the picture.

7 Remember that the bond of love grows even stronger after you've survived difficult times.

Teenage child

1 Set good examples through your actions. Listen attentively and let your teen know your love is unconditional. Resist complaining, nagging or criticizing.

2 Give clear guidelines. Explain the reasons behind them and the consequences of failure to abide by them.

3 If your teen disobeys the guidelines, reaffirm the reasons behind the guidelines and hold him or her responsible for the consequences.

4 Choose your battles carefully. Is blue hair really worth arguing about? Also, make sure to notice and affirm positive behavior in your teen.

5 Communicate openly about the many peer-related challenges, including alcohol, drugs, smoking and sex.

6 Encourage your teen to get a part-time job to learn financial responsibility.

7 Give your teen space and time to figure things out. Allow him or her to make mistakes. It's part of the learning process.

Tips

If you find yourself being judgmental toward the other person, you are not on a road to reconciliation. Adopt an attitude of understanding, instead of judging, if you truly want to improve your relationship.

Listen carefully to the body language and emotions of the other person. The real reason for his or her distress may be too difficult to put into words. If you listen only to the spoken words, you'll miss the underlying problem.

Be careful not to be preoccupied with solving the other person's dilemma or with dispensing unsolicited advice. Sometimes a person just needs an empathetic listener, not a problem solver.

In-laws

1 Reach an agreement with your spouse that you are going to work on repairing your in-law relationship as a united couple.

2 Make a list of past events that have injured the relationship. Forgive and forget, but also learn from the events.

3 Set clear boundaries as a couple about what is acceptable behavior for your in-laws. Communicate these boundaries to your in-laws when necessary.

4 Take time to get to know your in-laws. With knowledge comes greater understanding of these people and their behavior.

5 Be polite and treat your in-laws with dignity and respect even if you don't like them.

6 Learn to accept advice from your in-laws graciously even if you have no intention of following it: "Thank you for your thoughtful suggestion."

7 Always give your in-laws another chance. Set new limits if necessary after a negative encounter, but keep the bond alive.

Troublesome neighbor

1 Explain to the neighbor in person how he or she is causing a problem. If you feel concerned for your safety, bring a friend and have the encounter in an area you consider safe.

2 Suggest several solutions that take both your needs and your neighbor's into account.

3 Listen attentively to your neighbor's version of events. If the neighbor becomes argumentative or threatening, end the encounter immediately. Do not engage your neighbor in an argument. Report any threats of bodily harm to the police.

4 After you have listened to your neighbor, confirm that your neighbor agrees to one of the solutions. Be sure to thank him or her for cooperating.

5 If the neighbor neglects your request, decide whether you can tolerate rude behavior to keep peace in the neighborhood.

6 If you can't tolerate it, contact the landlord, neighborhood-watch representative or cooperative board. Call the police or city hall as a last resort.

Warning

Chronic or explosive arguments with loved ones may be a sign of anger-management problems or substance abuse. Seek appropriate therapy if necessary.

Physical contact, sexual assault or demeaning attacks during an argument are inexcusable. Seek help from a domestic abuse shelter or from law enforcement if you are a victim of physical, sexual or mental abuse.

Harboring anger, desires for revenge or hatred against another person will eat away at your own well-being. Find it in yourself to forgive others.

48 Salvage a Bad Date

An occasional bad date is par for the course in the world of dating. Assess the situation before you write off this person forever. Is your date being rude? Or do you have nothing in common? Is excessive nervousness the problem? Here are some guidelines.

Steps

During the date

1 Meet for coffee or lunch if you're apprehensive about a date. It's easier to suffer through a quick meal than it is to suffer through an evening date that lasts several hours.

2 If your date is being rude, obnoxious or abusive, leave. You don't have to give this person the time of day.

3 If you and your date have nothing in common, endure the date but end it as soon as it is polite to do so. You needn't extend the date with after-dinner drinks if that was not in the original plan.

4 If the two of you are merely nervous, muddle through the nervousness. Some couples claim their first date was awful because they were both addled with nervousness.

5 If you inadvertently insult your date, apologize and drop the subject. Depending on the severity of your insult, your date might forgive and forget. If not, the relationship was probably doomed anyway.

6 Treat the other person with dignity. Conversely, demand the same from your date. Never do anything that makes you feel uncomfortable in an effort to impress your date.

The morning after

1 Avoid beating yourself up if a date went wrong. File it away in your mind as a life experience and congratulate yourself for braving the dating circuit.

2 Call up a friend so you can share the excruciating details of the date and hopefully find some humor in it.

3 Do something fun to forget about the date. Jog, shoot hoops, eat ice cream or watch a movie.

4 Be honest yet kind if the person calls you with an invitation for a second date and you aren't interested: "I enjoyed our evening together, but I don't think we are the right fit."

5 If you like the person despite the disaster date, give him or her a second chance. Laughing about the awkwardness of the first date might help both of you relax and get to know each other.

Tip

A first date is an opportunity for two people to get acquainted. Plan an activity that reveals an aspect of your character and helps you relax. Go to a baseball game, visit an art exhibit, or meet for knishes at your favorite knish shop.

Warning

Avoid situations during a first date that could lead to date rape. Meet in public areas and do not get drunk. Firmly but politely decline an invitation to go into your date's apartment.

Avoid sharing personal information, such as your home address and phone number, until you get to know the person better and feel comfortable sharing this information. Opt for communicating via e-mail instead.

49 Get Rid of a Hangover

The party's over and now you're in a regrettable state—queasy, headachy and miserable. Alcohol dehydrates your body, so a hangover is actually a form of mild dehydration.

Steps

1 To rehydrate your body, drink water like the fish you were the night before.

2 Eat mild foods, since your stomach right now is quite sensitive. Bananas, rice, applesauce and toast or soda crackers (BRAT) are all good options.

3 Check the label before you take a pain reliever to reduce any hangover-induced aches. Some pain relievers, including aceta-minophen, aspirin and naproxen sodium, should not be used when alcohol is still in your system.

4 Rest to allow your body to recover from your revelry.

5 If alcohol has affected your relationship with others, your per-formance at work or your health, you are exhibiting signs of alcoholism. Visit www.alcoholics-anonymous.org to learn more.

What You'll Need

- Mild foods

Tips

Drink lots of water and eat some bread or crackers before going to sleep if you expect to have a hangover in the morning. It may help.

Practice moderation. It's not healthy to drink to the point of dehydrating your body.

50 Stop Hiccups

Hiccups result from involuntary spasms of the diaphragm. Many people get them after meals, and they can go on for hours if not brought to a halt. These tricks can bring a case of the hiccups to a welcome end. Success varies depending on the individual's response and the sev-erity of the hiccups. Find the technique that works best for you and stick with it.

Steps

1 Hold your breath for 30 seconds and then release it.

2 Breathe into a paper bag five times in a row.

3 Sip 10 consecutive gulps slowly from a glass of water without stopping to take a breath.

4 Immerse your face in ice-cold water for 30 seconds.

5 Swallow a teaspoon of dry white granulated sugar.

6 If you began hiccuping after taking a medication, seek medical help. Also see a doctor if the hiccups don't stop after 24 hours (3 hours for young children) of if they are extremely painful.

What You'll Need

- Paper bag
- Granulated sugar

51 Mend a Broken Heart

People may say no one ever died of a broken heart, but when you're suffering from one, it sure doesn't feel that way—at least initially. These suggestions may help you navigate the painfully troubled waters of a relationship that has ended.

TIME FRAME	WHAT TO DO
Day 1	● Breathe. All you can do is survive this first and difficult day. Take one day at a time. ● Give yourself permission to mourn. Call in sick at work, sleep all day, eat too much ice cream, sob. ● Congratulate yourself for being human: It is only when you open yourself to love that your heart can break. ● Develop and repeat a helpful mantra to get you through the initial shock and pain, such as "This too shall pass" or "I will survive."
Day 2	● Reach out to a close friend or family member. It helps to share your thoughts with others. ● Watch a movie to distract yourself. Choose a comedy that has cheered you up in the past. Or watch a movie that's guaranteed to make you sob—it may surprise you how good that feels.
Week 1	● Force yourself to go out even if you are feeling despondent. Take yourself out for a cup of coffee or go on a long walk. ● Express your emotions in a way that comes naturally. Write in a journal, paint, sculpt or play music. ● Do daily cardiovascular exercise—the endorphins will give your spirits an immediate lift. ● Resist the urge to call your ex. Instead, write a letter. Don't mail it. ● Go out of town for the weekend to distance yourself from the temptation to call your ex. Visit an old friend or go back home to your roots. A change of environment does wonders for the spirit. ● Put everything that reminds you of your ex in a box and seal it. Throw it away, donate it to charity or ask a friend to hold on to it indefinitely.
Week 2	● Surround yourself with friends. This may mean reaching out to people you fell out of touch with during the relationship. ● Make lists to help you regain your confidence and identity: a list of your friends, of things you like, of what you want to accomplish in the next decade. ● Spoil yourself: Get a new hairstyle, have a spa day or go shopping. ● Resist the urge to call your ex.

TIME FRAME	WHAT TO DO
Week 3	• Assess the experience. Have you learned anything about yourself? Does the experience make you more empathetic to others who've suffered a hardship?
	• Begin an activity that will fill your time, distract your mind and rebuild your confidence. Train for a marathon, take up yoga or learn a new language.
	• Resist the urge to call your ex.
	• Volunteer your time at a local homeless shelter, soup kitchen or tutoring center. It will take your mind off your own woes and keep your suffering in perspective.
Week 4	• Continue regular socializing and exercising. While socializing, though, make sure you don't depend on alcohol or drugs to dull the pain.
	• Call your ex if you feel it would be helpful. Resist if you merely want to say hurtful things.
	• Consider dating other people, but be wary of rebound relationships.
	• Understand that you will need to experience and process sadness, anger, guilt and fear to fully heal. Burying or ignoring these emotions will thwart the healing process. Write, cry, share the feelings with friends.
Months 3 to 6	• Force yourself to go on dates. You'll be surprised to discover that your heart can still flutter over someone. It's part of the healing process.
	• Consult a psychiatrist if you are experiencing symptoms of depression, such as lack of appetite, insomnia or too much sleeping, low self-esteem, and an inability to concentrate or carry out routine tasks. Ask a friend or physician to recommend one who is experienced in treating depression.
	• Remember that healing is a process that takes time. Expect waves of sadness, anger, guilt or fear even after you think you are over it. Give your heart time to heal.
One year and beyond	• Compartmentalize the experience in your memory: "My heart was broken once. It really hurt and I'm glad it's over."
	• Reach out to your ex if you want to re-establish a friendship. Do not harbor secret ambitions of winning him or her back. You'll only set yourself up for another heartbreak.

52 Mend a Family Feud

While money or differing lifestyles or priorities might be the impetus behind a family feud, at the root of the problem is a failure to communicate. Try these steps to mend a rift.

Steps

Introspection

1 Allow yourself time and space to calm down if you had a recent argument and you're full of anger.

2 Swallow your pride and decide that you definitely want to mend the relationship. Think about the undesirable outcomes if you do not mend it.

3 Examine your own role in the feud. Did you do or say things because you felt hurt and wanted to lash back?

4 Try to understand the other person and why he or she has acted in a hurtful way. Fight the urge to judge the person.

5 Forgive and forget. Holding a grudge will only eat you up inside.

Face-to-face discussion

1 Choose a private location to talk to the relative, preferably in person. The dinner table is not the place to discuss family feuds.

2 Apologize for anything you did that caused this person harm. Take responsibility for your actions. Do not assign blame to the other person.

3 Explain why the relationship is important and affirm your love for the other person.

4 Listen to his or her response. Do your best to understand the person's position on the matter as you listen.

5 If the person says things you find hurtful, resist reacting with anger. Say instead, "I'm sorry you feel that way."

Follow-up

1 Give your relative time and space to come around. This is a good opportunity for you to work on attaining the virtue of patience.

2 Let your actions and words demonstrate the sincerity of your peace offering. Refuse to speak poorly of them and continue to reach out.

3 Forgive and forget, but don't be a fool. If a relative never repays loans, don't lend him or her money. If a relative repeatedly insults you, contact him or her by mail, not in person or by phone.

4 If your efforts do not work and the feud threatens to break up your immediate family, seek help from a professional family counselor.

Tips

Clear, detailed wills and careful estate planning can minimize potential feuds in the aftermath of a family patriarch's or matriarch's death.

If a family member has abused you physically, emotionally or sexually, you do not need to mend relations with that person.

Warning

Keep money or business separate from family as much as possible. If you decide to loan money to a family member, either make it a legally binding contract or don't expect payment in the future.

53 Treat a Small Cut or Scrape

However small the "owie," it can still hurt quite a lot (like the notoriously painful paper cut), and it requires your attention to avoid any risk of infection. When you've got a small cut or light abrasion, follow the steps below to make it feel—and heal—better. Seek medical help if the cut is bleeding profusely, is very deep, involves the eye area or causes concern.

Steps

1 Have the person sit down if he or she is feeling weak.

2 Make sure the victim has had a tetanus shot within the last 10 years, especially if the wound is deep, dirty, involves an animal bite or is a puncture wound.

3 Before you touch the area, wash your hands with soap and water.

4 Apply light pressure to the area with sterile gauze to encourage blotting. It takes 5 to 8 minutes for bleeding to stop on a minor cut or abrasion.

5 Clean the area with soap and water. Remove any dirt or debris.

6 Allow the wound to air-dry before you apply a sterile adhesive bandage.

7 Use butterfly bandages or narrow adhesive strips on small cuts, especially on the face. These bandages pull the skin together to promote healing and minimize scars.

8 If the cut or scratch is on a knee, elbow or other joint, use an adhesive bandage designed to be flexible so that it can withstand lots of movement. This is especially useful for athletes, manual laborers and rambunctious children.

9 Replace the bandage every one to two days or after a bath or shower.

10 See a physician if the cut or scrape becomes swollen or irritated, or if the skin around it turns warm or red. The wound may be infected.

What You'll Need

- Soap
- Sterile gauze
- Adhesive bandages
- Butterfly bandages

Tips

Resist the urge to pick at the scab, which can lead to scarring and infection.

If the cut is on a prominent location on the face and you are worried about long-term scarring, visit a certified plastic surgeon. A plastic surgeon can use multiple, tiny sutures to reduce or eliminate scarring.

54 Fix Hair Disasters

A stylish new hairdo can do wonders for one's self-esteem. Conversely, a poorly shorn or styled head can make even confident, self-assured people feel sheepish. While it might take Sigmund Freud to explain the reasons for this, these remedies may restore your lovely locks—and perhaps your self-esteem.

PROBLEM	SOLUTIONS
Bad haircut	• Do not attempt to fix it yourself. • Return to the salon or barbershop and demand a new haircut by a different stylist or barber free of charge. • Or go to a reputable salon, explain your dilemma and request a remedial haircut. • Or consider using a wig, hair extensions or hair additions while you wait for the haircut to grow out.
Bad hair day	• Wet down hair with warm water, add styling mousse or gel, then restyle. • If restyling is not an option, cover hair with a hat or scarf. • Opt for the slicked-back look if a hat or scarf is unsuitable. Wet hair, add gel or mousse, pull hair into a ponytail. Allow to air-dry.
Bad dye job	• If hair is undercolored because you panicked and rinsed too early, reapply dye and leave on for time required minus time you already had it on. • If you chose the wrong color or overcolored your hair, consider using a color-removal product, available at salons and beauty supply stores. • Understand that hair-coloring professionals recommend visiting a reputable salon that specializes in hair coloring to correct bad dye jobs.
Botched perm	• If your home perm did not take, wait three days before you visit a salon to have a professional stylist perm your hair. • If the perm is overdone, apply a deep conditioner to hair from scalp to the ends. Leave it on for 15 minutes. Rinse and set hair in large curlers. If that doesn't fix it, have a professional stylist relax your overpermed hair.
Chlorine-green hair	• Use a hair product designed to remove green from hair, available at salons, beauty supply stores and drugstores. • For swimming, apply leave-in conditioner to hair and wear a swim cap to prevent further greening. • Shampoo and rinse hair immediately after swimming. • Monitor and reduce copper levels in pool water, which cause greening. • If hair is dyed or permed and turns green, visit a reputable salon to have it corrected.

PROBLEM	SOLUTIONS
Dandruff	• Wash hair with an over-the-counter shampoo designed to fight dandruff. Switch brands if shampoo becomes ineffective after several weeks of use. • Consult a dermatologist in extreme cases.
Gum in hair	• Rub peanut butter into hair and around gum and slowly work gum out of hair. Oil counters gum's stickiness. Shampoo thoroughly afterward. Mayonnaise and butter also work, but not as well as peanut butter.
Hair loss	• Understand that there is little one can do to prevent hair loss if it's hereditary. • Use hair products for sensitive hair to avoid unnecessary wear and tear. • Visit a dermatologist to learn about cosmetic options, including toupees, weaves and transplants. • Remember that stress, lack of protein, medication, hormones, pregnancy, disease and poor hair hygiene contribute to hair loss. • Be wary of products claiming to stop hair loss; results vary widely. • Sudden, smooth, round bald spots on scalp or beard are called alopecia areata. Wait for them to disappear (usually 6 to 12 months) or visit a dermatologist for treatment.
Head lice	• Cover your work area with towels to prevent contamination of upholstery or carpets. • Working under bright light, partition hair into sections and comb through hair with a fine-tooth comb (ideally a lice comb, available at drugstores). Remove lice (reddish-brown) and nits (white or clear) as you comb. Use mayonnaise to smother lice and nits while you comb. Repeat combings for two weeks. • Boil the comb after you use it to sanitize it for future use. • Wash towels, sheets, pillowcases, hats and other contaminated clothing in the washer with hot water. Use a hot setting to dry the items in the dryer. Vacuum contaminated fabric, upholstery or carpeting. • Use an anti-lice shampoo if you prefer, but remember that these products contain pesticides. Consult your doctor before using anti-lice products if you are pregnant, allergic or have pre-existing medical conditions. Avoid treatments containing lindane, which has caused neurological damage in children.

55 Treat a Bleeding Nose

Though they're not usually serious, nosebleeds can be very alarming. Most nosebleeds occur when blood vessels in the nasal passage rupture. Because children's nasal blood vessels are more delicate, they are more susceptible to nosebleeds than adults are. Help your little patient remain calm by using a relaxed, soothing approach. Here's how to stop the flow.

Steps

1 Have the person with the nosebleed sit down and lean forward so the blood does not flow down the respiratory passage.

2 Press a tissue or cold compress against the nostrils below the bone to encourage clotting.

3 Have the person with the nosebleed keep his or her nostrils pinched together for 15 minutes without letting go.

4 Replace the tissue or compress with a new one if it becomes soaked with blood.

5 Leave a bowl next to the person so that he or she can spit out any blood that drips down the throat.

6 Remove the tissue or compress slowly. If bleeding persists, continue pinching the nose for another 5 minutes.

7 After bleeding stops, wash away any blood with warm water. Apply a small amount of petroleum jelly inside the nostrils to moisturize the area.

8 Make sure the person does not sniff or blow the nose for several hours afterward, as this could cause another nosebleed.

9 If the nosebleed originates in the back of the nose and does not respond to treatment, seek medical attention. This type of nosebleed, called a "posterior" nosebleed, is common in older people and potentially very serious.

10 Visit a doctor or an emergency room immediately if bleeding does not stop or if the patient is weak, pale or experiencing an elevated heart rate. Keep the patient leaning forward with the nose pinched on the way to the doctor's office or hospital.

What You'll Need

- Tissue or cold compress
- Bowl
- Petroleum jelly

Tips

An ice pack across the bridge of the nose can restrict blood vessels and aid clotting.

Children who are prone to getting nosebleeds typically outgrow this tendency. In the meantime, make sure they keep their fingers or any other objects out of the nose, to prevent scratching and rupturing blood vessels.

Understand that dry air, irritation due to a cold or sinus problems, or extreme stress can cause a bloody nose.

56 Beat the Monday Morning Blues

There's actually a scientific explanation behind those dreaded Monday morning blues. Our internal clocks naturally operate on a day that is longer than 24 hours. By the time Monday rolls around each week, we've built up a sleep deficit of at least an hour. Of course, the weekend revelries and facing another work week don't help matters. Here are some tips to make Monday mornings a little easier.

Steps

1 If you can, sleep in an extra hour on Monday mornings. Going to bed early on Sunday night doesn't always help because most people will remain awake until their usual bedtime.

2 If you can't sleep in by a full hour (and most of us can't), take action Sunday night to shorten your morning preparation time so that you can set the alarm for 15 minutes later than usual. Wash your hair, pack lunches, lay out your outfit or pack your briefcase on Sunday night.

3 Hop out of bed the moment you wake up on Monday morning. Lingering in that downy comforter will only draw out the agony.

4 End your shower with a jolt of cold water to tear yourself out of your grogginess. Or exercise in the morning to get your blood pumping and to release those feel-good endorphins.

5 Get out in the sunlight. Bright light tells your body that it is indeed the morning and helps reset your internal clock.

6 Drink coffee or another caffeine beverage. Although it's not healthy to drink caffeine to the point of addiction, caffeine, when used in moderation, can give your Monday mornings that much-needed oomph and alertness.

7 Anticipate your Monday morning on Friday afternoon. Fight the temptation to race away from a messy desk. Clean up your desk and leave yourself a to-do list to make Monday morning a little more tolerable.

Tips

Take comfort in knowing that you are not alone in feeling miserable on Monday morning. There are millions of folks out there feeling the same way.

Warning

If you are constantly feeling blue or depressed, seek psychiatric help. Ask your family doctor or a close friend to recommend a psychiatrist who is experienced in handling depression. Some universities offer psychiatric services at a reduced cost as a way to train psychiatric students and interns.

57 Get Out of a Fix

Preparation and prevention are the best strategies for a potentially threatening situation. File away the following suggestions for unforeseen emergencies. Keep in mind that as a general rule of thumb, calmness and clear thinking are your best allies in a difficult fix.

PROBLEM	SOLUTIONS
Lost in the wilderness	• Prepare beforehand. Bring extra food, water and clothing; a compass and a topographical map; and a flashlight, whistle, pocket knife, small mirror, first-aid kit and waterproof matches.
	• Give someone your itinerary before you depart.
	• Stay put as soon as you realize you're lost. That will make it easier for search-and-rescue teams to find you.
	• Stay calm and develop a plan to keep yourself sheltered and hydrated.
	• Protect yourself from the elements. Dehydration and hypothermia are the leading causes of death in the wilderness. Rest in the shade if it's extremely hot. Wear a hat, gloves and warm clothing in the cold. Avoid excess sweating.
	• Find or build a shelter before nightfall. Sleep in an enclosed area (a tree trunk or cave) to retain body heat. Build a shelter with branches and logs or build a snow cave. Hang brightly colored gear above the shelter to alert searchers.
	• Signal for help. Any signal in threes (whistles, shouts, mirror reflections, smoke) indicates distress. Make a large "X" or "SOS" in a clearing or on a hill to signal aircraft. Use rocks, branches or brightly colored gear.
Hostile dog	• Never approach a dog that's showing signs of aggression: growling, barking, ears erect or flattened, raised fur, erect tail or snarling with teeth bared. Also, do not approach a dog that is confined or tied up even if he looks friendly.
	• Do not approach a dog that is sleeping or unaware of your presence. If you surprise or spook a dog, he may respond hostilely.
	• If a dog is acting hostile, walk away slowly and avoid eye contact. Making eye contact with a dog is considered aggressive behavior. Avoid sudden movement. If you are running or jogging, stop and walk away slowly.
	• If the dog lurches toward you, stand firm and say "No" or "Stay" in a low voice. If he attacks, adopt a protective stance. Put one leg in front of the other for maximum stability and cover your neck with your arm.
	• Kick or punch the dog in the eyes, nose, rib cage or groin. Or yank and twist his ears. If you have a purse or backpack, stick it in his mouth.
	• If you are knocked to the ground, curl up in a fetal position. Protect your face, ears and neck with your arms.
	• If a dog bites you, visit a doctor and get a rabies test.

PROBLEM	SOLUTIONS
Car breakdown or accident	• Be prepared. Carry flares, a triangular reflector, fire extinguisher, first-aid kit, flashlight, blankets, water, tire gauge, tire jack and jumper cables in your car.
	• Pull far off onto a shoulder for safety or exit a freeway if possible. If involved in an accident, wave the other driver over to a safe spot. If you have a flat tire, drive to a safe shoulder even if it means ruining the wheel rims. Safety is your first priority.
	• If the car won't move, remain in it unless it's safer to evacuate. Never exit a vehicle at a busy intersection or on a highway.
	• Turn on your hazard lights. Put up a triangular reflector or flares to alert other drivers.
	• Call police or roadside assistance using a cell phone or an emergency roadside phone. Use a road marker to give your precise location. Or, if you have the necessary tools and knowledge, repair your vehicle. Allow time for the engine to cool down if it has become overheated.
	• If you were involved in an accident, do not attempt to remove a person from a vehicle when there may be back, neck or head injuries unless that person is in imminent danger.
	• Exchange insurance information, driver's license information and license plate numbers with anyone else involved in the accident. Get the names and phone numbers of witnesses in case there is a dispute in the future.
Robbery or car-jacking	• If you suspect someone is following you, go to a well-lit, populated area, ideally a police station.
	• If confronted, hand over your wallet or car without a struggle, whether your assailant is armed or not. Do not make any sudden movements and do not try to negotiate with the assailant.
	• Make careful note of the thief's physical appearance, such as hair and eye color, height, weight, build and any distinguishing marks.
	• Memorize the make, model, color and license-plate number of the get-away car. Note the thief's direction of departure.
	• Contact the police immediately to make a report while your memory is still fresh.
	• Call your credit-card companies or banks to report stolen cards.
	• If you are visiting an area with a high crime rate, carry a "dummy" wallet in an outer pocket that you can hand over to a thief. Keep some small bills and useless plastic cards in the dummy wallet.

58 Extract a Broken Key

Faulty manufacturing or wear and tear sometimes causes keys to break off in the lock. If the key is not stuck too far in, you may be able to extract it without calling a locksmith—and without having to wait around for hours on a rainy day.

Steps

1 If a bit of the broken key is sticking out of the lock, grasp it firmly with needle-nose pliers and pull it out.

2 If the broken end of the key is visible but you can't grasp it with pliers, try the following superglue method.

3 Use a toothpick to apply a tiny amount of superglue to the broken edge of the key's head.

4 Insert the head into the lock so the broken edges of the key come together. Be extremely careful not to let the glue come into contact with any part of the lock.

5 Hold the key in place firmly for at least 3 minutes to allow the glue to dry and bond the broken pieces.

6 Carefully extract the key from the lock. Avoid unnecessary twisting or turning because this will strain the superglue bond.

7 Call a locksmith if you can't extract the key with either method. Locksmiths have a key-extractor tool designed specifically for this predicament.

What You'll Need

- Needle-nose pliers
- Superglue
- Toothpick

Tips

If you get superglue on your fingers, see 41 Get Superglue Off Your Skin.

You can use a large or medium clamp instead of needle-nose pliers.

59 Retrieve Keys Locked Inside a Car

Locking yourself out of a car can really put a dent in your day. If you have left a window slightly ajar or if your car is an older model, try these tips to break in and retrieve your keys.

Steps

1 Straighten out a wire hanger. Then bend one end of the hanger to form either a hook or a triangular handle.

2 If the car is an older model, pry open a window by slipping a putty knife between the window and the door.

3 Slip the bent wire hanger through the window opening.

4 Maneuver the hanger down along the window. Attempt to either pull up the door lock or push the lock button, depending on your car's lock style.

5 If your car is a newer model, you'll have to call a locksmith or tow truck. Your attempts to break into it could cause permanent damage.

What You'll Need

- Wire hanger
- Putty knife

Tip

For security reasons, most cars built after the mid-1980s are impervious to wire hangers and even the common slim jim, a long piece of metal used to jimmy car locks.

60 Get Better Seats

Want the best seat in the house? You'll need to invest some time or money, but it'll be worth it when you're sitting front row and center. Follow these tips and tricks to score better seats.

Steps

1 Review a seating map of the venue prior to buying preassigned seating tickets. Some venues have seating maps online. Most city guides and phone directories also contain this information.

2 Donate to the organization or become a sponsor if you are attending a community-based event, such as theater or opera. Donors or sponsors often get priority seating.

3 Buy season tickets every year. Most organizations reward loyal, regular patrons with great seats. Share season tickets with a group of people if you don't want to attend all of the games or performances.

4 Buy the tickets as soon as they become available to ensure that you have a good selection of seats.

5 If the event is general admission, show up as early as possible to nab the best seats.

6 If you expect an event to sell out quickly, form a tag team with a friend. Have one person stand in line at a ticket outlet while the other attempts to buy the tickets online. Or you can use a cell phone to call for tickets while you stand in line.

7 Find out if your company has any spare corporate tickets for the event. Corporations tend to purchase better seats than general admission ones.

8 Use a reputable ticket broker or an Internet auction site for hard-to-come-by seats. Be prepared to pay—these tickets will cost more than their face value.

9 Check with the box office several hours before the event. Sometimes returned or unsold tickets become available at the last minute.

Tips

Once a ticket has been purchased, it may be difficult (if not impossible) to change to a better seat, especially if the venue is sold out. Check with a seating usher or the box office. If a seat is broken or your view of the event is obscured, ask to speak to a manager at the box office and request a remedy.

Radio stations give away excellent concert seats and backstage passes. Listen early in the morning or late at night when the audience is smaller, and use multiple phone lines on automatic redial to increase your chances of winning.

61 Fix a Billing Mistake

With credit fraud running rampant these days, it pays to check your billing statements every month for mistakes or fraudulent charges. If you spot an error on a credit-card bill, follow these procedures, which reflect the guidelines of the Fair Credit Billing Act.

Steps

Credit-card accounts

1 Write to the creditor to inform it of the error within 60 days of receiving the bill. Include your name, address, account number and copies of the relevant sales receipts or documentation.

2 Make a copy of the letter for your files and send it via certified mail to the billing inquiries department. Request a return receipt from the post office so you have proof that the creditor received your letter.

3 Pay the undisputed amount plus the interest for the undisputed amount.

4 Expect the creditor to either fix the error or respond to your letter within 30 days. The creditor must resolve the dispute within two billing cycles (or 90 days) of receiving your letter.

5 Understand that the creditor cannot take legal action against you, threaten your credit rating or report your account as delinquent while the error is in dispute. The creditor can report to credit-rating agencies that you are disputing a bill.

6 If the creditor agrees that it was an error, it must let you know this in writing and reverse the charges related to the error, including any finance charges and late fees.

7 If the creditor decides there was no error, it must inform you of that decision in writing and tell you how much you owe and why. You will be expected to pay any finance charges that accrued during the dispute.

8 If you want to continue disputing the charge, write to the creditor within 10 days. Ask it to send you documentation that supports the decision, including a sales receipt from the original vendor. The creditor is allowed to begin collection procedures. It can report you to credit bureaus, but must indicate that you are disputing the claim and must let you know that it is reporting you.

9 If a creditor fails to abide by the Fair Credit Billing Act, you do not need to repay the disputed amount. You can also sue the creditor for breaking the law.

Other bills

1 Point out the mistake to the billing party—say, a merchant or contractor—and ask the biller to fix it. Supply a copy of a price quote or agreement if one exists.

Tips

The Fair Credit Billing Act does not cover disputes over the price of goods or services unless certain restrictions apply. Consult the Federal Trade Commission.

Save credit-card receipts so you have evidence of the amount you agreed to pay.

When you make a complaint, remind the creditor or vendor that you are a good customer. Many companies will write off disputes under $50 to maintain good customer relations.

For onetime purchases, such as services provided by a carpenter or mechanic, always get an itemized quote in writing before any work starts, to avoid future disputes over the bill.

2 If the biller refuses to fix the error, put the request in writing and mail it to the business's owner or manager via certified mail. Keep a copy for your files.

3 If the biller still refuses to fix the error, file a complaint with the Better Business Bureau (www.bbb.org), which will help you resolve the dispute. Supply documentation of your efforts to fix the error. The Better Business Bureau will not handle price disputes unless they involve misrepresentation by the seller.

4 If the biller belongs to a guild or union, file a complaint with that organization as well. Make sure to include the biller's membership number when you file the complaint.

Warning

If you are a victim of fraud, deception or unfair business practices, file a complaint with the Federal Trade Commission. Call (800) FTC-HELP or go to www.ftc.gov to file a complaint online.

62 Fix a Bad Grade

A bad grade can devastate a student who plans to apply to colleges, scholarships or graduate schools, in terms of both self-esteem and future prospects. Here are some suggestions for dealing with low or failing grades.

Steps

1 If you feel you've received a grade in error, ask the teacher to review it. Or if you misunderstood an assignment, ask if you can redo it. Visit during regular office hours and remain calm while you discuss the matter.

2 If you deserved the poor grade, ask the teacher if you can do an extra-credit assignment to make up for your performance. Ask to retake the test if you have a legitimate excuse, such as an illness or a death in the family.

3 If you are doing poorly in a class, check with the registrar's office to see if you can take the class on a pass or no-pass basis, or drop it entirely, to avoid marring your transcript with a bad grade.

4 Visit the registrar's office if the grade is already on your transcript. Ask if the school has a policy on retaking classes; some schools allow this. The bad grade will remain on your transcript, but your grade point average (GPA) will not include it.

5 Petition the registrar's office if you feel you received a low grade in error or unfairly. Follow the registrar's guidelines when you file the petition.

6 Ask a counselor in the registrar's office if you can do anything else. Some schools will drop the lowest grade on your transcript, although this is highly unusual.

Tips

A bad grade is not the end of the world. Some admissions officers will overlook one bad grade on a transcript if it is clearly an aberration.

Let admissions officers know if extenuating circumstances, such as a death in the family, explain a bad grade.

Hire a tutor if you can't keep up with the rest of the class on a specific subject. The extra help will improve your scores.

63 Fix Bad Credit

Living with debt or bad credit can be very stressful, but help is closer than you realize. Improving your credit rating requires that you take positive action and change your attitude toward money.

Steps

1 Request a copy of your credit report from a credit bureau. If there is an error, write to the bureau and ask it to fix the mistake. It might also help to contact the creditor who reported the error. Some creditors will contact the bureau on your behalf.

2 If the bad marks on your credit report result from outstanding debts, repay them as quickly as possible. Pay off those with the highest interest rates first.

3 If your debts are overwhelming, contact a nonprofit credit-counseling organization to work out a debt-consolidation plan. A counselor will help you consolidate your debts and will contact your debtors on your behalf to reduce or eliminate finance charges. This can reduce your monthly payments by up to 40 percent.

4 Steer clear of any services that offer you credit-repair or debt-consolidation loans. These companies will plunge you further into debt. Be suspicious of any company that advertises aggressively or sends unsolicited mail or e-mail.

5 Close your credit accounts and cut up the cards. Sell valuables or liquidate assets that will help you repay your debts. Buy the bare essentials (food and gas) and use the rest of your earnings to pay off your consolidated debts.

6 Work with your credit counselor to repay all of your debts. Meanwhile, live a life that will help you re-establish good credit. Pay rent and utilities or mortgages promptly, keep the same residence and job, maintain savings and checking accounts, set a budget and stick to it.

7 Once you have repaid your debts, apply for a new credit card to build a good credit history. It might be easier initially to get a department-store or gasoline credit card or one from an employee credit union.

8 Promptly pay off the balance of the credit card monthly to build good credit. Use the card responsibly.

9 If you don't qualify for a regular credit card, apply for a secured one. With a secured credit card, you fund an account up front and then "charge" expenses on it. This card will show up as a credit card on your credit report and, if used responsibly, can help you build a good credit history.

What You'll Need

- Credit report
- Credit counselor
- Debt-consolidation plan
- New credit card

Tips

Get a copy of your credit report once a year even if you think you have good credit. You may find errors that will damage your credit rating.

Filing for bankruptcy is always an option, although your credit history will reflect it for 7 to 10 years, making it very difficult for you to get a car or home loan in the future.

Creditors agree to reduce or eliminate interest rates under a debt-consolidation plan because it saves them the expense of collection efforts and increases their chances of recouping the balance.

Every application you make for a credit card shows up on your credit report, and multiple applications can hurt your credit rating. To avoid this, use an online service that matches you with credit-card companies that will extend credit to you. Search online for "credit card finder" or "credit card search."

64 Recover From Jet Lag

Maybe you pictured taking the Louvre by storm the minute you stepped off that plane in Paris, but though your mind's willing, your body's not. When you travel to a new time zone, your internal clock needs time to adjust. Insomnia, fatigue, lack of appetite at meals and a ravenous appetite at the wrong times are all signs of jet lag.

Steps

1 Drink plenty of water as you travel to your destination and after you arrive. If you are dehydrated, it will take you longer to adapt to the new time zone.

2 Sleep on the plane to be alert and awake if you will be arriving in the morning or early afternoon. Stay awake on the plane to be sleepy upon arrival if you'll reach your destination in the evening or at night.

3 If you arrive at your final destination in the morning, try to stay awake all day. Drink small amounts of coffee, tea or caffeinated soda to wake you up (too much caffeine will further disrupt your sleep cycle). Keep napping to a minimum.

4 If you arrive in the evening, go to sleep at your normal bedtime according to the new time zone. That is, if your bedtime at home is 11 p.m., go to bed at that time in your new location. You may want to ask your doctor to recommend an over-the-counter sleeping aid.

5 If your trip is shorter than 48 hours, schedule meetings according to your home time zone. If the new time zone is 3 hours ahead of your normal time, schedule late morning or afternoon meetings when you will be awake and alert. For example, a 1 p.m. meeting is at 10 a.m. according to your internal clock.

6 Expose yourself to bright light and exercise in the morning in the new time zone. This helps reset your internal clock.

7 Eat small meals throughout the day while you adjust to the new mealtimes. Keep a snack by your bed if your regular dinnertime occurs in the middle of the night in the new time zone.

8 Give your body time to make the switch. If you feel very drowsy during the day, take a nap for up to one hour, but make sure it's before evening. Avoid pushing yourself too hard during the first few days.

Tips

To minimize the effects of jet lag, start adjusting your internal clock before you depart. Go to sleep an hour earlier or later on the days leading up to your departure.

Generally, it is more difficult to adjust to a time zone when you are traveling east, because you must wake up and go to sleep earlier than you're used to.

65 Resuscitate an Unconscious Person

When performing cardiopulmonary resuscitation (CPR), remember your ABCs: Check the *airway* first for obstructions, then check for *breathing* and finally for *circulation*.

Steps

Assisted breathing

1 Tell somebody to call 911. If a neck, head or back injury may be involved, do not move the unconscious person unless he or she is in imminent danger. Wait for medical help to arrive.

2 Use two fingers to check the airway. Clear any visible foreign objects from the mouth. Remove loose dentures or retainers.

3 Lay the victim on a hard, flat surface. Tilt the head back by placing one hand on the forehead and one on the chin. Place your head near the victim's mouth to listen or feel for breathing; watch to see if the chest is rising and falling.

4 If the victim is not breathing, close the nostrils with your thumb and index finger. Keep the victim's head tilted back with your other hand on the chin. Take a deep breath and seal your mouth over the victim's mouth (see A). For small children, cover both mouth and nose. Exhale two full breaths, each lasting 1½ to 2 seconds for an adult or a child over 8; 1 to 1½ seconds for children ages 1 to 8. Remove your mouth between breaths to allow the victim to exhale.

5 Watch the chest to see if it is rising with each breath. If it is not, make sure you've tilted the head back enough. If an object is lodged in the airway, perform the Heimlich maneuver (see 66 Stop Someone From Choking).

6 Check the pulse: Keep one hand on the forehead while you put two fingers (not your thumb) on the neck alongside the Adam's apple (see B). Press down 5 to 10 seconds to feel for a pulse.

7 If you feel a pulse, continue with the breathing: two breaths every 5 seconds for adults and children over 8 (12 breaths per minute),

Tips

Stay calm and act quickly; every second counts. Continue CPR until help arrives.

If the victim vomits, turn the head to the side, use two fingers to clear out the mouth, and continue resuscitation efforts.

If you have assistance, one person can do chest compressions while the other person handles breathing. Alternate five compressions and one breath. The person doing the breathing should check for a pulse between breaths.

Enroll in CPR classes to learn the proper procedures in person, especially if you work with children or the elderly or if you are expecting a baby. Contact a local branch of the American Heart Association or the American Red Cross to find out about courses.

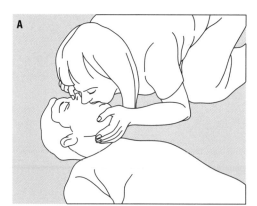

A

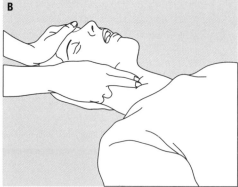

B

or two breaths every 3 seconds for children ages 1 to 8 (20 breaths per minute).

8 Breathe in deeply between each breath. Make sure the victim's chest depresses in exhalation between breaths. Continue until help arrives or until the victim resumes breathing independently.

Chest compressions

1 If you don't feel a pulse, begin chest compressions. Find the breastbone (in the center of the chest where the ribs meet). Measure two fingers' width above the bottom of the breastbone. Put the heel of your hand there. Kneel next to the victim and place your other hand on top of the first one. Interlock your fingers to provide extra force (see C). For children ages 1 to 8, use only one hand for compressions.

2 Keep your elbows locked straight and your shoulders directly above your hands as you gently push onto the breastbone with the heel of your hand (see D). Push the chest down 1½ to 2 inches (4 to 5 cm) in 15 rapid yet smooth thrusts for adults and children over 8; 1 to 1½ inches (2.5 to 4 cm) five times for children ages 1 to 8. Allow the chest to rise between thrusts but do not remove your hand from the chest. Count aloud as you go.

3 Breathe two breaths into the victim's mouth using the process described in "Assisted breathing," opposite page.

4 Alternate 15 chest compressions and two breaths four times for adults and children over 8; five compressions and one breath 20 times for children ages 1 to 8. Then quickly check for a pulse.

5 If you don't feel a pulse, continue rotating between 15 compressions and two breaths—about 80 to 100 compressions per minute—for adults and children over 8; five compressions and one breath for children ages 1 to 8.

6 Check the pulse every minute or so. Continue until the victim has a pulse and resumes breathing or until medical help arrives.

Warning

Do not perform CPR on a victim who is still breathing or chest compressions on a victim who has a pulse. You risk causing greater injury.

A person should receive professional training from a certified instructor prior to administering CPR. These instructions are not intended to replace CPR courses.

Resuscitating an unconscious infant (younger than 12 months) requires quite different techniques. Ask your pediatrician or healthcare provider to recommend a certified infant CPR course.

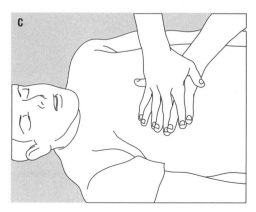

C

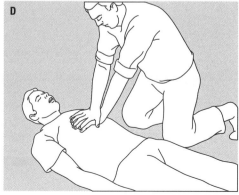

D

66 Stop Someone From Choking

A meal can turn into a sudden emergency when a food particle becomes trapped in a person's airway, making it impossible for him to breathe or speak. Sometimes the individual will put his hand on his throat as a signal to others. Here's how to perform the Heimlich maneuver on an adult or child over one year of age.

Steps

1 Stand behind the victim and wrap your arms around him.

2 Place your fist with the thumb against the victim's upper abdomen, above the navel but below the ribs and breastbone. Clasp the other hand over the fist.

3 Push your fist forcefully into the abdomen with a quick upward and inward thrust (see A). This pushes air from the lungs up into the windpipe to dislodge the foreign object.

4 Repeat several times if necessary.

5 If the victim passes out, hold his tongue with one hand while you reach two fingers from the other hand into the back of the throat. Remove the foreign object if possible. Make sure not to push it farther down into the throat.

6 If you can't remove the object, lay the person on his back and straddle him. Place the heel of your hand on the abdomen with your other hand on top of it. With your elbows locked straight, push forcefully with a quick downward and forward thrust (see B). Attempt to clear the airway with several thrusts.

7 Seek medical attention for the victim after performing the Heimlich maneuver to ensure that it didn't cause any internal damage.

Tips

If the victim is pregnant or obese, place your fist over the breastbone (the bone in the middle of the chest) and perform the upward thrusts.

If you choke while alone, perform the thrusts on yourself. Or you can force the edge of a chair or railing into your abdomen to push air from your lungs into your windpipe.

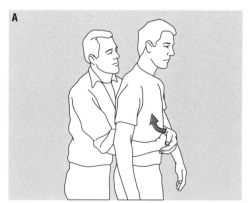

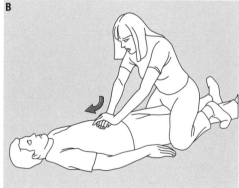

67 Stop an Ant Invasion

On a rainy day, you may see hordes of ants marching into your house. They're searching for dry shelter, food and water, and who can blame them even if they're unwelcome guests? Here's how to ward off these industrious fellows.

Steps

1 Follow the ant line to its source. It might be a window, molding crevice or floor crack.

2 Form a temporary barrier at the source with boric acid or laundry detergent in powder form.

3 Remove any food the ants have attacked and discard it in a garbage can outside your house.

4 If the ants have invaded the kitchen garbage can, bring it outside, hose it down and wash it with dishwashing liquid and water.

5 Put food the ants have not found in zipper-lock plastic bags or in plastic containers with sealable lids. Or put these items in the refrigerator.

6 Remember that ants can penetrate metal-threaded lids on glass jars. Seal these jars in zipper-lock plastic bags. Glass jars are immune from ants only when sealed with a rubber gasket.

7 Seal all food items in your cupboards, especially sugar, honey, maple syrup, grains, cereals, cookies, jams and breads.

8 Once you've secured the food, vacuum up the ant line, along with a bit of cornstarch, which helps suffocate them inside the bag. Or wash them away with dishwashing liquid, water and a rag if you prefer.

9 Use dishwashing liquid and hot water to wash the area around the ant line and erase any scent of the trail.

10 Seal the area where the ants entered; caulk windows and cracks and weather-strip doors (see 114 Fix a Drafty Door). Apply duct tape or petroleum jelly over holes as a temporary fix.

11 Go outside and see if you can determine where the ants entered the house. If they used a branch as a bridge to the house, trim it.

12 Check the area in an hour. If you see any single ants, or scouts, searching the area, squash them. They're scoping out the area for future invasions.

13 If you wish to wipe out the ant population, use ant traps that contain boric acid. The returning ants poison the entire colony. Ants play a beneficial role in gardens, however, so only do this if absolutely necessary.

What You'll Need

- Boric acid or laundry detergent (powder)
- Dishwashing liquid
- Zipper-lock bags
- Plastic storage containers with sealable lids
- Vacuum
- Cornstarch
- Rag
- Caulk, weather-stripping, duct tape or petroleum jelly
- Ant traps

Tips

Some natural ant deterrents include crumbled bay leaves, cinnamon, peppermint leaves and cayenne pepper.

If an indoor plant is infested with ants, bring it outside and flood it several times with a hose to remove them.

Insecticidal sprays kill only the ants you spray—a very small percentage of the colony—and won't prevent future invasions. If you use a spray, keep children and pets away from sprayed areas.

Warning

Carpenter ants, which are large with smooth backs, burrow into wood and cause structural damage. Keep piles of decaying wood away from the house as this attracts them.

68 Stabilize a Christmas Tree

Your kitten may not seem quite so cute after she's managed to topple the tree. Stabilize a Christmas tree before you adorn it with your precious ornaments. People (and pets) have been known to do crazy things in the frenzy of the holidays.

Steps

1 Buy a tree stand that is stable, sturdy and large enough to accommodate the tree you plan to buy.

2 Before you bring the tree inside, measure the height of the room where you plan to display it. Keep the tree soaking in a bucket of water while you measure.

3 Saw off the top or bottom of the tree so it doesn't exceed the height of the room. Remove at least ½ inch (12 mm) from the bottom so the tree can absorb moisture.

4 Bring the tree inside. Have one person hold it upright while the other person screws the tree stand into the trunk.

5 Step back and examine the tree. If it is leaning to one side, adjust and retighten the screws.

6 Grab the trunk and shake it gently to make sure it's screwed in tightly. Tighten if necessary.

7 Anchor the tree into the ceiling if the tree is over 7 feet (2 m) or if a household cat is likely to climb it. Install a hook in the ceiling. Tie the treetop to the hook with twine or wire.

8 If you're using slats of wood instead of a tree stand to hold the base, have one person hold the tree upright while another person slips magazines underneath the uneven slats until the tree is stabilized.

9 Keep the tree away from heat sources (fireplaces, heater vents and televisions) and make sure it does not block any doors or windows you'd use in an emergency.

10 To reduce the chances of a fire, check the water level of the tree stand daily so the tree does not dry out. Never leave a lighted tree unattended.

What You'll Need

- Tree stand
- Tape measure
- Bucket
- Saw
- Ceiling hook
- Twine or wire
- Magazines

Tips

If the tree topples after you have decorated it, have one or more people hold it in place while one person adjusts the screws on the tree stand.

For problems with holiday lights, see 202 Troubleshoot Holiday Lighting.

69 Rescue an Item From the Sink

You gasp in dismay as your ring goes down the drain—but all's not lost. If you have a bucket and channel-type pliers or a wrench, you may be able to rescue precious jewelry or even a contact lens. A sink drain has a U-shaped pipe underneath it, called the P-trap, which captures most items that fall in.

Steps

1 Shut off the faucet immediately so the object does not flow past the P-trap.

2 Look underneath the sink to locate the P-trap. In most cases, the P-trap is easily accessible. If it is not, you might need to call a plumber.

3 Note that some older sinks have a drain plug at the bottom of the P-trap. If your sink has this, you will still need to remove the P-trap to retrieve your item. This drain plug, intended to aid cleaning the P-trap, is probably too small for your dropped item to fit through.

4 Move a bucket beneath the P-trap to capture any debris that flows out after you remove it.

5 Use the channel-type pliers or a wrench to loosen the P-trap's slip nuts (see 184 Clear a Clogged Sink or Tub). Tape the ends of the pliers to prevent scratching of chromed pipes.

6 Once you've loosened the slip nuts, unscrew them by hand.

7 Allow the contents of the P-trap to fall into the bucket as you remove it. Hair, dirt and slime gather in the P-trap, so expect a fair amount of icky sludge to drain out of it.

8 Don rubber gloves and search the dirty water in the bucket for the item you dropped.

9 If you can't find the item, wash out the P-trap with hot, soapy water and a scrub pad to remove buildup that might be hiding your item.

10 Once you have found the item, replace the P-trap and tighten the slip nuts.

11 If you've dropped an item down a sink that has a garbage disposal, exercise extreme caution. If the item is visible, use a wooden spoon or tongs to retrieve the item from the garbage disposal. If the item was caught in the grinder, it's probably a goner. Contact a plumber.

12 If the item you've dropped is magnetic, try dangling a magnet tied to a string down the drain to retrieve the item. While most jewelry is not magnetic, sometimes a steel clasp will provide the necessary magnetism to make this work.

What You'll Need

- Bucket
- Channel-type pliers or wrench
- Tape for pliers
- Rubber gloves
- Soap
- Scrub pad
- Wooden spoon or tongs
- Magnet and string

Tips

Use a mesh drain guard to prevent future loss of valuables down the sink. And keep a ring holder near the sink if you remove your rings to wash dishes.

Keep in mind that periodic removal and cleaning of the P-trap can help prevent clogged or sluggish sink drains. Also, if the P-trap is leaky or corroded, you might want to replace it.

70 Fix Improper Use of Pronouns

Pronouns are useful little words that replace nouns in sentences. Unfortunately, they are misused almost as frequently as they are used. Here's how to employ pronouns correctly.

Steps

1 Remember that you should use subjective personal pronouns (I, you, we, he, she, they) when the pronoun is the subject of the sentence: "I am hungry."

2 Use objective personal pronouns (me, you, us, him, her, them) when the pronoun is the object of the sentence: "Give it to him."

3 Turn a sentence around if you are confused about whether a pronoun is the subject or object:

"The best swimmer is him." *"Him is the best swimmer."* (Wrong)

"The best swimmer is he." (Correct)

4 Or fill in the implied words in a sentence if you are in doubt about correct usage:

"She is stronger than me." *"She is stronger than me am."* (Wrong)

"She is stronger than I." (Correct)

5 Exercise extra caution when using conjunctions with pronouns. Remove *and* to verify that you have used a pronoun correctly:

"Joe is going skating with Sue and I." *"Joe is going skating with I."* (Wrong)

"Joe is going skating with Sue and me." (Correct)

"Dan and me are going to the store." *"Me is going to the store."* (Wrong)

"Dan and I are going to the store." (Correct)

6 Answer "This is he (or she)" when you identify yourself on the telephone:

Caller 1: "Is Lucy Peters there?"

Caller 2: "This is she." ("*She is this,*" not "*Her is this.*")

7 Remember to use the relative pronoun *whom* when the pronoun is the object of the verb in a sentence rather than the active subject. This is a very common error:

"Who do you like?" *"You like who?"* (Wrong)

"Whom do you like?" (Correct)

"Sara is the one whom likes cats." "*whom likes cats*" (Wrong)

"Sara is the one who likes cats." (Correct)

Tips

When writing, make sure the pronoun is not so far from the referent that the reader loses the connection. This is particularly important when a sentence begins with a pronoun.

Using proper grammar is more important in a formal or professional environment. Many people slip into a vernacular or slang when they are hanging out with their friends—a linguistic form of relaxation.

8 Try not to overcorrect yourself in the effort to improve your usage of pronouns:

"We invited Bill, whom likes baseball more than us." (Wrong)

"We invited Bill, whom likes baseball more than us like baseball." (Doubly wrong)

"We invited Bill, who likes baseball more than we do." (Correct)

71 Fix a Run-On Sentence

Clarity and conciseness in writing is a beautiful thing. Sometimes we get so tangled up in what we are trying to say that we write monstrously long and convoluted phrases. Here's how to untangle a run-on sentence.

Steps

1 Determine whether the sentence is indeed a run-on. Suspect a run-on if the sentence contains more than 25 words and has multiple clauses: "Thales, who was the first Greek philosopher-scientist, developed geological and astronomical theories that have been outdated for thousands of years, and yet his wisdom endures, such as his timeless adage that the most difficult thing one can do is 'to know oneself.'"

2 Isolate the verbs and conjunctions in the sentence. In our example, these would be *developed, endures* and *and.*

3 Delete the conjunctions and change verb tenses (if necessary) to form two or more sentences: "Thales, the first Greek philosopher-scientist, developed geological and astronomical theories that have been outdated for thousands of years. His wisdom endures, however, including his timeless adage that the most difficult thing is 'to know oneself.'"

4 Add a transitional word or phrase if necessary to tie the sentences together. In the above case, the word *however* emphasizes the difference between Thales's outdated teachings and his wisdom.

5 Read the sentences aloud to make sure they are concise and clear. If you trip over any wording or phrases, you probably need to split up the sentences even more.

Tips

Tighten up your writing as you review it by deleting unnecessary words. Excessive use of the words *which* and *that* often accompany sloppy writing and run-on sentences.

Some of America's most acclaimed writers, including Walt Whitman and William Faulkner, have written whopper run-on sentences. Unless you are writing to achieve a certain literary effect, however, it is best to avoid run-ons.

72 Fix Misuse of the Word *Good*

Why is a nice little word like *good* so troublesome to so many people? Separate yourself from the ungrammatical masses and learn how to use this word correctly.

Steps

1 Remember that *good* is an adjective and *well* is an adverb. One exception to this rule is that you can use *well* as an adjective to refer to health or general well-being.

2 Realize that when you respond "I'm good" to the question "How are you?" you are telling the person that you are beneficial, kind, favorable or perhaps virtuous (depending on how the listener interprets your answer).

3 Correct yourself by responding "I'm well, thank you," which gives a more precise (and polite) response to the person's inquiry.

4 Realize that the ebullient, upbeat response "I'm great" to the question "How are you?" is literally a conceited answer. An astute listener might wonder why you feel it necessary to express to him or her how great you are.

5 Exercise extra caution when you are using the word *good* as an adverb. It's acceptable to do so only when the verb links the subject to the adverb. Common linking verbs include those of being and of sensing: *be, feel, look, seem, taste* and *smell*.
"He skates really good." (Wrong)
"He skates very well." (Correct)
"This apple tastes good." (Correct because *taste* is a linking verb)

6 The comparative superlative forms of *good* are *better* and *best,* respectively: "The apple is good, but the pear is better and the melon is best."

7 Remember that *good* can also be used as a noun when it refers to a beneficial or advantageous situation. For example, "This medicine is for your own good" or "He contributes daily to the common good."

8 Refrain from correcting other people when they misuse *good* unless you are the person's parent or teacher. Instead, set a good example by using *good* properly when you speak.

9 Exercise extra caution when speaking in a formal setting or when writing. These are the times when it is imperative to use proper grammar.

Tips

"I'm good" is accepted as common usage in spoken English to mean "I'm *well* or *healthy*." However, if you wish to speak precisely, it is better to respond "I am well" when someone inquires about your health or well-being.

If you do not feel well, it is preferable to reply "I am not well." The responses "I am bad" or "I feel bad" have a variety of possible interpretations. "I feel poorly" is also an acceptable response.

73 Fix Your Dog or Cat

Unless you are a breeder, neutering or spaying is a humane and ethical element of caring for your pet. It reduces many health risks and ensures that your pet will not contribute to the overpopulation of animal shelters.

Steps

1 Buy a pet carrier and train your pet to ride in it. If your dog is too large for a carrier, teach him to ride in the backseat of the car. Provide yummy treats after a drive so the pet has positive associations with car rides. This will make trips to the veterinarian's office much easier.

2 Bring your pet to a reputable veterinarian. Word of mouth is the best way to find a good vet. The veterinarian will tell you when your pet is old enough for neutering or spaying. It might be as early as eight weeks.

3 Follow any presurgery instructions the veterinarian provides.

4 Act calmly and lovingly as you bring your pet in for surgery. Your attitude can soothe your furry friend.

5 After the surgery, administer any pain-management medications to your pet according to your vet's instructions.

6 Call your veterinarian's office the following day. A diligent vet will want a post-op update.

7 Monitor your pet closely for the next 24 hours. Contact your vet immediately if you see symptoms of possible complications (vomiting, failure to eat, weakness, bleeding or swelling).

8 If your pet is chewing or licking the incision, ask your veterinarian about getting a special collar to prevent this.

9 Keep your pet indoors for a few days while he or she heals, to reduce the risk of torn sutures or infection. Understand that females will typically take a longer time to mend since an ovario-hysterectomy is a more involved surgery than a castration is.

10 Schedule a return visit to your veterinarian when it is time to have the sutures removed.

What You'll Need

- Pet carrier
- Pet treats
- Patience and compassion

Tips

Neutering a male will reduce aggressive behavior significantly. An unneutered male is more likely to get in fights or run away.

Spaying or neutering reduces the likelihood of certain types of cancer. Spaying also protects females from the risks associated with pregnancy.

Programs exist to help low-income pet owners pay for neutering or spaying. Inquire at a local animal shelter or humane society.

Correct Bad Behavior in Dogs

A poorly trained dog can embarrass its owner and offend other people—or even make them feel threatened. To raise a well-behaved dog, enroll him or her in an obedience class at a young age. Here are some pointers on how to handle common dog problems. Many of these instructions encourage the

PROBLEM	POSSIBLE CAUSES	SOLUTIONS
Begging	Natural instinct; improper social-ization; boredom; desire for your attention	• Feed dog on regular schedule with no snacks between meals. • Never feed dog from dinner table. • Ignore dog while he's begging, or say "no" firmly.
Biting	Natural instinct; improper social-ization; puppy is teething; dog feels threatened; dog is injured; dog has been abused; dog is in heat	• If puppy bites or nips, say "no" firmly and use shake can. • Provide chew toys for teething puppy. • If child teases dog, teach child to treat dog kindly. Do not leave child unattended with dog. • Put muzzle on dog that is injured and in pain to prevent biting. • If dog is over 10 months old, have dog trainer or vet evaluate her to determine whether it's safe to keep her.
Chasing cars	Natural hunting instinct; dog is protecting territory; dog dislikes cars; dog wants to fol-low owner	• Keep dog in secured yard where street is not accessible. • On walks, keep dog on leash. When he chases car, yank firmly on leash as it becomes taut and say "no." • Lavish praise on dog when he resists chasing cars. • Exercise dog regularly to reduce pent-up energy.
Chewing	Natural teething process in pup-pies; boredom; separation anxiety; undernourishment; lack of exercise; thunderstorms	• Provide plenty of chew toys as alternate chewing outlet, especially for puppies. Vary chew toys for older dogs. • Spray bitter apple (available at pet stores) on items dog likes to chew. Home remedies include hot pepper sauce, vinegar and hot mustard, as well as alum mixed with water. • Say "no" firmly and use shake can if you catch dog in act. • Exercise dog daily to relieve excess energy and anxiety. • Consult veterinarian if diet is problem. • Don't leave dog alone during thunderstorms.

use of a shake can, a soda can filled with dry beans, coins or pebbles that you rattle sharply when a dog misbehaves.

PROBLEM	POSSIBLE CAUSES	SOLUTIONS
Digging through trash can	Hunger; boredom; attracted to odor	Store trash can in area inaccessible to dog, or use can with sealed lid. Spray bitter apple (available at pet stores) on trash can. Home remedies include hot pepper sauce, vinegar and hot mustard, as well as alum mixed with water. Or place shake cans on top of trash can to startle snooping dog and to alert you if you are in hearing range.
Digging up lawn	Natural sheltering instinct; desire to escape yard; boredom; separation anxiety; moles or rabbits; desire to cool off in hot weather	Discourage it early on; it's tough habit to break, especially in terriers. Provide doggy toys to entertain dog in your absence. Provide kiddie pool if dog is digging hole to cool off in hot weather. Exercise dog daily to burn off excess energy and anxiety. Confine dog to area of yard where digging is acceptable if you can't stop her.
Eating stools	Undernourishment; stress; boredom; poor hygienic conditions	Clean up stool as soon as dog has eliminated it. Feed dog special food (available through vets) that makes feces undesirable. Exercise and play with dog daily to relieve stress and boredom. Keep dog on leash during walks. Yank at leash and say "no" firmly if he tries to eat stools. Consult veterinarian if you suspect malnourishment.
Excessive barking	Separation anxiety; boredom; fear; frustration; territorial aggression; hunger or thirst; thunderstorms	Treat underlying problem (see "Separation anxiety," next page.) Exercise and play with dog daily to reduce excess anxiety and energy. Train dog to know boundaries of yard and narrow area she feels territorial about. Do not leave dog alone during thunderstorms.

(continued on next page)

PROBLEM	POSSIBLE CAUSES	SOLUTIONS
Fighting with other dogs	Natural territorial instinct; instinct to dominate pack; improper socialization	Enroll dog in obedience courses. Keep dog on leash during walk. Yank leash and say "no" firmly if he growls at another dog. Never try to break up dog fight with your hands. Hose dogs off, throw jacket on them or try to distract them with loud noise.
Jumping on people	Improper socialization; dog is eager to greet person with a kiss	Consistently discourage at early age with firm "no." Ignore dog and avoid eye contact when she jumps on you to discourage such behavior. Tell dog to "sit" and reward her with affection and treats when she obeys. Exercise dog daily to reduce excess energy.
Mounting	High sex drive; nervousness; improper socialization	Neuter male dogs. Spray dog with squirt gun or water sprayer when he mounts and say "no" firmly. Exercise dog daily to reduce pent-up sexual energy.
Separation anxiety	Fear of being alone; overdependence on owner	Leave dog only for short intervals. Gradually increase intervals to allow her to adjust. Don't make fuss when you leave, which will excite her. Act calm and subdued. Play soothing music to help her relax in your absence. Hire pet-sitter to visit while you are at work. Provide doggy toys or put treat inside series of cardboard boxes so she can entertain herself by finding treat while you are gone. Don't punish dog for misbehaving (chewing, urinating, barking) in your absence. This will only increase her anxiety. Exercise and play with dog daily to reduce anxiety and promote canine bliss.

75 Remove Skunk Odor From Your Dog

Though you'll find sprays and rinses at pet stores for removing skunk stinks, you rarely have the luxury of running to the store when a skunk strikes. Battle the odor with this homemade remedy.

Steps

1 Keep your dog outside if possible. It could take weeks to remove this noxious odor from your house.

2 Check her eyes. Skunk spray can irritate them. If they are red and irritated, add eye drops designed for humans or olive oil to her eyes to relieve the irritation.

3 Don rubber gloves and wash the dog thoroughly with dog shampoo. Rinse and dry her.

4 Douse her with tomato juice, which diminishes the stench. Use enough to soak the fur thoroughly. It might take several cans. Allow the tomato juice to soak in for 10 to 20 minutes.

5 Rinse out the tomato juice. Reapply it if the odor lingers.

What You'll Need

- Eye drops or olive oil
- Rubber gloves
- Dog shampoo
- Tomato juice

Tip

Keep skunks away by using garbage cans with tight-fitting lids and by bringing pet food indoors at night.

76 Get a Cat Out of a Tree

It is important to remain calm if your kitten or cat gets caught in a tree. She is probably quite freaked out, and you, as the owner, need to help her calm down.

Steps

1 Avoid mass panic. Given time and privacy, the cat will likely find a way down on her own. (Exceptions are if the cat is injured or if she has a leash wrapped around her neck; go to step 4 in those instances.)

2 If several hours have passed, try to lure the cat down by opening a can of her favorite food underneath the tree. Call out her name in a calm, reassuring voice.

3 Lean a wooden ladder up against the tree near the cat so she can climb down. Leave her alone with the ladder for at least 15 minutes so she can climb down on her own.

4 If the cat is too freaked out to use the ladder, put on work gloves and a thick coat to protect yourself and climb up the ladder to retrieve her. Make sure the ladder is stable before you climb it.

5 Grab the cat by the nape of the neck to reduce your chances of getting scratched and to induce calmness in the cat.

6 If your efforts only send the cat farther up the tree, call an animal shelter or a local humane society. A professional animal handler can rescue the cat quite quickly.

What You'll Need

- Cat food
- Wooden ladder
- Work gloves and thick coat

Tips

Do not leave the cat stuck in the tree overnight. She'll be terrified and might fall victim to a night predator such as a raccoon or an owl.

If a dog has chased the cat up the tree, make sure he is removed from the premises so the cat feels secure enough to climb down.

77 Correct Bad Behavior in Cats

Unlike dogs, cats don't need obedience classes to develop good manners. If you are consistent in your regulations and generous in your affection, most cats will reward you with good behavior. If a cat suddenly begins misbehaving, there's usually an underlying cause, such as separation anxiety, stress in the household, sickness or injury.

PROBLEM	POSSIBLE CAUSES	SOLUTIONS
Aggressive behavior (scratching, biting and hissing)	Natural instinct; improper socialization; fear; irritation; injury or illness	• Say "no" and discontinue petting if cat becomes aggressive. Avoid roughhouse play. • Leave cat alone if he displays signs of aggression (tail flickers, ears flatten or cat hisses). • Avoid petting cat in certain area of body if it triggers aggressive responses. • Reward cat with treats and affection for good behavior. • Bring cat to veterinarian if injured or ill.
Begging	Natural instinct; improper socialization; hunger; desire for attention	• Feed cat right before you eat to distract her. Cats like to sleep after they eat. • Never feed cat from dinner table. Be consistent. • Ignore cat while she's begging or say "no" firmly.
Catching mice, birds and squirrels	Natural hunting instinct	• Understand that it's a natural instinct that provides cat exercise and stimulation. • Be preventive: Don't leave birdseed or birdhouse where cat can reach it. Supervise cat outside. • Play with cat using chase toy to provide alternate forms of stimulation and exercise.
Cater-wauling	Mating call; desire for affection; anxiety; injury or illness; cat is stuck somewhere	• Spay or neuter cat to reduce sexual pursuits. • Provide cat plenty of petting and affection to decrease feelings of loneliness. • Bring cat to veterinarian if you suspect cat is injured or ill, especially if cat wails while trying to relieve himself. • Rescue cat from vent or elsewhere if necessary.

PROBLEM	POSSIBLE CAUSES	SOLUTIONS
Fighting with other cats	Natural territorial instinct; desire to dominate other cats	Spay or neuter cat to reduce sexual drive. Keep cat indoors if fights occur at night with neighborhood cats. Provide cats with separate space if fights occur between two cats in same household. Never break up cat fight with your hands. Spray them with hose, throw jacket on them or use loud noise to distract them.
Jumping up on kitchen counters or stove	Improper socialization; hunger; curiosity	Put food items away to remove incentive. Place double-sided sticky tape on counters to adhere to cat's paws. Cats don't like this. Place cans filled with coins along counter edge to startle cat and alert you.
Jumping up on furniture and beds	Improper socialization; cat wants to be elevated to see things; cat wants a comfy nesting spot; cat wants company	Provide an alternate nesting spot, preferably elevated. Rub catnip into it to attract cat. Place obstructions (boxes or pots) on cat's favorite nesting spot or spray it with bitter-apple cat repellent. Say "no" firmly and remove cat when she jumps on furniture or bed. Be consistent. Provide cat plenty of affection when she behaves well.
Plant eating	Hunger; desire to induce vomiting; curiosity	Move plant to inaccessible area. Spray plant with bitter-apple cat repellent or hot pepper sauce. Provide cat grass (available at some grocery stores, pet stores, nurseries) as substitute. Surround plant with double-sided sticky tape.
Scratching furniture, curtains or carpets	Natural instinct to shed old claws; natural instinct to mark territory	Spray area with bitter-apple cat repellent or hot pepper sauce. Cover area with aluminum foil. Put scratching post next to area cat has been scratching. Rub post with catnip to attract cat. Trim cat's nails to reduce damage.

(continued on next page)

PROBLEM	POSSIBLE CAUSES	SOLUTIONS
Spraying	Natural instinct to mark territory; cat feels threatened; separation anxiety	• Spay or neuter cat to decrease territorial instincts. • Determine underlying cause. If cat sprays near window, he probably spotted another cat. Close curtains or drapes. • Provide safe nesting space if cat feels threatened by other household pets. • Don't leave dirty laundry around if cat sprays clothing that has owner's scent. This indicates overdependence on owner. • Wash sprayed area with citrus-based cleaner to remove scent and prevent future sprayings. • Provide lots of petting and affection to reassure cat. • Do not punish cat. He will not understand why you are punishing him; it will increase his anxiety.
Urinating and defecating in house	Dirty litter box; dissatisfaction with litter type or location of litter box; separation anxiety; illness	• Check litter box. • Change litter type or brand if cat displays aversion to it. • Make sure litter box is conveniently located and provides suitable privacy. • If cat keeps relieving herself in same spot, move litter box to that spot temporarily. Gradually move box back to its original location. • If cat stops using litter box when you travel, hire pet-sitter who will spend time with cat. This indicates separation anxiety. • Bring cat to veterinarian if you suspect she is ill. She might be having bladder-control problems.
Wool-sucking	Unknown, possibly oral fixation or nutritional deficit; common in Siamese cats	• Keep wool items out of cat's reach. Provide chew toys as alternate. • Increase fiber in diet or try feeding cat romaine lettuce. • Jury-rig closet with motion-triggered alarm (such as cans filled with coins) to startle wool-seeking cat and to alert you.

78 Treat a Cat for Matted Fur

Grooming your cat regularly with a brush or comb will reduce the occurrence of mats in the fur. Unfortunately, many cats wind up with matted fur because they hate to be groomed. Here's how to deal with the problem, which occurs most often in longhairs.

Steps

1 Attempt to remove the fur mat after the cat has eaten. Cats tend to be more relaxed after meals.

2 Adopt a calm and soothing demeanor as you approach the cat. Have your manicure scissors hidden in your pocket as you pet the cat.

3 Once the cat is relaxed, try to work out the fur mat with your fingers. Pull out the scissors if that doesn't work.

4 Snip down the middle of the fur mat, far from the skin. It's quite easy to snip the skin accidentally on longhaired cats, so work carefully.

5 Slowly work apart the fur mat with your fingers. Snip away a little more if necessary. Reassure the cat in a soothing voice as you snip. If she becomes upset, stop and come back to the task later.

6 Once you've worked apart the fur mat and it's clearly away from the skin, cut it off.

7 Reward the cat's cooperation with a kitty treat.

8 If the cat has several fur mats, remove them at separate times. The cat will quickly lose her patience after you remove the first fur mat. Build trust with a gentle approach and kitty treats to make future encounters easier.

9 Bring the cat to a professional groomer if the cat is unapproachable, if the fur mat is in a delicate area or if the mats are extremely tangled.

10 Purchase a hair-ball treatment at a pet store to help your cat eliminate a troublesome hair ball. Or feed the cat butter or a can of oily sardines.

What You'll Need

- Manicure scissors
- Kitty treats
- Hair-ball treatment

Tip

If a cat is vomiting hair balls, it is a sign that he needs more grooming. Comb or brush Kitty at least once a week to remove excess fur, more in shedding season. Cats ingest their fur while they groom themselves.

Warning

If a cat is retching for days, stops eating or is constipated, bring him to a veterinarian. It could indicate that a major hair ball is blocking the digestive tract.

If a cat stops grooming, bring him to the veterinarian. This is a common sign of underlying illness.

ORING • FIX BAD HABITS • REPAIR A BROKEN EYEGLASS FRAME • REPOSITION A SLIPPED CONTACT LENS • FIX A RUN IN STOCKINGS • JO
EAKOUT • REPAIR A TORN FINGERNAIL • FIX CHIPPED NAIL POLISH • FIX A STUCK ZIPPER • FIND A LOST CONTACT LENS • ELIMINATE BAD
Y THAT STICKS • STOP TELEMARKETERS AND JUNK MAIL • GET SUPERGLUE OFF YOUR SKIN • EXTRACT A SPLINTER • SOOTHE A SUNBURN
IANGOVER • STOP HICCUPS • MEND A BROKEN HEART • MEND A FAMILY FEUD • TREAT A SMALL CUT OR SCRAPE • FIX HAIR DISASTERS •
TTER SEATS • FIX A BILLING MISTAKE • FIX A BAD GRADE • FIX BAD CREDIT • RECOVER FROM JET LAG • RESUSCITATE AN UNCONSCIOUS
PRONOUNS • FIX A RUN-ON SENTENCE • FIX MISUSE OF THE WORD GOOD • FIX YOUR DOG OR CAT • CORRECT BAD BEHAVIOR IN DOGS •
SSING BUTTON • REMOVE LINT FROM CLOTHING • FIX A DRAWSTRING ON SWEATPANTS • REPAIR A HEM • REPAIR LEATHER GOODS • MEND
UNDER YOUR CASHMERE • FIX A SWEATER THAT HAS SHRUNK • FIX A SWEATER THAT HAS STRETCHED • FIX A HOLE IN A POCKET • FIX A H
LING FROM CLOTHING • FIX A FRAYED BUTTONHOLE • REMOVE DARK SCUFFS FROM SHOES • TREAT STAINS ON LEATHER • PROTECT SUE
IET SQUEAKY HINGES • TROUBLESHOOT LOCK PROBLEMS • TIGHTEN A LOOSE DOORKNOB • TIGHTEN A LOOSE DOOR HINGE • FIX A BIN
PLACE CRACKED TILE • TROUBLESHOOT MOLD ON INTERIOR WALLS • REPLACE CRACKED TILE GROUT IN A TUB OR SHOWER • FIX A DRAI
NDS • TROUBLESHOOT WINDOW SHADE PROBLEMS • FIX BROKEN GLASS IN A WINDOW • REPAIR A WINDOW SCREEN • REPAIR ALUMINUM
MAGED PLASTER • REPAIR WALL COVERINGS • TOUCH UP PAINTED WALLS • TROUBLESHOOT INTERIOR-PAINT PROBLEMS • SOLVE A LEAD
RDWOOD FLOOR • RESTORE A DULL, WORN WOOD FLOOR • TOUCH UP WOOD-FLOOR FINISHES • REPAIR DAMAGED SHEET-VINYL FLOORI
USE • CHILDPROOF YOUR HOME • PREVENT ICE DAMS • CURE A FAULTY FIREPLACE DRAW • START A FIRE IN A COLD CHIMNEY • FIX A WO
AL A GARAGE FLOOR • REFINISH A GARAGE OR BASEMENT FLOOR • CONTROL ROOF LEAKS • REDIRECT RAINWATER FROM A DOWNSPOU
MAGED ASPHALT SHINGLE • PATCH A FLAT OR LOW-PITCHED ROOF • REPAIR ROOF FLASHING • TROUBLESHOOT EXTERIOR-PAINT PROBLE
W WATER PRESSURE • FIX LEAKING PIPES • STOP A TOILET FROM RUNNING • FIX A LEAKY TOILET TANK • FIX A STOPPED-UP TOILET • STO
OGGED SINK OR TUB • REPAIR A TUB-AND-SHOWER VALVE • REPAIR CHIPPED FIXTURES • QUIET NOISY PIPES • DEFROST YOUR PIPES • DI
NSUMPTION • REPLACE A RECEPTACLE • FIX AN ELECTRICAL PLUG • REPLACE A LIGHT FIXTURE • INSTALL A NEW DIMMER • FIX A LAMP •
ORBELL • FIX A WOBBLY OVERHEAD FAN • ADJUST WATER-HEATER TEMPERATURE • RELIGHT A WATER-HEATER PILOT LIGHT • TROUBLESH
MAKER • GET RID OF MICROWAVE SMELLS • FIX A REFRIGERATOR THAT COOLS POORLY • FIX A GAS OVEN THAT HEATS POORLY • CLEAN
HWASHER PROBLEMS • CORRECT AN OVERFLOWING DISHWASHER • FIX A LEAKY DISHWASHER • FIX A DISHWASHER THAT FILLS SLOWLY
VASHING MACHINE THAT FILLS SLOWLY • FIX A WASHING MACHINE THAT "WALKS" ACROSS THE FLOOR • FIX A CLOTHES DRYER THAT DRI
YOUR VACUUM CLEANER • REPLACE VACUUM CLEANER BRUSHES • TROUBLESHOOT A PORTABLE AIR CONDITIONER • FIX A WINDOW AIR
OCESSOR • FIX A TOASTER • DIAGNOSE MICROWAVE OVEN PROBLEMS • TROUBLESHOOT A GAS GRILL • FIX A TRASH COMPACTOR • REP
ART • TROUBLESHOOT A CRASHING COMPUTER • CLEAN UP LAPTOP SPILLS • FIX BAD SECTORS ON A HARD DISK • QUIT A FROZEN PC AF
ECTED COMPUTER • IMPROVE YOUR COMPUTER'S MEMORY • GET RID OF E-MAIL SPAM • CHANGE A LASER PRINTER CARTRIDGE • FIX A F
URE OUT WHY A PRINTER WON'T PRINT • FIX SPELLING AND GRAMMAR ERRORS • RECALL AN E-MAIL IN MICROSOFT OUTLOOK • DIAGNO
ES • TROUBLESHOOT A PALM OS PDA • RESET A PALM OS PDA • REMOVE FINGERPRINTS FROM A CAMERA LENS • TROUBLESHOOT A CD-
VAGE A VIDEOCASSETTE • TROUBLESHOOT A DVD PLAYER • STRENGTHEN FM RADIO RECEPTION • STRENGTHEN AM RADIO RECEPTION
AMMED SLIDE PROJECTOR • GET BETTER SPEAKER SOUND • TROUBLESHOOT A DIGITAL CAMCORDER • TROUBLESHOOT A DIGITAL CAM
HTBULB • FIX A BROKEN WINEGLASS STEM • FIX BLEMISHED WOOD FURNITURE • REPAIR GOUGES IN FURNITURE • RESTORE FURNITURE
MOUFLAGE A DOG-SCRATCHED DOOR • REPAIR A SPLIT CARPET SEAM • RID CARPETS OF PET ODORS • REINFORCE A SAGGING SHELF •
NTS OF CHAIRS AND TABLES • REUPHOLSTER A DROP-IN CHAIR SEAT • REVIVE A CANE SEAT • REINFORCE A WEAK BED FRAME • FIX UP A
TTERY • REPAIR CHIPPED OR CRACKED CHINA • UNCLUTTER YOUR HOME • CLEAN CRAYON FROM A WALL • GET WAX OFF A TABLECLOTH
INS • REMOVE CHEWING GUM FROM CARPETING • REMOVE BLEACH SPOTS FROM CARPETING • REMOVE PET STAINS • ELIMINATE WINE
INS FROM TILE GROUT • REMOVE MILDEW FROM WALLS AND CEILINGS • DISINFECT A TOILET BOWL • REMOVE FIREPLACE GRIME • GET
EAN OIL SPOTS FROM A GARAGE OR DRIVEWAY • REMOVE STAINS FROM BRICK • WASH AN OUTDOOR GRILL • FIX A FALLEN SOUFFLÉ • R
SCUE OVERPROOFED YEAST DOUGH • FIX YOUR KID LUNCH • GET RID OF TAP-WATER MINERAL DEPOSITS • CALIBRATE A MEAT THERMOM
UCE • RESCUE A BROKEN SAUCE • REMOVE FAT FROM SOUPS AND SAUCES • FIX LUMPY GRAVY • SUBSTITUTE MISSING INGREDIENTS • F
RNED RICE • REMOVE COOKING ODORS • FINISH UNDERCOOKED MEAT • SALVAGE AN UNDERCOOKED TURKEY • FIX AN OVERSEASONED
ALE BREAD • SMOOTH SEIZED CHOCOLATE • SOFTEN HARDENED SUGARS OR COOKIES • FIX BREAKFAST FOR YOUR SWEETHEART • MEN
GGING TOOLS • RESTORE A BROKEN FLOWERPOT • SHARPEN PRUNING CLIPPERS • REMOVE RUST FROM TOOLS • REVIVE WILTING CUT F
T RID OF RAMPANT BRAMBLES • TROUBLESHOOT BROWN SPOTS ON A LAWN • CONTROL MAJOR GARDEN PESTS • RID YOUR GARDEN O
NPERFORMING COMPOST PILE • FIX BAD SOIL • SHORE UP A RAISED GARDEN BED • REMOVE A DEAD OR DISEASED TREE LIMB • TROUB
AINAGE • TROUBLESHOOT ROSE DISEASES • IDENTIFY AND CORRECT SOIL DEFICIENCIES IN ROSES • TROUBLESHOOT ROSE PESTS • OV
MAGED DECK BOARDS • REPAIR DECK RAILINGS • STRENGTHEN DECK JOISTS • FIX A RUSTY IRON RAILING • REPAIR A GATE • REPAIR A
ACKED OR DAMAGED CONCRETE • IMPROVE THE LOOK OF REPAIRED CONCRETE • REPAIR AN ASPHALT DRIVEWAY • REVIVE WOODEN OU
RDEN PONDS • CLEAN SWIMMING POOL WATER • TROUBLESHOOT HOT TUBS AND SPAS • REPLACE BRICKS IN WALKWAYS AND PATIOS •
R WITH JUMPER CABLES • SHUT OFF A CAR ALARM THAT WON'T QUIT • FREE A CAR STUCK ON ICE OR SNOW • DE-ICE YOUR WINDSHIEL
RN-SIGNAL COVER • FIX A CAR FUSE • FIX DASHBOARD LIGHTS THAT WON'T LIGHT • REMOVE CAR SMELLS • CHECK TIRE PRESSURE • IN
PROPERLY INSTALLED CHILD CAR SEAT • TROUBLESHOOT LEAKING OIL • CHECK AND ADD POWER-STEERING FLUID • CHECK AND ADD C
OKEN EXHAUST PIPE • CHECK AND ADD ENGINE OIL • CHECK AND ADD BRAKE FLUID • CHECK AND ADD FLUID TO YOUR AUTOMATIC TR
UBLESHOOT A WINDSHIELD-WASHER PUMP • REPAIR MINOR DENTS • CHANGE A HUBCAP • FIX AN IGNITION KEY THAT WON'T TURN • C

EMORY • FIX AN ELECTRIC CAN OPENER THAT DROPS THE CAN • TROUBLESHOOT A CELL PHONE • KEEP MIRRORS FROM FOGGING • ZAP
KEEP A SHAVING NICK FROM BLEEDING • GET RID OF SPLIT ENDS • UNTANGLE HAIR SNARLS • FIX FRIZZY HAIR • FIX BLEEDING LIPSTICK
ICKY SOCIAL SITUATION • FIX A BAD REPUTATION • CLEAN LIPSTICK FROM A COLLAR • FIX A BAD RELATIONSHIP • SALVAGE A BAD DATE
LEEDING NOSE • BEAT THE MONDAY MORNING BLUES • GET OUT OF A FIX • EXTRACT A BROKEN KEY • RETRIEVE KEYS LOCKED INSIDE A
STOP SOMEONE FROM CHOKING • STOP AN ANT INVASION • STABILIZE A CHRISTMAS TREE • RESCUE AN ITEM FROM THE DRAIN • FIX IMP
SKUNK ODOR FROM YOUR DOG • GET A CAT OUT OF A TREE • CORRECT BAD BEHAVIOR IN CATS • TREAT A CAT FOR MATTED FUR • REPLA
EAM • TREAT MILDEW DAMAGE • GET STATIC OUT OF YOUR LAUNDRY • DEAL WITH A CLOTHES-MOTH INFESTATION • FIX A SEPARATED ZIP
UR SOCK • TREAT MIXED-WASH ACCIDENTS • TAKE WRINKLES OUT OF CLOTHING • FIX A HOLE IN JEANS • REPAIR A SNAG IN A SWEATER
TAINS • WASH SNEAKERS • PICK UP A DROPPED STITCH IN KNITTING • RESTRING BEADS • FRESHEN SMELLY SHOES • FIX A SAGGING CLO
R • FIX A RUBBING DOOR • FIX A DRAFTY DOOR • TUNE UP SLIDING DOORS • FIX A SHOWER DOOR • SEAL WALL JOINTS AROUND A TUB O
W • REPAIR A FAULTY WINDOW CRANK • REPAIR VERTICAL BLINDS • REPAIR VENETIAN BLINDS OR MINIBLINDS • REPAIR WOOD OR PLASTI
CREEN WINDOWS • INSTALL NEW SASH CORDS IN WINDOWS • FIX A TIGHT OR LOOSE WINDOW SASH • REPAIR MINOR DRYWALL DAMAGE
OBLEM • REPLACE A DAMAGED CEILING TILE • REPLACE A WOOD FLOORBOARD • QUIET SQUEAKING FLOORS • REPAIR A WATER-DAMAGE
R A VINYL-TILE FLOOR • SILENCE SQUEAKY   STER • REPLACE CAULKING ON THE OUTSIDE OF
NG STOVE • REPAIR AND PREVENT WOOD RO   TCH A GUTTER LEAK • TROUBLESHOOT A WET BA
AGGING GUTTER • UNCLOG GUTTERS AND D   • REPAIR A CRACKED OR SPLIT WOOD SHINGLE
ARAGE-DOOR TENSION • TROUBLESHOOT A   ITES • LOOSEN A RUSTY NUT OR BOLT • TROUBL
NK SWEATING • FIX FLUSHING PROBLEMS •   FAUCET • FIX A STOPPER THAT DOESN'T SEAL • C
JMP PUMP PROBLEMS • TROUBLESHOOT ELE   USE • SWAP A FAULTY LIGHT SWITCH • REDUCE F
HOOT FLUORESCENT LIGHTING • FIX A LOW   E THERMOSTAT • TROUBLESHOOT HOLIDAY LIGH
TING SYSTEM • REFRESH A SMELLY REFRIGE   EMS • FIX A LEAKING REFRIGERATOR • REPAIR A C
CTIONING GAS BURNER • REPAIR A RANGE H   FIX AN ELECTRIC OVEN THAT HEATS POORLY • D
P YOUR APPLIANCES • CONTROL GARBAGE   E DISPOSAL • DIAGNOSE WASHING MACHINE PRO
• FIX A HAIR DRYER • TROUBLESHOOT A CLO   AT SPUTTERS • FIX AN IRON THAT LEAVES SPOTS
NER • FIX A DEHUMIDIFIER • REPAIR A CONS   DER • HANDLE A MIXER THAT OVERHEATS • REPAI
IG MACHINE • TROUBLESHOOT SMOKE ALAR   OARD SPILLS • TROUBLESHOOT A COMPUTER TH
• REMOVE A WINDOWS PROGRAM • SPEED U   OUSE • REPLACE YOUR PC'S BATTERY • CLEAN A
AT FAILS ITS SELF-TEST • CORRECT MONITOR   PAPER JAM • TROUBLESHOOT A RECURRING PRIN
ONE MODEM PROBLEMS • TROUBLESHOOT   REEN GLARE • GET TOP-NOTCH SCANS • RECOVE
ESTORE A CD • REPAIR A WARPED CD • CLE   • EXTRACT A JAMMED VIDEOTAPE • ADJUST VCF
OTE CONTROL • FIX AUDIOCASSETTES • FIX   OT A CASSETTE DECK • REPLACE BROKEN RABBI
BLESHOOT A CD PLAYER • REPLACE A HEAD   RASS • SHINE SILVER SAFELY • REMOVE A BROKE
PLACE A BROKEN TOWEL ROD • REMOVE ST   FOR NATURAL DISASTERS • FIX A FRAYED CARPE
BORING BATHROOM • REPLACE A SHOWER   NACE FILTER • REPAIR A BROKEN SLIDING DRAWE
OD CHAIR • FIX A WOBBLY WOOD CHAIR • SP   OR CRACKED PORCELAIN • REPAIR CHIPPED OR C
WAX FROM CARPETING • GET RID OF CEILIN

Clothing

M A RUG OR TABLECLOTH • REMOVE BURN N   NITURE • STRIP WAX BUILDUP FROM FLOORS • R
DORANT STAINS • ELIMINATE CIGARETTE ODOR • RESTORE SHINE TO YOUR JEWELRY • WASH DIRTY WINDOWS • REMOVE GRIME FROM M
UMBLED CAKE • FIX A PERFECT CUP OF TEA • PATCH A TORN PIE CRUST • KEEP A PIE CRUST FROM GETTING SOGGY • FIX DOUGH THAT
A DULL KNIFE • REMOVE RUST FROM A CAST-IRON PAN • REPAIR LAMINATE COUNTERTOPS • REMOVE STAINS FROM A STONE COUNTERTO
R CHOLESTEROL • TREAT BURNED POTS AND PANS • RESCUE A BURNED CAKE OR PIE • PUT OUT A KITCHEN FIRE • REMOVE THE BITTER
AN UNDERSEASONED DISH • REMOVE OVEN SPILLS • CLEAN UP OIL SPILLS • FIX A DRINK FOR ANY OCCASION • DISENTANGLE PASTA • R
J CUTTING BOARD • KEEP MIXING BOWL STEADY • FIX GARDEN TOOL HANDLES • REPAIR A LEAKY HOSE NOZZLE • MEND A LEAKY HOS
HARPEN A POWER MOWER BLADE • SHARPEN PUSH MOWER BLADES • REPAIR BALD SPOTS ON GRASS • RID YOUR GRASS OF DOG URINE
OUBLESHOOT HERBS • TROUBLESHOOT HOUSEPLANTS • OVERCOME SHADE PROBLEMS • RID SOIL OF PESTS AND DISEASES • REVIVE A
EES AND SHRUBS • REPAIR A LEAKING IRRIGATION SYSTEM • UNCLOG A SPRINKLER SYSTEM • CLEAN A CLOGGED DRIP SYSTEM • FIX PO
JGUS DISEASES IN ROSES • REPAIR DECK STEPS • RENOVATE A WEATHERED DECK • TIGHTEN LOOSE DECKING • REMOVE DECK STAINS
E • LEVEL AND SMOOTH A GRAVEL PATH • FIX A POTHOLE IN A DIRT OR GRAVEL DRIVEWAY • REPLACE PATIO STONES, TILES AND PAVERS
NITURE • RESTORE WEATHERED METAL FURNITURE • REPAIR CHAIR STRAPS AND WEBBING • REVIVE RUSTED IRON FURNITURE • TROUBL
LLED CAR • SHUT OFF A JAMMED HORN • CHANGE YOUR CAR'S BATTERY • TROUBLESHOOT A CAR THAT WON'T START • FIX A FLAT TIRE
RNED-OUT SIGNAL BULB • FIX A BURNED-OUT HEADLIGHT • ADJUST HEADLIGHTS • FIX A STUCK BRAKE LIGHT • REPLACE A BROKEN TAIL
TIRES • FIX A STUCK CONVERTIBLE TOP • DIAGNOSE A LEAK INSIDE YOUR CAR • REPLACE YOUR AIR FILTER • HANDLE A FAULTY REPAIR
OOL AN OVERHEATED ENGINE • REPLACE A LEAKING RADIATOR HOSE • CHANGE YOUR WIPER BLADES • ADD WINDSHIELD-WASHER FLUI
• TROUBLESHOOT YOUR BRAKES • ADD BRAKE FLUID TO THE CLUTCH MASTER CYLINDER • TROUBLESHOOT DASHBOARD WARNING LIC
SPARK-PLUG WIRES • DIAGNOSE CAR SMELLS • CLEAN THE OUTSIDE OF YOUR CAR • RESTORE YOUR CAR'S SHINE • WASH THE INTERI

79 Replace a Missing Button

Luckily, one of the most common clothing-repair chores—sewing on a button—is also one of the easiest. Even if you don't know the difference between a sewing machine and a can opener, you can complete this simple task in a few minutes.

Steps

1 If you haven't saved the missing button, look for a spare attached to the garment lining. If there's no spare, take the garment to the fabric store to buy a button that looks as much like the others as possible.

2 Thread the needle with thread the same color as the kind attaching the other buttons. Cut a piece of thread about a foot (30 cm) long, pass one end through the eye of the needle, and tie the two loose ends into a knot. Double-knot if you wish.

3 Place the button on the garment at the right place. Sometimes needle holes or bits of thread mark the location of the original button.

4 Starting on the inside of the garment (the side that doesn't show), push the needle up through the fabric and through one of the holes in the button.

5 Now push your needle back down through the fabric through a different hole in the button (see A). (If the button has more than two holes, follow the stitching used on the other buttons.)

6 Repeat steps 4 and 5 six to eight times. The last few times, leave the thread loop on the inside of the garment a little bit loose instead of pulling the thread taut.

7 With the needle on the inside of the garment, make your finishing knot: Pull the needle through the loose loops you made at step 6 a few times and tug gently (see B).

8 Snip off the extra thread, close to the knot you just made.

What You'll Need

- Needle
- Thread
- Scissors
- Button

Tips

If you save in your sewing kit extra buttons that come with clothing and buttons that have popped off, you'll always have a button handy when you need it.

Some buttons have a little loop, or shank, on their underside rather than holes in the middle. Not to worry. Just follow the same steps, except at steps 4 and 5 you're just continually making a loop through the shank rather than through different button holes.

A

B
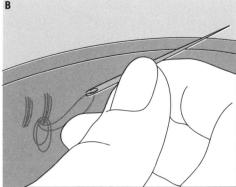

80 Remove Lint From Clothing

Light-colored clothing may show more dirt, but dark garments are lint magnets. Pet owners know that animal hair is another irritating culprit that attaches itself to clothing. The solution for this unsightly problem is simple.

Steps

1 Lay out the garment on a bed or any clean surface.

2 Place several fingers together and wrap either masking tape or cellophane tape around them. Make sure the sticky side faces outward.

3 Pat the lint-covered areas of the garment with the sticky tape.

4 Replace the tape with a fresh supply when you notice that it's covered with fuzz and lint; if it's no longer sticky, it won't be effective anymore.

What You'll Need

- Masking tape or cellophane tape

Tip

It's best to "de-lint" before donning the garment so that you can make sure you've removed lint from the front and back.

81 Fix a Drawstring on Sweatpants

If the drawstring on your sweatpants is broken or has slipped out, you don't have to spring for a new pair. This quick fix requires only moderately deft hands and a few household items.

Steps

1 Call your local fabric store to find out if it sells cord that can be used as a drawstring; alternatively, use an extra-long shoelace. Be sure it's at least 12 inches (30 cm) longer than the sweatpants' full waist size.

2 If the drawstring is broken, pull out both pieces.

3 Knot one end of the new drawstring—the end that will not be pulled through the waistband.

4 Attach a safety pin securely to the other end. The pin should be as large as possible, but small enough to slide through the opening and the elasticized waistband.

5 Push and pull the safety pin through the waistband by repeating the motion of using one hand to scrunch up the fabric and the other hand to pull it taut.

6 When the safety pin, to which the drawstring is still attached, has gone all the way around the waistband and reappears, remove the pin and knot the drawstring so that it can't slip out. The operation is complete.

What You'll Need

- Drawstring or extra-long shoelace
- Safety pin

Tip

Don't try to repair a broken drawstring unless the break is very near the end of the string. It will be too weak when it's reknotted or mended.

82 Repair a Hem

A few quick stitches can take care of a kicked-out hem on a pair of pants or a skirt. This is one repair that proves the cliché "A stitch in time saves nine," so find your sewing kit and get to work.

Steps

1 Use a ruler or measuring tape to measure the hem at a spot where it hasn't pulled out.

2 Where the hem needs to be repaired, turn it under the same width. Pin it into place with straight pins (see A).

3 Thread the needle with thread the same color as that used in the rest of the hem. Cut a piece of thread about 18 inches (45 cm) long, pass one end through the eye of the needle, and tie the two loose ends into a knot.

4 Working on the inside of the garment (the side that doesn't show), start stitching about ½ inch (12 mm) before where the hem has begun to pull out, using the blind hemstitch (see steps 5 through 7).

5 Make a small horizontal stitch in the fabric, picking up only a few threads from the right side of the fabric, so it will be barely noticeable when you're wearing the garment.

6 Take the next stitch, this time a little bit larger, in the folded hem, about ¼ inch (6 mm) from the first stitch (see B). Don't pull the stitches too tightly or the fabric will pucker.

7 Repeat steps 5 and 6 until you've crossed the distance of the pulled hem plus about ½ inch (12 mm).

8 Tie a knot in the thread, and snip off the thread with the scissors.

What You'll Need

- Ruler or measuring tape
- Straight pins
- Thread
- Needle
- Scissors

Tips

If you have a sewing machine equipped with a blind hemstitch feature, you can use it instead of doing steps 4 through 7 by hand.

Ideally a hem is almost invisible when you're wearing the garment. To accomplish this, take the tiniest stitch possible when stitching through to the right side of the fabric.

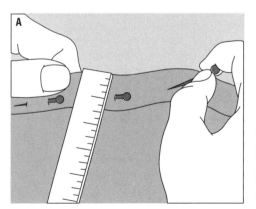

A

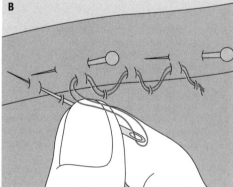

B

83 Repair Leather Goods

The durability and texture of leather make it an appealing material for jackets, gloves, purses and luggage. These same qualities, though, make leather difficult to repair. Here's how to handle minor fixes.

Steps

1 If the damage consists of a small hole or rip in the leather (under 1½ inches/4 cm), make a patch to repair it. Use sharp scissors to cut out a circle around the hole or rip that is just large enough to remove the rough edges. Avoid making the hole any larger than necessary.

2 Place paper underneath the circle and trace the circle onto the paper.

3 Cut the circle out of the paper and use this circle as a guide to cut out a circle from a leather swatch that matches the material you are repairing. For small leather patches on a garment, you sometimes can cut out a swatch from a pocket or interior lining. If not, shop at fabric stores or upholstery shops to find replacement leather swatches. Or you can go online to find leather suppliers.

4 Place the leather circle into the hole on a smooth, hard surface—it should fit in nicely. Use a hammer with a smooth head to gently pound the backside of the leather so that the circle lays flat and is not too thick.

5 Cut out a linen patch that is at least 1 inch (2.5 cm) larger all around than the leather circle.

6 Use garment glue to adhere the leather circle onto the middle of the linen patch. Then adhere the linen patch to the back side of the leather garment or bag you are repairing so that the circle fits perfectly into the hole.

7 Place the repaired leather under a heavy weight, such as phone books, for an hour to allow the patch to dry smoothly into place.

8 If you want to repair a smooth, clean cut in leather, fold together the two smooth edges and use a slanting stitch on the back side of the leather to sew it together. Keep the stitches far apart, because heavy stitching can weaken leather. Use a heavy-duty needle and polyester or silk thread; cotton thread is too weak.

9 Use a combination of a linen patch and stitching for repairs in areas that will sustain a lot of wear and tear or strain, such as elbows or armpits.

10 If the damage is severe, consult a tailor or luggage repair professional. They have the tools necessary to make more drastic repairs.

What You'll Need

- Sharp scissors
- Paper and pencil
- Replacement leather swatch
- Hammer with smooth head
- Linen patch
- Garment glue
- Phone books
- Heavy-duty needle
- Polyester or silk thread

Tips

To repair a snag in leather, use clear nail polish to smooth the snag into place against the leather. Do not use clear nail polish to repair snags on suede.

To remove small scratches or cracks, apply leather conditioner (available at hardware, upholstery, auto supply and saddlery stores). Leather conditioner makes leather smooth and supple and can remove imperfections due to dryness. If leather conditioner doesn't remove a scratch, try using a shoe polish that matches the leather color. Always test in an inconspicuous spot beforehand.

See also 101 Treat Stains on Leather.

84 Mend a Split Seam

Whether it's in a sleeve, a pant leg or the bodice of a blouse, the principles for repairing a split seam are the same.

Steps

1 With the garment inside out, pick out any bits of loose thread from the splitting seam.

2 Still working with the garment inside out, match the edges of the fabric together where the seam is coming apart. Pin into place (see A).

3 Thread a needle with thread that resembles the rest of the thread in the garment as much as possible. Tie a knot in the end of the thread.

4 Starting 1 inch (2.5 cm) to the right of where the seam is coming apart, begin stitching the fabric together from right to left using a backstitch. Pull your needle up through both layers of fabric. Then insert the needle ⅛ inch (3 mm) to the right of the spot where the thread came out and push the needle down through both layers of fabric. Pull the needle back up through the fabric, this time ⅛ inch (3 mm) to the left of the spot where the thread originally came out (see B).

5 Continue with this backstitch, bringing the needle up through the fabric half a stitch behind the previous stitch, until you've reached the spot 1 inch (2.5 cm) to the left of where the seam is ripped.

6 Tie a knot in the thread, and snip off the thread with scissors.

What You'll Need

- Straight pins
- Needle
- Thread
- Scissors

Tips

For a stronger repair, after you've backstitched across the split seam, begin stitching in the opposite direction over the stitches you just made, returning to the spot where you began.

If you're continually splitting the seams of a garment, it's probably too tight. A tailor might be able to open the seam and restitch it so you have more breathing room.

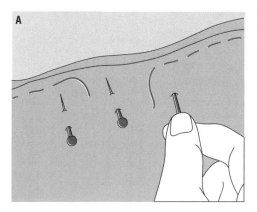

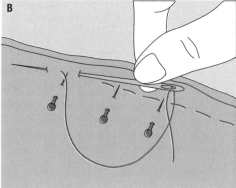

85 Treat Mildew Damage

Mildew is happiest in damp, dark places where air can't circulate, so your closet can be a prime breeding ground for the fungus, which likes leather and most fabrics. When you notice mildew on clothes or accessories, get rid of it as quickly as possible; in addition to being an allergen, it smells terrible and is unsightly.

Steps

1 Pour undiluted white distilled vinegar into a spray bottle. Vinegar has a high success rate for getting rid of mildew, and it also eliminates the bad odor.

2 Spray the vinegar onto the affected area of the garment or accessory.

3 Let the vinegar work its magic for several hours, ideally outside in the sun.

4 If you're dealing with a garment, wash it only after the sight and smell of the fungus is gone. Use warm, sudsy water, and hang the garment to dry in a clean, dry place.

What You'll Need

- White distilled vinegar
- Spray bottle

Tip

Liquid chlorine bleach also kills mildew. Check the tags on your garment to find out if it's safe to bleach them. Other acidic substances like lemon juice or grapefruit juice can also combat mildew damage.

86 Get Static Out of Your Laundry

If you find that your clothes snap, crackle and pop alarmingly, or that you generate a spark with every step, try these simple remedies to minimize static cling.

Steps

1 If you're already wearing the clothes that suffer from static cling, wet your hands slightly and brush them over the surface of your clothing.

2 While doing laundry, separate the synthetic fabrics, especially nylon, from the natural fabrics when putting clothes into the dryer. A load of all-natural fabrics, like cotton, will rarely develop static.

3 Remove your clothes from the dryer when they are just barely dry; overdrying is the No. 1 cause of static.

4 If you still notice static when you remove the clothes from the dryer, dampen your hands slightly before folding the laundry.

5 If all else fails, toss a fabric-softener sheet into the dryer before drying the next time you do laundry.

6 For really stubborn clothing—like nylon slips that bunch up underneath your skirt—rub a fabric-softener sheet on the surface of the fabric. This coats it with a waxy antistatic film.

What You'll Need

- Fabric-softener sheet

Warning

Some people are sensitive to the perfumes and dyes in fabric-softener sheets, and others are concerned about the potential environmental impact of the sheets, so try out the low-impact (and free) steps first.

87 Deal With a Clothes-Moth Infestation

These creepy little crawlies can chew their way through your clothing, wool carpets or even the felt in your piano. When you first discover signs of infestation, take immediate steps to prevent further damage.

Steps

1 Locate the source of the infestation. Use a flashlight to inspect clothing and carpets for telltale signs of moth infestation such as holes in clothing or other woolen items, moth larvae, or silk webs spun by the larvae. (If you find dried skins from larvae or sandlike droppings, they're likely from carpet beetles rather than moths. Clothes moths typically like dark, secluded places and may be found under furniture, in carpets or in boxes of stored clothing.)

2 Thoroughly clean the infested area with soapy water.

3 Vacuum the infested area, and continue to vacuum it regularly, disposing of the vacuum bags promptly, since they may contain the moths' eggs or larvae.

4 Dry-clean all the items you suspect may have become infested with moths, or launder them in hot water. Even if you don't see any moths, there may be larvae embedded in the clothing that need to be removed.

5 If the items are going into long-term storage, place them in a sealed, airtight container along with cedar chips or mothballs. If you're using mothballs, wrap them in paper so your clothes don't become discolored from contact with the chemicals. (Note that cedar chips are not 100 percent effective and must be sanded every year or refreshed with cedar oil in order to increase the odor they give off. Mothballs are more effective but can impart an unpleasant odor to your clothing.)

6 Moth larvae typically feed on wool or other fibers derived from an animal (feathers, fur, felt), but they can also be attracted to sweat, hair or oils embedded in other fabrics, so clean all items well before putting them in storage.

7 If the items are not going into long-term storage and it's not practical to put them in an airtight container, distribute some cedar chips or mothballs among them. Then, at least once a year, brush the items and expose them to sunlight to discourage further infestations.

What You'll Need

- Flashlight
- Soap
- Vacuum
- Sealed, airtight container
- Cedar chips or mothballs

Tip

Garments with moth holes can be repaired by a professional experienced in reweaving, but be sure to have the item dry-cleaned first. The cleaning should kill any moth larvae remaining in the garment.

Warning

Mothballs are one of the leading causes of childhood poisoning, so always keep them out of the reach of children, and read the precautions on the package.

88 Fix a Separated Zipper

A separated zipper can make getting in and out of your clothes a struggle. Try these steps to get your zipper back in working order. See 31 Fix a Stuck Zipper and 532 Unjam a Sleeping-Bag Zipper for more zipper tips.

Steps

1 With a small pair of pliers (needle-nose pliers work best), pry off the zipper's metal stop, the little band at the bottom of the zipper that stops the slider when you open the zipper (see A). If you don't have needle-nose pliers, you might be able to pry off the stop with a screwdriver or even a blunt kitchen knife.

2 Once you've removed the stop, move the slider all the way to the bottom of the zipper, just below the bottommost teeth.

3 Realign the zipper's teeth so that they mesh smoothly.

4 Move the slider up to the top of the zipper, zipping it completely.

5 Thread a needle with strong thread. Tie a knot at the end of the thread.

6 Starting with your thread on the back side of the zipper, make six or seven stitches across the bottom of the zipper where the old stop was, creating a new stop out of thread (see B).

7 With your thread on the back side of the zipper, tie a knot in the thread and snip it off with your scissors.

What You'll Need

- Small pair of pliers (needle-nose are best)
- Needle
- Strong thread
- Scissors

Tip

If the zipper is merely sticky and not separated, try rubbing a candle along the teeth of the zipper, then zipping and unzipping it several times. This quick fix will often make the zipper work more smoothly.

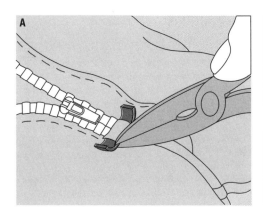

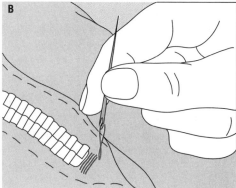

89 Launder Your Cashmere

Contrary to popular opinion, hand washings won't ruin a cashmere sweater—in fact, it will last longer and smell fresher than if you take it to the dry cleaner.

Steps

1 Read the garment's care label to make sure it can be hand-washed. Some sweaters have trim or finishes that do require dry cleaning.

2 Use a detergent that's safe for delicate fabrics.

3 Pour detergent in a clean sink, measuring out the amount suggested on the bottle. By adding the detergent before the water, you'll make sure it's evenly dispersed once you fill the sink.

4 Fill the sink with cool to lukewarm water.

5 Place the sweater in the sink. Swish it around and lightly squish the suds through the fabric. Leave the sweater in the sink for about 15 minutes.

6 Let the sudsy water drain out of the sink. Fill the sink with clean water that's cool to lukewarm.

7 Squeeze the sweater gently in the clean water. Repeat, refilling the sink with clean water as necessary, until you've removed all the soap from the sweater.

8 Lightly squeeze (but don't wring) the sweater to begin removing the water.

9 Roll the sweater in a bath towel, pushing down on the towel to press out more water. If the sweater is fairly large, you may need to use a second towel after the first one becomes soaked through.

10 Unroll the sweater, and reshape it to its proper size.

11 Place the sweater flat on a dry towel, on a drying rack if possible. Keep it away from direct sun to protect the color.

12 Flip the sweater once or twice a day if necessary so that it air-dries thoroughly.

What You'll Need

- Detergent designed for fragile fabrics
- At least two towels
- Drying rack

Tip

If you don't have a detergent made for fine fabrics, such as Lanowash or Woolite, baby shampoo makes a fine substitute.

90 Fix a Sweater That Has Shrunk

When your sweater has shrunk more than a size or two, you might as well cut off the arms and use it to keep Fluffy warm next winter. But if your sweater has become just a bit too snug, try these steps to return it to its original size.

Steps

1 Mix 2 tbsp. baby shampoo into a sink full of warm water. The shampoo will relax natural fibers like wool.

2 Soak the sweater in the shampoo-and-water mixture for 15 minutes.

3 Without rinsing the sweater, take it out of the soapy water and roll it in a towel to remove as much moisture as possible.

4 Spread the sweater onto a large corkboard, pulling it into the size and shape you want. Fasten the sweater to the corkboard using pins, being careful not to snag the sweater.

5 Return to the sweater every several hours, restretching and repinning it as necessary, until the sweater is dry.

What You'll Need

- Baby shampoo
- Towel
- Large corkboard
- Pins

Tip

To avoid shrinkage in the first place, don't machine-wash your sweater unless the label specifically says you can. Even if you use cold water, the agitation may cause the sweater to shrink.

91 Fix a Sweater That Has Stretched

If the arms of your sweater are long enough for a monkey, or maybe the whole thing is a size too large, you might be able to get it back down to size. The following techniques work best with wool sweaters.

Steps

1 Fill the sink with warm water. Soak the sweater in the water for 10 to 15 minutes.

2 Take the sweater out of the water and roll it in a towel to remove as much moisture as possible.

3 Spread the sweater on a towel placed on a flat surface, scrunching the sweater into the size and shape you want.

4 Return to the sweater every several hours, rescrunching it as necessary, until the sweater is dry.

5 If the above steps haven't fixed the problem, you can try tumbling the sweater in the dryer on low heat, checking it every few minutes to see if it's the right size. If you're not careful, however, you can end up ruining the sweater, and at best drying it will likely weaken the fibers.

What You'll Need

- Towels

Tip

To avoid stretching out your sweaters, store them flat rather than on hangers.

92 Fix a Hole in a Pocket

There are almost as many kinds of pockets as there are types of garments—patch pockets and inside pockets, in-seam and slashed, lined and unlined. Though each presents slightly different challenges, the following basic techniques will work for almost any pocket that hangs inside the garment. So before you lose any more loose change, try these simple repairs.

Steps

1 Turn the pocket inside out. Determine whether the hole was caused by a ripped seam or by a hole in the fabric of the pocket itself.

Fixing a hole in a pocket seam

1 Pick out any bits of loose thread from the split seam.

2 Match the raw edges of the fabric together where the seam is coming apart. Pin the fabric into place.

3 Thread a needle with thread that matches the color of the inside of the pocket. Tie a knot at the end of the thread.

4 Starting ½ inch (12 mm) to the right of where the seam is coming apart, begin stitching the fabric together from right to left using a whipstitch (see A): Pull the needle up through both layers of fabric with the needle at a slant, just a few threads from the edge. Loop the needle over the top of the seam to the back side of the fabric.

What You'll Need

- Straight pins
- Needle
- Thread
- Scissors
- Fabric to cover the hole
- Iron

Tip

These techniques will work even if the garment is lined and you don't have easy access to the back side of the pocket fabric. If you can get to the back side of the pocket fabric, you can make a less conspicuous repair.

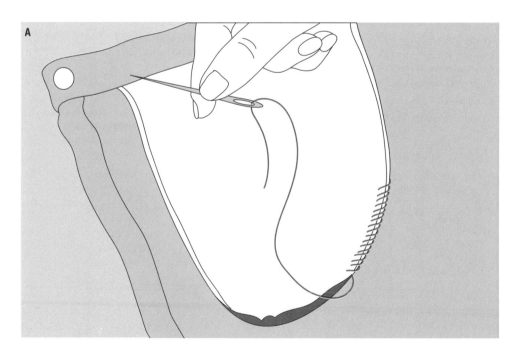

A

5 Repeat the whipstitch, making about 15 stitches per inch (2.5 cm), until you've reached the point ½ inch (12 mm) to the left of where the seam is coming apart. It won't be pretty, but the whip-stitch is strong, and the thread will be hidden inside the pocket when you're done.

6 Tie a knot in the thread, and snip off the thread with scissors.

Fixing a hole in the pocket fabric

1 Cut a patch large enough to cover the hole with ¾ inch (2 cm) extra fabric all around. You can use any fabric of similar weight to the pocket lining.

2 Turn the edges of the patch under ¼ inch (6 mm), ironing the wrong sides together, so you have a patch that is ½ inch (12 mm) larger than the hole on every side (see B).

3 Center the patch over the hole in the pocket, and pin it into place with straight pins.

4 Fold the pocket fabric level with one edge of the patch and whipstitch the edges together, making about 10 to 15 stitches per inch (2.5 cm).

5 When you reach the corner, refold the pocket fabric and continue stitching the next side, until all sides are stitched.

6 Tie a small knot and snip off the extra thread, close to the knot you just made.

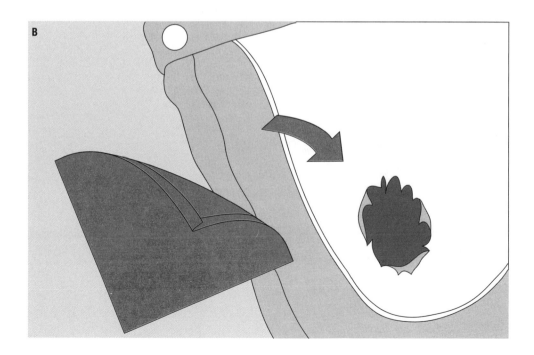

B

93 Fix a Hole in Your Sock

Your big toe is poking out of one of your socks? Practice this skill our grandmothers knew, and learn how satisfying it is to darn.

Steps

1 Carefully insert a lightbulb (or another round, smooth object) into the sock where the hole is. This will give you a smooth surface to work on.

2 Thread a darning needle with thread that's similar in color and weight to the fabric of the sock. Don't knot the thread.

3 Trim the ragged threads around the edges of the sock hole, being careful not to make the hole any bigger.

4 Imagine a circle (or oval) drawn around the hole in the sock, about ¼ inch (6 mm) larger than the hole on every side. With your needle and thread, stitch around this circle using a simple run-ning stitch, your needle piercing the fabric down, then up, about every ⅛ inch (3 mm). Complete the circle and add five more stitches (see A). Clip off the remaining thread.

5 Rethread the darning needle with another length of thread (again, don't knot it). Starting at the top of the hole, just outside the circle you've stitched, make a series of vertical lines all the way across the hole. Where there is fabric, weave your needle through the fabric in a running stitch. Where there is no fabric, your thread will simply lie flat across the hole. Continue stitching parallel vertical lines all the way across the hole (see B).

6 When you've covered the hole with vertical lines, make horizontal stitches, weaving your needle under and over the vertical lines you just made (see C).

7 Once the entire area has been filled up, make another six or seven running stitches (simple up-and-down stitches) in the sock outside the darning area. This will hold the stitches in place.

8 Clip off the remaining thread.

What You'll Need

- Lightbulb (or other smooth, round object)
- Darning needle
- Thread
- Scissors

Tips

The thread you usually use for sewing is probably too thin for this task. Look for embroidery cotton or wool-nylon thread, which is more likely to match the weight of the sock fabric.

For easier darning, do this repair when the sock begins to show wear but hasn't developed a hole yet.

Warning

Don't pull your stitches too tight or the fabric is likely to pucker.

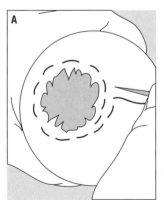

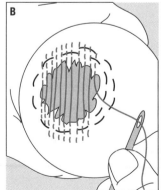

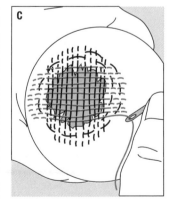

94 Treat Mixed-Wash Accidents

Who hasn't accidentally tossed a soon-to-be bleeding garment into a load of laundry? When clothing dye runs and your garments pick up the wrong colors in the wash, there's good news: It's often possible to get the stains out.

Steps

1 Act quickly before the stain sets. It's much easier to remove a new stain than an old one.

2 Rinse the stained clothing immediately with cold water. Then wash the garment in cold water using liquid detergent.

3 If step 2 doesn't do the trick, soak the garment in a diluted solution of all-fabric bleach. Chlorine bleach isn't advisable unless you're certain it's safe for the fabric.

4 Wash the garment in detergent, and use bleach that you've tested on the fabric. To test your fabric, mix a small spoonful of bleach in ¼ cup (2 fl oz/60 ml) water. Place a couple of drops of the solution on a part of the fabric that doesn't show. If you don't see any color change or bleeding after a minute, the bleach is OK to use.

5 Be patient—up to five washings may be required.

What You'll Need

- Liquid detergent
- Non-chlorine bleach

Tip

If you need to rewash the garment in a machine with bleach, keep in mind that bleach works best in hot water. Warm water is the second choice, and cold water is the least effective option.

95 Take Wrinkles Out of Clothing

Ironing isn't the only way to get rid of wrinkles. If you're traveling without your iron or are just too lazy to drag out the ironing board, your clothes don't have to look like you've slept in them. Some people are sensitive to the perfumes and dyes in fabric-softener sheets, and others are concerned about the potential environmental impact of the sheets, so try out these low-impact (and free) steps first.

Steps

1 If you haven't yet taken a shower, give your clothes a good shake and hang them in the bathroom near the shower. The steam from the shower will relax the wrinkles.

2 If this doesn't solve the problem, dampen your hands slightly and run them over the surface of the garment, smoothing out the wrinkles as you go. Wait a few minutes, allowing the garment to dry. Alternatively, use a spray bottle filled with water to mist the garment lightly instead of wetting your hands.

3 If these steps still haven't fixed the problem, dampen the garment slightly and place it in the dryer with a fabric-softener sheet (check the garment's label first to see if it's safe to put in the dryer). Tumble dry for a few minutes until the wrinkles fall out.

What You'll Need

- Spray bottle
- Fabric-softener sheet

Tip

To avoid wrinkles in the first place, don't overload the dryer, and remove the clothes from the machine when they are just barely dry.

96 Fix a Hole in Jeans

Don't throw away those comfy jeans just because they make a ripping sound every time you move. You can probably preserve your modesty with a strategically placed patch.

Steps

1 Head to a fabric store to buy an iron-on patch large enough to cover the hole. With scissors, trim the patch so that it is about ½ inch (12 mm) larger than the hole in every direction (see A).

2 Center the patch over the hole and pin it in place.

3 Using an iron, press the patch onto the jeans according to the instructions on the package.

4 Thread a needle with strong thread and tie a knot.

5 To reinforce the patch, fold the jeans level with one edge of the patch, and whipstitch the edge of the patch to the jeans, making about 10 stitches per inch (2.5 cm). Pull the needle up through both layers of fabric, the jeans and the patch, with the needle at a slant, just a few threads from the edge. Loop the needle over the top of the edge to the back side of the jeans.

6 When you reach the corner, refold the jeans and continue stitching the next side until all sides are stitched (see B).

7 Tie a small knot on the inside of the jeans. Snip off the extra thread, close to the knot you just made.

What You'll Need

- Iron-on patch
- Scissors
- Straight pins
- Iron
- Needle
- Thread

Tips

If you're short on time, you can simply iron on the patch without sewing it, or vice versa, but since patches on jeans are typically subject to a lot of stress, it's best to do both steps.

If you use the sew-only method, you can use any sort of decorative fabric you'd like instead of a denim patch, though strong fabrics work best.

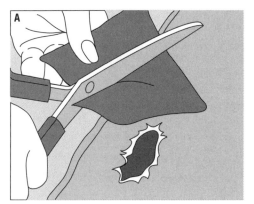

97 Repair a Snag in a Sweater

If your favorite sweater has sprouted a big hole, you should take it to a professional for reweaving. But if it's got nothing more than a small snag or unraveling thread, you can keep the sweater from unraveling further with this simple repair.

Steps

1 Insert a very small crochet hook (about a size 5) from the back side of the sweater through to the front at the site of the snag.

2 Use the hook to pull the loose yarn through to the back side of the garment.

3 Turn the sweater inside out.

4 Use the crochet hook to make a loop out of the loose yarn, then pull the loose end through the loop, creating a knot on the inside of the sweater.

5 Dab the end of the loose yarn with liquid ravel preventer (sold under the brand name Fray Check), available at fabric and hobby stores. In a pinch you can use a small dab of clear nail polish instead.

6 After the ravel preventer has dried, turn the sweater right-side out and gently stretch it to smooth out any bunching that the snag might have caused.

What You'll Need

- Very small crochet hook (about a size 5)
- Liquid ravel preventer

Tip

If you don't have a crochet hook handy, you can probably use a needle, a long, thin letter opener, or even the cap of a pen to pull the loose yarn through the sweater. Just be careful not to snag more threads or poke another hole in the sweater.

98 Remove Pilling From Clothing

When your coats, sweaters or blankets begin to pill—that is, they're showing those unsightly little fuzzies common to knitted, woven or napped fabrics—this is the safest method for removal.

Steps

1 Buy a small comb, designed for this purpose, at a fabric store. The comb is much smaller than any hair comb you could find, and it has stiff, tiny teeth about ⅛ inch (3 mm) long.

2 Lay the clothing or blanket on a flat surface.

3 Hold the fabric taut with one hand. With the comb in the other hand, use a brisk but gentle stroke to remove the fuzz.

4 Repeat as often as necessary.

What You'll Need

- Sweater/fabric comb

Tip

Experienced "de-pillers" advise against using a razor because of the possibility of accidentally cutting the fabric. The same risk applies to the use of scissors.

99 Fix a Frayed Buttonhole

Fraying buttonhole threads not only make a garment look untidy, but they also may lead to your buttons' popping open at the slightest provocation. You don't need a fancy sewing machine with a buttonhole feature to fix this problem. Follow these steps to do a simple dress-maker's buttonhole stitch.

Steps

1 With a seam ripper, carefully remove all the threads from the frayed buttonhole.

2 Choose thread that matches as closely as possible the button-hole thread you just picked out.

3 Cut a piece of the thread about 18 inches (45 cm) long, pass one end through the eye of a needle, and tie the two loose ends into a knot to create a double length of thread.

4 Holding the fabric right-side up with the buttonhole horizontal, begin stitching at the inside bottom edge of the buttonhole (the side farthest from the edge of the garment). Starting from the reverse side of the fabric, pull your needle up through all layers of the fabric at the same distance below the slit as the previous stitching was (you should be able to follow the line where the old stitching used to be).

5 Push your needle back down through the buttonhole slit.

6 Pull the needle back up through all layers of the fabric, just to the right of the first stitch, but this time stop when the needle is still piercing the fabric and the tip of the needle protrudes from the fabric ½ inch (12 mm) or so.

7 With your fingers, loop the thread clockwise around the needle, first under the eye end of the needle, then under the tip end (see A).

8 Pull the needle the rest of the way up through the fabric, creating a knot against the edge of the buttonhole slit.

Tip

If the buttonhole has barely begun to fray, you can keep it from fraying further and avoid having to repair it by dabbing it with a bit of liquid ravel preventer (sold under the brand name Fray Check), available at fabric and hobby stores.

A

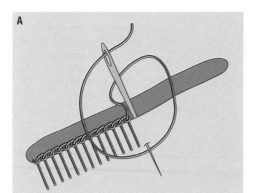

B

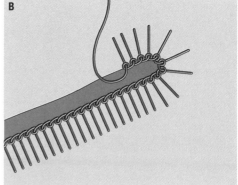

9 Repeat steps 5 through 8, working along the edge of the button-hole from left to right, keeping the stitches close together so that you can't see any fabric between the knots.

10 When you reach the outer edge of the buttonhole, continue creating the same knots around the end of the buttonhole (see B). Pull the knots tight and adjust them with your thumb-nail so that they don't overlap, to keep the buttonhole from looking lumpy.

11 Continue creating these knots along the top and left edges of the buttonhole until you reach the point where you started.

12 Stitch through the first knot you made to finish encircling the buttonhole slit.

13 With the needle on the reverse side of the garment, make a finishing knot, pulling your needle through a few of the stitches you made at the beginning of the repair.

14 Snip off the extra thread, close to the knot you just made.

100 Remove Dark Scuffs From Shoes

Light scuffs on leather shoes can usually be handled with a coat of shoe polish. But dark scuffs, especially on lighter-colored shoes, call for refinishing. With a few supplies from the shoe repair shop, you can do it yourself.

Steps

1 Purchase a refinishing spray such as Nulife at a shoe repair shop. Take the shoes with you so that you can match them to the color chart.

2 Use masking tape to mask off the sole and heel of the shoes. Only the leather upper should be exposed.

3 Find a well-ventilated area to work in. Using a light-colored cloth, wash the leather with leather preparer. Let dry. Repeat until the leather has a dull, even finish.

4 Apply the refinishing spray to the shoe. Spray it on evenly and lightly. Repeat until the leather has an even color, allowing it to dry between coats.

5 Remove the tape. Polish the shoes with cream polish and a soft, clean cloth.

What You'll Need

- Shoe refinishing spray
- Masking tape
- Light-colored cloth
- Leather preparer
- Cream shoe polish
- Soft, clean cloth

Tip

Help prevent scuffs by pol-ishing your shoes regularly. Cream shoe polish is a good choice, because it comes in a wide range of colors and has staying power.

101 Treat Stains on Leather

Here are basic guidelines for treating stains on leather clothing, shoes and furniture, and they apply to all gradations of the material. However, cleaning can alter the color or appearance of leather, so when in doubt, consult a leather-cleaning professional.

MILDEW

1 Mix 1 cup (8 fl oz/250 ml) rubbing alcohol with 1 cup (8 fl oz/250 ml) water.

2 Moisten a cloth with the mixture and wipe the affected area. Leave to dry.

INK

1 Spray the affected area with hairspray, then wipe it off with a clean cloth.

2 Ink can be extremely difficult to remove, so you may need to consult a leather-cleaning professional.

WATER

1 Allow a soaked leather garment to dry slowly and naturally.

2 Keep the item away from heat sources, and restore its softness with a leather conditioner after it's dry.

3 For soaked leather shoes, insert shoe trees and let air-dry.

GREASE

1 Blot excess grease with a clean cloth.

2 Sprinkle talcum powder or cornstarch on the affected area.

3 Let sit for at least 4 hours, then wipe off the powder.

PROTEIN (BLOOD, URINE)

1 Blot excess moisture with a clean, damp cloth.

2 Allow item to dry slowly, away from a heat source.

GUM

1 Rub with a plastic bag of ice cubes to harden the gum, and then pull off the gum.

2 For any residual gum, heat the area with a hair dryer and rub off the gum with a clean cloth.

SALT STAINS

1 Mix a solution of 3 parts vinegar to 1 part water.

2 Moisten a cloth with the vinegar solution and dab on the affected area.

DISCOLORATION

1 For leather garments, gloves and bags that are discolored, use a leather spray designed to restore color. These products are sold at shoe repair shops; choose the color that most closely matches.

102 Protect Suede From Stains

While stains on suede do not necessarily spell disaster, preventive care is the best way to keep your delicate suede items looking fabulous. Just think of the indelicate sport of football and its famous saying: "The best defense is a good offense."

Steps

1 Spray a recently purchased or recently cleaned suede item with one of the many products that protect against water damage and other stains. As with any fabric, test a small, unseen patch first.

2 Wear a scarf to protect the collar of a suede garment. The scarf can shield suede from hair products, sweat and makeup stains.

3 Store suede items so that they can breathe. Avoid plastic bags, which prevent air circulation, and opt for a pillowcase instead to protect clothing from dust. When traveling, store shoes in cotton flannel shoe bags instead of plastic bags.

4 Keep suede away from light, which will fade the color, and damp conditions, which can encourage growth of damaging mold and mildew.

5 If suede clothes or shoes get wet, soak up excess moisture with a clean towel. Then allow the suede to dry naturally; do not use a heat source to speed up the process. After the item dries, restore the nap (the raised fibers typical of suede) with a suede brush.

6 Use a nail file to remove dry mud and scuff marks on suede shoes. Gently file away the stain with delicate strokes. A suede brush also works to remove dirt on shoes and clothing.

7 Remove oil stains on suede by rubbing talcum powder or corn-meal directly on the spot. After several hours, brush off the powder. Repeat if necessary.

8 Recondition suede shoes with products designed for that pur-pose. Such products can also be used on suede clothing, unless the manufacturer's instructions specifically state otherwise. Make sure the item is clean first.

9 Keep in mind that major stains will probably require professional care. Take your suede item to someone who specializes in leather and suede; inexperienced dry cleaners or cobblers can cause more harm than good.

What You'll Need

- Suede protector spray
- Scarf
- Pillowcase
- Cotton flannel shoe bags
- Towel
- Suede brush
- Nail file
- Talcum powder or cornmeal
- Reconditioning products

Tip

Rubbing suede with a nail file not only cleans it but also raises the nap. Holding your suede item above a steam-ing kettle is another method for raising the nap.

Warning

While many suede garments these days are washable, remember that animal skins can shrink a great deal when washed. Read the instruc-tions on the label carefully.

103 Wash Sneakers

Do you wash your workout clothes regularly but leave your shoes languishing in the locker until they smell up the locker room? Your shoes, too, should be cleaned regularly to keep them looking good and smelling sweet.

Steps

1 Remove the laces and any inserts from the shoes.

2 Throw the laces in with a load of laundry, and then let them air-dry.

3 Mix up a solution of mild soap and water (dishwashing soap or Ivory soap flakes work well). If the shoes are very heavily soiled, you might want to buy a cleaner specifically designed for athletic shoes instead. Check the bottle's label to make sure it is appropriate for all the materials—whether nylon, leather, vinyl, canvas or rubber—your shoes are made of.

4 With a soft-bristle brush and the soapy water or shoe cleaner, clean the inserts and the shoes, inside and out. Then use clean water to rinse the shoes and the inserts well with clean water.

5 Wipe off the excess moisture with paper towels.

6 With paper towels, stuff the shoes to soak up moisture and preserve their shape.

7 Place the shoes and the inserts on a waterproof surface in a well-ventilated room to dry, replacing the paper towels if necessary as they become soaked through.

8 Put the laces and the inserts back into the shoes once all the parts are completely dry.

9 Sprinkle a bit of baking soda inside the shoes to keep them smelling fresh.

10 Allowing your shoes to dry out thoroughly between wearings will lengthen their life considerably.

What You'll Need

- Soft-bristle brush
- Mild soap or athletic shoe cleaner
- Paper towels
- Baking soda

Tips

Throwing your shoes in the washing machine is a last-ditch way to clean a particularly grubby pair. But unless your shoes were marketed as "washable," the heat, agitation and thorough soaking they receive could ruin them, so don't try this unless you're otherwise ready to throw them out anyway.

See 106 Freshen Smelly Shoes for more tips.

104 Pick Up a Dropped Stitch in Knitting

If you drop a stitch while knitting, you don't need to live with a gap in your garment, or even laboriously pull out all the rows back to the dropped stitch. You can retrieve the dropped stitch or stitches with a crochet hook, and no one will be the wiser. When you notice a slipped stitch, fix it immediately: Left alone, the dropped stitch can continue to unravel down the work and create many more dropped stitches to fix.

Steps

1 Continue knitting until you are directly above the spot where the dropped stitch occurs. The spot where the stitch or stitches are dropped will resemble a ladder, with horizontal bits of yarn instead of the usual vertical loops.

2 Insert a crochet hook from front to back through the loop of the bottommost dropped stitch.

3 With the hook, catch the bottommost horizontal piece of yarn and pull it through the loop of the dropped stitch (see illustration). Continue pulling it in front of and over the next horizontal piece of yarn. This will create a new loop stitch.

4 Unhook the crochet hook from that piece of yarn.

5 If you have dropped more than one stitch, repeat steps 2 through 4 until you have picked up all the dropped stitches.

6 When you've picked up the last dropped stitch, slip that stitch onto your left knitting needle and continue knitting as usual.

What You'll Need

- Crochet hook

Tip

These instructions are for fixing a dropped stitch on the knit side. If you're working from the purl side, simply reverse the crochet hook at step 2, inserting it from back to front.

Warning

The picked-up stitches will typically be a bit tighter than the surrounding stitches, but will generally relax with time or when you block the garment.

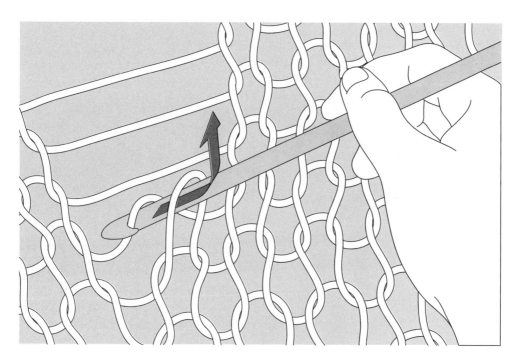

105 Restring Beads

Though there are many techniques for stringing a necklace, these basic steps will work for almost any set of beads.

Steps

1 Place the beads you're restringing on a flat, soft surface, such as a towel or a piece of folded fabric, to keep the beads from rolling every which way. (If you plan to do this regularly, you might want to invest in a bead board—a wooden or plastic board with storage compartments and grooves for laying out your beads.)

2 Determine in what order you'd like the beads restrung, and arrange them in that pattern on your flat surface. (If possible, keep the beads on their original string before restringing so you can maintain their original arrangement.)

3 With scissors, cut a piece of beading thread long enough for the necklace with about 6 inches (15 cm) to spare. A standard necklace is typically 18 to 20 inches (45 to 50 cm), a choker 14 to 16 inches (35 to 40 cm).

4 Spread a bit of craft glue along 1 inch (2.5 cm) of one end of the beading thread and let it dry. This will stiffen the thread and make it easier to string the beads.

5 Tie a knot close to the opposite end of the string (see A).

6 Dab the knot with a tiny bit of the craft glue and let it dry. A toothpick is often helpful for dabbing glue on the knot, where you want to use as little glue as possible.

7 Cut off the excess thread close to the knot.

8 String the unknotted end of the thread through the top of one of the bead tips (sometimes also called "bell tips") (see B), pulling the knot that you just made into the cup of the bead tip.

What You'll Need

- Towel or piece of folded fabric
- Scissors
- Beading thread
- Craft glue
- Toothpick
- Two bead tips
- Jewelry clasp
- Flat-nose pliers

Tips

Beading thread comes in silk, cotton and nylon varieties. Any type can be used for this project, but choose the heaviest thread that will fit through the holes in your beads without fraying.

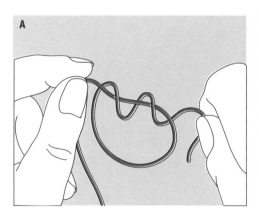

A

B

9   String all of the beads onto the beading thread in the order that you want them.

10 After all the beads are on the thread, string the thread through the bottom of the remaining bead tip so that the open end of the bead tip faces away from the beads.

11 Tie a knot in the unknotted end of the thread.

12 Dab the knot with a bit of the craft glue, and tuck the knot into the cup of the bead tip. Cut off any excess thread.

13 Attach one end of the jewelry clasp to one of the bead tips, using flat-nose pliers to wrap the hook of the bead tip around the loop of the jewelry clasp.

14 Attach the other half of the jewelry clasp to the other bead tip, again using the flat-nose pliers to wrap the bead tip's hook around the jewelry clasp.

When restringing very expensive or delicate items, such as pearls or rare gemstones, it's best to make a knotted necklace, with a small knot separating each bead, which will keep the beads from scattering if the necklace breaks as well as prevent damage from the beads rubbing together. Invest in a bead cord knotter, available at bead stores, and ask for advice on how to use it.

106 Freshen Smelly Shoes

Odor-causing bacteria thrive in dark, damp spaces, which makes your sweaty tennies an ideal habitat. You'll need to wipe out the smelly bacterial population to achieve truly odor-free shoes.

Steps

1 Examine the shoes. Are the insoles damp and causing the odor? Remove them and dry them. Or replace them with insoles formulated to kill bacterial growth, available at drugstores.

2 If the shoes are slightly damp, place them in the sun or near a heater and allow to dry thoroughly. Remove laces and lift the shoes' tongues to fully air out the shoes.

3 Put the shoes in a zipper-lock plastic bag and place them in the freezer overnight. The freezing temperatures will kill most odor-causing bacteria.

4 If odor remains after the freezing, pour baking soda into the shoes and leave it in overnight to absorb the odors. Or use products designed to remove shoe odor, which are available at supermarkets and drugstores.

5 If all else fails, go to a pet store and purchase an odor remover such as Nature's Miracle that contains enzymes or bacteria. The enzymes and bacteria in these products literally eat away the source of the bad odors. Follow the instructions carefully as you apply the product to your shoes.

What You'll Need

- Odor-controlling insoles
- Zipper-lock plastic bag
- Baking soda or shoe odor products
- Odor remover with enzymes or bacteria

Tips

Dry shoes thoroughly after they become wet to prevent smelly bacterial growth.

If your feet sweat a lot, wear lightweight cotton socks that allow your feet to breathe. You can also try odor-absorbing foot powder. And invest in two pairs of athletic shoes so that your shoes can dry out.

OOKED PICTURE • UNPLUG A STUCK AEROSOL CAN • GIVE BARBIE A MAKEOVER • DEAL WITH A STUCK WINE CORK • REPAIR A BOOK •
ORING • FIX BAD HABITS • REPAIR A BROKEN EYEGLASS FRAME • REPOSITION A SLIPPED CONTACT LENS • FIX A RUN IN STOCKINGS • JO
EAKOUT • REPAIR A TORN FINGERNAIL • FIX CHIPPED NAIL POLISH • FIX A STUCK ZIPPER • FIND A LOST CONTACT LENS • ELIMINATE BAD
Y THAT STICKS • STOP TELEMARKETERS AND JUNK MAIL • GET SUPERGLUE OFF YOUR SKIN • EXTRACT A SPLINTER • SOOTHE A SUNBURN
HANGOVER • STOP HICCUPS • MEND A BROKEN HEART • MEND A FAMILY FEUD • TREAT A SMALL CUT OR SCRAPE • FIX HAIR DISASTERS •
TTER SEATS • FIX A BILLING MISTAKE • FIX A BAD GRADE • FIX BAD CREDIT • RECOVER FROM JET LAG • RESUSCITATE AN UNCONSCIOUS
PRONOUNS • FIX A RUN-ON SENTENCE • FIX MISUSE OF THE WORD GOOD • FIX YOUR DOG OR CAT • CORRECT BAD BEHAVIOR IN DOGS
SSING BUTTON • REMOVE LINT FROM CLOTHING • FIX A DRAWSTRING ON SWEATPANTS • REPAIR A HEM • REPAIR LEATHER GOODS • MEN
UNDER YOUR CASHMERE • FIX A SWEATER THAT HAS SHRUNK • FIX A SWEATER THAT HAS STRETCHED • FIX A HOLE IN A POCKET • FIX A I
LING FROM CLOTHING • FIX A FRAYED BUTTONHOLE • REMOVE DARK SCUFFS FROM SHOES • TREAT STAINS ON LEATHER • PROTECT SUE
IET SQUEAKY HINGES • TROUBLESHOOT LOCK PROBLEMS • TIGHTEN A LOOSE DOORKNOB • TIGHTEN A LOOSE DOOR HINGE • FIX A BIN
PLACE CRACKED TILE • TROUBLESHOOT MOLD ON INTERIOR WALLS • REPLACE CRACKED TILE GROUT IN A TUB OR SHOWER • FIX A DRA
NDS • TROUBLESHOOT WINDOW SHADE PROBLEMS • FIX BROKEN GLASS IN A WINDOW • REPAIR A WINDOW SCREEN • REPAIR ALUMINUN
MAGED PLASTER • REPAIR WALL COVERINGS • TOUCH UP PAINTED WALLS • TROUBLESHOOT INTERIOR-PAINT PROBLEMS • SOLVE A LEAD
RDWOOD FLOOR • RESTORE A DULL, WORN WOOD FLOOR • TOUCH UP WOOD-FLOOR FINISHES • REPAIR DAMAGED SHEET-VINYL FLOOR
USE • CHILDPROOF YOUR HOME • PREVENT ICE DAMS • CURE A FAULTY FIREPLACE DRAW • START A FIRE IN A COLD CHIMNEY • FIX A WO
AL A GARAGE FLOOR • REFINISH A GARAGE OR BASEMENT FLOOR • CONTROL ROOF LEAKS • REDIRECT RAINWATER FROM A DOWNSPOU
MAGED ASPHALT SHINGLE • PATCH A FLAT OR LOW-PITCHED ROOF • REPAIR ROOF FLASHING • TROUBLESHOOT EXTERIOR-PAINT PROBLE
W WATER PRESSURE • FIX LEAKING PIPES • STOP A TOILET FROM RUNNING • FIX A LEAKY TOILET TANK • FIX A STOPPED-UP TOILET • STO
OGGED SINK OR TUB • REPAIR A TUB-AND-SHOWER VALVE • REPAIR CHIPPED FIXTURES • QUIET NOISY PIPES • DEFROST YOUR PIPES • D
NSUMPTION • REPLACE A RECEPTACLE • FIX AN ELECTRICAL PLUG • REPLACE A LIGHT FIXTURE • INSTALL A NEW DIMMER • FIX A LAMP •
OORBELL • FIX A WOBBLY OVERHEAD FAN • ADJUST WATER-HEATER TEMPERATURE • RELIGHT A WATER-HEATER PILOT LIGHT • TROUBLESH
E MAKER • GET RID OF MICROWAVE SMELLS • FIX A REFRIGERATOR THAT COOLS POORLY • FIX A GAS OVEN THAT HEATS POORLY • CLEAN
SHWASHER PROBLEMS • CORRECT AN OVERFLOWING DISHWASHER • FIX A LEAKY DISHWASHER • FIX A DISHWASHER THAT FILLS SLOWLY
WASHING MACHINE THAT FILLS SLOWLY • FIX A WASHING MACHINE THAT "WALKS" ACROSS THE FLOOR • FIX A CLOTHES DRYER THAT DRI
, YOUR VACUUM CLEANER • REPLACE VACUUM CLEANER BRUSHES • TROUBLESHOOT A PORTABLE AIR CONDITIONER • FIX A WINDOW AI
OCESSOR • FIX A TOASTER • DIAGNOSE MICROWAVE OVEN PROBLEMS • TROUBLESHOOT A GAS GRILL • FIX A TRASH COMPACTOR • REF
ART • TROUBLESHOOT A CRASHING COMPUTER • CLEAN UP LAPTOP SPILLS • FIX BAD SECTORS ON A HARD DISK • QUIT A FROZEN PC AT
FECTED COMPUTER • IMPROVE YOUR COMPUTER'S MEMORY • GET RID OF E-MAIL SPAM • CHANGE A LASER PRINTER CARTRIDGE • FIX A
GURE OUT WHY A PRINTER WON'T PRINT • FIX SPELLING AND GRAMMAR ERRORS • RECALL AN E-MAIL IN MICROSOFT OUTLOOK • DIAGNO
LES • TROUBLESHOOT A PALM OS PDA • RESET A PALM OS PDA • REMOVE FINGERPRINTS FROM A CAMERA LENS • TROUBLESHOOT A CD
LVAGE A VIDEOCASSETTE • TROUBLESHOOT A DVD PLAYER • STRENGTHEN FM RADIO RECEPTION • STRENGTHEN AM RADIO RECEPTION
IAMMED SLIDE PROJECTOR • GET BETTER SPEAKER SOUND • TROUBLESHOOT A DIGITAL CAMCORDER • TROUBLESHOOT A DIGITAL CAM
GHTBULB • FIX A BROKEN WINEGLASS STEM • FIX BLEMISHED WOOD FURNITURE • REPAIR GOUGES IN FURNITURE • RESTORE FURNITURE
MOUFLAGE A DOG-SCRATCHED DOOR • REPAIR A SPLIT CARPET SEAM • RID CARPETS OF PET ODORS • REINFORCE A SAGGING SHELF •
INTS OF CHAIRS AND TABLES • REUPHOLSTER A DROP-IN CHAIR SEAT • REVIVE A CANE SEAT • REINFORCE A WEAK BED FRAME • FIX UP
TTERY • REPAIR CHIPPED OR CRACKED CHINA • UNCLUTTER YOUR HOME • CLEAN CRAYON FROM A WALL • GET WAX OFF A TABLECLOT
AINS • REMOVE CHEWING GUM FROM CARPETING • REMOVE BLEACH SPOTS FROM CARPETING • REMOVE PET STAINS • ELIMINATE WINE
AINS FROM TILE GROUT • REMOVE MILDEW FROM WALLS AND CEILINGS • DISINFECT A TOILET BOWL • REMOVE FIREPLACE GRIME • GET
EAN OIL SPOTS FROM A GARAGE OR DRIVEWAY • REMOVE STAINS FROM BRICK • WASH AN OUTDOOR GRILL • FIX A FALLEN SOUFFLÉ • F
SCUE OVERPROOFED YEAST DOUGH • FIX YOUR KID LUNCH • GET RID OF TAP-WATER MINERAL DEPOSITS • CALIBRATE A MEAT THERMOM
UCE • RESCUE A BROKEN SAUCE • REMOVE FAT FROM SOUPS AND SAUCES • FIX LUMPY GRAVY • SUBSTITUTE MISSING INGREDIENTS •
RNED RICE • REMOVE COOKING ODORS • FINISH UNDERCOOKED MEAT • SALVAGE AN UNDERCOOKED TURKEY • FIX AN OVERSEASONED
ALE BREAD • SMOOTH SEIZED CHOCOLATE • SOFTEN HARDENED SUGARS OR COOKIES • FIX BREAKFAST FOR YOUR SWEETHEART • MEN
GGING TOOLS • RESTORE A BROKEN FLOWERPOT • SHARPEN PRUNING CLIPPERS • REMOVE RUST FROM TOOLS • REVIVE WILTING CUT F
ET RID OF RAMPANT BRAMBLES • TROUBLESHOOT BROWN SPOTS ON A LAWN • CONTROL MAJOR GARDEN PESTS • RID YOUR GARDEN C
ONPERFORMING COMPOST PILE • FIX BAD SOIL • SHORE UP A RAISED GARDEN BED • REMOVE A DEAD OR DISEASED TREE LIMB • TROUE
RAINAGE • TROUBLESHOOT ROSE DISEASES • IDENTIFY AND CORRECT SOIL DEFICIENCIES IN ROSES • TROUBLESHOOT ROSE PESTS • OV
MAGED DECK BOARDS • REPAIR DECK RAILINGS • STRENGTHEN DECK JOISTS • FIX A RUSTY IRON RAILING • REPAIR A GATE • REPAIR A
RACKED OR DAMAGED CONCRETE • IMPROVE THE LOOK OF REPAIRED CONCRETE • REPAIR AN ASPHALT DRIVEWAY • REVIVE WOODEN O
ARDEN PONDS • CLEAN SWIMMING POOL WATER • TROUBLESHOOT HOT TUBS AND SPAS • REPLACE BRICKS IN WALKWAYS AND PATIOS •
AR WITH JUMPER CABLES • SHUT OFF A CAR ALARM THAT WON'T QUIT • FREE A CAR STUCK ON ICE OR SNOW • DE-ICE YOUR WINDSHIEL
RN-SIGNAL COVER • FIX A CAR FUSE • FIX DASHBOARD LIGHTS THAT WON'T LIGHT • REMOVE CAR SMELLS • CHECK TIRE PRESSURE • IN
PROPERLY INSTALLED CHILD CAR SEAT • TROUBLESHOOT LEAKING OIL • CHECK AND ADD POWER-STEERING FLUID • CHECK AND ADD C
ROKEN EXHAUST PIPE • CHECK AND ADD ENGINE OIL • CHECK AND ADD BRAKE FLUID • CHECK AND ADD FLUID TO YOUR AUTOMATIC TI

MORY • FIX AN ELECTRIC CAN OPENER THAT DROPS THE CAN • TROUBLESHOOT A CELL PHONE • KEEP MIRRORS FROM FOGGING • ZAP A
EEP A SHAVING NICK FROM BLEEDING • GET RID OF SPLIT ENDS • UNTANGLE HAIR SNARLS • FIX FRIZZY HAIR • FIX BLEEDING LIPSTICK •
CKY SOCIAL SITUATION • FIX A BAD REPUTATION • CLEAN LIPSTICK FROM A COLLAR • FIX A BAD RELATIONSHIP • SALVAGE A BAD DATE •
EEDING NOSE • BEAT THE MONDAY MORNING BLUES • GET OUT OF A FIX • EXTRACT A BROKEN KEY • RETRIEVE KEYS LOCKED INSIDE A C
TOP SOMEONE FROM CHOKING • STOP AN ANT INVASION • STABILIZE A CHRISTMAS TREE • RESCUE AN ITEM FROM THE DRAIN • FIX IMPR
KUNK ODOR FROM YOUR DOG • GET A CAT OUT OF A TREE • CORRECT BAD BEHAVIOR IN CATS • TREAT A CAT FOR MATTED FUR • REPLA
AM • TREAT MILDEW DAMAGE • GET STATIC OUT OF YOUR LAUNDRY • DEAL WITH A CLOTHES-MOTH INFESTATION • FIX A SEPARATED ZIPF
R SOCK • TREAT MIXED-WASH ACCIDENTS • TAKE WRINKLES OUT OF CLOTHING • FIX A HOLE IN JEANS • REPAIR A SNAG IN A SWEATER •
AINS • WASH SNEAKERS • PICK UP A DROPPED STITCH IN KNITTING • RESTRING BEADS • FRESHEN SMELLY SHOES • FIX A SAGGING CLOS
• FIX A RUBBING DOOR • FIX A DRAFTY DOOR • TUNE UP SLIDING DOORS • FIX A SHOWER DOOR • SEAL WALL JOINTS AROUND A TUB OF
/ • REPAIR A FAULTY WINDOW CRANK • REPAIR VERTICAL BLINDS • REPAIR VENETIAN BLINDS OR MINIBLINDS • REPAIR WOOD OR PLASTIC
REEN WINDOWS • INSTALL NEW SASH CORDS IN WINDOWS • FIX A TIGHT OR LOOSE WINDOW SASH • REPAIR MINOR DRYWALL DAMAGE •
BLEM • REPLACE A DAMAGED CEILING TILE • REPLACE A WOOD FLOORBOARD • QUIET SQUEAKING FLOORS • REPAIR A WATER-DAMAGED
A VINYL-TILE FLOOR • SILENCE SQUEAKY ... STER • REPLACE CAULKING ON THE OUTSIDE OF Y
G STOVE • REPAIR AND PREVENT WOOD RO ... TCH A GUTTER LEAK • TROUBLESHOOT A WET BAS
GGING GUTTER • UNCLOG GUTTERS AND D ... T • REPAIR A CRACKED OR SPLIT WOOD SHINGLE •
RAGE-DOOR TENSION • TROUBLESHOOT A ... TES • LOOSEN A RUSTY NUT OR BOLT • TROUBLE
K SWEATING • FIX FLUSHING PROBLEMS • ... FAUCET • FIX A STOPPER THAT DOESN'T SEAL • CL
MP PUMP PROBLEMS • TROUBLESHOOT ELE ... USE • SWAP A FAULTY LIGHT SWITCH • REDUCE EN
OOT FLUORESCENT LIGHTING • FIX A LOW ... E THERMOSTAT • TROUBLESHOOT HOLIDAY LIGHT
ING SYSTEM • REFRESH A SMELLY REFRIGE ... MS • FIX A LEAKING REFRIGERATOR • REPAIR A CL
TIONING GAS BURNER • REPAIR A RANGE ... FIX AN ELECTRIC OVEN THAT HEATS POORLY • DIA
YOUR APPLIANCES • CONTROL GARBAGE ... E DISPOSAL • DIAGNOSE WASHING MACHINE PROE
FIX A HAIR DRYER • TROUBLESHOOT A CLO ... AT SPUTTERS • FIX AN IRON THAT LEAVES SPOTS O
ER • FIX A DEHUMIDIFIER • REPAIR A CONS ... DER • HANDLE A MIXER THAT OVERHEATS • REPAIR
MACHINE • TROUBLESHOOT SMOKE ALAR ... ARD SPILLS • TROUBLESHOOT A COMPUTER THA
REMOVE A WINDOWS PROGRAM • SPEED ... OUSE • REPLACE YOUR PC'S BATTERY • CLEAN A
FAILS ITS SELF-TEST • CORRECT MONITOR ... APER JAM • TROUBLESHOOT A RECURRING PRINT
NE MODEM PROBLEMS • TROUBLESHOOT A ... REEN GLARE • GET TOP-NOTCH SCANS • RECOVER
STORE A CD • REPAIR A WARPED CD • CLE ... • EXTRACT A JAMMED VIDEOTAPE • ADJUST VCR
TE CONTROL • FIX AUDIOCASSETTES • FIX ... OT A CASSETTE DECK • REPLACE BROKEN RABBIT
LESHOOT A CD PLAYER • REPLACE A HEAD ... RASS • SHINE SILVER SAFELY • REMOVE A BROKEN
LACE A BROKEN TOWEL ROD • REMOVE ST ... FOR NATURAL DISASTERS • FIX A FRAYED CARPET
BORING BATHROOM • REPLACE A SHOWER ... NACE FILTER • REPAIR A BROKEN SLIDING DRAWEF
D CHAIR • FIX A WOBBLY WOOD CHAIR • SE ... OR CRACKED PORCELAIN • REPAIR CHIPPED OR CF
AX FROM CARPETING • GET RID OF CEILIN ... MOVE MYSTERY STAINS FROM CLOTHING • REMOV
A RUG OR TABLECLOTH • REMOVE BURN ... NITURE • STRIP WAX BUILDUP FROM FLOORS • REI
DRANT STAINS • ELIMINATE CIGARETTE ODOR • RESTORE SHINE TO YOUR JEWELRY • WASH DIRTY WINDOWS • REMOVE GRIME FROM MIN

Home Repair

MBLED CAKE • FIX A PERFECT CUP OF TEA • PATCH A TORN PIE CRUST • KEEP A PIE CRUST FROM GETTING SOGGY • FIX DOUGH THAT W
DULL KNIFE • REMOVE RUST FROM A CAST-IRON PAN • REPAIR LAMINATE COUNTERTOPS • REMOVE STAINS FROM A STONE COUNTERTOF
CHOLESTEROL • TREAT BURNED POTS AND PANS • RESCUE A BURNED CAKE OR PIE • PUT OUT A KITCHEN FIRE • REMOVE THE BITTERN
N UNDERSEASONED DISH • REMOVE OVEN SPILLS • CLEAN UP OIL SPILLS • FIX A DRINK FOR ANY OCCASION • DISENTANGLE PASTA • REI
CUTTING BOARD • KEEP A MIXING BOWL STEADY • FIX GARDEN TOOL HANDLES • REPAIR A LEAKY HOSE NOZZLE • MEND A LEAKY HOSE
ARPEN A POWER MOWER BLADE • SHARPEN PUSH MOWER BLADES • REPAIR BALD SPOTS ON GRASS • RID YOUR GRASS OF DOG URINE
UBLESHOOT HERBS • TROUBLESHOOT HOUSEPLANTS • OVERCOME SHADE PROBLEMS • RID SOIL OF PESTS AND DISEASES • REVIVE A
ES AND SHRUBS • REPAIR A LEAKING IRRIGATION SYSTEM • UNCLOG A SPRINKLER SYSTEM • CLEAN A CLOGGED DRIP SYSTEM • FIX POC
GUS DISEASES IN ROSES • REPAIR DECK STEPS • RENOVATE A WEATHERED DECK • TIGHTEN LOOSE DECKING • REMOVE DECK STAINS • F
• LEVEL AND SMOOTH A GRAVEL PATH • FIX A POTHOLE IN A DIRT OR GRAVEL DRIVEWAY • REPLACE PATIO STONES, TILES AND PAVERS •
TURE • RESTORE WEATHERED METAL FURNITURE • REPAIR CHAIR STRAPS AND WEBBING • REVIVE RUSTED IRON FURNITURE • TROUBLE
ED CAR • SHUT OFF A JAMMED HORN • CHANGE YOUR CAR'S BATTERY • TROUBLESHOOT A CAR THAT WON'T START • FIX A FLAT TIRE •
IED-OUT SIGNAL BULB • FIX A BURNED-OUT HEADLIGHT • ADJUST HEADLIGHTS • FIX A STUCK BRAKE LIGHT • REPLACE A BROKEN TAILL
RES • FIX A STUCK CONVERTIBLE TOP • DIAGNOSE A LEAK INSIDE YOUR CAR • REPLACE YOUR AIR FILTER • HANDLE A FAULTY REPAIR •
OL AN OVERHEATED ENGINE • REPLACE A LEAKING RADIATOR HOSE • CHANGE YOUR WIPER BLADES • ADD WINDSHIELD-WASHER FLUID
TROUBLESHOOT YOUR BRAKES • ADD BRAKE FLUID TO THE CLUTCH MASTER CYLINDER • TROUBLESHOOT DASHBOARD WARNING LIGH
SPARK-PLUG WIRES • DIAGNOSE CAR SMELLS • CLEAN THE OUTSIDE OF YOUR CAR • RESTORE YOUR CAR'S SHINE • WASH THE INTERIOR

107 Fix a Sagging Closet Rod

If a closet rod is sagging, either it's too thin for the weight it supports or it's spanning too wide a space. You don't have to give all your clothes to charity, though. The fix is quick and easy, and as a bonus you can make good on your New Year's resolution to clean the closet.

Steps

Replace an undersize rod

1 If the sag is modest, replace an undersize wood pole with a thicker rod. Standard-size closet rods range from 1 1/16 inches (27 mm) to 1 5/8 inches (41 mm) in diameter.

2 Lift the rod out of the U-shaped pole socket.

3 Use the existing rod as a guide for cutting the new rod to length with a saw.

4 Set the new rod in the sockets.

Add a support

1 Locate a stud on the rear wall near midspan. To do this, shine a bright light at a low angle across the wall and baseboard while looking for the slight indentations that indicate a fastener location. Tap at this location. If the stud is there, the wall will feel firmer when you tap and you'll hear a dull rather than a hollow sound.

2 Hold a rod bracket over the stud and up against the closet shelf. If the new bracket is not in line with the pole sockets, move the pole sockets in or out as needed to align everything.

3 Mark the bracket mounting holes on the wall and on the underside of the closet shelf.

4 Drive a nail partway into the wall at the marked locations to verify the presence of a stud. If you don't find a stud there, tap to either side until you hit one, then again drive a nail to confirm.

5 Drive screws through the bracket into the wall. If you don't own a drill with a driver, bore a pilot hole for the screw with a drill and use a screwdriver to install the screws.

What You'll Need

- Replacement rod
- Saw
- Rod bracket
- Hammer
- Nails
- Drill, driver and bit
- Screws
- Screwdriver

Warning

Anytime you drill or screw into a wall, you risk encountering either an electric cable or some kind of pipe. Work slowly, listening and feeling for any unexpected sounds or resistance.

108 Quiet Squeaky Hinges

Hinges make noise because of friction, which is caused by a rusty hinge pin or out-of-alignment hinges. You can silence that annoying noise with a quick fix.

Steps

1 Tap a nail into the hole under the hinge pin to knock the pin partially out. Place the tip of a screwdriver under the pin's head and tap on the screwdriver with the palm of your hand or a hammer until the pin is loose enough to pull out.

2 Use No. 0000 steel wool, a fine emery cloth or an abrasive cleaning pad to scrub dirt and rust off the hinge pin and leaves.

3 Lubricate all parts with an oil or spray lubricant such as WD-40 and wipe off any excess.

4 Reinstall the hinge, tapping it in with a hammer. Repeat the procedure for the remaining hinge(s).

5 If you still hear squeaking, remove all the hinge pins and then remove the door and hold it against the hinges to see if any hinges are misaligned.

6 If the misalignment is minor, tap the hinge leaf up or down as needed to align it with the leaf on the door. You should also tap the leaf on the door so you move each hinge a little rather than moving one a lot. Reinstall the door.

7 In extreme cases you may need to remove the hinge and then chisel out the mortise to move the hinge. If this is the case, plug the old screw holes with wood filler. Mix a two-part wood filler according to the manufacturer's instructions and press it into the holes with a putty knife.

8 When the filler is hard, position the hinge and drill new pilot holes. To avoid the tendency for a drill bit to wander off center, use a self-centering bit or self-centering punch to start the hole. Its convex surface fits into the concave recesses in the hinge.

9 If moving the hinge results in a noticeable gap along one edge, mask the face of the hinge with tape to protect it, and apply additional wood filler to fill the gap.

10 When the filler dries, remove the hinge, sand and touch up with paint, and reinstall the hinge.

What You'll Need

- Nail
- Screwdriver
- Hammer
- No. 0000 steel wool, fine emery cloth or abrasive cleaning pad
- Oil or spray lubricant
- Wood chisel
- Wood filler
- Putty knife
- Drill and bit
- Painter's masking tape
- Sandpaper
- Touch-up paint

Tip

When removing a door, start with the bottom hinge and work your way up.

109 Troubleshoot Lock Problems

Have a problem with a door that won't lock or latch properly? These difficulties fall into two general categories: those related to the lock set or key, and those related to the door's frame and latch assembly.

Steps

If the lock mechanism is broken

1 If the key turns but doesn't operate the lock bolt, the lock mechanism is broken. Remove the mechanism to have it repaired, or replace the lock set yourself.

2 To remove a mortise lock-set cylinder for repair (see illustration for 110 Tighten a Loose Doorknob), remove the deadbolt knob by loosening the setscrew in the sleeve of the knob using a standard screwdriver or Allen (hex) wrench, or by removing any mounting screws. Then, on the faceplate, loosen the setscrew opposite the lock cylinder and unscrew the lock cylinder.

3 To remove the rest of a mortise lock set, take off the interior knob, the exterior handle and any trim. Remove the faceplate and strike plate by removing their screws.

4 To replace a mortise lock set with one that has the same dimensions, reverse the procedure in step 3, making sure to follow the detailed instructions that the new unit will probably include.

5 To remove cylinder and tubular lock sets, locate a slot on the shaft of the knob. Depress and hold down the protruding spring clip with a screwdriver (or a thumbnail) as you pull the knob straight out (see A). Or, if there is no slot, loosen the two machine screws in the face of the rose. If there's a mounting plate, loosen (or sometimes remove) the two machine screws to take out the cylinder (see B).

6 To replace the lock set, reverse the procedure in step 5. If you cannot reuse the strike plate (or prefer not to), unscrew it. Position the new one to check the fit in the mortise (recess).

What You'll Need

- Screwdrivers
- Allen (hex) wrench
- Replacement lock set
- Wood putty and putty knife
- Sandpaper
- Primer and paint, or stain and varnish
- Wood chisel
- Graphite powder or silicone spray
- Lock de-icer or hair dryer
- Drill
- ⅞-inch (22-mm) spade drill bit
- Vise

Tips

If you must drive a distance to have a key cut, you may want to remove the lock set and bring it, so you won't have to make another trip if the new key doesn't work.

You can stain some types of wood putty by either mixing the powder with the stain or applying the stain to the cured putty—an important step in repairing doors with a natural-wood finish that the putty must match.

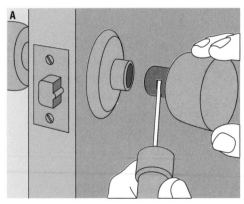

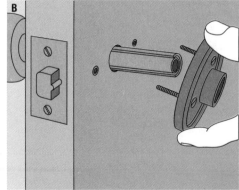

7 If the mortise is too large, install the strike plate temporarily and fill the excess mortise with wood putty. When the putty is hard, remove the plate to sand the putty smooth and touch up the finish (use either primer and paint or stain and varnish).

8 If the mortise is too small, trace the plate's perimeter on the wood and use a sharp chisel to extend the mortise. First make vertical cuts at the perimeter with the bevel side facing inward. Then, with the bevel flat on the already mortised area and the chisel at a low angle, chisel out wood up to the perimeter cut.

Other lock-set problems

1 If a replacement key won't turn, it may have been cut poorly. Check the lock set's operation using the original key. If the replacement key is faulty, take it back to the store where you had it cut and ask for another.

2 If the key turns but only with effort, lubricate the lock mechanism with graphite powder or silicone spray by injecting the lubricant into the keyway. Work the key or thumb latch back and forth to distribute the lubricant.

3 If lubricating fails, the tumblers in the lock cylinder might be damaged. Remove the lock cylinder or lock set and bring it to a locksmith for a minor repair.

4 If the key either does not fit into the lock or won't turn, and you've been having wet, freezing weather, the lock is likely frozen. Spray a lock de-icer into the key slot or warm it with a hair dryer.

5 If a latch bolt doesn't extend fully, the mortise for it might not be deep enough. Remove the strike plate and bore the hole deeper; the hole has a ⅞-inch (22-mm) diameter, so you'll need a spade drill bit that size.

6 If you have to push against the door to make it latch, weather-stripping may be pressing against the door. Reposition the weather-stripping; adjust the strike plate's position; or remove the strike plate, put it in a vise to file off the offending portion, and reinstall it.

7 If a latch bolt bumps into the bottom edge of the hole in the strike plate, tighten the hinges (see 112 Fix a Binding Door). If that doesn't fix the problem, adjust or file the strike plate as described in step 6, above.

Leave the protective plastic film on the strike plate until you've completed the work, especially if you need to apply putty.

When you putty a strike-plate mortise, make sure the putty does not extend onto the plate.

If you need to bring a lock cylinder or lock set in for repair, bring one of the original keys.

Warning

Heating a key over a flame to insert it in a frozen lock may work, but it can make the key more likely to break in the future, and you may burn your fingers unless you grasp the key with pliers.

110 Tighten a Loose Doorknob

If your doorknobs feel a little loose and jiggly, you may need to tighten either the lock set (for most modern doorknobs) or the knob itself (on older mortise-style passage locks, pictured below).

Steps

1 If you have a modern cylindrical or tubular lock set with a loose knob, see 109 Troubleshoot Lock Problems. These knobs either snap onto a cylinder or are integrated into the lock set, so you need to tighten the lock set itself.

2 If you have a mortise-style lock and lock set (see illustration), follow these steps. These lock sets (both interior and entry models), once the standard, are now rarely used. The knobs thread onto the ends of a square spindle with rounded, threaded corners. A setscrew, located in the knob's sleeve, tightens down on the square face of the spindle, preventing the knob from turning on the spindle when operated.

3 Loosen the setscrew in the sleeve of one knob with a standard screwdriver or in some cases an Allen (hex) wrench.

4 Unscrew the knob to expose the spindle and access the setscrew on the other knob. Make sure the setscrew is very tight.

What You'll Need

- Screwdriver or Allen (hex) wrench

Tips

You can remove the knobs on a passage lock, which has no locks on either side, from either side of the door. With an entry lock set, you must remove the inside knob first.

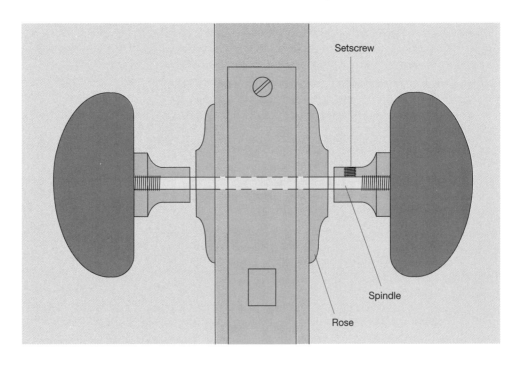

Setscrew

Spindle

Rose

5 Turn the knob until one of the spindle's flat sides is directly on top. Press the knob toward the door and hold it tightly against the trim (the rose) as you thread the other knob onto the spindle.

6 Make sure the knob is contacting the trim, but is not tight; then turn the knob slightly one way or the other as needed to align the setscrew with any flat face of the spindle. Then screw in the setscrew until it's very tight.

7 Test the knob's operation. It should turn freely but not loosely. To adjust the position of the knob, repeat the above procedure as needed, turning the knob onto the spindle more or less.

Match the screwdriver tip to the size of the setscrew slot. If it's too large, you can't drive the screw in all the way; if it's too small, you can't exert adequate tightening force.

111 Tighten a Loose Door Hinge

A heavy door puts a constant strain on the hinges, particularly the top one. This can loosen the screws and eventually enlarge the holes so the screws just spin when you try to tighten them. Here's what to do if you're facing this problem.

Steps

1 Tighten a loose hinge screw with a screwdriver as soon as you notice it. Otherwise the screw's movement will likely strip the hole or cause the door to bind and mar the finish on its frame and edge.

2 If the screw turns but doesn't tighten, the hole is already stripped. For lightweight interior doors, you can probably get away with the following quick fix. Open the door wide and wedge something under the door to take the weight off the hinge. Remove the loose screw and any other screw holding that hinge leaf. Dip a couple of cardboard matches in wood glue or white glue and insert them into the stripped hole. Reinstall the hinge.

3 An even better option is a variation on this idea: Plug the hole with glue-covered wood matches, a golf tee, or a wood shaving cut from the corner of a board with a utility knife. Reinstall the hinge using all the holes except the plugged one. Allow that hole to dry for several hours, cut off any wood that sticks out, and carefully drill a pilot hole in the center. Then drive in the remaining screw.

4 The most effective option, especially for the top hinge of a heavy door, is to replace the existing screw with one at least 2½ inches (6 cm) long. (If you have such a screw handy, it's also the easiest approach.) This long screw will penetrate the frame behind the doorjamb, creating a secure connection.

What You'll Need

- Screwdriver
- Item for wedging under door
- Cardboard matches
- Wood glue or white glue
- Wood matches, golf tee or wood shaving
- Utility knife
- Drill and bit
- Long screws

Tips

Replace standard slotted screws with Phillips-head screws whenever you put in new ones.

If you use a drill with a screw-driving bit, adjust the clutch so you won't strip or break off a screw.

112 Fix a Binding Door

Wood doors that once fit perfectly may bind due to loose hinges, seasonal expansion of the door or, in rare cases, settling of the house. Fixes range from simple to complex, depending on the problem's extent and cause. If planing is required and you don't own a jack plane or larger power plane, consider renting one for the task.

Steps

Tightening loose hinges

1 If the hinges are loose, especially the top one, the door will likely bind near the top of the opposite jamb. Use a screwdriver to tighten any loose screws.

2 If a screw turns but doesn't tighten, replace the existing screw with a longer one that will penetrate the frame or go deeper into the door. Alternatively, plug the screw hole with small slivers of wood (matches, toothpicks and so forth) dipped in glue, then reinstall the screw (this approach is adequate only for lightweight interior doors).

Adjusting hinge-mortise depth

1 If the door binds at the hinge side just before it closes, place a layer of noncorrugated cardboard under the hinges to shim them. Either fix one hinge leaf at a time in place, or remove the door and do all of the hinges at once.

2 To remove a door, support its weight on wood shims and then tap a nail into the hole under each hinge pin to drive the pin out a little. Tap the pins out the rest of the way with a hammer and screwdriver placed under the head of the pin.

3 If the door binds on the lock side and the hinge leaves project above the wood surface, deepen each mortise with a hammer and chisel. Cut the perimeter with the chisel vertical and its beveled side facing the mortise. Then make numerous consistent, shallow cuts spaced about ³⁄₁₆ inch (5 mm) apart over the entire mortise, with the chisel held at a slight angle, bevel side down. Lay the chisel nearly flat to scrape out the small pieces and smooth the bottom of the mortise (see A).

Door is too large for opening

1 If the door fits in winter but not in summer or in damp weather, when it expands, inspect its underside with a mirror for visible breaks in the paint or varnish. If the finish is not completely sealed, wait until the weather is dry and the door isn't binding, then apply a new finish. Use a paint pad that allows you to paint the bottom edge of a door without removing the door (sold at paint stores), or remove the door to brush it on.

What You'll Need

- Screwdriver
- Long hinge screws or small pieces of wood
- Wood glue
- Noncorrugated cardboard
- Tapered wood shims
- Nail
- Hammer
- Wood chisel
- Small mirror
- Primer and paint, or stain and varnish
- Paint pad or paintbrush
- Carpenter's square and spirit level
- Door jig
- Jack or power plane
- Carpenter's scribe (compass)
- Sanding block and sandpaper

Tips

Remove hinges starting from the bottom and moving up.

Scrape the paint out of the screw slots of painted-over hinges and screws. Attempting to remove a paint-clogged screw usually strips it.

Before you plane a painted door's edge, use a paint scraper to remove as much paint as you can. Paint destroys the sharp edge of your planer very quickly.

Often the direction of the wood grain makes a plane dig deeply into the wood in one direction but cut more smoothly in the other direction.

2 For more severe problems with a door that doesn't seal properly, plane it. First test the jamb with a carpenter's square and spirit level to see if it's square and plumb.

3 Only if the jamb is out of square and you don't want to remove the casing to correct the problem should you plane the door's strike edge. Plane the edge near the top or bottom as needed to create a consistent gap all around the door. If the door binds near the handle, plane the hinge side.

4 If the jamb is square, close the door and set a carpenter's scribe to the widest gap dimension, or about ³⁄₁₆ inch (5 mm) minimum. Hold it perpendicular to the door with its metal point against the jamb's edge and its pencil on the door's face, and draw a line parallel to the jamb along the entire length of the hinge side of the door.

5 Remove the door and stand it on its edge in a door jig to remove the hinges. To make a door jig, nail two triangular pieces of 2-by-4 wood to the wide edge of a longer 2-by-4. Space the triangular pieces about 2 inches (5 cm) apart. Then do the same with another 2-by-4. Stand the door on the 2-by-4s between the plywood, and tap in a shingle tip or other shim (see B).

6 Using the scribed line on the other side of the door as a reference, remove material from the edge with a jack (see B) or power plane. To remove an even amount, use long strokes from end to end. To achieve a taper, start planing where you need to remove the most wood. With each successive stroke, extend the cut more.

7 Finish with one or two light passes over the full length and chisel the hinge mortises deeper as needed. Install the hinges and hang the door to test the fit. When it's right, remove the door and hinges for sanding and finishing. Allow paint or finish to dry before you hang the door.

Warning

Exterior wood doors are usually very heavy. Get a helper when removing or hanging a heavy door.

Wear eye protection throughout the process and ear protection when using a power plane.

A

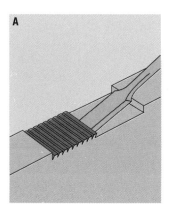

B

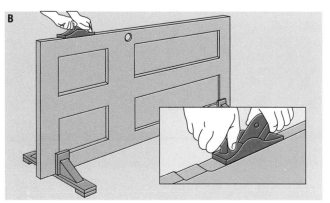

113 Fix a Rubbing Door

The constant rubbing of a door against your carpet or floor may mar those surfaces. Trimming the bottom of the door can prevent this damage and allow the door to open smoothly. A handsaw guided by a straight board works, but a guided circular saw—the method described below—is generally more accurate and easier to use.

Steps

1 If the door is on its hinges, close it and place a board on the floor up against the door to trace a line on the door parallel to the floor (see A). Ideally use a ½-inch (12-mm) thick board to mark a cut line ½ inch (12 mm) above the flooring; but if you use a ¾-inch (2-cm) board, just subtract the difference.

2 If you can't install the door because, for example, you've recently put in thick carpeting, measure from the top of the door opening to the floor at each side of the opening. Subtract ⅝ inch (15 mm) from each measurement. Put the door on sawhorses or a work-bench and transfer the measurements to the door, then draw a straight line between them. Assuming there's a ⅛-inch (3-mm) gap above the door, this allows for a ½-inch (12-mm) gap under it after you cut along this line.

3 To prevent the circular saw's blade from chipping a veneered door or the vertical stiles on a solid wood door, cut through the veneer or score the wood stiles along your cut line with several passes of a utility knife.

4 Clamp a straightedge on the door to guide a circular saw's cut. Complete the cut (see B).

5 Use a sanding block with medium and then fine sandpaper to round over and smooth the cut edges. Seal the bottom edge of the door with varnish or primer and paint to limit expansion, contraction and warping caused by changes in humidity.

What You'll Need

- Board
- Tape measure
- Straightedge
- Sawhorses or workbench
- Retractable utility knife with blades
- Clamp
- Circular saw
- Sanding block
- Sandpaper
- Varnish, or primer and paint

Warning

Wear eye protection such as goggles when using a circular saw.

Avoid dangerous circular-saw kickback. Clamp the door and straightedge guide into place so you can use two hands for cutting and you don't overreach.

Use padded clamps or insert a scrap of wood between the clamp and the door to protect the finish.

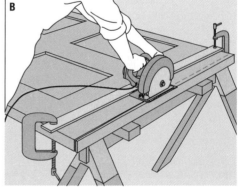

114 **Fix a Drafty Door**

Your energy savings will typically reimburse the full cost of weather-stripping materials within a year, and it's easy to install yourself.

Steps

Seal the doorsill

1 Measure the width of your door and cut the weather-stripping (sweep, door bottom or threshold type) to length. Depending on the material, use a fine metal-cutting blade in a hacksaw, tin snips, a woodcutting saw or a utility knife.

2 For a sweep (see A), close the door and position the sweep so it contacts the sill. For a door bottom (see B), verify that the gap under the door is within the prescribed limits; open the door to slide on a U-shaped door bottom and close it, or position an L-shaped one on the closed door. For a threshold (see C), notch it to fit against the side jambs when its gasket is centered under the door.

3 Mark the mounting-hole locations (usually slotted) on the door for a sweep or door bottom, and on the sill for a threshold. (Remove the gasket to access the screws.)

4 Remove a threshold to caulk under it unless it has vinyl seals in its feet, then reposition it.

5 Install screws in the center of any slotted mounting holes, and adjust the sweep or door bottom before driving in the screws.

Seal the jambs

1 For peel-and-stick V-shaped vinyl, thoroughly clean the surface where you're applying the product. Position the product according to the diagram on the package, mark and cut pieces to length, and notch the one for the strike side to fit around the door strike.

2 Install the vinyl with the specified fasteners, which may include tacks, staples, 4d finishing nails or just an adhesive backing.

What You'll Need

- Tape measure
- Weather-stripping (sweep, door bottom or threshold type)
- Hacksaw, tin snips, wood-cutting saw or utility knife
- Screwdriver
- Caulk and applicator
- Hammer
- V-shaped vinyl weather-stripping and specified fasteners
- Cleaning supplies

Tips

If you buy a threshold with a gasket, get the adjustable type. Otherwise it's difficult to achieve a precise fit.

To make it easier to start a screw without marring the door, start the hole with an awl or drill a pilot hole.

Miter the corners of spring-metal and V-strip weather-stripping so that they don't interfere with each other, and test-fit the two pieces before installing either one.

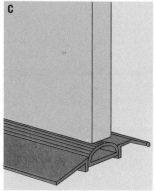

115 Tune Up Sliding Doors

Sliding doors should glide easily and close evenly against a jamb. This is true of an exterior slider and its screen door as well as of interior bypassing sliders and pocket doors. Here's how to handle adjustments.

Steps

Exterior sliders

1 Remove the door to repair a bent track and to inspect, lubricate and clean the rollers in the underside. Slide the operating panel into a half-open position. From indoors, lift the door up into the top track as far as it will go. Tilt the bottom out toward you and lower the door to the floor.

2 If the outside edge of the track is bent inward and rubbing against the door, tap it out with a block of wood and hammer. If it needs additional straightening, cut a block of wood to fit tightly in the channel and then hammer another block of wood against the outside face of the track (see A).

3 Clean the tracks with a stiff brush or sponge and some soap and water, then clean and lubricate the rollers located in the bottom of the door. (You shouldn't oil or otherwise lubricate the lower track of a sliding door. It's unnecessary, and the lubricant collects dirt.)

4 Reinstall the door panel. With the door almost closed, look for an even gap between the door and the jamb. Adjust if needed.

5 To adjust one side of the door up or down as needed, insert a pry bar under the end of the door. Placing a small wood block under the bar for leverage, lift the door up while you turn the adjustment screw (see B), or hold the door up with a wedge.

6 Locate the wheel-height adjustment screws in the end (or sometimes the face) of the bottom rail. Turn these clockwise or counterclockwise to lower or raise the wheel, which in turn will align the door with the jamb.

What You'll Need

- Block of wood
- Hammer
- Stiff brush or sponge
- Soap
- Lubricant
- Pry bar
- Small wood block or wooden wedge
- Screwdriver
- Open-ended wrench
- Hacksaw blade
- Hammer
- Nail set
- Touch-up paint and supplies

Tip

Adjusting the right side of a sliding door up or the left side down produces the same results. Decide whether you want the door higher or lower, and let that determine how you level it. For a narrow gap across the top, you'll want it higher, but to engage a floor guide, you'll want it lower.

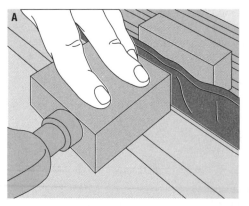

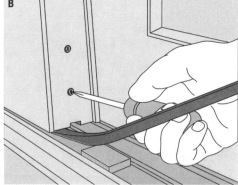

Interior bypassing closet doors

1 With the closet light on and a screwdriver in hand, go inside the closet and close the door to observe how it meets the jamb.

2 Turn the adjusting screw, located on the back of each roller bracket, until you've aligned the door and jamb. Some cam-type assemblies adjust as you turn the screw. With other types, loosening the screw allows you to raise or lower the door via a slot in the hardware, then lock it into place by retightening the screw. You adjust still others by turning a hanger bolt from the trolley with an open-ended wrench (see "Pocket doors," below).

3 If the door meets the jamb evenly but rubs against the carpet, or conversely if the bottom of the door is too high to engage the floor guides, raise or lower both sides equally to achieve the desired height.

Pocket doors

1 The door brackets on the top of the door hook onto hanger bolts suspended from a pair of two- or four-wheel trolleys that ride in the track. To access the hanger bolt for adjustment, remove the stop and the split (two-piece) head jamb on one side of the door. This can be quite tricky or easy, depending on how the door fastens together. If you see screws, remove them.

2 If you don't see any screws, carefully pry off the stop and look again for screws that may secure the split jamb to the frame of the pocket door. (Look for putty indentations that might indicate the location of the screws.)

3 If the casing is nailed to the jamb, it shouldn't be. Pry the pieces apart enough to cut the nails with a hacksaw blade, or drive each nail through the casing with a nail set and hammer.

4 Use an open-ended wrench to turn the hanger bolt and level the door. (If you don't have the thin open-ended wrench required to adjust the locknut on a four-wheel trolley, you can lift the door off the trolley, adjust the nut and rehang it. Test and repeat as needed.)

5 When you've properly adjusted the door, tighten the locknut, then reinstall the trim and touch up the paint as needed.

Warning

Removing and reinstalling a heavy glass sliding-door panel is awkward at best. Mishandling one may result in broken toes or a broken door. It's much easier and safer to have one person on each end for this task.

Place a throw or other padding on the floor where you plan to rest a glass sliding panel you've removed.

Avoid laying a glass door flat, which can damage the insulated glass seal. Stand it on its end or edge.

116 Fix a Shower Door

Once installed, a shower door requires little maintenance other than frequent cleaning and occasionally tightening a screw. You can easily take care of the few problems that may arise.

Steps

Cleaning a shower door

1 To minimize soap-scum buildup, use a squeegee after you shower to clean the glass, especially if it's clear, and clean the glass regularly with a cleaner designed for bathroom surfaces.

2 To avoid unsightly hard-water stains, scrub the glass *at least* every other month with a nonabrasive powder cleaner and a white polishing pad. Don't use the green or red ones; they're too abrasive. To speed up the job, buy white polishing pads that fit palm sanders.

Sealing leaks at the sill and jambs

1 Scrape off any old caulk with a single-edge razor held at a very low angle. Work carefully to avoid scratching the surfaces.

2 Clean all surfaces with a bathroom cleaner. If you see mildew, use a cleaner that contains a mildewcide, or simply sponge on a 50-50 solution of water and bleach and allow it to sit for 15 minutes. Rinse well.

3 When the surfaces are dry, cut the tip off a caulking cartridge's nozzle at a 45-degree angle with a utility knife. Avoid cutting too much off the tip of the caulking cartridge. Too large a hole will deposit too much caulk, making for a messy caulk joint.

4 To seal any leaks between the metal sill and the tub or shower pan, apply clear caulk on the exterior side of the track with a caulking gun. (In most cases you must leave the inside joint open to allow water to drain out of the track into the tub or shower.) It's best to use a caulking gun with a quick-release trigger and lift it away as soon as you reach the end of the joint so the residual pressure won't deposit excess caulk.

5 To seal any leaks between the metal jambs and the walls, apply caulk on the inside where it will be less noticeable.

6 Smooth and seal the caulk into each joint in a single pass with a wetted fingertip immediately after application.

Rehanging a bypassing shower panel

1 Stand outside the shower for an exterior panel and inside for an interior one. Tilt the bottom of the panel toward you. Lift the panel up into the head so the wheels are suspended above the track. Tilt the bottom inward as you lower it into the lower track or (on some models) the guide.

What You'll Need

- Squeegee
- Bathroom cleaner
- Nonabrasive powder cleaner
- White polishing pad
- Single-edge razor
- Mildewcide or bleach
- Sponge
- Clear caulk
- Utility knife
- Caulking gun

Tips

Some people prefer to use caulk in squeezable tubes. With small tubes you often waste less, and you may find it easier to stop the caulk at the end of a run.

Use a nonabrasive cleaner. Never use scouring pads or abrasive powder on glass, metal or tile.

See also 317 Replace a Shower-Door Sweep.

Warning

If a door falls off its track, chances are you may not have much (if anything) on. Avoid handling the glass door any more than necessary until you at least get some shoes on.

117 Seal Wall Joints Around a Tub or Shower

You're much better off maintaining the caulk joints around a tub or shower base than cleaning up the mess that results when water penetrates that protective barrier.

Steps

1 In areas where the caulk is still bonded, use a plastic putty knife or (with porcelain tubs only) a single-edge razor to break the bonds between the caulk and the fixture and between the caulk and wall. Hold the putty knife at an angle, with the pointed corner at the edge of the caulk; hold the razor blade at a low angle, with its edge on the tub or wall surface, and push it into the caulk.

2 Use a flathead screwdriver to scrape out loose caulk. Push the tip into the joint and pull the blade through the caulk. To give yourself greater control, hold the blade in your left hand if you are right-handed (the reverse if you are left-handed), and keep that hand in contact with the tub or shower base as you pull the tool along the joint. For very dry, stubborn caulk, use a chemical for caulk softening and removal, such as 3M Caulk Remover, as directed by the manufacturer.

3 Repeat steps 1 and 2 as needed until the joint is open and there is no caulk on either the fixture or the wall surface. You may find an excess of caulk on the wall near the fixture, well outside the joint, left over from previous attempts to repair caulk or from too-heavy application of caulk. Remove all of this.

4 Use a hair dryer or heat gun at a low setting to dry out the joint.

5 Use a vacuum with a pointed attachment, an old toothbrush or another small brush to remove any loose bits of caulk from the joint. Apply painter's masking tape to the wall surface and the tub or shower pan immediately adjacent to the joint.

6 Hold the tip of your caulk tube or cartridge against a cutting board and cut off the tip at a 45-degree angle with a utility knife, removing about ¼ inch (6 mm) to create a ⅛-inch (3-mm) hole.

7 Holding the caulk tube at an angle, squeeze caulk into the joint until you've slightly overfilled it, then run the tube along the joint. Adjust the pressure, the speed or both to get the desired result.

8 Smooth the joint. Use a plastic caulk-smoothing tool designed specifically for this task, or use the wetted tip of your finger. Ideally you should do this in a single pass, but you'll likely have to pause because your fingertip is leaving an excess of caulk outside the joint, or because you need to add caulk in some places.

9 Remove the masking tape immediately after smoothing the caulk, and smooth the joint again with a wet, soapy finger. Wait overnight before using the tub or shower, or at least as long as indicated on the caulk label.

What You'll Need

- Plastic putty knife or single-edge razor
- Flathead screwdriver
- Caulk-removing and -softening chemical
- Hair dryer or heat gun
- Vacuum with pointed attachment, toothbrush or small brush
- Painter's masking tape
- Tub-and-tile caulk
- Cutting board
- Utility knife
- Caulk-smoothing tool

Tips

Don't use grout to fill the joint between the tub and the wall. The different rates of expansion of these dissimilar materials, as well as movement caused by the weight of water in a tub, require a permanently flexible joint filler.

Avoid patch jobs. Failure in one location indicates the likelihood of future problems. While it may be possible to caulk over failed sections, the bond between new and old caulk usually fails, and the results are unattractive.

Use only caulk designated for tub and tile use, which is formulated for mildew resistance.

Warning

Metal tools can easily scratch or chip the surfaces of tubs and shower bases.

118 Replace Cracked Tile

You may be replacing a cracked tile, removing an unwanted fixture from a tiled surface, or installing some beautiful decorative tiles from Portugal to liven up your kitchen or bathroom. In all cases, the procedure for replacing a tile is the same.

Steps

1 To remove the existing tile, scrape grout out of the joint around the tile with a grout saw (see 120 Replace Cracked Tile Grout in a Tub or Shower).

2 Break up the tile with a hammer and cold chisel so you can remove a piece and get under the edge of the remaining pieces (or the adjoining tiles, if you are removing more than one), then pry them up with a stiff putty knife.

3 Remove the tile pieces and use an old chisel, a stiff putty knife or a paint scraper to scrape out the old adhesive (see A) so you have a relatively smooth, level surface for the new tile.

4 Spread the entire back of the replacement tile with a light coat of tile adhesive (see B). Then scrape off the adhesive that's within ¼ inch (6 mm) of the perimeter so it won't fill the grout joint.

5 Press the tile firmly into place so it's level (flush) with the surrounding tiles. Let the adhesive set overnight or as directed by the manufacturer before grouting.

6 Grout and seal the joints as in 120 Replace Cracked Tile Grout in a Tub or Shower, except that if you're dealing with a small area, you can use a fingertip or squeegee to apply the grout. Use sanded grout for floor tiles or tiles with wide joints, and unsanded grout for wall tiles.

What You'll Need

- Grout saw
- Hammer
- Cold chisel
- Stiff putty knife
- Chisel or paint scraper
- Replacement tile
- Tile adhesive
- Grout
- Squeegee

Warning

Wear eye protection such as goggles when hammering or removing the damaged tile.

Avoid hammering too hard or you may damage the substrate, crack the grout or even damage adjoining tiles.

119 Troubleshoot Mold on Interior Walls

Do you see indoor condensation and the unsightly appearance of mold and mildew on your walls? Warm and moist air, inadequate wall insulation, improper wall construction and lack of ventilation are at the heart of this issue.

Steps

Exhaust excessive moist air

1 Install an exhaust fan in bathrooms. If you have access from above (an attic), install the fan in the ceiling and vent it out the nearest attic wall. If there is no wall within the limits suggested by the fan's manufacturer, vent the fan through a roof.

2 If you have a bathroom fan, operate it for 20 minutes after showering. Replace the standard switch with a timer control to make this easier (see 192 Swap a Faulty Light Switch).

3 Cut down the bathroom door if the gap underneath is much less than 1 inch (2.5 cm). You need that much to provide adequate air for the exhaust fan. See 113 Fix a Rubbing Door.

4 Vent clothes dryers to outdoors. You can easily install through-wall kits in most walls. Use rigid aluminum duct, which is easy to cut, assemble and connect.

5 Vent kitchen fans to outdoors and use them whenever you boil water, wash dishes or run the dishwasher.

Tighten a leaky exterior wall

1 Seal switch and receptacle outlets with foam gaskets (energy savers).

2 Caulk joints between floors and walls and around the inside and outside of windows or exterior walls.

3 If there is no vapor retarder (polyethylene sheeting or facing on insulation), make sure there are two coats of good-quality paint on the walls. To see if an exterior wall has a vapor retarder, remove an electrical outlet cover to explore the outside of the box.

4 In bathrooms the problem may be so bad that as a last resort you must remove finished walls to install a proper retarder.

5 Insulate the walls and/or ceilings (see a related problem and the solution in 150 Prevent Ice Dams).

Remove existing mold

1 When you feel you've resolved the problem, wash the affected surfaces with a homemade bleach solution; see 346 Remove Mildew From Walls and Ceilings.

What You'll Need

- Exhaust fan
- Timer control
- Duct and vent materials
- Foam gaskets
- Caulk and applicator
- Vapor retarder
- Insulation
- Bleach

Tips

Vapor retarders and sealants prevent moist interior air from penetrating exterior walls on its way to drier outdoor air.

The maximum length for an exhaust fan's vent—typically 20 feet (6 m)—varies according to fan rating, vent size and type, and other factors.

You can adapt some recirculating kitchen-hood fans to vent outdoors.

Warning

Never use plastic ducts to vent a clothes dryer. Although widely sold for this purpose, they can melt and create a fire hazard.

120 Replace Cracked Tile Grout in a Tub or Shower

Attend to cracked or crumbling grout joints as soon as they appear. Water getting behind the tiles can ruin the tile job and cause costly damage. The process described below assumes you need to regrout the entire area. More often you only have to work on a few damaged areas. Regardless, it is a four-day job—one day to regrout and recaulk, two days of curing time and one day for sealing.

Steps

Remove the plumbing trim

1 Remove the tub spout. One type slips over a copper pipe: Loosen the setscrew on the underside with an Allen (hex) wrench and pull off the spout. The other type threads onto an iron pipe: Twist it off either by hand or with groove-joint pliers. Pad the spout first with a rag to avoid marring its finish.

2 Remove the faucet handle(s). Pop off any decorative cap that covers the handle screw with a knife or an awl. Then remove the screw and pull off the handle.

3 Remove the faucet trim. First unscrew or pull off the cylindrical sleeve from the valve. Then unscrew or pull off the flange that covers the hole in the tile. Slide the trim around the shower arm away from the wall.

Remove the grout and clean

1 Use a grout saw (some have teeth and others have an abrasive coating on the blade) to remove as much grout from the joint as you can (see A). Work very carefully to avoid scratching the tile.

2 Remove the caulk joint between the tile and the tub or shower pan (see 117 Seal Wall Joints Around a Tub or Shower).

3 Vacuum with a wand attachment to suck all loose material out of the joints. Sponge on a 50-50 bleach-and-water solution to kill any mildew. Hand-rinse well, and wipe the surface dry with a towel.

What You'll Need

- Allen (hex) wrench or groove-joint pliers
- Rag
- Knife or awl
- Screwdriver
- Grout saw
- Vacuum with wand attachment
- Bleach
- Towel
- Unsanded grout
- Bucket
- Electric drill with paint-mixing attachment
- Rubber float (grout trowel)
- Grout sponge
- Soft cotton cloth
- Green abrasive pad
- Silicone grout sealer
- Rubber gloves
- Goggles

Tips

Dremel's Grout Removal attachment kit for electric rotary tools guides the cutter along grout joints for fast grout removal—a modest investment that makes a big job much easier.

Mix and apply the grout

1 Mix enough unsanded grout to do one wall at a time. Slowly add water to the powder in a bucket. Mix with a paint-mixing drill attachment until you reach the right consistency. The grout should be just stiff enough so it won't pour out of the container without a push. Wait 10 minutes and remix.

2 Spread the grout diagonally across the tile with a rubber float (a grout trowel) held at a 45-degree angle (see B). Press firmly and go over the surface several times to pack the joints. Finish by striking off any excess with the float held at a 90-degree angle.

3 When the grout is dry but still crumbly, use a screwdriver to scrape it out of the joint between the tile and the tub or shower pan, as you will be caulking it.

Clean and seal the surface

1 Before you wet-clean the tile, allow the grout to set up for a few minutes. As soon as you can wipe grout off the surface using a damp (not wet) grout sponge without pulling grout out of the joint, clean until only a light haze of grout remains (see C). Use light, diagonal strokes, and rinse and wring out the sponge often.

2 Clean and shape the joints by wiping parallel to them. Remove the grout until its level is just below the tile's rounded edges. If any voids appear in the process, press in a dab of grout with the float, the sponge or a fingertip (see D), and wait about 10 minutes.

3 Wipe off the grout haze with a soft, dry cotton cloth. Dampen the sponge if needed, or use a green (mild) abrasive pad to scrub off any stubborn spots.

4 Caulk the tub or shower joint (see 117 Seal Wall Joints Around a Tub or Shower).

5 After 48 hours, apply a grout sealer, following the instructions on the label.

Protect the floor of the shower or tub with an old blanket or a canvas drop cloth, and put tape over the drain to keep out debris.

If a metal tub spout is stuck, insert a large screwdriver or the handle of a pair of pliers into the spout opening to twist it off.

Warning

Wear eye protection, such as goggles, and rubber gloves.

Do not allow grout to cure on the surface of the tile. It won't come off.

Grout sealer inevitably gets on the tub floor and is very slippery. Move carefully and clean spills promptly with soapy water.

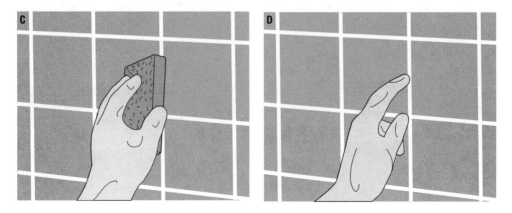

121 Fix a Drafty Window

The icy winds of winter may be bent on finding a way into your house, but you're equally determined to stop them and stay toasty warm. Here's how you can keep cold drafts from getting in via a poorly insulated window. Spring-metal or V-shaped vinyl weather-stripping works very well and is almost invisible.

Steps

Weather-stripping a double-hung window

1 Review the installation diagrams to determine the exact location and orientation for the product you're using.

2 Clean all surfaces well, especially if you'll be using adhesive-backed weather-stripping.

3 To seal the channels, cut lengths of V-shaped or other spring-type weather-stripping about 1 inch (2.5 cm) longer than the height of each sash. Use tin snips or a hacksaw, or (for vinyl only) a utility knife.

4 Open the sash fully and slip one end of the strip behind it (see A). Then continue back down to the sill for the lower sash channel, or up to the head jamb for the upper sash channel.

5 To secure the strip, either peel off the tape and press the self-adhering type into place, or hammer in the small nails provided for metal types.

6 To seal the window at the horizontal rails where the two sashes meet when closed, cut a length of weather-stripping equal to the sash's width.

7 Partially open both sashes so you can access the front edge of the horizontal meeting rail on the upper sash. Install the weather-stripping on that rail with the point of the V facing up (see B) or the nailing flange at the top.

What You'll Need

- Cleaning supplies
- Weather-stripping or storm-window kit
- Tape measure
- Tin snips or hacksaw
- Utility knife
- Tack hammer
- Scissors
- Single-edge razor
- Hair dryer

Tips

Nailable metal is more durable than vinyl, which comes in both peel-and-stick and nailable forms.

Gaskets seal well and install easily, but they're often unsightly and don't last.

You never want to paint over weather-stripping, so now's the time to touch up or paint the surfaces where you're installing strips.

A sliding window is like a double-hung unit turned on its side, so you weather-strip it in a similar fashion.

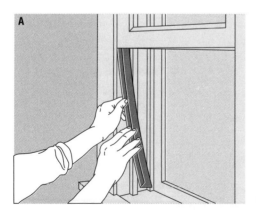

8 Cut and install additional strips equal to the sash's width to seal any gap between the top of the upper sash and the head jamb as well as between the bottom of the lower sash and the sill. Secure the strips to the top of the upper sash and to the bottom of the lower sash.

Weather-stripping a casement window

1 Measure the window's perimeter and cut four pieces of spring-metal or V-shaped vinyl weather-stripping to fit.

2 Position each piece as shown in the manufacturer's installation diagrams (with either the nailing flange or the point of the V facing outward).

3 Either nail or peel and press to apply the weather-stripping.

Installing a plastic-film storm window

1 If you won't be opening the window often or at all in wintertime, consider installing virtually invisible storm windows (made of plastic film) that cover the entire window. These seal out drafts and add an insulating layer. You install reusable types in permanent moldings and tape in the temporary types.

2 Clean the surface well.

3 Cut adhesive-backed tape to fit the perimeter of the area you will cover, and then press it into place.

4 Remove the protective paper from the top strip.

5 Cut the plastic film with a razor or scissors so it will extend beyond the tape about 2 inches (5 cm) on all sides.

6 Pull the film taut across the top, just enough to straighten, not stretch, it. Then press it onto the tape.

7 Repeat the procedure at the bottom and then at the sides. Do one strip at a time to prevent the plastic from coming into contact with the adhesive until you are ready.

8 Use a hair dryer on a low setting to warm the film. This shrinks it and pulls out any wrinkles.

9 Carefully trim the excess with a single-edge razor blade or sharp utility knife.

Miter the corners of spring-metal and V-shaped vinyl weather-stripping so they don't collide, and test-fit the two pieces before installing either one.

To avoid smashed fingers when driving in the tiny nails that secure spring-metal weather-stripping, hold the nails with long-nose pliers.

Peel-and-stick vinyl may not adhere well for long, but you can tack or staple it if it comes loose.

To reduce tension on spring-metal weather-stripping, flatten it with a block of wood and a hammer.

To increase tension on spring-metal weather-stripping, insert a screwdriver under it, pry it up and slide the screwdriver along the strip's length.

For greater efficiency, easier installation and less vulnerability to weather and dirt, install plastic films inside wherever they won't interfere with the shades or blinds.

122 Repair a Faulty Window Crank

Don't put up with a struggle every time you open or close a casement window. Restoring it so it works like new is easy. Procrastinating may result in damage to the mechanism and the added cost of replacement parts.

Steps

1 Open the window and, working from outside if necessary, disengage the arm from the track. In some models you must remove the screws that attach the arm to the sash.

2 From inside, remove the mounting screws that secure the hardware to the window.

3 If there are no visible screws, remove the handle by loosening the setscrew that holds it onto the shaft and lift off the snap-on plastic cover to access the screws.

4 If there is no such cover, use a trim pry bar to remove the trim that extends from side to side and is notched around the gearbox (see Tips). There may or may not be nails.

5 Clean the gearbox with a soft wire brush and a solvent such as kerosene.

6 Operate the mechanism to make sure the gears mesh properly and aren't worn. If a replacement is required, contact the window manufacturer. Most windows do not have the manufacturer's name printed on the hardware or window, but if you look carefully at the metal spacer between the panes of an insulated unit, you'll probably find the name there. Or bring the old part to a window or lumber dealer who can identify and order it for you.

7 Working from outside, clean the track on the sash's underside with the same brush and solvent to remove dirt-caked grease.

8 Lubricate the window operator with a little light household oil and reinstall it, reversing the removal procedure in steps 1 through 4. Do the same if you are installing a replacement part.

9 Lubricate the track on the sash's underside with white grease.

10 Reattach the arm to the sash and operate the window crank.

11 Wipe any excess grease off the track with paper towels.

What You'll Need

- Screwdriver
- Trim pry bar
- Soft wire brush
- Grease and oil solvent
- Replacement crank
- Household oil
- White grease
- Paper towels

Tips

To remove wood trim, first break any paint sealing the joints using the tip of a utility knife. This will make the piece easier to remove without damage. Work very carefully to avoid cutting into the wood or injuring yourself.

If you don't want to reinstall the old part until a new one comes in, just push the window closed from outside, and have someone engage the sash lock from inside.

Warning

Use caution if you must lean out a window or work on a ladder to disengage the arm and clean the track.

123 Repair Vertical Blinds

It's easy to repair vertical blinds, although any work on the head rails is best left to the factory's experts.

Steps

1 To remove a vane for replacement or cleaning, open the blind, lift the vane up off the hook on the holder or carrier, and bend the vane out to open the holder and down to pull it out (see A).

2 For vinyl or aluminum vanes with a spacer chain, remove the screw or tie-down clip that secures the end of the chain. Feed the chain out through the vane you're removing and as many others as necessary to get to the damaged vane.

3 For fabric vanes, disconnect the spacer-chain connector from one side of the vane weight and pull the weight out of its pocket in the bottom of the vane (see A).

4 To install a vane, orient its curve in the same direction as those of the other vanes. Grasp the vane near the top and gently push it up into the holder, then down to lock it into place.

5 For vinyl or aluminum vanes, thread the chain through the holes in the replacement vane and subsequently through all other vanes between the replaced vane and the chain-anchor point. To maintain the proper spacing, cut a piece of cardboard to the appropriate length, using the existing spacing as a guide. Insert the cardboard between the last installed vane and the one you're installing next (see B).

6 For fabric vanes, reinsert the vane weight (clip side up) into the pocket of the vane and clip the spacer-chain connector to it.

7 For head-rail repairs, such as cord and hanger replacement, remove all vanes as described in steps 1 through 3 and disconnect the head rail from the mounting brackets so you can bring it in for professional repair. Typically you must rotate an arm on a mounting to unlock the head rail. Have a helper at the other end hold the blind so it doesn't fall.

What You'll Need

- Screwdriver
- Cardboard
- Scissors or utility knife
- Replacement vanes

Tips

Keep in mind that most DIY repairs on vertical blinds void the warranty.

To clean your vertical blinds, consult the manufacturer's instructions.

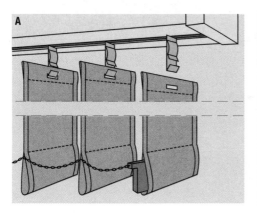

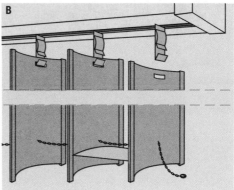

124 Repair Venetian Blinds or Miniblinds

You probably open and close your window blinds every morning and evening, so any problem with their operation becomes a daily source of annoyance. Try these steps. Keep in mind that most do-it-yourself repairs on blinds void the warranty.

Steps

1 Lower the blind and adjust the slats to the open position using the tilt cord or wand.

2 Unclip and remove the blind from its brackets. Lay it flat on a large table or other work surface. Follow the steps below as far as your repair requires.

3 Remove any end caps and the cover on the bottom rail to expose the knots or clips that secure the ends of the lift cord and ladder tape or string ladders.

4 If you are replacing the ladders, disconnect them. Otherwise just disconnect the two lift-cord ends, which are clipped or tied to the rail.

5 Pull both lift cords up through the slats as far as needed to remove any damaged slats and feed new ones onto the ladders. Thread the cords back down and secure them to the bottom rail. Then install the cover and end caps.

6 If you are replacing the ladders or lift cords, pull the cords up to the head box.

What You'll Need

- Large table or other work surface
- Replacement slats
- Replacement lift cords and ladder tape or ladder string
- Scissors or utility knife

Tips

If you are replacing venetian-blind cords, you may also cut the replacement into two pieces at least as long as the originals (one is longer than the other), and tie or tape them to the ends of the old cords so you pull the new ones through as you pull the old ones out.

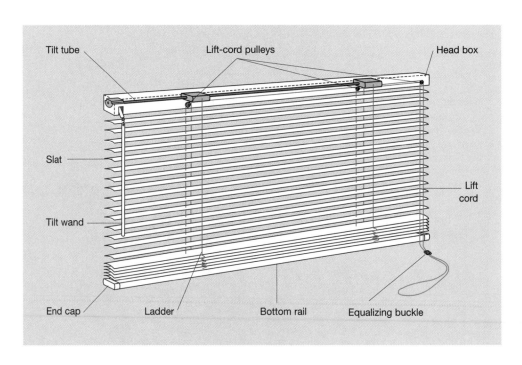

7 To replace the ladders, disconnect them from the tilt tube in the head box and slide them off the sides of the slats. Slide the slats into the new ladders and attach the ladders to the tilt tube and bottom rail. Thread the lift cords through the slats, alternating back and forth between the ladder rungs, and secure them to the bottom rail.

8 To replace a lift-cord, pull both ends up into the head box, over the pulleys, down and out. If you don't have another assembled blind to refer to, sketch a simple diagram before taking them out.

9 Feed the two ends of a new lift cord back into the head box and over the first pulley. Direct one end over the next pulley and the other one across the head box to the far pulley. Feed both cords down through the slats to the bottom rail and secure them. Install any cover or end caps.

10 Hang the blind.

11 If you've installed new cords, level the bottom rail. Depending on the model, either adjust the lift-cord equalizing buckle or knot the two cords together just above the tassel when the bottom bar is level. Cut the cords, if necessary.

A lift cord on a venetian blind may be two separate cords or one that is looped at the grasped end.

While the cords are out, give the slats a good cleaning. It will never be easier!

125 **Repair Wood or Plastic Roll-Up Blinds**

Repairs on wood or plastic roll-up blinds are typically limited to replacing a worn or rotted cord.

Steps

1 Remove the blind. Usually you just lift it off the screws it is hooked over, but you may need to loosen or remove screws.

2 Using a utility knife, cut the lift cord at the point where it is attached to the head box.

3 Using the old cord as a guide, cut a new cord that is 3 to 4 inches (7.5 to 10 cm) longer than the old cord.

4 Roll up the blind by hand. Tie the two ends of the new cord to the head box, and feed the cord around the blind and over the respective pulleys.

5 Slip the equalizing buckle (from the old cord) over the pooled end, and rehang the blind.

6 Adjust the buckle until the blind hangs level.

What You'll Need

- Screwdriver
- Utility knife
- Replacement cord

Tip

Sun-bleached wooden blinds can be refreshed with paint or stain.

126 Troubleshoot Window Shade Problems

Problems with shades are a cinch to resolve, and the repairs don't cost a cent. Whether you're troubleshooting a new shade you've installed or trying to resolve a problem with an old one, you'll find the solutions below.

PROBLEM	POSSIBLE CAUSE	SOLUTIONS
Shade won't roll up completely	Too little spring tension	1 Roll shade down and remove it from brackets, blade end first. 2 Roll nearly all of shade around roller by hand. 3 Reinstall shade and test. 4 If more tension is required, repeat procedure.
Shade rolls up too slowly	Too little spring tension	1 Roll shade down and remove it from brackets, blade end first. 2 Roll about half of shade around roller by hand. 3 Reinstall shade and test. 4 If more tension is required, repeat procedure. 5 If less tension is required, see "Shade rolls up too fast," below.
Shade rolls up too fast	Too much spring tension	1 Roll shade up and remove it from brackets, blade end first. 2 Unroll about half of shade by hand. 3 Reinstall shade and test. 4 If less tension is required, repeat procedure. 5 If more tension is required, see "Shade rolls up too slowly," above.
Shade falls out of brackets	Shade too narrow	1 For outside mount, remove shade from brackets, blade end first; bend each bracket inward slightly with pliers; or reposition one bracket. 2 For inside mount, pry out one or both brackets with tip of standard screwdriver, enough to slip cardboard shim behind bracket; tap bracket nails back in.

PROBLEM	POSSIBLE CAUSE	SOLUTIONS
Shade won't lock in desired position	Stuck pawl	1 Roll shade up fully to reduce tension on spring; remove shade from brackets, blade end first; unroll shade by hand and reinstall it. 2 Roll it up again as needed to release all tension. 3 Blow, brush or use a toothpick to remove any dirt in the pawl (the little arm that engages ratchet teeth in blade end of shade). It must move freely. 4 Lubricate pawl with graphite powder (lock lubricant) or brief squirt of WD-40. Have cloth handy to protect shade from overspray and to wipe off excess. 5 Test operation. If it still doesn't work, replace shade.
Shade binds	Shade too wide	1 For outside mount, remove shade and grasp each bracket with pliers to bend it outward; or remove and reposition bracket. 2 For inside mount, tap each bracket to flatten it slightly. 3 If necessary, drill small hole of ⅛-inch (3-mm) diameter in window frame as recess for stationary pin (easier than shortening pin). 4 Remove shade and bring it to store to have it cut shorter (typically done at no charge).
Shade wobbles	Stationary pin bent	1 Remove shade. 2 Grasp pin with pliers and bend it straight.
Warning	When adjusting tension, use the methods suggested here. Never try to wind the spring by grasping the blade end with pliers and twisting it. The blade can spin violently and cause injury.	

127 Fix Broken Glass in a Window

That ill-flung baseball or confused bird always seems to find your window. If it broke a single-pane window, you're in luck—this is usually a straightforward task, as long as the window is on a ground floor and the sash is removable.

Steps

Replacing single-pane window glass

1 Remove the window sash and place it flat on a worktable to remove what's left of the glass. Lay a towel over the glass to break it and carefully wiggle out the pieces.

2 Remove the glazing compound on the glass perimeter. Old glazing compound may be hardened and difficult to remove, or so brittle it practically falls off. Use a glazier's tool, an old chisel or flathead screwdriver, or a putty knife to pry and scrape out the compound. Pull out any glazing points (small metal fasteners that hold the glass in place) with long-nose pliers (see A).

3 Brush a fast-drying paint primer on any bare wood exposed while removing the old compound. This seal prevents too-dry wood from absorbing all the glazing compound's oils.

4 If you need to buy glass, measure the opening it will fill, then have the store clerk cut a replacement pane ⅛ inch (3 mm) shorter and narrower than those dimensions.

5 If you have a piece of glass handy that requires cutting to fit, place it on a thin rug or other firm, padded surface. Lay a metal straightedge, square or ruler over the glass at the cut line and use a glass cutter to score from edge to edge with one continuous, firm stroke. Then position the scored line on the glass over the edge of a table or board. Snap the overhanging portion downward sharply to complete the cut.

What You'll Need

- Towel
- Glazier's tool or stiff putty knife
- Chisel or flathead screwdriver
- Long-nose pliers
- Fast-drying paint primer
- Small paintbrush
- Tape measure
- Replacement glass
- Metal straightedge, square or ruler
- Glass cutter
- Silicone or siliconized acrylic caulk
- Glazing compound
- Glazing points
- Glass cleaner
- Exterior trim paint
- Tape or liquid masking
- Single-edge razor

Tips

Make vertical cuts by rolling the blade of a putty knife into the joint between the sash and the glazing compound. This breaks the joint cleanly and prevents accidental damage to the sash.

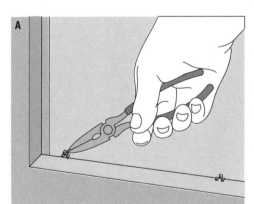

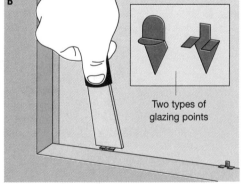

Two types of glazing points

6 For a weatherproof and watertight seal on the exterior, apply a thin bead of caulk on the frame perimeter as a setting bed before installing the glass. Alternatively, use a thin coat of glazing compound and press it into place with a putty knife.

7 Put the new pane in the frame, pressing just hard enough to bed it in the compound or caulk.

8 Place at least two glazing points on the glass with the points facing the frame along each side, about 2 inches (5 cm) in from each corner; use additional points so the maximum span between them is 8 inches (20 cm). Press the points into the wood using a glazier's tool or putty knife (see B).

9 Roll a handful of glazing compound between your hands until it is soft and pliable. Then roll it out on a flat surface to form a rope of ⅜-inch (1-cm) diameter and press it into the corner between the glass and the wood frame with your fingertips (see C).

10 Use a glazier's tool or stiff putty knife to press the compound firmly into place against the glass and the wood frame (see D). Angle and cock the tool as needed so the beveled compound fills the gap but projects above the wood when viewed from inside. Finish each side with one long continuous stroke.

11 Scrape off any excess compound with the same tool or knife and clean the glass carefully without disturbing the compound.

12 Put the sash back in and allow the glazing compound to dry for a week or more.

13 Paint over the glazing with exterior trim paint to seal and protect it from the weather. Mask the glass with tape or liquid masking and paint it freehand. Paint about ⅛ inch (3 mm) out onto the glass to form a watertight seal (see Tips).

14 Scrape off any excess paint on the glass with a single-edge razor in a holder. Try to leave the thin edge of paint on the glass to maintain the seal.

To maintain the proper ⅛-inch (3-mm) paint seal on the glass, either use Wagner's Glass Mask, which includes a liquid masking system and special scraper (available at many paint and home centers); or hold a wide spackle knife or scraper against the wood muntin as you scrape the paint off the glass.

When double-pane or insulated windows break, or the seal fails and the inside surface fogs up, you must replace the entire sash, including the glass and the frame around it.

Warning

Wear heavy work gloves and proper eye protection, such as goggles.

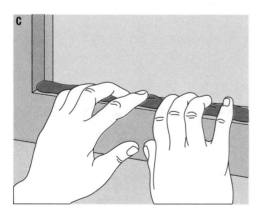

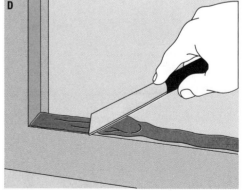

128 Repair a Window Screen

If there's a hole anywhere in a screen, a mosquito will find it ... and then you! Short of replacing a damaged window screen entirely, you can try several quick fixes that will keep the little buggers out until you have time for a proper repair. Stores offer rescreening services, but you can easily do it yourself and save some money.

Steps

Quick fixes for small holes

1 Flatten any wires that stick up around the hole and realign the screen wires as best you can with any small pointed tool, such as an awl, nail, needle or tiny screwdriver. Spread clear silicone caulk or epoxy adhesive over the tear.

2 To make a patch, cut a small square of screening with shears; remove three or four strands of wire from each side. Place the patch on a board so the ends of the wires overhang, and bend them down to a 90-degree angle. Repeat for all sides. Place the patch upside down on a hard surface. Remove the screen sash and lay the damaged area of the screen over the patch. Press down on the screen so the bent wires project through, and bend the wires over with a wood block (see A).

3 Use wire strands removed from a piece of screening to "darn" between the sound strands and across the hole. (No needle is required; your fingers will do the job.) Turn the screen over after each "stitch" to bend the wire flat.

Replacing a screen installed in splines

1 Remove the screen sash.

2 Use an awl or nail point to pry out one end of the vinyl spline that holds the screen in the sash's channels. Slowly pull out the spline and then the screen.

3 For large or flimsy screen frames, tack some ¼-inch (6-mm) plywood stops into your workbench so you have one centered

What You'll Need

- Small pointed tool
- Clear silicone caulk or epoxy adhesive
- Fiberglass or aluminum screening
- Board
- Shears
- Wood block
- Awl or nail
- ¼-inch (6-mm) plywood stops
- Screen roller
- Flathead screwdriver
- Utility knife and new blades
- Vinyl spline

Tips

You may save money in the long run by buying a roll of screening. The unit cost is less, and you'll avoid another trip to the store if you accidentally tear the screen during installation or future repairs.

Choose screening material that matches the type (aluminum or fiberglass) and color of your existing screens.

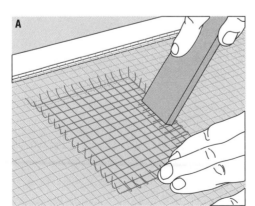

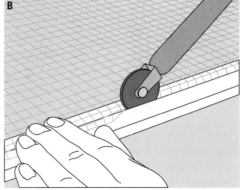

on each of the frame's inside edges when you place the screen over the stops. This prevents distortion of the sash as you roll in the screening.

4 Lay new screening over the sash so it overlaps all sides by at least 1 inch (2.5 cm) and cut it with shears.

5 If you are using aluminum screening, roll the screen into the channel on one side of the sash using the convex wheel of a screen roller (see B). Press against the center of the screen to keep it from shifting. To avoid cutting the screen, roll lightly at first, and then more firmly to press in the screen in stages. Roll in the spline (see step 6) before rolling in more screening. If you are using fiberglass screening, skip step 6 and roll in the screen and spline simultaneously.

6 Starting about 1 inch (2.5 cm) in from a corner, press the spline into place with your fingers as you roll it into the channel with the concave side of the roller (see C). Roll lightly at first to avoid stretching the spline and to maintain control. For fiberglass screening, roll the screen and spline into the channel at the same time.

7 As the spline approaches each corner, use shears to make a diagonal relief cut from the outside corner of the overlapping screening to the inside corner of the sash.

8 Work your way around the screen frame. As you roll one side, hold the opposite side of the screen slightly taut.

9 Use the tip of a screwdriver to press in the spline at each corner (the round roller can't roll right up to the inside corners).

10 Cut off excess screen with a sharp utility knife when the spline is all in (see D). To avoid accidentally cutting the screen, angle the blade toward the outside of the frame; cut slowly and steadily.

11 Reinstall the screen sash.

Bring a sample of the old spline (or better yet, the screen frame itself) with you when you go to purchase materials. Spline diameters vary and sizing is critical.

If you are repairing more than one screen, do the larger ones first. Then if you accidentally cut the screen during installation, you can use the damaged piece for a smaller screen.

Make sure the screening's horizontal and vertical patterns align correctly with the frame.

Warning

If you pull the screen too tight when rolling in the screen or spline, you may cut the screening or distort the frame.

When cutting off excess screening, hold the frame securely with your other hand but keep it a safe distance from the blade.

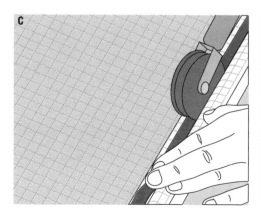

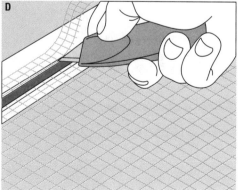

129 Repair Aluminum Storm/Screen Windows

Self-storing storm/screen windows will give you years of useful service with minimal maintenance, keeping your home insulated in cold weather and breezy when it's hot. The few repairs you may need to do are inexpensive.

Steps

Keep screens clean

1 Remove screens yearly. Lay them on a flat surface to clean them with a soft-bristle brush. Then stand them up to rinse them with a fine spray from a garden hose.

2 Clean the outside of storm windows from the ground, using a garden-hose cleaning attachment.

3 Remove the storm windows from the inside for simultaneous interior and exterior cleaning. Typically you'll need to do this less often because the inside surface is protected.

Prevent excessive condensation

1 Inspect the small vent holes, usually located between the bottom of the aluminum frame and the exterior wood windowsill (or sometimes cut into the frame itself). They must be open to allow the escape of moisture-laden air from indoors and proper drainage when storm windows are open.

2 Use an awl to open holes clogged with dirt, paint or caulk.

Replace cracked, scratched or broken glazing

1 Remove the screen sash or storm sash.

2 Remove the glazing (glass or sometimes acrylic plastic). If metal keys inside the frame secure the corners, remove the screws to take out one or two corners (see A). If the corners are crimped (see B), use an awl to remove the vinyl splines that secure the glazing.

What You'll Need

- Soft-bristle brush
- Garden hose with spray nozzle and cleaning attachment
- Awl
- Screwdriver
- Replacement glazing
- Stiff-bristle brush
- No. 0000 steel wool
- Cleaning cloths
- Silicone-lubricant spray
- Gel for dissolving aluminum oxidation
- Scraper or old chisel
- Mineral spirits or tack cloth
- Primer for galvanized metal
- Paintbrush
- Siliconized exterior latex caulk and caulking gun
- Acrylic-latex exterior trim paint

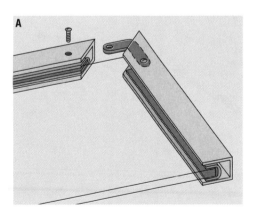

A

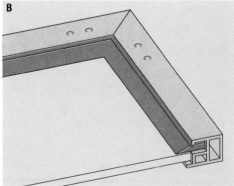

B

3 Install new glazing that's ⅟₁₆ inch (2 mm) smaller than the inside frame dimension to allow for expansion and contraction. Lay the glazing vinyl onto the glass and press it into the frame; assemble the corners. Or for crimped frames, lay the glass in the frame and press the vinyl weather seal into the joint between the glass and frame.

Make the sash slide more easily

1 Remove the sash and clean the channels with a stiff-bristle brush. Clean the sash frames with No. 0000 steel wool to remove dirt and oxidation.

2 Wipe the sides of the sash using a cloth sprayed with silicone lubricant before reinstalling the sash.

Update the sash's look with paint

1 Remove the screen sash or storm sash.

2 Use No. 0000 steel wool to remove light oxidation from the frame's outside face (and inside, if you plan to paint it or just want to spruce up its appearance). To remove excessive oxidation, brush on gel formulated to dissolve aluminum oxidation.

3 Remove any old, dried caulk along the frame's perimeter with a scraper or an old screwdriver or chisel.

4 Wipe the frame clean using a cloth slightly dampened with mineral spirits or a tack cloth. A tack cloth is a slightly sticky cloth used to remove fine dust from surfaces just prior to painting.

5 Apply a primer formulated for galvanized metal with a brush. When the first coat dries as directed for recoating, apply a second coat over any surfaces not fully coated.

6 When the primer has fully dried, use a caulking gun to caulk the perimeter with siliconized exterior latex caulk. Don't caulk over the vent holes.

7 When the caulk has cured (see its label for the time required), apply two topcoats of 100 percent acrylic-latex exterior trim paint. Use only 100 percent acrylic-latex paint for a topcoat. It's superior to the less expensive ones made with other binders, and many brands now offer lifetime warranties.

Tips

In cold climates, cleaning screens and windows just before winter maximizes the amount of solar heat that gets into your house, reducing your heating bill.

Clean any paint or caulk from the vent holes if you paint the frames.

Warning

Set your ladder on firm soil. Use a board if necessary to prevent its feet from sinking or to level it.

Wear gloves to protect your hands when replacing glass and when scrubbing the frames with steel wool.

Never paint the sash frames or the channels, or the windows will no longer operate smoothly (or at all).

Do not use any primer on aluminum other than one formulated for galvanized metal, regardless of what the label or salesperson says. It will not bond as well (or maybe not at all).

130 Install New Sash Cords in Windows

A broken sash cord makes a single- or double-hung window very diffi-cult to open. Propping the window open creates a household hazard, especially for curious young children. Generally you're best off replac-ing all the cords, even if only one is broken.

Steps

Remove the sash

1 Lay down a drop cloth.

2 Pry off the window stops with a trim pry bar. Sand off any rough edges and use a trim-size nail puller to pull nails out of the trim's back side and/or the window frame.

3 Move the sash and pull out any tacks that hold down metal weather-stripping in the frame channels.

4 Tilt the lower sash out to remove the (usually knotted) ends of the sash cords attached to it. If the cord still suspends a weight, hold onto the cord as you lower the weight. Then cut off the knot with a utility knife and allow the cord to fall into the weight cavity.

5 Score painted-over joints and parting strips with the utility knife, then pry them out with locking pliers, starting at the bottom and working up carefully. Repeat steps 3 and 4 for the upper sash.

What You'll Need

- Drop cloth
- Trim pry bar
- Sandpaper
- Trim-size nail puller
- Utility knife
- Locking pliers
- Screwdriver
- Pliers or coat hanger
- Sash cord
- 4d finishing nails
- 1-inch (2.5-cm) wire nails
- Hammer
- Nail set
- Caulk
- Paint and paintbrush

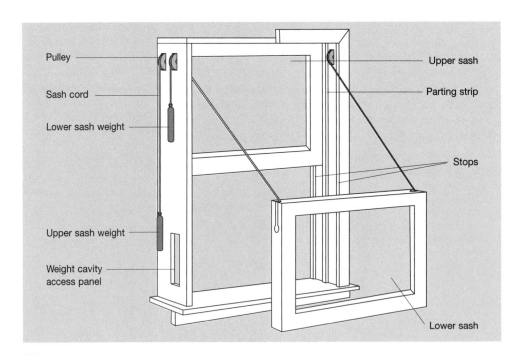

Replace the cords

1 Remove the screw that secures the weight cavity's access panel and lift out the panel.

2 Reach inside with pliers, a coat hanger bent into a hook, or your hand to grasp the cord and lift out the weight (see A).

3 Untie the cord from the weight or cut the cord with a utility knife. Cut a new sash cord that is about 6 inches (15 cm) longer than the old one.

4 Tie a knot at the very end of the cord to keep it from falling into the pulley opening. Insert the other end into the opening above the pulley. Push the cord into the cavity until you can see it, then pull it out of the access opening.

5 Double-knot the cord to the weight so it will end up the same length as the old one, then cut off any excess. Repeat steps 1 through 4 for the other cords.

Reinstall the sash

1 Start with the upper sash. Press the knotted end of the sash cords into the recessed area in the sash's edge (see B). Drive a 4d finishing nail through the knot and into the sash.

2 Place the weather-stripping on the sides of the sash before tilting the sash into the window frame. Then position the sash so you can tack the weather-stripping in place with two wire nails.

3 Tap the parting strips back into the frame channels.

4 Repeat steps 1 through 3 to reinstall the lower sash. Reinstall the window stops with 4d finishing nails, then set the nails and caulk over them. Apply touch-up paint as required.

Tips

To minimize damage to the trim and avoid having to repaint, score the painted-over joints between the window trim and the frame before attempting to pry them apart.

Pad the jaws of the locking pliers with cloth or tape to avoid damaging the parting strip when you pull it out.

If a weight is still attached to a sash cord, clamp locking pliers or a C-clamp onto the cord at the pulley to hold it in place while you remove the cord from the sash.

Scrape any paint out of the slot in a screw head before you try to twist it out, or you may strip the slot.

To make sure the knots don't come loose someday, put a little wood glue on them.

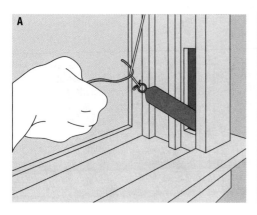

A

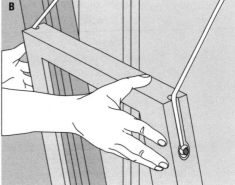

B

131 Fix a Tight or Loose Window Sash

If your double-hung windows are too loose, they may rattle in the wind, admit street noise and leak large volumes of air, causing drafts and wasting your precious energy dollars. Too tight, and you'll find them difficult or impossible to open and close. Finding the right balance is easy.

Steps

Free a stuck window

1 Try a sharp blow to the center rail, near the locking point, with the palm of your hand or a rubber mallet. That can break the bonds that sometimes form between painted surfaces, in this case the two rails.

2 If that fails, try tapping a wood block against the sides of the sash to break a similar bond between the stops and sash. Be gentle; too hard a tap can crack the glass.

3 If the problem is a painted-over joint, it's best to cut it, either with a window zipper (a serrated-blade tool designed for this purpose) or with any flat-blade tool, such as a putty knife or spackle knife. Hold the blade flat against the face of the sash and push the blade's edge into the joint as you draw the tool along the surface. A utility knife is harder to control.

Adjust the friction

1 Lubricate the channels of a too-tight sash with candle wax or talcum power, which also effectively keeps painted surfaces from sticking together.

2 If the windows have V-shaped spring-metal weather-stripping in the channels, you can decrease tension by hammering the strip flatter with a block of wood and hammer (see A). You increase friction by prying the V open with a screwdriver. In both cases, have the sash in its fully open position.

What You'll Need

- Rubber mallet
- Wood block
- Window zipper, putty knife or spackle knife
- Candle wax or talcum powder
- Hammer
- Screwdriver
- Window weather-stripping kit
- Sharp paint scraper
- Sandpaper
- Primer, paint and paint-brush
- Fiberglass insulation
- Flexible stick or rod
- Sharp chisel
- Nails
- Safety glasses

Tips

When nailing in window stops, insert a flexible putty knife between the stop and the sash (next to where you're driving in the nail) to maintain the proper distance between them.

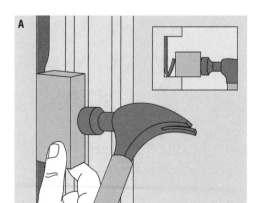

3 If you have an old, loose window that lacks weather-stripping, you can kill two birds with one stone by installing weather-stripping. Some types mount in the channels, some mount on the stops and against the sash, and some mount between the stops and the sash. Follow the directions on the package.

Remove paint buildup

1 If there is too much paint buildup on the sash or stops, you need to make more room. Start by using a sharp paint scraper to remove excess paint from the faces of the channel moldings: namely, the window (interior) stop, parting strip (middle) and blind (exterior) stop. Raise and lower the sash as needed.

2 On a lower sash, you can usually fix the problem by removing the window stop, then scraping and sanding the edge that faces the window before reinstalling the stop. The blind (exterior) stop for an upper sash is often locked into place with casing (trim), and you can't move it in or out to adjust friction.

3 If that fails, remove both sashes from the inside (see 130 Install New Sash Cords in Windows). Scrape, sand or strip off all the paint to the bare wood. Repaint the sash, and reinstall it when the paint is completely dry.

Install new friction channels

1 Lastly, you can install new friction channels, which have the added advantage of eliminating uninsulated weight cavities. The weight cavities in a home account for tremendous heat loss in cold climates. First remove the sashes and any weights and pulleys (see 130 Install New Sash Cords in Windows).

2 Stuff fiberglass insulation into the access openings for the weight cavities. Push the material up to the top first, using a flexible stick or rod, and then work your way down.

3 Use a hammer and a very sharp chisel to notch the ends of the top parting strip for the new channels.

4 Place the sashes between the two channels and tilt that assembly into the opening, bottom first, from the inside (see B).

5 Reinstall the interior stops, following the manufacturer's instructions for adjusting tension. Basically, the harder you press the stops against the sash before nailing them into place, the more friction you create.

6 If you find that the windows are too loose after you've installed the stops, you can increase the tension by hammering a wood block against the stop at the nail locations. Drive in a few more nails when the tension is just right.

Keep your paint scraper's blades sharp by frequently touching up the edge with a metal file.

If you are installing new sash channels and the weight pulleys are painted into place, as is often the case, you can hammer the pulleys into the opening.

Warning

Wear safety glasses for most of these tasks.

132 Repair Minor Drywall Damage

Dings happen—and fasteners pop. Maybe that contractor you hired didn't do such a great job of applying the drywall (he didn't press it firmly against the wall when installing the fasteners), or maybe he used cut-rate framing lumber. Never fear. You can repair gouges and popped nails or screws inexpensively yourself.

Steps

Filling tiny holes

1 Apply a dab of caulk with your fingertip or apply premixed interior spackling compound, available in very small cans, with a putty knife. Fill the hole but don't leave any residue on the surrounding surface.

2 If the compound shrinks as it dries, leaving a dimple, apply another coat. When the compound is dry, touch up the paint.

Repairing a small hole or gouge

1 Place an appropriate quantity of premixed joint compound, available in 1- and 5-gallon (4-l and 19-l) sizes, into a metal bread pan or onto a hawk (see Warning).

2 Pick up a small quantity of compound on the corner of a spackle knife and spread it over the damaged area. Hold the knife on the wall at a low angle and draw it across the compound horizontally; then wipe the knife clean on the edge of the pan and make a second pass vertically.

3 When the first coat dries (it will turn from gray to bright white), apply a second coat, but use more compound and extend it a little beyond the first coat. In the rare case when two coats are not enough, apply a third coat.

4 When the patch is dry, sand lightly and apply primer over the repaired surface before applying a paint topcoat.

What You'll Need

- Caulk or spackling compound
- Putty knife
- Touch-up paint and paintbrush
- Premixed joint compound
- Metal bread pan or hawk
- Spackle knife
- Sandpaper
- Primer
- Drywall screws (coarse thread)
- Screwdriver or electric drill and driver
- Hammer
- Joint tape
- Utility knife
- Drywall-reinforcing tape (paper or fiberglass)
- Drywall (see Tips)
- Drywall saw
- Drywall clips
- 1¼-inch (3-cm) Type W drywall screws
- Long-nose pliers

Tips

When embedding joint tape, don't press so hard that you squeeze out all the compound, or the joint is likely to fail.

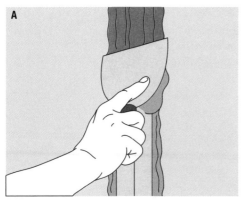

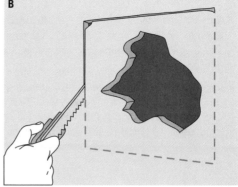

Repairing popped fasteners

1 Press firmly against the surface as you drive in one drywall screw on each side of the popped fastener (just above and below it on a wall, or in line with the ceiling joist) with a screwdriver or an electric drill and driver.

2 Drive in the popped fastener tight to the drywall with a hammer or screwdriver. Remove any loose drywall but try not to tear off the paper facing. Apply joint compound and smooth it over as described in "Repairing a small hole or gouge," opposite page.

Repairing larger damaged areas

1 Apply joint tape wherever the paper facing is badly damaged or missing. To embed paper tape, cover the damaged area with a thin layer of joint compound, press the paper into the compound and smooth it by drawing a clean spackle knife across it with firm pressure. If you're using adhesive-backed fiberglass tape, just press it onto the drywall.

2 When the first coat is dry, scrape off any dry bits on the surface and apply a second and third coat (see A) as described in "Repairing a small hole or gouge," opposite page.

Patching a large hole

1 Cut a drywall patch. Place it over the damaged area to trace it. Cut along your lines with a drywall saw (see B) or by making repeated passes with a utility knife. Remove the damaged pieces and clean up the cut with a utility knife.

2 Install drywall clips near the four corners of the opening. Slip them over the drywall (narrow spring tabs out) and secure them with 1¼-inch (3-cm) Type W drywall screws (see C). Position and screw the patch to the clips (see D).

3 Grasp the clip tabs with long-nose pliers and twist to break them off below the surface. Tape and finish the seams as described in "Repairing larger damaged areas," above.

Drive screws so they dimple the surface but don't break through the paper facing.

Ask a drywall supplier for a broken piece of drywall, or use a patch kit that includes all the materials you need.

If you don't have drywall clips, bridge the back of the opening with a board 4 inches (10 cm) longer than the opening. Secure the board to the drywall and the patch to the board.

Warning

Take care when using a saw to cut out damaged drywall. To avoid cutting into wiring or piping, enlarge the hole with a hammer as needed to explore under the surface.

Never work directly out of a bucket of compound. Doing so inevitably contaminates the material. Instead, transfer batches of material into a bread pan or onto a hawk, an aluminum square with a handle mounted on its underside.

C
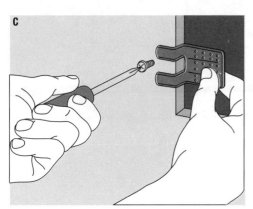

D
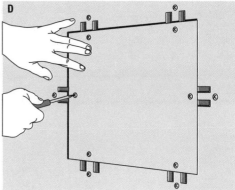

133 Repair Damaged Plaster

Plaster repairs can seem daunting, especially when you've attempted to patch a crack and it reappears within a year. Here's how to make repairs that last.

Steps

Fill tiny holes

1 Use a putty knife to apply spackling compound, available in small cans for touch-ups. Let dry. If the first coat shrinks as it dries and leaves a slight indentation, apply a second coat.

2 Sand lightly with fine sandpaper. Touch up with primer and paint.

Repair loose plaster

1 Remove any small, loose chunks of plaster and patch the holes (see "Fill holes and areas where plaster is missing," opposite page). Reattach larger sections of plaster with screws and plaster washers, spaced a few inches (about 7 cm) apart, using a drill and driver. For large, loose areas, install the washers in concentric rings, starting where the plaster is firmly attached and working inward. Cover the area with joint compound (opposite page).

2 To reinforce plaster along large cracks, install screws every 6 inches (15 cm) on both sides of the crack and about 1 inch (2.5 cm) away from it (see A). Drill pilot holes with a ⅛-inch (3-mm) masonry drill bit. Cover the area with joint compound (see opposite page).

What You'll Need

- Putty knife
- Spackling compound
- Fine sandpaper
- Primer
- Touch-up paint and paint-brush
- Plaster washers with screws
- Drill and driver
- ⅛-inch (3-mm) masonry bit
- Setting-type joint compound
- Bucket
- Potato masher, paint-mixing drill attachment or paddle mixer
- Mud pan
- 6-inch (15-cm) spackle knife
- Drywall
- Coarse-threaded drywall screws
- Paper drywall-reinforcing tape

A

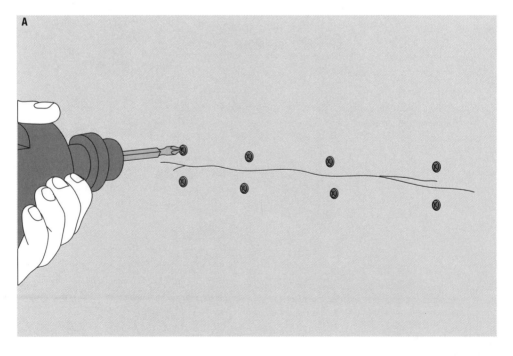

Mix compound

1 Use a setting-type joint compound such as Durabond 90 for all repairs other than tiny holes. Mix the compound in a bucket with water according to the directions. Depending on the quantity, use a potato masher, paint-mixing drill attachment or paddle mixer.

2 Transfer a working supply of the compound into a mud pan, a drywall specialty item.

Fill holes and areas where plaster is missing

1 Fill a hole with compound to within ⅛ inch (3 mm) of the surface using a 6-inch (15-cm) spackle knife. Then scratch the wet compound in a crisscross pattern with the edge of your knife. When the scratched coat dries, apply a leveling coat.

2 For larger areas of missing plaster, measure a piece of drywall to fit the hole, cut the piece out with a utility knife, then screw it to the lath (see B). Apply the compound in two stages and extend it about 2 inches (5 cm) onto the surrounding surface. Embed paper drywall-reinforcing tape in the compound and smooth with a spackle knife or wide trowel (see C).

3 Apply two or three additional coats of compound, allowing complete drying between coats and feathering each coat over a wider area than the preceding one. Drying time varies according to the type of compound as well as the humidity and ventilation.

4 Use a pole sander or a similar pad sander with very fine (150-grit) sandpaper to smooth the compound after it has dried.

Repair hairline cracks

1 Apply a thin coat of compound on the wall along the crack.

2 Embed paper drywall-reinforcing tape in the compound immediately and smooth with a spackle knife.

3 Continue as described in steps 3 and 4 of "Fill holes and areas where plaster is missing," above.

- Utility knife and tape measure
- Pole sander or pad sander
- 150-grit sandpaper
- Dust mask

Tips

Setting compounds dry very fast and hard. Don't mix more than you can use in the time indicated on the packaging (30, 45, 60 or 90 minutes), and don't allow the compound to dry on your tools.

Don't use fiberglass mesh tape or premixed joint compound. Although they are easier to work with, repairs made with them won't last.

Warning

Wear a dust mask and, if sanding overhead or high on walls, goggles.

Don't use a household vacuum for plaster dust, which is so fine that it gets past filters and into the motor.

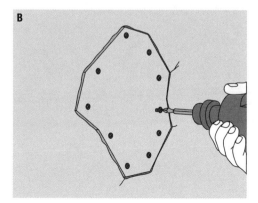

B

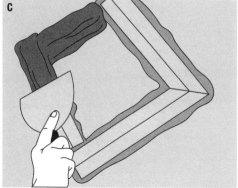

C

134 Repair Wall Coverings

Though they're a beautiful, practical and durable way to dress up a room, wall coverings occasionally need minor repairs where adhesive bonds have failed or damage has occurred. To avoid more problems, tackle these simple repairs promptly.

Steps

Fix a bubble

1 Using a sharp single-edge razor, utility knife or mat knife, cut a slit through the bubble.

2 Use a glue syringe to inject premixed wallpaper adhesive into the slit under the paper (see A).

3 Distribute the adhesive evenly with your fingertip, then wipe gently with a damp sponge. Sponge toward the slit at first to squeeze out excess adhesive. Then rinse and wring out the sponge, and wipe parallel to the slit to clean off any adhesive on the wall covering.

Fix a loose seam

1 Lift the edge of the wall covering to inject, spread and smooth adhesive as in "Fix a bubble," above.

2 After about 15 minutes, lightly roll the repaired seam with a seam roller.

Patch damaged wall covering

1 Using scissors, cut a generous patch from the wall covering you saved from the initial installation. (If you don't have any leftover wall covering and can't obtain new material that matches well, remove some from an inconspicuous location, such as behind a cabinet.)

2 Remove any loose, torn wall covering and tape the patch over the area, carefully aligning the patterns.

What You'll Need

- Single-edge razor, utility knife with new blade or mat knife
- Wallpaper adhesive
- Glue or adhesive syringe
- Sponge
- Seam roller
- Leftover wall covering
- Scissors
- Straightedge
- Tape

Tips

Wallpaper adhesive is great for any small repair.

When cutting wallpaper as required to fix a bubble or install a patch, cut on a pattern line so the repair's seam will be less noticeable.

A knife with a snap-off blade is particularly appropriate for light-duty cutting that requires a very sharp edge, as is the case here.

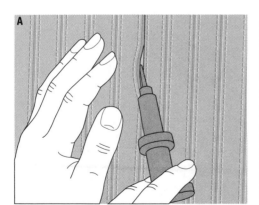

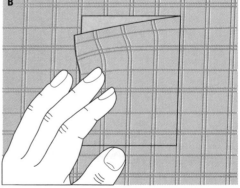

3 Cut through both wall-covering layers with a utility knife, using a straightedge to guide cuts made on linear patterns and cutting freehand on nonlinear patterns.

4 Save the cut-out patch; remove the taped portion left on the wall and remove the cut-out section of the original wallpaper.

5 Use a damp sponge to clean and smooth the substrate.

6 Apply adhesive to the back of the patch and place it on the wall, carefully aligning any patterns (see B). Smooth it into place with a damp sponge.

7 Wait about 15 minutes to roll the seams lightly with a seam roller.

135 Touch Up Painted Walls

There's no need to put up with a marred wall or postpone a small wall repair just because you're not ready to paint the whole room. Try these techniques. The results may not be perfect, but only you (and maybe that aunt with the magnifying glass) will notice.

Steps

1 For marred surfaces, try cleaning first. Good-quality paint can withstand some scrubbing. First try a sponge and dishwashing liquid, and if that fails, try a little household cleanser. In the worst case, the finish will be a bit duller, but you can burnish it with a soft cloth or touch it up with paint.

2 If you have made a spackling repair or are trying to cover a stain that won't scrub off, apply stain-killing wall primer over stains using a paint roller. Let dry. Apply the normal amount of paint over the repair area. Then feather the edges into the surrounding wall with a nearly dry roller by rolling out from the center with numerous light strokes. Lift the roller off the surface as you roll.

3 Apply a topcoat in the same manner, extending the paint to a loosely defined shape at least 6 square feet (.5 square m) in area. Clean your tools and judge how well the touched-up area blends with the surrounding area when it's dry.

Warning

When cutting wallpaper installed on drywall, avoid pressing too hard, or you'll cut through the drywall's paper facing.

What You'll Need

- Sponge
- Dishwashing liquid or household cleanser
- Stain-killing wall primer
- Soft cloth
- Paint roller pan, roller and best-quality roller cover(s)
- Touch-up topcoat paint

Tip

Don't let a quick paint touch-up turn into a disaster. Move furnishings that might get spattered, and protect your floors with a drop cloth.

136 Troubleshoot Interior-Paint Problems

There's only one thing worse than seeing the paint job you worked so hard on fail—that's repainting and seeing it fail again. Save yourself some heartbreak by addressing the cause(s) of that initial problem before you pick up a brush. (See also 169 Troubleshoot Exterior-Paint Problems.)

PROBLEM	POSSIBLE CAUSES	SOLUTIONS
Mildew (tiny black or gray spots or areas)	Excessive dampness and lack of air circulation; painting over improperly cleaned mildewed surface; failure to apply primer on wood	• Increase air circulation by using kitchen and bath fans. • Before painting, wash affected surfaces with 1-to-3 solution of bleach and water. Wait 15 minutes, rinse well. • Use mildewproof paint.
Blistering (air pockets bubble paint)	Exposing freshly applied latex paint to excessive dampness, such as showering too soon in newly painted bathroom; moisture coming through wall	• If blisters go all the way to substrate (bare wood, drywall), find and address moisture problem. • If only upper layer is blistered, scrape off blisters, sand to feather hard edges, repaint.
Cracking or flaking (initial fine cracks, then flaking)	Overthinning or overspreading paint; inadequate surface preparation; failure to apply primer on wood	• Scrape or wire-brush off loose paint; sand to feather hard edges. • Apply high-quality primer and topcoat.
Lapping (darker, denser color where strokes overlap)	Failure to maintain a wet edge; likely to occur on too-porous surface	• Prime porous surface; allow primer to dry thoroughly before applying topcoat. • Work in smaller areas; always maintain wet edge by painting from wet areas into dry, unpainted areas.

PROBLEM	POSSIBLE CAUSES	SOLUTIONS
Picture framing (uneven color or texture around windows, doors, corners)	Different application rates for brush, pad and roller	Use less paint when rolling or more when brushing. Use edging pad instead of brush to approximate spread rate and texture; cut in small section at a time to maintain wet edge, then roll over as much of cut-in area as possible.
Shiny or dull spots	Improper priming or failure to prime; uneven spread rate or poor technique	Use primer or sealer to achieve uniform porosity on surface (say, between joint compound and paper surface of drywall). Apply another coat. Always maintain wet edge by painting from wet areas into dry, unpainted areas.
Roller marks (paint bears traces of roller)	Improper roller cover for surface texture; poor-quality paint or roller cover; poor rolling technique	Use only best-quality roller covers; match nap length to surface texture. Dampen new roller cover before using it. Work in 3-foot-square (.3-m-square) sections; apply paint in shape of W, then fill in and complete area with light, parallel strokes.
Leaching (brown or soapy deposits)	Latex paint tends to do this in high-moisture areas, especially bathrooms	Wash surface with detergent-and-water solution. May take two or three times before all material has leached out of paint.

137 Solve a Lead-Paint Problem

About 75 percent of houses built before 1978 contain lead paint. If you have one of these homes, you need to understand the risks associated with lead. Avoid doing anything that might abrade or break a painted surface (inside or outside) until you know whether it contains lead. If you're doing permitted work yourself, make sure that you know—and follow—the proper procedures and precautions.

Steps

Determine if you have lead paint

1 Test painted surfaces for lead. You can rely on positive results from chemical lead-test kits, but if you get a negative result, collect and send samples to a lab for testing or have a professional test using an X-ray fluorescence machine.

2 Inform yourself! Start by reading "Protect Your Family From Lead in Your Home" and "Reducing Lead Hazards When Remodeling Your Home." Call the National Lead Information Service at (800) 424-5323 or download these brochures at www.epa.gov/lead.

Limit contamination during projects

1 Turn off air-conditioning and forced-air heating systems.

2 Move everything you can out of the work area. Cover and seal in plastic anything you can't move. For example, move furnishings out of a room and cover the floor with plastic.

3 Seal the work area with plastic and duct tape.

4 Take steps to control dust, such as misting work surfaces with water.

Clean up and retest

1 To clean, you will need a vacuum cleaner with a High Efficiency Particulate Air (HEPA) filter, buckets, disposal bags and more. Test for lead again after completing a major project.

Protect your health

1 Keep away everyone who does not need to be in the work area, especially children and pregnant women, who are more vulnerable to lead contamination.

2 Wear personal protection gear, including, for example, a respirator with HEPA filters that's approved by NIOSH (National Institute for Occupational Safety and Health), protective clothing and goggles.

What You'll Need

- Chemical lead-test kit
- EPA booklets on lead
- Plastic sheets
- Duct tape
- HEPA vacuum cleaner
- Buckets, disposal bags, and other cleaning and disposal equipment and supplies
- Personal protection gear

Tips

Everyday actions, such as opening and closing windows and doors, generate lead-contaminated dust.

Ordinary paint will not seal lead-based paint. Special encapsulating paint is required.

Check the yellow pages under "Lead Inspection and Control" for licensed, certified professionals who do lead-paint removal and control.

138 Replace a Damaged Ceiling Tile

Maybe an overflowing bathtub or an exploding pot of spaghetti sauce has damaged some ceiling tiles beyond repair. You'll find them easy to replace, especially if they're the suspended type.

Steps

Suspended ceiling tile

1 Press up on the tile to pop it out of the track. Lift up the tile and tilt it at an angle as needed to remove it.

2 If the tile is less than full size, use the damaged tile to cut the replacement tile to size with a utility knife guided by a straight-edge. Or use a measuring tape to determine the correct size.

3 Reverse the removal procedure to install the tile.

Interlocking tile

1 Cut out the center of the damaged tile to about 1 inch (2.5 cm) from the perimeter with a utility knife. Make additional cuts per-pendicular to each side, up to the joints with adjoining tiles, to remove the remaining pieces.

2 Pull out any nails or staples with a nail puller or pliers, or drive them in flush with a hammer. For tiles installed with adhesive, use a putty knife, paint scraper or old chisel to remove any adhe-sive residue from the furring strips or the original ceiling (in the absence of furring strips).

3 Cut the tongues off the new tile with a utility knife (see A). If you are replacing a partial tile, use a straightedge and a utility knife to cut it to size.

4 Use a caulking gun to apply panel adhesive to the furring strip (or to put four dabs on the back of the tile if you're attaching it directly to the ceiling). Press the tile into place (see B). Alterna-tively, nail the tile to the wood strapping with 4d finishing nails, countersink the nails with a nail set and hammer, and fill the holes with acrylic caulk.

What You'll Need

- Replacement ceiling tile(s)
- Utility knife with new blade
- Straightedge
- Measuring tape
- Nail puller or pliers
- Hammer
- Putty knife, paint scraper or old chisel
- Caulking gun
- Panel adhesive
- 4d finishing nails
- Nail set
- Acrylic caulk
- Goggles

Warning

Some ceiling tiles manufac-tured prior to mid-1970 con-tain asbestos. Before you work on a ceiling that old, contact your regional EPA office, state environmental office or local health depart-ment for advice on testing and handling. See also www.epa.gov/iaq/pubs/asbestos.html.

Wear goggles when cutting or handling overhead tiles to protect your eyes from falling dust and fibers.

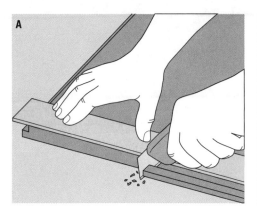

A

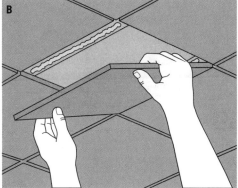

B

139 Replace a Wood Floorboard

A gleaming wood floor can transform a house's looks, but it does require some maintenance. When you can't effectively repair or disguise stains, gouges and other wood-floor damage with touch-ups, putty or the screen-and-overcoat method (see 142 Restore a Dull, Worn Wood Floor), you can replace individual strips or planks.

Steps

Removing one or more strips

1 Determine which strips you'll remove entirely and which have damaged portions you'll need to cut out. Use a carpenter's square to mark the latter boards for crosscutting.

2 For strip floors, use a spade bit in an electric drill to bore pairs of holes with a ¾-inch (2-cm) diameter at the ends of the boards you're removing (see A).

3 With the cut depth on a circular saw set equal to the flooring's thickness, make plunge cuts between the holes.

4 Pry out the strip between the cuts and the groove-edge piece (see B). To pry away the remaining strip, which is nailed through its tongue, drive an old chisel into the strip at its center, angled away from the adjacent strip. With the tongue and groove held apart, use a pry bar to pull out the strip.

5 Crosscut at your cut lines with a circular saw, using a plunge cut as necessary (see Tips). Guide all crosscuts with a square or straightedge to ensure that they're square.

6 To complete the cuts, drive a very sharp chisel into the saw kerf with the flat side of the chisel against the cut line.

What You'll Need

- Carpenter's square or straightedge
- Electric drill with ¾-inch (2-cm) spade bit
- Circular saw with flooring blade and trim blades
- Wood chisels
- Pry bar
- Speed square or miter saw
- Hammer
- Spiral flooring nails
- Nail set
- Belt and random-orbit sanders with abrasive belts and discs
- Sanding block and sandpaper
- Painter's masking tape
- Stain, sealer and finish
- Cloth
- Polyurethane
- Varnish brush
- No. 0000 steel wool
- Tack cloth
- Floor-buffing machine

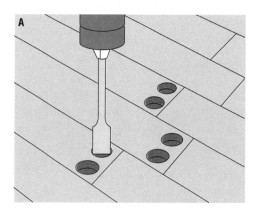

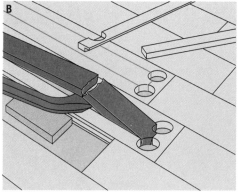

Install new floorboards

1 Install the first strip's tongue over an exposed groove. Cut the strip to length from the tongue end. Guide all crosscuts with a speed square or use a miter saw.

2 Tap in the strip with a hammer, then blind-nail (at an angle) spiral flooring nails into the tongue so that they will be hidden from view. To avoid damaging the wood, use a nail set to drive the nail the last ¼ inch (6 mm).

3 When you get to the last strip, cut the bottom lip of the tongue off the side and the end, then cut it to length. Tilt the strip to insert its tongue into the existing groove. Nail down the strip's face and countersink the heads with a nail set.

Finish the repair area only

1 Sand the replacement strips and the strips immediately adjacent to them using a belt sander with 60-grit belts until you cannot feel the joints when you move your hand across them. Sand with the grain.

2 Continue sanding with 80-grit and 100-grit belts. Then sand with 120-grit discs on a random-orbit sander, up to but not onto adjacent strips. Switch to a hand-sanding block to sand up to the edges of all unsanded adjacent strips.

3 Mask off the finished flooring using painter's masking tape.

4 If the existing floor is stained, apply stain with a cloth. It is very difficult to lighten a too-dark floor, so start light and mix in more dark stain as needed, or leave the stain on the wood long enough to achieve the desired results. If the floor is natural, apply a clear penetrating sealer.

5 Wipe off all excess stain or sealer with a soft cloth and allow it to dry for 24 hours before applying a finish.

6 Apply the same finish as on the original floor, or if you don't know what that finish is, apply polyurethane with a comparable gloss. Use a professional-quality varnish brush. When the first coat is ready for recoating (see the label), degloss the surface with No. 0000 steel wool, wipe the floor with a tack cloth and apply a second coat.

7 When the second coat dries, remove the tape. Using a floor-buffing machine over the whole floor or at least around the repair area may help even the overall sheen. If you're not satisfied with the results, either screen and overcoat the entire floor (see 142 Restore a Dull, Worn Wood Floor) or completely refinish it.

Tips

Stagger end joints at least 1 foot (30 cm) apart.

Use a black marker to apply an X to strips or sections you're removing. Once the dust starts flying and the strips get covered with sawdust, mistakes can happen.

Although you can use other types of blades, flooring blades are designed to hold up when they encounter an occasional nail.

To make a plunge cut, rest the nose of the saw shoe (base) on the floor, retract and hold back the blade guard and turn on the saw. Slowly tilt the saw down. When the shoe is flat on the floor, push forward to make the cut.

Drill pilot holes for face nails to avoid splitting the wood.

Warning

Dangerous kickback can occur if you are not very careful when using a circular saw. Use two hands for optimal control, plunge slowly, never back up, and avoid twisting the blade during a cut.

140 Quiet Squeaking Floors

So that squeaky floorboard makes it hard to walk to the bathroom in the middle of the night without waking the entire household? Then you've got to fix it. The cure for an annoying floor squeak depends on what layer is squeaking, what type of finish the flooring has and whether you have access to the floor from below.

Steps

Repairing squeaks from below

1 Locate the squeak from below by looking for any gap or movement of the subfloor when someone above steps on the squeaky area. If you notice either, you have a couple of options: Spread construction adhesive on a tapered shim and tap it into the gap, just until it's snug (too tight a fit will make things worse). Or put a bead of adhesive on the top edge and one face of a short 2-by-4 with a caulking gun, then fasten the 2-by-4 to the joist, angling 12d common nails upward so you draw the board tight against the subfloor.

2 If the subfloor is tight under a nailed-down hardwood floor, put as substantial a weight as you can, 200 lbs. (90 kg) or more, directly on the squeaking floorboard(s). From below, drill numerous closely spaced clearance holes, 1 to 2 inches (2.5 to 5 cm) apart, through the subfloor and drill pilot holes into the hardwood flooring. Drive in an appropriate-length sheet-metal screw, ¼ inch (6 mm) shy of the total thickness of the wood.

Working from above

1 Locate the joists. Typically this is easier to do from below. Tap the ceiling while listening for a dull (versus a hollow) sound; use an electronic stud finder or drive exploratory nails to locate one joist. Then, assuming a 16-inch (40-cm) center-to-center joist spacing, locate the others.

2 Measure the distance from the wall to the center of the relevant joist(s) downstairs. This measurement must be *very accurate*. Use it to mark the joist location on the floor upstairs with masking tape.

3 If you have hardwood floors, concentrate a very heavy weight on the loose board, then drive a spiral flooring nail at an angle through the floor and into the joist; or use a special fastening system called Counter Snap, in which the screw breaks off just below the surface for a nearly invisible repair (see Tips).

4 Drive in additional fasteners as needed; countersink the nails with a nail set. Fill the holes with a color-matched wax-putty stick or crayon, then buff off the extra wax with a dry cloth.

5 If you have carpeting installed over an underlayment, use a special fastening system called Squeeeeek No More (see Tips). Its screw also snaps off just below the floor surface, so you can install it right through carpeting without damage.

What You'll Need

- Shim packet
- Construction-adhesive cartridge
- Caulking gun
- 2-by-4
- 12d common nails
- Drill with driver, drill bits, and countersinks
- Sheet-metal screws
- Screwdriver
- Electronic stud finder
- Measuring tape
- Masking tape
- Spiral flooring nails
- Counter Snap kit
- Nail set
- Wax-putty stick or crayon
- Cloth
- Squeeeeek No More kit

Tips

Sheet-metal screws work well for tightening floors from below because the coarse thread grabs well and the head does not allow it to go in too deeply.

Spiral flooring nails have superior holding power, though they're not quite as strong as screws.

Squeeeeek No More and Counter Snap are unique systems made by O'Berry Enterprises. You can reach them at (800) 459-8428 or www.oberry-enterprises.com.

Warning

Don't screw up into a finished floor until you have determined the thickness of the subfloor, any underlayment and the finished flooring.

141 Repair a Water-Damaged Hardwood Floor

Wood and water just don't mix. Sealed and waxed floors may become stained if water sits on their surface for more than a few minutes. Here's how to repair the damage.

Steps

Removing white stains from a surface finish

1 To remove a smoky white haze or a white spot, buff the finish with a soft cotton cloth and a very mild abrasive, such as whitening toothpaste, auto-polishing compound, or tobacco ash mixed with mineral oil, until the stain disappears (see A).

Removing black or white water stains from wood

1 Mask off the surrounding boards with painter's masking tape.

2 First remove any wax or surface finish. Use fine steel wool to remove wax, and sandpaper to remove a surface finish. Depending on the size of the repair area, hand-sand with a rubber sanding block (see B) or machine-sand with a random-orbit sander. In both cases, start with 80- or even 60-grit abrasive and sand to 100-grit. Sand just *up* to the edges of unaffected boards.

3 Mix oxalic acid crystals (available at paint or hardware stores) in 1 cup (8 fl oz/250 ml) or so of hot water and stir to dissolve them. Keep adding crystals until they won't dissolve anymore.

4 Pour, brush or sponge the solution on the stained area. When it is completely dry, brush off the crystals and repeat the process until the stain is gone.

5 Stain or seal, then refinish the affected area (see 139 Replace a Wood Floorboard). Or, if the touch-up stands out too much, use the screen-and-overcoat method to restore the entire floor (see 142 Restore a Dull, Worn Wood Floor).

What You'll Need

- Soft cotton cloths
- Very mild abrasive
- Painter's masking tape
- Fine steel wool
- Rubber sanding block or random-orbit sander
- Sandpaper
- Oxalic acid crystals
- Brush or sponge
- Rubber gloves
- Goggles

Tip

Choose the least aggressive approach that yields the desired results.

Warning

Using excessive or concentrated pressure when buffing out a stain with even a mild abrasive can mar the finish.

Carefully follow all safety advice on oxalic acid packaging, such as wearing rubber gloves and goggles.

A

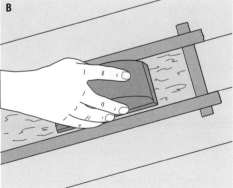

B

142 Restore a Dull, Worn Wood Floor

You may think that when a polyurethane or varnish finish on a hard-wood floor becomes dull, scratched and worn, your only recourse is to call in a professional to sand the floors down to the bare wood and refinish. But there's a simpler approach, well within the capabilities of a do-it-yourselfer—the screen-and-overcoat technique. If your wood floors are prefinished, consult the manufacturer for safety and finish recommendations.

Steps

Prepare the room

1 Move all furniture and wall decorations out of the room.

2 Install a box fan in a window within the room, and open a window across the room and just outside the room. With the fan set to exhaust, the negative pressure keeps dust from moving outside the room.

3 Just in case, cover furniture in adjoining rooms with lightweight plastic drop cloths.

Screen the floor

1 Install an abrasive pad on the rubberized wheel of a floor polisher to practice in the center of the room until you are comfortable controlling the machine.

2 Install a 100-grit abrasive screen on the polisher and sand the floor. Go back and forth across the floor in overlapping passes from one end of the room to the other.

3 Sweep, vacuum and inspect the floor. All the finish should be dull, wear patterns should no longer be noticeable, and any scratches and stains should be gone. Repeat the sanding as necessary.

4 Using a random-orbit electric sander, sand areas at the perimeter where the polisher missed. Use a rubber sanding block with fine sandpaper (or a sanding sponge), sanding with the grain, on areas the sander couldn't reach.

Remove all dust

1 Sweep, vacuum, dust and then vacuum again to clean the room (floors, walls, baseboards) and eliminate all dust.

2 Using a soft cloth slightly dampened with mineral spirits, wipe down the entire floor, turning and shaking out the cloth often.

3 Turn the fan off and vacuum one final time, using the floor brush on large areas and the pointed wand at the perimeter and in cracks.

What You'll Need

- Box fan
- Plastic drop cloths
- Rented floor polisher
- Abrasive pad
- 100-grit abrasive screens
- Soft-bristle push broom
- Vacuum with floor-brush and wand attachments
- Random-orbit electric sander
- Abrasive discs for sander
- Fine sandpaper and rubber sanding block or sanding sponge
- Soft cloths
- Mineral spirits
- Angled sash brush
- Varnish brush
- Finish
- Dust mask or respirator

Tips

Pick up plenty of 100-grit screens. You can return what you don't use.

Coarser-grit screens are available for more aggressive sanding of floors in worse condition.

Don't walk on a sanded floor in bare or stocking feet. Skin oils and moisture can prevent proper bonding and cause staining.

Apply the finish

1 Using a professional-quality angled sash brush, cut in a band of finish 3 inches (7.5 cm) wide along the baseboard on one wall and about 2 feet (60 cm) down the sides.

2 Using a professional-quality varnish brush 5 inches (13 cm) wide, apply an even coat of finish. Work across the room, following the direction of the flooring planks, coating about a 2-foot (60-cm) strip at a time. Cut in more along the walls as needed.

Tips for preventing damage to wood floors

- In your kitchen, place small, washable area rugs in front of the stove, sink and refrigerator. Heavy traffic, spills and dropped items will be less likely to damage the floor.

- Wipe up spills immediately with a dry cloth or paper towel. Use a slightly damp mop or cloth, if necessary, but dry the floor immediately after.

- Keep dirt, especially gritty sand, out of the house. Choose exterior mats that are most effective at removing dirt, and add throw rugs inside to catch any remaining dirt. Regularly shake out, hose off or otherwise clean the mats and area rugs.

- Set up a convenient place for people to slip off dirty or wet shoes just inside the most commonly used family entrance.

- Acknowledge that you can't keep all dirt out. Vacuum often to remove dirt that slips by your defenses.

- Protect wood floors from excessive sunlight, which can cause colors to fade or finishes to fail. Exterior awnings, drapes, window tinting or area rugs may all be helpful solutions.

- Install and frequently clean fabric glides on chairs, tables and other furniture legs. Pay special attention to clean or vacuum the glides on chairs often, and replace them about once a year, depending on use.

Warning

Wear a tight-fitting dust mask or respirator when sanding and sweeping.

Follow all safety guidelines recommended by the finish's manufacturer.

143 Touch Up Wood-Floor Finishes

Modern wood-floor finishes can take quite a bit of abuse, but accidents do happen. You can try to camouflage scratches and other minor damage on an otherwise beautiful floor. If the results don't satisfy you or if you can't make certain areas blend in, a screening and overcoat may help. Some situations require complete refinishing.

Steps

Fixing a surface-coated floor

1 For a small, relatively inconspicuous area on a surface-coated or film-forming floor, try cleaning with very fine steel wool followed by paste wax.

2 If that fails, apply a little of the same finish directly on the scratch with an artist's brush. If possible, contact the manufacturer of a factory-finished floor or the installer of a site-finished floor to determine the finish. Or use polyurethane with a comparable sheen.

3 Put a cloth lightly dampened with mineral spirits over your fingertip, and immediately wipe off the excess finish before it dries.

4 When the finish is dry, buff well with a soft cloth.

5 If the scratch has penetrated a stained floor and removed an area of stain, touch up the stain before you apply finish. Wipe or brush on stain, allow it to penetrate for a few minutes and wipe it off. Or use a furniture stick or floor touch-up marker that approximates the floor stain's color. Allow overnight drying before finishing.

6 If the repair is too obvious, the next step is to refinish the entire affected strip. Use steel wool or fine sandpaper on a sanding block that's narrower than the floorboard to remove layers of the finish. Brush on polyurethane, being careful not to get any on surrounding strips.

Fixing a waxed floor

1 Depending on the depth of the scratch or other damage, use steel wool, a cabinet scraper, or even fine sandpaper on a sanding block to remove the finish, along with the scratch.

2 Wipe on a matching stain (or a clear sealer on an unstained floor). You can stain more to darken the area, but it's very hard to lighten stained wood, so start on the light side.

3 Waxed floors are forgiving, so you can try many times and extend the repair to the entire strip, as for a polyurethane floor, until you get the results you want. When the color is right, wax the repair area, and then wax a wider area for a uniform sheen.

What You'll Need

- Very fine steel wool
- Paste wax
- Artist's brush
- Polyurethane or other finish
- Cloths
- Mineral spirits
- Stain, furniture stick or floor touch-up marker
- Fine sandpaper
- Sanding block
- Cabinet scraper
- Varnish brush

Tips

Manufacturers of factory-finished flooring may sell color-matched repair kits. Contact them for additional guidance before attempting any repairs.

To make your own sanding block, put self-adhering felt on a block of wood cut to the desired size.

Before sanding a strip, cover the adjacent strip with a board that you either tape to the floor or kneel on so you avoid accidentally sanding that strip.

Similarly, put painter's masking tape on adjacent strips when applying stain or finish.

Warning

Read and heed safety warnings on finishing products; some are flammable or toxic.

144 Repair Damaged Sheet-Vinyl Flooring

Vinyl-floor manufacturers typically offer extensive stain-removal guides, but if your sheet flooring is permanently stained or damaged, you can cut out the damaged area and patch it.

Steps

Patching a fully adhered floor

1 Cut an oversize patch of flooring saved from the installation with a utility knife (see A). If you don't have any, you can cut some from a hidden area. Use tape to place the patch over the soiled area after carefully aligning the patch's pattern with the floor's.

2 With a straightedge as a guide, slice through the two layers (see B). Use a new blade and a firm stroke to assure a single, clean cut. Lift off the patch and pry up the adhered damaged section with a stiff-blade putty knife. Scrape off *all* adhesive from the substrate with a chisel. Don't damage the seam edges.

3 Test-fit the patch. Apply adhesive to it with a notched $\frac{1}{16}$-inch (2-mm) disposable spreader and press the patch into place with a rolling pin. Wipe up any adhesive that squirts from the seam. After 30 minutes, apply the recommended seam coater or sealer with the applicator provided. Don't walk near the repair for 24 hours.

Patching a perimeter-fastened floor

1 Apply reinforced masking tape 2 inches (5 cm) wide on the outside edge of the pattern you're removing to limit shrinkage when you make the cut. Double-cut as described above, and vacuum the underlayment in and around the cutout section.

2 Lift up the flooring to apply a *light* coat of adhesive 4 inches (10 cm) wide and centered on the seam. Firmly press the flooring into the adhesive and roll it with a rolling pin. Level the seam with a wallpaper roller.

3 After 30 minutes, apply the recommended seam coater or sealer with the applicator provided.

What You'll Need

- Utility knife with new blades
- Flooring material
- Reinforced masking tape
- Straightedge
- Stiff-blade putty knife
- Chisel
- Adhesive and notched $\frac{1}{16}$-inch (2-mm) disposable spreader
- Rolling pin
- Seam coater or sealer
- Vacuum
- Wallpaper roller

Warning

Some vinyl tile, tile backing and adhesive installed prior to the mid-1970s may contain dangerous asbestos. If your floor is this old, obtain a copy of the booklet "Asbestos in Your Home" by calling the Environmental Protection Agency at (202) 554-1404 or downloading it from www.epa.gov/iaq/pubs/asbestos.html.

Seam sealers are very flammable. Extinguish all flames, including pilot lights in the area, and open windows and doors for ventilation.

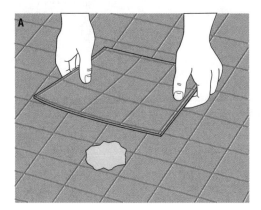

145 Repair a Vinyl-Tile Floor

Tiles coming loose or looking scratched and scuffed? You can re-adhere loose vinyl tiles and replace or patch damaged ones. If you don't have any leftover tiles and you can't get replacements, remove a tile from an inconspicuous area such as a closet floor. Use it for the repair, and fill the empty square with a new tile that's as close a match as you can get.

Steps

Replace a damaged tile

1 Cover the damaged tile with aluminum foil and warm it with an iron on a moderate temperature setting.

2 With a 3-inch (7.5-cm) scraper or stiff putty knife, pry up the tile and scrape all adhesive off the substrate. When you scrape the substrate, start at the edge of a remaining tile and scrape toward the center.

3 After test-fitting the new tile, spread fresh adhesive on the floor with a ⅛-inch (3-mm) notched trowel.

4 Place the new tile and push it in with a rolling pin.

5 Remove any stray adhesive using a cloth moistened with water or the tile manufacturer's recommended solvent.

6 Cover the tile with a board and a heavy weight for at least 8 hours.

Fix a loose or curling tile

1 If a tile is attached but curls up at a corner or edge, warm the curled area (using aluminum foil and an iron as described in step 1, above) to make it flexible and to soften the adhesive.

2 Raise the tile just enough to spread the bottom or the floor with fresh adhesive using a putty knife or plastic spreader.

3 Press the tile into place and roll toward that edge to force out any excess adhesive.

4 Clean and weight the tile as described in "Replace a damaged tile," above.

Repair a small hole

1 Mask the area up to and around the hole to about 2 inches (5 cm) with painter's masking tape.

2 Color a two-part clear epoxy to match the tile with artist's acrylic paint. Use as little paint as possible and mix the ingredients on a clean scrap of board with a putty knife.

3 Spread the mixture in the hole and level it with a plastic spreader or putty knife.

What You'll Need

- Aluminum foil
- Iron
- 3-inch (7.5-cm) scraper or stiff putty knife
- Adhesive
- ⅛-inch (3-mm) notched trowel
- Rolling pin
- Cloth
- Solvent
- Board
- Heavy weight
- Plastic spreader
- Painter's masking tape
- Clear epoxy
- Artist's acrylic paint
- Clean scrap of board

Tip

The same foil-and-heating trick makes it easier to remove dry adhesive.

Warning

Some vinyl tile, tile backing and adhesive installed prior to the mid-1970s may contain dangerous asbestos. If your floor is this old, obtain a copy of the booklet "Asbestos in Your Home" by calling the Environmental Protection Agency at (202) 554-1404 or download it from www.epa.gov/iaq/pubs/asbestos.html.

146 Silence Squeaky Stairs

Squeak, squeak, squeak ... it can really get to you after a while, so why not fix that troublesome tread? If you have access to the underside of a squeaky stair, you can make an easy, invisible and effective repair. It's only slightly more difficult from above, and with the right fasteners and a crayon for cover-up, no one will notice the repair.

Steps

Working from below

1 For squeaks at the nose of the tread, cut short lengths of ¾-inch (2-cm) quarter-round molding, coat them with wood glue, and toenail them into the inside corner formed by the tread and riser (see A).

2 For squeaks at the rear of the tread, use a countersink bit to bore a pilot hole through the back of the riser into the tread. Then drive in a 2-inch (5-cm) screw to join the two parts and eliminate any friction. Install additional screws as needed.

Working from above

1 For a squeak at the nose of the tread, nail the tread into the top of the riser. To make nailing easier, bore a pilot hole slightly smaller than the nail's diameter through the tread. Drive one or more pair of nails about 2 inches (5 cm) apart and at opposing 45-degree angles for maximum holding power (see B).

2 Alternatively, use Squeeeeek No More (for carpeted stairs) or Counter Snap (for hardwood stairs) fastening systems (see Tip). The trim screws in both systems break off just below the surface, leaving only a tiny hole, and Squeeeeek No More screws go right through the carpet without damaging it.

3 Fill any holes with color-matched wax-filler sticks or crayons, and buff any wax residue off the face with a dry cloth.

4 Put graphite or talcum power into the crack at the rear of the tread to stop squeaks there.

What You'll Need

- Quarter-round molding
- Saw or utility knife
- Wood glue
- Drill and driver with countersink bit
- 2-inch (5-cr⁻ʼ coarse-thread drywall screws
- 4d finishing nails
- Hammer
- Squeeeeek No More or Counter Snap kits
- Wax-filler sticks or crayons
- Cloth
- Graphite or talcum powder

Tip

Squeeeeek No More and Counter Snap are unique systems made by O'Berry Enterprises. You can reach them at (800) 459-8428 or www.oberry-enterprises.com.

Warning

Toenail (angle) nails so they won't penetrate the face of the tread or riser.

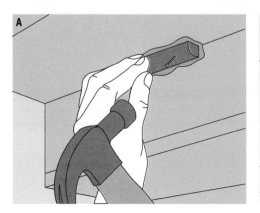

A

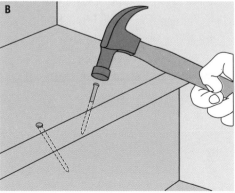

B

147 Repair a Loose or Broken Baluster

Your grand staircase makes a less-than-grand impression if it's got a broken baluster. Replacing, tightening or repairing a baluster is easy if you understand how it's secured. The bottom end is dovetailed and locked into the edge of the tread before the nosing is applied; or it's doweled and inserted in a hole as it's tilted into place for nailing at the top. The top is toenailed to the railing.

Steps

Remove a baluster for replacement or repair

1 To remove a dovetailed baluster, pry off the cove molding and nosing (see A). (Insert a trim pry bar into the joint on the nosing's underside so the trim will cover any mar.) Then tap out the baluster with a block of wood. To disconnect the top, drive the top end in the upstairs direction with a wood block and hammer.

2 To remove a doweled baluster, disconnect the top. Then pull or pry up on the baluster to lift out the doweled end.

Glue together a broken baluster

1 Remove the baluster and use padded clamps to draw the pieces together and test the fit.

2 Use a glue injector if the baluster is just cracked. If it's completely broken, apply wood glue to the break with a brush.

3 Squeeze the break closed carefully and apply pressure with a padded clamp every 6 inches (15 cm).

What You'll Need

- Trim pry bar
- Hammer
- Scraps of wood
- Padded clamps
- Glue injector or brush
- Wood glue
- Cloth
- Electric drill
- Drill bits
- Construction or panel adhesive
- 4d finishing nails
- Nail set
- Caulk or putty
- Caulking gun
- Wax-filler stick

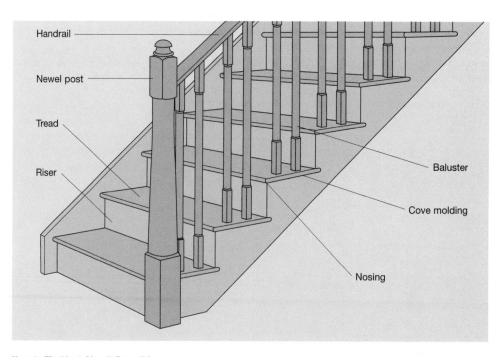

Handrail

Newel post

Tread

Riser

Baluster

Cove molding

Nosing

4 Wipe off excess glue with a damp cloth. Allow the glue to cure overnight before touching up the finish as needed and reinstalling the baluster.

Install a repaired or replacement baluster

1 Drill two new pilot holes for nails at the top, angling them slightly toward each other so you will be able to drive them in without hitting the adjacent baluster.

2 Test-fit the baluster. If the dowel or dovetail joint at the bottom fits tightly, apply wood glue and insert the end of the baluster into the tread. If the joint is loose, use construction or panel adhesive instead of glue to fill the gaps.

3 Drive 4d finishing nails into the new pilot holes to secure the top to the underside of the rail.

4 Countersink the nails with a nail set, and fill the holes with caulk or putty if you are painting, or wax filler if the baluster has a clear finish.

Tighten a loose baluster

1 If the baluster is loose at the bottom, remove and reinstall it using construction adhesive in the joint (see "Install a repaired or replacement baluster," above).

2 A quicker but less reliable way to tighten a baluster that's loose at the bottom is to drill two pilot holes, then drive two nails through the baluster and into the tread.

3 If the baluster is loose at the top, drill two pilot holes through the top of the baluster, then drive two nails into the baluster's upstairs face (see B).

4 Countersink the nailheads with a nail set, and fill the holes.

Tip

You may be able to determine whether a baluster is doweled or dovetailed by slipping a playing card between the tread and the baluster and "feeling" for a round or rectangular shape on the recessed pin.

Warning

Always wear eye protection when cutting, hammering or drilling.

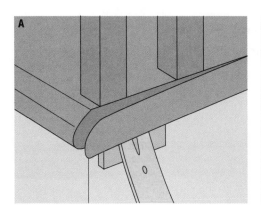

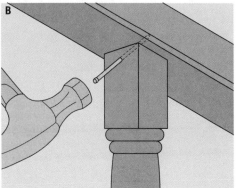

148 Replace Caulking on the Outside of Your House

Caulk and other sealants safeguard your house against rain and snow at vulnerable points such as cracks and open joints, wherever flashing and other approaches can't do the job. Keep the weather outside where it belongs by making sure your exterior caulking stays in good shape.

Steps

Sealing joints around windows and doors

1 Scrape out old caulk using a painter's five-in-one tool, a stiff putty knife or another similar tool.

2 Use a putty knife to scrape off any caulk that remains on the surface or walls of the joint.

3 For very dry, stubborn caulk, use a caulk softening and removal chemical, such as 3M Caulk Remover, as directed by the manufacturer.

4 Allow the cleaned joint to dry for a day or more unless the product is approved for wet applications.

5 Press an open-cell foam backer rod into joints wider than ¼ inch (6 mm) or deeper than ½ inch (12 mm) so the joint is about half as deep as it is wide. Never fill a deep joint. Doing so wastes caulk and makes a good, permanent bond less likely.

6 To avoid getting caulk on adjacent surfaces, apply painter's masking tape. While this may not be practical for large areas, it's an option for highly visible areas or for surfaces that caulk might ruin.

7 Cut about ⅜ inch (1 cm) off the caulking cartridge's nozzle at a 45-degree angle with a utility knife. The goal is to get a hole ³⁄₁₆ inch (5 mm) across to produce a bead of that diameter.

8 Press the caulk into the joint, adjusting both the rate of application and the amount of pressure to apply enough caulk so you slightly overfill the joint. Some experts say it's better to push rather than pull, but you can achieve excellent results either way.

9 Smooth the joint with a wetted fingertip or smoothing tool.

Sealing joints in other locations

1 For masonry chimney and siding joints, always use backer rods and choose a caulk that is designed to adhere to masonry and that matches the color of the cement grout. Mask the chimney; caulk won't easily come off porous surfaces.

What You'll Need

- Painter's five-in-one tool or stiff putty knife
- Caulk softening and removal chemical
- Open-cell foam backer rod
- Painter's masking tape
- Utility knife
- Exterior caulk and gun
- Smoothing tool
- Polyurethane sealant
- Expanding foam

Tips

Most sealants don't bond to wet surfaces and bond better to primed wood than bare wood.

Keep paper towels and a wet cloth or sponge handy to clean your smoothing finger and wet it for the next task.

A finger is easy to use for smoothing and it's always handy. On rough or splintered surfaces, however, use an ice-pop stick, a caulk-smoothing tool, metal flashing or an old putty knife cut or ground to a suitable shape.

2 For horizontal joints between a house and concrete slabs, such as those in a patio, walk or driveway, always use a backer rod. Self-leveling polyurethane sealants, although very messy to work with, offer superior protection.

3 For joints between a foundation and the wall above it, use expanding foam. The gap here is often too difficult to access with the tip of a caulking tube. The foam expands to fill the gap and better seal against air infiltration and pests.

Seal any gaps between dissimilar materials (foundation and wall, chimney and siding) and along the perimeter of penetrations (wire, pipe, vent, fan, air conditioner, mail slot and so forth). Fill cracks in the exterior siding and trim.

Caulking tips

- If you plan to paint, use paintable caulk. Paint does not bond well to silicone caulk.

- Caulk may not adhere to paint or stain that contains wax, stearate, silicone, or paraffin-based oil. Verify the compatibility of your caulk and paint.

- Caulk bonds best when gaps are between $^3/_{16}$ inch (5 mm) and $^1/_2$ inch (12 mm) wide, when they are as half as deep as they are wide, and when the caulk adheres only to the joint walls (not to the bottom or rear surface).

- Do not caulk the joints between aluminum or plastic siding and windows or doors. The channels provide the necessary seal.

- Clear silicone caulk does not bond well with unfinished cedar siding, shingles and trim. Use a copolymer rubber-based clear sealant, such as Lexel (available from Sashco Sealants, www.sashcosealants.com).

- The primary purpose of exterior caulk is to keep water out. Caulking for energy efficiency also requires that you seal wall penetrations indoors.

- Caulking guns with a thumb-activated quick-release trigger are easier and less messy to use.

- Caulking guns with an open frame are easier to keep clean than the partially enclosed type.

- Ideally, the hole in the tip of the caulk tube should be as wide as the gap you're filling. A smaller hole is OK but slower; a larger one makes a mess.

- Wrap the end of a partially used caulking tube in plastic and secure it with a rubber band to prevent caulk from drying out in the nozzle.

149 Childproof Your Home

Take measures to protect your child from common household dangers before you bring a newborn home from the hospital. After that, review your safety measures every six months to make sure your child has not outgrown or outsmarted any of them. Remember that no safety device outweighs the

AREA	CHILDPROOFING STEPS TO TAKE
Overall precautions	Install outlet covers and plates on outlets to prevent electrocution.
	Install smoke detectors in every bedroom and in kitchen.
	Use window guards, window stops or safety netting to prevent kids from falling out windows. Make sure adult or older child can remove safety devices to use window as emergency exit.
	Remove window blind cords that have loops, which can cause strangulation. Buy safety tassels to replace cord loops. (Or simply cut looped cords in half.)
	Keep children out of dangerous rooms (bathrooms, garage, office) with door-knob covers and door locks. Place slide lock or hook-and-eye latch high on door, out of child's reach.
	Use cordless phone to remain mobile with kids around. Have at least one cell phone in house for use in emergencies when there is no electricity.
	Post emergency numbers next to all phones, including numbers for poison control center, nearest emergency room and pediatrician.
	If your house has chipped or flaking lead paint, hire professional to remove it.
	Install safety latches on all cupboards and airtight containers, including refrigerators, chests or coolers, where child could become trapped and suffocate.
Kitchen	Install safety latches on cupboards within child's reach. Remember that safety latches are not fail-proof. Store knives, sharp objects and heavy pans out of child's reach.
	Store detergents, soaps, alcohol and other hazardous items out of reach.
	Keep breakables, especially fine china, in secured cupboard out of reach.
	Use back burners when cooking, and turn handles away from counter edge.
	Leave appliances unplugged when not in use, especially the toaster. Keep electrical cords coiled and out of reach.
	Always put iron away when not in use; never leave it on ironing board, where child could tug the cord.
	Equip faucets with anti-scalding devices. Never have hot drinks near children.
	Remove tablecloths, which can be pulled down, along with anything on them.
	Always latch trash compactor and dishwasher.
	Keep stairs and step stools away from counters to prevent unauthorized exploring.
	Keep fire extinguisher in kitchen but not close to any heat sources.
	Make sure trash can has lid and is inaccessible to children.

importance of adult supervision. The safety devices mentioned below are available at most hardware stores, drugstores and baby stores.

AREA	CHILDPROOFING STEPS TO TAKE
	• Have a safe cupboard for child to explore while you are cooking. Fill with wooden spoons, plastic cups and lids, and other harmless items. • Use safety gate to keep kids out of kitchen when you are not there.
Bathroom	• Set water heater to 120°F (49°C) to prevent scalding; install anti-scalding devices on faucets and shower heads. • Keep toilet seat cover closed to prevent drowning; install lid-lock for extra safety. • Keep hair dryers, curling irons, electric shavers and other electric devices unplugged and out of reach. Don't plug in anything near bathtub. • Install safety latches on cupboards; keep medications, toiletries and cleaning supplies out of reach. Store medication in original containers. • Keep sharp objects out of reach (razors, manicure scissors and clippers). • Place nonslip stickers in bathtub and rubber guard over bathtub faucet to prevent injury. Place nonskid bathmat on floor to prevent slipping. • Install GFCI (ground fault circuit interrupters) on all outlets. • Remove lower locks on bathroom door to prevent accidental locking by child.
Living room	• Place bumpers on all sharp corners and edges of furniture. Remove any glasstop tables. • Make sure area rugs have nonslip pads. • Place indoor plants out of reach. • Secure bookshelves, TV and other furniture against walls to prevent tipping. • Keep remote controls, CDs and videos out of reach. • Remove any frayed or unnecessary extension cords. • Place any breakables or table lamps out of reach of children. • Install fireplace grill; keep matches and fireplace tools out of reach. • Keep recliner chair closed unless in use by adult; moveable parts can trap child.
Stairs and hallway	• Install safety gates at top and bottom of stairs. Gates that screw into wall are more secure than those that use pressure. Don't use accordion-type gates, which can cause strangulation. • Remove any clutter or toys near stairs to prevent tripping. • Install handrails along entire length of stairs if not there already.

(continued on next page)

AREA	CHILDPROOFING STEPS TO TAKE
Nursery	• Make sure crib, playpen and other baby furniture are not near windows, dangling cords, heater vents, wall hangings or sharp objects.
	• Use crib mattress that is firm and fits snugly into crib; do not place stuffed animals, blankets, comforters, pillows or other bedding in crib.
	• Examine crib: Slats should be no more than 2⅜ inches (6 cm) apart; posts in corners should be short (at most ¹⁄₁₆ inch/2 mm) unless it is a canopy crib; decorative cutouts should be smaller than a baby's head.
	• Examine playpen: Mesh should be less than ¾ inch (2 cm) and/or slats should be no wider than 2⅜ inches (6 cm) apart.
	• Make sure diaper changing table has safety strap, and changing supplies are within your reach.
	• Install carpeting under changing table and crib to soften any accidental fall.
Bedrooms	• Install carbon monoxide detectors in any rooms where people sleep.
	• Secure chest of drawers, bookcases and other furniture to prevent toppling.
	• Inspect toys for small or detachable parts. Dispose of broken or dangerous toys or toys that are heavy enough to cause injury to child.
	• Do not leave balloons or plastic bags (even filled ones) near children; both can cause suffocation.
	• Install safety rails on bunkbeds and make sure ladders are firmly attached.
Garage and yard	• Keep all toxins out of reach of children. Install safety latches on lower cupboards. Use door locks or safety gates to keep children out of garages.
	• Test to make sure garage door reverses automatically if there is an obstruction.
	• Keep children away from exercise equipment at all times.
	• Inspect outdoor play structures (jungle gyms, playhouses, slides) for loose screws, sharp edges, splintered wood and small removable parts that are choking hazards. Make sure such structures are stable and secure.
	• Keep children away from barbecue grills, especially when in use.
	• Fix any loose bricks or pathway cracks that can cause tripping.
	• Place stickers on sliding glass doors so children won't walk into them.
	• Keep any firearms unloaded and securely locked away. Store ammunition in a locked area separate from any guns.
	• Remember that children can drown in 2 inches (5 cm) of water. Protect them from ponds, wells, kiddy pools and deep puddles.
	• Install slide or hook-and-eye latch locks on all doors leading outdoors so children cannot go outside unattended.
	• Install fence with locking gate around swimming pool.

150 **Prevent Ice Dams**

When a large amount of snow accumulates on a roof, heat loss from insufficient insulation and poor attic ventilation can melt the snow from the underside. As the water reaches the roof edge, where it's colder, it forms a dam. The dammed water backs up under the roofing and leaks into your home. The best way to prevent thawing from the underside is to maintain a cold roof.

Steps

Maintain a cold roof

1 The most significant area for heat loss in a room below an attic is usually the ceiling, especially in the area adjacent to the outside wall. Inspect the ceiling insulation with a flashlight, then take steps to maximize it.

2 Maintain an open channel through which cold air can pass from soffit vents to the attic. Attach insulation baffles made for this purpose on the underside of the roof sheathing. The channel also allows you to insulate over the top of the wall and compress extra insulation into this restricted area.

3 Use caulk or expanding foam (available in cans) to seal gaps around pipes or electric cables that penetrate the top plates of the walls in rooms below. Weather-strip the attic door, or insulate and weather-strip pull-down attic stairs.

4 Seal and cover recessed light fixtures (Type IC only) with insulation (see Warning).

5 Keep attic vents open so the heat that inevitably escapes from living areas into the attic can go out the vent before it warms the roof. The size of attic-vent openings typically must be at least 1/150 of the attic's floor area.

Create a second line of defense

1 Install thermostatically controlled electric heat tapes (wires) in a zigzag pattern along the lower roof edge and into the gutters. Installing the wires is easy—they clip onto the shingles—but you'll need to install an exterior, weatherproof GFCI (ground fault circuit interrupter) receptacle outlet near one end of the roof edge. Typically an electrician or homeowner with electrical savvy can tap into an attic outlet to feed the new boxes on the low end of a gable wall.

2 Or accept the inevitable and install a nailable waterproof membrane that extends at least 24 inches (60 cm) up the roof from a point directly above the inside of the exterior wall. A roof with a 24-inch (60-cm) overhang would require coverage at least 54 inches (137 cm) wide. Although the best time to do this is when you're reroofing, you can remove lower courses of asphalt roofing for a retrofit.

What You'll Need

- Flashlight
- Insulation baffles
- Caulk or expanding foam
- Caulking gun
- Door weather-stripping
- Utility knife
- Attic-stair insulation kit and weather-stripping
- Attic-ceiling insulation
- Electric heat tapes
- Weatherproof outlet box with weather cover
- GFCI receptacle
- Roofing membrane and related roofing materials and tools

Tips

Cold drafts from electrical outlets in rooms below an attic indicate the presence of an attic opening in the top of the wall.

Snow guards keep snow and ice from dislodging, sliding off the roof and damaging the gutter.

When you're using an outdoor outlet for more than short-term use, such as powering a tool, you must equip it with a cover that protects it from weather.

Warning

Insulating light fixtures that aren't Type IC without providing the necessary space between the insulation and the housing causes overheating and fires.

151 Cure a Faulty Fireplace Draw

When a fireplace spills smoke into a room, it's at best annoying and at worst hazardous to your health. Considering the great enjoyment (not to mention the resale value) a working fireplace adds to your home, it's good news that you have a choice of effective solutions, ranging in cost from nothing to $2,000 or $3,000.

Steps

Determine the cause

1 If a fireplace spills smoke into the house only on windy days, the problem is downdraft, resulting from a too-short chimney or environmental situations beyond your control. Consider extending the chimney or installing a wind-deflecting chimney cap or fan.

2 Flow reversals typically occur when the operation of exhaust fans, including those for clothes dryers, causes negative pressure in a tightly closed house. Either open a window or install an air-intake kit to supply the needed combustion air. A leaky attic in a multistory house can create a chimney effect and cause chronic depressurization. The solution is to seal all openings between the living space and the attic.

3 Inadequate flow can occur when the size of the fireplace opening is too large for the size or length of the flue. Compare your flue's dimensions with the standards published in architectural manuals, available in the reference section of most public libraries. Solutions range from reducing the size of the opening with a metal smoke guard to major projects such as installing a fireplace insert, rebuilding the firebox, adding to chimney height or installing a chimney fan.

Implement the cure

1 Install a wind cap. Consult a chimney professional who can install a wind-diverting chimney cap. Although the installation itself is relatively simple, working safely at a chimney top isn't, and some suppliers will only sell products to professionals.

2 Install a chimney fan. The demanding conditions these fans must endure, such as extreme heat and corrosive flue gases, make them very expensive (about $2,000 installed), but they are guaranteed to solve the problem.

3 Increase the height of the chimney. A chimney must be 2 feet (60 cm) higher than a roof or any other structure within 10 feet (3 m). If your chimney is not high enough, consult a mason to extend a masonry chimney or an appropriate professional to extend a metal chimney.

What You'll Need

- Materials and tools related to the chosen solution
- Yellow pages, to locate a professional

Tips

Test for depressurization by opening a window in the fireplace room, waiting about an hour, and starting a fire. If smoke still spills into the room, depressurization isn't the issue.

Deal with licensed, experienced professionals only and obtain references.

Make sure you have the necessary permits and inspections.

4 Reline to enlarge a flue. If the flue in an old chimney is too small, there may be enough room between the flue and the brick to knock out the existing flue and install a new one. A metal liner for a single-flue chimney costs roughly $2,000, and a solid flue, which is poured around a form lowered into the chimney, costs $500 to $1,000 more. Both are professional installations.

5 Install an intake air vent in the firebox. Remove firebrick and exterior brick or stone facing, then drill a hole for a stainless steel vent that extends from outdoors right into the fireplace. Alternatively, you can install some models into the ash pit below the firebox and admit air through a special floor vent.

6 A much easier alternative for do-it-yourselfers is to install an air-intake vent through the wall of the room. Although the vent itself is available only through fireplace shops, the installation is identical to that of a dryer vent, a common DIY project.

7 Lower the lintel with a metal shield, such as SmokeGuard. This shield, available in several widths, heights and finishes from fireplace shops, snaps into place. Some glass doors for fireplaces may also effectively lower the lintel.

8 If the convenience, energy efficiency and appearance of a gas fireplace appeals to you, installing a sealed-combustion gas-fireplace insert will resolve any draft problem.

152 Start a Fire in a Cold Chimney

Avoid smoking up your home when you first light a fire in a cold fireplace. The trick is to create a torch with rolled-up newspaper and use it to warm up the smoke chamber before starting your fire.

Steps

1 Open the damper fully. Start preparing the fire as you normally would with adequate paper, kindling and seasoned firewood.

2 Slightly open a window in the room where the fireplace is located.

3 Roll a few sheets of newspaper to form a torch. It should be tightly twisted on the end you hold and loose on the end you will light.

4 Light the torch and hold it up to the damper to heat the smoke chamber.

5 When the chimney seems to draw well, light the fire.

Warning

Depressurization can increase radon infiltration and cause carbon monoxide poisoning from combustion appliances such as water heaters, furnaces and boilers.

Due to the sometimes high costs and considerable risks involved with modifying a fireplace or chimney, never act without consulting a professional and your local building department.

What You'll Need

- Fire-starting materials
- Newspaper
- Gloves

Warning

Wear gloves to protect your hand from falling burning embers, and don't look up into the chimney while warming it.

153 Fix a Wood-Burning Stove

Promptly fixing any problems with your wood-burning stove is essential for your personal safety. It also maximizes energy efficiency and minimizes air pollution.

Steps

Replace a corroded stove connector

1 Measure the existing components and purchase the necessary stovepipe, connectors and installation materials and tools.

2 Remove screws (or nuts and bolts) at the appliance collar, stovepipe joints and flue connection. If stainless-steel rivets were used, drill them out using a bit slightly larger than the hole in the rivet. (You may need to grasp the rivet with pliers or push against it with a screwdriver to keep it from spinning as you drill.)

3 When you've removed all fasteners, disassemble the connector.

4 If any cutting is required, open the pipe seam (if it's not already open) by pressing in on it. Use straight-cutting metal snips to make the cut. Snap the pipe back together, pressing in to engage the seam and releasing to lock it.

5 If any crimping is necessary, place a crimping tool over the end of the pipe and squeeze tightly. Move the tool over a jaw's width and crimp again. Repeat this procedure around the pipe (see A).

6 Assemble the connector and then secure all joints with self-tapping ¼-inch (6-mm) sheet-metal screws. Use three equally spaced screws at each pipe connection, and secure the pipe to the appliance collar and flue in the same manner as the old pipe. Drill pilot holes for the screws and twist them in with a screwdriver or drill and driver.

Inspect, clean or replace a catalytic combustor

1 Remove the combustor (see B). Access varies, but it's always easy. You may access it from inside or by removing a plate on the outside, and you may need a screwdriver or other hand tool.

2 Use a soft paintbrush or a vacuum to remove fly ash or soot. Boil a 50-50 solution of white vinegar and distilled water in a pot large enough to submerge the combustor (or pour boiling water into such a container). Reduce the heat and gently lower in the combustor to soak for 30 minutes. Loop wire or string through the combustor to form a handle. Rinse it twice for 15 minutes in clean, boiled distilled water. Wait 24 hours or dry it completely in a 300°F (150°C) oven for an hour.

What You'll Need

- Tape measure
- Stovepipe, connectors, and installation materials and tools
- Screwdriver, pliers and wrenches
- Electric drill and driver, drill bits
- Straight-cutting metal snips
- Crimping tool
- Self-tapping ¼-inch (6-mm) sheet-metal screws
- Paintbrush or vacuum
- White vinegar and distilled water
- Large metal pot
- Wire or string
- Replacement catalytic combustor
- Wire brush
- High-temperature cement cartridge
- Caulking gun
- Glass-fiber door gasket

Tips

You must use double-wall stainless Type L vent pipe when you can't meet the necessary clearances from combustibles for single-wall stovepipe.

To prevent liquid creosote from leaking out of a connector, plan the pipe assembly so the crimped end will face downward on vertical sections.

3 Burn off any creosote. Reinstall the combustor and burn a fire at higher than normal temperatures for 30 minutes, but no higher than 1,700°F (927°C).

4 Combustors typically last 12,000 hours (five to six years). If yours is due for replacement (indicated by severe peeling of the catalyst coating, random thermal cracking or missing pieces), replace it.

Replace a door gasket

1 Pry and scrape out the old gasket with an old screwdriver and clean the door's surface with a wire brush.

2 Apply a bead of high-temperature cement using a caulking gun. Embed the replacement glass-fiber door-gasket rope. Close and secure the door to allow the required curing time as directed on the label.

Prevent chimney fires

1 Have connectors and chimney flues cleaned when creosote buildup reaches ¼ inch (6 mm), or ⅛ inch (3 mm) for creosote in a tarlike form. Many factors affect the rate of buildup. Frequent inspection and past experience is the only way to determine if cleaning needs to be done monthly, yearly or on some other schedule.

2 If your flue needs cleaning, call a certified chimney sweep. Chimney cleaning is a complex process that involves far more than brushing out the flue and vacuuming up the mess. Preliminary and final inspections spot problems and potentially dangerous situations, and the task requires numerous inside preparations.

Warning

Consult your local building department before making changes to a wood stove's installation; for example, repositioning it or changing to another type of connector.

Burning creosote off a combustor can cause a fire if the chimney is dirty. Always inspect and clean the chimney before this procedure.

Reinstalling and using a still-wet combustor can ruin it.

Never burn trash in a wood-burning stove. The corrosive by-products drastically speed the failure of stovepipe connectors, internal parts of the stove and catalytic combustors.

Never remove the protective sleeve on a catalytic combustor. The ceramic combustor is very fragile once it has been used.

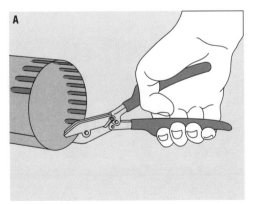

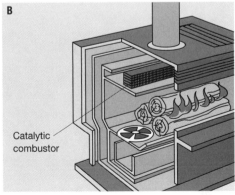

Catalytic combustor

154 Repair and Prevent Wood Rot

Rot occurs whenever water gets into cracks or penetrates a wood finish and can't dry out. Seal these cracks and maintain the finish to protect wood's beauty and integrity. Consult a pro for structural rot repairs, but you can tackle small ones yourself.

Steps

Repair decayed wood

1 Use a wood chisel, an electric drill with a spade bit, or another tool appropriate for the situation to remove all wet, loose and unsound wood.

2 Probe the surrounding area with an awl. If it feels as solid as unaffected areas, drill numerous closely spaced holes of ⅛-inch (3-mm) diameter in the wood and inject a liquid wood hardener as directed by the manufacturer.

3 Mix two-part epoxy or polyester wood filler as directed. Mix only what you can apply and shape in a few minutes. Once the material hardens—and it does so quickly—you must throw it away.

4 Fill the hole or build up the affected area with the wood filler, using a putty knife or flexible plastic spreader (see A). Press hard to work the initial layer into the surface for a good bond.

5 Clean off the applicator and mixing container immediately.

6 Use a rasp tool to roughly shape or level excess filler as soon as the filler sets up, but before it dries completely (see B).

7 Use medium or coarse sandpaper to further shape and blend the patch when the filler is completely dry. On flat surfaces, use a rubber sanding block or power sander. On contoured surfaces, use wood dowels or other appropriate shapes to back the sandpaper.

What You'll Need

- Wood chisel or electric drill with spade bit
- Awl
- Drill and bits
- Liquid wood hardener
- Epoxy or polyester wood filler
- Mixing container
- Putty knife or plastic spreader
- Rasp tool
- Sandpaper
- Rubber sanding block or power sander
- Wood dowels
- Primer
- Paint and paintbrush

Tips

Epoxy dries very fast and is very hard to remove—good points, except when it comes to you and your tools. Clean up as you go along.

Build up deep holes in layers about ½ inch (12 mm) thick. Slightly overfill a flat surface.

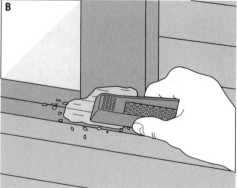

8 Blow off the dust and apply freshly mixed filler to fill any remaining depressions or pinholes, or to build up more material as needed to attain the desired shape.

9 Use medium, then fine sandpaper to smooth the patch and feather it into the surrounding wood.

10 Touch up the patched area with primer and paint.

Take preventive steps

1 Use naturally decay-resistant or treated lumber for decks and other outdoor structures. Never allow untreated lumber posts or lumber to rest directly on concrete.

2 Clean joints between deck boards or between a deck and a house so debris and dirt won't retain moisture.

3 Inspect for peeling paint or other paint failures, especially near joints, such as mitered trim corners at roof eaves or where window and door casings contact sills.

4 Probe these areas with an awl to search for soft or wet, spongy wood (wood that resists being probed is sound).

5 Seal cracks with caulk. If possible, use screws to close any open miter joints. Bore pilot holes for the screws to avoid splitting the wood, and then inject adhesive caulk into the joint before driving in the screws.

6 Sand any bare wood and apply wood preservative before you apply a primer. Caulk joints after priming and before the top coating. Preservative greatly increases the likelihood of a better, longer-lasting paint bond.

7 Create ventilation through trimmed posts or columns by providing space for air to circulate between the trim and the floor surface and an outlet vent at the top. In some cases, this requires cutting ½ inch (12 mm) off the bottom of the trim. Lay a board that's ½-inch (12-mm) thick on the floor against the post and rest a handsaw on the board as you make the cut. Use small metal louvers pressed into drilled holes to vent the tops of posts or columns.

8 Avoid positioning outdoor sheds, such as one for trash cans, against wood siding. Elevate sheds above the ground on concrete blocks or short sections of 6-by-6-inch (15-by-15-cm) pressure-treated posts.

9 Make sure crawl-space vents remain open, especially during the summer, or add vents where there are none.

Shape the filler with whatever tools seem appropriate on contoured surfaces or corners.

Rasps come in a wide variety of shapes for flat and contoured surfaces.

Rasping is not required, but sanding off a lot of hard, dried material takes more time and effort.

Drive nails into large damaged areas and let the heads stick up a little so they will be embedded in the filler but lie below the finished surface.

You can cut, shape, smooth and drill into cured epoxy just as you can wood.

Warning

Read warning labels and wear goggles, gloves, a dust mask and any other recommended protective equipment while working.

155 Fix Crumbling Chimney Mortar

Avoid extensive, costly damage to a masonry chimney. Maintain the mortar joints by tuck-pointing (repointing) them, and make sure the chimney crown remains sealed against water.

Steps

Tuck-pointing masonry joints

1 Work from the bottom up to remove loose mortar a few feet (a meter or so) at a time. Set up ladders or scaffolding if necessary. Use a mason's hammer and chisel, a scraper and similar hand tools for difficult-to-reach areas. For extensive tuck-pointing, rent an electric grinder with a tuck-pointing attachment and blades.

2 Mix water into a packaged mortar mix as directed on the label, using a cement-mixing container and hoe.

3 Apply the mortar by first loading the bottom side of a square mason's trowel (or a board) with mortar (see A). Then, holding the trowel against the chimney just below the joint you're filling, slice off a portion of the mortar with a pointing trowel and pack it into the joint.

4 When the joints in an area are all full, strike off the excess by slicing through the mortar with a brick trowel held flat against the bricks.

5 Compress, shape and smooth the joint. Run a jointing tool across the joints for concave and V joints (see B). Or use the tip of a pointing trowel to create a 30-degree bevel from the underside of the upper course to the edge of the lower course. Knock off any excess and move up to the next section.

6 When the joints have set up, clean the face of the brick with a soft brush.

What You'll Need

- Ladders or scaffolding
- Mason's hammer and chisel
- Scraper
- Grinder with tuck-pointing attachment and blades
- Mortar mix
- Cement-mixing container and hoe
- Square mason's trowel or board
- Pointing trowel
- Brick trowel
- Jointing tool
- Soft brush
- Crown repair and sealing material
- High-temperature caulk and caulking gun

Tip

For very minor tuck-pointing repairs, use mortar-patching material in caulking-gun cartridges.

Repairing a chimney crown

1 If a traditional crown made of portland cement and sand is badly eroded or cracked, replace it with a modern (crown-sealer) system. These coatings, which you can apply with a trowel (following the manufacturer's instructions), remain flexible and provide a far superior water seal. If the crown has some cracks and is beginning to show wear, or even if a masonry crown is in good condition, consider using this material as part of an overall chimney repair.

2 Seal joints between the clay flue's liner and the crown with high-temperature caulk.

156 Patch a Gutter Leak

When it rains, it pours—right down the side of your house, if you have a leaky gutter. These leaks generally occur at connections between gutter sections or gutters and downspouts. Very old metal gutters (especially steel ones) may corrode all the way through. For all repairs, start with a well-cleaned gutter.

Steps

1 To patch a hole, scrub the inside of the gutter around the hole with steel wool or an abrasive pad, using a ladder if necessary.

2 Cut a patch from metal flashing using metal snips. Make the patch a little larger than the corroded area.

3 Using a putty knife, coat the back of the metal patch with asphalt flashing cement (or gutter patch), and press it into place.

4 Smooth any adhesive that oozes out at the edges with a gloved finger.

5 To seal leaks at joints, you can try to clean and caulk, but usually the better approach is to disassemble the gutter as needed to remove the leaking connector. Then clean mating surfaces and caulk as you reassemble. Cut the tip off your caulking cartridge with a utility knife and insert the cartridge into a caulking gun to apply.

What You'll Need

- Gloves
- Steel wool or abrasive pad
- Ladder
- Metal flashing
- Metal snips
- Putty knife
- Asphalt flashing cement and cartridge, or gutter patch
- Utility knife
- Caulking cartridge and gun

Warning

Flashing cement is difficult to clean off your hands without solvents, so wear disposable gloves.

157 Troubleshoot a Wet Basement

Take care of water seeping into the basement before it damages stored items or fills the family room with mildew. Controlling the water's source is always preferable to attempting to block its entry. You can fix the vast majority of wet basements by controlling roof water and surface drainage.

Steps

Evaluate the water's source

1 Observe when water enters: If it occurs within an hour or so of heavy rain, the cure lies in controlling surface and roof water.

2 If seepage happens only after days of heavy rain, the problem may be a swelled aquifer. If leaks persist for several days after the rain stops, the source is likely related to the presence of a high water table (the top of an aquifer), an uphill spring or a perched water table (a small underground pond). A rising water table usually penetrates everywhere at once. Springs and perched water tables may enter along one wall.

3 If water is unrelated to either the weather or seasonal changes in the water table, it might stem from a broken water service. Test this by shutting off the house main and observing the meter at the street, or contact the local water utility for assistance.

Correct an improper grade

1 Scrape away loamy topsoil, then add soil or rearrange dirt as needed, using digging tools, an iron rake and a wheelbarrow. The grade should slope away from the foundation at least 1 inch per foot (2.5 cm per 30 cm) for a distance of about 3 feet (1 m) minimum but preferably 10 feet (3 m), and leave at least 8 inches (20 cm) of foundation exposed under the siding, more in snowy climates.

2 If this involves a great deal of work and transplanting, consider having a professional excavator and landscaper do the work.

3 Plant grass next to the foundation and locate planting beds 5 to 6 feet (1.5 to 2 m) away from the building; or plant ground cover with a thick root system (which draws water out of the soil) rather than putting mulch (which holds water in) around the foundation.

Clear a clogged foundation or footing drains

1 If clean-outs (access pipes that allow auguring, flushing and other cleaning tasks) are provided, attempt to flush the system yourself by inserting a garden hose.

2 Otherwise consult a drain-cleaning professional.

What You'll Need

- Fill and topsoil
- Digging tools, iron rake and wheelbarrow
- Grass or ground cover
- Garden hose and nozzle
- Pressure washer, scraper, steel brush, compressed air or other wall-cleaning tools
- Brick or pointing trowel
- Hydraulic cement
- Foundation coating, backfill and applicator or brush

Tips

You can resolve some groundwater problems with grading and drainage work, or control them with a sump (pit) pump. Evaluating the problem and designing a solution requires consultation with professionals.

Plugging holes and filling cracks from the inside is rarely successful, especially if there's hydrostatic pressure on the wall.

Interior dewatering that requires drilling holes in foundation walls and interior wall sealants at best get rid of dampness, not water.

Seal foundation cracks and holes

1 Excavate the area to access the crack or hole from the outside.

2 Use a pressure washer, scraper, steel brush, compressed air and/or other approaches and tools to clean the wall area in and around the leak thoroughly.

3 Use a brick or pointing trowel to pack large voids with hydraulic cement, which you can apply to a wet surface. When it dries after a few days, brush on foundation coating and backfill.

A 1,000-square-foot (93-square-m) roof will collect about 250 gallons (950 l) of water in a 2-inch (5-cm) rainfall. With four downspouts, that's about 63 gallons (240 l) to deal with at each location.

PROBLEM	POSSIBLE CAUSES	SOLUTIONS
Excessive roof water	Faulty or missing gutters; downspouts empty next to foundation	Install roof gutters where there are none. Repair leaky or disconnected gutter (see 156 Patch a Gutter Leak). Level sagging gutters (see 162 Fix a Sagging Gutter). Clean clogged gutters and downspouts (see 163 Unclog Gutters and Downspouts). Add downspouts if clean gutters overflow. Direct downspout water away from house (see 161 Redirect Rainwater From a Downspout).
Plumbing issues	Broken water main, floor-drain or sewer connection; clogged floor drain; sump discharge pipe drains too close to house	Evaluate and excavate to make repairs. Have plumber evaluate any floor-drain or -sewer connections; install ball-type backwater valve in floor drain (allows drainage but blocks backflow). Have drain service clear drain clogs. Extend drainpipe for sump-pump discharge.
Foundation issues	Faulty parging; missing cove at footing-and-wall junction; damaged or missing damp-proofing; cracked masonry block or concrete; clogged, missing or improperly drained foundation-footing drain	Excavation and exterior repairs are costly and advisable only after roof and surface-water controls have failed, or for localized leaks, such as at utility entrance. Have professional inject epoxy to repair holes and cracks after cementing larger voids. Depending on design and access points, some foundation drains can be professionally cleaned. Have interior footing drains, sump pump installed.

(continued on next page)

PROBLEM	POSSIBLE CAUSES	SOLUTIONS
Groundwater issues	High water table, spring	Install sump pump with baseboard-style dewatering system.
Poor drainage	Grade level or slopes toward house; too porous soil adjacent to foundation; animal holes near or under foundations; settling next to foundation and under porches due to poor fill or backfill practices; window well settled below grade; leaves on window well floor; patio or driveway slopes toward house; patio or driveway connection at foundation not flashed or caulked	Fill voids, animal holes near foundations, under porches. Regrade so ground slopes down 1 inch per foot (2.5 cm per 30 cm) for distance of 10 feet (3 m) from house. Avoid planting immediately adjacent to foundation or before ground has had time to settle after new construction. Cap soil within 3 feet (1 m) of foundation. Provide drainage for window wells and exterior stairwells to downhill, above-ground location. Extend window well and add tamped soil near foundation. Install sump pump, direct drain water to sump. Enlarge drywell to handle more water from drains. Clear clogs from window well and exterior stairwell drains. Install plastic rain cover on window well. Intersect hillsides uphill from house with swales to redirect water. Recap patio or drive to correct improper slope. Seal patio or foundation joint with polyurethane caulk (see 148 Replace Caulking on the Outside of Your House).

158 Seal a Garage Floor

Sealing a concrete garage floor protects it from road salt, eliminates concrete dust, makes it easier to sweep and prevents stains. It's also a great primer if you want to paint the floor.

Steps

1 Use a hose to scrub the floor with commercial concrete cleaner and degreaser according to the manufacturer's instructions.

2 In stained areas, let the cleaner soak in for up to 30 minutes, and repeat the application as needed for stubborn stains.

3 When the floor is dry, put the sealer in a large paint tray. Use a brush to cut in the perimeter and then roll the rest with a medium-nap paint roller, equipped with a long handle. Work your way out of the garage. Apply generously but roll out all puddles. Sealer will stain surfaces, so apply it carefully and mask other areas when spraying.

4 Clean up tools with warm soapy water immediately and allow the sealer to dry as directed by the manufacturer. Do not apply a second coat.

What You'll Need

- Garden hose and nozzle
- Concrete cleaner and degreaser
- Stiff brush and bucket
- Concrete sealer
- Large paint tray
- Paintbrush
- Paint roller with long handle and medium-nap roller cover
- Painter's masking tape

Warning

Read product cautions and directions, ventilate the room, and wear protection such as goggles and a respirator mask.

159 Refinish a Garage or Basement Floor

Painting has all the benefits of sealing and then some. This technique is especially nice if you use your garage as a screened summer room.

Steps

1 Prepare and seal the floor as directed in 158 Seal a Garage Floor, above.

2 Mix a two-part epoxy paint that is designed for use on concrete floors according to the manufacturer's instructions. Mix only what you plan to use, and allow the mixed paint to rest for the specified time before application.

3 Mask any baseboard trim, floor drains and posts that you don't want to paint.

4 Use a paintbrush or trim pad to cut in paint along the edges.

5 Use a roller with a long handle attachment to apply the rest of the paint.

6 Some paint kits come with paint chips, which add a decorative element and provide a nonslip terrazzo-like finish. Sprinkle such chips on the wet finish before moving on to the next area.

What You'll Need

- Epoxy concrete floor paint
- Mixing container
- Painter's masking tape
- Paintbrush or trim pad
- Paint roller with long handle attachment
- Paint tray and medium-nap roller cover

Tip

Don't walk on the floor for at least 12 hours, and don't park cars or lawn tractors on it for a week.

160 Control Roof Leaks

Treat a leaking roof as an emergency, because it can wreak havoc in your house in a very short time. Attend to any signs of a roof leak, such as water entry, stains or mold, immediately to limit damage. Locate the leak from inside and then take steps to control the damage until you can have a suitable outside inspection and repair done.

Steps

Locate the leak from inside

1 The first and perhaps most obvious place to look for a roof leak is directly above the leak in a ceiling or exterior wall. Use a flashlight to inspect the attic floor over the leak while it's raining. Look for standing water, water stains, mold, wet insulation or other exposed insulation.

2 Examine the underside of the roof for wetness or mold around points of penetration (plumbing vents, chimneys), wherever different roof planes intersect (valleys) and near dormers. These symptoms indicate holes in the flashing or faulty flashing installation.

3 A leak away from such locations suggests a problem in the roofing material. Keep in mind that water may travel sideways before passing through a joint in the roof sheathing, and may travel in a horizontal joint before falling on the floor or ceiling.

4 Take measurements from points inside that you can also locate from outside. Measure down from a ridge and horizontally from the center of a valley or sidewall; or measure distances from a chimney or other point of penetration.

5 If your ceiling is attached to roof rafters, as would be the case for a cathedral ceiling, all you can do from inside is take the measurements that will help you locate the leak externally, and attempt to control the damage internally.

Control the damage

1 Water can travel on the underside of sheathing or down roof rafters before dropping off in one or more places. To control where it falls, tack a piece of string into the stream of water and let it hang into a bucket. The water will tend to follow the string.

2 Poke or drill a hole in your ceiling to let the water through. This technique prevents the water from spreading across the top of the ceiling to other areas; it prevents the ceiling from becoming saturated, eliminating the chance of collapse and often the need for replacement; and it allows you to collect water from below using the string-and-bucket method.

What You'll Need

- Powerful flashlight
- Long tape measure
- Bucket and string
- Screwdriver or drill and drill bit
- Extension ladder
- Binoculars
- Roof ladder
- Flashing cement and putty knife

Tips

Don't walk on a very hot or an old and dried-out roof, as this may damage it.

You can rent a roof ladder—a single ladder that hooks over the ridge and lies on the roof—or buy attachments to install on your own ladder.

For related repairs, see 164 Repair a Leaking Skylight, 167 Patch a Flat or Low-Pitched Roof, 168 Repair Roof Flashing and 150 Prevent Ice Dams.

Locate the leak from outside

1 Using any measurements or other information you gathered indoors, make your initial outdoor observations from a ladder and/or using binoculars. Do not walk on a pitched roof during rain or as long as the roof is wet. A wood roof is particularly treacherous.

2 Look for leaves and other debris slowing the natural downward flow of water, as often happens in valleys and adjacent to or above any roof penetration or dormer. If there is snow on the roof, an ice dam may have formed at the roof's lower edge, causing water to back up under overlapping layers of roofing materials. Remove the obstruction if you can get to it safely.

3 If or when you can safely get close enough, examine metal flashings for corrosion or open joints where they connect to a chimney or other roof penetration. You can temporarily patch metal flashings, but replacement is the only permanent solution. Typically, you can replace cracked or dried-out rubber gaskets on plumbing vents.

4 Pay particular attention to any areas already covered with black flashing cement; these indicate locations of previously repaired leaks. Look for pinholes or cracks, which often occur as the material ages. Make temporary repairs by applying flashing cement with a putty knife.

5 If or when you can safely get close enough, inspect attachment points for any antenna, satellite dish or other object screwed or nailed into the roof. A dab of roof flashing in good condition should cover each fastener. The best solution is to avoid mounting anything on your roof in the first place.

6 If you determined from inside that your leak is midroof and therefore not related to flashing, look for damaged or missing asphalt shingles. On wood roofs, look for cracked or badly cupped or warped shingles or shakes. Look for joints in one course that fall less than 1½ inches (4 cm) to the left or right of a joint in the course below. Flat or nearly flat roofs generally require very close inspection to locate damaged or badly worn areas.

Warning

For safety, lay down catwalks in an unfloored attic, making sure the ends of boards fall over framing members. Distributing your weight more evenly can also prevent nail pops in drywall ceilings.

To avoid roof damage or risk of injury or even death resulting from a fall, never walk on a wet roof, and stay off any roof unless absolutely necessary.

161 Redirect Rainwater From a Downspout

Your house would probably be better off without gutters if they simply dump water in concentrated areas right next to its foundation. That's what happens when downspouts terminate with only an elbow or a splash block at the bottom. You'll find some effective solutions below.

Steps

Add a surface extension

1 If foundation plantings or ground cover camouflage the downspouts, add a length of horizontal downspout, PVC or flexible drainpipe to the bottom of the existing downspout to extend it at least 5 to 6 feet (1.5 to 2 m) away from the house.

2 If necessary, drive downspout-extension stakes into the ground to support and hold metal extensions in place, and place a rock or concrete splash block at the end to reduce soil erosion (see A).

Install a manual hinged extension

1 You can make a hinged extension, which tilts up and out of the way when not in use (see B). Remove the elbow (if any) at the bottom of the downspout.

2 Cut the end off a length of downspout at a 45-degree angle using a hacksaw with a fine-tooth blade.

3 Join the cut end to the bottom of the downspout with a hinge. Drill pilot holes for ¼-inch (6-mm) aluminum sheet-metal screws or rivets.

4 Alternatively, you can purchase a kit that has the hinge already riveted to two short lengths of downspout, which just slip into or over your downspout and extension. Or purchase a preassembled extension with a hinge and a short section that slips over your downspout. In both cases, secure the connections with ¼-inch (6-mm) aluminum sheet-metal screws or rivets installed in drilled pilot holes.

What You'll Need

- Desired extension product(s) or components
- Hacksaw with fine-tooth blade
- Hinge
- Drill and drill bit
- Aluminum sheet-metal screws and screwdriver or rivet tool and short aluminum rivets
- Digging shovel with long handle

Tips

Downspout filters, which attach near the end of a downspout before it enters an extension, have an opening in front of an angled grate that catches leaves but allows water to run through.

When sawing through a downspout, use a miter box or sandwich the downspout between two boards and use their ends to guide your saw.

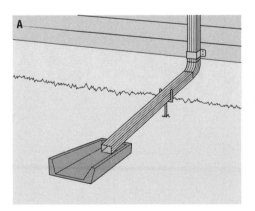

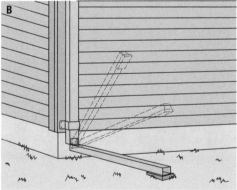

Install an automatic extension

1 Installation procedures vary with the system, but typically you must shorten the downspout. You can do so with the downspout in place, or remove and reinstall it. Slip the downspout into the end of the extension device.

2 Mount the device to the wall with screws as directed by the manufacturer. For stone, brick and other masonry walls, drill a hole for masonry anchors that will accept the mounting screws. The weight of the water collecting in the extension eventually lowers it to the ground, and it springs back up slowly as the rain stops.

Install an underground extension

1 Use a digging shovel with a long handle to dig a trench for an underground pipe, the Cadillac of downspout extensions.

2 Put an elbow and a drain adapter on the house end of a 4-inch (10-cm) PVC or flexible drainpipe. Connect it to the downspout, extending one or the other as needed.

3 Insert the other end into a catch basin or surface bubbler. The bubbler's grate (green, brown or black) lies flush with the surface and allows water to spill harmlessly on the ground.

4 Alternatively, direct the pipe into a gravel drywell (see C). Dig a hole at least 4 feet (1 m) deep, line it with landscape fabric and fill it with gravel to within 1 or 2 feet (30 to 60 cm) of the surface, embedding the pipe near the top. Cover with more fabric and then topsoil.

A drywell can be as deep or wide as needed. The size primarily depends on soil porosity. You may need more or less topsoil over it, depending on landscaping requirements.

Warning

The cut edges of metal downspouts are very sharp. Be careful when making any cuts with saws or snips, and file to remove burrs and dull the edges.

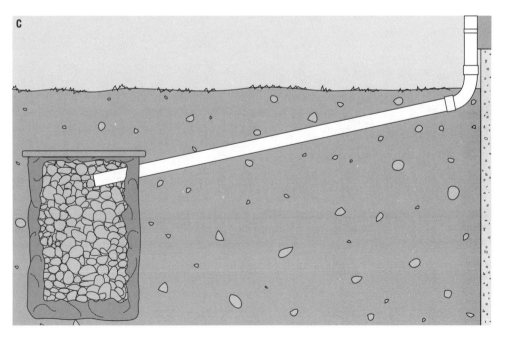

C

162 Fix a Sagging Gutter

If a gutter sags too much, it looks unsightly, and if the sag is in the wrong direction, water collects, giving mosquitoes a breeding ground and creating leaks. It's standard to pitch gutters 1/16 inch per foot (2 mm per 30 cm) toward the nearest downspout, but even a level gutter will drain. Assuming that the spikes, brackets or hangers are installed correctly, most commonly a gutter sags due to ice and snow damage or because a ladder has bent or dislodged its supports.

Steps

If the gutter is supported by spikes (see A)

1 Straighten a bent spike by pushing up on the gutter at that location with a pry bar (you'll likely need a ladder to reach it); or remove a nailed gutter spike for replacement by locking the head of the spike firmly in a pair of locking pliers, then tapping the side of the jaws with a hammer to pull the spike out.

2 Replace a spike that has fallen out or been removed with a threaded gutter spike. For a tighter fit, press a few wood slivers coated with exterior adhesive or epoxy into the nail hole first.

If the gutter is supported by hangers or brackets (see B)

1 Remove the gutter by unclipping the brackets and disconnecting it from the downspout(s). This is definitely a job for two or more people.

2 Replace the damaged bracket. Fill the old screw holes with caulk or exterior putty and let dry. Install the new bracket at approximately the same height and position as the old one. Repeat as needed for other brackets and tighten any loose screws before reinstalling the gutter.

What You'll Need

- Ladder(s)
- Pry bar
- Threaded gutter spikes
- Locking pliers
- Hammer
- Wood slivers
- Exterior adhesive or epoxy
- Caulk or exterior putty
- Screwdriver or drill and driver
- Replacement brackets
- Nail puller
- Roofing nails or exterior screws

Tips

Assuming that your building is reasonably level, measure up from the bottom of a fascia board to level or pitch a gutter.

Leaning a ladder against an aluminum gutter may ruin it. Use a standoff ladder attachment.

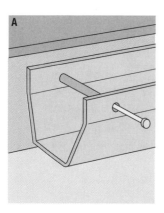
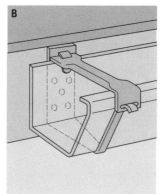
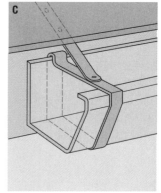

If the gutter is supported by hangers or straps (see C)

1 If the strap is bent down, press down on it about 1 inch (2.5 cm) up the roof from the edge of the shingle it lies under, or from the surface to which it's nailed. Then pull up just below the point of the bend.

2 If the bracket has pulled out of the roof or needs replacing, and the roofing is asphalt shingles, disconnect the bracket from the gutter and carefully pry up the shingle to remove the nails (or screws), or drive new fasteners through the strap into the roof.

If the gutter is supported by concealed brackets

1 Remove the mounting screw to replace a damaged bracket.

163 Unclog Gutters and Downspouts

Clogged gutters often allow enormous quantities of water to fall right next to your house's foundation. This can cause structural damage and lead to wet or damp basements, dirty or stained siding, leaks and rot at the roof's edge, and iced-over walkways in winter—all of which you'll want to avoid.

Steps

1 If a downspout feeds into an underground pipe, disconnect it before cleaning so debris won't clog that pipe or the drywell into which it typically empties. Use a ladder with a standoff bracket to access the downspout. (Leaning a ladder against an aluminum gutter may ruin it.)

2 Clean the gutters and remove any clogs at the downspout that you can reach from the ladder. When you're cleaning by hand, wear heavy-duty rubber gloves and hang a large bucket for debris on your ladder using a painter's hook or an S-hook.

3 If the downspout is clogged, try gently inserting the end of a hose into the downspout from the bottom and turning it on fully; if it's clear, do the same from the top. Don't try to force the hose past bends. It may damage the downspout or get stuck.

4 If that fails, disassemble the downspout at the bends by removing the retaining screws. Then clear the clogs, which are usually located at bends. Reassemble and rinse gutters.

Warning

The distance from the foot of the ladder to the house wall should be about one-quarter the distance from the ground to where the ladder leans against the house.

What You'll Need

- Ladder with standoff bracket
- Heavy-duty rubber gloves
- Large bucket
- Painter's hook or S-hook
- Garden hose with nozzle
- Screwdriver

Warning

Keep one hand on the ladder and don't overreach. Keep the trunk of your body within the ladder rails.

164 Repair a Leaking Skylight

Skylights are supposed to bring light into your life, not rain on your parade—but sometimes they do spring a leak. In the event that your skylight starts leaking, here's how to analyze the problem and make a few of the simpler repairs yourself.

Steps

Analyze the leak

1 Verify that the supposed leak is not actually excessive condensation that has moved along the underside of the glass toward the edge and then dripped down the side of the interior opening. This is most likely in very cold climates, in single-glazed skylights, and in damp locations such as bathrooms, kitchens and greenhouse rooms. You will probably need a ladder.

2 Verify that the skylight is fully closed and that any weather seals are in good condition (pliable, not deformed or torn). Problems typically occur when skylights are located in very high ceilings and it's hard to see if they are fully closed.

3 Ask yourself: Does the leak occur only in winter, in fall, or when there is snow or ice on the roof? If the answer to any of these questions is yes, look behind the skylight for leaves, ice, snow or other debris that might be blocking the downhill flow of water and causing it to back up under the shingles.

4 Look carefully at the roofing or flashing on vents and other penetrations further up the roof. A leak there can travel quite a distance before finding its way to an indoor opening at the skylight.

If a manufactured skylight leaks

1 Most skylights have integral flashing or a special flashing kit that is specifically designed for the skylight and roofing material. Obtain the installation instructions for the skylight's make and model.

2 Refer to the installation literature to verify that the unit is installed according to instructions. Inspect with a flashlight and mirror, and pry up a few shingles (but don't damage them).

3 If it is not installed correctly, and you know the company or builder that did the job, contact that company to fix it. Otherwise correct the installation yourself or hire a professional recommended by the manufacturer's local dealer.

4 If the visible portion of the installation appears to match the instructions, inspect the flashing for defects or damage.

What You'll Need

- Ladder
- Mirror
- Flashlight

Tips

Whether you do the reinstallation or hire a pro, incorporate a layer of nailable membrane in the new installation, especially on shallow pitched roofs and in snowy climates.

Used hemmed edges (folded back, not raw edges) on all flashing.

If a custom skylight leaks

1 Inspect a custom skylight (typically nonopening) for proper flashing details, including the following:

- Soldered top flashing wraps around the corners and extends at least 6 inches (15 cm) under the roofing at the top and 4 inches (10 cm) at the sides.

- Soldered (or folded) base flashing wraps around the lower corners and extends at least 4 inches (10 cm) under the shingles at the sides and 4 inches (10 cm) over the shingles below.

- Step flashing interwoven with shingles on the sides extends at least 3 inches (7.5 cm) up the curb sides and 4 inches (10 cm) onto the roof, and overlaps the next piece by at least 2 inches (5 cm).

- Counter flashing that's sealed or bonded to the skylight and soldered at the corners extends down all sides to within 1 inch (2.5 cm) of the roof.

- Roofing should extend to the flashing on the sides and top. Gaps tend to collect debris that traps and slows water flow.

Inspect for damage

1 Examine exposed flashing carefully for corrosion, pinholes and other damage. Carefully bend up the roof to see as far under it as possible with the help of a mirror and flashlight.

2 Examine previous "temporary" repairs made with caulk, flashing cement or other sealants. Look for cracks and holes, dry or brittle sealants and peeling. Either remove old sealant and apply a new layer, or make a more reliable repair.

Make needed repairs

1 Patch damaged flashing as described in 156 Patch a Gutter Leak.

2 If you are an experienced do-it-yourselfer with roofing skills and feel comfortable working on roofs, remove the roof and flashing as necessary to correct a faulty installation or replace damaged flashing. Otherwise hire a competent professional.

Warning

To avoid damaging a roof or risking injury or even death from a fall, never walk on a wet roof.

To avoid injury or roof damage, observe proper ladder and roof safety, and use a roof ladder (a rental item) where possible.

165 Repair a Cracked or Split Wood Shingle

Properly installed shingles provide three layers of protection, but when a shingle cracks and the crack falls right over a joint, a leak may occur. A prompt repair can save you money and lots of trouble.

Steps

Setting up ladders and equipment

1 Position an extension ladder so the bottom is out from the house about one-quarter the distance from the ground to the roof edge, and so the top extends several feet (about a meter) above the roof edge.

2 Hook a roof ladder over the ridge and secure a rope from the top of the ladder to a solid anchor point on the opposite side of the house, such as a tree or a deck railing.

Removing and replacing the shingle

1 Split the cracked shingle into numerous pieces with a hammer and chisel. Then wiggle the split pieces back and forth as you pull them down and out. Saw off the nails that secured it with a hacksaw blade (see A).

2 Measure the gap for the replacement shingle and cut one about ⅜ inch (1 cm) narrower to allow for expansion when the shingle gets wet.

3 Tap the shingle into place until it hits the nails (a dent appears at each nail). Measure how much farther the shingle would have to go to align with the others. Then pull out the shingle and, at each dent, cut slots as long as your measurement with a utility knife or saw.

4 Tap the shingle to within ½ inch (12 mm) of its final position. Drive two shingle nails at a 45-degree angle into the shingle, just below the course above it (see B). Use a nail set to complete the nailing. Drive the new shingle up the remaining ½ inch (12 mm) with a hammer and a block of wood.

What You'll Need

- Extension and roof ladders
- Long safety rope
- Hammer and chisel
- Hacksaw
- Measuring tape
- Replacement shingle
- Utility knife or saw
- Shingle nails
- Nail set
- Wood block

Warning

To minimize the chance of both personal injury and damage to shingles, never walk on a wood roof. Wood roofs are slippery when wet; loose shingles often pull out when stepped on; and brittle, warped or loose shingles are easily damaged. Always work from a roof ladder and do not overreach.

166 Replace a Damaged Asphalt Shingle

Timely replacement of a damaged roof shingle can prevent further leak damage or extend the life of a roof that's just beginning to fail. Hopefully your roofer left behind a partial bundle for repair purposes.

Steps

1 See "Setting up ladders and equipment," opposite page, to set up ladder safely.

2 Tap a large, flat pry bar under the damaged shingle just above the gap between tabs until you hit a nail. Center the tool's nail-pulling slot on the nail, tap the bar in a bit more, and press down on the other end to pry the nail partly out. Then place a block of wood under the bar just down the roof from the nail to act as a fulcrum, and pry out the nail the rest of the way.

3 Continue to remove all nails that secure shingles directly above the damaged shingle and that also penetrate the top edge of the damaged shingle.

4 Pull out the damaged shingle and slip in the replacement (see A).

5 Align the replacement shingle and lift the shingle above it as needed to nail the new one into place with 1-inch (2.5-cm) roofing nails (see B).

6 Replace any nails that you removed from the shingles above.

7 Dab roofing cement over all the nail heads that you couldn't remove without breaking the shingle, as far up as it should go (just above the notch).

8 Use a putty knife to spread a little roofing cement under each shingle tab that you lifted during the repair, and press each shingle down to adhere it to the one below.

What You'll Need

- Extension and roof ladders
- Long safety rope
- Flat pry bar
- Wood block
- Hammer
- Replacement shingle
- Roofing nails
- Roofing cement
- Putty knife

Warning

Don't attempt repairs that require walking on a steep or wet roof.

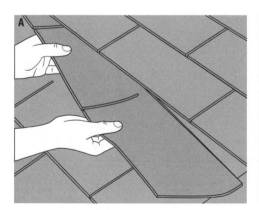

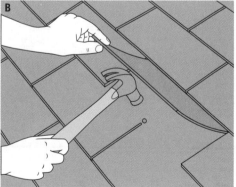

167 Patch a Flat or Low-Pitched Roof

Flat-roof patches are temporary fixes. You should plan to replace them with a permanent repair as soon as is practical, unless you'll be reroofing in the next year or so.

Steps

1 Brush aside the existing gravel (in a built-up roofing system) and scrape off any that remains in the area you're patching. For double-coverage roll-roof systems without gravel, just brush and/or blow off dirt, loose materials and dust.

2 Trowel plastic roof cement over the damaged area and about 6 inches (15 cm) around it using a disposable trowel or wide putty knife (see A).

3 Immediately embed a layer of fiberglass cloth into the cement, pressing it lightly with the trowel or wide putty knife.

4 Apply a second layer of cement over the fabric (see B).

5 Allow the patch to dry and preferably withstand the test of another rainstorm before you cover it with gravel.

Repairing in the rain

1 In the case of sudden damage—caused by, say, a fallen tree limb or a storm that blows loose an object anchored to the roof—make an immediate repair, even in the rain, to limit interior damage. Use a roof cement formulated for application on a wet roof.

Repairing a rubber roof

1 Clean the damaged area with window cleaner, then wipe it using a cloth dampened with white gas or splice-cleaning fluid (available from a roofing supplier).

2 Cut the tip off a caulking gun and use it to apply butyl or poly-urethane sealant to the tear or hole, then smooth the sealant with a trowel. Alternatively, use a peel-and-stick roofing tape and apply weight to press it firmly into place.

What You'll Need

- Brush
- Disposable trowel or wide putty knife
- Plastic roof cement
- Fiberglass reinforcing cloth
- Window cleaner
- Cloth
- White gas or splice-cleaning fluid
- Butyl or polyurethane sealant, or peel-and-stick roofing tape
- Caulking gun
- Utility knife

Warning

Never make a repair if there is any danger of lightning.

Walk and work carefully on a built-up roof to avoid damaging it.

Protect your hands with rubber gloves when cleaning a rubber roof or work gloves when installing a roof patch.

168 Repair Roof Flashing

Whenever it's practical to replace damaged roof flashing, do so. In an emergency or when replacement is too difficult or expensive, use a patch and inspect it annually. Typically, you can use this method for step flashing, which interlaces with shingles where they meet a wall or other vertical surface (see 164 Repair a Leaking Skylight). However, it's not practical to repair flashing at the valley where two roof planes intersect.

Steps

Insert new step flashing

1 Install new step flashing over the damaged step flashing (you'll likely need a ladder). Cut the flashing with tin snips, bend it in half at a 90-degree angle; slip the vertical half up under the siding or trim on the wall; slide it up the roof under the shingle and on top of or under the damaged piece. Adhere it using dabs of asphalt flashing cement under and over it.

Replace plumbing-vent flashing

1 Look for the leak. A plumbing vent can leak between the collar and the pipe, through the collar, or through the plastic or metal pan that fits under the course of shingles above the pipe and on top of the course below.

2 For leaks between the pipe and collar or through the collar, replace the collar or slip a repair collar over the pipe on top of the existing one.

3 For flashing leaks, install new vent flashing. Remove the shingles above the flashing (see 166 Replace a Damaged Asphalt Shingle), and install it according to the manufacturer's instructions, usually with finishing nails.

Repair chimney flashing

1 If the step flashing is corroded, insert step flashing as described in "Insert new step flashing," above. If the counter flashing is corroded, patch it until you can have it replaced professionally.

2 If the mortar joint where counter flashing is embedded is deteriorating, repoint the joint (see 155 Fix Crumbling Chimney Mortar).

Patch open-valley or other exposed flashing

1 Clean the damaged area with steel wool.

2 Apply asphalt cement. In valleys, embed a flashing patch as described in 156 Patch a Gutter Leak.

What You'll Need

- Flashing
- Ladders
- Tin snips
- Asphalt flashing cement (ASTM D4586)
- Collar
- Hammer
- Galvanized finishing nails
- Steel wool

Tip

Step flashing should extend at least 4 inches (10 cm) out onto the roof and ideally 2 to 4 inches (5 to 10 cm) up behind the siding, trim or counter flashing.

Warning

To avoid injury or roof damage, observe proper ladder and roof safety, and use a roof ladder (a rental item) where possible. See "Setting up ladders and equipment" in 165 Repair a Cracked or Split Wood Shingle.

Don't mix metals when nailing flashing or where new and existing flashing contact. The electrolysis generated causes rapid corrosion.

The cut edges of metal flashing are very sharp, so wear work gloves.

169 Troubleshoot Exterior-Paint Problems

Exterior paint is subjected to extremes in temperature, air pollution, expansion and contraction of building materials, mold growth and a host of other problems related to improper preparation and application. Understanding the causes of failure can help you correct an existing problem or avoid one in the future. (See also 136 Troubleshoot Interior-Paint Problems.)

PROBLEM	POSSIBLE CAUSES	SOLUTIONS
Mildew (tiny black or gray spots or areas)	Excessive dampness and lack of air circulation; painting over improperly cleaned mildewed surface; failure to apply primer on wood	• Cut down or prune tree branches within 15 feet (5 m) of house. • Before painting, wash affected surfaces with 1-to-3 solution of bleach and water. Wait 15 minutes, rinse well. • Use mildewproof paint or paint that contains mildewcide additive.
Rust staining (rusting nail heads bleeding through paint)	Using nongalvanized or inferior-quality galvanized nails; sanding good-quality galvanized nails during paint preparation	• Sand rust off nail heads; countersink nails; dab water repellent in holes; spot-prime nail heads; fill hole with exterior latex or siliconized-acrylic caulk.
Tannin staining (brown stains in painted wood)	Typical in redwood and cedar, or at knots; aggravated by moisture from interior escaping through walls	• Resolve interior moisture problems such as leaks, bathrooms without fans, absence of vapor retarder. • Apply alkyd-based primer or top-quality acrylic-latex primer. • Topcoat with two applications of 100 percent acrylic-latex paint.
Chalking (fine powder on surface easily rubs off on your hand)	Normal to some degree; excessive amount indicates use of inferior, highly pigmented paint or interior paint outdoors	• Remove chalk with stiff brush and water or house-washing solution; rinse well. • If chalking is still present, apply primer and repaint.

PROBLEM	POSSIBLE CAUSES	SOLUTIONS
Alligatoring (cracked pattern in paint, resembling alligator skin)	Applying hard finish such as alkyd enamel over flexible finish such as latex paint or primer; applying topcoat before primer is dry; end of life span for oil-based paint.	• Remove all paint down to bare wood; apply primer and one or two topcoats of paint.
Wrinkles (ripples in paint surface)	Applying paint to hot or dirty surface, or before first coat has fully dried; exposing freshly painted siding to rain	• Scrape or sand to remove all loose paint and to feather edges smooth. • Prime bare spots and apply two top coats, allowing plenty of drying time.
Peeling and bubbling (all or some layers of paint peel off and bubble)	Moisture getting into wood at unpainted joints or coming through from interior; inadequate surface preparation	• Maintain exterior caulk (see 148 Replace Caulking on the Outside of Your House). • Pressure-wash house exterior before painting; scrape, wire brush and/or sand to remove all poorly adhered paint. Apply primer to bare spots. Locate source of interior moisture and resolve problem.
Wax bleed (dirty stains coming through finish on hardboard siding)	Use of improper or low-quality primer and paint	• Remove stains with hot, soapy water and scrub brush or steam cleaner. • Apply alkyd-based primer followed by two topcoats of 100 percent acrylic-latex paint.

170 Fix Garage-Door Tension

You want an overhead garage door to operate easily and safely, neither putting undue strain on a garage door opener (or you) nor crashing down when it closes. To achieve this goal, set the tension correctly and make sure the sides are balanced. A test and adjustment is all that's usually required, but you may need to replace the springs.

Steps

Test and adjust the tension

1 Disconnect any door opener and position the door half open (you may need a stepladder). It should be level and stay put, and you should be able to raise or lower it from this position with very little coaxing.

2 To adjust the spring tension, open the door fully to relieve all spring tension and clamp a wood block, locking pliers or a similar stop onto the tracks just below the bottom rollers to hold it open.

3 Disconnect the lifting cable from the brace near the bend in the track and move it to a hole closer to or farther from the door to increase or decrease tension. Cables either hook to or tie to a fitting on their end; that fitting in turn hooks into holes in the bracket.

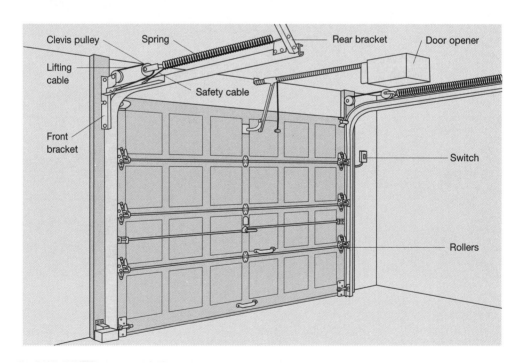

4 Remove the stops, retest and readjust as necessary. Once the door remains level, you must make any further adjustments equally on both sides.

5 If the lifting cable is hooked to the hole closest to the door and still needs more tension, shorten the cable. Disconnect the cable or loosen it enough so you can feed more cable through the fitting. With the cable shortened and securely reattached to the fitting, hook it on the bracket and adjust the tension.

6 If you have shortened the cable to the point where more shortening would create tension with the door in the open position, the springs are worn and need replacing. Springs are rated according to the number of pounds they can properly support, so you need to weigh your door in this case.

Weigh the door

1 Raise the door to relieve all tension and block the door open as described in "Test and adjust the tension," opposite page. If you haven't already done so, move your car out of the garage.

2 Disconnect the safety-cable springs from the track support at the rear of the garage. The cable is usually bolted, so you'll use a wrench to disconnect it; the springs may be attached to a hook or equipped with brackets bolted to the track support.

3 With one person on each side, raise the door a bit to remove the stop blocks and lower it to the floor. Garage doors can weigh hundreds of pounds, so work with a helper. Lift the door and insert a bathroom scale under the center of the door, then lower the door onto the scale.

4 If the door's weight exceeds the capacity of your scale, place the scale inside the door and rest a 2-by-4 on the scale and on a block of wood outside the door. Lower the door onto the 2-by-4 and double the weight measurement to determine the required spring capacity.

Replace a tension spring

1 If you have not already done so, support the door in its open position, remove the safety cable and spring from the rear track support, and disconnect the lifting cable from the bracket as described in "Weigh the door," above.

2 Disassemble and remove the front bracket and clevis-pulley assembly and the rear brackets from the old spring. Reattach them to the new spring.

3 Feed the safety cable through the spring and reattach it to the rear track support with a nut and bolt. Feed the lifting cable through the clevis pulley, reattach it to the fitting, hook it onto the bracket and adjust the tension.

Work on one side at a time. That way, if you can't figure out how to reassemble something, you can always look at the other side for guidance.

Place shims under the outside end of the bathroom scale as needed to level it for a more accurate reading.

Warning

Torsion spring controls, installed parallel to and above the door, may be found on some heavy, wide residential doors. These require professional service due to the extreme danger involved in making adjustments.

Wear leather work gloves when handling springs, pulleys and cables to avoid being pinched or cut.

Wear safety goggles or glasses to protect your eyes from injury and dirt when working with overhead cables.

Be careful when removing a spring. Although there is no tension, the spring can pinch an ungloved hand. If the heavy spring falls out of your hand, it could easily injure someone or cause damage.

Never reinstall a spring without the safety cable. It passes through each spring to hold it in place in case the lifting cable or the spring itself breaks.

171 Troubleshoot a Garage-Door Opener

For your convenience and safety, frequently test and maintain your door and opener. Make any needed repairs immediately or deactivate the opener until you can.

Steps

Check the door's operation

1 Disengage the opener for manual door operation.

2 Check the door's balance (see 170 Fix Garage-Door Tension) and test it for smooth operation.

3 Straighten misaligned tracks: Loosen the screws that secure track brackets to the opening, or the bolts that secure tracks to brackets. Adjust the bracket or track. Then tighten the fasteners to lock the track into place.

4 Clean the tracks with a soft brush or rag. They shouldn't be greasy. Spray on an automotive degreaser and wipe them clean with a rag.

5 Clean and then lubricate roller-wheel bearings and axles or hinge pins with light oil.

Test and adjust the safety reverse

1 Open the door and place a 2-by-4 on the floor in the center of the door opening, then activate the door.

2 If the door does not reverse when it hits the board, adjust the close limit per your owner's manual.

Troubleshoot a photocell system

1 Attempt to reset the system. Shut off and then restore power to the opener, either at the house's circuit-breaker panel or at the opener's plug; or momentarily connect the two screws on the sending module with a wire or any metal tool.

2 Inspect the wiring between the opener and the photocell modules for damage or loose connections. Or remove the modules and wire them to the opener with new short-wire leads. If they work, replace the wiring.

3 If the wiring is good, either the modules or the main sequencer board in the opener are defective.

What You'll Need

- Screwdriver
- Socket and/or open-end wrenches
- Soft brush
- Automotive degreaser
- Rags
- Oiling can and light oil
- 2-by-4
- Wire or metal tool
- Switch wire

Tips

Tracks should not be lubricated. The lubricant just collects dirt.

Install the receiving sensor for a photocell system on the side least likely to have direct sun.

PROBLEM	POSSIBLE CAUSES	SOLUTIONS
Opener does not run at all	• No power	• Plug lamp or tool in to test for power. If receptacle has no power, check house circuit breaker or fuse.
	• Loose wires	• Unplug opener to inspect 120-volt wiring connections.
	• Excessive cycling tripped motor protection	• Wait 10 to 15 minutes for auto reset or to press reset per manual.
	• System locked for "vacation"	• Unlock it.
	• Lightning damage	• Use GFCI (ground fault circuit interrupter) receptacle and ground door tracks to rod to prevent recurrence.
Wall switch does not work but remote does	• Faulty switch wiring	• Check connections; disconnect switch wires at opener and wire direction across terminals. Repair or replace wire.
Remote does not work but wall switch does	• Loose or damaged wiring to photocell system	• Check photocells and wiring for loose connections or damage.
	• Improper remote coding	• Reprogram per manual.
	• Dead or weak battery	• Test or replace battery.
	• Antenna out of position	• Reposition or coil antenna wire at opener.
Door starts on its own	• Intermittent short	• Look for cut wire insulation at staples. Repair with electrical tape or replace wiring.
	• Outside signals	• Erase codes and reprogram remote per manual.
Door stops before closing fully	• Down limit out of adjustment	• Adjust per manual.
Door starts to close but reverses	• Inadequate close force	• Adjust per manual.
	• Problem with safety-reverse system	• See "Test and adjust the safety reverse," opposite page.
	• If door closes to floor and reverses, and problem is seasonal, concrete may be moving up and down with varying temperatures	• Make seasonal adjustments of close travel and follow with safety-reverse system test.

(continued on next page)

PROBLEM	POSSIBLE CAUSES	SOLUTIONS
Door closes but won't open	Stuck open-limit switch or loose wiring	Inspect or replace open-limit switch and check wiring to open-limit switch.
	Inadequate open force	Adjust per manual.
	Door needs adjustment or maintenance, or door is binding due to expansion in hot, humid weather	Check operation without opener.
Door opens but won't close	Problem with safety-reverse system	Test and adjust safety-reverse system according to owner's manual.
	Stuck close-limit switch or loose wiring	Inspect or replace open-limit switch and check wiring to open-limit switch.
	Inadequate close force	Adjust per manual.
Door starts up but stops before it is completely open	Door needs adjustment or maintenance, or door is binding due to expansion in hot, humid weather	Check operation without opener.
	Improper open-limit switch setting	Adjust open-limit switch according to owner's manual.
	Inadequate open force	Check adjustment.
Opener runs briefly, but door does not move; lights flash	Lights flash when system senses obstruction	Make sure door is engaged with opener.
	Improper open- or close-limit force settings	Check open- and close-force adjustments according to owner's manual.
	Burned drive belt	Replace drive belt.
	Faulty circuit board or faulty capacitor (especially if opener hums)	Replace faulty board or capacitor (or call for service).
	Severely out-of-balance door	Test opener with door disengaged.
Noisy operation	Door out of balance; tracks misaligned or dirty	Make sure door is in good repair, properly lubricated and balanced.
	Inherently noisy metal wheels	Replace metal wheels with nylon ones.

172 Get Rid of Termites

Termites can destroy structural framing in short order. Learn the signs of infestation, inspect every year or two and consult a professional to confirm your suspicions. Above all, be persistent—your enemy is!

Steps

Make a thorough inspection

1 In warm months, you may spot dry-wood termites when they swarm and come out of hidden infested areas.

2 Look for structural wood damage at the first-floor level, especially where the foundation meets the walls and below exterior doors. First search carefully with a flashlight. The damage may not be visible, so thump the wood with the heel of a large screwdriver and probe with a heavy-duty awl in search of hollowed-out wood.

3 Look for very small tan, reddish-brown or black droppings.

4 Inspect the foundation walls inside and out in search of mud tubes. Subterranean termites live in the soil and close to a moisture source but feed on structural wood members, which they access by building mud passageways extending from the soil to the wood.

Confirm your suspicions

1 If you find a problem (or enough evidence to suspect one), call a professional to confirm your suspicions and discuss options for elimination, control, prevention, treating existing wood and making repairs using naturally termite-resistant or treated lumber.

Work on prevention yourself

1 Repair any water leaks or dripping outside faucets.

2 Control roof water by correcting gutter problems. See 156 Patch a Gutter Leak, 161 Redirect Rainwater From a Downspout and 163 Unclog Gutters and Downspouts.

3 Correct grading and other drainage problems near the foundation. See 157 Troubleshoot a Wet Basement.

4 Remove or elevate all wood in direct contact with soil, such as a stack of firewood.

5 Inspect, repair or cover all foundation vents with insect screening.

6 Caulk your home's exterior to fill all cracks, especially between the foundation and house walls.

What You'll Need

- Bright flashlight
- Large screwdriver
- Sturdy awl
- Insect screening
- Caulk and applicator

Tips

Call in the pros for treatment and structural repairs.

Replace white light bulbs, which attract insects, with yellow or pale-amber ones in your outdoor fixtures.

Although any treatment should last about five years, provided there are no untreated gaps in the chemical barrier, inspections every two years are recommended.

Warning

Know your enemy. Learn about insect behavior, their eating and nesting habits, and the signs of their presence.

ORING • FIX BAD HABITS • REPAIR A BROKEN EYEGLASS FRAME • REPOSITION A SLIPPED CONTACT LENS • FIX A RUN IN STOCKINGS • JO
EAKOUT • REPAIR A TORN FINGERNAIL • FIX CHIPPED NAIL POLISH • FIX A STUCK ZIPPER • FIND A LOST CONTACT LENS • ELIMINATE BAD
Y THAT STICKS • STOP TELEMARKETERS AND JUNK MAIL • GET SUPERGLUE OFF YOUR SKIN • EXTRACT A SPLINTER • SOOTHE A SUNBURI
HANGOVER • STOP HICCUPS • MEND A BROKEN HEART • MEND A FAMILY FEUD • TREAT A SMALL CUT OR SCRAPE • FIX HAIR DISASTERS •
TTER SEATS • FIX A BILLING MISTAKE • FIX A BAD GRADE • FIX BAD CREDIT • RECOVER FROM JET LAG • RESUSCITATE AN UNCONSCIOUS
PRONOUNS • FIX A RUN-ON SENTENCE • FIX MISUSE OF THE WORD GOOD • FIX YOUR DOG OR CAT • CORRECT BAD BEHAVIOR IN DOGS
SSING BUTTON • REMOVE LINT FROM CLOTHING • FIX A DRAWSTRING ON SWEATPANTS • REPAIR A HEM • REPAIR LEATHER GOODS • MEN
UNDER YOUR CASHMERE • FIX A SWEATER THAT HAS SHRUNK • FIX A SWEATER THAT HAS STRETCHED • FIX A HOLE IN A POCKET • FIX A
LING FROM CLOTHING • FIX A FRAYED BUTTONHOLE • REMOVE DARK SCUFFS FROM SHOES • TREAT STAINS ON LEATHER • PROTECT SUE
JIET SQUEAKY HINGES • TROUBLESHOOT LOCK PROBLEMS • TIGHTEN A LOOSE DOORKNOB • TIGHTEN A LOOSE DOOR HINGE • FIX A BIN
PLACE CRACKED TILE • TROUBLESHOOT MOLD ON INTERIOR WALLS • REPLACE CRACKED TILE GROUT IN A TUB OR SHOWER • FIX A DRA
INDS • TROUBLESHOOT WINDOW SHADE PROBLEMS • FIX BROKEN GLASS IN A WINDOW • REPAIR A WINDOW SCREEN • REPAIR ALUMINU
MAGED PLASTER • REPAIR WALL COVERINGS • TOUCH UP PAINTED WALLS • TROUBLESHOOT INTERIOR-PAINT PROBLEMS • SOLVE A LEAF
RDWOOD FLOOR • RESTORE A DULL, WORN WOOD FLOOR • TOUCH UP WOOD-FLOOR FINISHES • REPAIR DAMAGED SHEET-VINYL FLOOR
JUSE • CHILDPROOF YOUR HOME • PREVENT ICE DAMS • CURE A FAULTY FIREPLACE DRAW • START A FIRE IN A COLD CHIMNEY • FIX A W
AL A GARAGE FLOOR • REFINISH A GARAGE OR BASEMENT FLOOR • CONTROL ROOF LEAKS • REDIRECT RAINWATER FROM A DOWNSPOL
MAGED ASPHALT SHINGLE • PATCH A FLAT OR LOW-PITCHED ROOF • REPAIR ROOF FLASHING • TROUBLESHOOT EXTERIOR-PAINT PROBL
W WATER PRESSURE • FIX LEAKING PIPES • STOP A TOILET FROM RUNNING • FIX A LEAKY TOILET TANK • FIX A STOPPED-UP TOILET • STC
OGGED SINK OR TUB • REPAIR A TUB-AND-SHOWER VALVE • REPAIR CHIPPED FIXTURES • QUIET NOISY PIPES • DEFROST YOUR PIPES • D
ONSUMPTION • REPLACE A RECEPTACLE • FIX AN ELECTRICAL PLUG • REPLACE A LIGHT FIXTURE • INSTALL A NEW DIMMER • FIX A LAMP
OORBELL • FIX A WOBBLY OVERHEAD FAN • ADJUST WATER-HEATER TEMPERATURE • RELIGHT A WATER-HEATER PILOT LIGHT • TROUBLES
E MAKER • GET RID OF MICROWAVE SMELLS • FIX A REFRIGERATOR THAT COOLS POORLY • FIX A GAS OVEN THAT HEATS POORLY • CLEAN
SHWASHER PROBLEMS • CORRECT AN OVERFLOWING DISHWASHER • FIX A LEAKY DISHWASHER • FIX A DISHWASHER THAT FILLS SLOWLY
WASHING MACHINE THAT FILLS SLOWLY • FIX A WASHING MACHINE THAT "WALKS" ACROSS THE FLOOR • FIX A CLOTHES DRYER THAT DR
K YOUR VACUUM CLEANER • REPLACE VACUUM CLEANER BRUSHES • TROUBLESHOOT A PORTABLE AIR CONDITIONER • FIX A WINDOW A
OCESSOR • FIX A TOASTER • DIAGNOSE MICROWAVE OVEN PROBLEMS • TROUBLESHOOT A GAS GRILL • FIX A TRASH COMPACTOR • REF
ART • TROUBLESHOOT A CRASHING COMPUTER • CLEAN UP LAPTOP SPILLS • FIX BAD SECTORS ON A HARD DISK • QUIT A FROZEN PC A
FECTED COMPUTER • IMPROVE YOUR COMPUTER'S MEMORY • GET RID OF E-MAIL SPAM • CHANGE A LASER PRINTER CARTRIDGE • FIX A
GURE OUT WHY A PRINTER WON'T PRINT • FIX SPELLING AND GRAMMAR ERRORS • RECALL AN E-MAIL IN MICROSOFT OUTLOOK • DIAGN
LES • TROUBLESHOOT A PALM OS PDA • RESET A PALM OS PDA • REMOVE FINGERPRINTS FROM A CAMERA LENS • TROUBLESHOOT A CD
LVAGE A VIDEOCASSETTE • TROUBLESHOOT A DVD PLAYER • STRENGTHEN FM RADIO RECEPTION • STRENGTHEN AM RADIO RECEPTION
JAMMED SLIDE PROJECTOR • GET BETTER SPEAKER SOUND • TROUBLESHOOT A DIGITAL CAMCORDER • TROUBLESHOOT A DIGITAL CAM
GHTBULB • FIX A BROKEN WINEGLASS STEM • FIX BLEMISHED WOOD FURNITURE • REPAIR GOUGES IN FURNITURE • RESTORE FURNITUR
AMOUFLAGE A DOG-SCRATCHED DOOR • REPAIR A SPLIT CARPET SEAM • RID CARPETS OF PET ODORS • REINFORCE A SAGGING SHELF
DINTS OF CHAIRS AND TABLES • REUPHOLSTER A DROP-IN CHAIR SEAT • REVIVE A CANE SEAT • REINFORCE A WEAK BED FRAME • FIX UP
OTTERY • REPAIR CHIPPED OR CRACKED CHINA • UNCLUTTER YOUR HOME • CLEAN CRAYON FROM A WALL • GET WAX OFF A TABLECLOT
AINS • REMOVE CHEWING GUM FROM CARPETING • REMOVE BLEACH SPOTS FROM CARPETING • REMOVE PET STAINS • ELIMINATE WINE
AINS FROM TILE GROUT • REMOVE MILDEW FROM WALLS AND CEILINGS • DISINFECT A TOILET BOWL • REMOVE FIREPLACE GRIME • GET
LEAN OIL SPOTS FROM A GARAGE OR DRIVEWAY • REMOVE STAINS FROM BRICK • WASH AN OUTDOOR GRILL • FIX A FALLEN SOUFFLÉ • F
SCUE OVERPROOFED YEAST DOUGH • FIX YOUR KID LUNCH • GET RID OF TAP-WATER MINERAL DEPOSITS • CALIBRATE A MEAT THERMO
AUCE • RESCUE A BROKEN SAUCE • REMOVE FAT FROM SOUPS AND SAUCES • FIX LUMPY GRAVY • SUBSTITUTE MISSING INGREDIENTS •
JRNED RICE • REMOVE COOKING ODORS • FINISH UNDERCOOKED MEAT • SALVAGE AN UNDERCOOKED TURKEY • FIX AN OVERSEASONE
ALE BREAD • SMOOTH SEIZED CHOCOLATE • SOFTEN HARDENED SUGARS OR COOKIES • FIX BREAKFAST FOR YOUR SWEETHEART • MEN
GGING TOOLS • RESTORE A BROKEN FLOWERPOT • SHARPEN PRUNING CLIPPERS • REMOVE RUST FROM TOOLS • REVIVE WILTING CUT
ET RID OF RAMPANT BRAMBLES • TROUBLESHOOT BROWN SPOTS ON A LAWN • CONTROL MAJOR GARDEN PESTS • RID YOUR GARDEN C
ONPERFORMING COMPOST PILE • FIX BAD SOIL • SHORE UP A RAISED GARDEN BED • REMOVE A DEAD OR DISEASED TREE LIMB • TROUE
RAINAGE • TROUBLESHOOT ROSE DISEASES • IDENTIFY AND CORRECT SOIL DEFICIENCIES IN ROSES • TROUBLESHOOT ROSE PESTS • OV
AMAGED DECK BOARDS • REPAIR DECK RAILINGS • STRENGTHEN DECK JOISTS • FIX A RUSTY IRON RAILING • REPAIR A GATE • REPAIR A
RACKED OR DAMAGED CONCRETE • IMPROVE THE LOOK OF REPAIRED CONCRETE • REPAIR AN ASPHALT DRIVEWAY • REVIVE WOODEN C
ARDEN PONDS • CLEAN SWIMMING POOL WATER • TROUBLESHOOT HOT TUBS AND SPAS • REPLACE BRICKS IN WALKWAYS AND PATIOS
AR WITH JUMPER CABLES • SHUT OFF A CAR ALARM THAT WON'T QUIT • FREE A CAR STUCK ON ICE OR SNOW • DE-ICE YOUR WINDSHIEL
JRN-SIGNAL COVER • FIX A CAR FUSE • FIX DASHBOARD LIGHTS THAT WON'T LIGHT • REMOVE CAR SMELLS • CHECK TIRE PRESSURE • IN
PROPERLY INSTALLED CHILD CAR SEAT • TROUBLESHOOT LEAKING OIL • CHECK AND ADD POWER-STEERING FLUID • CHECK AND ADD C
ROKEN EXHAUST PIPE • CHECK AND ADD ENGINE OIL • CHECK AND ADD BRAKE FLUID • CHECK AND ADD FLUID TO YOUR AUTOMATIC T
OUBLESHOOT A WINDSHIELD-WASHER PUMP • REPAIR MINOR DENTS • CHANGE A HUBCAP • FIX AN IGNITION KEY THAT WON'T TURN • C

MORY • FIX AN ELECTRIC CAN OPENER THAT DROPS THE CAN • TROUBLESHOOT A CELL PHONE • KEEP MIRRORS FROM FOGGING • ZAP A
EEP A SHAVING NICK FROM BLEEDING • GET RID OF SPLIT ENDS • UNTANGLE HAIR SNARLS • FIX FRIZZY HAIR • FIX BLEEDING LIPSTICK •
CKY SOCIAL SITUATION • FIX A BAD REPUTATION • CLEAN LIPSTICK FROM A COLLAR • FIX A BAD RELATIONSHIP • SALVAGE A BAD DATE •
EEDING NOSE • BEAT THE MONDAY MORNING BLUES • GET OUT OF A FIX • EXTRACT A BROKEN KEY • RETRIEVE KEYS LOCKED INSIDE A C
TOP SOMEONE FROM CHOKING • STOP AN ANT INVASION • STABILIZE A CHRISTMAS TREE • RESCUE AN ITEM FROM THE DRAIN • FIX IMPF
KUNK ODOR FROM YOUR DOG • GET A CAT OUT OF A TREE • CORRECT BAD BEHAVIOR IN CATS • TREAT A CAT FOR MATTED FUR • REPLA
EAM • TREAT MILDEW DAMAGE • GET STATIC OUT OF YOUR LAUNDRY • DEAL WITH A CLOTHES-MOTH INFESTATION • FIX A SEPARATED ZIP
UR SOCK • TREAT MIXED-WASH ACCIDENTS • TAKE WRINKLES OUT OF CLOTHING • FIX A HOLE IN JEANS • REPAIR A SNAG IN A SWEATER •
TAINS • WASH SNEAKERS • PICK UP A DROPPED STITCH IN KNITTING • RESTRING BEADS • FRESHEN SMELLY SHOES • FIX A SAGGING CLO
• FIX A RUBBING DOOR • FIX A DRAFTY DOOR • TUNE UP SLIDING DOORS • FIX A SHOWER DOOR • SEAL WALL JOINTS AROUND A TUB O
V • REPAIR A FAULTY WINDOW CRANK • REPAIR VERTICAL BLINDS • REPAIR VENETIAN BLINDS OR MINIBLINDS • REPAIR WOOD OR PLASTIC
REEN WINDOWS • INSTALL NEW SASH CORDS IN WINDOWS • FIX A TIGHT OR LOOSE WINDOW SASH • REPAIR MINOR DRYWALL DAMAGE •
BLEM • REPLACE A DAMAGED CEILING TILE • REPLACE A WOOD FLOORBOARD • QUIET SQUEAKING FLOORS • REPAIR A WATER-DAMAGED
R A VINYL-TILE FLOOR • SILENCE SQUEAKY _____ STER • REPLACE CAULKING ON THE OUTSIDE OF
NG STOVE • REPAIR AND PREVENT WOOD RO_____ TCH A GUTTER LEAK • TROUBLESHOOT A WET BAS
GGING GUTTER • UNCLOG GUTTERS AND D_____ • REPAIR A CRACKED OR SPLIT WOOD SHINGLE •
RAGE-DOOR TENSION • TROUBLESHOOT A_____ ITES • LOOSEN A RUSTY NUT OR BOLT • TROUBLE
NK SWEATING • FIX FLUSHING PROBLEMS •_____ FAUCET • FIX A STOPPER THAT DOESN'T SEAL • C
MP PUMP PROBLEMS • TROUBLESHOOT ELE_____ USE • SWAP A FAULTY LIGHT SWITCH • REDUCE E
HOOT FLUORESCENT LIGHTING • FIX A LOW_____ E THERMOSTAT • TROUBLESHOOT HOLIDAY LIGHT
TING SYSTEM • REFRESH A SMELLY REFRIGE_____ EMS • FIX A LEAKING REFRIGERATOR • REPAIR A C
TIONING GAS BURNER • REPAIR A RANGE H_____ FIX AN ELECTRIC OVEN THAT HEATS POORLY • DIA
R YOUR APPLIANCES • CONTROL GARBAGE_____ E DISPOSAL • DIAGNOSE WASHING MACHINE PRO
FIX A HAIR DRYER • TROUBLESHOOT A CLO_____ AT SPUTTERS • FIX AN IRON THAT LEAVES SPOTS O
ER • FIX A DEHUMIDIFIER • REPAIR A CONS_____ DER • HANDLE A MIXER THAT OVERHEATS • REPAIR
G MACHINE • TROUBLESHOOT SMOKE ALAR_____ OARD SPILLS • TROUBLESHOOT A COMPUTER THA
REMOVE A WINDOWS PROGRAM • SPEED U_____ OUSE • REPLACE YOUR PC'S BATTERY • CLEAN A
T FAILS ITS SELF-TEST • CORRECT MONITOR_____ PAPER JAM • TROUBLESHOOT A RECURRING PRINT
NE MODEM PROBLEMS • TROUBLESHOOT A_____ REEN GLARE • GET TOP-NOTCH SCANS • RECOVE
STORE A CD • REPAIR A WARPED CD • CLE_____ • EXTRACT A JAMMED VIDEOTAPE • ADJUST VCR
TE CONTROL • FIX AUDIOCASSETTES • FIX_____ OT A CASSETTE DECK • REPLACE BROKEN RABBIT
LESHOOT A CD PLAYER • REPLACE A HEAD_____ RASS • SHINE SILVER SAFELY • REMOVE A BROKEN
PLACE A BROKEN TOWEL ROD • REMOVE ST_____ FOR NATURAL DISASTERS • FIX A FRAYED CARPE
BORING BATHROOM • REPLACE A SHOWER_____ NACE FILTER • REPAIR A BROKEN SLIDING DRAWE
D CHAIR • FIX A WOBBLY WOOD CHAIR • SF_____ OR CRACKED PORCELAIN • REPAIR CHIPPED OR C
WAX FROM CARPETING • GET RID OF CEILIN_____ MOVE MYSTERY STAINS FROM CLOTHING • REMOV

Plumbing & Electrical

A RUG OR TABLECLOTH • REMOVE BURN _____ NITURE • STRIP WAX BUILDUP FROM FLOORS • RE
ORANT STAINS • ELIMINATE CIGARETTE ODOR • RESTORE SHINE TO YOUR JEWELRY • WASH DIRTY WINDOWS • REMOVE GRIME FROM MIF
MBLED CAKE • FIX A PERFECT CUP OF TEA • PATCH A TORN PIE CRUST • KEEP A PIE CRUST FROM GETTING SOGGY • FIX DOUGH THAT W
DULL KNIFE • REMOVE RUST FROM A CAST-IRON PAN • REPAIR LAMINATE COUNTERTOPS • REMOVE STAINS FROM A STONE COUNTERTO
CHOLESTEROL • TREAT BURNED POTS AND PANS • RESCUE A BURNED CAKE OR PIE • PUT OUT A KITCHEN FIRE • REMOVE THE BITTERN
N UNDERSEASONED DISH • REMOVE OVEN SPILLS • CLEAN UP OIL SPILLS • FIX A DRINK FOR ANY OCCASION • DISENTANGLE PASTA • RE
CUTTING BOARD • KEEP A MIXING BOWL STEADY • FIX GARDEN TOOL HANDLES • REPAIR A LEAKY HOSE NOZZLE • MEND A LEAKY HOSE
ARPEN A POWER MOWER BLADE • SHARPEN PUSH MOWER BLADES • REPAIR BALD SPOTS ON GRASS • RID YOUR GRASS OF DOG URINE
OUBLESHOOT HERBS • TROUBLESHOOT HOUSEPLANTS • OVERCOME SHADE PROBLEMS • RID SOIL OF PESTS AND DISEASES • REVIVE A
ES AND SHRUBS • REPAIR A LEAKING IRRIGATION SYSTEM • UNCLOG A SPRINKLER SYSTEM • CLEAN A CLOGGED DRIP SYSTEM • FIX POC
GUS DISEASES IN ROSES • REPAIR DECK STEPS • RENOVATE A WEATHERED DECK • TIGHTEN LOOSE DECKING • REMOVE DECK STAINS •
• LEVEL AND SMOOTH A GRAVEL PATH • FIX A POTHOLE IN A DIRT OR GRAVEL DRIVEWAY • REPLACE PATIO STONES, TILES AND PAVERS
ITURE • RESTORE WEATHERED METAL FURNITURE • REPAIR CHAIR STRAPS AND WEBBING • REVIVE RUSTED IRON FURNITURE • TROUBLE
LED CAR • SHUT OFF A JAMMED HORN • CHANGE YOUR CAR'S BATTERY • TROUBLESHOOT A CAR THAT WON'T START • FIX A FLAT TIRE •
NED-OUT SIGNAL BULB • FIX A BURNED-OUT HEADLIGHT • ADJUST HEADLIGHTS • FIX A STUCK BRAKE LIGHT • REPLACE A BROKEN BRAKE
IRES • FIX A STUCK CONVERTIBLE TOP • DIAGNOSE A LEAK INSIDE YOUR CAR • REPLACE YOUR AIR FILTER • HANDLE A FAULTY REPAIR •
OL AN OVERHEATED ENGINE • REPLACE A LEAKING RADIATOR HOSE • CHANGE YOUR WIPER BLADES • ADD WINDSHIELD-WASHER FLUID
• TROUBLESHOOT YOUR BRAKES • ADD BRAKE FLUID TO THE CLUTCH MASTER CYLINDER • TROUBLESHOOT DASHBOARD WARNING LIGH
SPARK-PLUG WIRES • DIAGNOSE CAR SMELLS • CLEAN THE OUTSIDE OF YOUR CAR • RESTORE YOUR CAR'S SHINE • WASH THE INTERIO

173 Loosen a Rusty Nut or Bolt

A nut or bolt that's frozen in place is bad enough, but three things are even worse: damaging the corners of a bolt or nut so they end up rounded and hard to turn, breaking off a bolt while attempting to free it, and smashing your knuckles. Here's how to get it unstuck safely.

Steps

1 Heat the connection with a propane torch if you can do so without any risk of damage or fire. It helps draw penetrating oil into the threads (see step 2).

2 Apply a liberal amount of penetrating oil in and around the joint, then wait … and wait … and wait. It can take anywhere from 10 minutes to several hours to loosen the joint.

3 Strike the head of the bolt or nut with a cold chisel to shock the connection.

4 Apply an open-ended wrench or socket of the *proper size,* and rap its handle sharply with a rubber or wood mallet.

What You'll Need

- Propane torch
- Penetrating oil
- Cold chisel
- Open-ended wrench or socket
- Rubber or wood mallet
- Work gloves

Warning

Wear heavy work gloves and use heat, lubricant, shock and leverage rather than uncontrolled brute force.

174 Troubleshoot Low Water Pressure

Low water pressure can make all sorts of little tasks, from taking a shower to washing the dishes, less efficient (not to mention less pleasant). Inadequate pressure at a faucet may result from clogs and corrosion in pipes and in-line devices, or from low water volume or delivery pressure. Only after determining the cause can you and your plumber evaluate the solutions. Here's a diagnostic guide.

Steps

1 If the problem is limited to a fixture, try unscrewing any in-line device, such as a faucet aerator or showerhead, by hand or with pliers, and rinsing off or replacing clogged or corroded screens and parts on an in-line device such as a faucet aerator or showerhead.

2 If the problem is that the supply lines feeding a branch (say, in an addition) are too small, increase their pipe size.

3 If the problem is inadequate flow to the entire house, as might occur when you add new fixtures to an existing system, increase the size of the main supply pipe from the water meter to the house.

4 If the problem is inadequate pressure—for example, at the end of a municipal system or from a well located downhill—install a booster pump.

What You'll Need

- Tools as required for disassembly and replacement of parts

Tips

Soak showerheads in a vinegar-and-water solution to dissolve mineral deposits.

When you install an irrigation system that includes backflow prevention in an existing home, you may see a significant loss of water pressure.

Water pipes made of galvanized steel, found in some very old homes, become clogged over time. Replacement is the only effective solution.

175 Fix Leaking Pipes

When a pipe springs a leak, the situation can get out of control fast. You don't want spraying water to wreak havoc and lead to huge repair bills. Here are quick fixes to control the damage and keep your water running while you're arranging for a proper repair.

Steps

1 Turn off the water at the main valve.

2 Open the faucets on the water line to relieve pressure. For all but clamp-type repairs, you must drain water from the pipe by opening the faucets or bleed valves located *below* the leak.

Superfast fixes

1 Wrap a piece of rubber around the leaking joint, then apply a stainless-steel hose clamp (see A). Tighten the clamp with a screwdriver or socket wrench. If you don't have a hose clamp, use another type, such as a C-clamp, to secure the rubber over the leak.

2 Soak water-activated fiberglass-resin tape (sold in a repair kit for just this purpose) in water, wrap it around the leak and smooth it with gloved hands. Allow it to cure as directed before restoring the water.

3 For leaks around fittings, dry the surface, mix two-part epoxy putty and apply it over and around the leak (see B). Allow curing time as directed before restoring the water.

4 For leaks in PVC (polyvinyl chloride) or PB (polybutylene) plastic pipes, use a hacksaw or pipe cutter with a plastic-cutting wheel to cut out a section of pipe long enough to allow you to slip in a compression coupling. Tighten the coupling by hand and snug it with pliers.

What You'll Need

- Rubber sheet
- Stainless-steel hose clamp or C-clamp
- Screwdriver or socket wrench
- Fiberglass-tape repair kit
- Disposable gloves
- Two-part epoxy putty
- Putty knife
- Hacksaw or pipe cutter with plastic cutting wheel
- Compression coupling
- Pliers

Tip

You can't make emergency repairs if you don't have the materials on hand, so make sure you're stocked up.

Warning

Work carefully with hot-water lines to avoid injury or burns.

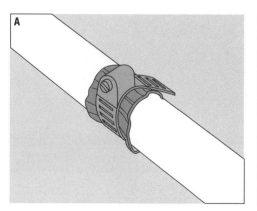

A

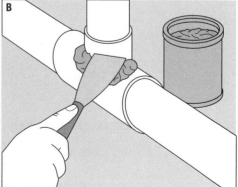

B

176 Stop a Toilet From Running

The sound of running water is audible all the way from your bedroom, and it's keeping you awake. Time to say good-night to toilet troubles. If you see water flowing into the overflow tube when the toilet runs, the problem lies in the fill valve. If water is leaking from the tank into the bowl, the problem is with the flush-valve assembly.

Steps

When water runs into an overflow pipe

1 First, check the float ball. If it is submerged more than halfway in the water, it is waterlogged and can't rise high enough to shut off the fill valve. Replace the ball.

2 Check the guide arm to make sure it's not binding on the inside of the tank or the overflow tube. If it is, straighten the guide arm.

3 If the float ball and guide arm are operating properly, adjust the water level by bending the guide arm or turning the adjustment screws on the fill valve. Flush the toilet and recheck the water level. When it is adjusted correctly, the water level will be even with the fill line on the tank or overflow tube (see 180 Fix Flushing Problems).

4 Service or replace the fill valve. Turn off the water supply and flush. Open the fill valve, rinse the parts and replace any worn seals. On plunger types, loosen the thumbscrews to slide out the

What You'll Need

- Replacement parts
- Screwdrivers
- Sponge
- Spud wrench
- Channel-type pliers
- Abrasive pad

Tips

To test whether water is leaking from the tank into the bowl, put a few drops of food coloring into the tank and see if it gets into the bowl.

A worn flapper or ball is the most common cause of tank leakage.

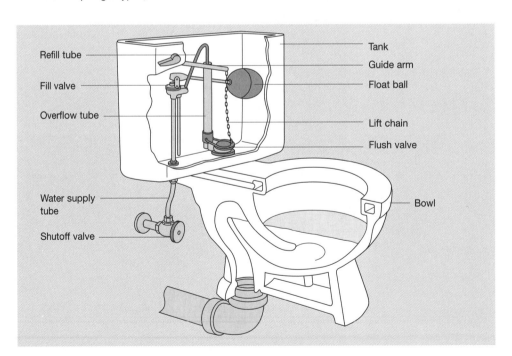

- Refill tube
- Fill valve
- Overflow tube
- Water supply tube
- Shutoff valve
- Tank
- Guide arm
- Float ball
- Lift chain
- Flush valve
- Bowl

float arm and lift out the plunger. On diaphragm types, remove the top screws. On float-cup types, remove the cap and push down on the top assembly as you unscrew it. To replace a fill valve, sponge out the tank, remove the refill tube and then disconnect the water-supply tube's coupling nut and the mounting nut with channel-type pliers. Reverse the procedure to install. Check the manufacturer's instructions to locate the fill valve's critical level, which must be a minimum of 1 inch (2.5 cm) higher than the top of the overflow tube. Most replacement fill valves are adjustable in height.

Avoid the use of blueing or other sanitizing products that contain chlorine, which can damage rubber components (including float balls, flappers and fill-valve seals) and may void the manufacturer's warranty.

When water leaks from the tank into the bowl

1 Clean the valve seat with an abrasive pad and the flapper or ball with a sponge. To replace a worn flapper, lift it off the lugs and hook on a new one.

2 To replace a valve seat (the large opening between the tank and bowl), first disconnect the water supply and use a screwdriver and pliers to remove the bolts that secure the tank to the bowl.

3 Turn the tank over to remove the spud washer. Use a spud wrench to remove the locking nut on the flush valve.

4 Reverse the procedure to install new parts and to reinstall the tank and water supply.

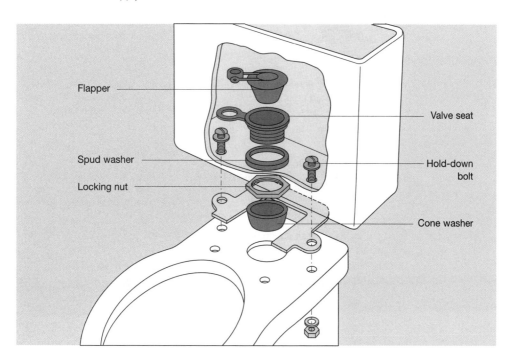

Flapper

Valve seat

Spud washer

Hold-down bolt

Locking nut

Cone washer

177 Fix a Leaky Toilet Tank

Unattended toilet-tank leaks can damage flooring and subflooring, and in more severe cases even the ceilings and framing below, so avoid procrastination when faced with this problem. If the problem is excessive condensation on the tank, see 179 Stop Toilet-Tank Sweating.

Steps

1 First, tighten all connections. If the leak persists, determine the leak's source by drying everything with a towel, then looking and feeling for water.

For leaks at the fill valve

1 Turn off the water supply to the toilet, flush to drain the tank and sponge out any remaining water.

2 Use a wrench to disconnect the supply-tube coupling nut and remove the fill valve's mounting nut (see illustration in 176 Stop a Toilet From Running).

3 Lift out the fill valve to clean the gasket and washer. If either is damaged or dried out, replace it.

4 Reseat the valve, carefully centering it in the hole and holding it vertical as you tighten the mounting nut about a half turn past the point of full contact.

5 Reinstall the water-supply tube and turn on the water to test it. If necessary, tighten the mounting nut a little more.

For leaks at the flush valve

1 Drain the tank and supply-tube coupling as described in step 1, above. Remove the tank's mounting bolts using a large standard screwdriver on the bolt and either a socket wrench or channel-type pliers on the nut (see illustration in 176 Stop a Toilet From Running). Lift off the tank.

2 With the tank upside down, pull or twist off the rubber spud washer and use a spud wrench to unscrew the large locking nut from the flush valve.

3 Lay the tank on its side and remove the flush valve.

4 Remove the beveled cone washer from the flush valve. Clean it and the spud washer with a soapy sponge (or replace them if they are in poor condition).

5 Reverse the procedure to reinstall the tank. Make sure the beveled side of the cone washer is facing the tank's inside and the beveled side of the spud washer is facing the bowl.

What You'll Need

- Towel
- Large sponge
- Adjustable wrench
- Replacement parts
- Large standard screwdriver
- Socket wrench or channel-type pliers
- Spud wrench

Tips

Leaks that appear to come from either the fill valve or the flush valve may actually be passing through hairline tank cracks at those locations. If so, you need to replace the tank or possibly the entire toilet.

When you remove the tank to work on it, place it on a bath mat or similar padding to protect both the flooring and the tank.

When you reinstall the tank, it's helpful to have someone hold it level and plumb as you tighten the bolts.

Warning

Don't overtighten the mounting bolts on the tank. You could crack the porcelain.

178 Fix a Stopped-Up Toilet

Most clogs result from an excess of tissue—a problem that's easily resolved. Partial clogs usually require a closet auger. If the problem is in the drain line and out of reach, you may need a longer snake or a professional drain-line service.

Steps

For tissue clogs

1 Fill a bucket or other container with about 2 gallons (8 l) of water. Pour it all at once into the center of the bowl. In most cases, this will take care of the problem.

2 If that fails, position a plunger over the opening so it makes the best seal possible. Move the plunger up and down vigorously, using very short strokes so it maintains contact with the bowl.

For stubborn clogs or other obstacles

1 Use a closet auger to reach and pull out clogs that lie beyond the trapway, to remove an obstacle other than excessive tissue, or to clear a clog that remains after you've tried the methods above.

2 Insert the auger into the opening at the bottom of the bowl and push it in slowly until you feel soft resistance. Keep pushing, but start turning the handle clockwise to screw the end into the clog (see below). Keep turning as you draw the clog back into the bowl.

3 Remove or break up the clog and flush the toilet to test it.

What You'll Need

- Bucket
- Plunger
- Closet auger

Tips

If the bowl is near overflowing, wait until the water level goes down before using the water bucket or plunger method.

Plungers are fine for clearing clogs caused by tissues. If another foreign object is the problem, the plunger may just push the clog out of reach but not out of the drain. Your best bet in this case is to use an auger.

Oval plungers generally make a better seal than bell-shaped ones.

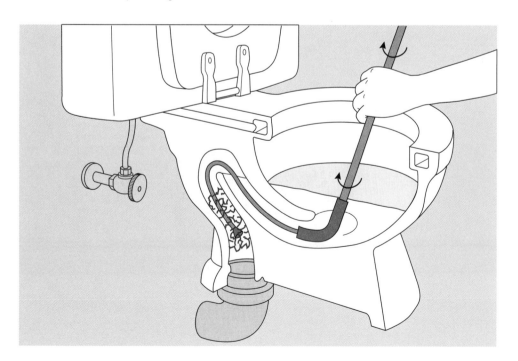

179 Stop Toilet-Tank Sweating

Condensation on a toilet can be so severe that you may think it's sprung a leak, and the water can seep through the floor and cause damage. First try insulating the tank. If that doesn't work (or if insulation won't fit), have your plumber install a tempering valve and turn it on during humid months.

Steps

Insulate the tank

1 Drain the tank. Turn off the water at the shutoff valve, remove the tank cover, flush the toilet and hold open the tank stopper or flapper to drain as much water as possible. Use a large sponge to remove any remaining water, and dry the tank with a towel.

2 Use a tape measure to get the dimensions of the tank walls, then use a utility knife to cut appropriate-size sections of foam from a tank-insulating kit. Test-fit the sections and spread adhesive on the tank walls to adhere the foam as directed (see illustration).

Install a tempering valve

1 Have your plumber install a tempering (mixing) valve between the cold-water pipe and the shutoff, and extend a hot-water line from under a sink to the valve. Install a separate shutoff on the hot-water line to the tempering valve so you can turn it off when it's not needed.

What You'll Need

- Large sponge
- Towel
- Tank-insulating kit (adhesive included)
- Tape measure
- Utility knife
- Tempering valve, tubing, related fittings, supplies and tools

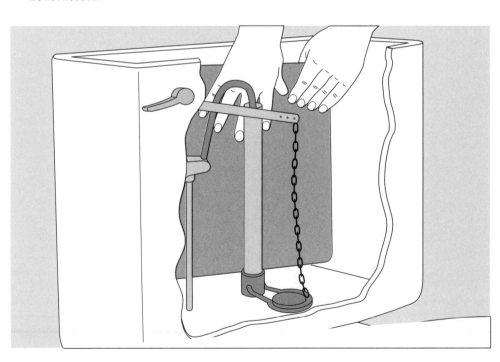

180 Fix Flushing Problems

Water-saving toilets tend to experience flushing problems. The following simple service should improve performance. If it doesn't work, the vent pipe may be obstructed (see 181 Clear a Clogged Plumbing Vent).

Steps

1 Fully open the water supply's shutoff valve to assure that there is adequate water pressure and volume.

2 Clear any obstruction in the toilet trapway. Push a closet auger into the bowl opening until you feel an obstruction. Turn clockwise to screw the auger into the obstruction and draw it out.

3 Use a mirror to inspect the holes on the rim's underside during a flush. Clear any clogged holes with a piece of copper wire.

4 Adjust the water level until it's at the water line marked on the tank or overflow tube. Flush to test. To adjust water levels on plunger- or diaphragm-type fill valves with a float ball, either turn the adjustment screws on those models that have them or use both hands to bend the arm—down to lower the water level, up to raise it. For floatless models, turn the adjustment screw about a half turn at a time. For float-cup fill valves, pinch the spring clip to raise or lower the float.

What You'll Need

- Closet auger
- Small mirror and copper wire
- Screwdriver

Tips

Wear rubber gloves to protect your hands.

At the proper height, the water level should be no more than ½ inch (12 mm) below the top of the overflow tube. If the tube's too long, cut it with a hacksaw. Some tubes unscrew. If yours doesn't, remove the flush valve to make the cut.

181 Clear a Clogged Plumbing Vent

If your plumbing fixtures drain slowly, the problem may be a clogged vent. This happens when vents are improperly located and when birds or animals deposit debris in the vent where it exits the roof.

Steps

1 Set up an extension ladder to access the roof below the vent. Typically the vent consists of a metal or plastic pipe 3 to 4 inches (7.5 to 10 cm) in diameter that extends about 1 to 2 feet (30 to 60 cm) above the roof surface, usually above a bathroom.

2 Install a roof ladder so you can work next to the vent. This single ladder hooks over the ridge and extends to the access ladder, allowing you to work safely and prevent damaging the roof.

3 Shine a bright light down the vent pipe to look for leaves, nesting materials or other debris you may be able to remove from above.

4 Put a garden hose into the vent and turn on the water. Listen for water backing up and a sudden whoosh when the weight of the water forces the clog into and down the drain. Or feed the hose down into the vent as you would a plumber's snake to dislodge a clog that's not solid enough to dam water.

What You'll Need

- Extension ladder
- Roof ladder
- Bright flashlight
- Garden hose and nozzle

Warning

Never walk on a wet or steeply pitched roof or on any roof surface that seems unsafe to you.

Tie a safety line to a solid anchor point on the opposite side and extend it over the ridge and along the ladder.

182 Fix a Faucet

Drip, drip, drip . . . when you've had enough of that repetitive sound, it's time to fix a leaky faucet. And you'll save money on your water bill. Today's sinks commonly use one of the faucet types shown below. Dual-handled faucets utilize either a traditional compression valve, which seals by pressing a washer against a valve seat, or more reliable stem assemblies with ceramic or stainless-steel discs that slide over the inlet opening. Single-handle faucets have ball, cartridge or ceramic-disc valves.

Steps

1 Before removing any parts other than a handle, turn off the water with the shutoff valves under the sink, or the branch lines or main shutoffs (hot and cold) for a tub faucet. Then open the faucet to drain it.

2 If you don't have an exploded parts diagram for your faucet, obtain one from the manufacturer (online, by fax or by mail). If you're using a repair kit, follow its instructions carefully. Otherwise, disassemble the faucet to determine its type, laying out the parts in the exact order of removal.

3 After a repair, always turn the faucet to the On position and slowly open both shutoff valves. When the water is flowing without air, turn off the faucet.

What You'll Need

- Replacement kit or parts
- Nail file or other thin blade
- Tape-padded screwdriver
- Handle puller
- Adjustable wrench
- Open-ended wrench or locking pliers
- Utility knife
- Mild abrasive pad
- Seat wrench
- Pipe-joint compound
- Seat-dressing tool
- Repair-kit wrench
- Tape-padded channel-type pliers
- Old toothbrush

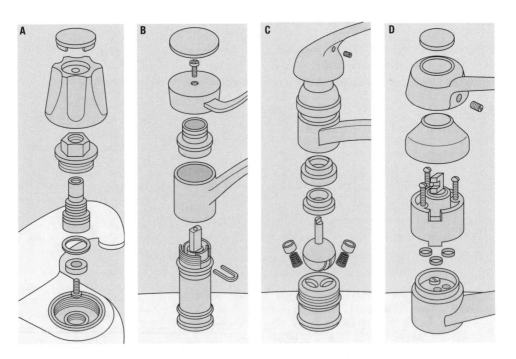

Fixing a compression faucet (see A)

1 To stop a spout drip or handle leak, pry off the cap from the faucet's top with a nail file or other thin blade to access and remove the handle screw and handle.

2 If the handle is stuck and you can't pry it off with a large tape-padded screwdriver, use a handle puller. This tool's arms hook under the handle and pull it up as you turn the threaded shaft down onto the top of the faucet spindle.

3 To stop a handle leak, turn on the water and try tightening the packing nut with an adjustable wrench. If that fails, shut off the water and continue to the next step.

4 Remove the packing nut with an open-ended wrench of the correct size or with locking pliers. Cut off the O-ring around the base of the spindle with a utility knife and roll on a new one. Or in some models, unscrew the threaded spindle from the packing nut, then replace the pack string that's wound clockwise around the spindle just below the packing nut.

5 To repair a spout drip, remove the stem screw and washer from the bottom of the stem assembly and replace the washer. Insert a mild abrasive pad into the open valve and rub back and forth to clean the valve seat. Also stick your finger into the open valve to feel for any rough edges indicating damage.

6 If a removable seat is damaged or corroded, replace it. Insert a seat wrench into the hole to unscrew it (turn counterclockwise). Coat the threads of the new seat with pipe-joint compound before screwing it in.

7 Resurface a damaged nonremovable seat with a seat-dressing tool, which threads into the valve. As you turn the T-handle shaft, a cutter head resurfaces the seat.

Repairing a cartridge faucet (see B)

1 To stop a spout drip or a leak at the base of the faucet, first pry off the cap on top of the faucet with a nail file to access and remove the handle screw. Lift off the handle.

2 If it's a leak at the faucet base, next remove the retainer ring with channel-type pliers and wiggle the spout up and off the faucet body. Cut off the O-rings and roll on identical replacements.

3 If it's a spout drip, look on the outside of the faucet for a retainer clip that holds the cartridge in place and pull it off. Or with some types, turn a nut counterclockwise with an adjustable wrench or channel-type pliers and remove it.

Tips

Close the sink stopper to prevent parts from falling down the drain, and protect the sink and countertops with an old towel.

Pad the jaws of the wrench with plastic tape to avoid marring the faucet's finish.

Many leading manufacturers offer exploded diagrams to aid in repairing or replacing parts for all faucets, available online or by fax or mail.

The new washer may stop a leak in a compression faucet for only a short time if you fail to resurface a damaged valve seat.

(continued on next page)

4 Grasp the cartridge with pliers and pull it straight out. Cut off the O-rings and roll on identical replacements.

5 Reassemble the faucet and test. If it still drips, replace the cartridge.

6 To replace a worn cartridge, first note its orientation. The most common type has a flat side that faces front. If you fail to install the new one the same way, you'll reverse the hot and cold orientation. Reinstall the retainer clip snugly in its slot.

7 Press the spout back on and screw on the retaining ring by hand, then snug it with a wrench. Reinstall the handle and snap on the index cap.

Fixing a ball faucet (see C)

1 If water leaks at the handle, leave the water on and tighten the adjusting ring. Use a provided repair-kit wrench or tape-padded channel-type pliers.

2 If the leak persists, turn off the water and remove the handle setscrew and handle. Remove the adjusting ring and replace the plastic or ceramic cam and the seal between it and the ball.

3 To stop spout drips, lift out the ball, remove the rubber inlet seals and springs, and clean the ball and inlet openings. Install new seals and springs, and reposition the ball so its slot fits over an aligning pin between the water inlets.

4 To stop leaks at the base of the spout, lift off the spout to replace the O-rings around the faucet body. Use a utility knife to cut off the old ones; clean the faucet body before you roll on identical replacements.

Fixing a ceramic-disc faucet (see D)

1 If a faucet with a ceramic-disc valve leaks, it's usually because of dirty seals. Disassemble it for cleaning. Remove the handle setscrew's cap, the setscrew and the handle. Lift off the cap and remove the screws that secure the cylinder below it. Lift out the cylinder and turn it over to pull out the neoprene seals carefully.

2 Clean the cylinder, the water-inlet openings in the cartridge, and the faucet body and neoprene seals with an old, soft toothbrush or a mild abrasive pad under running water.

3 Reassemble and test. If the leak persists, contact the manufacturer for warranty information before purchasing a replacement cartridge and seals.

Tips (continued)

Apply penetrating oil to stubborn parts. Trying to remove a part with force alone can cause injury or damage.

With a valve open, turn the water back on just enough to flush out any dirt that might cause a leak.

To prevent damage to the O-rings, lubricate them with heatproof grease.

183 Fix a Stopper That Doesn't Seal

A minor adjustment and a few minutes of your time are all it takes to make a tub or sink stopper work properly. See 184 Clear a Clogged Sink or Tub for more illustrations.

Steps

Adjust a pop-up tub drain (see A)

1 Raise the lever and pull the stopper out of the drain opening.

2 If the stopper itself is adjustable, turn the stopper head clockwise and reinsert it for a test. If it won't seal when turned in fully, unscrew it halfway and proceed to the next step.

3 For nonadjustable stoppers, remove the cover-plate screws and lift out the trip-lever assembly. Use a wrench or pliers to loosen the locknut on the threaded lift rod and turn the lift rod clockwise three to four times. Tighten the locknut before you reinstall the trip-lever assembly and stopper for a test.

Adjust a plunger tub drain (see B)

1 Remove the cover-plate screws and lift out the plunger assembly.

2 Loosen the locknut on the threaded lift rod and turn the rod clockwise three to four times. Tighten the locknut before you reinstall the plunger assembly for a test.

Adjust a pop-up sink stopper

1 If a sink won't hold water, look up behind the sink (with a flashlight if needed) to identify the following parts: a pivot rod that connects to the back of the drain pipe, a perforated strap (a clevis), and a screw that locks the strap onto the stopper rod. See illustration C in 184 Clear a Clogged Sink or Tub.

2 To make a stopper seal, hold the stopper rod with one hand (or have a helper hold it down from above). Loosen the clevis screw with pliers and slide the clevis up the rod a little. Tighten the screw and test the seal.

What You'll Need

- Screwdriver
- Wrench
- Pliers
- Flashlight

Tips

Place an old towel on the floor of the tub before you remove a trip-lever or plunger assembly. This protects the tub from accidental damage and prevents the loss of a screw down the drain.

While you have the cover plate off, inspect the foam gasket. If it is dried out, remove the screws that secure the drain assembly to the tub, then pull out the old gasket and replace it.

Warning

Wear goggles when adjusting a sink stopper that's overhead.

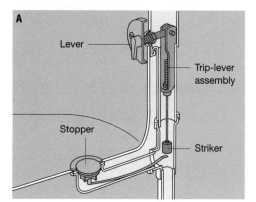

A
Lever — Trip-lever assembly
Stopper — Striker

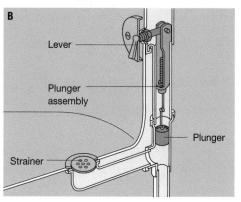

B
Lever — Plunger assembly
Strainer — Plunger

184 Clear a Clogged Sink or Tub

Clogs usually build slowly, so if you act fast you'll find the clog just inches away.

Steps

Try this first

1 If the clog is not right at the tub or sink stopper, or if you have a plunger-type drain system, pour a large pot full of boiling water into the tub or sink to melt away a soap or hair clog.

Clearing a tub clog

1 Take out the screws that secure the drain assembly's cover plate and lift out the assembly. Remove any hair clogs and clean the mechanism with an old toothbrush or a soft wire brush, then lubricate it with heatproof grease.

2 If the clog is in the drain line, use a hand auger, which is better than a plunger because it pulls the clog out rather than pushing it down the drain. Push the cable into the overflow drain's opening, past the bend at the top of the pipe, until you feel soft resistance. Then screw the auger into the clog and try to pull it out.

3 If you must use a plunger, plug the overflow opening with a wet rag so the force of the plunger is directed at the clog. Put some water in the tub and plunge away. Flush the cleared line with boiling water.

Clearing a sink clog

1 Place a dishpan under the trap to catch spilled water. If the trap is the removable type, loosen the two couplings with channel-type pliers (see A). Slide the trap off, dumping the water into the dishpan. Clean it with a bottle brush (see B).

2 If the trap is welded or glued and has a clean-out plug at the bottom, remove the plug with pliers and pull out the clog.

What You'll Need

- Large cooking pot
- Screwdriver
- Old toothbrush or soft wire brush
- Heatproof grease
- Hand auger
- Plunger
- Rag
- Dishpan
- Channel-type pliers
- Bottle brush
- Replacement trap

Tips

Wear rubber gloves when handling clog materials.

If possible, try to remove the clog rather than force it down the drain, where it will be more difficult to access. Remove accessible clogs before plunging, and screw out resistant clogs with an auger.

If all else fails, try using drain-clearing chemicals according to the manufacturer's instructions.

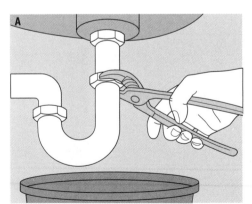

3 If a nonremovable trap doesn't have clean-outs, insert an auger through the drain and draw out the clog. To access the drain, remove the stopper. Lift it out, or turn it 90 degrees and then lift. With other models, remove the drain stopper's pivot rod, which screws into the back of the tailpipe drain just below the sink.

4 If the clog appears to extend into the drain line, insert the auger into the drain line or trap clean-out. Push it past any pipe bends until you feel soft resistance. Screw the auger into the clog and keep turning as you pull it out.

5 Flush the line with boiling water.

Using a plunger

1 To plunge a sink, remove the stopper as directed in step 3, above.

2 If the sink has an overflow opening, stuff a wet rag into the opening so the force of the plunger is directed at the clog.

3 Position the plunger over the opening. Add a few inches of water, then plunge up and down vigorously, but with short strokes so you maintain contact with the basin.

4 To plunge a shower drain, remove the strainer and any visible clogs. Then cover the opening, add water and plug as for a sink.

5 To clear a tub clog, lift out the stopper, if there is one, and stuff a wet rag into the overflow opening in the bottom of the drain assembly's cover plate. Then position the plunger, add water and plunge as described in step 3.

Lay a towel down in the tub to protect it from dropped tools and metal parts, and to prevent anything from going down the drain.

Do not try to auger a drain line through the drain hole.

If the foam gasket between the back side of the tub and the fitting at the top of the drain assembly is dry or disintegrating, replace it. Remove the two screws that secure the drain to the tub so you can pull out the old gasket and slip in the new one.

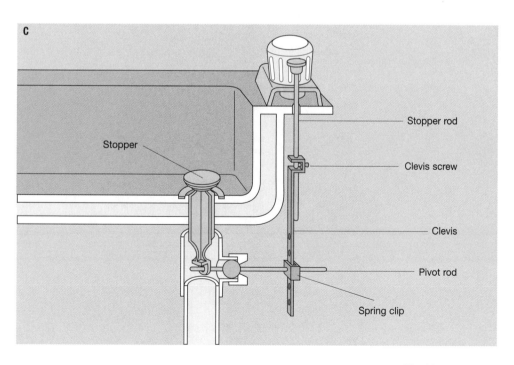

C
Stopper rod
Stopper
Clevis screw
Clevis
Pivot rod
Spring clip

Plumbing & Electrical

185 Repair a Tub-and-Shower Valve

You repair a two-handled shower valve just as you would a compression or cartridge faucet in a sink (see 182 Fix a Faucet), except that you might need a deep socket wrench to remove a valve stem that's recessed in the wall. The repairs for ball and disc faucets also work for those types of shower valves. Here's how to fix a single-handle, cartridge-style tub-and-shower valve.

Steps

Access the valve

1 Pop off the valve cap with the point of a nail file or a similar tool to expose the handle screw. Remove the screw and pull off the handle.

2 To remove a lever handle, look for a setscrew (a small cap may conceal it as well) and loosen it (it may have a hex or a slotted head).

3 Remove the escutcheon (cover plate). Depending on the model, you may need to remove other parts between the handle and the valve body. Lay out the parts in order of removal or label them so you can replace them the same way.

4 If the valve has stop-check valves—large plugs with slotted heads in T-fittings on the hot and cold feeds that lead to the valve—close these by turning them clockwise. If the valve does not have shutoffs or if they're inaccessible, shut off the hot and cold water to this branch or to the entire house if necessary.

What You'll Need

- Nail file or other pointed tool
- Screwdriver(s)
- Allen (hex) wrench
- Adjustable or channel-type wrench
- Locking pliers
- Rag
- Old toothbrush
- Cartridge repair kit

Tips

Cover the drain opening to prevent accidental loss of any small parts you drop.

Cover the floor of the tub or shower to protect it against damage from a dropped tool.

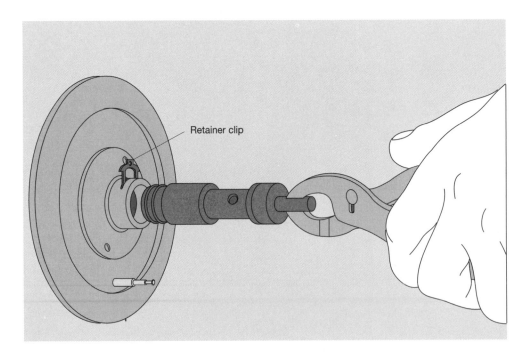

Retainer clip

Remove, repair or replace cartridge parts

1 Pull off the U-shaped retainer clip (see illustration, opposite page). Or use an adjustable or channel-type wrench to remove the nut that locks the cartridge into the valve body.

2 Grasp the cartridge with locking pliers or a similar tool and pull it straight out (see illustration, opposite page).

3 Open a water line momentarily to flush out any dirt in the valve body that might cause a leak. Stuff a dry rag under and around the valve to keep water out of the wall opening.

4 Clean the cartridge with an old, soft toothbrush and replace the O-ring at the base of the stem. Reinstall to test.

5 If the problem persists, purchase a cartridge repair kit, which will include the cartridge, a full set of O-rings and grease. Install it according to the manufacturer's instructions.

186 Repair Chipped Fixtures

Using materials you probably have around your house, you can do a pretty good job of disguising chips in bath and kitchen fixtures.

Steps

To repair a large chip

1 Test-fit any broken piece. If you have the entire piece, clean the surfaces you'll be mating. Dry them with a hair dryer. Clean them again with denatured alcohol or nail-polish remover.

2 Mix and apply two-part 5-minute epoxy adhesive to the fixture and carefully press the chip into place. Scrape off any excess with a single-edge razor before it sets. Apply masking tape if necessary to hold it in place, but don't disturb its alignment.

To fill and color a small chip

1 Clean and dry the surface with a hair dryer, and clean it again with denatured alcohol. Mask the area immediately around the damaged area with painter's masking tape. Press down firmly.

2 Test-mix very small quantities of oil-based hobby paint to create a color that matches the fixture. When you have a good match, mix a slow-acting, two-part clear epoxy on a clean surface with a toothpick, and stir in the paint to color the epoxy.

3 Use a putty knife to apply and smooth the colored resin to fill the hole until it's level with the surrounding area. After 48 hours, you can remove the masking tape and use the fixture.

What You'll Need

- Cleaning supplies
- Hair dryer
- Denatured alcohol or nail-polish remover
- Two-part 5-minute epoxy adhesive
- Single-edge razor
- Painter's masking tape
- Oil-based hobby paint
- Two-part clear epoxy
- Toothpick
- Putty knife

Tip

If you have most but not all of a large chip, glue it back in using colored epoxy, which will fill any gaps.

Warning

Ventilate the area well when using solvents and epoxy.

187 Quiet Noisy Pipes

The squeaking and banging you're hearing probably results from too loose or tight a fit as your pipes pass over or through wood framing. This is especially likely for heating and hot-water pipes. When shutting a faucet or other valve suddenly stops fast-flowing water, the shock (called water hammer) creates a loud bang.

Steps

For pipes that contact wood framing

1 Water pressure in excess of 50 lbs. per square inch (psi), or 3.5 kg per square cm, can cause noisy pipes. Test for excessive pressure by attaching a pressure gauge to an outdoor faucet. Some gauges mark the high point reached over any period of time. Control excessive pressure by having a pressure regulator installed on your water system.

2 Secure loose pipes to framing with straps or hangers as needed to prevent movement.

3 Remove any pipes that fit tightly into holes drilled through framing members. Enlarge the holes (usually you do so with a drill bit larger than the one originally used), then reconnect the pipes.

4 Cushion copper pipes where they contact framing or framing hardware. Cut short lengths of foam pipe insulation and remove any straps or hangers so you can wrap the insulation around the pipe (you may need a nail puller). Reinstall the straps or hangers with a hammer or other appropriate tool.

For a loud water hammer

1 The air-cushioning chambers that codes require for most fixtures and appliances, typically a short length of capped pipe that extends up from the water pipe, is probably waterlogged (filled with water rather than air). To restore air to the chambers, shut off the water main, open the faucets and drain both hot and cold water from the system. Turn the water back on, closing faucets as soon as water is flowing without air.

2 If any plumbing fixture or washing machine lacks an air chamber, drain the water lines to install one on the hot and cold lines. Ideally, you should install the air chamber immediately inside the wall behind the fixture or machine. If you must cut out drywall, see 132 Repair Minor Drywall Damage.

3 Cut out a short section of pipe, as close as possible to the faucet, and install a T-fitting, a nipple (a very short length of pipe) and a reducer fitting that will allow you to connect a 1-foot (30-cm) length of pipe larger than the supply pipe. Install a cap fitting to complete the air chamber.

What You'll Need

- Pressure gauge
- Straps or hangers
- Drill and drill bits
- Foam pipe insulation
- Hammer
- Nail puller
- Pipe cutter
- Plumbing tools, pipe and fittings or commercial air chamber, solder or fittings appropriate for pipe system

Tips

Excessive water pressure can damage any appliance that connects to a water line.

Special water-cushioning devices that contain air bladders are superior to pipe chambers because they won't become waterlogged.

Warning

Don't ignore a banging water hammer. It can do considerable damage to your home's hot and cold pipe system.

188 Defrost Your Pipes

Burst pipes are bad news for your home and everything it contains. Both metal and plastic water pipes may burst if you allow the water within them to freeze. When your pipes freeze, act fast and chances are you won't need to call a plumber—or your insurance agent.

Steps

Thawing house water lines

1 To relieve any pressure and determine how extensive the problem is, open all faucets. If only one fixture is not working, you can assume that the pipe is frozen somewhere between that fixture and the line that leads to others. Locate where uninsulated water lines pass through an uninsulated space. Examine pipes adjacent to uninsulated foundation walls or in or adjacent to exterior walls, especially within sink and vanity cabinets, where the closed doors partially block room heat.

2 If the frozen pipe is a hot-water line, open a hot-water faucet. The moving water may thaw the pipes. If it is a cold-water line, open a cold-water faucet. If it is both or you're not sure, open both the hot and cold faucets. Keep opening faucets until the water flows freely or until you've opened them all.

3 Warm the pipes slowly wherever you have access to them. Work from an open faucet toward the frozen area. Possible approaches include hair dryers, heat lamps, towels soaked in hot water, electric heat tapes wrapped around pipes, and space heaters. If the frozen pipes extend into walls or floors, heating the pipe adjacent to where it enters and exits the wall will eventually thaw the section within the wall. Also turn up the heat in the room.

4 Let the water run for a minute or two. Then turn the faucet(s) off. Look for leaks everywhere you can see. Listen very carefully for hissing sounds where hidden pipes pass through walls or floors.

Dealing with frozen heating pipes

1 Frozen hydronic (hot-water) heating pipes present problems best addressed by a plumber. Your best bet in the meantime is to turn off the heating system's water supply, which will prevent a major flood in the event that a burst pipe thaws. Do not turn off the boiler if you have more than one heating zone on your thermostat, since another zone may be working.

2 Relieve any excess pressure in the system. Follow the same procedure you would to drain a waterlogged expansion tank: Shut the valve to the expansion tank. Attach a garden hose to the hose bib on the tank and extend the other end to a drain. Open the hose bib to drain the tank. Then close the hose bib and open the valve to the tank.

What You'll Need

- Heat sources
- Garden hose
- Patience

Tips

To limit possible flooding from a frozen pipe that may already be broken, locate the shutoff for the affected branch or shut off the water main (located where the water pipe enters the house from the street or a well).

Once you have resolved the problem, take steps to prevent reoccurrence: Always maintain heat at no less than 55°F (13°C); open vanity and sink-cabinet doors on exceptionally cold nights; insulate pipes that pass through unheated areas, especially those adjacent to foundation walls; shut interior valves to outside hose bibs and open the outside faucet; replace standard hose bibs with freeze-proof models.

Warning

Never use an ungrounded electrical device near metal pipes or water, or while standing on a concrete floor.

Avoid using torches or heat guns, which create a risk of fire. Too much heat can also generate steam, which in turn can increase pressure inside the pipe and cause it to burst.

189 Diagnose Sump Pump Problems

Sump pumps usually purr along for years without a glitch. When problems do occur, you can generally identify and repair them easily if you know what to look for (see chart, opposite page). The following steps describe how to handle the two most common problems.

Steps

Install or replace a check valve

1 To add a check valve to a line that doesn't have one, purchase a valve no smaller in diameter than the existing drain pipe and any required couplings or adapters. Use a hacksaw or pipe cutter to cut out a section of pipe to accommodate them. Deburr the cut edges with a metal file or utility knife. Go to step 3.

2 To remove a check valve secured with a flexible coupling or adapter, loosen the steel strap with a flathead screwdriver and twist it off. If it is welded or glued together, cut the pipe with a hacksaw. If the valve was incorrectly installed and you need to reverse it, leave about 2 inches (5 cm) of pipe on each end of the valve. Otherwise cut close to the valve and discard it.

3 To install a new valve, slide one flexible coupling over the pipe that connects to the pump and another over the pipe that connects to the drain. Insert the valve with the direction-of-flow arrow facing away from the pump. To reinstall a valve after reversing its direction of flow, slide the coupling over the pipe stubs on the valve and tighten the straps.

What You'll Need

- Check valve and couplings or adapters
- Hacksaw or pipe cutter
- Metal file or utility knife
- Flathead screwdriver
- Wrench

Warning

Always unplug a pump before cleaning or working on it or making adjustments.

Put on rubber boots if you must walk on a wet floor to unplug the pump.

Be sure that the pump is on its own grounded 15-A circuit and that the plug's grounding prong is intact.

A sump-pit cover is recommended for safety.

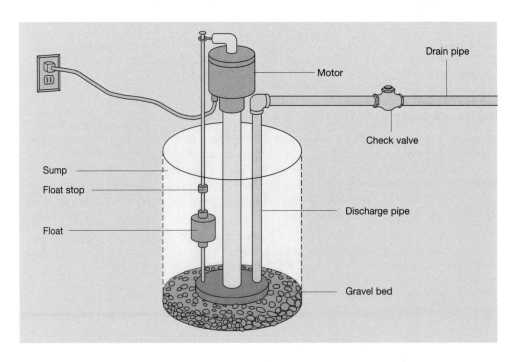

Clean a screen and free a jammed impeller

1 Unplug and disconnect the pump from the discharge piping, then lift it out of the sump.

2 Remove the housing to access the screen and impeller; typically it snaps or bolts into place, so you may need a wrench. Remove any debris, rinse the screen and carefully pry out any obstacle jamming the impeller. Clean the sump pit before reinstalling pump.

PROBLEM	POSSIBLE CAUSES	SOLUTIONS
Pump does not start or run	Blown fuse or tripped breaker	If blown, replace with proper size fuse or reset breaker.
	Faulty GFCI receptacle	Test GFCI (ground fault circuit interrupter) receptacle.
	Poor connection at switch or damaged cord	Tighten connection or replace damaged cord.
	Low line voltage	If voltage is under 108 volts, check wiring size.
Pump starts but trips breaker or blows fuse	Defective float switch	Test and replace float switch.
	Impeller bound	If impeller will not turn, remove housing and remove blockage.
	Float movement possibly obstructed	Make sure float moves freely up and down float rod.
Pump operates but does not deliver water or delivers too little water	Water level too low	Add water to test.
	Defective motor windings	Contact factory.
	Undersize fuse or breaker	Have electrician install correct breaker.
	Other appliances on circuit	Rewire to give pump its own circuit.
	Inadequate wiring or extension cord	Check wiring size and do not use extension cord.
	Defective motor or switch	Contact factory for repair or replacement.
	Plugged impeller or screen	Remove pump and clean impeller or screen.
	Check valve faulty or installed backward	Reverse position of check valve.
	Airlocked pump	If pump has weep hole between pump and check valve, make sure it is clear. If pump has no weep hole, refer to manual or contact company to determine if one is required; if so, drill one of 3/16-inch (5-mm) diameter.
	Piping too small	Increase outlet pipes so they're equal to or one size greater than discharge opening.

190 Troubleshoot Electrical Problems

All those electrical devices in your house require an unbroken supply of power from your utility company. Here are the basic tests you may need to conduct if you run into an interruption in power or an appliance stops working.

Steps

Reset a circuit breaker

1 When a circuit breaker trips, it moves about midway between the full-on and full-off positions, and it will move back and forth a little when you wiggle it.

2 To reset a tripped breaker, push it to the full-off position (opposite all the other breakers in its column), then to the full-on position, and then let go immediately. If it trips again or does not stay in the On position, push it to the full-off position and tape it over until you've resolved whatever's causing it to trip.

Test a live receptacle

1 Plug the two probes of a continuity tester into the two vertical slots. If there is power, the tester will glow. Test both halves. Some receptacles are powered by two separate circuits.

2 Alternatively, plug a neon tester into the receptacle. It analyzes the wiring, and its lights identify the problem.

Test for power at an open outlet box

1 Shut off power to the circuit at the service panel. Remove the outlet cover and remove the device (a switch or receptacle), or bend out the connected wires and keep the ends apart.

2 Test a device by probing each terminal screw with one lead from a neon tester and probing a metal outlet box or bare grounding wire with the other lead.

3 Test connected wires by removing the wire nut enough to expose bare wire, then probing that wire and either a metal outlet box or the bare grounding wire. Repeat the process for every wire connection.

Test a device for continuity

1 Make sure the wire or device isn't live. Use a neon tester on wiring, or unplug or disconnect a device.

2 Clip one lead onto one terminal of a switch, for example, and probe the other terminal. The tester should light with the switch in the On position and, just as important, should *not* light in the Off position.

What You'll Need

- Tape
- Continuity tester
- Neon tester
- Screwdriver

Tips

Test a continuity tester's battery and bulb by touching the probe and clip together momentarily. The bulb should light.

A circuit breaker may have a red indicator that signals it has been tripped.

Warning

If a breaker tripped due to a tool or machinery overload, make sure you've switched off or unplugged that tool before restoring power.

Never use a continuity tester until you have verified that there's no current in the line.

If you know of or suspect an unresolved problem that has caused the breaker to trip, do not attempt to reset it until you've investigated and corrected the situation.

PROBLEM	POSSIBLE CAUSES	SOLUTIONS
Plugged-in device not working	If device is light fixture, bulb may be out	Replace bulb with working one or test suspect bulb in working lamp.
	Faulty device	Test device in working receptacle. If it works, test for power. If not, inspect the plug, cord, switch, internal wiring connections, fuses, safety shutoff or reset button, other electrical contacts (see 192 Swap a Faulty Light Switch, 195 Fix an Electrical Plug, 196 Replace a Light Fixture, 198 Fix a Lamp, 202 Troubleshoot Holiday Lighting).
	No power at receptacle	Test receptacle with neon tester by inserting probes into two receptacle slots. Light should glow.
Hard-wired device not working	No power coming into outlet	Test for power at problem outlet (see "Test for power at an open outlet box," opposite page); inspect previous (upstream) outlet for faulty or loose connections (only if series wiring); if outlet is only outlet on circuit, see "No power in particular circuit," below.
	Faulty or improper wiring connections within outlet box	Shut power to circuit and access outlet for inspection. Verify that connections are properly made and tight.
	Wall switch off, faulty or has faulty wiring	Make sure wall switch, timer or other control is on; turn power off to inspect connections; remove switch to test continuity (see "Test a device for continuity," opposite page).
	Faulty device	If outlet is powered, unplug device to inspect, as applies, for problems in its switch, internal wiring connections, internal fuses, safety shutoff or reset button, other electrical contacts.
No power in entire house	Off-premises power failure	Contact power company or neighbors.
	Main circuit breaker tripped or fuse blown	At the main service panel, see if main breaker has tripped (see "Reset a circuit breaker," opposite page) or remove and test main fuse (see 191 Replace a Blown Fuse).
No power in particular circuit	Branch circuit breaker tripped or fuse blown	Resolve known cause and reset circuit (see "Reset a circuit breaker," opposite page).
No power in half of duplex receptacle	That half is wall-switched	If there is a switch, verify that it's on and that connections are tight. Test switch with continuity tester.
	Link between two halves removed	Remove receptacle to determine if two silver terminals and two brass terminals are connected.

191 Replace a Blown Fuse

The next time someone turns on the hair dryer, microwave and toaster oven all at once and sends your house's circuits into a tizzy, be prepared. If you live in an older home with electrical circuits protected by fuses, keep replacements on hand.

Steps

Identify and test a blown fuse

1 Open the door to your service panel and examine it with a flashlight to identify the blown fuse. Typically lights are on 15-A circuits. Receptacles may be either 15 A (for 14-gauge wiring) or 20 A (for 12-gauge wiring). A large fixed appliance, such as an electric range or a water heater, should be on its own circuit, protected by fuses as specified by the appliance manufacturer (see the appliance's rating plate for amp requirements). In addition, one or more main fuses protect service lines coming from your power utility.

2 For light and receptacle circuits, look for a break or blackened area visible through the glass of a screw-in plug fuse. If all the fuses look good, identify the fuse according to the circuit label (map) printed on the door or next to each fuse.

3 If the circuits are not mapped, locate the fuse by trial and error: Remove the fuses one at a time and either insert a new fuse to test the circuit, or touch the pointed probe of a continuity tester to the fuse's tip and the clip to its threaded shaft. If the tester does not glow, the fuse is bad.

4 For fuse blocks, which protect an electric stove and the main circuit, pull straight out on the handle, then remove the individual cartridge fuses from the block using a cartridge-fuse puller. Test the fuses with a continuity tester by probing the two ends.

Install a new fuse

1 Screw in a new plug fuse, or install a new cartridge fuse in the fuse block and press the block back in. The replacement should always have the same rating as the original.

2 If all of the circuits have stopped working, remove and test the cartridge fuses in the main fuse block, usually located at the top left (occasionally it's reversed with the stove circuit on the top right). Replace any faulty ones.

Replace a fuse holder

1 More often than not the problem with cartridge fuses is related to loose clips or rivets in the fuse block or fuse box, not the fuse itself. Replace a faulty cartridge or have an electrician make other necessary repairs.

What You'll Need

- Flashlight
- Continuity tester
- Cartridge-fuse puller
- Replacement fuses
- Replacement fuse holders

Tips

Always keep a flashlight handy in case the lights near the circuit panel are not operating. It can be very dangerous to feel around.

Test the tester by touching the probe to the clip to make sure the light glows.

If a fuse element is burned in the middle and the ends are intact, an overloaded circuit is the cause. Remove the appliance from that circuit.

If the element appears to have exploded and has blackened the underside of the glass, a short is at fault. Investigate the cause of the short at the appliance, receptacle or wiring.

Warning

A circuit board with fuses pulled out is dangerous— you run the risk of potentially fatal shock. Use great care and never insert anything but a fuse into the open spaces.

192 Swap a Faulty Light Switch

If a light switch sparks or fails to work, if it makes too much noise or if you just want to change the color or style, swapping an old switch for a new one is easy. Spend the extra money for commercial-grade switches and receptacles. They are safer and last longer. See also 197 Install a New Dimmer.

Steps

1 Switch off power to the circuit at the main service panel.

2 Remove the cover plate over the switch, unscrew the switch from the box and pull it out carefully.

3 Test each terminal with one lead of a neon tester and probe a metal outlet box or bare grounding wire with the other. The tester should not glow.

4 Loosen or remove the screws to disconnect the insulated wires and any bare grounding wire.

5 If the wires are not nicked or damaged, insert them clockwise under the same terminals on the new switch and tighten the terminal screws.

What You'll Need

- Screwdriver
- Neon tester
- New switch

Warning

Often you'll see other wires in the switch box, and they may be live. Normally you can pull out the switch and make the change while keeping well away from these wires. If not, you must test all the wires for power (see 190 Troubleshoot Electrical Problems).

193 Reduce Energy Consumption

The incandescent lightbulb should be a called a "heat bulb," because 90 percent of the electricity we put into it comes out as heat. Light is only the byproduct. Changing to compact fluorescent lamps (CFLs) will save about $70 per bulb. To maximize the benefits and reduce the chance of buying a bulb that won't fit, take the following approach.

Steps

1 Take a lighting inventory of your home. Write down the fixture location, number of bulbs and wattage, size limitations (measured from end to end), control needs such as dimmability or three-way, and any other requirements such as outdoor use.

2 Review lighting manufacturers' catalogs, which are widely available online or by calling toll-free customer-service departments.

3 Write down suitable compact fluorescent lamp substitutes for the fixtures on your inventory list. For the greatest payback, make bulbs used more than 4 hours a day your priority.

4 Shop your list at local sources such as home centers and lighting stores. For your remaining lightbulb needs, search the Internet.

What You'll Need

- Paper and pencil
- Tape measure
- Lighting catalogs

Tip

CFL models now include reflectors, three-ways, globes, dimmables, bug lights, outdoor floods and many other styles. You should be able to replace one-third to one-half the lights in your home.

194 Replace a Receptacle

For safety's sake, you want all the receptacles in your house to stay in perfect working condition. Replacing a receptacle that no longer holds a plug securely, or replacing an ungrounded receptacle with a grounded one, is a relatively easy task.

Steps

Shut off power to the circuit

1 Locate the receptacle's circuit breaker (or its fuse, on older systems).

2 If the panel doesn't have a circuit map, identify the circuit by plugging a lamp or radio into the receptacle and turning off 15-A or 20-A breakers or fuses one by one until the power at the receptacle goes off.

3 Remove the cover plate and the two screws that secure the receptacle to the outlet box.

4 Identify what type of receptacle and cabling you have. In most cases, one cable goes into the box and one comes out. You'll find the receptacle at the end of the line if only one cable goes into the box. Less often, two cables (each on a separate circuit) may power each half of a duplex receptacle, and other cables may pass through or terminate in the outlet box. A receptacle that's wired in series will not work if the wiring at a receptacle between it and the service panel is disconnected. Type NM (non-metallic, plastic-sheathed) cable has at least two conductors (insulated wires)—one black (hot) and one white (neutral)—and one bare copper grounding wire. Grounded receptacles should only be used with grounded systems.

5 Use a neon tester to verify that the receptacle doesn't have any power by probing a metal box or grounding wire with one lead and touching each terminal with the other lead.

6 If either two black wires or one black and one red wire connect to the two brass-screw terminals on one side of the receptacle, and the slotted metal tab between the top and bottom brass-screw terminals has been removed, two circuits are feeding the receptacle. Make sure to shut off both of these circuit breakers.

Swap an old receptacle for a new one

1 Carefully pull the receptacle out of the box (see illustration) and note how it is wired or make a diagram.

2 Loosen or remove the terminal screws on the receptacle as needed to disconnect the wires.

3 Attach the insulated wires to the new receptacle as they were attached to the old one. Connect any black or red wires (hot) under the brass-screw terminals; connect any white wires (neutral) under the silver-screw terminals.

What You'll Need

- Lamp or radio
- Screwdriver
- Neon tester
- Electrician's pliers
- Wire nuts

Tips

Before you shut off the power, make sure you've shut down any computer on the circuit.

If there is any chance someone might turn on the breaker while you're working, put tape over the breaker or tape a note to the service panel.

Always use receptacles that have screw terminals, and use the screw terminals on receptacles that also have push-in connections on the back. The latter aren't as reliable and may not meet code approval in your jurisdiction.

Wire connectors are color coded for the maximum or minimum number of wires of a particular gauge you can join with the device. Be sure to use the appropriate one.

Wrap a conductor or grounding wire clockwise two-thirds to three-quarters of the way around a terminal screw so that when you tighten the screw, the wire tends to wrap tighter around the terminal and not get pushed out from under it.

4 If you are using Type NM cable and only one cable enters the box, connect its bare ground wire to the ground terminal on the receptacle, which usually has a green terminal screw.

5 If you are using Type NM cable and more than one cable is present, connect all grounding wires and a separate length of bare wire (called a jumper) by twisting the wire ends together with electrician's pliers and twisting on a wire nut. Secure the other end of the jumper under the receptacle's ground-terminal screw.

6 If you are using metal boxes and Type NM cable, you must ground the receptacle to the box in one of two ways. You can install a jumper wire, called a pigtail, under the ground-terminal screw on the receptacle and under a grounding screw on the box. Or you can use a special receptacle with a spring-type grounding strap, which you ground by screwing it into the box.

7 If you are using armor-clad cable, the cable grounds the box itself, but you need to ground the receptacle to the box via a terminal screw or by using a receptacle that has a spring-type grounding strap. If the cable has a thin aluminum wire, you shouldn't connect it to anything.

8 Bend the wires back into the box, then attach the receptacle and its cover plate. Restore power.

To tighten a screw terminal, turn the screw until it's in full contact with the wire, and then make an additional half turn.

If your home is wired with aluminum rather than copper wiring, you must use fixtures and wire connectors that Underwriters Laboratories (UL) has approved for use with aluminum and copper (Type CO/ALR).

Warning

Don't leave bare wires exposed. The screw or connector should cover them.

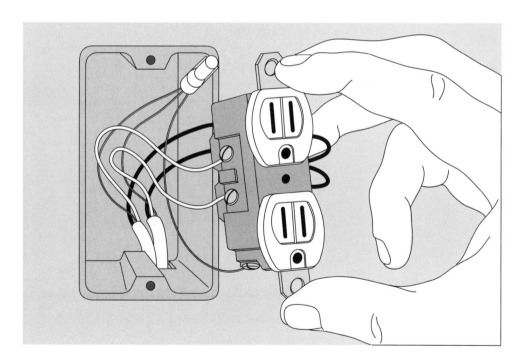

195 Fix an Electrical Plug

A plug with a cracked or broken housing, a missing insulating cover or loose, badly bent prongs may present a fire or shock hazard or both; unplug it immediately and replace it. You might also want to swap a standard plug for one of a different color or a flatter one that takes up less room behind furniture.

Steps

Installing a terminal-screw plug

1 Assuming that you don't mind losing a little cord length, cut the old plug off with wire cutters rather than trying to disassemble it.

2 Open the new plug according to the instructions. Some snap on and off the cord, and others screw together.

3 Insert about 6 inches (15 cm) of the cord through the plug's housing.

4 For a lamp or flat heater cord, split apart the two wires if they're not already split. Start the cut with a utility knife and then tear 2 inches (5 cm) apart by hand.

5 For a round cord, such as those used for some appliances and machinery, strip off the outer insulation. Make a 1-inch (2.5-cm) cut lengthwise at the cord's end; grasp the insulation to tear open about 3 inches (7.5 cm), scoring the surface with a utility knife as needed; and cut off the outer insulation at the top of the tear, being careful not to nick the wire insulation.

6 Unless the plug body is equipped with a clamp or another strain-relief connector, tie the two wires together using an Underwriters knot (see A).

7 Determine how much wire must be exposed to reach and wrap around the terminal screws, then cut off any excess with wire cutters/strippers.

What You'll Need

- Wire cutters/strippers
- Utility knife
- New plug and/or cord
- Standard screwdriver and/or nut driver
- Masking tape and pen

Tips

Choose a polarized plug for a lamp, or when wiring a nonpolarized plug for one, mark the prong connected to the ribbed wire with a permanent marker. Plug the cord in so the marked prong fits into the receptacle's wide slot.

To make a lamp with a nonpolarized plug safer, determine which prong is connected to the shell, and make sure that prong plugs into the receptacle's wide slot.

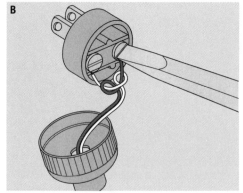

8 Remove ½ inch (12 mm) of the wire insulation with wire cutters/ strippers, using the stripper hole that corresponds to the gauge of wire you are stripping.

9 Twist the wire strands together and bend them to form a loop, then wrap each loop clockwise under the appropriate terminal screw (see B).

10 For an ungrounded (two-prong) plug, attach the white or ribbed wire under the silver terminal screw or to the terminal on the wider prong, and attach the black wire (hot) under the brass terminal screw or to the terminal on the narrower prong.

11 When an appliance or tool requires a three-prong grounded plug, connect the grounding wire (green) under the green terminal screw on the grounding prong; attach the black wire (hot) under the brass terminal screw and the white wire (neutral) under the silver terminal screw.

12 Tighten any cord clamp or other strain-relief connector.

Installing a quick-connecting flat-cord plug

1 To install a quick- or self-connecting flat-wire plug, cut the end of the cord with wire cutters.

2 Installation varies. Either open an arm on the plug body, insert the cord and press the arm closed; or pull the terminal block and prong assembly out of the plug shell, feed the cord through the shell and into the terminal block, squeeze the prongs and push the two parts of the plug back together.

Installing a 240-V plug

1 Appliances requiring 240 volts utilize cords with molded plugs and pigtails. Unplug the appliance and open the wiring-box cover with a screwdriver or nut driver.

2 Write "left," "center" and "right" on short lengths of masking tape and wrap these around the wires to identify the connection points. Remove and save the terminal screws.

3 Purchase an identical cord and connect its pigtails under the terminal screws, using the old cord as a guide. Reinstall the wiring-box cover.

The National Electrical Code no longer permits plugs with removable insulating covers that fit over the prongs. Compliant terminal plugs are all wired from the back.

To close the arm fully on some quick-connect plugs, you may need to push it against a hard surface.

Don't replace a plug on a portable tool. Replace the whole cord with one that has a molded plug. Why? Even if a replacement plug could handle the abuse, it's more likely to get caught on work pieces, which might cause an accident.

Warning

Always use a grounding plug to replace one of that style, or on an appliance or tool that requires grounding.

196 Replace a Light Fixture

Maybe that old sconce or chandelier is broken beyond repair, or perhaps you're just tired of its leftover-from-the-last-century look. You can usually replace faulty sockets or wiring in light fixtures (see 198 Fix a Lamp), but if this isn't possible or you want to make a change, replace the entire fixture.

Steps

1 Start by turning off the power to the fixture's circuit at the service panel.

2 When you remove the fixture base on a wall or ceiling-mounted fixture, or the cover plate on a strip fluorescent fixture, test the wiring to verify that the power is indeed off. Probe each set of insulated wires with one lead of a neon tester and the metal box or grounding wire with the other. If the tester lights, the power is still on.

3 Remove the screws or cap nuts that secure a globe or glass light shade.

4 Remove the screws or cap nuts that secure the fixture, fixture body or canopy to the outlet box. Support the full weight of a heavy fixture during this step and the next. Get help for a heavy one, especially if you are working overhead from a ladder.

5 With the wiring in the outlet box now accessible, repeat the power test described in step 2. When you've confirmed that there's no power in the outlet box, remove the wire connectors that join the fixture wires to the house. If the fixture body is grounded, remove the screw or nut that secures the grounding (green) wire.

6 You must secure fixtures that weigh over 50 lbs. (23 kg) independently of the electrical box. If you have access from above, install wood bridging between the joists above the box. Then screw the box into the bridging from below. If you don't have access to install a support from above, purchase retrofit mounting hardware for a ceiling fan and install it according to the manufacturer's instructions.

7 Compare new mounting-hole requirements with the existing provisions at the outlet box. If necessary, purchase a new mounting strap or a universal mounting plate, which will accommodate virtually any fixture.

8 Connect the new fixture to the same wires that connected the old fixture, and mount the fixture to the box with screws or cap nuts as required. Create a loop in the wires with long-nose pliers, then wrap them clockwise under a terminal screw. Or use electrician's pliers to twist the wires from a prewired fixture together with the house wires, then secure them with wire nuts. Cut off excess with wire cutters.

What You'll Need

- Neon tester
- Screwdriver
- Ladder
- Wood bridging
- Fixture and mounting hardware
- Long-nose pliers or electrician's pliers
- Wire cutters
- Wire nuts

Tips

Depending on the switching and other unrelated wiring, you may find other cables coming into the box and other wire-nut connections, but you shouldn't have to disturb them.

Buy a new mounting strap if the existing one does not have a threaded hole in the middle and your fixture requires it, or if the threaded screw holes in the old strap don't work for the new light fixture.

Warning

Wear goggles, especially when working overhead.

197 Install a New Dimmer

With a dimmer, you can adjust light levels to create just the right light-ing to suit your mood and enhance your home's atmosphere. Equally important, dimmers save energy and make bulbs last much longer than they would at constant full power.

Steps

1 Shut off the circuit at the main service panel and remove the housing over the switch. Unscrew the switch and lift it out. If the box is metal, be particularly careful not to let the screw terminals on the side of the switch touch the box.

2 Test for power with a neon tester, probing one switch terminal and the bare grounding wire; repeat the test for the other termi-nal (see A). Proceed if the test light doesn't glow.

3 Cut off the wires at the switch terminals using wire cutters/strip-pers, and strip about ½ inch (12 mm) of insulation off the two cut switch wires.

4 Wire the dimmer. A dimmer with two black wires has no polarity, so twist each dimmer wire together with either one of the switch wires and screw on a wire nut (see B). If the dimmer has a green wire, connect it to the grounding wire.

5 If a dimmer has black and red wires, wire the black one to the incoming power (line) and red to the lights (load). To identify the wires, pull both switch wires out of the box; if you have a plastic outlet box, pull out the bare wires, too. Keep them well apart from each other. Have someone restore power. Use a neon tester to probe one switch wire and the bare wire (or the metal box). If the tester glows, that is the line, and the other wire is the load.

What You'll Need

- Screwdriver
- Neon tester
- Wire cutters/strippers
- Dimmer with wire nuts

Tips

Make sure the dimmer is rated for at least the maxi-mum rated wattage of all the light fixtures it will control.

If two switches in different locations control a light, only one of them can be a dim-mer switch.

To replace a three-way switch, attach the common lead to the wire connected to the darkest screw on the old switch.

Only fluorescent lights with special ballasts can be dimmed; low-voltage lighting requires special dimmers.

A
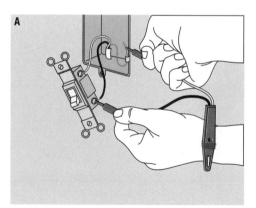

B
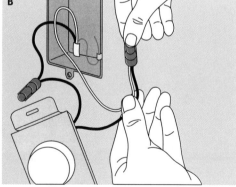

198 Fix a Lamp

The most common problem with lamps is a faulty socket or switch within that socket. Loose or faulty wiring comes next.

Steps

Determine the cause

1 Unplug the lamp to inspect the plug and cord for any visible damage. To replace a damaged plug, see 195 Fix an Electrical Plug. To replace a cord, see "Rewire a lamp," opposite page.

2 If you don't see any damage, remove the shade and bulb, slide up the sleeves that fit over the harp holder and squeeze the arms together to remove the harp. Depress the socket's shell just above its base with your thumb to disengage the clips that hold the two pieces together while you rock out the shell.

3 Clip a continuity tester to one of the plug prongs and probe each of the socket's screw terminals with the pointed lead. Repeat for the other prong. If the test light does not go on once for each test, replace the cord.

4 Test the socket by clipping a continuity tester's lead to the threaded shell and probing the metal tab at the bottom of the socket with the other lead, then operating the switch. The test light should go on when the switch is in one position but not the other, except in the case of a three-way switch, which has three On positions and one Off position. Replace a faulty socket.

What You'll Need

- Continuity tester
- Standard screwdriver
- Wire strippers/cutters
- Lamp cord
- Electrical tape
- Lamp socket only or complete socket assembly

Tips

While the instructions here refer specifically to incandescent table lamps, the principles are the same for all table, floor and desk lamps.

You may see the word *press* stamped at the location where you press to remove a socket shell. Use pliers if thumb pressure is not enough.

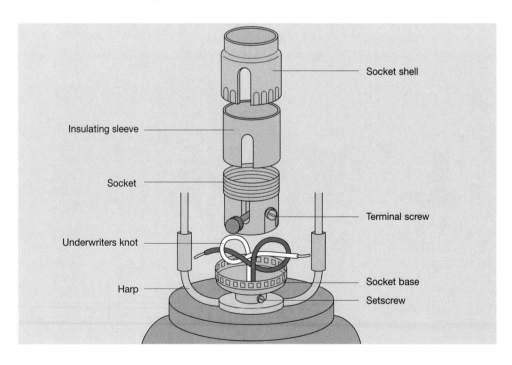

Socket shell

Insulating sleeve

Socket

Terminal screw

Underwriters knot

Socket base

Harp

Setscrew

Rewire a lamp

1 With the socket taken apart (see illustration), loosen the terminal screws to disconnect the wires and untie the Underwriters knot. Also remove the felt cover (if any) from the bottom of the lamp.

2 If the cord travels through anything longer than a short threaded nipple extending from one end of the lamp to the other, cut the cord at the bottom of the lamp, leaving 6 inches (15 cm) exposed; you'll need the old cord to pull the new one through the lamp.

3 Split apart the wires on the old and new cords so you can strip about 1 inch (2.5 cm) of insulation off each wire.

4 Twist each wire from the new cord onto the ends of the existing wires. Tape the splice and use the old cord to pull the new cord into the lamp.

5 If the cord travels a very short distance, simply pull the old cord out from the bottom of the lamp and feed in the new one. Then split apart the wires to strip off the insulation.

6 Tie a knot in the cord just inside the hole in the lamp base, and feed the cord out through any hole in the base to install the plug (see 195 Fix an Electrical Plug). If you are using a cord with a molded plug, you must tie this knot after threading it through any holes in the lamp base but before feeding it through the lamp.

7 Tie an Underwriters knot (see illustration) in the end of the new cord, leaving just enough wire after the knot to wrap around the socket terminals. If you leave too much, there won't be room for the excess wire inside the socket base.

8 Twist the loose wire strands and cut off the excess so ½ inch (12 mm) of wire is exposed.

9 Wrap the cord's neutral wire (white) clockwise around the silver terminal screw and tighten the screw. Secure the hot wire (black) under the brass terminal screw.

Replace a lamp socket

1 To replace the lamp's socket assembly, loosen any setscrew in the socket base and twist off the socket base and harp holder from the nipple.

2 Remove the new socket's shell from its base and screw the harp holder and new base onto the threaded nipple at the top of the lamp.

3 To replace just the lamp socket, leave the existing socket base and harp on the lamp and install a new socket.

4 Wire the socket using the existing cord or a new one as described in "Rewire a lamp," above.

Look closely at the cord. One wire is ribbed to identify it as neutral. On a cord with a polarized molded plug, this wire connects to the wider plug prong. If you are installing your own plug (see 195 Replace a Plug), follow this convention.

Feeding new cords into some floor lamps and desk lamps is easier if you first tie string to one wire of the old cord instead of twisting the wires together.

Lubricate a cord you're pulling through tight curves with a lubricant sold at electrical-supply outlets for "fished" wires and cables.

If you are replacing a socket, use the switch type you want—chain, push, rotating, on-off or three-way.

Warning

The Underwriters knot keeps a cord from being jerked out of its terminal, protecting you against a possible electrical short or shock.

Polarized plugs have a wide neutral prong and can only plug one way into a receptacle. In a properly wired lamp, the polarized plug ensures that the hot wire energizes the metal tab at the bottom of the socket, which is less exposed to fingers than is the threaded shell.

199 Troubleshoot Fluorescent Lighting

The most likely culprits when a fluorescent fixture does not work (or flickers, or fails to start every time) are a worn-out tube or bulb or a faulty socket connection.

Steps

Check a tube and its sockets

1 Remove the diffuser, if any, to access the tube or bulb; twist the tube to remove it (you may need a ladder). Replace a worn-out fluorescent bulb that's blackened at the ends or that has bent or broken pins.

2 Make sure that the socket is not cracked or broken, that it is tightly secured to the fixture housing and that the metal contacts hold the tube securely in the socket.

3 In very humid climates, the pins and contacts can oxidize. Clean them with contact cleaner and a cloth or cotton swab. Don't use sandpaper or other abrasives, which can ruin protective coatings.

4 Old fixtures may have a small cylindrical device, called a starter, that screws into the fixture just below one end of the lamp. To remove and replace it with a matching starter, press in and turn it as you would a childproof cap.

What You'll Need

- Ladder
- Replacement tubes or bulbs
- Contact cleaner
- Cloth or cotton swab
- Replacement starter, sockets, ballast and/or fixture
- Screwdriver
- Neon tester
- Wire cutters/strippers
- Tape and pen
- Drill and drill bits

Tips

Some light gray coloring at the end of a used fluorescent bulb is normal.

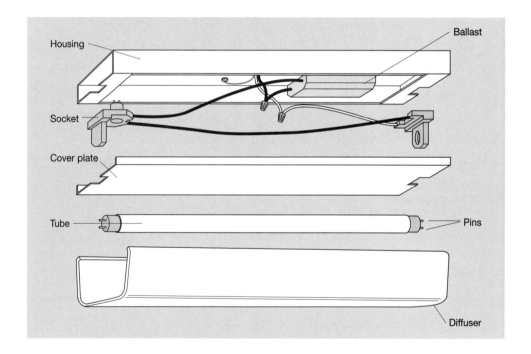

Housing

Ballast

Socket

Cover plate

Tube

Pins

Diffuser

Replace a faulty socket

1 Shut off power to the circuit at the main service panel; remove the tube(s) and the cover plate, which is typically secured at one end by a clip and at the other by a screw.

2 Double-check that the power is off using a neon tester. Probe under the wire connector on the black or red wire connections with one lead, and to the bare ground wire or metal box with the other.

3 Unhook or unscrew the faulty socket from the fixture housing.

4 Use wire cutters/strippers to cut off the wires at the socket and strip off about ½ inch (12 mm) of insulation from the ends of the two wires using the 14-gauge hole.

5 Wire the replacement socket by pressing the ends of the wires into push-in terminals or wrapping them clockwise under the screw terminals and tightening the screws.

6 Snap or screw in the socket and test the light. If it still doesn't work, replace the ballast or the entire fixture, depending on the value of the fixture and the cost of a replacement ballast.

Replace a fixture

1 Having tested to confirm the power is off (see "Replace a faulty socket," above), disconnect the house wiring (black, white and bare-copper wires) that feed the fixture.

2 Tape together and label any wires grouped under a single connector; this will make rewiring easier.

3 Remove the mounting screws unless they fit into keyhole openings, in which case simply loosen them.

4 Lower the fixture enough to access the cable clamp that secures that cable to the fixture, then pull out the wires. Or remove the nut that secures the cable clamp to the fixture housing.

5 Compare the mounting-hole locations on the new fixture with those on the one you're replacing. Drill new holes as necessary.

6 Secure the cable clamp to the new fixture and attach the fixture to the ceiling with screws.

7 Rewire with wire connectors. Reinstall the cover, lamps and diffuser, if any.

If any wire at a terminal connection sticks out from under a screw head, remove it to cut off excess wire, then reinstall it.

If your fixture is in an unheated garage and it's cold out, a standard fluorescent fixture may turn on or brighten slowly. Special cold-weather ballasts can fix the problem, but they're costly.

The heavy pins on single-pin 8-foot (2.4-m) lamps are much more reliable than those on dual-pin models, so if you need an 8-foot (2.4-m) fixture, choose that type.

Warning

Don't remove the cover until you have shut off the power. That could cause a hidden loose wire to short.

200 Fix a Low-Voltage Thermostat

While low-voltage thermostats are very reliable and rarely defective, thermostat-related problems, such as faulty wires or loose connections, may cause a failure in your heating or cooling system. The problems are easy to identify, and just as easy to fix by making the appropriate repair or by replacing a faulty thermostat.

Steps

1 Turn off the power to heating and/or cooling systems at the main service panel or system shutoff switch.

2 Remove the thermostat. On some models, remove the cover plate and then unscrew the thermostat body from a wired base plate secured to the wall. Other models plug into the base plate without screws.

3 Remove any dust from the thermostat and base plate with a soft artist's brush.

4 Check for broken, frayed or corroded wires and loose wire connections. Tighten any loose connections. Use wire cutters/strippers to cut damaged wires and strip off about ½ inch (12 mm) of insulation, then reconnect the wires.

5 Restore the power to test the thermostat. Consult the manual for your thermostat and disconnect the power wire (usually red), then touch it to the terminal for the heat (the terminal marked as W with white wire from heater's transformer).

What You'll Need

- Screwdriver
- Artist's brush
- Wire cutters/strippers
- Neon tester
- Replacement thermostat
- Tape and pen
- Level or plumb line
- Batteries

Tips

If you don't have the installation instructions for your thermostat, go online to the manufacturer's Web site and download them, or call to have them faxed or mailed.

Make sure disconnected thermostat wires don't slip inside the wall. Pull them out a bit and either tape them to the wall, bend them or loop them around a pencil.

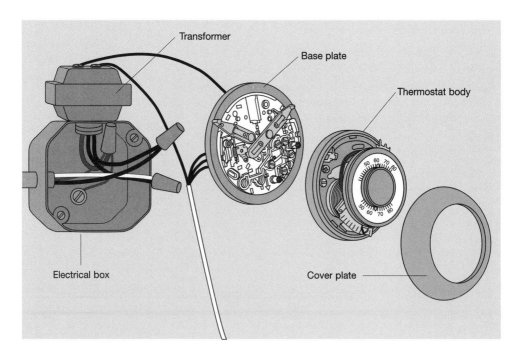

Transformer

Base plate

Thermostat body

Electrical box

Cover plate

6 Similarly bypass the thermostat to check its cooling function by touching the disconnected power wire (red) to the terminal for the cooling system (typically yellow).

7 If one or both systems fail to start, turn off their power, then identify (see step 8) and replace any faulty wires between the thermostat and the low-voltage transformer(s) at the heating or air-conditioning units.

8 One way to test thermostat wires—on your heating system, for example—is to disconnect the wires from the thermostat and transformer, wire them together at one end, and test for continuity at the other end by clipping a continuity tester to one wire and probing the other wire. If the tester fails to light, replace the wires.

9 Check for loose low-voltage wire connections at the transformer or loose line-voltage connections to the transformer (see 203 Fix a Doorbell).

10 If both systems activate, replace the faulty thermostat (see below).

Replace a thermostat

1 Choose a thermostat suitable for your particular system. Read the thermostat labeling and/or consult with a knowledgeable salesperson or HVAC (heating, ventilating and air-conditioning) service professional.

2 Shut off the power to your heating and/or cooling systems at the main service panel or system shutoff switch.

3 Remove the old thermostat as described on the opposite page.

4 Disconnect all wires from the base plate one at a time and tape a label on each that identifies its terminal connections (R, Y, W and so forth).

5 If the new thermostat base does not cover the old mounting holes, either patch them and touch up the paint (see 132 Repair Minor Drywall Damage) or install the cover ring that the new unit may provide.

6 Mount the new thermostat to the wall, leveling it according to the manufacturer's instructions. Typically, you can align notches with a level or plumb line on the wall, or place a small level on leveling posts at the base or its edge.

7 Use the wiring chart provided in the installation instructions to connect the labeled wires to the appropriate terminals, removing the tape as you make the connections.

8 If applicable, install batteries and program the thermostat.

9 Attach the thermostat to the base and restore power.

If you're replacing a thermostat, choose a programmable model that allows nighttime setback for heating or daytime setback for cooling. This could save up to a third of your energy bill.

Unless power is required for low-voltage testing, always shut the power off and follow the manufacturer's wiring instructions. Accidental wire contact or improper connections may damage the thermostat.

Warning

While low-voltage wiring cannot hurt you, it can startle you, and that may cause an injury. Work with the power off whenever possible.

201 Fix a Line-Voltage Thermostat

You don't have to humor a capricious thermostat by walking around wrapped in a blanket. Here's a problem you can likely fix yourself.

Steps

1 Turn off the power to the heater at your main circuit panel. Remove the thermostat cover plate. Remove the mounting screws and carefully pull the thermostat away from the wall or heater, and the wires out of the box (see illustration).

2 Remove one wire nut at a time to test for power with a neon or continuity tester. Probe the grounding wire with one lead and each uncovered set of wires with the other lead. Proceed if the test light does not glow in any test.

3 Identify the house wires that connect to the wires identified on the thermostat as *line*. Typically they're red. Mark some masking tape with the word *line* and put it on these house wires. Disconnect all wires to remove the thermostat.

4 Place the thermostat on a table and tape down the wires so you'll have a hand free to rotate the tester knob. Use a continuity tester to test the thermostat. Clip a lead onto a black wire; probe the red wire on the same side of the thermostat while rotating the dial through all the On positions. The tester should remain lighted. Repeat for the other set of red and black wires.

5 Replace the thermostat if it's defective. Reinstall a working one and call a professional to service the heating element.

What You'll Need

- Screwdriver
- Neon or continuity tester
- Masking tape and pen
- Replacement thermostat

Tip

Test the tester. Touch the probe of a continuity tester to its tip; it should light if the battery and its own connections are working.

Warning

Never remove a thermostat or any electrical device until you have shut off the power to the circuit.

Always double-check that power is really off by testing all the wires in an outlet box.

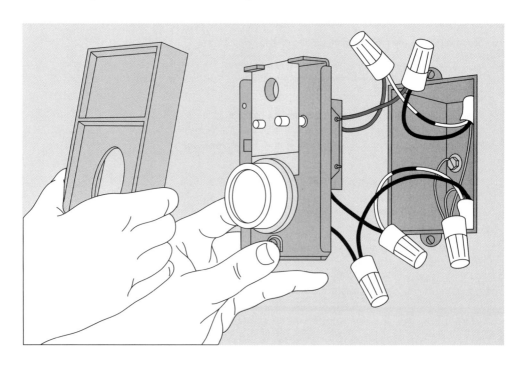

202 Troubleshoot Holiday Lighting

Those little twinkling lights are so inexpensive that you may be inclined to buy a new set. But you can easily avoid making yet another trip to the store when you're already busy. The following tips will help you locate and fix the problem.

Steps

1 To check for and fix a bad plug connection, unplug and plug the nonworking strand, or plug it directly into a wall socket or working extension cord. If this doesn't work, keep looking for the problem.

2 To fix unwanted blinking, look for clear bulbs with a red tip or a different-looking base (these are blinker bulbs), and replace any you find. If that fails to solve the problem, go on to the next step.

3 To locate a missing, broken or burned-out bulb for replacement, check the nonworking strand from end to end, looking for a missing bulb and examining each bulb for visible damage or blackness.

4 To locate a loose bulb, tap each bulb to see which one flickers or causes the strand to flicker. Unplug it for reinsertion, but while it's out inspect the wire at the base of the bulb and the bulb itself for damage. If it's damaged, replace it; otherwise plug it back in securely.

5 To locate and replace a bad bulb in a strand that won't light, use a bulb that you know works and substitute it for the first bulb on the string; continue down the line, replacing each bulb with the previous socket's bulb until the strand lights.

6 To locate a bulb with a broken or misaligned wire in a strand that flickers, hold one end of the lighted strand on the floor. Starting at that end, run your other hand over the strand until you hit a bulb that causes a flicker (or until you need to reposition your hands). Remove that bulb and the next few. Replace any that have a damaged wire, or straighten the wire and reinsert the bulb.

7 To locate a blown plug fuse, plug a working light set into the one that doesn't work. If the test set doesn't light up, replace the fuse in the nonworking strand (if it's replaceable) or replace the strand.

8 To solve shorts caused by water in sockets, make sure the lights are not sitting in water or located where water from a roof or gutter can spill on them.

What You'll Need

- Replacement bulbs
- Replacement fuses

Tip

Don't throw away a bulb you think has caused a problem until you have retested the strand.

Warning

Handling a broken bulb can cause a shock, so it's best to unplug the strand once you've located the problem.

203 Fix a Doorbell

If your doorbell stops working, you may inadvertently miss deliveries or leave dinner guests standing on the doorstep for a while. All you need to avoid this situation is a simple tool or two. The most common causes of malfunction—loose wiring and worn-out switches—are the easiest to fix, requiring only a screwdriver. Troubleshooting other problems may require an inexpensive multitester.

Steps

1 If you have another doorbell button, test it. If it works, the transformer has power, and its half of the chime is working.

Troubleshoot a doorbell switch

1 Unscrew the switch from the house and pull it away to tighten any loose wires.

2 If that fails, bypass the switch by shorting across the terminals with a screwdriver blade or by removing the two wires and touching them together. If the bell rings, replace the switch. If not, twist the two wires together and move on to the next step.

3 Connect the two wires to the two terminals; push the wires back into the wall and screw on the switch. If new mounting holes are required, start the holes with an awl and drive in the screws.

Troubleshoot a transformer

1 Locate the transformer, and inspect and tighten low-voltage wire connections to it.

2 If neither doorbell works, use a multitester set to the 50-volt AC range to test the transformer. Touch the probes to the two terminals. If the reading is within 2 volts of the transformer's rating, troubleshoot the chime. If not, go on to the next step.

3 Shut off the power to the transformer's circuit at the service panel, and remove the outlet-box cover. To test for power, pull out the black circuit wire and remove the wire nut. Probe the black and grounding wires with a neon tester. Repeat the test for white and grounding wires. Tighten any loose connections.

4 To replace a faulty transformer, remove the low-voltage wires. When there is more than one wire at a terminal, tape them together for easier rewiring.

5 Shut off the power to the doorbell circuit at the main service panel. Remove the outlet-box cover and disconnect the wires from the old transformer, then disconnect it from the box or the box's cover.

6 Attach and wire the replacement. Connect the transformer's green wire to the bare grounded wire and its other two wires to the black and white circuit wires. Attach the outlet-box cover and secure each low-voltage wire or set of wires under a terminal.

What You'll Need

- Screwdriver
- Replacement parts and wire as required
- Awl
- Neon tester
- Multitester
- Tape
- Wire staples
- Hammer or stapler

Tips

An inexpensive digital autoranging multitester is very easy to use and comes with detailed instructions.

If you have trouble fishing new wire through an inaccessible cavity, don't pull too hard or you may damage the wire. Try splicing and taping a new wire to the old one at that point. Hopefully the damaged section is not inside the cavity.

Before deciding to replace a chime, depress the plunger to make sure it isn't stuck. If it is, clean it with alcohol and a cotton swab.

Troubleshoot a chime

1 Remove the chime cover, which may snap or screw onto the base, and inspect all wiring connections.

2 If the connections look good, set a multitester to the 50-volt AC range, then touch one probe to the transformer terminal and the other to the nonworking front or rear terminal. If it fails the test, replace the faulty wiring (see "Replace doorbell wiring," below). If the chime has power but neither doorbell works, replace the chime (go on to steps 3 and 4).

3 To replace a chime, remove its cover. Disconnect and label the wires for easier rewiring. Remove the mounting screws and the old chime.

4 Thread the wires into the back of the new chime and mount it to the wall with the provided screws and anchors. Attach low-voltage wires to their respective terminals and replace the cover.

Replace doorbell wiring

1 Disconnect the faulty wire at both ends and loosen or remove all accessible wire staples.

2 Twist together one end of the existing wire to an end of the new wiring and tape the splice, using very little tape. Pull the existing wire to draw the new wire through holes, staples and wall or ceiling cavities. Pull it through one section at a time rather than all at once. Staple as needed.

Warning

All the wiring in a doorbell is low-voltage and safe except the 120-volt connection to the transformer.

Multitesters are easy to use, but using them to test 120-volt or 240-volt circuits when you've set them for low voltage is very dangerous. Read instructions and double-check settings before you probe.

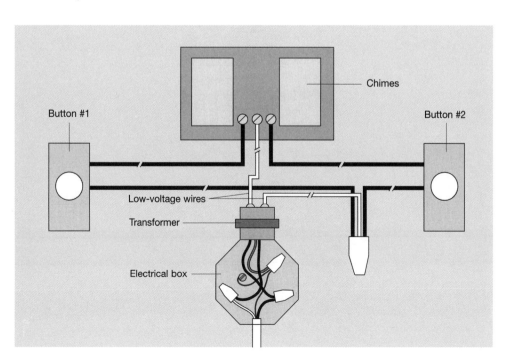

Chimes

Button #1

Button #2

Low-voltage wires

Transformer

Electrical box

204 Fix a Wobbly Overhead Fan

When a ceiling fan wobbles, the vibration can damage the fan and shorten its life. Usually you can trace the problem to one of three sources: The fan isn't securely fastened to the ceiling, the blades are unbalanced or the blades are warped.

Steps

Securing the fan

1 Standing on a stepladder, grasp the fan body and try to shake it. If it moves easily, the screws that hold the fan to the junction box may be loose.

2 While a helper supports the fan, remove the screws from the canopy. The fan will now be free from the ceiling, so your helper must hold it securely.

3 Tighten the screws that hold the ceiling plate to the junction box.

4 Reinstall the canopy.

Balancing the blades

1 Attach a clothespin to the edge of a blade, about halfway from the end. Start the fan on slow speed and check to see if the wobble disappears. If it doesn't, move the clothespin to another blade and repeat. Continue until you've tested all the blades. If the fan stops wobbling at any point, the last blade tested is unbalanced.

What You'll Need

- Stepladder
- Screwdriver
- Clothespin
- Weight kit, or epoxy and coins
- Adjustable pliers
- Replacement blade

Tip

If your unit continues to wobble despite your taking these steps, have an electrician check the junction box. Heavy fans require sturdy boxes to support the weight.

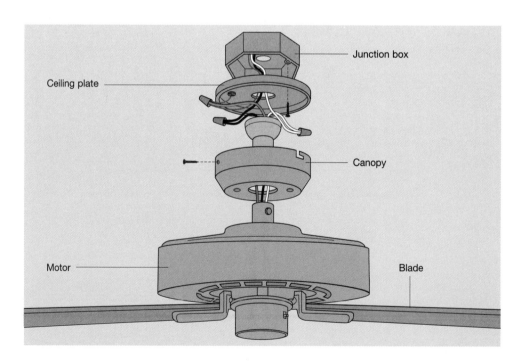

2 Balance the problem blade by attaching a weight to the middle of the top edge, about halfway from the end of the blade. You can buy a weight kit, or use epoxy to glue one or more coins to the blade. Experiment to determine how much weight you need to add.

Fixing warped blades

1 Remove the blades one at a time, using a screwdriver and, if necessary, adjustable pliers to hold any retaining nuts. Lay each blade on a flat surface. If a blade won't lie flat, it is warped.

2 Obtain a replacement from the manufacturer or a dealer (take the old blade with you so you can get one that's the same length and weight) and install it.

205 Adjust Water-Heater Temperature

Once you and the rest of your household have agreed on what temperature is "just right," the next step is convincing your water heater to stay there. This may simply require an easy thermostat adjustment, or you may need to call in a professional for repair or replacement.

Steps

Water too hot or too cold

1 Adjust the thermostat incrementally until you've achieved the desired temperature.

2 If you are unable to adjust the temperature, the thermostat is faulty. Have a plumber replace it.

Insufficient hot water

1 Adjust the thermostat incrementally until you've achieved the desired temperature.

2 Connect a garden hose to the drain valve. Open the valve until the water runs clear to flush sediment from the bottom of the tank every year.

3 Run hot water from a faucet first thing in the morning to activate the heater and bring the water back up to its set temperature before showering.

4 Have a plumber replace a too-small water heater or add a super-insulated hot-water storage tank.

What You'll Need

- Garden hose

Tip

For efficient operation, dishwashers typically require water that's at least 120°F (49°C), or at the Hot setting on water heaters that don't display degrees.

Warning

If steam or boiling water is coming from a valve, immediately shut off the power (for an electric heater) or the gas line (for a gas unit). Then call for professional help.

206 Relight a Water-Heater Pilot Light

If you have shut off your water heater for draining or repairs or to conserve fuel while away on a trip, you must relight the pilot manually.

Steps

1 Set the gas-control knob to the Off position and turn the thermostat to its lowest setting (typically clockwise in both cases). Wait 5 minutes for any gas to clear. If after 5 minutes you smell gas, do not proceed. Call the utility company for immediate service.

2 Open or remove the outer and inner access covers for the burning chamber using a wrench or pliers. Use a flashlight to locate the end of the pilot-light tube that extends from the gas-control valve into the burning chamber. Adjust your position so you can comfortably reach this point with a wooden match and see what you are doing.

3 Turn the control knob to the pilot position and immediately hold a match near the end of the pilot-light tube. Depress and hold the reset button on the gas-control valve (see illustration). Remove the match as soon as the pilot lights, but keep the button depressed for about a minute.

4 If the pilot does not remain lighted, repeat all these steps. Otherwise, turn the gas cock on the control valve to the On position, set the thermostat to the desired temperature and replace the access panels.

What You'll Need

- Wrench or pliers
- Flashlight
- Wooden matches

Warning

If the control knob does not pop up when you release it, call for immediate service.

Watch out for sharp sheet-metal edges when lighting the pilot; better yet, wear work gloves.

Keep your face away from the burning chamber when lighting the pilot, turning the control knob or adjusting the thermostat.

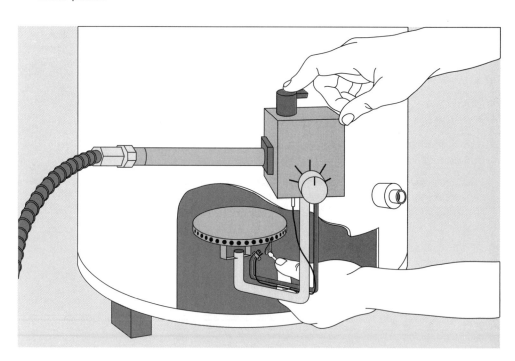

207 Troubleshoot a Heating System

Problems with modern heating systems are rare, but when they occur, you want to fix them quickly, before your household's population freezes in place. You can usually troubleshoot and correct the most common ones yourself; contact a professional for other problems. Always consult the manuals for your heating system and thermostat when you're making repairs yourself.

PROBLEM	CAUSES	SOLUTIONS
No heat	Thermostat switch in wrong position	Set thermostat switch to heat setting or to desired temperature for electric heat.
	No 120-volt power to heater	Turn on furnace or boiler power switch, or check fuse on circuit breaker.
	No low-voltage power to thermostat or no 120-volt power to its transformer	On low-voltage systems, test transformer and its wiring connections (see 203 Fix a Doorbell).
	Defective thermostat or connections	Repair or replace thermostat (see 200 Fix a Low-Voltage Thermostat).
	Pilot out on gas heater	Relight pilot according to manufacturer's instructions.
	Flame-sensing element on oil-fired system has shut off burner	Press reset button on heating unit once. If that fails, call for service.
	No fuel	Check fuel levels.
Furnace cycles on and off frequently or creates excessive temperature swings	Improperly adjusted heat anticipator	Increase amount of time furnace is turned on to reduce excessive cycling by turning anticipator lever counterclockwise; decrease time to reduce temperature swings by turning lever clockwise.
Thermometer and thermostat readings differ	Thermostat out of level	Adjust level (see 200 Fix a Low-Voltage Thermostat).
	Thermometer out of calibration	Test thermometer with another thermometer. Recalibrate inaccurate thermometer according to manufacturer's instructions.
	Thermostat out of calibration	If thermometer is correct, recalibrate thermostat according to manufacturer's instructions.

CDOALD FIXTURE • UNREGISTERED ISSUE • SOMEONE • JO
NORING • FIX BAD HABITS • REPAIR A BROKEN EYEGLASS FRAME • REPOSITION A SLIPPED CONTACT LENS • FIX A RUN IN STOCKINGS • JO
BEAKOUT • REPAIR A TORN FINGERNAIL • FIX CHIPPED NAIL POLISH • FIX A STUCK ZIPPER • FIND A LOST CONTACT LENS • ELIMINATE BAD
LY THAT STICKS • STOP TELEMARKETERS AND JUNK MAIL • GET SUPERGLUE OFF YOUR SKIN • EXTRACT A SPLINTER • SOOTHE A SUNBURN
HANGOVER • STOP HICCUPS • MEND A BROKEN HEART • MEND A FAMILY FEUD • TREAT A SMALL CUT OR SCRAPE • FIX HAIR DISASTERS •
TTER SEATS • FIX A BILLING MISTAKE • FIX A BAD GRADE • FIX BAD CREDIT • RECOVER FROM JET LAG • RESUSCITATE AN UNCONSCIOUS
F PRONOUNS • FIX A RUN-ON SENTENCE • FIX MISUSE OF THE WORD GOOD • FIX YOUR DOG OR CAT • CORRECT BAD BEHAVIOR IN DOGS
SSING BUTTON • REMOVE LINT FROM CLOTHING • FIX A DRAWSTRING ON SWEATPANTS • REPAIR A HEM • REPAIR LEATHER GOODS • MEN
UNDER YOUR CASHMERE • FIX A SWEATER THAT HAS SHRUNK • FIX A SWEATER THAT HAS STRETCHED • FIX A HOLE IN A POCKET • FIX A I
LLING FROM CLOTHING • FIX A FRAYED BUTTONHOLE • REMOVE DARK SCUFFS FROM SHOES • TREAT STAINS ON LEATHER • PROTECT SUE
JIET SQUEAKY HINGES • TROUBLESHOOT LOCK PROBLEMS • TIGHTEN A LOOSE DOORKNOB • TIGHTEN A LOOSE DOOR HINGE • FIX A BIN
PLACE CRACKED TILE • TROUBLESHOOT MOLD ON INTERIOR WALLS • REPLACE CRACKED TILE GROUT IN A TUB OR SHOWER • FIX A DRA
INDS • TROUBLESHOOT WINDOW SHADE PROBLEMS • FIX BROKEN GLASS IN A WINDOW • REPAIR A WINDOW SCREEN • REPAIR ALUMINU
AMAGED PLASTER • REPAIR WALL COVERINGS • TOUCH UP PAINTED WALLS • TROUBLESHOOT INTERIOR-PAINT PROBLEMS • SOLVE A LEAD
ARDWOOD FLOOR • RESTORE A DULL, WORN WOOD FLOOR • TOUCH UP WOOD-FLOOR FINISHES • REPAIR DAMAGED SHEET-VINYL FLOOR
OUSE • CHILDPROOF YOUR HOME • PREVENT ICE DAMS • CURE A FAULTY FIREPLACE DRAW • START A FIRE IN A COLD CHIMNEY • FIX A W
AL A GARAGE FLOOR • REFINISH A GARAGE OR BASEMENT FLOOR • CONTROL ROOF LEAKS • REDIRECT RAINWATER FROM A DOWNSPOI
AMAGED ASPHALT SHINGLE • PATCH A FLAT OR LOW-PITCHED ROOF • REPAIR ROOF FLASHING • TROUBLESHOOT EXTERIOR-PAINT PROBL
OW WATER PRESSURE • FIX LEAKING PIPES • STOP A TOILET FROM RUNNING • FIX A LEAKY TOILET TANK • FIX A STOPPED-UP TOILET • STC
LOGGED SINK OR TUB • REPAIR A TUB-AND-SHOWER VALVE • REPAIR CHIPPED FIXTURES • QUIET NOISY PIPES • DEFROST YOUR PIPES • D
ONSUMPTION • REPLACE A RECEPTACLE • FIX AN ELECTRICAL PLUG • REPLACE A LIGHT FIXTURE • INSTALL A NEW DIMMER • FIX A LAMP •
OORBELL • FIX A WOBBLY OVERHEAD FAN • ADJUST WATER-HEATER TEMPERATURE • RELIGHT A WATER-HEATER PILOT LIGHT • TROUBLESI
E MAKER • GET RID OF MICROWAVE SMELLS • FIX A REFRIGERATOR THAT COOLS POORLY • FIX A GAS OVEN THAT HEATS POORLY • CLEAN
SHWASHER PROBLEMS • CORRECT AN OVERFLOWING DISHWASHER • FIX A LEAKY DISHWASHER • FIX A DISHWASHER THAT FILLS SLOWLY
WASHING MACHINE THAT FILLS SLOWLY • FIX A WASHING MACHINE THAT "WALKS" ACROSS THE FLOOR • FIX A CLOTHES DRYER THAT DRI
K YOUR VACUUM CLEANER • REPLACE VACUUM CLEANER BRUSHES • TROUBLESHOOT A PORTABLE AIR CONDITIONER • FIX A WINDOW AI
ROCESSOR • FIX A TOASTER • DIAGNOSE MICROWAVE OVEN PROBLEMS • TROUBLESHOOT A GAS GRILL • FIX A TRASH COMPACTOR • REF
ART • TROUBLESHOOT A CRASHING COMPUTER • CLEAN UP LAPTOP SPILLS • FIX BAD SECTORS ON A HARD DISK • QUIT A FROZEN PC A
FECTED COMPUTER • IMPROVE YOUR COMPUTER'S MEMORY • GET RID OF E-MAIL SPAM • CHANGE A LASER PRINTER CARTRIDGE • FIX A
GURE OUT WHY A PRINTER WON'T PRINT • FIX SPELLING AND GRAMMAR ERRORS • RECALL AN E-MAIL IN MICROSOFT OUTLOOK • DIAGNO
LES • TROUBLESHOOT A PALM OS PDA • RESET A PALM OS PDA • REMOVE FINGERPRINTS FROM A CAMERA LENS • TROUBLESHOOT A CD
ALVAGE A VIDEOCASSETTE • TROUBLESHOOT A DVD PLAYER • STRENGTHEN FM RADIO RECEPTION • STRENGTHEN AM RADIO RECEPTION
JAMMED SLIDE PROJECTOR • GET BETTER SPEAKER SOUND • TROUBLESHOOT A DIGITAL CAMCORDER • TROUBLESHOOT A DIGITAL CAM
GHTBULB • FIX A BROKEN WINEGLASS STEM • FIX BLEMISHED WOOD FURNITURE • REPAIR GOUGES IN FURNITURE • RESTORE FURNITURE
AMOUFLAGE A DOG-SCRATCHED DOOR • REPAIR A SPLIT CARPET SEAM • RID CARPETS OF PET ODORS • REINFORCE A SAGGING SHELF •
OINTS OF CHAIRS AND TABLES • REUPHOLSTER A DROP-IN CHAIR SEAT • REVIVE A CANE SEAT • REINFORCE A WEAK BED FRAME • FIX UP
OTTERY • REPAIR CHIPPED OR CRACKED CHINA • UNCLUTTER YOUR HOME • CLEAN CRAYON FROM A WALL • GET WAX OFF A TABLECLOT
TAINS • REMOVE CHEWING GUM FROM CARPETING • REMOVE BLEACH SPOTS FROM CARPETING • REMOVE PET STAINS • ELIMINATE WINE
TAINS FROM TILE GROUT • REMOVE MILDEW FROM WALLS AND CEILINGS • DISINFECT A TOILET BOWL • REMOVE FIREPLACE GRIME • GET
LEAN OIL SPOTS FROM A GARAGE OR DRIVEWAY • REMOVE STAINS FROM BRICK • WASH AN OUTDOOR GRILL • FIX A FALLEN SOUFFLÉ • F
ESCUE OVERPROOFED YEAST DOUGH • FIX YOUR KID LUNCH • GET RID OF TAP-WATER MINERAL DEPOSITS • CALIBRATE A MEAT THERMO
AUCE • RESCUE A BROKEN SAUCE • REMOVE FAT FROM SOUPS AND SAUCES • FIX LUMPY GRAVY • SUBSTITUTE MISSING INGREDIENTS •
URNED RICE • REMOVE COOKING ODORS • FINISH UNDERCOOKED MEAT • SALVAGE AN UNDERCOOKED TURKEY • FIX AN OVERSEASONE
TALE BREAD • SMOOTH SEIZED CHOCOLATE • SOFTEN HARDENED SUGARS OR COOKIES • FIX BREAKFAST FOR YOUR SWEETHEART • MEN
GGING TOOLS • RESTORE A BROKEN FLOWERPOT • SHARPEN PRUNING CLIPPERS • REMOVE RUST FROM TOOLS • REVIVE WILTING CUT F
ET RID OF RAMPANT BRAMBLES • TROUBLESHOOT BROWN SPOTS ON A LAWN • CONTROL MAJOR GARDEN PESTS • RID YOUR GARDEN C
ONPERFORMING COMPOST PILE • FIX BAD SOIL • SHORE UP A RAISED GARDEN BED • REMOVE A DEAD OR DISEASED TREE LIMB • TROUE
RAINAGE • TROUBLESHOOT ROSE DISEASES • IDENTIFY AND CORRECT SOIL DEFICIENCIES IN ROSES • TROUBLESHOOT ROSE PESTS • OV
AMAGED DECK BOARDS • REPAIR DECK RAILINGS • STRENGTHEN DECK JOISTS • FIX A RUSTY IRON RAILING • REPAIR A GATE • REPAIR A
RACKED OR DAMAGED CONCRETE • IMPROVE THE LOOK OF REPAIRED CONCRETE • REPAIR AN ASPHALT DRIVEWAY • REVIVE WOODEN O
ARDEN PONDS • CLEAN SWIMMING POOL WATER • TROUBLESHOOT HOT TUBS AND SPAS • REPLACE BRICKS IN WALKWAYS AND PATIOS •
AR WITH JUMPER CABLES • SHUT OFF A CAR ALARM THAT WON'T QUIT • FREE A CAR STUCK ON ICE OR SNOW • DE-ICE YOUR WINDSHIEL
URN-SIGNAL COVER • FIX A CAR FUSE • FIX DASHBOARD LIGHTS THAT WON'T LIGHT • REMOVE CAR SMELLS • CHECK TIRE PRESSURE • IN
IPROPERLY INSTALLED CHILD CAR SEAT • TROUBLESHOOT LEAKING OIL • CHECK AND ADD POWER-STEERING FLUID • CHECK AND ADD C
ROKEN EXHAUST PIPE • CHECK AND ADD ENGINE OIL • CHECK AND ADD BRAKE FLUID • CHECK AND ADD FLUID TO YOUR AUTOMATIC T
ROUBLESHOOT A WINDSHIELD-WASHER PUMP • REPAIR MINOR DENTS • CHANGE A HUBCAP • FIX AN IGNITION KEY THAT WON'T TURN •

Appliances

R GUITAR • GET RID OF RED-EYE IN PHOTOGRAPHS • REDUCE PUFFINESS AROUND YOUR EYES • REMOVE A SPECK FROM YOUR EYE •
MORY • FIX AN ELECTRIC CAN OPENER THAT DROPS THE CAN • TROUBLESHOOT A CELL PHONE • KEEP MIRRORS FROM FOGGING • ZAP
KEEP A SHAVING NICK FROM BLEEDING • GET RID OF SPLIT ENDS • UNTANGLE HAIR SNARLS • FIX FRIZZY HAIR • FIX BLEEDING LIPSTICK •
ICKY SOCIAL SITUATION • FIX A BAD REPUTATION • CLEAN LIPSTICK FROM A COLLAR • FIX A BAD RELATIONSHIP • SALVAGE A BAD DATE •
EEDING NOSE • BEAT THE MONDAY MORNING BLUES • GET OUT OF A FIX • EXTRACT A BROKEN KEY • RETRIEVE KEYS LOCKED INSIDE A C
TOP SOMEONE FROM CHOKING • STOP AN ANT INVASION • STABILIZE A CHRISTMAS TREE • RESCUE AN ITEM FROM THE DRAIN • FIX IMPE
KUNK ODOR FROM YOUR DOG • GET A CAT OUT OF A TREE • CORRECT BAD BEHAVIOR IN CATS • TREAT A CAT FOR MATTED FUR • REPLA
EAM • TREAT MILDEW DAMAGE • GET STATIC OUT OF YOUR LAUNDRY • DEAL WITH A CLOTHES-MOTH INFESTATION • FIX A SEPARATED ZIP
UR SOCK • TREAT MIXED-WASH ACCIDENTS • TAKE WRINKLES OUT OF CLOTHING • FIX A HOLE IN JEANS • REPAIR A SNAG IN A SWEATER •
TAINS • WASH SNEAKERS • PICK UP A DROPPED STITCH IN KNITTING • RESTRING BEADS • FRESHEN SMELLY SHOES • FIX A SAGGING CLO
• FIX A RUBBING DOOR • FIX A DRAFTY DOOR • TUNE UP SLIDING DOORS • FIX A SHOWER DOOR • SEAL WALL JOINTS AROUND A TUB O
W • REPAIR A FAULTY WINDOW CRANK • REPAIR VERTICAL BLINDS • REPAIR VENETIAN BLINDS OR MINIBLINDS • REPAIR WOOD OR PLASTIC
CREEN WINDOWS • INSTALL NEW SASH CORDS IN WINDOWS • FIX A TIGHT OR LOOSE WINDOW SASH • REPAIR MINOR DRYWALL DAMAGE •
BLEM • REPLACE A DAMAGED CEILING TILE • REPLACE A WOOD FLOORBOARD • QUIET SQUEAKING FLOORS • REPAIR A WATER-DAMAGE
R A VINYL-TILE FLOOR • SILENCE SQUEAKY S[...]STER • REPLACE CAULKING ON THE OUTSIDE OF
NG STOVE • REPAIR AND PREVENT WOOD RO[...]TCH A GUTTER LEAK • TROUBLESHOOT A WET BA
GGING GUTTER • UNCLOG GUTTERS AND D[...] • REPAIR A CRACKED OR SPLIT WOOD SHINGLE •
ARAGE-DOOR TENSION • TROUBLESHOOT A [...]ITES • LOOSEN A RUSTY NUT OR BOLT • TROUBLE
NK SWEATING • FIX FLUSHING PROBLEMS •[...]FAUCET • FIX A STOPPER THAT DOESN'T SEAL • C
MP PUMP PROBLEMS • TROUBLESHOOT ELE[...]USE • SWAP A FAULTY LIGHT SWITCH • REDUCE E
HOOT FLUORESCENT LIGHTING • FIX A LOW[...]E THERMOSTAT • TROUBLESHOOT HOLIDAY LIGHT
TING SYSTEM • REFRESH A SMELLY REFRIGE[...]MS • FIX A LEAKING REFRIGERATOR • REPAIR A C
CTIONING GAS BURNER • REPAIR A RANGE H[...]FIX AN ELECTRIC OVEN THAT HEATS POORLY • DIA
P YOUR APPLIANCES • CONTROL GARBAGE [...]E DISPOSAL • DIAGNOSE WASHING MACHINE PRO
FIX A HAIR DRYER • TROUBLESHOOT A CLO[...]AT SPUTTERS • FIX AN IRON THAT LEAVES SPOTS C
NER • FIX A DEHUMIDIFIER • REPAIR A CONS[...]DER • HANDLE A MIXER THAT OVERHEATS • REPAIF
G MACHINE • TROUBLESHOOT SMOKE ALAR[...]OARD SPILLS • TROUBLESHOOT A COMPUTER THA
REMOVE A WINDOWS PROGRAM • SPEED U[...]OUSE • REPLACE YOUR PC'S BATTERY • CLEAN A
T FAILS ITS SELF-TEST • CORRECT MONITOR[...]APER JAM • TROUBLESHOOT A RECURRING PRIN
ONE MODEM PROBLEMS • TROUBLESHOOT A[...]REEN GLARE • GET TOP-NOTCH SCANS • RECOVE
ESTORE A CD • REPAIR A WARPED CD • CLE[...] • EXTRACT A JAMMED VIDEOTAPE • ADJUST VCR
OTE CONTROL • FIX AUDIOCASSETTES • FIX[...]OT A CASSETTE DECK • REPLACE BROKEN RABBIT
BLESHOOT A CD PLAYER • REPLACE A HEAD[...]RASS • SHINE SILVER SAFELY • REMOVE A BROKEN
PLACE A BROKEN TOWEL ROD • REMOVE ST[...]E FOR NATURAL DISASTERS • FIX A FRAYED CARPE
BORING BATHROOM • REPLACE A SHOWER[...]NACE FILTER • REPAIR A BROKEN SLIDING DRAWE
D CHAIR • FIX A WOBBLY WOOD CHAIR • SF[...]OR CRACKED PORCELAIN • REPAIR CHIPPED OR C
WAX FROM CARPETING • GET RID OF CEILIN[...]MOVE MYSTERY STAINS FROM CLOTHING • REMOV
A RUG OR TABLECLOTH • REMOVE BURN M[...]NITURE • STRIP WAX BUILDUP FROM FLOORS • RE
ODORANT STAINS • ELIMINATE CIGARETTE ODOR • RESTORE SHINE TO YOUR JEWELRY • WASH DIRTY WINDOWS • REMOVE GRIME FROM MIN
UMBLED CAKE • FIX A PERFECT CUP OF TEA • PATCH A TORN PIE CRUST • KEEP A PIE CRUST FROM GETTING SOGGY • FIX DOUGH THAT W
DULL KNIFE • REMOVE RUST FROM A CAST-IRON PAN • REPAIR LAMINATE COUNTERTOPS • REMOVE STAINS FROM A STONE COUNTERTO
R CHOLESTEROL • TREAT BURNED POTS AND PANS • RESCUE A BURNED CAKE OR PIE • PUT OUT A KITCHEN FIRE • REMOVE THE BITTERN
N UNDERSEASONED DISH • REMOVE OVEN SPILLS • CLEAN UP OIL SPILLS • FIX A DRINK FOR ANY OCCASION • DISENTANGLE PASTA • RE
CUTTING BOARD • KEEP A MIXING BOWL STEADY • FIX GARDEN TOOL HANDLES • REPAIR A LEAKY HOSE NOZZLE • MEND A LEAKY HOSI
ARPEN A POWER MOWER BLADE • SHARPEN PUSH MOWER BLADES • REPAIR BALD SPOTS ON GRASS • RID YOUR GRASS OF DOG URINE
OUBLESHOOT HERBS • TROUBLESHOOT HOUSEPLANTS • OVERCOME SHADE PROBLEMS • RID SOIL OF PESTS AND DISEASES • REVIVE A
EES AND SHRUBS • REPAIR A LEAKING IRRIGATION SYSTEM • UNCLOG A SPRINKLER SYSTEM • CLEAN A CLOGGED DRIP SYSTEM • FIX PO
GUS DISEASES IN ROSES • REPAIR DECK STEPS • RENOVATE A WEATHERED DECK • TIGHTEN LOOSE DECKING • REMOVE DECK STAINS •
E • LEVEL AND SMOOTH A GRAVEL PATH • FIX A POTHOLE IN A DIRT OR GRAVEL DRIVEWAY • REPLACE PATIO STONES, TILES AND PAVERS
NITURE • RESTORE WEATHERED METAL FURNITURE • REPAIR CHAIR STRAPS AND WEBBING • REVIVE RUSTED IRON FURNITURE • TROUBLE
LED CAR • SHUT OFF A JAMMED HORN • CHANGE YOUR CAR'S BATTERY • TROUBLESHOOT A CAR THAT WON'T START • FIX A FLAT TIRE •
NED-OUT SIGNAL BULB • FIX A BURNED-OUT HEADLIGHT • ADJUST HEADLIGHTS • FIX A STUCK BRAKE LIGHT • REPLACE A BROKEN TAIL
TIRES • FIX A STUCK CONVERTIBLE TOP • DIAGNOSE A LEAK INSIDE YOUR CAR • REPLACE YOUR AIR FILTER • HANDLE A FAULTY REPAIR •
OOL AN OVERHEATED ENGINE • REPLACE A LEAKING RADIATOR HOSE • CHANGE YOUR WIPER BLADES • ADD WINDSHIELD-WASHER FLUID
• TROUBLESHOOT YOUR BRAKES • ADD BRAKE FLUID TO THE CLUTCH MASTER CYLINDER • TROUBLESHOOT DASHBOARD WARNING LIG
SPARK-PLUG WIRES • DIAGNOSE CAR SMELLS • CLEAN THE OUTSIDE OF YOUR CAR • RESTORE YOUR CAR'S SHINE • WASH THE INTERIOR

208 Refresh a Smelly Refrigerator

Is something fouling the air around your refrigerator? Assuming it's not a long-forgotten dish left inside, there are two common causes: mold growing inside the drip pan, or dust overheating on the condenser coils.

Steps

Cleaning a drip pan

1 Remove the grill along the bottom of your refrigerator. Locate the drip pan, using a flashlight if necessary. The pan should be sitting on a set of black condenser coils.

2 Remove the pan and wash it. Use a mixture of warm, soapy water and bleach to kill the mold.

3 Reinstall the pan and the grill.

Cleaning the condenser coils

1 Locate the coils. They look like thin, black radiators and may be underneath the fridge or attached to the back.

2 If the coils are on the back, pull the refrigerator away from the wall, then vacuum the dusty coils, using the brush and crevice attachments. Reinstall the refrigerator grill.

3 If the coils are underneath, pull off the grill and remove the drip pan. Vacuum the dusty coils, using the crevice attachment to get between them (see illustration). Take care not to damage the delicate coils. Reinstall the refrigerator grill.

What You'll Need

- Flashlight
- Sponge
- Bucket
- Soap
- Bleach
- Vacuum and attachments

Tips

To clean coils thoroughly, buy a condenser coil brush. Sold at home centers and appliance stores, these long, thin brushes are designed to fit into tight spots.

Your refrigerator's electrical parts can produce an acrid smell if they malfunction. If the strategies suggested here don't cure your problem, ask a professional to check your system.

209 Diagnose Refrigerator Problems

When your fridge malfunctions, you need answers quickly. Otherwise, you could end up losing hundreds of dollars' worth of food. This list of possible causes and solutions will help you analyze your problem. See also 208 Refresh a Smelly Refrigerator, 210 Fix a Leaking Refrigerator, 211 Repair a Clogged Ice Maker and 213 Fix a Refrigerator That Cools Poorly.

PROBLEM	CAUSE	SOLUTION
Fridge won't run	No power	Check power cord. Reset circuit breaker.
	Thermostat turned off	Adjust thermostat.
	Faulty thermostat	Call a professional.
Fridge won't cool or cools poorly	Thermostat turned down	Adjust thermostat.
	Compressor has overheated due to dust buildup on condenser coils	Vacuum condenser coils.
	Bad condenser fan	Call a professional.
	Ice buildup on evaporator coils due to bad defrost heater	Call a professional.
	Worn-out door gaskets	Replace gaskets.
Squealing sound inside	Failing evaporator-coil fan	Call a professional.
Squealing sound underneath	Failing condenser-coil fan	Call a professional.
Water leaks from machine	Cracked or misaligned drain pan	Replace pan or align it under drain tube.
	Plugged defrost drain	Clean drain.
	Water filter for ice maker is leaking	Tighten fittings or replace filter.
	Water-supply line to ice maker is leaking	Tighten fittings or replace line.
	Ice-maker inlet valve is leaking	Tighten fittings. If it still leaks, call a professional.
	Water tube to ice-maker tray has slipped out of position	Realign water tube.
Fridge too cold	Bad thermostat	Call a professional.
Frost buildup in freezer	Bad defrost heater	Call a professional.

210 Fix a Leaking Refrigerator

Water on the floor around a refrigerator is enough to make anyone nervous. But often there's a simple reason for the problem—and an easy cure. The key is locating the source.

Steps

Analyzing the likely source

1 Move the refrigerator out from the wall and look for the location of the leak.

2 Check the side panels and the seals around the door for beads of "sweat." This could indicate a condensation problem.

3 Check the floor. A puddle there could indicate a missing or cracked drip pan, or a leak in the water line that feeds your ice maker.

4 Check for water seeping from the front of the freezer or the refrigerator. This could indicate your defrost drain is plugged or your ice maker is leaking.

Fixing a condensation problem

1 Check that the doors shut correctly. Hold each door about halfway open, then let go. If the doors don't shut completely, adjust the screw legs on the front of the refrigerator so the unit tilts back a bit. With adjustable pliers, turn each leg one revolution clockwise. Recheck the doors and, if necessary, repeat the process until they shut securely.

2 Inspect the door gaskets. Look for debris that may keep the doors from shutting. Also check for cracks or gaps in the gaskets that could allow the cold air to seep out. If you find debris, clean the gaskets with warm, soapy water. If you find cracks or gaps, you'll need to replace the gaskets (see 213 Fix a Refrigerator That Cools Poorly).

3 If your refrigerator is equipped with a door-frame heater that evaporates condensation, make sure the heater is turned on. The switch should be located with your other refrigerator controls.

Fixing a drip-pan problem

1 Pull off the grill that runs along the bottom of your refrigerator.

2 Locate the drip pan, using a flashlight if necessary. The pan should be sitting on top of a set of black condenser coils and directly below a drain tube that carries water from your freezer when it is in defrost mode.

What You'll Need

- Adjustable pliers
- Soap
- Replacement parts
- Flashlight
- Screwdriver
- Meat baster
- Nut driver and socket
- Adjustable wrench

Tips

To keep door gaskets clean and supple, wash them twice a year with warm, soapy water, then coat them with a light film of petroleum jelly.

Some refrigerators have an internal defrost drain that is meant to be serviced by a professional. If you can't find your drain, call a pro.

3 Place the drip pan in your sink and fill it with water to test for leaks. If it leaks, order a replacement from your appliance dealer.

4 If the drip pan doesn't leak, clean it with warm, soapy water, then reinstall the pan and the refrigerator grill.

Fixing a clogged defrost drain

1 Locate the defrost drain. It should be a round hole or a channel running under the vegetable and fruit bins in the refrigerator or along the floor of the freezer compartment.

2 Inspect the drain for clogs and remove any debris. If necessary, use a small screwdriver to break up debris that's trapped in the drain hole.

3 Fill a meat baster with hot water and force it through the drain to make sure the clog is gone. If the drain is operating properly, the hot water will fill the drip pan.

Fixing a leaky ice maker

1 Pull the refrigerator away from the wall and locate the copper water-supply line. It runs from the house water line to the refrigerator water-supply valve. (To get to the supply valve, you may have to use a screwdriver or a nut driver and socket to remove your refrigerator's back access panel.)

2 Inspect the copper supply line, the supply valve, and the plastic supply tube that runs from the other side of the supply valve to the back of the ice maker.

3 If a connection is leaking, tighten it with an adjustable wrench. If either the copper supply line or the plastic supply tube is leaking, you need to replace it.

4 Turn off the water supply. The valve may be under the kitchen sink or connected to a cold-water pipe in your basement.

5 Remove the faulty line and take it to a hardware store to get an exact replacement.

6 Install the new line, tighten the connections with the adjustable wrench and turn the water back on.

Warning

To prevent possible electrical shock, always unplug your refrigerator before working on it.

Put carpet scraps or another soft material under the front legs before pulling your refrigerator away from the wall. Otherwise, the legs could damage the flooring.

211 Repair a Clogged Ice Maker

When your ice maker produces small or hollow cubes, it's a sign the unit isn't getting enough water. The cause could be a faulty thermostat or a bad water-inlet valve—problems you may want a professional to fix. Or if you're lucky, you may just have a clog in the water-supply system. You can handle that yourself following these steps.

Steps

Dealing with a damaged water line

1 Pull the refrigerator out from the wall and unplug it.

2 Turn off the water-supply valve. The valve may be under the kitchen sink or connected to a cold-water pipe in your basement.

3 Inspect the water-supply line that runs to the refrigerator, looking for crimps or kinks.

4 Carefully straighten any problem areas you find, using just hand pressure. If you can't remove the crimps and kinks, replace the water line.

5 Disconnect the line from the refrigerator and from the water-supply valve, using an adjustable wrench.

6 Buy a replacement line at your appliance store and install it, tightening the connections firmly to prevent leaks.

Checking and replacing a water filter

1 Turn off the water, unplug the refrigerator and pull it away from the wall.

2 Locate the water filter, if your ice maker has one. It will look like a canister or cylinder and will be attached to the water-supply line.

3 Using the adjustable wrench, disconnect the end of the filter that runs to the refrigerator while leaving the other end of the filter attached to the water-supply line.

4 Hold the filter over a bucket and ask a helper to turn on the water-supply valve. If water flows freely, the filter is good. If water dribbles or doesn't flow at all, the filter needs to be replaced.

5 Turn off the water-supply valve and disconnect the filter from the water-supply line, using your adjustable wrench.

6 Buy a replacement filter at your appliance store and install it. Tighten the connections firmly to prevent leaks.

What You'll Need

- Replacement parts
- Adjustable wrench
- Bucket
- Screwdriver, or nut driver and socket

Tips

If your ice maker itself is faulty, think twice before having it rebuilt. Often replacement parts are so expensive, you're better off buying a new unit.

Still have problems with your ice? Check the freezer temperature. It must be 5°F (–15°C) or colder for the ice maker to work properly.

Warning

To prevent possible electrical shock, always unplug your refrigerator before working on it.

Put carpet scraps or another soft material under the front legs before pulling your refrigerator away from the wall. Otherwise, the legs could damage the flooring.

Cleaning a clogged inlet valve

1 Turn off the water, unplug the refrigerator and pull it away from the wall.

2 Remove the bottom access panel on the back of the refrigerator, using a screwdriver or a nut driver and socket.

3 Remove the water inlet valve using the nut driver and socket.

4 Disassemble the valve and clean the screen, using the tools and steps outlined in 222 Fix a Dishwasher That Fills Slowly.

212 Get Rid of Microwave Smells

Given the wide range of foods that get passed through it, your microwave oven can get a little smelly from time to time. Usually you can eliminate odors by giving the oven a good cleaning.

Steps

1 Unplug the oven and unfasten the cabinet body, using a screwdriver. The body should be attached along the back as well as along the sides or bottom.

2 Slide the cabinet body back slightly to clear any internal brackets, then lift it off.

3 Clean the oven, using a vacuum with plastic crevice attachment. Vacuum the fan and other internal parts, then vacuum the vents underneath the oven, on the back and inside the chamber.

4 Reassemble the oven and plug it in.

5 Fill a small bowl with a 50-50 mixture of water and white vinegar, then set it in the oven and turn the oven on high for 5 minutes. When the mixture boils, it will remove stubborn smells inside the vents and loosen food particles on the oven walls.

6 Wipe down the oven walls with a clean sponge.

What You'll Need

- Screwdriver
- Vacuum with plastic crevice attachment
- Small bowl
- White vinegar
- Sponge

Tip

Occasionally, electrical parts will burn and produce a foul smell. If so, unplug your oven and call a professional.

Warning

Never put your hands or any metal object inside the cabinet. You could get shocked.

213 Fix a Refrigerator That Cools Poorly

Are the foods in your refrigerator spoiling quickly? Do your drinks feel warm? You could have a bad compressor or condenser fan, which means calling in a professional. But if you're lucky, the problem may just be dirty coils or troublesome door gaskets. To clean the coils, see 208 Refresh a Smelly Refrigerator. To fix the gaskets, follow these steps.

Steps

Inspecting and cleaning a door gasket

1 Inspect the gasket for dirt or debris that could prevent it from sealing. If you find any, remove the large debris, then wash the gasket, using a scrub brush and warm, soapy water.

2 Check the gasket for cracks or tears that can let cold air escape. If you find any, replace the gasket. If the gasket appears to be solid, go on to step 3.

3 Check the seal: Open the door, insert a dollar bill partway and shut the door on the bill. Try to pull out the bill. You should feel some resistance. Repeat the test at several points around each door. If the bill slips out easily, replace the gasket.

Replacing a door gasket

1 Remove the old gasket. It is held to the refrigerator by screws and a retainer strip that runs around all four sides of the door. Lift the lip of the gasket so you can see the screws. Loosen but do not remove the screws, using a screwdriver or a nut driver and socket. Pull the gasket from the retainer strip.

2 Buy a replacement gasket—and a package of cord caulk—at an appliance store.

3 Prepare the new gasket for installation: Soak it in warm water to soften it. Then place a 2-inch (5-cm) strip of cord caulk at each corner of the door where the gasket will sit. This will keep the gasket from curling at the corners when it's installed.

4 Install the new gasket: Slip the bead on the back of the gasket under the retainer strip. Tighten the retainer screws. Do the top and the bottom, then the sides. Make sure the gasket is straight and flat when you're done.

5 Close the door and check that the new gasket is touching on all four sides. If it isn't, the door has twisted while the gasket screws were loose, and you'll need to adjust it.

6 To adjust the door, loosen the retainer screws slightly, then grab the door at opposite corners and push or pull to remove the twist. Tighten the screws, then shut the door and recheck alignment. If the door still appears warped, repeat the process.

What You'll Need

- Scrub brush
- Soap
- Dollar bill
- Screwdriver, or nut driver and socket
- Replacement gasket
- Cord caulk

Tips

Before removing a gasket, empty the shelves on the door. This will reduce the likelihood that the door will warp when you loosen the retainer screws.

Dirt and debris can quickly collect in the grooves in your door gaskets. To keep them sealing properly, check them every few months.

214 Fix a Gas Oven That Heats Poorly

A gas oven that heats unevenly or won't get up to temperature may
have a faulty thermostat or clogged burner ports. To adjust the thermostat, see 218 Fix an Electric Oven That Heats Poorly.

Steps

1 Remove the oven door. It may just lift up and off the hinge arms,
or you may have to unscrew it from the hinges.

2 Spread several sheets of newspaper on the bottom pan to absorb
soap and water that may spill during cleaning.

3 Locate the upper burner, attached to the roof of the oven.
Remove the burner cover, if there is one. Use a screwdriver or
a nut driver and socket, as required.

4 Clean the burner flame openings, using a scrub brush and warm,
soapy water to remove the surface grime, and the end of a paper
clip to poke out dirt that has collected in the openings (see illustration). If the surface grime is particularly stubborn, spray with
oven cleaner and let it sit for 15 minutes. Then rewash the burner
with warm, soapy water, and again clear the flame openings with
your paper clip.

5 Remove the newspaper and lift out the bottom pan. The lower
burner will be underneath. Clean the lower burner, following the
same procedure described in step 4.

6 Wipe up any water or dirt that collects under the burner. Let all
the parts dry thoroughly, then reassemble the oven.

What You'll Need

- Screwdriver, or nut driver
  and socket
- Old newspaper
- Scrub brush
- Soap
- Paper clip
- Oven cleaner

Tips

The flames from your oven
burner should be blue. If
yours are yellow, the air-gas
mixture may be out of
adjustment. Ask a profes-
sional to correct it.

Never cover the bottom pan
with aluminum foil to collect
drips. You might cover air
openings and hinder the
oven's ability to heat evenly.

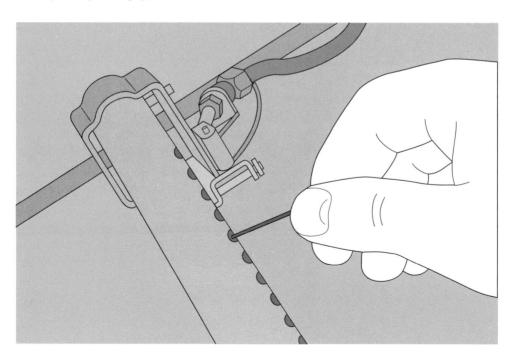

215 Clean a Malfunctioning Gas Burner

Most of the time, when a gas burner refuses to light or runs poorly when lit, the cause is dirt or grease. Fine particles of dirt or grease spatters can clog the flame openings on the burner, or can plug the pilot light that starts the burner. Here's how to handle both problems.

Steps

1 Turn off the gas to the stove. Lift the cooktop so you can access the burner parts. On some stoves, you just need to lift the corners to raise the cooktop; on others you have to push the top backward first, then lift. Prop the cooktop open, using the brace that is attached to the inside of it.

2 Remove the burner unit by lifting up the back end of the unit and sliding the front end off the gas-supply lines.

3 Wash the burner unit in warm, soapy water, using a scrub brush to remove any grease that may be blocking the openings. Let the unit dry upside down in a dish rack before moving to step 4.

4 Clear the flame openings, using a straight pin or needle to poke out any dirt or debris (see A).

5 Clear the flash tube openings, using a needle or piece of fine wire, such as one strand from a piece of twisted electrical wire.

6 Clean the pilot opening, using a straight pin or needle (see B). Take care not to enlarge the opening. If you do, the pilot may not run right.

7 Reinstall the parts, turn on the gas to the stove, and relight the pilot light with a match. Test the burner.

What You'll Need

- Scrub brush
- Soap
- Dish rack
- Straight pin or needle
- Fine wire

Tips

If your stove hasn't been used in a while, check the orifice tube to the burner. Sometimes spider webs will block the flow of gas.

If your stove has an electronic igniter instead of a pilot light and the igniter isn't working, call a professional to replace it.

A
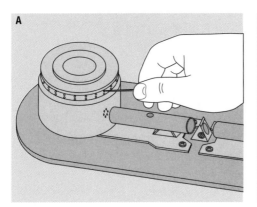

B
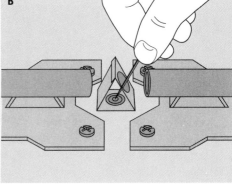

216 **Repair a Range Hood**

A range hood that doesn't adequately remove smoke and smells from your kitchen is usually suffering from one of a few common problems: The grease filter or some part of the exhaust ductwork may be clogged, or the fan may be bad. Neither of these repairs should take you much time.

Steps

Unclogging the exhaust system

1 Remove the grease filter by sliding it out of its clips.

2 Submerge the filter in a plastic pan filled with hot, soapy water and ½ cup (4 fl oz/125 ml) ammonia. Let it soak for at least 15 minutes. If it's still dirty, soak it again, then rinse it thoroughly and set it aside to dry.

3 Remove the exhaust fan. Unplug the fan, then use a screwdriver or a nut driver and socket to take out the screws that attach it to the hood.

4 Clean the fan blades with an old toothbrush dipped into the ammonia-water mixture (see Warning).

5 Clean the inside of the exhaust ductwork, using a plumber's snake with a heavy rag tied around the end. Push the snake through the ductwork. Soak the rag in the ammonia and water mixture, then run it through the ductwork. Rinse out the rag and repeat the operation until the duct appears to be clean.

6 Clean the exhaust hood that's attached to the outside of your house. Use the old toothbrush and the ammonia-water mixture to loosen the grit and grime around the flapper plate. Make sure the plate moves freely when you're done. If it sticks closed, it can prevent the exhaust hood from working.

7 Reinstall the grease filter.

Replacing the fan motor

1 Remove the grease filter by sliding it out of its clips.

2 Turn on the fan and inspect the motor. It needs to be replaced if it hums rather than turns, turns very slowly, runs for a short time then stalls, or feels very hot and won't turn.

3 Disconnect and remove the fan, following step 3, above.

4 Take the fan to an appliance store to get an exact replacement.

5 Install the new fan.

What You'll Need

- Plastic pan
- Soap
- Ammonia
- Screwdriver, or nut driver and socket
- Old toothbrush
- Plumber's snake
- Heavy rag
- Replacement fan

Tips

Never put a grease filter in your dishwasher to clean it. You could end up with a film of hard-to-remove grease on the dishwasher walls.

Clean your grease filter monthly. It's your first line of defense against grease and grime that can damage the fan motor and plug the ductwork.

Warning

When cleaning the blades on the exhaust fan, take care not to wet the motor. The water could short-circuit the motor when you reinstall it.

217 Fix an Electric-Range Element

Has one burner on your electric stove suddenly stopped burning? Don't worry. Usually this is a problem you can solve quickly, once you've used the process of elimination to figure out what's wrong. One safety note—always unplug the stove between each repair step to avoid shock.

Steps

Identifying the problem

1 Inspect the faulty element to determine whether it plugs into a receptacle, as most do, or is wired directly. If it plugs in, move on to step 2. It the element is direct-wired, move on to step 4.

2 Remove the plug-in element and inspect the prongs: Lift up the front of the element, then pull the element straight out (see illustration). Check to see if the prongs are burned, pitted or otherwise damaged. If they are, you'll need to replace the element and the receptacle.

3 If the prongs are clean, test the element: First reinstall it in the receptacle and turn on the burner—sometimes an element just needs to be reseated to work right. If it still doesn't heat, turn off the burner, exchange the element with another of the same size and test. If the burner works now, the original element needs to be replaced.

What You'll Need

- Flathead screwdriver
- Replacement parts
- Masking tape and pen
- Wire cutters
- Wire strippers
- Wire nuts

Tips

If these steps don't identify your problem, ask a profes-sional to check the surface switch that controls the faulty element. Occasionally it can go bad.

If the entire stove won't work and the power is on, check the stove fuse. It may be near the surface controls or under the cooktop.

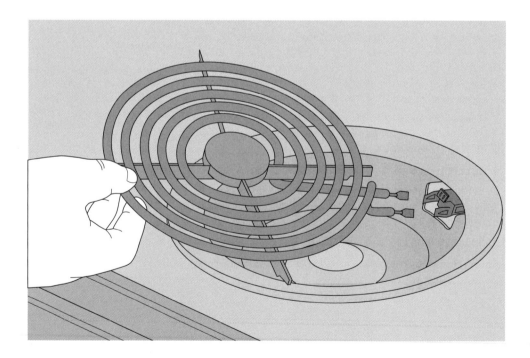

4 If the element is direct-wired, lift the front of the element and pull it out until you see a white porcelain insulator with clips on each side.

5 Open the insulator. Wedge a flathead screwdriver under the side of one clip and gently pry. This will pop the clip off. Repeat to remove the other clip. Then separate the two halves of the insulator.

6 Remove the screws that hold the element to its wiring, using a screwdriver. Exchange the element for another of the same size. Reassemble both elements so no bare wires are left exposed, then turn on the burner. If the new element works, the original one needs to be replaced.

Warning

Always unplug your stove between each repair step to protect yourself from accidental shock.

Replacing an element

1 Take the faulty element to a hardware or appliance store and buy a replacement.

2 Install the new element in the stove. For a plug-in element, just plug it into the receptacle. For a direct-wired element, screw the new element to its wiring, reassemble the two halves of the porcelain insulator, and snap the clips in place.

3 Test the element to make sure it's operating.

Replacing a receptacle

1 Disconnect the old receptacle. If it is screwed to the cooktop, use a screwdriver to disconnect it. If it is held in place by a spring steel clamp, spread the clamp and pull out the receptacle.

2 Lift the cooktop so you can access the receptacle wiring. On some stoves, you just need to lift the corners to raise the cooktop; on others, you have to push the top backward first, then lift. Prop the top open, using the brace that is attached to the inside of the cooktop.

3 Remove the receptacle. Wrap the wires with masking tape and label them so you can install the new receptacle correctly, then cut the wires. Take the receptacle to a hardware or appliance store to get a replacement.

4 Install the new receptacle. Strip the ends of the wires with a wire stripper, then twist the wires together and twist on wire nuts to hold them together. Reinstall the receptacle in the cooktop and install the element.

If your oven won't get up to temperature or leaves your food half-cooked, it's likely that either the thermostat needs to be adjusted or one of the elements has gone bad. Both fixes take little more than a screwdriver and a few minutes of your time.

Steps

Testing and adjusting the thermostat

1 Place an oven thermometer inside the oven and shut the door.

2 Turn on the oven, set it for 350°F (180°C) and let it heat for 30 minutes.

3 Check the thermometer. Most thermostats are accurate to within 25°F (14°C). If yours is off by more than 50°F (28°C), the thermostat is bad and you will need to have a professional replace it. If your thermostat is off by less than 50°F (28°C), adjust the thermostat.

4 Locate the adjustment screw. On some thermostats, the adjustment screw is on the back of the thermostat knob; on others it's inside the thermostat shaft.

5 To make a temperature adjustment on the back of a knob, remove the knob and loosen the retaining screws on the back, using a Phillips screwdriver. Turn the center disk toward "Hotter" or "Raise" to increase the temperature, or toward "Cooler" or "Lower" to decrease the temperature. Tighten the screws, reinstall the knob and test the oven. Readjust the knob if necessary.

6 To make a temperature adjustment inside the shaft, remove the knob and slip a thin flathead screwdriver into the knob until it engages the adjustment screw in the bottom. Turn the screwdriver clockwise to raise the temperature, counterclockwise to lower it. Each quarter-turn will move the temperature about 25°F (14°C). When you're done, reinstall the knob and test the oven. Readjust the temperature if necessary.

Replacing a faulty element

1 Identify the bad element. Set the oven to broil and check the upper element. Then turn it to bake and check the lower one. Both elements should turn bright orange if they're operating correctly. If one is cold, it needs to be replaced. If they both seem to heat up, look for signs that one is damaged. It may appear to be melted in one spot, or one spot may not turn as bright a color as other parts.

What You'll Need

- Oven thermometer
- Phillips and flathead screwdrivers
- Nut driver and socket
- Masking tape and pen
- Replacement oven element

Tips

If you find it hard to reach to the back of the oven, lift off the oven door.

Oven still won't work? Ask a professional to check the oven-door safety switch. A faulty switch can prevent the oven from heating.

2 Turn off power to the oven at the circuit-breaker panel, leave the oven door open, and let the oven sit until the elements are cool to the touch.

3 Loosen the bad element. Use a screwdriver or a nut driver and socket to remove the screws that hold the element-support bracket to the oven's back wall. Slip the element out of the brackets that hold it in place, and pull it forward until you can access the wiring (see illustration).

4 Disconnect the wiring. Wrap each wire with masking tape, and label them so you can install the new element correctly. Then unscrew the element from its wiring.

5 Take the element to an appliance store and buy a replacement.

6 Install the new element. Screw the element to its wiring, slip the element into its brackets, and screw the element-support bracket to the back of the oven.

7 Turn on the power and test the new element.

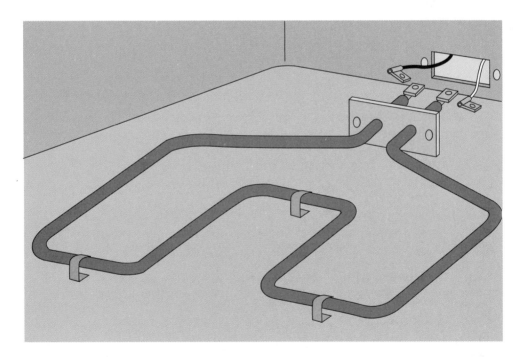

219 Diagnose Dishwasher Problems

In the grand scheme of things, a dishwasher is a fairly simple machine. It doesn't have a clutch like a washing machine, nor a drive belt like a dryer. Still, the parts can malfunction from time to time. Here's how to analyze what's troubling your dishwasher. See also 220 Correct an Overflowing Dishwasher, 221 Fix a Leaky Dishwasher and 222 Fix a Dishwasher That Fills Slowly.

PROBLEM	CAUSE	SOLUTION
Dishwasher won't start	No power to machine	Check plug on portable machine. Reset circuit breaker on wired-in machine.
	Door isn't closed	Close and latch door.
	Motor has failed	Call a professional.
Machine cleans poorly	Spray head is blocked	Check for utensils or pot handles that may be hanging below the bottom rack and interfering with motion of spray head.
	Spray head is clogged	Clean holes with toothpick.
	Water temperature is too low	Check temperature at hot water faucet with meat thermometer. If below 120°F (49°C), turn up thermostat on hot water heater.
Dishwasher overflows or leaks	Float switch is jammed or malfunctioning	Clean float shaft so float moves freely. If necessary, replace float switch.
	Machine isn't level	Adjust feet to level machine.
	Broken door gasket	Replace gasket.
	Loose hoses or fittings	Tighten hoses and water-supply-line fitting.
	Pump or motor seal leaks	Call a professional.
Dishwasher fills slowly	Water strainer is partially clogged	Clean water strainer.
Dishwasher won't fill	Inlet valve or float switch is malfunctioning	Clean or replace valve or float switch.
	Water strainer is clogged	Clean water strainer
Dishwasher won't drain	Drain screen is clogged	Remove food debris from drain screen.
	Drain hose is clogged	Unhook each end of hose to locate clog, then clean.

220 Correct an Overflowing Dishwasher

When a dishwasher overflows, the float switch assembly is the most likely cause. The float itself may be sticking, or the electrical switch that turns the water on and off may be malfunctioning. Neither is difficult to fix.

Steps

Cleaning the float

1 Open the dishwasher door and locate the float switch. It should be a cylinder-shaped piece of plastic and may be set to one side along the front of the cabinet or near the sprayer head in the middle of the machine.

2 Check the float to make sure it moves freely up and down on its shaft. (You may have to unscrew and remove a protective cap to get to the float.) If the float sticks, you'll need to clean away any debris or mineral deposits that are causing it to jam.

3 Pull the float off the shaft, then clean the inside of the float with a bottle brush. Clean the shaft with a scrub brush.

4 Reinstall the float and check that it moves smoothly.

5 Set the dishwasher to fill, and check to see if it overflows. If it still malfunctions, you need to replace the float switch.

Replacing the float switch

1 Turn off power to the dishwasher by unplugging it or turning off the circuit breaker.

2 Remove the service panel that runs along the bottom front edge of the dishwasher. If it is screwed to the dishwasher, remove the screws with a screwdriver. If the panel hangs on hooks, pull the panel out and swing it up to get it off the hooks.

3 Locate the float switch. Wrap each wire with masking tape and label each so you can reinstall them correctly on the new switch. Then remove the wires with needle-nose pliers.

4 Remove the old switch, using a screwdriver or a nut driver and socket to loosen the fasteners.

5 Take the switch to an appliance store and purchase an exact replacement.

6 Install the new switch and attach the wires.

7 Replace the service panel, turn on the power and test the machine.

What You'll Need

- Bottle brush
- Scrub brush
- Screwdriver
- Masking tape and pen
- Needle-nose pliers
- Nut driver and socket
- Replacement float switch

Tips

To melt mineral deposits that can jam the float, pour a cup of white vinegar in the empty dishwasher and run it through a cycle.

If your dishwasher won't fill, also check the float switch assembly. The unit can stick in the Off position, too, preventing water from entering the machine.

221 Fix a Leaky Dishwasher

Is there a puddle in front of your dishwasher? Often this is a relatively easy problem to solve. At best, all you need to do is tighten a few fittings or level the dishwasher so water doesn't slosh out when the machine is running. At worst, you may need to replace a door gasket.

Steps

Tightening the fittings

1 Remove the service panel that runs along the front of the dishwasher just below the door. If it is screwed in place, remove the screws with a screwdriver. If the panel hangs on hooks, pull the panel out and swing it up to remove it from the hooks.

2 Check the end of the drain hose that connects to the dishwasher. If it's leaking, tighten the clamp with a screwdriver.

3 Check the drain hose connection to the kitchen sink drain. Again, if it's leaking, tighten the clamp with a screwdriver.

4 Check for leaks around the water-inlet valve. If necessary, use an adjustable wrench to tighten the compression fitting that connects the water-supply line to the valve. If the fill hose is leaking, replace the spring clamp that is on the hose with a worm-drive hose clamp. It produces more clamping pressure. Use adjustable pliers to compress the spring clamp so you can pull the clamp and hose off the valve. Remove the spring clamp from the hose. Buy a worm-drive clamp at your hardware store, then install it and tighten it with a screwdriver.

What You'll Need

- Screwdriver
- Adjustable wrench
- Worm-drive hose clamp
- Adjustable pliers
- Small level
- Replacement door gasket

Tips

If your dishwasher has an air gap, which prevents dirty water from re-entering the machine, clean it regularly. Otherwise, it could overflow and leak.

Always use detergent that's made for your dishwasher. Dishwashing liquids and other soaps can create excessive suds that will leak from the machine.

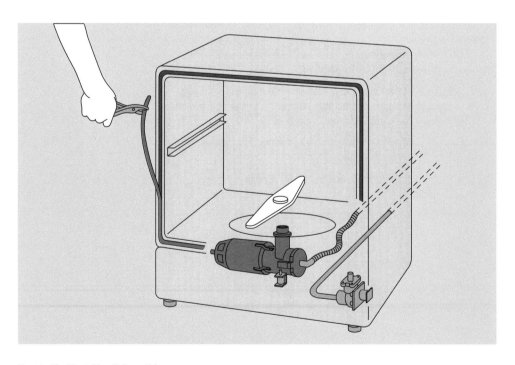

Leveling the machine

1 Remove the front access panel (see step 1, opposite page). This will give you access to the dishwasher's adjustable feet.

2 Open the door completely and remove the bottom dish rack.

3 Unscrew the dishwasher from the kitchen countertop so the dishwasher can move freely as you adjust the feet.

4 Check to see if the dishwasher is level side to side. Place a small level inside the dishwasher so it's sitting on the bottom pan and facing parallel to the front lip of the dishwasher. If the dishwasher is not level, use adjustable pliers to turn one of the dishwasher's front feet up or down until you hit level.

5 Check to see if the dishwasher is level front to back. Turn the level perpendicular to the door, and place it on one of the bottom ledges that run along the side of the cabinet. Check the level again. If the dishwasher isn't level, use your adjustable pliers to turn the back feet up or down until you hit level.

6 Reattach the dishwasher to the countertop and reinstall the front access panel.

Fixing a leaking door

1 Inspect the door gasket. As it ages, the gasket can crack or become hard, preventing it from sealing completely.

2 If the gasket appears solid, adjust the door latch so the door seals tightly. Loosen the screw that holds the door latch to the cabinet. Push the latch in slightly and retighten the screw. Test the door and readjust the latch if necessary.

3 Replace the gasket if water continues to leak after you've tightened the latch. Most gaskets are held by compression in a groove on the door or on the dishwasher cabinet.

4 Pull the old gasket out of its groove, using adjustable pliers (see illustration). Take the gasket to an appliance store to get a replacement.

5 Soak the new gasket in warm water to soften it, then press it into the groove. Start at the top, then work your way down the sides and across the bottom.

Occasionally, the main seal between the dishwasher cabinet and the pump fails. If your dishwasher leaks at this spot, have a professional replace the seal.

222 Fix a Dishwasher That Fills Slowly

Your dishwasher is equipped with an intake screen that filters out rust and other debris that could damage the pump and other delicate parts. Sometimes, though, the intake screen collects so much debris that it slows the flow of water to the dishwasher. When that happens, you need to remove and clean the screen.

Steps

1 Shut off the power and water to the dishwasher. Flip the circuit breaker at the main panel, then close the water valve. If you can't find a dedicated valve under your sink, shut off the home's main water valve.

2 Remove the service panel from the bottom of the dishwasher. If it is screwed to the dishwasher, remove the screws with a screwdriver. If the panel hangs on hooks, pull the panel out and swing it up to remove it from the hooks.

3 Locate the inlet valve. It should be near the front and will have two water lines and a pair of wires connected to it (see A).

4 Disconnect the water lines. Use an adjustable wrench to remove the fitting from the water-supply tube. Use adjustable pliers to compress the hose clamp on the fill hose, then slide the clamp up a couple of inches (about 5 cm) so you can remove the hose.

5 Wrap the wires with masking tape; label each so you can reinstall them correctly. Remove the wires with needle-nose pliers.

6 Remove the screws that hold the valve to the dishwasher, using a nut driver and socket. Remove the four bolts that hold the inlet fitting to the valve, using a nut driver and socket or an adjustable wrench. Then pull the fitting off the valve. The screen will be underneath.

7 Use a small screwdriver to gently pry the screen out (see B), then clean it with an old toothbrush.

8 Reassemble the valve and reinstall it, then turn the power and water back on.

What You'll Need

- Screwdriver
- Adjustable wrench
- Adjustable pliers
- Masking tape and pen
- Needle-nose pliers
- Nut driver and socket
- Small screwdriver for prying
- Old toothbrush

Tips

If your intake screen is coated with hard-to-remove mineral deposits, soak it overnight in a bowl of white vinegar to dissolve the minerals.

If your dishwasher won't fill at all, the inlet valve could be bad. To replace the old valve, use the steps outlined on this page.

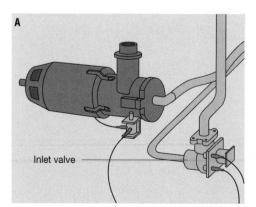

A

Inlet valve

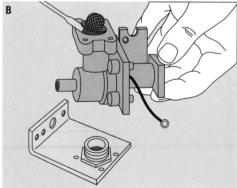

B

223 Touch Up Your Appliances

In a busy kitchen, it's hard not to scratch and scuff appliances. Simple touch-ups will help keep them looking like new.

Steps

1 Sand the damaged area lightly with fine-grit sandpaper. Roughen the area to be painted and remove any rust, but avoid sanding the surrounding surface.

2 Clean the area thoroughly with a rag dampened with paint thinner. Let dry.

3 Paint over scratches with appliance touch-up paint, using the bottle's applicator brush or another fine-tip paintbrush. Let dry overnight. (Touch-up paint fades and peels from surfaces that are exposed to high temperatures, so use it only on appliances that do not heat.)

4 Fill nicks by building up thin layers of paint. Allow each layer to dry completely before painting the next layer.

What You'll Need

- Fine-grit sandpaper (280- to 320-grit)
- Rag
- Paint thinner
- Appliance touch-up paint
- Fine-tip paintbrush

Tip

You can buy appliance touch-up paint at hardware or home improvement stores.

224 Control Garbage Disposal Odors

A garbage disposal is supposed to *eliminate* odors by chopping up garbage and sending it down the drain. But occasionally the disposal itself becomes the source of smells. If the smell is caused by garbage collecting inside a jammed disposal, see 225 Fix a Jammed Garbage Disposal. Otherwise, the steps here should fix the problem.

Steps

1 Inspect the black rubber cover that fits in the disposal. Sometimes bits of garbage collect under the flaps and create a smell.

2 Clean the rubber cover, if necessary. If yours lifts out, remove it and clean away debris with a scrub brush and warm, soapy water. If your rubber cover is installed permanently, lift up each flap and clean it with soapy water and an old toothbrush.

3 Deodorize the disposal. Cut a lemon in half and drop the fruit and a handful of baking soda into the disposal. Turn on the cold water faucet and then the disposal. The unit will clean itself as it grinds up the mixture.

What You'll Need

- Scrub brush
- Soap
- Old toothbrush
- Lemon
- Baking soda

Warning

If you need to work anywhere near a garbage disposal's blades, shut off the switch or turn off the circuit breaker first.

225 Fix a Jammed Garbage Disposal

Garbage disposals are simple machines—basically a motor and a fly-wheel with impeller arms that spin and shred whatever they touch. Sometimes, though, the machine can jam on a bottle top or other debris, or trip a circuit breaker when it's overloaded. If that happens, you just need to take a quick step or two to repair it.

Steps

1 Turn the garbage disposal on and off quickly and check to see if it has power. If it hums, the power is on but the impeller is jammed. Move on to step 3. If it doesn't hum, it may have over-heated and tripped a circuit breaker. Move on to step 2.

2 Restore power to the machine. Most disposals have an overload switch that trips when the motor starts to overheat. To reset the switch, look for a small red button on the bottom of the housing, and if it's there, push it in (see A). If your disposal doesn't have an overload switch or the machine still won't run after you reset the switch, reset the circuit breaker that serves the disposal.

3 Clear the jam from underneath. On many disposals, you can insert a ¼-inch (6-mm) Allen (hex) wrench into the bottom of the housing and manually move the motor shaft and flywheel to dislodge the jam. If your disposal has an opening for an Allen (hex) wrench, insert the wrench and move it back and forth until the motor and flywheel turn freely.

4 Clear the jam from above. Press the end of a short broomstick against one of the impellers, and jab in one direction and then the other until the jam breaks loose (see B).

5 Remove the debris. Turn off the circuit breaker that controls the garbage disposal. Reach inside with a pair of long-nose pliers and pull out whatever jammed the machine.

6 Turn on the cold water—this hardens any grease inside and helps the disposal chop it up—and run the disposal until all the remain-ing garbage is gone.

What You'll Need

- ¼-inch (6-mm) Allen (hex) wrench
- Short broomstick
- Long-nose pliers

Tips

Never use a chemical drain cleaner to try to clear debris from the garbage disposal. The caustic chemicals can damage gaskets and other parts.

To avoid jams, keep the opening to your disposal covered with a rubber strainer when not in use.

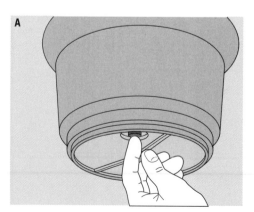

A

B

226 Diagnose Washing Machine Problems

Are washing machine problems leaving you—well, agitated? Don't fret. Many times the cause is something simple. And fixing it is just a matter of a little tightening here, replacing the odd part there. See also 227 Fix a Washing Machine That Fills Slowly and 228 Fix a Washing Machine That "Walks" Across the Floor.

PROBLEM	CAUSE	SOLUTION
Washer won't start	No power to machine	Check to see if plug is in socket. Reset circuit breaker.
	Defective lid switch	Call a professional.
Washer has power but tub won't turn	Motor may be overheated	Let washer cool for 30 minutes. If it still won't restart, call a professional.
	Motor or transmission may have failed	Call a professional.
	Drive belt may have broken	Call a professional.
Washer won't drain	Drain hose is clogged or kinked	Clean out drain hose and straighten any kinks.
	Drain hose fits too tightly in standpipe	Standpipe must be minimum of 1¼ inches (3 cm) in diameter to provide air so water drains.
	Clothing is stuck in the drain pump, or the drain pump has failed	Call a professional.
Washer won't fill or fills slowly	Faucets only partially open	Turn faucet handles counterclockwise as far as possible.
	Fill hoses are kinked	Straighten hoses.
	Water strainers are clogged	Turn off water, remove hoses and clean strainers.
Washer leaks	Loose hose connections	Tighten connections at faucets and washer.
	Hoses have failed	Turn off water at faucets and install new hoses.
	Drain hose has disconnected	Reseat drain hose in drain.
	Main tub seal has failed	Call a professional.
Washer is noisy	Load is unbalanced	Redistribute heavy items.
	Machine isn't level	Adjust feet.
Washer overfills	Water-inlet valve or switch is defective.	Call a professional.

227 Fix a Washing Machine That Fills Slowly

When a washing machine fills slowly, the problem is usually something simple. You may have a kink in the hose that runs from the faucet to the washer. But most often, a clogged intake screen is the reason. Clean it and your washer will be back in action.

Steps

1 Turn off the water faucets that feed the machine.

2 Unplug the washer and pull it far enough away from the wall that you can get behind it to work.

3 Remove each water-supply hose, using adjustable pliers. Start at the end that connects to the inlet valve on the back of the washer (see A). Hold a small bucket under each hose as you remove it to collect any water that's left in the hose. Then remove each hose where it connects to a faucet.

4 Locate the screens. Most washers have intake screens in the hose ports on the back of the machine. But your machine also may have aftermarket screens. They'll be inside the hose couplings, in the ends that attach to the faucets.

5 Gently pry out the screens using a small flathead screwdriver (see B). Take care not to dent them.

6 Clean the screens, using an old toothbrush.

7 Reinstall the screens, using the tip of your screwdriver to push them firmly into place.

8 Reinstall the hoses and tighten the couplings securely.

9 Turn on the water to check for leaks, then plug in the machine and push it back into position.

What You'll Need

- Adjustable pliers
- Small bucket
- Small flathead screwdriver
- Old toothbrush

Tips

If your inlet screens are clogged with hardened mineral deposits, soak them overnight in a bowl of white vinegar to dissolve the minerals.

If your machine refuses to fill at all, it's likely the inlet valve itself is bad. Call a professional to replace it.

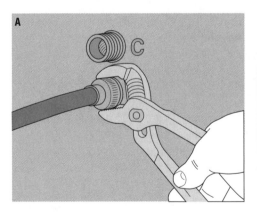

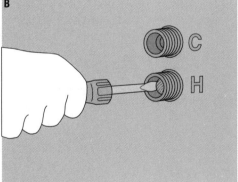

228 Fix a Washing Machine That "Walks" Across the Floor

Does your washing machine seem possessed with the spirit of John Travolta during his *Saturday Night Fever* days? It's likely that one or more of the machine's feet aren't touching the floor and it is rocking as it washes. To fix the problem, you just need to level the machine.

Steps

1 Tilt the machine forward so the back feet are 3 to 4 inches (7.5 to 10 cm) off the ground, then set it back down. The back feet usually are self-leveling—just raising and lowering the machine like this will cause the feet to re-level themselves.

2 Place a sturdy 2-by-4 wood block under the center of the washer to prop it up so you can access the front feet. You might have to move the washer out from the wall so that you can tilt it up enough to install the block.

3 Loosen the locknut on each foot, using an adjustable wrench. Once the locknuts are loose, you can adjust the feet.

4 Remove the wood block, and if you moved the washer, set it back into position against the wall.

5 Place a carpenter's level across the front of the washer and check to see if the machine is level side to side. If it isn't, use adjustable pliers to rotate one front foot or the other until the washer is level.

6 Place your level perpendicular to the front of the machine and check to see if the washer is level in this direction. If it is off, readjust each front foot by the same number of turns until you reach level.

7 Put the washer back on the wood block and retighten the locknuts, then if necessary, push it back against the wall.

What You'll Need

- 2-by-4 wood block
- Adjustable wrench
- Carpenter's level
- Adjustable pliers

Tips

It's better to adjust the feet so they end up shorter, rather than longer. The closer the machine is to the floor, the less likely it is to vibrate and shake.

If your machine still "walks" after you've leveled it, it could be that the floor under the machine is weak. Have a carpenter check it.

229 Fix a Clothes Dryer That Dries Slowly

Does your dryer take forever to dry? While the problem could be something simple, like a kink in the vent hose, or complex, like a broken heating element, a more likely cause is excessive lint. When lint collects in your machine, it reduces air flow, slowing drying time significantly. And lint on electrical parts can shorten their lives or cause a fire. The solution? A good vacuuming.

Steps

Cleaning the ductwork

1 Pull the dryer out from the wall and unplug it.

2 Disconnect the clamps that hold the vent hose to the dryer and the vent duct, using adjustable pliers or a screwdriver.

3 Take the hose outdoors where you can stretch it out and clean it.

4 Loosen the lint inside the hose, using a plumber's snake with a heavy rag tied around the end. Push the snake and rag back and forth through the hose.

5 Vacuum up the loose lint, using a vacuum and attachments. Then, if lint still appears to be stuck to the hose, repeat the process.

6 Clean the ductwork that runs to your outside exhaust hood. If you have a long run of ductwork, you may have to take it apart to clean it thoroughly. Otherwise, use the plumber's snake and rag.

7 Clean the exhaust hood that's attached to the outside of your house. Use an old toothbrush to loosen the lint and your vacuum to collect it. Take extra time cleaning the flapper plate and make sure it moves freely when you're done. If the flapper sticks when it's shut, the dryer won't be able to exhaust properly.

Cleaning inside the machine

1 Open the filter slot—it's either on top of the machine or inside the door—and take out the removable filter.

2 Vacuum around and inside the filter slot, using your vacuum and crevice attachment. Vacuum the removable filter, too.

3 Remove the dryer's back panel, using a nut driver and socket.

4 Vacuum inside the back of the machine. Then vacuum the vents on the back panel.

What You'll Need

- Adjustable pliers or screwdriver
- Plumber's snake
- Heavy rag
- Vacuum with attachments
- Old toothbrush
- Nut driver and socket
- Thin screwdriver or putty knife

Tips

Lint is more likely to collect in a long run of ductwork. If yours is over 12 feet (3.5 m) long, try to reroute and shorten it.

Packing too many clothes in your dryer also can slow drying time significantly. Fill the dryer loosely rather than jamming it with clothes.

5 Remove the service panel that runs along the front of the dryer, just below the door. It should be held in place by two clips along the top edge of the panel. To free the clips, slip a thin screwdriver or a putty knife between the top of the panel and the bottom of the door and pry. Pull the top of the panel forward, then lift it off the hooks that hold the bottom to the machine. Set it aside.

6 Vacuum inside the bottom of the dryer. Make sure to vacuum the motor and pulley.

7 Reinstall the front and back panels.

8 Reinstall the vent hose.

9 Plug in the machine.

230 **Fix a Hair Dryer**

The parts in a hair dryer are subject to dust and high heat during the natural course of operating. So it's no surprise that those two trouble-makers are often to blame when a hair dryer runs poorly or stops altogether. Often, all it needs is a good cleaning and lubrication.

Steps

1 Disassemble the housing, using a screwdriver.

2 Clean the heating element. With tweezers, extract any hair or lint, then use an old toothbrush to remove dust.

3 Clean the inside and outside of the intake vent and filter, using an old toothbrush to loosen the grit, and a vacuum with crevice attachment to remove it.

4 Vacuum the rest of the interior, including the fan, motor and switches. Use the tweezers to remove any hair that's wound around the motor or other parts.

5 Spray the switches with electrical-contact cleaner to remove grit that may be preventing them from operating correctly.

6 Oil the bushings at both ends of the motor with one drop of machine oil.

7 Reassemble the hair dryer.

What You'll Need

- Screwdriver
- Tweezers
- Old toothbrush
- Vacuum with crevice attachment
- Electrical-contact cleaner
- Machine oil

Warning

Be gentle when cleaning around the hair dryer's heating element. The wire in the element is fragile and can break easily.

Always unplug your hair dryer before working on it to avoid electric shock.

231 Troubleshoot a Clothes Dryer

Dryers are hardy machines that can run for years. Even when something does go wrong, the problem may be something simple, like lint buildup. Check this list for possible causes and solutions. See also 229 Fix a Clothes Dryer That Dries Slowly.

PROBLEM	CAUSE	SOLUTION
Dryer won't start	No power to machine	Check plug. Reset circuit breaker.
	Door isn't closed	Close door.
	Door switch is bad	Call a professional.
Drum won't turn	Drive belt has failed	Call a professional.
	Motor has failed	Call a professional.
	Thermal fuse that protects motor is bad	Call a professional.
Dryer dries slowly	Lint filter is clogged	Clean filter.
	Exhaust duct is clogged	Clean duct.
	Kink in exhaust duct	Straighten duct.
	Dryer overloaded	Remove some clothes.
	Bad door gasket	Replace gasket.
Dryer won't heat	Gas-supply problem (on gas-powered machines)	Call a professional.
	Igniter is bad (on gas-powered machines)	Call a professional.
	Electric heating coil has failed (on electric dryers)	Call a professional.
	Defective thermostat	Call a professional.
Excess humidity in air	Duct has come loose from dryer	Reattach and tighten clamp.
	Hole in exhaust hose	Replace duct.
Dryer squeals or rumbles when running	Drive-belt idler pulley needs to be replaced	Call a professional.
	Rollers that support drum need lubrication or replacement	Call a professional.
	Blower wheel clogged with lint	Vacuum blower.
Dryer overheats	Defective thermostat or clogged internal vent	Call a professional.

232 Correct a Steam Iron That Sputters

If your iron sputters when it should be steaming, it's often because minerals from your water have hardened and clogged the steam jets and spray nozzle. Here's an easy cure.

Steps

1 Unplug the iron and let it cool.

2 Scrape any visible mineral deposits from the jets on the bottom of the iron, using a toothpick or the tip of a small ice pick.

3 Clean the spray nozzle with a fine needle.

4 Fill the iron with equal parts white vinegar and distilled water. Place an oven rack over your sink and position the iron on top, with the steam vents facing down. Plug in the iron and turn it to the steam setting. Run it until the steam stops.

5 Fill the iron with plain distilled water and repeat the process.

What You'll Need

- Toothpick or small ice pick
- Fine needle
- White vinegar
- Distilled water
- Oven rack

Tip

To prevent mineral buildup in your iron, always use distilled water.

233 Fix an Iron That Leaves Spots on Fabric

When an iron leaves stains on your clothes, the cause could be rust inside the steam chamber or dirt on the ironing surface.

Steps

1 Scrub the ironing surface with a wet cloth covered with a mild abrasive such as baking soda or table salt.

2 Wipe the ironing surface with a clean, damp cloth to remove the residue.

3 Fill the iron with equal parts white vinegar and distilled water. Place an oven rack over your sink and position the iron on top, with the steam vents facing down. Plug in the iron and turn it to the steam setting. Run it until the steam stops.

4 Fill the iron with plain distilled water and repeat the process.

5 To prevent spots in the future, after ironing, empty any leftover water while the iron is still hot. That way, the heat will dry out the steam chamber and prevent any metal particles in the water from rusting.

What You'll Need

- Cloths
- Baking soda or table salt
- White vinegar
- Distilled water
- Oven rack

234 Fix Your Vacuum Cleaner

If your vacuum runs but still leaves dirt behind, the culprit could be the drive belt or an obstruction. If the agitator brush slips or won't turn, the belt is bad and needs to be replaced. If suction is weak when you place your hand over the vacuum hose, some part is blocked.

Steps

Replacing a drive belt

1 Unplug the machine and flip it over so you can access the agitator brush.

2 Unscrew the bottom plate that holds the brush in place, using a screwdriver.

3 Lift out the brush by pulling the roller ends out of the slots in the vacuum base. If the drive belt isn't completely broken, one end will be wrapped around the agitator brush, the other around the motor drive shaft. Slide the belt off of each part. Take it to a hardware store to get a replacement.

4 Inspect the agitator brush before installing the new belt. Sometimes thread or hair will wrap around the ends or elsewhere on the brush roller. This can prevent the agitator from turning and cause a belt to fail prematurely. Cut any thread or hair with a sharp knife and pull it off.

What You'll Need

- Screwdriver
- Replacement drive belt
- Sharp knife
- Broomstick

Tips

For peak performance, always empty your vacuum cleaner when the bag or canister gets about three-quarters full. Beyond that, dirt and debris can hinder suction.

Inspect your hoses once or twice a year. A hole or slit in a hose can cut suction dramatically.

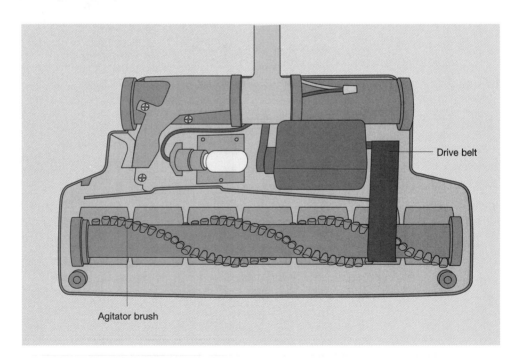

Drive belt

Agitator brush

5 Install the new belt. Slide one end over the agitator brush and the other over the drive shaft. Then reinstall the agitator brush. You may have to pull on the agitator brush to stretch the new belt a bit so the roller ends fit into the vacuum base.

6 Reinstall the bottom plate.

Clearing an obstruction

1 Inspect the hose, wand and cleaning tools to locate the obstruction. Debris often collects where one part plugs into another, or where the hose connects to the main vacuum housing. Remove the parts one at a time and remove any debris you find.

2 Clear any hidden obstructions by pushing a broom handle through the hose and wands.

3 Reassemble all the parts.

235 Replace Vacuum Cleaner Brushes

The bristles on your vacuum cleaner's agitator brush are designed to beat the rug and lift out dirt. But over time they wear out from this constant pounding. You can test your brushes and replace them if necessary using these steps.

Steps

1 Unplug the vacuum cleaner and flip it over so you can access the agitator brush.

2 Lay a ruler across the vacuum's bottom plate and move it back and forth while turning the agitator brush by hand. If the bristles touch the edge of the ruler, they are good. If not, they need to be replaced.

3 Remove the agitator brush (see 234 Fix a Vacuum Cleaner, "Replacing a drive belt," steps 2 and 3, opposite page).

4 Take the agitator brush to an appliance store to buy the replacement part. On some machines, the bristles are permanently attached to the agitator and you'll have to replace the whole unit. Other machines have replaceable bristles that fit into slots in each side of the agitator brush; you can buy replacements and slide them into place.

5 Install the new or refurbished agitator brush (see 234 Fix a Vacuum Cleaner, "Replacing a drive belt," steps 5 and 6, above).

What You'll Need

- Ruler
- Screwdriver
- Replacement agitator brush or bristles

Tip

To keep the bristles on your vacuum from becoming clogged with hair, thread and other debris, regularly clean them with an old comb.

If you return home after a long day and find your air conditioner out of order, it can leave you hot in more ways than one. Once you've determined what's wrong, getting the unit running right may be just a matter of making one or two small repairs. See also 237 Fix a Window Air Conditioner.

PROBLEM	CAUSE	SOLUTION
Unit won't run	Power is off	Check wall plug. Check circuit breaker.
	Bad thermostat	Call a professional.
A/C unit won't cool air	Dirty filter	Remove grill and clean filter.
	Clogged evaporator coils or clogged condenser coils	Vacuum coils. If necessary, scrub coils lightly with old toothbrush. Take care not to bend fins.
	Shrub or other obstacle blocking air flow	Trim obstacle or move air conditioner to other location.
	Bad fan motor	Call a professional.
	Bad compressor	Call a professional.
Unit won't blow air	Bad fan motor	Call a professional.
Machine leaks	Drain plug clogged, preventing condensed water from escaping	Clear clog with screwdriver.
	Improper installation	Unit should be installed so it tilts slightly to the outside to let water drain.
Ice forms on coils	Dirty air filter	Clean filter.
	Outside temperature below 60°F (16°C)	Defrost the coil by turning selector switch to Fan position. Let run until ice melts.
Rattling noise inside unit	Condenser fan or evaporator fan is loose, hitting coils or housing	Remove cabinet, reposition fan and tighten screw at center of fan.

237 Fix a Window Air Conditioner

When a window air conditioner cools poorly, it doesn't necessarily mean you're in for an expensive trip to the repair shop. It could be the machine just needs a good cleaning and some tender care.

Steps

1 Remove the front grill. Pry it off with a putty knife if it's held by clips, or use a screwdriver if it is screwed in place.

2 Unplug the air conditioner, slide it out of the window cabinet and set it on a sturdy table. You may need a helper to move the air conditioner if it's heavy.

3 Locate the mesh filter. It covers the radiator-like fins on the machine's evaporator coils.

4 Remove the filter, and wash it and the grill in a mixture of warm, soapy water and bleach—this will remove any mold. Shake out the excess water and set the filter and grill in your dish drain to dry.

5 Vacuum the evaporator coils thoroughly, using a vacuum with brush attachment. Remove any stubborn dirt with a plastic scrub brush.

6 Inspect the fins on the coils. If any fins are bent or flattened, buy a fin comb from an appliance store and run the comb up or down the fins to straighten them.

7 Turn the air conditioner around so the back is facing you. You will see a second set of coils—the machine's condenser coils.

8 Vacuum these coils thoroughly, using the vacuum and brush attachment. Remove any stubborn dirt with a plastic scrub brush.

9 Inspect the fins on the condenser coils, and if any are bent, use the fin comb to straighten them.

10 Remove any dirt or lint from inside the unit, using the vacuum and crevice attachment. Make sure you clean the fan blades, too, using the vacuum and brush attachment.

11 Put the air conditioner back into the window cabinet.

12 Reinstall the filter and front grill, and plug in the machine.

What You'll Need

- Putty knife or screwdriver
- Bleach
- Soap
- Vacuum and attachments
- Plastic scrub brush
- Fin comb

Tips

Having a hard time vacuuming dust deep inside the coils? Take the air conditioner outside and use a leaf blower to blow the dust away.

Clean the filter monthly when the air conditioner is running. The machine will cool better, and you'll cut energy consumption 5 to 15 percent.

Warning

Take extra care when working around the fins on the evaporator and condenser coils. They are extremely delicate and bend easily.

238 Fix a Dehumidifier

A dehumidifier is really just an air conditioner working in reverse—it's subject to the same problems and cured by the same repairs. So if your dehumidifier won't pull moisture from the air, the problem could be a simple one that often stops an air conditioner from cooling: The filter and coils are clogged with dirt. The solution? Give it a thorough cleaning.

Steps

1 Unplug the dehumidifier, then remove and empty the water-holding tank.

2 Remove the front and back grills. You'll have to either use a putty knife and pry between the top of the grill and the cabinet body to release the catches, or use a screwdriver to unscrew the fasteners.

3 Remove the mesh filter, if your machine has one. It may be attached to the front grill or set in a track in front of the evaporator coils.

4 Clean the filter with a mixture of warm, soapy water and bleach. The bleach will kill any mold or mildew, so it won't be blown around the room when the machine is running.

5 Clean the evaporator coils, using a vacuum with brush attachment. Remove any stubborn dirt with a scrub brush and a household spray cleaner, such as Formula 409. Scrub lightly so you don't bend the fins covering the coils.

6 Inspect the fins. If they are flattened or bent, buy a fin comb at your appliance store and use it to comb up or down on the fins to straighten them.

7 Clean the condenser coils, using the vacuum and brush attachment. Again, remove any stubborn dirt with the scrub brush and spray cleaner.

8 Inspect the fins covering these coils. If they are flattened or bent, use the fin comb to straighten them.

9 Unfasten the cabinet body so you can get access to the interior parts. Use a screwdriver to remove the screws along each side of the bottom of the cabinet. Also check the control panel and the plastic drain tray that directs water into the holding tank. If any screws are holding these parts to the cabinet, remove them.

10 Remove the cabinet body. Grab each side, pull out slightly and then lift the body off the unit.

11 Clean the fan blade and the other parts inside the cabinet, using the vacuum and crevice attachment.

12 Reassemble the dehumidifier, reinstall the water-holding tank and plug in the unit.

What You'll Need

- Putty knife
- Screwdriver
- Soap
- Bleach
- Vacuum and attachments
- Scrub brush
- Household spray cleaner
- Fin comb

Tips

Clean the water-holding tank with bleach at least once a month. Otherwise, mold may grow and be blown around when the dehumidifier runs.

If your dehumidifier seems to be running well, yet still won't draw moisture from the air, check the room temperature. Dehumidifiers won't work efficiently below 65°F (18°C).

239 Repair a Console Humidifier

A console humidifier that fails to humidify a room could have a bad humidistat, fan switch or float switch—problems that take specialized equipment to diagnose. But before you call in a pro, it's worth your time to test the fan motor and float assembly, since repairing them is something you can handle on your own.

Steps

Testing and fixing the fan

1 Test the fan motor. While the machine is plugged in and full of water, turn both the humidistat knob and fan-control knob to high. If the fan hums but does not turn, or turns slowly, the motor needs to be replaced. If the fan won't move, you may have a bad switch somewhere. Call a professional.

2 To replace a bad fan motor, unplug the machine and disconnect the fan wires from the switch panel. You may have to pry apart a plug, use needle-nose pliers to pull the connectors off the switch, or unscrew the connectors.

3 Remove the old motor from its housing, using a Phillips screwdriver or a nut driver and socket.

4 Remove the fan blade from the motor. Use adjustable pliers to open the spring clamp at the center of the fan blade, and then slip the clamp off. Use a flathead screwdriver to gently pry off the blade, then set it aside.

5 Take the motor to an appliance store to buy a replacement.

6 Install the fan blade on the new motor, then install the motor and reattach the wires.

Testing and fixing the float assembly

1 Locate the empty tank float assembly. This assembly consists of a switch, a connecting rod (on some units) and some type of float. It's supposed to shut down the machine when the water reservoir is low, but if the float jams in the down position, the dehumidifier won't turn on.

2 Check the float and connecting rod, if there is one. If the parts are bent and touching the cabinet, use gentle hand pressure to straighten them so they move freely. If your dehumidifier has a float switch that is triggered by the filter housing moving up and down, make sure the housing is centered in its tracks and moves freely. Clean any debris and dirt out of the channels, using a scrub brush.

3 Check that the float connecting rod is contacting the float switch. If it isn't, bend the end of the rod so it touches the switch.

What You'll Need

- Needle-nose pliers
- Phillips screwdriver, or nut driver and socket
- Adjustable pliers
- Flathead screwdriver
- Replacement fan motor
- Scrub brush

Tips

To prevent bacteria and dust from collecting in your humidifier and then being blown around the room, clean the water reservoir and fan monthly.

To keep your fan motor running smoothly, lubricate it with a few drops of machine oil every few months.

240 Troubleshoot a Blender

The last thing you need while you're making mayonnaise or serving up smoothies is for your blender to go on the blink. Here are some ways to get it crushing and puréeing again.

Steps

1 Make sure the blender is plugged in properly and that the circuit breaker has not been tripped.

2 Check that the jar is fully engaged with the base.

3 Remove the blender jar from the base, and check that the blade moves freely. If not, disassemble the blade and ring. Check for obstructions or misalignment.

4 If the blender is not puréeing well, check that there are no air pockets in the food surrounding the spinning blade. To get rid of any air pockets, turn off the blender and press the food down with a long spoon.

5 If you've been using the blender for a long period of time and it stops working, it may have overheated. Turn it off and let it cool for 10 to 20 minutes before trying again.

6 You may have a blown fuse or a worn-out motor. If the blender has multiple speeds but now works only at full speed, the triax (or variable-speed control) is broken. Contact the manufacturer for parts and instructions.

What You'll Need

- Long spoon

Tip

You may need to add a little liquid to help blend the food more smoothly.

241 Handle a Mixer That Overheats

Mixing dough can be hard work; even electric mixers get tired now and then. For such times, some mixers have reset buttons. If your handheld or countertop mixer doesn't have one, here are a few ways to get it whirring smoothly again.

Tip

Higher-wattage mixers are less likely to overheat. A 350-watt countertop mixer should be powerful enough to knead dough for one loaf of bread, but you'll need at least 450 watts for kneading two loaves at a time.

Steps

1 As soon as you smell an acrid, burning odor, turn off the mixer and let it cool for 10 to 20 minutes before turning it on again.

2 If the mixer continues to overheat, split the batter or dough into smaller batches. Mix them separately.

3 Run the mixer for shorter periods and let the mixer cool between each one.

4 If the mixer no longer starts, you may have blown a fuse. Call the manufacturer to ask for parts and directions or for the location of the nearest service center.

242 Repair a Food Processor

If your food processor stops dead in mid-chop, turns erratically or begins making a grinding noise, there's a good chance the drive belt or the drive gear is the cause. You can fix either problem with a pair of screwdrivers and, if need be, a replacement part or two.

Steps

Dealing with a worn or broken belt

1 Unscrew the machine's base, using a screwdriver. You may need to pry off the rubber feet to access some of the screws.

2 Inspect the drive belt (see A). If it is slack, loosen the screws holding the motor assembly (see B), and follow step 4 to increase the belt's tension. If the belt is broken, get a replacement from an appliance store or the manufacturer.

3 Install the new belt. Loosen the screws holding the motor assembly, and shift the drive gear toward the reduction gear so you can slip the belt over each gear.

4 Shift the drive gear away from the reduction gear to increase the belt's tension, then tighten the motor-assembly screws.

Dealing with a worn drive gear

1 Inspect the drive gear. If the teeth are worn, you need to replace it. Remove the drive belt as described above to access the gear.

2 Remove the gear, using an Allen (hex) wrench to loosen the setscrew in the side. Then buy a replacement from an appliance store or the manufacturer.

3 Slide the new gear onto the drive shaft, and align it so the center is parallel to the center of the reduction gear. Tighten the setscrew with the Allen (hex) wrench.

4 Replace the belt, and increase the tension as directed in step 4, above.

5 Reinstall the base and any rubber feet you removed.

What You'll Need

- Screwdriver
- Replacement parts
- Allen (hex) wrench

Tip

If the drive gear is hard to remove, tap it gently with a hammer to loosen it, then pry it off with a flathead screwdriver.

Warning

To avoid electric shock and prevent your fingers from getting jammed in moving parts, always unplug your food processor before disassembling it.

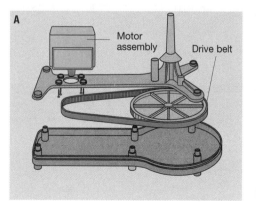

A — Motor assembly, Drive belt

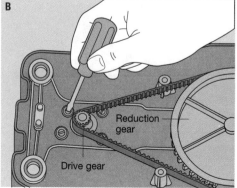

B — Reduction gear, Drive gear

243 Fix a Toaster

Given how inexpensive the average toaster is, it's not worth putting a lot of time and money into repairing one if it refuses to heat up. But before you consign yours to the scrap heap, there are a couple of quick things you can check that might just put it back into operation.

Steps

1 Pull out the plug.

2 Turn it over and remove the screws in the bottom, using a screwdriver (see A). On a toaster with a metal body and plastic end caps, just remove the screws that connect the bottom to the front end cap. On a toaster with a full plastic body, remove the screws that hold the entire cabinet body in place.

3 Pull the knob off the carriage lever. This is the part that lowers the toast into the toaster.

4 Remove the front end cap or the cabinet body as needed to get to the electric contacts.

5 Locate the electric contacts. They'll be below and in line with the carriage lever.

6 Inspect the contacts. If they are burnt or pitted, clean them with fine sandpaper, then move to step 7. If one set of contacts is melted together or appears to be seriously damaged, replace the toaster.

7 Depress the toast carriage lever and check to see if the two sets of contacts touch firmly. If they don't, you'll have to adjust them, as in step 8.

8 Use needle-nose pliers to grab the movable contacts. Slightly bend them up and away from the fixed contacts (see B). That way, when you depress the carriage lever, it will apply more pressure to the movable contacts and press them firmly against the fixed contacts.

9 Reassemble the toaster and test it.

What You'll Need

- Screwdriver
- Fine sandpaper
- Needle-nose pliers

Tips

If you have a new toaster that is controlled by an electronic circuit board, you're better off letting a professional repair it.

If following these steps doesn't fix your problem, you probably have a bad electric cord or a damaged heating element. If so, replace the toaster.

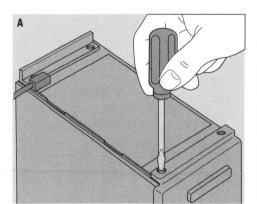

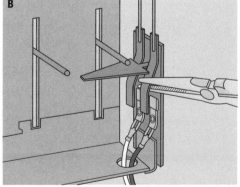

244 Diagnose Microwave Oven Problems

Once you become dependent on such a timesaving appliance, you'll need to know how to fix common problems. Avoid opening the microwave cabinet; doing so can be dangerous, and many manufacturers will void your warranty. See also 212 Get Rid of Microwave Smells.

PROBLEM	SOLUTIONS
Microwave doesn't activate	• Make sure microwave is plugged in properly. • Check that door closes completely and its latch is aligned. • Check that interlock switch in door works properly (required for activating microwave). • Replace a blown fuse if it's accessible, or contact a service technician.
Carousel won't turn	• Inspect plastic coupling beneath tray. • Check ring and roller assembly for misalignment or debris. • Make sure that tray is sitting properly on turning mechanism. • If carousel motor is broken, contact a service technician.
You see lightning inside the oven chamber	• Make sure there's no aluminum foil or metal trim on dishware. • Food residue or burned spots can cause electrical arcing. Clean chamber thoroughly. Replace wave-guide cover if burned or carbonized. • Sand away burn spots, and smooth rough metal edges. • Touch up spots with microwave interior paint if necessary. • If chamber has burn holes, contact a service technician.
Touch pad does not work or works erratically	• If touch pad has gotten wet, then allow to dry for several days. Avoid spraying cleaning liquid near touch pad. • Check for insect infestation. Insects (cockroaches most frequently) will appear under clear surface of touch pad or under readout window; they like the warmth of the circuit boards. • Place window mesh over vent to keep insects out.
Microwave activates but won't heat food	• If you hear an unusual buzzing noise, the magnetron (the component that actually generates the microwaves) or other electronic module may be broken. This is not easily fixed; contact a service technician.
Warning	Microwave ovens are high in voltage and can seriously shock you, even after you've unplugged them. Do not open the microwave cabinet or other sealed areas; contact a service technician or consider buying a new microwave oven.

245 Troubleshoot a Gas Grill

A gas grill offers plenty of outdoor entertainment as well as trouble-free cooking. To keep it simple, fun and safe, be sure to catch problems as soon as you notice them. Read your owner's manual to review your grill's components. See also 356 Wash an Outdoor Grill.

PROBLEM	SOLUTIONS
Burners won't light	• Be sure you still have gas in tank.
	• Check that propane tank valve is open.
	• Straighten kinks or sharp turns in hose.
	• Check venturi tubes frequently. Spiders like to build nests in them. Slip tubes off gas lines and clean with pipe cleaner or small bottlebrush. Wash with soapy water if needed.
	• Check that orifices are clear. Remove and clean them gently with small brush or stiff wire. Do not enlarge their holes.
	• Make sure there are no obstructions in gas line. Close gas valve and remove hose. Clear out any residue.
	• Check that electrode is aligned and has proper amount of gap. Make sure there are no cracks in the ceramic.
Grill doesn't heat well	• Adjust air shutters or venturi tubes.
	• Test gas tank fittings for leaks. Mix 1 tbsp. dishwashing liquid and 1 cup (8 fl oz/250 ml) water. Slowly open propane tank valve, keeping grill's gas valve closed. Spray soapy water over all fittings and hoses. Bubbles indicate a leak. Turn off gas and tighten or replace leaking parts.
	• Clear venturi tubes and orifices as above. Make sure they're properly aligned.
	• Check that control knobs are locking and unlocking properly. The knob's spring-lock mechanism and valve stem need to be properly aligned for control of gas flow. Replace them if necessary.
Flames blow out on the low setting	• A cold grill may be the cause. Let it heat up on high setting for 5 minutes before turning to low.
	• Adjust shutters or venturi tubes for better combustion.
	• Increase low flame setting according to manufacturer's instructions.
Flame burns yellow	• Adjust air shutter.
	• Check for spider webs in the venturi tubes. Clean them as above.
	• See if there are seasonings or salt on the burners. Wash them with soapy water.
	• Check for oil film on burners. Operate grill on high setting for 10 minutes to burn it away.
Warning	Do not operate the grill without its orifices in place: This is an extremely dangerous fire hazard.

246 Fix a Trash Compactor

If your trash compactor's motor is working but the machine won't flatten your trash, you could have a broken or stretched drive chain or drive belt. Tightening the belt or replacing it is a snap.

Steps

1 Unscrew the compactor from your kitchen counter, using a screwdriver.

2 Lay the unit on its side and locate the drive chain or belt. It will be under a cover plate on the top or bottom of the machine.

3 Remove the cover plate, using a nut driver and socket. You'll see the drive gear, one or more power screw sprockets, and a drive chain or drive belt.

4 Inspect the chain or belt. If it appears slack, you just need to increase the tension as explained in step 7. If it's broken, buy a replacement at an appliance store, then go on to step 5.

5 Loosen the motor mount bolts, using a socket wrench and socket (see A). Then push the mount toward the power screw sprocket(s). This will make it easier to fit the new chain or belt in place.

6 Slip the chain or belt over the sprockets (see B). On trash compactors with two power screws, you may have to unbolt the power screws from the frame and slide them out of the unit a bit to install the chain or belt.

7 Push the motor mount away from the power screw sprocket(s) to increase the tension on the drive chain or belt. Tighten the motor mount bolts and check the tension. You should have no more than ½ inch (12 mm) of flex. Loosen the bolts and increase the tension again if necessary.

8 Reinstall the cover plate, and screw the compactor to the counter.

What You'll Need

- Screwdriver
- Nut driver and socket
- Replacement drive belt or drive chain
- Socket wrench and socket

Tips

A drive chain or belt that's extremely loose can spin and damage gears and sprockets. Check the tension on your belt or chain yearly.

If your compactor won't run at all, the drive motor or drawer safety switch may be bad. Call a professional to check and replace them.

Warning

Always unplug your trash compactor before working on it.

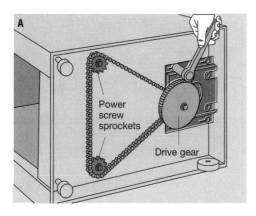

A

Power screw sprockets

Drive gear

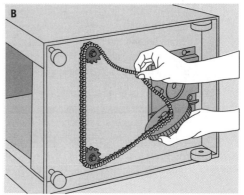

B

247 Repair a Sewing Machine

Sewing machines are heavy-duty appliances that can stand up to years of use. And when one stops working, often the machine just needs a good cleaning and oiling, or replacement of a simple part like the drive belt.

Steps

Cleaning and oiling the machine

1 Unfasten the top, bottom, side and handwheel covers, using a screwdriver. Set the covers aside.

2 Remove the plate that covers the thread bobbin. If it is screwed in place, use a screwdriver. If it is held by a clip or magnet, use a small flathead screwdriver to pry up the plate.

3 Thoroughly clean inside all the openings, using a vacuum with crevice attachment. Remove any stubborn lint, and use tweezers to take out any thread that is wound around the parts.

4 Clean the teeth on the gears, using the tip of a round toothpick to loosen the grime. Vacuum to remove it.

5 Lubricate all the moving parts. Use white lithium grease on the gears, and sewing machine oil on the other parts.

6 Reassemble the machine and plug it in.

Tightening or replacing the drive belt

1 Remove the top cover, bottom cover and handwheel cover, using a screwdriver to take out the screws.

2 Inspect the drive belt. If it is slack, use your screwdriver to loosen the screws that hold the motor in place, then follow step 4, below, to increase the belt's tension. If the belt is cracked or broken, get a replacement from your sewing machine supplier.

3 Install the new belt. Loosen the motor-mounting screws, and shift the motor toward the handwheel so you can slip the belt over the parts.

4 Shift the motor away from the handwheel to increase the belt's tension, then tighten the motor-mounting screws and check the tension. The belt should flex no more than ½ inch (12 mm). If it is too loose, increase the tension.

5 Reinstall the covers and plug in the machine.

What You'll Need

- Small flathead screwdriver
- Vacuum with crevice attachment
- Tweezers
- Round toothpick
- White lithium grease
- Sewing machine oil
- Replacement drive belt

Tips

Over-oiling a sewing machine will encourage grime buildup and can lead to premature part failure. Apply just one drop of oil to each location.

To keep your sewing machine operating smoothly, clean and oil it after every 8 to 10 hours of operation.

Warning

To avoid electric shock and prevent your fingers from getting jammed between moving parts, always unplug your machine before working on it.

248 Troubleshoot Smoke Alarms

A smoke alarm is one of those appliances you want to troubleshoot *before* it breaks down. Otherwise, it may fail to sound when you need it most. Test your alarm monthly to ensure it's working: Depress the test button to see if it sounds, then hold a smoldering candle near the sensor. To perform a smoke test on an alarm that's mounted on a vertical wall, use a piece of paper to fan the smoke into the alarm.

PROBLEM	CAUSE	SOLUTION
Alarm chirps	Weak battery	Replace battery. (It's best to replace battery yearly.)
	Loose connections on alarm powered by house current	Tighten connections.
	Dust or dead insects clogging sensors	Clean in and around alarm with vacuum and brush attachment.
Alarm fails to sound when tested	Dust or dead insects clogging sensors	Vacuum alarm.
Alarm fails to sound after cleaning	Malfunctioning alarm	Replace alarm.
	Deteriorated sensors due to age	Replace alarm. (It should be replaced after 10 years anyway.)
Alarm sounds when there is no sign of smoke	Detector improperly located	Install at least 20 feet (6 m) from ovens and furnaces, and 10 feet (3 m) from areas of high humidity like bathrooms.
	Dust from heating system triggering alarm	This can happen when the heat is turned on for the first time during the year. Vacuum the alarm and replace the air filter on the heating system.
	Faulty wiring on AC-powered units	Call an electrician.
	Detector improperly located	Do not install in dusty locations such as attic or garage.
	Faulty wiring	Replace alarm.
	Faulty detector	Replace alarm.
Alarm fails to sound	Dead battery on battery-powered units	Replace battery.

ORING • FIX BAD HABITS • REPAIR A BROKEN EYEGLASS FRAME • REPOSITION A SLIPPED CONTACT LENS • FIX A RUN IN STOCKINGS • JC
EAKOUT • REPAIR A TORN FINGERNAIL • FIX CHIPPED NAIL POLISH • FIX A STUCK ZIPPER • FIND A LOST CONTACT LENS • ELIMINATE BAD
Y THAT STICKS • STOP TELEMARKETERS AND JUNK MAIL • GET SUPERGLUE OFF YOUR SKIN • EXTRACT A SPLINTER • SOOTHE A SUNBURN
HANGOVER • STOP HICCUPS • MEND A BROKEN HEART • MEND A FAMILY FEUD • TREAT A SMALL CUT OR SCRAPE • FIX HAIR DISASTERS •
TTER SEATS • FIX A BILLING MISTAKE • FIX A BAD GRADE • FIX BAD CREDIT • RECOVER FROM JET LAG • RESUSCITATE AN UNCONSCIOUS
PRONOUNS • FIX A RUN-ON SENTENCE • FIX MISUSE OF THE WORD GOOD • FIX YOUR DOG OR CAT • CORRECT BAD BEHAVIOR IN DOGS
SSING BUTTON • REMOVE LINT FROM CLOTHING • FIX A DRAWSTRING ON SWEATPANTS • REPAIR A HEM • REPAIR LEATHER GOODS • MEN
UNDER YOUR CASHMERE • FIX A SWEATER THAT HAS SHRUNK • FIX A SWEATER THAT HAS STRETCHED • FIX A HOLE IN A POCKET • FIX A
LLING FROM CLOTHING • FIX A FRAYED BUTTONHOLE • REMOVE DARK SCUFFS FROM SHOES • TREAT STAINS ON LEATHER • PROTECT SUE
JIET SQUEAKY HINGES • TROUBLESHOOT LOCK PROBLEMS • TIGHTEN A LOOSE DOORKNOB • TIGHTEN A LOOSE DOOR HINGE • FIX A BIN
PLACE CRACKED TILE • TROUBLESHOOT MOLD ON INTERIOR WALLS • REPLACE CRACKED TILE GROUT IN A TUB OR SHOWER • FIX A DRA
INDS • TROUBLESHOOT WINDOW SHADE PROBLEMS • FIX BROKEN GLASS IN A WINDOW • REPAIR A WINDOW SCREEN • REPAIR ALUMINU
AMAGED PLASTER • REPAIR WALL COVERINGS • TOUCH UP PAINTED WALLS • TROUBLESHOOT INTERIOR-PAINT PROBLEMS • SOLVE A LEAD
ARDWOOD FLOOR • RESTORE A DULL, WORN WOOD FLOOR • TOUCH UP WOOD-FLOOR FINISHES • REPAIR DAMAGED SHEET-VINYL FLOOR
OUSE • CHILDPROOF YOUR HOME • PREVENT ICE DAMS • CURE A FAULTY FIREPLACE DRAW • START A FIRE IN A COLD CHIMNEY • FIX A W
AL A GARAGE FLOOR • REFINISH A GARAGE OR BASEMENT FLOOR • CONTROL ROOF LEAKS • REDIRECT RAINWATER FROM A DOWNSPOL
AMAGED ASPHALT SHINGLE • PATCH A FLAT OR LOW-PITCHED ROOF • REPAIR ROOF FLASHING • TROUBLESHOOT EXTERIOR-PAINT PROBL
W WATER PRESSURE • FIX LEAKING PIPES • STOP A TOILET FROM RUNNING • FIX A LEAKY TOILET TANK • FIX A STOPPED-UP TOILET • STC
OGGED SINK OR TUB • REPAIR A TUB-AND-SHOWER VALVE • REPAIR CHIPPED FIXTURES • QUIET NOISY PIPES • DEFROST YOUR PIPES • D
ONSUMPTION • REPLACE A RECEPTACLE • FIX AN ELECTRICAL PLUG • REPLACE A LIGHT FIXTURE • INSTALL A NEW DIMMER • FIX A LAMP
OORBELL • FIX A WOBBLY OVERHEAD FAN • ADJUST WATER-HEATER TEMPERATURE • RELIGHT A WATER-HEATER PILOT LIGHT • TROUBLES
E MAKER • GET RID OF MICROWAVE SMELLS • FIX A REFRIGERATOR THAT COOLS POORLY • FIX A GAS OVEN THAT HEATS POORLY • CLEAN
SHWASHER PROBLEMS • CORRECT AN OVERFLOWING DISHWASHER • FIX A LEAKY DISHWASHER • FIX A DISHWASHER THAT FILLS SLOWLY
WASHING MACHINE THAT FILLS SLOWLY • FIX A WASHING MACHINE THAT "WALKS" ACROSS THE FLOOR • FIX A CLOTHES DRYER THAT DRI
K YOUR VACUUM CLEANER • REPLACE VACUUM CLEANER BRUSHES • TROUBLESHOOT A PORTABLE AIR CONDITIONER • FIX A WINDOW AI
ROCESSOR • FIX A TOASTER • DIAGNOSE MICROWAVE OVEN PROBLEMS • TROUBLESHOOT A GAS GRILL • FIX A TRASH COMPACTOR • REF
ART • TROUBLESHOOT A CRASHING COMPUTER • CLEAN UP LAPTOP SPILLS • FIX BAD SECTORS ON A HARD DISK • QUIT A FROZEN PC A
FECTED COMPUTER • IMPROVE YOUR COMPUTER'S MEMORY • GET RID OF E-MAIL SPAM • CHANGE A LASER PRINTER CARTRIDGE • FIX A
GURE OUT WHY A PRINTER WON'T PRINT • FIX SPELLING AND GRAMMAR ERRORS • RECALL AN E-MAIL IN MICROSOFT OUTLOOK • DIAGNO
LES • TROUBLESHOOT A PALM OS PDA • RESET A PALM OS PDA • REMOVE FINGERPRINTS FROM A CAMERA LENS • TROUBLESHOOT A CD
ALVAGE A VIDEOCASSETTE • TROUBLESHOOT A DVD PLAYER • STRENGTHEN FM RADIO RECEPTION • STRENGTHEN AM RADIO RECEPTION
JAMMED SLIDE PROJECTOR • GET BETTER SPEAKER SOUND • TROUBLESHOOT A DIGITAL CAMCORDER • TROUBLESHOOT A DIGITAL CAM
GHTBULB • FIX A BROKEN WINEGLASS STEM • FIX BLEMISHED WOOD FURNITURE • REPAIR GOUGES IN FURNITURE • RESTORE FURNITURE
AMOUFLAGE A DOG-SCRATCHED DOOR • REPAIR A SPLIT CARPET SEAM • RID CARPETS OF PET ODORS • REINFORCE A SAGGING SHELF •
OINTS OF CHAIRS AND TABLES • REUPHOLSTER A DROP-IN CHAIR SEAT • REVIVE A CANE SEAT • REINFORCE A WEAK BED FRAME • FIX UP
OTTERY • REPAIR CHIPPED OR CRACKED CHINA • UNCLUTTER YOUR HOME • CLEAN CRAYON FROM A WALL • GET WAX OFF A TABLECLOT
AINS • REMOVE CHEWING GUM FROM CARPETING • REMOVE BLEACH SPOTS FROM CARPETING • REMOVE PET STAINS • ELIMINATE WINE
AINS FROM TILE GROUT • REMOVE MILDEW FROM WALLS AND CEILINGS • DISINFECT A TOILET BOWL • REMOVE FIREPLACE GRIME • GET
EAN OIL SPOTS FROM A GARAGE OR DRIVEWAY • REMOVE STAINS FROM BRICK • WASH AN OUTDOOR GRILL • FIX A FALLEN SOUFFLÉ • F
SCUE OVERPROOFED YEAST DOUGH • FIX YOUR KID LUNCH • GET RID OF TAP-WATER MINERAL DEPOSITS • CALIBRATE A MEAT THERMON
UCE • RESCUE A BROKEN SAUCE • REMOVE FAT FROM SOUPS AND SAUCES • FIX LUMPY GRAVY • SUBSTITUTE MISSING INGREDIENTS • F
JRNED RICE • REMOVE COOKING ODORS • FINISH UNDERCOOKED MEAT • SALVAGE AN UNDERCOOKED TURKEY • FIX AN OVERSEASONEL
ALE BREAD • SMOOTH SEIZED CHOCOLATE • SOFTEN HARDENED SUGARS OR COOKIES • FIX BREAKFAST FOR YOUR SWEETHEART • MEN
GGING TOOLS • RESTORE A BROKEN FLOWERPOT • SHARPEN PRUNING CLIPPERS • REMOVE RUST FROM TOOLS • REVIVE WILTING CUT F
ET RID OF RAMPANT BRAMBLES • TROUBLESHOOT BROWN SPOTS ON A LAWN • CONTROL MAJOR GARDEN PESTS • RID YOUR GARDEN O
ONPERFORMING COMPOST PILE • FIX BAD SOIL • SHORE UP A RAISED GARDEN BED • REMOVE A DEAD OR DISEASED TREE LIMB • TROUB
RAINAGE • TROUBLESHOOT ROSE DISEASES • IDENTIFY AND CORRECT SOIL DEFICIENCIES IN ROSES • TROUBLESHOOT ROSE PESTS • OV
AMAGED DECK BOARDS • REPAIR DECK RAILINGS • STRENGTHEN DECK JOISTS • FIX A RUSTY IRON RAILING • REPAIR A GATE • REPAIR A
RACKED OR DAMAGED CONCRETE • IMPROVE THE LOOK OF REPAIRED CONCRETE • REPAIR AN ASPHALT DRIVEWAY • REVIVE WOODEN OL
ARDEN PONDS • CLEAN SWIMMING POOL WATER • TROUBLESHOOT HOT TUBS AND SPAS • REPLACE BRICKS IN WALKWAYS AND PATIOS •
AR WITH JUMPER CABLES • SHUT OFF A CAR ALARM THAT WON'T QUIT • FREE A CAR STUCK ON ICE OR SNOW • DE-ICE YOUR WINDSHIEL
RN-SIGNAL COVER • FIX A CAR FUSE • FIX DASHBOARD LIGHTS THAT WON'T LIGHT • REMOVE CAR SMELLS • CHECK TIRE PRESSURE • IN
PROPERLY INSTALLED CHILD CAR SEAT • TROUBLESHOOT LEAKING OIL • CHECK AND ADD POWER-STEERING FLUID • CHECK AND ADD C
ROKEN EXHAUST PIPE • CHECK AND ADD ENGINE OIL • CHECK AND ADD BRAKE FLUID • CHECK AND ADD FLUID TO YOUR AUTOMATIC TR
OUBLESHOOT A WINDSHIELD-WASHER PUMP • REPAIR MINOR DENTS • CHANGE A HUBCAP • FIX AN IGNITION KEY THAT WON'T TURN • C

MORY • FIX AN ELECTRIC CAN OPENER THAT DROPS THE CAN • TROUBLESHOOT A CELL PHONE • KEEP MIRRORS FROM FOGGING • ZAP A
EEP A SHAVING NICK FROM BLEEDING • GET RID OF SPLIT ENDS • UNTANGLE HAIR SNARLS • FIX FRIZZY HAIR • FIX BLEEDING LIPSTICK •
CKY SOCIAL SITUATION • FIX A BAD REPUTATION • CLEAN LIPSTICK FROM A COLLAR • FIX A BAD RELATIONSHIP • SALVAGE A BAD DATE •
EEDING NOSE • BEAT THE MONDAY MORNING BLUES • GET OUT OF A FIX • EXTRACT A BROKEN KEY • RETRIEVE KEYS LOCKED INSIDE A C
TOP SOMEONE FROM CHOKING • STOP AN ANT INVASION • STABILIZE A CHRISTMAS TREE • RESCUE AN ITEM FROM THE DRAIN • FIX IMPR
KUNK ODOR FROM YOUR DOG • GET A CAT OUT OF A TREE • CORRECT BAD BEHAVIOR IN CATS • TREAT A CAT FOR MATTED FUR • REPLAC
EAM • TREAT MILDEW DAMAGE • GET STATIC OUT OF YOUR LAUNDRY • DEAL WITH A CLOTHES-MOTH INFESTATION • FIX A SEPARATED ZIPP
R SOCK • TREAT MIXED-WASH ACCIDENTS • TAKE WRINKLES OUT OF CLOTHING • FIX A HOLE IN JEANS • REPAIR A SNAG IN A SWEATER •
AINS • WASH SNEAKERS • PICK UP A DROPPED STITCH IN KNITTING • RESTRING BEADS • FRESHEN SMELLY SHOES • FIX A SAGGING CLOS
• FIX A RUBBING DOOR • FIX A DRAFTY DOOR • TUNE UP SLIDING DOORS • FIX A SHOWER DOOR • SEAL WALL JOINTS AROUND A TUB OF
• REPAIR A FAULTY WINDOW CRANK • REPAIR VERTICAL BLINDS • REPAIR VENETIAN BLINDS OR MINIBLINDS • REPAIR WOOD OR PLASTIC
REEN WINDOWS • INSTALL NEW SASH CORDS IN WINDOWS • FIX A TIGHT OR LOOSE WINDOW SASH • REPAIR MINOR DRYWALL DAMAGE •
BLEM • REPLACE A DAMAGED CEILING TILE • REPLACE A WOOD FLOORBOARD • QUIET SQUEAKING FLOORS • REPAIR A WATER-DAMAGED
R A VINYL-TILE FLOOR • SILENCE SQUEAKY ... STER • REPLACE CAULKING ON THE OUTSIDE OF Y
G STOVE • REPAIR AND PREVENT WOOD RO ... TCH A GUTTER LEAK • TROUBLESHOOT A WET BAS
GGING GUTTER • UNCLOG GUTTERS AND D ... • REPAIR A CRACKED OR SPLIT WOOD SHINGLE •
RAGE-DOOR TENSION • TROUBLESHOOT A ... ITES • LOOSEN A RUSTY NUT OR BOLT • TROUBLE
K SWEATING • FIX FLUSHING PROBLEMS • ... FAUCET • FIX A STOPPER THAT DOESN'T SEAL • CL
MP PUMP PROBLEMS • TROUBLESHOOT ELE ... USE • SWAP A FAULTY LIGHT SWITCH • REDUCE EN
OOT FLUORESCENT LIGHTING • FIX A LOW ... E THERMOSTAT • TROUBLESHOOT HOLIDAY LIGHT
ING SYSTEM • REFRESH A SMELLY REFRIGE ... EMS • FIX A LEAKING REFRIGERATOR • REPAIR A CL
TIONING GAS BURNER • REPAIR A RANGE H ... FIX AN ELECTRIC OVEN THAT HEATS POORLY • DIA
YOUR APPLIANCES • CONTROL GARBAGE ... E DISPOSAL • DIAGNOSE WASHING MACHINE PROB
FIX A HAIR DRYER • TROUBLESHOOT A CLO ... AT SPUTTERS • FIX AN IRON THAT LEAVES SPOTS O
ER • FIX A DEHUMIDIFIER • REPAIR A CONS ... DER • HANDLE A MIXER THAT OVERHEATS • REPAIR
G MACHINE • TROUBLESHOOT SMOKE ALAR ... OARD SPILLS • TROUBLESHOOT A COMPUTER THA
REMOVE A WINDOWS PROGRAM • SPEED U ... OUSE • REPLACE YOUR PC'S BATTERY • CLEAN A
T FAILS ITS SELF-TEST • CORRECT MONITOR ... PAPER JAM • TROUBLESHOOT A RECURRING PRINT
NE MODEM PROBLEMS • TROUBLESHOOT A ... REEN GLARE • GET TOP-NOTCH SCANS • RECOVER
STORE A CD • REPAIR A WARPED CD • CLE ... • EXTRACT A JAMMED VIDEOTAPE • ADJUST VCR
TE CONTROL • FIX AUDIOCASSETTES • FIX ... OT A CASSETTE DECK • REPLACE BROKEN RABBIT
LESHOOT A CD PLAYER • REPLACE A HEAD ... RASS • SHINE SILVER SAFELY • REMOVE A BROKEN

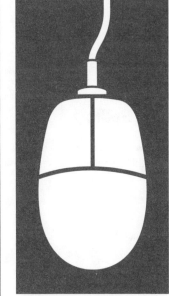

**Computers &
Home Electronics**

LACE A BROKEN TOWEL ROD • REMOVE ST ... FOR NATURAL DISASTERS • FIX A FRAYED CARPET
BORING BATHROOM • REPLACE A SHOWER ... NACE FILTER • REPAIR A BROKEN SLIDING DRAWE
D CHAIR • FIX A WOBBLY WOOD CHAIR • S ... OR CRACKED PORCELAIN • REPAIR CHIPPED OR C
WAX FROM CARPETING • GET RID OF CEILIN ... MOVE MYSTERY STAINS FROM CLOTHING • REMOV
A RUG OR TABLECLOTH • REMOVE BURN M ... NITURE • STRIP WAX BUILDUP FROM FLOORS • RE
ORANT STAINS • ELIMINATE CIGARETTE ODOR • RESTORE SHINE TO YOUR JEWELRY • WASH DIRTY WINDOWS • REMOVE GRIME FROM MIN
MBLED CAKE • FIX A PERFECT CUP OF TEA • PATCH A TORN PIE CRUST • KEEP A PIE CRUST FROM GETTING SOGGY • FIX DOUGH THAT W
DULL KNIFE • REMOVE RUST FROM A CAST-IRON PAN • REPAIR LAMINATE COUNTERTOPS • REMOVE STAINS FROM A STONE COUNTERTOP
CHOLESTEROL • TREAT BURNED POTS AND PANS • RESCUE A BURNED CAKE OR PIE • PUT OUT A KITCHEN FIRE • REMOVE THE BITTERN
N UNDERSEASONED DISH • REMOVE OVEN SPILLS • CLEAN UP OIL SPILLS • FIX A DRINK FOR ANY OCCASION • DISENTANGLE PASTA • RE
CUTTING BOARD • KEEP A MIXING BOWL STEADY • FIX GARDEN TOOL HANDLES • REPAIR A LEAKY HOSE NOZZLE • MEND A LEAKY HOSE
ARPEN A POWER MOWER BLADE • SHARPEN PUSH MOWER BLADES • REPAIR BALD SPOTS ON GRASS • RID YOUR GRASS OF DOG URINE
UBLESHOOT HERBS • TROUBLESHOOT HOUSEPLANTS • OVERCOME SHADE PROBLEMS • RID SOIL OF PESTS AND DISEASES • REVIVE A
ES AND SHRUBS • REPAIR A LEAKING IRRIGATION SYSTEM • UNCLOG A SPRINKLER SYSTEM • CLEAN A CLOGGED DRIP SYSTEM • FIX PO
GUS DISEASES IN ROSES • REPAIR DECK STEPS • RENOVATE A WEATHERED DECK • TIGHTEN LOOSE DECKING • REMOVE DECK STAINS •
• LEVEL AND SMOOTH A GRAVEL PATH • FIX A POTHOLE IN A DIRT OR GRAVEL DRIVEWAY • REPLACE PATIO STONES, TILES AND PAVERS •
ITURE • RESTORE WEATHERED METAL FURNITURE • REPAIR CHAIR STRAPS AND WEBBING • REVIVE RUSTED IRON FURNITURE • TROUBLE
LED CAR • SHUT OFF A JAMMED HORN • CHANGE YOUR CAR'S BATTERY • TROUBLESHOOT A CAR THAT WON'T START • FIX A FLAT TIRE •
NED-OUT SIGNAL BULB • FIX A BURNED-OUT HEADLIGHT • ADJUST HEADLIGHTS • FIX A STUCK BRAKE LIGHT • REPLACE A BROKEN TAILL
IRES • FIX A STUCK CONVERTIBLE TOP • DIAGNOSE A LEAK INSIDE YOUR CAR • REPLACE YOUR AIR FILTER • HANDLE A FAULTY REPAIR •
OL AN OVERHEATED ENGINE • REPLACE A LEAKING RADIATOR HOSE • CHANGE YOUR WIPER BLADES • ADD WINDSHIELD-WASHER FLUID
• TROUBLESHOOT YOUR BRAKES • ADD BRAKE FLUID TO THE CLUTCH MASTER CYLINDER • TROUBLESHOOT DASHBOARD WARNING LIGHT
SPARK-PLUG WIRES • DIAGNOSE CAR SMELLS • CLEAN THE OUTSIDE OF YOUR CAR • RESTORE YOUR CAR'S SHINE • WASH THE INTERIOR

249 Fix Date and Time

If your PC has the wrong date and time setting, then all the files you create and save will have the wrong dates on them as well. Here's the quickest and easiest way to manually set your clock and calendar to the correct time in Windows.

Steps

1 On the right side of the Taskbar at the bottom of your Windows screen, double-click directly on the time. The Date/Time control panel will automatically open.

2 To set the date, click on the correct day, month and year.

3 To set the time, enter the correct time in the box.

4 To set your time zone, click on the Time Zone tab, then select the correct zone from the drop-down menu.

Tip

You can use the Regional Settings control panel to change the format that Windows uses to display the date and time—if, say, you prefer European date formats.

250 Clean Up Keyboard Spills

Science can't explain it, but soft drinks and coffee are undeniably attracted to computer keyboards. Put them in proximity and they're bound to interact messily sooner or later.

Steps

1 Unplug the keyboard.

2 If you spilled water, turn the keyboard over and let it drain and dry out for at least 24 hours.

3 If you spilled something sticky, try prying the small key caps off of the keyboard with a flathead screwdriver to get better access to the mess. Don't remove the spacebar, the Enter key or other large key caps. (Take a picture of the keyboard layout, or make a quick sketch of it, before you remove any keys so you can put them back where you found them.)

4 Gently clean the keyboard with a wet cotton swab.

5 Replace the key caps after rinsing them and letting them dry.

6 Let everything dry for at least 24 hours before plugging the keyboard back in.

What You'll Need

- Flathead screwdriver
- Cotton swabs

Tips

Keyboards are not expensive. If you've had a bad spill, it might be easier to buy a new one than take the time to clean one.

Laptop computer spills are more serious. See 253 Clean Up Laptop Spills.

251 Troubleshoot a Computer That Won't Start

A computer that won't start is both alarming and infuriating, especially if you're on a deadline or you haven't been backing up all your data. Don't panic, though. This problem often has a simple solution.

Steps

1 If your desktop computer does nothing at all when you try to start it, first check that the power cable is securely plugged in at the back of the computer as well as into a working power outlet. It's amazing how often this is the case.

2 If you're starting from a button on the keyboard, make sure the keyboard is connected to the computer.

3 If the computer is plugged into a surge protector, see if the surge protector has a reset switch that you can push. (If it doesn't have a reset switch and the problem is with the surge protector, it will need to be replaced.) Try plugging a lamp or other device into one of the surge protector's outlets to make sure it's working.

4 If you can hear the computer's fan or hard-disk drive, or if you can see indicator lights on the main unit but the monitor stays dark, make sure that the monitor is connected to a working power source, that it's turned on and that it's securely connected to the computer via the video cable.

5 If the monitor and computer have power but the computer displays a "Non-system disk or disk error" message, check to make sure you didn't leave a disk in the A: drive. If you did, eject it and restart the computer.

6 If the operating system still won't start even though the computer and monitor have power, try restarting with a Windows startup disk in the A: drive or, if you've got a Macintosh, with a Mac OS disc in the CD-ROM drive. (You can start a Mac from the CD-ROM drive by holding down the C key while starting up. On older Macs, pre-G3, you need to press the Command-Opt-Shift-Delete combination.) Many newer PCs can also start from the CD-ROM drive, so it's worth trying if you don't have a startup disk.

7 If the operating system then starts, your problem is probably with the startup hard drive or with the operating system installed on it. If you can't fix the drive, you'll have to replace it. (See also 254 Fix Bad Sectors on a Hard Disk and 275 Recover Lost Files.)

What You'll Need

- A startup disk or a CD-ROM with the operating system on it

Tips

If you've got a laptop computer that suddenly refuses to start up, it's possible that the battery drained too low while the computer was in sleep mode. Try plugging in the power cord to see if the laptop will wake up.

If you don't have an emergency Windows startup disk, you can create one with the Add/Remove Programs control panel. Select the Startup Disk tab and click on Create Disk. (You'll need a blank, formatted floppy disk.)

252 Troubleshoot a Crashing Computer

During World War II they were called "gremlins"—tiny demons responsible for seemingly inexplicable aircraft problems. Today, gremlins prefer personal computers, which often seem to crash if you so much as give them a funny look. Although a crash-proof computer has yet to be built (just ask NASA), you can rid yours of most gremlins with a little patient troubleshooting.

Steps

Check for a software conflict

1 If an older program suddenly stops working properly after you install a new program, try reinstalling the older program, which may have had some of its files overwritten by the new one.

2 If your computer crashes after you install a new program, when both it and an older program are running, check with the publishers of the programs to see if there are updates that address the conflict.

3 If you've installed a new program and start getting crashes that don't seem to be related to running any other program, try uninstalling the new program. (See 256 Remove a Windows Program.) If crashes continue, reinstall the operating system.

Check for a hardware conflict

1 If your computer starts crashing after you add a new piece of hardware, remove the hardware and uninstall whatever software you installed with it. (See 256 Remove a Windows Program.)

2 If removing the hardware solves the problem, contact the manufacturer or visit its Web site to see if there's a later driver version that fixes the problem.

3 If removing the hardware doesn't solve the problem, it's possible that some Windows files were changed when you installed the drivers, which are the files that enable a particular piece of hardware. You'll need to reinstall Windows.

Check for overheating

1 Take note of seemingly random computer crashes. If they tend to occur after the computer has been running for a while, they could be the result of overheating. As computers get faster, they have a tendency to run hotter.

2 Check to make sure the vents in the computer case aren't blocked and there's good air circulation around the computer.

3 If your computer has a fan, remove the computer case with a screwdriver, then turn on the computer briefly to see if the fan is turning. If it isn't, you'll need to replace it or the power supply.

What You'll Need

- Screwdriver
- Can of compressed air
- Virus-protection software
- Patience

Tips

Anytime you suspect a problem is being caused by a particular piece of hardware or software, make sure you have the most recent version. You probably aren't the first person to experience a conflict, so there's a good chance that a fix has been posted on the Internet.

If you have a PC without a good virus-protection program, you're practically begging for trouble. Get one and keep it up-to-date.

Although most computer viruses cause obvious symptoms, some may operate sneakily in the background.

4 If the inside of the computer case looks like Oklahoma during the Dust Bowl, clean things up by turning off the computer and using a can of compressed air (available at electronics stores) to blow dust off of circuit boards, chips, the fan and anything else that looks dirty. Vacuums and dust rags are a bad idea, however, because they can build up static charges and zap your chips.

Check for a virus

1 If you have virus-protection software, make sure it has been updated recently. New viruses appear daily.

2 If you don't have virus-protection software, invest in a program that can scan and clean your hard drive.

253 Clean Up Laptop Spills

Spilling coffee on your laptop will not only ruin your morning, it can ruin your computer. Act quickly if this happens, because it only takes seconds for liquids to destroy the hard drive of a laptop computer.

Steps

1 Shut down the computer immediately.

2 Wipe up any liquid. Tilt the computer to the side to drain any liquids.

3 Remove any removable parts from the laptop, including the power cord, printer and mouse cables, the floppy drive, CD drive, modem cards and battery. Do not disassemble the laptop body to remove internal parts.

4 Once the parts are removed, gently lift the computer and turn it to the side and upside down to drain any liquid. Tilt the computer in a variety of directions to verify that there are no pools of liquid lurking, but be careful not to shake it or handle it roughly.

5 Repeat with the floppy drive and other removable parts.

6 Use a hair dryer on a cool setting to dry the laptop and its parts if you can.

7 Allow the computer and its removable parts to dry for 24 hours before you reassemble it and turn it back on. (If you are under a tight deadline, let the laptop dry for at least an hour before you reassemble it.)

8 If the computer does not work properly or does not turn on, bring it to a computer repair professional, although the damage might be irreparable. Spills are one of the leading causes of laptop deaths.

Warning

If you open your computer case to blow the dust out, be careful not to touch anything that can be damaged by static electricity.

What You'll Need

- Paper towels
- Hair dryer

Tips

Back up any files you have on a laptop as a precaution. Accidents do happen.

For spills on PCs, see 250 Clean Up Keyboard Spills.

Warning

Do not attempt to remove key caps from a laptop unless the owner's manual provides instructions on how to do so.

254 Fix Bad Sectors on a Hard Disk

The minute your computer's hard disk starts to act flaky, make sure you have an up-to-date backup. Then you can do some simple diagnostics and repairs. Both Windows and Mac OS come with built-in hard-disk utility software that scans your hard disk for errors and attempts to fix them.

Steps

For Windows

1 Double-click on My Computer to open the My Computer window.

2 Select the disk that you want to diagnose and repair.

3 Choose Properties from the File menu. You should see the Properties window for the drive that you selected.

4 Choose the Tools tab.

5 Click the Check Now button under Error Checking Status.

6 Depending on your version of Windows, choose either "Thorough" or "Scan for and Attempt Recovery of Bad Sectors."

7 Click on Start.

For Mac OS

1 If you're running Mac OS 9.2 or an earlier version, search your hard drive for a file called Disk First Aid. You can use this Apple-supplied utility to verify and repair disk errors.

2 If Disk First Aid says it can verify but not repair your disk because it's the startup disk, you should restart your Mac from the System CD-ROM disc that came with your computer. Hold down the C key during startup to force the Mac to start from the CD-ROM. Older Macs, pre-G3, need to press the Command-Opt-Shift-Delete combination.

3 If Disk First Aid fails to fix all the problems it detected the first time you run it, try running it a few more times

4 If you're running Mac OS X, you'll find that Disk First Aid has been made part of the Disk Utility program, which you'll find in the Utilities folder in the Applications folder. Click on the First Aid tab after launching Disk Utility.

Tip

Third-party hard-disk utilities do a more thorough job of diagnosis and repair than the software that comes with Windows or Mac OS, but they work much better if you install them before you have a problem.

255 Quit a Frozen PC Application

Fish swim, birds fly and software crashes. The program that never chokes has yet to be written. If your screen suffers the dreaded freeze, though, you might be able to escape by keeping your cool and pressing the right keys.

Steps

1 Take a break and get a cup of coffee. Sometimes a program that seems irrevocably frozen is just temporarily stalled.

2 Once you're convinced that the program really is stuck, it's time to attempt a graceful exit. On a Windows PC, press Ctrl+Alt+Delete. In addition, if you're running Windows NT or 2000, click on Task Manager. On a Macintosh, press Command-Option-Escape.

3 In Windows, select the program you want to quit from the Close Program dialog box or Application list box. The program will probably display the words "Not Responding." Choose End Task. On a Mac, click on the Force Quit button in the dialog box.

4 After the program shuts down, save your work in any other open applications, restart your computer, then restart the program.

5 If you can't shut down the program, use the computer's reset button, if it has one. Laptop owners should consult their manuals for finding the reset "paperclip" hole.

Warning

Unplugging the computer from its power source should be only a last resort. It's like stopping your car by driving into a wall.

Be careful with Ctrl+Alt+Delete. If you press it twice in succession, your computer will restart without asking you to save your work.

256 Remove a Windows Program

If you want to uninstall a Windows program from your computer, just deleting the application or its folder will result in lots of extra files and potential headaches. Use the Install/Uninstall control panel instead.

Steps

1 From your Start menu, choose Settings, then Control Panel.

2 Double-click on the Add/Remove Programs icon in the Control Panel.

3 Choose the Install/Uninstall tab.

4 Select the program you want to uninstall from the list and click on Add/Remove.

5 Windows Me comes with a Maintenance wizard that includes a Disk Cleanup function. You can use it to uninstall unneeded programs as part of a regular disk-maintenance routine. Similar third-party programs are available for earlier versions of Windows.

Warning

Be extremely wary of deleting any file from your hard-disk drive without knowing exactly what it is and what it does. You might render Windows or one of your programs inoperative.

257 Speed Up a Hard-Disk Drive

No one ever bought a car or a computer because it could go slower. If your hard-disk drive seems to take forever to go about its business, or if it's having trouble keeping up with your CD-R burning software, chances are it's time for a tune-up and defragmentation.

Steps

For Windows

1 Close any open applications. Disable antivirus utilities, screen savers and other background programs. Make sure you've quit all programs in Windows by pressing Ctrl+Alt+Delete once (don't press it twice or you'll restart the computer).

2 Windows will show you a list of applications running. Highlight each application (one at a time) and click on End Task to close each one.

3 Double-click on My Computer to open the My Computer window.

4 Select the hard disk that you want to defragment.

5 Choose Properties from the shortcut File menu. You should see the Properties window for the drive that you selected.

6 Choose the Tools tab.

7 Click the Defragment Now button.

For Mac OS

1 Apple doesn't supply a disk-defragmentation program with Mac OS, although most third-party disk utility programs include one.

2 If you don't opt for a third-party utility program, you can do a partial defragmentation by copying as many files as possible to a backup disk. Don't include the System Folder.

3 Once the files are safely copied, then delete them from the original disk.

4 Copy the backed-up files back to the original disk.

Tip

Check heavily used disks for fragmentation on a regular basis, as part of a regular maintenance routine (the Maintenance Wizard in later versions of Windows can help you set one up).

Warning

Disk defragmentation is dangerous to your data and should never be undertaken without first backing up all data and then performing a general diagnostic routine. (See 254 Fix Bad Sectors on a Hard Disk.)

258 Clean and Fix a Mouse

Computer mice have been around longer than personal computers, and the basic design doesn't look like it's going away anytime soon. When your mouse starts acting up or stops working altogether, it may just need some simple maintenance.

Steps

Cleaning the mouse

1 Unplug your mouse and flip it over to see what kind it is. The most common type is mechanical; it has a small rubber ball on its underside that rolls on the desk or mouse pad. These kind of mice are notorious for attracting and retaining crud. If your mouse has no ball but a small light, it's optical, so you can skip ahead to step 6.

2 If your mouse has a rubber ball, you can probably release it by rotating a locking ring that holds it in place. Look for an arrow telling you which way to push or twist the locking ring (see A).

3 Remove the ball and carefully clean it with a lint-free cloth or soap and water. Dry it carefully.

4 If you find crud in the mouse case too, scrape it off with a toothpick (see B) or, if you're desperate, a fingernail.

5 Put the mouse back together.

6 Clean your optical mouse occasionally with distilled rubbing alcohol and a paper towel. This type of mouse stays clean longer.

Other possible mouse problems

1 Check the mouse connection at the back of the PC. Is the cable plugged firmly into the correct port? Most newer PCs have a port labeled for the mouse.

2 If the mouse cable looks damaged, borrow a mouse from someone else's computer and see if it works with yours. If it does, then your mouse needs to be replaced.

What You'll Need

- Clean, lint-free cloth or soap
- Toothpick
- Distilled rubbing alcohol
- Paper towel

Tip

Occasionally washing your mouse pad with a mild soap-and-water solution will help keep your mouse from getting dirty in the first place.

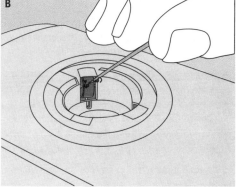

259 Replace Your PC's Battery

All Windows PCs contain a small battery that powers a chip, which in turn stores important system data called the CMOS settings. If that battery runs down, when you attempt to start up the computer you'll get errors such as "Invalid system settings—Run Setup" or "CMOS checksum error." If you aren't ready to buy a new PC, it's time to put in a new battery.

Steps

Restore the CMOS settings

1 If you've never made a backup copy of your CMOS settings (by using a backup utility program such as Norton Utilities or by printing a hardcopy out on paper), look them up in the printed documentation for your system or call the vendor of your PC. Restoring your CMOS settings from a backup will help determine whether the battery is the problem.

2 If you're using a backup utility to restore the CMOS settings, insert the emergency startup disk and follow the prompts.

3 Use the Setup utility that's built into your PC's BIOS to re-enter your CMOS settings manually. Restart your computer and wait for a screen that tells you what key or key combination to press for Setup.

4 If re-entering or restoring your CMOS settings solves your problem, then it's possible your battery is fine and the settings were corrupted by a virus or some other anomaly. If, however, your PC "forgets" the CMOS settings you just re-entered or restored after you turn the machine off (and then back on), you probably have a bad battery.

Locate the dead battery

1 Turn off your PC.

2 Before opening your PC case, put on a grounding wrist strap to prevent discharging static electricity onto any sensitive components. In fact, throughout this procedure it's a good idea to frequently touch something metal (other than your PC) that's resting on the ground, to make sure you discharge any static electricity.

3 Open the PC. For most PCs, this entails removing a few screws with a Phillips screwdriver and sliding the case off.

4 Locate the battery on your PC's motherboard. This is trickier than it sounds because PC manufacturers have used many different types of batteries for CMOS settings. The most common are lithium, like the kind in watches, but they could also be a pair of AA batteries. Or they could look like two cylinders encased in red plastic: a silver box or a red and black box.

5 Draw a picture of the battery, showing its exact position on the motherboard.

What You'll Need

- Electronic or printed backup copy of CMOS settings
- Backup utility
- Replacement battery
- Grounding wrist strap
- Phillips screwdriver

Tips

If you have trouble spotting your battery, try removing expansion cards or cables that might be obscuring it.

You can and should recycle lithium batteries, the most common type in PCs. To find out how, contact your local recycling center.

Remove and replace the battery

1 Examine the battery carefully to see how it's attached to the motherboard. Most likely, the battery is attached by a clip or with Velcro. Some older PCs might have the battery soldered to the motherboard. Unless you're confident with a soldering iron, don't attempt to replace one of these.

2 After you've removed the battery, take it to an electronics store to match it with a replacement.

3 Replace the new battery in exactly the same position as the old one, referring to your drawing (see Warning).

4 Restart your PC and re-enter or restore the CMOS settings.

Warning

If you don't connect the new battery in exactly the same way you found the original, you could destroy your entire motherboard.

260 Clean a Virus-Infected Computer

Computer viruses are insidious, sneaky and—like their biological counterparts—constantly mutating. If you think your computer has been infected, the only safe course of action is to use a good anti-virus program.

Steps

1 As soon as you suspect that your computer has a virus, remove your computer from any networks it might be on, as well as from the Internet, so that you don't inadvertently spread the bug to others. Unplug your network cable if you have to.

2 If you have virus-scanning (anti-virus) software installed, run it.

3 If you don't have anti-virus software, you'll need to obtain some. If you can't get it from a network administrator or download it from an uninfected computer, you can mail-order it from a retailer.

4 Start your computer (still not connected to a network) and follow the instructions that came with the anti-virus software.

5 Keep running the virus-scanning software until your computer comes up clean.

6 Reconnect your computer to the Internet and check with the anti-virus software's publisher to make sure you have the latest updates. If not, download them now.

7 After updating the anti-virus software, run it again until your computer comes up clean.

What You'll Need

- Anti-virus software

Tips

There's no substitute for prevention. Good anti-virus software more than pays for itself as long as you keep it up-to-date.

Common sense also goes a long way toward keeping your computer clean. Never open an attachment from someone you don't know, and be suspicious of odd attachments from people you do know (a virus may have mailed itself to you from their computer).

261 Improve Your Computer's Memory

Computers are greedy for memory, and if you give them more, they will reward you with fewer crashes and slowdowns. Fortunately, increasing your RAM is relatively easy and by far the most cost-effective upgrade you can make.

Steps

1 If you don't already know, find out how much random-access memory (RAM) you currently have installed: On a Windows PC, check the System control panel in Windows. On a Macintosh, check About This Computer under the Apple menu.

2 Check your PC's documentation, visit the manufacturer's Web site or contact the manufacturer to learn the following: the maximum amount of RAM your PC can handle (in many cases, it will be double or more the amount that came with the machine); what type, speed and category of RAM is installed (so you'll know what kind to buy); and where the new RAM chips should be installed on the motherboard.

3 If the slots for the RAM chips are not easily accessible, or if you aren't comfortable opening your computer case, you may want to hire a technician to do the installation.

4 Purchase your upgrade RAM from a vendor that will give you a money-back guarantee. The vendor should also be willing to help you determine exactly what kind of chips you need for your system.

5 Before starting the upgrade, back up your data files.

6 Turn off the computer and open the case. This will probably involve removing some screws.

7 Before touching anything on the machine, discharge any static electricity built up on your person by touching a grounded piece of metal. Many memory vendors sell an inexpensive grounding wrist strap designed to make this procedure safer (for your PC, not you!).

8 Locate the empty sockets where the upgrade chip(s) will go. Handle the chip(s) carefully and by the edges only. Different types of chips have different sockets. The most common types require that you push the chip straight down with firm but gentle force. Chips are designed to fit only the correct socket, so be careful not to force them.

9 Once the chip(s) are seated, close the PC and restart.

What You'll Need

- Information about your PC's current RAM
- Upgrade RAM chips
- Screwdriver
- Grounding wrist strap

Tips

Memory is so cheap these days that it may make sense to replace some of the chips that came with your PC with higher-capacity ones.

If your PC fails to recognize new memory after you've installed more than one new chip, try reinstalling the chips in a different order.

Warning

Static electricity is your sworn enemy when it comes to handling and installing chips. Don't perform the upgrade in your favorite wool shirt or on a shag carpet.

262 Get Rid of E-mail Spam

Unsolicited junk e-mail, or spam, is an unwelcome and often offensive byproduct of the Internet's success. Although there's no guarantee you can avoid all spam, there are ways to avoid looking at most of it.

Steps

Basic prevention

1 If you're already getting spam messages, check with your Internet service provider to see whether it has a spam-prevention option that scans your incoming e-mail for known spammers.

2 If you're lucky enough not to be getting spam now, then sign up for a second (free) e-mail address from a service such as Yahoo or Hotmail. Use this address exclusively for e-commerce, mailing-list subscriptions and bulletin-board postings of any kind. Reserve your main e-mail address for private e-mail to and from friends.

Rule filtering

1 Create an e-mail folder called Suspected Spam.

2 Use the filtering feature in your e-mail program to create rules that redirect spam messages to your Suspected Spam folder. Most spam is not addressed to its recipient by name.

3 Define a rule for incoming mail that says, "If my name appears in the To: or cc: field, then move this message to the Inbox." The procedure for defining rules varies among e-mail programs, so you should consult your program's Help feature to learn exactly how this works.

4 Define individual rules to catch e-mail that isn't addressed to you personally but that you nevertheless want to receive, such as messages from lists you've subscribed to. Have these rules redirect the relevant messages to the Inbox or to special folders that you have created for mail from those sources—for instance: "If the Sender field includes 'MyList,' then send this message to the MyList folder."

6 Define a final rule that sends all other e-mail that hasn't already been redirected by one of your other rules to the Suspected Spam box. For instance, a rule that says, "If the Sender field isn't 'XYXYXYXYY,' then move this message to the Suspected Spam folder" would work as a catchall.

Tip

Never reply to a spam message, even to request that your name be removed from the list. That just tells the spammers that your address is valid.

263 Change a Laser Printer Cartridge

Most laser printers deliver thousands of pages before the toner cartridge runs out of gas. But when those telltale streaked pages start showing up, it's time for the old toner-cartridge switcheroo.

Steps

1 If your toner cartridge starts to die in the middle of an important job with no replacement on hand, you can squeeze out a few more good pages by removing it and gently rocking it back and forth to redistribute the remaining toner powder.

2 Turn off the printer and disconnect the power cord.

3 Remove any paper trays.

4 Open the cover on the printer. If you're not sure how it opens, consult the manual that came with your printer or the directions packaged with your replacement cartridge.

5 Rest one hand on top of your printer. With the other hand, grasp the toner cartridge and pull upward until the cartridge unlocks and releases.

6 Set the cartridge aside and open the bag that contains the replacement cartridge.

7 Install the replacement cartridge in the printer, following the instructions that were packaged with it.

8 Place the old cartridge in the bag and box that the new one came in so you can mail it back to the manufacturer for recycling. Many manufacturers will pay the postage for returning used cartridges.

9 If your new toner cartridge starts out printing lightly or unevenly, you can speed the break-in process by printing a couple of pages of solid black (to do that, draw a black box in Microsoft Word or another application).

What You'll Need

- Replacement toner cartridge

Warning

Toner cartridges are sensitive to light, so don't leave a new one sitting in a pool of sunlight while you make a sandwich.

264 Fix a Printer That Fails Its Self-Test

If your printer produces nothing but blank pages (or no pages at all) when you run its self-test, then there's something wrong with the printer rather than your computer. You might need to take it in for professional repairs, but try one of these easy fixes first.

Steps

1 If you're setting up the printer or changing the toner or ink cartridge for the first time, double-check the instructions to make sure that you installed the cartridge correctly and, for new printers, that you have removed all the pieces of cardboard or plastic packing material.

2 Check to see whether paper is feeding from the paper tray. If it's not leaving the tray at all, try feeding a page manually (if that's an option) or using a different paper tray. Sometimes a problem with the tray can be traced to a broken spring or a piece of plastic.

3 If paper is feeding from the tray but jamming in the printer, examine where the jam is occurring and then inspect the printer carefully to see if you can find what is causing the problem. A piece of paper, for instance, might be blocking the paper path.

4 If paper is feeding through the printer but coming out blank, check to see whether the printer is out of toner or ink. A defective toner or ink cartridge could be the problem.

265 Correct Monitor Resolution on PCs

The monitor is your window on the virtual world. Make sure you've got the best view possible in Windows. Your eyes will thank you.

Steps

1 Go to Start, Settings, then Control Panel.

2 In the Control Panel window, double-click on the Display icon.

3 Click on the Settings tab.

4 In the Desktop or Screen Area, adjust the slider control higher or lower with your mouse to reach the setting you want. Then click on Apply.

5 The Display Properties dialog box will appear and explain that your monitor might flicker. Some combinations of video cards and Windows versions will require that the computer reboot and will ask if you wish to do so. In either case, click on OK to proceed.

6 If you're happy with the new settings, click on Yes to keep them. If not, click on No and your old settings will return, or click on Cancel to readjust the settings.

Tip

Higher resolutions are usually easier on the eyes because images appear sharper and more finely detailed.

266 Clear a Printer Paper Jam

The flashing error code that indicates a jammed printer is the digital-age equivalent of a flat tire. Sooner or later it happens to everyone, so you'd better know how to get things moving again if you want to finish your print job.

Steps

1 Turn the printer off and on to see if it can automatically clear some or all of the jam. Many printers provide an error-code listing on the front panel display for the area where the jam occurred. If your printer shows an error code, be sure and check the printer manual to see if that identifies the area of the printer where the jam occurred.

2 Turn off the printer.

3 Remove any paper trays. Inspect them for wrinkled or damaged paper.

4 Open any other doors that give access to the printer's paper path and to the toner or ink cartridge.

5 If necessary, remove the toner or ink cartridge. Place it in a bag or away from light to avoid damaging it.

6 If you find a piece of jammed paper, remove it by holding it with both hands and pulling firmly (see A). The goal is to keep the paper from tearing. If several pieces are jammed together, try pulling out the middle piece first to loosen the jam.

7 If the paper does tear, try rotating the roller gears manually to free the paper (see B). Don't force anything, though.

8 Replace the toner or ink cartridge and paper trays, close any doors you opened and turn the printer back on.

9 If the printer paper jam message still appears, then there is still some paper in the printer. Reinspect the paper path.

Tip

If you get toner or ink on your clothing, wipe it off with a dry cloth and then launder the clothing in cold water.

Warning

Watch out for loose toner or ink on jammed paper, and do your best to avoid spilling it on yourself or the printer. If a little bit of loose toner or ink gets in the printer, though, it should clear after a few sheets are printed.

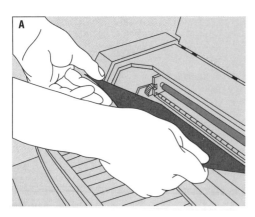

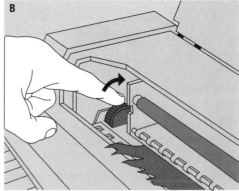

267 Troubleshoot a Recurring Printer Jam

There are a variety of things that can gum up the gears of a printer and cause recurring jams. Though you might be tempted to solve the problem by tossing your printer out the window, here are some more effective approaches to diagnosing and solving the problem.

Steps

1 Inspect the paper trays to make sure they are not overloaded. To determine if this is the problem, do a test print with only one piece of paper loaded in the paper tray. (If this turns out to be the problem, keep the paper tray half-full in the future.)

2 Check that the type of paper being used falls within the printer manufacturer's recommendations. For example, paper designed for ink-jet printers doesn't necessarily work well in laser printers. High-quality, bonded paper will cause paper jams in some printers; look for bonded paper that is "laser and ink-jet compatible."

3 If someone has recently printed labels on this printer, check to see if a label has come unglued from a sheet and become stuck inside the printer.

4 Check the gears and rollers for stuck shreds of torn paper from previous jams. Turn off the printer before you attempt to remove the bits of paper.

5 If you have a laser printer, inspect the printer's paper rollers. They should be smooth but not shiny. Rollers that are cracked or glazed are a frequent cause of paper jams and should be replaced by a technician.

6 If you have a laser printer, try cleaning the printer's paper rollers with a lint-free cloth and isopropyl alcohol (available at electronics shops or drugstores).

7 Try changing the toner or ink cartridge.

8 If you hear a clinking sound during printing, your printer probably has a broken gear and needs to be serviced by a technician.

What You'll Need

- Lint-free cloth
- Isopropyl alcohol

Tips

Occasionally cleaning your laser printer rollers with a lint-free cloth and isopropyl alcohol will extend their life and make them less likely to cause jams.

If you reuse paper to print on the back side, make sure that the paper is not torn, wrinkled or dog-eared. Tears, wrinkles or bends in paper can cause paper jams.

268 Figure Out Why a Windows Printer Won't Print

If your printer turns out perfect pages when you have it perform a self-test, but all you get is an error code when you try to print from Windows, you've got a communication problem. Here's how to get your PC and printer talking again.

Steps

Check your printer cable

1 Make sure your printer cable is securely connected between the PC and printer. The cable should be less than 10 feet (3 m) long.

2 Check for any bent pins on the printer cable. If you find any, straighten them with needle-nose pliers.

3 If you aren't sure about your cable, try swapping it with one from another printer. If the printer suddenly starts working, you know that your original cable is defective.

4 If you're replacing a parallel cable, be sure to get an IEEE 1284 (look at the packaging label or ask a salesperson). Older cables often won't work in newer printers, even though they might look like they should.

Update and reload your drivers

1 Check the Web site for your printer's manufacturer and download the latest version of the driver software for your printer.

2 Open the Printers folder through the Start, Settings menus.

3 Right-click on the icon for your printer.

4 Choose Delete.

5 Double-click on the Add Printer icon in the Printers folder.

6 Follow the Add Printer wizard directions to reinstall the driver software.

Verify printer properties

1 Open the Printers folder through the Start, Settings menus.

2 Right-click on the icon for your printer, then select Properties.

3 Verify that all of your printer's properties are configured as recommended by your printer's manufacturer. You can look up these guidelines in the documentation that came with your printer or, if you've misplaced it, on the manufacturer's Web site.

What You'll Need

- Needle-nose pliers

Tips

Simply turning off the printer for a few seconds to clear its memory can cure a surprising number of printer problems.

Windows 95, Windows 98 and Windows Me include a Print Troubleshooter tool.

Try printing from a simple text-editing program such as Windows Notepad to rule out a problem with a particular application such as your word processor or graphics program.

Check your parallel port settings

1 Right-click on My Computer and select Properties (in Windows 2000, you'll need to then click on the Hardware tab).

2 Go to Device Manager.

3 Double-click on Ports (COM & LPT).

4 Double-click on Printer Port (LPT1) and select the Resources tab.

5 Check the "Conflicting device list" box for an interrupt request line (IRQ) conflict. No other device should be using the same IRQ as the printer port.

6 If you find a conflict, disable the offending device or assign it a new IRQ. To disable a device, find it in Device Manager, open its Properties dialog box, select the General tab and check "Disable in this hardware profile."

Remove temporary files and spool files

1 Windows must be off, so restart your computer to a DOS command prompt. In Windows 95, press F8 when you see the words "Starting Windows 95" appear, then choose Safe Mode Command Prompt Only from the Startup menu.

2 In Windows 98, restart your computer, press and hold down the Control key after your computer completes the Power-On Self-Test, then choose Safe Mode Command Prompt Only from the Startup menu.

3 At the command prompt, type the word "set," then press Enter.

4 Write down the location (the DOS file path) of the TEMP variable.

5 Change your directory to the folder you noted in step 4. For example, if TEMP is set to C:\Windows\Temp, you'll type "cd \windows\temp" and then press Enter.

6 Once you're in the Temp folder, you can delete any temporary files that might be there, by typing "del *.tmp" and then pressing Enter. Don't delete these files while Windows is running, because Windows 95/98 or a Windows-based program might be using one of them.

7 Type "cd \windows\spool\printers" and then press Enter to switch to the spool folder.

8 Delete any spool files you find here by typing "del *.spl" and then pressing Enter.

269 Fix Spelling and Grammar Errors

If computers are so smart, why can't they keep us from looking dumb? Nothing ruins the perception of your scintillating intelligence faster than an obvious spelling or grammar goof.

Steps

1 Use your word processor's spelling and grammar checking features, but don't rely on it completely because it will only get you part of the way there. Microsoft Word, for instance, wouldn't be able to spot the spelling mistake or the grammar and punctuation errors in the previous sentence.

2 Proofread everything of importance at least once on paper rather than on the computer screen.

3 Show important documents to someone whose expertise you trust. If they find a mistake, ask them to explain exactly what you did wrong.

4 If you've never read *The Elements of Style,* by William Strunk Jr. and E.B. White, pick up a copy. It's only about 100 pages and you can get it for less than $10 ($5 used).

What You'll Need

- *The Elements of Style,* by William Strunk Jr. and E.B. White

270 Recall an E-mail in Microsoft Outlook

Red-faced about an embarrassing e-mail you sent to your boss by mistake? Or perhaps you noticed a dumb misspelling just as you clicked the Send button. If you and your recipient are using Microsoft Outlook 97 or later, there's still a chance you can recall that message.

Steps

1 Go to the Sent Items folder in Outlook and open the message you want to recall.

2 Click on Recall This Message in the Tools menu.

3 If your message hasn't already been opened by the recipient, either delete the message or replace it with a new message.

4 If there are multiple recipients, you can request notification of whether the recall succeeded or failed for each one (at least you'll know whom to apologize to). Even if you successfully recall a message, the recipient may still know that you sent a message and then recalled it. So if you didn't replace it with a corrected message, you'll need to get your story straight as to why you recalled it.

Tip

Never send "loaded" e-mail messages immediately after you write them. Save them in a draft folder, then review them one more time before sending. Some e-mail programs also let you queue messages so that they're sent after a slight delay.

271 Diagnose Telephone Modem Problems

In spite of inroads made by cable and DSL, telephone modems are still the most popular way to connect to the Internet, and they're an essential element of every road warrior's portable computer. Sometimes, though, they just refuse to make the connection. The following tips apply to both Windows and Mac computers (except steps 9 and 10, which are for Windows users only).

Steps

1 Check your cable connections. If you have an external modem, check the serial cable between the computer and the modem. For both internal and external modems, check the phone cord connection.

2 Make sure the modem is turned on and has power. If you have an internal modem, you can try removing it and reseating it.

3 Check the phone line to make sure there's a dial tone. This is also a good time to make sure that a phone on the same line wasn't accidentally left off the hook. If your modem is on a dedicated phone line, connect a phone temporarily to check the line.

4 If the modem is dialing but failing to connect, double-check that the phone number entered in your Internet connection program is correct.

5 If you're using a notebook or laptop computer, make sure you don't still have a phone number entered for dialing out of a hotel or from a different area code.

6 Use a telephone to dial the access number or fax number that you're attempting to connect to, then listen to make sure there's a data signal at the other end.

7 Re-enter your password for the service you're trying to connect to. Passwords can accidentally get changed at the user end.

8 If you're dialing an Internet service provider (ISP), contact it to make sure it isn't experiencing system problems that are preventing you from connecting.

9 Test your modem in Windows by using the Modems control panel. Go to Start, Control Panel, Modems, then select the Diagnostics tab. Select the serial (COM) port your modem is installed on and click on More Info. Windows will perform diagnostic tests and show you a window that lists the commands that were sent to the modem and the responses.

10 If you recently upgraded your Windows system software and your modem stops working or returns an error message, visit Microsoft's Product Support Services pages (http://search.support.microsoft.com) to see if there are specific compatibility issues with your modem. Search on "modem troubleshooting."

Tip

If your modem shares a phone line with a phone that has call-waiting, incoming calls might disrupt the modem connection. To get around this, you can temporarily disable call-waiting by adding *70 to the modem command string. You can do this easily in Windows via the Modems control panel's Dialing Properties settings.

272 Troubleshoot an Internet Connection

Losing access to your e-mail and favorite Web sites can be as frustrating as picking up a dead telephone receiver. Although the problem may lie with your ISP, it's worth knowing how to troubleshoot your own end of the line, too.

Steps

If your modem isn't getting an answer from your ISP

1 Make sure that the cable is correctly connected to both a phone line and your modem and that, if you're using an external modem, it's connected to the PC.

2 Dial the access number for your Internet service provider (ISP) with a regular telephone and listen for a data tone. If you don't get one, then you have the wrong number or your ISP is down.

3 If your modem is internal, skip this step. Unplug the power cord from your modem and shut down your computer. Plug the modem back in and restart your computer.

4 If you have another modem cable that you can use to connect the computer to the modem, swap it with your current cable to rule out a bad cable.

If your connection is refused by your ISP

1 Make sure your username and password are still correct. These are usually entered through a connection program that your ISP provided. You will probably have to retype your password, as you won't be able to read it on-screen.

2 Locate the TCP/IP settings for your computer. In Windows, these are found in the Network and Dial-up Connection control panels. In Mac OS 9.2 and earlier, they're in the TCP/IP control panel. In Mac OS X, they're in the Network section of System Preferences.

3 Check that the host name and domain name information are correctly entered in the TCP/IP settings. This information should have been supplied by your ISP.

If your connection is accepted but you can't load Web pages or send e-mail

1 Call your ISP's support number to find out if you have been affected by a service outage.

2 Unplug the power from your modem (whether it's telephone, DSL or cable) for at least 10 seconds, shut down your computer, plug the modem back in and restart your computer.

Tips

A telephone modem works better if it's connected directly to the phone line without anything else—a fax machine, splitter or caller-ID box—intervening.

Print out a paper copy of your TCP/IP settings and keep it handy as a reference to check against when you have problems.

It's also wise to have the phone number for your ISP's technical support printed out or stored on your computer where you can find it without having online access.

If your connection seems too slow

1   Set your Windows computer to MS-DOS mode: Click on Start, Programs, MS-DOS Prompt.

2   Type "ping" followed by an Internet domain name—for example, www.google.com or www.yahoo.com. Macintosh users with OS X can use Apple's Network Utility program to "ping." Earlier versions of Mac OS don't have it built in, but freeware programs are available on the Web.

3   You should get a report saying how many milliseconds it took for your "ping" to reach the destination. A computer communicating with the Internet via a 56-KBps modem connection might typically have a 0.3-second (300-ms) or longer ping. Anything longer than 5 seconds (5,000 ms) indicates a problem with your connection that might be the fault of your ISP.

273 Get Rid of Screen Glare

Glare on your computer monitor is more than just an annoyance. It can leave you with eyestrain and a headache. Taking the shine off your screen should be an ergonomic priority.

Steps

1   Evaluate your computer setup to determine whether the monitor is optimally positioned. You don't want the screen to be facing a window, nor do you want to be facing a window yourself—a position that can cause eyestrain from too much light contrast. The ideal screen-to-window angle is 90 degrees.

2   Reduce the amount of bright sunlight in your workplace. Shades, blinds and draperies all help block sunlight. Even switching to a flat rather than glossy wall paint can help.

3   If you have a bright light source directly above your screen—the worst possible place and typical of many offices—try turning it off and placing a small desk lamp to one side of your computer instead.

4   If you can't avoid overhead light, you can construct an anti-glare hood for your monitor by taping together several sheets of black cardboard and using them to frame your monitor screen.

5   If you can't avoid bright light from a window (or if you think a hood looks too goofy), purchase an anti-glare screen to place over your monitor. Generally, the best ones are polarized or have a purplish optical coating.

What You'll Need

- Window covering
- Flat wall paint
- Desk lamp
- Black cardboard
- Cellophane or masking tape
- Anti-glare screen

Tips

Sometimes just adjusting the brightness and contrast on your monitor is enough to make the display more comfortable to view.

Polarized screens are not effective when used over a monitor with frosted or etched glass.

274 Get Top-Notch Scans

Scanners are a great way to transfer photographs to your computer, but getting the best results requires both skill and experience. The skills aren't tough to learn, though, and the experience can be fun.

Steps

1 If you're using a flatbed scanner, make sure the glass is clean and unsmudged. Use a glass-cleaning solution to get it as transparent as possible.

2 Consider your source material. Is it as sharp as possible? Scanning magazine photos will likely result in ugly moiré images with murky patterns in them.

3 Find out the resolution at which you will be using the final image. If it's going to be displayed on a computer screen, that's 72 dots per inch (dpi). An inexpensive ink-jet printer might be 90 dpi, while a color laser printer might be 300 or 600 dpi.

4 Set the resolution for your scan to be at least 1.5 times the resolution of your final output. For example, for a 90-dpi ink-jet printer, you'd set the scanning resolution to be at least 135 pixels per inch (ppi). Scanning at a higher resolution will produce large graphics files that make demands on processor speed and the hard disk, though, so don't set resolutions higher than necessary.

5 If your scanning or image-editing software provides a tool for adjusting the luminance (as opposed to simple brightness and contrast) of your images, then take the time to learn how to use it. This will provide much more precise control over what we think of as the brightness and contrast of an image.

6 Whenever possible, plan to scan your image at its final output size. If you have to change the size of an image later, the image-editing software will introduce fuzziness as a consequence of adding or removing pixels (called interpolation).

7 Almost all scanned images (and digital photos) can benefit from a certain amount of sharpening to compensate for fuzziness that is introduced during the image-acquisition process. The tool for this is called an Unsharp Mask (see Tips), and the best way to learn how to use it effectively is by trial and error, so have fun.

What You'll Need

- Glass cleaner

Tips

A good general tutorial on luminance controls can be found at www.scantips.com.

Always make the Unsharp Mask step the last thing you do before an image is ready for printing or posting online.

275 Recover Lost Files

Anyone who's ever used a computer for any length of time has experienced the stomach-dropping sensation of losing an important file through bad karma or injudicious use of the Delete key. Sometimes, though, what's lost can be found again.

Steps

If you accidentally deleted the file

1 Double-click on the Recycle Bin in Windows or the Trash on a Mac to see if the file is still there.

2 If you find the file, drag it to the desktop. To return the file to its original location in Windows, click on the file and select Restore from the drop-down menu.

3 If the file is no longer in the Recycle Bin or the Trash, look for a backup. If your PC is on a network that has regular backups, check with the system administrator to see if it's possible to retrieve a saved copy of the file.

4 Try using a commercial file-recovery utility that scans the disk for recognizable data (you can buy one for less than $100). When you delete a file, the operating system probably won't erase the actual bits from the disk until it needs them for something else; therefore, you may be able to recover some data.

5 If you decide to use a file-recovery utility, don't install it on the same disk that you're hoping to retrieve the file from, or you might overwrite the data you're trying to recover. Launch the software from a CD-ROM or a floppy disk. And if you download it directly from the Internet, don't download it onto the disk from which you deleted the file.

If your hard disk crashed

1 Try to repair the disk first with the disk-repair utility that came with your operating system. Both Microsoft and Apple supply such programs.

2 If that doesn't work, try a commercial disk-repair utility, although success with these is somewhat limited if you didn't install the software before you experienced the crash.

3 If a disk appears to be irreparable and if the data is valuable enough, you can send the entire disk to a specialty drive-recovery service that will disassemble it and retrieve as much data as possible. Expect to pay at least a couple hundred dollars, though (payable even when they don't recover anything). Is backing up regularly starting to sound like a good idea?

What You'll Need

- File-recovery software package

Tips

Eventually, all hard drives crash. If you can't back up your entire drive, at least back up the data that you wouldn't want to lose forever.

The efficacy of a file-recovery program increases enormously if it's installed ahead of time so that it can monitor a disk's directory information.

276 Troubleshoot a Palm OS PDA

If you've got one of the 20 million or so personal digital assistants (PDAs) that were sold with the Palm OS, then you've probably become addicted to having information at your fingertips. Suddenly losing that access can be a jolt. Better find out what the trouble is so you can get your life back.

Steps

Problems with HotSync synchronization

1 If you've never used HotSync Manager before, check the documentation that came with your PDA to see if there are known incompatibilities that might be affecting your system.

2 Check to make sure that the HotSync Manager application is running. In Windows, look for its icon (a red and blue circle with arrows) in the system tray of the Taskbar.

3 Make sure you have the right kind of connection, either serial or universal serial bus (USB), selected in HotSync Manager.

4 Quit HotSync Manager and restart it.

5 Lower the data-transfer rate by selecting SetUp in HotSync Manager's menu, then choosing the Local tab. This often works for laptops.

6 If you're using a serial connector, make sure the cradle is connected to a serial (COM) port that isn't being used by another device such as a modem or mouse.

7 If you're using a USB connector, make sure you have Windows 98 or later, and reinstall the PalmConnect USB system software to be sure you have the latest version. Also try removing other USB devices.

8 If you're using Mac OS 9.2 or earlier, go to the Chooser and make sure AppleTalk is turned off (Inactive). You should also disable any other software that uses the serial port.

Defective HotSync cradle contacts

1 Make sure that the System Sound is activated on your PDA. Go to Prefs in the Application screen and select General in the category list, then click the check box next to System Sound.

2 Inspect the cradle contacts to see if any of them look uneven.

Tips

If your PDA doesn't turn off with a single press of the on-off button, it's a sign that your batteries may be running down.

If you leave the PDA in its cradle when you aren't synchronizing, you'll run down the batteries faster.

3 Regardless of whether you can see any defects, place the PDA in the cradle and press it toward the connector.

4 With the PDA in this position, initiate a HotSync session. If HotSync now works (you'll hear the connection chime) and it previously didn't, then the cradle is defective and should be replaced.

You can't find your data after a HotSync session

1 Go to the Tools menu on your PDA.

2 Choose Users.

3 Make sure you have the correct username selected.

Beaming doesn't work

1 Make sure the infrared ports are pointed at each other and between 4 inches (10 cm) and 39 inches (100 cm) apart.

2 Try a soft reset of one or both PDAs (see 277 Reset a Palm OS PDA).

Stylus stops working

1 Perform a soft reset (see 277 Reset a Palm OS PDA).

2 Go to the Prefs application on the PDA and select Digitizer from the drop-down menu.

You've forgotten the user password

1 If you haven't recently backed up your PDA data by synchronizing, you may want to buy a Palm password-cracking program. You can find one on the Internet for about $30.

2 Otherwise, your only choice is to perform a hard reset and restore your data, if possible, by synchronizing with your PC (see 277 Reset a Palm OS PDA).

PDA seems dead

1 Install fresh batteries. Wait several minutes after the installation before restarting the PDA.

2 Try a soft reset and then a hard reset (see 277 Reset a Palm OS PDA).

277 Reset a Palm OS PDA

The Palm OS, which is what runs the popular Palm Pilot and Hand-spring personal digital assistants (PDAs), is pretty robust—but that doesn't mean it never crashes or freezes. If your PDA suddenly stops working, it's time to deliver a wake-up call in the form of a reset.

Steps

1 If you're sure your unit is frozen, turn it over so that the screen faces down.

2 Locate the reset hole, which is just large enough for you to insert the end of an unwound paper clip, and press gently for a "soft" reset. You don't have to use a paper clip if you've got something else that fits, but don't use anything sharp, such as a safety pin.

3 If the soft reset doesn't snap your PDA back to attention (you'll see a Welcome screen), the next step is a "warm" reset, which bypasses potentially troublesome system extensions. Repeat the reset procedure in step 2, but hold down the Page Up button on the front of your PDA while doing so.

4 If the warm reset doesn't result in a welcome screen, then your only recourse is a "hard" reset. The hard part about this is that you'll lose all the data and preferences in your PDA.

5 Before proceeding with the hard reset, replace the batteries in your PDA to make sure the old ones aren't just spent. Check also that the contrast isn't turned down.

6 Repeat the reset procedure in step 2, but this time hold down the power button while you reset. This should return your PDA to the way it came from the box.

What You'll Need

- Paper clip
- New batteries

Tips

If you have a metal stylus for your PDA, check to see if the top unscrews to reveal a probe that you can use instead of a paper clip.

Even if you don't use your PDA data on a PC, it's a good idea to synchronize with one frequently so that you can restore your data in the event that you're forced to do a hard reset.

278 Remove Fingerprints From a Camera Lens

If you're careful, you shouldn't need to clean your camera lens often. A little dust is unlikely to affect image quality, so don't become obsessive about it. Fingerprints, however, can damage the lens coating.

Steps

1 Start by using a sable artist's brush or a hand-squeeze dust blower to remove dust particles from the lens. Compressed air shouldn't be used for this purpose because it can damage the lens by suddenly lowering its temperature.

2 Put a small drop of lens-cleaning fluid on the end of a piece of cloth or lens-cleaning paper. Lightly wipe the lens with the cloth or paper in a circular motion.

3 Dry the lens with a fresh piece of cloth or lens-cleaning paper.

What You'll Need

- Sable artist's brush or hand-squeeze dust blower
- Lens-cleaning fluid
- Cloths or lens-cleaning paper

Warning

Never put lens-cleaning fluid directly on a lens.

279 Troubleshoot a CD-R Drive

When it works right, a CD-R drive provides a great way to back up data and burn audio CDs. When it acts up, it can seem like an expensive device for converting blank CDs into cheap DCs (drink coasters). Although it can be tough to pin down the problem, there's no shortage of potential fixes.

PROBLEM	SOLUTIONS
CD-R drive loses connection to computer while writing	• Try writing at slower speed and with all other applications closed. • Upgrading your operating system can confuse your CD-R drive. Check drive manufacturer's Web site for compatibility info on your system. • Download and install up-to-date drivers for CD-R drive. • If cables are defective or too long, try different, shorter cables. • For universal serial bus (USB) drive, try plugging it directly into USB port on computer rather than into hub. • For FireWire drive, connect drive to computer only after both drive and computer have been turned on. • Set CD-authoring software to Disc-at-Once if that option is available. • Make sure CD-R drive is isolated from loud noises and vibrations while writing. • Try different brand of blank CD media.
Drive reports buffer underruns while writing (PC isn't sending data fast enough to CD-R)	• Try writing at slower speed and with all other applications closed. • Shut down and restart computer and CD-R drive. Try writing another disc in simulation mode (most CD-writing software supports this) before trying to write another disc for real. • Set CD-authoring software to Disc-at-Once if that option is available. • Try different brand of blank CD media. • Create image of the CD and store it on your hard drive temporarily (check your CD-writing software documentation to see if it supports this feature). Then write to disc from this image. • If you still get underruns when writing from a disc image, you may need to defragment your hard-disk drive. (See 257 Speed Up a Hard-Disk Drive.) • If your drive is overheating, make sure the drive's fan is working (if it has one), and don't set the drive on top of another warm device.
Discs burned on your drive can't be read by other drives	• Try a different brand of CD-R media. Some drives like a particular brand, while others refuse to give it the time of day. • Make sure you have your CD-writing software set to "close the session" or "finalize" on discs you're writing. • Dust can affect your CD-R lens. You can clean the interior of the drive by blowing compressed air into it (with no disc inserted). You can also buy a standard audio CD player cleaning kit (see 299 Troubleshoot a CD Player).

280 Restore a CD

If a CD or CD-ROM gets scratched, it often becomes unplayable. Don't write off your favorite album or computer game yet, though.

Steps

1 Clean your disc so that you can see where the scratches are. Holding the disc by its edges, wash it with mild soap and water and pat it dry (don't rub it or you'll make more scratches). Sometimes this is enough to make a disc playable again.

2 Examine the clean disc carefully under a good light. Scratches that are likely to affect disc play run parallel to the edge of the disc. Vertical scratches that run between the center hole and the edge are usually not a problem.

3 For minor scratches, carefully clean the clear plastic that protects the aluminum inside the disc. Use a soft, damp cloth and a small amount of very mild abrasive cleaner—plain white tooth-paste, metal cleaner or plastic cleaner. The key is not to make new scratches. When polishing or cleaning, always rub gently from the inside of the disc to the outside (see illustration). That way, any scratches you make will be the harmless vertical kind.

5 After wiping away a scratch, clean the disc again, let it dry and try playing it again. If it still skips, repeat the process.

6 If your disc is severely scratched, try using a combination abra-sion and waxing technique with a commercial disc-repair solution.

What You'll Need

- Mild soap such as dishwashing liquid
- Soft cloth
- Very mild abrasive cleaner
- Commercial disc-repair solution

Tips

Make a digital copy of any repaired disc onto a CD-R in case it starts skipping again and further cleaning doesn't work.

Copy new CDs onto cas-settes, minidiscs or MP3 players to save wear and tear on your CD collection.

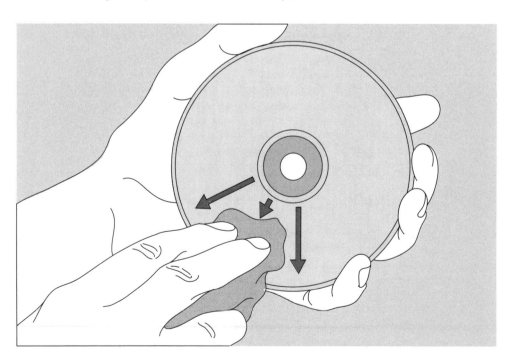

281 Repair a Warped CD

CDs are partly made of plastic, and if you accidentally leave one on your dashboard or in your car trunk (and you'd only do that by accident, right?), it could get more warped than your taste in music. Since CD players prefer perfectly flat discs, that's a problem—but one that may be fixable.

Steps

1 Inspect the CD for cracks. If the airtight seal is broken, then the aluminum inside the disc will corrode regardless of whether you can get the CD flat again. (See 280 Restore a CD.)

2 If the CD isn't cracked, clean it carefully with a soft cloth, making sure it's free of debris.

3 If the CD is only slightly warped, try sandwiching it between two pieces of ¼-inch (6-mm) window glass and pressing it beneath a 10-lb. (5-kg) stack of books for two or three days.

4 If the heavy books alone don't work, try warming up the disc to soften the plastic first. Place the disc in a zipper-lock plastic bag and immerse it in 100°F (38°C) water for 5 minutes. Repeat the book pressing.

5 If you succeed in flattening a warped disc, it's a smart idea to make a copy of it, in case the airtight seal was broken and the disc later starts to corrode.

What You'll Need

- Soft cloth
- Two sheets of ¼-inch (6-mm) window glass
- 10 lbs. (5 kg) of books
- Zipper-lock plastic bags

Warning

Attempting to play a warped or damaged disc could damage your CD player.

282 Clean VCR Heads

If you rent videotapes, there's a chance you'll get one that's been around the block a few too many times and leaves an oxide mess on your VCR's tape heads. The result is a snowy picture or—if your VCR has a video-mute feature—a plain blue screen, which is less interesting than at least half the shows on TV.

Steps

1 Play a new blank tape in your VCR. Most of the time this works to clean the heads and keep them from flaking additional oxide.

2 After an hour, remove the clean tape and try the VCR.

3 If the heads still aren't clean, try using a special head-cleaning tape (available at electronics stores). Buy one that uses a cleaning fluid; dry cleansers are more likely to damage the VCR heads.

4 To keep your heads clean longer, check rental tapes for obvious signs of damage before putting them in your VCR, and fast-forward past the first few minutes of any rental tape, which is where damage is most likely to occur.

What You'll Need

- New blank videotape
- Head-cleaning tape

Tip

Fast-forward and rewind your own tapes every two years to prevent sticking and potential flaking of oxide.

283 Diagnose VCR Problems

VCRs today are smaller, lighter and smarter, but they still have a heck of a lot of moving parts, and they suffer mightily if a child tries to load a peanut-butter-and-jelly sandwich into them. Follow these steps to keep your VCR in good health.

PROBLEM	SOLUTIONS
VCR display doesn't work at all or shows gibberish	• Reset VCR's CPU by unplugging it from wall, waiting several minutes, then plugging it back in. Just turning off power switch isn't enough.
VCR display works, but there's no picture or sound	• Check to see if a tape is jammed inside (see 284 Extract a Jammed Videotape, opposite page).
	• Try changing the video input and/or output source. Many VCRs have two ways to receive and send a video signal (coaxial and video direct). If that works, try changing the cable for the other method to see whether you need a new cable.
	• Clean tape heads (see 282 Clean VCR Heads).
	• Open VCR and inspect any belts that are accessible (see 284 Extract a Jammed Videotape). A drive belt may be broken or loose.
VCR plays but won't record	• Clean tape heads (see 282 Clean VCR Heads).
VCR shuts down shortly after startup	• Open VCR and inspect any belts that are accessible (see 284 Extract a Jammed Videotape). A drive belt may be broken or loose.
VCR display works, sound works, but video doesn't work or picture looks snowy	• Clean tape heads (see 282 Clean VCR Heads).
Picture and/or sound is intermittent or distorted	• Adjust tracking (see 285 Adjust VCR Tracking).
Sound from only one channel	• Replace audio cable.
VCR plays but can't find picture on TV	• Check cables between VCR and TV. Tighten if necessary.
	• Make sure VCR and TV remotes are set to Video or VCR. Look for TV/Video or TV/VCR button on both remotes.
	• Check channels 3 and 4 on TV and VCR. Sometimes VCR output is displayed on these channels.

284 Extract a Jammed Videotape

Most people never see the convoluted path that a videotape follows in a VCR, or else they'd have a lot more respect for these workhorses of the home-entertainment center. Still, tapes do jam—usually the day they're due back to the rental store. Before you grab a pair of pliers and ruin both the tape and your VCR, try these steps.

Steps

1 Make sure the VCR's CPU isn't just confused. Unplug the unit from the wall outlet and wait a few minutes before plugging it back in. Try ejecting.

2 If the CPU doesn't come back to life, unplug the unit from the wall. Then, with a Philips screwdriver, unscrew the top and bottom plates from the unit and remove them.

3 Look for any foreign objects, such as toy parts or cassette labels, that may be obstructing the tape-eject mechanism. If you find any, remove them and reassemble the VCR.

4 See if the tape is in the cassette shell or if it has been loaded onto the video-head drum.

5 If the tape is loaded onto the video drum, determine which shaft or pulley you can turn to unload the tape back into the cassette. If you can't get the tape wound back into the cassette, you should take the VCR into a shop.

6 Locate the cassette-loader motor. Turn the motor carefully in the direction that causes the cassette to lift up and out.

7 Reassemble the VCR.

What You'll Need

- Phillips screwdriver

Tip

If you reach a point where you feel uncomfortable or afraid you're going to force something, take your VCR into a shop and use the opportunity to have them clean the tape-drive path while removing the tape.

Warning

Don't plug the VCR back into the wall while you're in the middle of extracting a tape or while you have the top VCR plate (cover) off.

285 Adjust VCR Tracking

The weakest link in any VCR is the tape you just inserted into it. That Disney classic you picked up at the rental store may have been played 100 times (and that's just your kids). As the tape stretches with use, the picture gets distorted. Time to adjust the tracking.

Steps

1 Look on the front of the VCR for a tracking knob.

2 While the tape is playing, turn the knob to the left to see if the picture improves. If it does, leave it there.

3 If turning the knob to the left doesn't work, try turning it to the right to improve the picture.

4 When you're finished watching the video, return the knob to the central (neutral) position.

Tip

If you find that you constantly have to adjust tracking or that you can't get the picture to look right by adjusting the tracking—regardless of what tape you are playing—you may need to clean the tape heads (see 282 Clean VCR Heads).

286 Salvage a Videocassette

If you've got a favorite or irreplaceable videocassette that's been broken or damaged, resist the temptation to try splicing it. A poorly spliced videotape could ruin the video-head drum in your player. All is not lost, though, if you want to salvage the tape's contents.

Steps

1 Take out the five screws with a Phillips screwdriver from the bottom of two videocassettes—one you can sacrifice and the one that's been damaged.

2 Gently separate the tops and bottoms of the cassettes. Slice through the label (if any) on the side edge with a razor blade.

3 Study the way the tape threads through the cassette (see A). You'll need to remember this later.

4 Discard all of the tape from the sacrificed cassette, but keep all the other parts, including the reels.

5 Take the first section of the damaged tape (still on its reel) from the videocassette you want to save and transfer it to the shell of the sacrificed cassette. Attach it to the take-up reel with adhesive tape (see B).

6 Take the empty reel from the sacrificed cassette and transfer it to the shell of the cassette you're saving. Attach the second section of broken tape to this cassette.

7 Reassemble the cassette shells, being careful to thread the tape the way you found it. You now have two tapes that contain as much of your material as can be saved, with no midtape splice that could damage your video-head drum.

8 Copy the two tapes to a new videocassette and then throw them away.

What You'll Need

- A videocassette you can sacrifice
- Phillips screwdriver
- Razor blade
- Adhesive tape

Tips

Practice this videocassette repair technique on a couple of tapes you don't care about before you attempt to repair that irreplaceable tape of your sister's wedding.

If a tape breaks at one end, you can safely reattach it to the reel for the purpose of copying it, but you should still throw it away since it won't have the leader that the VCR's end sensor relies on to tell it to stop rewinding.

A

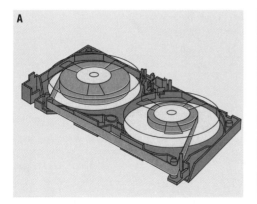

B

287 Troubleshoot a DVD Player

Although DVD players may look like their CD-playing cousins, they're run on a very different kind of optical technology. And thanks to the audio and video demands of movies, they're also more complicated to set up.

PROBLEM	SOLUTIONS
Intermittent or no sound, weak volume, poor sound quality	• Check audio connections to make sure they're secure. • Replace the cable connecting the DVD unit to your receiver. • Clean the contacts on the player and receiver with electronics-grade contact cleaner.
Video images breaking up or freezing	• Make sure DVD is clean and unscratched. • DVDs can be cleaned in the same way that CDs can, but they are more fragile and more sensitive to scratches than CDs are (see 280 Restore a CD).
DVD disc not recognized after loading	• Check that disc is loaded the correct way. • Check that disc is encoded for your geographical region. A disc from Europe (Region 2) will not play in a North American (Region 1) player. • Turn off player with disc inserted, unplug temporarily from wall outlet, plug back in and turn back on. • If your player has a transportation lock (usually a plastic screw on the bottom of the unit), make sure that it is not engaged. • If you have an older player, check with the manufacturer to see whether an update to the firmware is available. Many newer DVD titles with lots of special features are famous for causing problems on older players.
Movies playing with subtitles on	• Go to disc's menu and turn off subtitles. Some players will let you turn off subtitles by pressing the Subtitle button on the remote and then pressing 0 or clear.
Squished picture	• Check player's setup menu to make sure it's not set for a wide-screen TV if you don't have one.
CD-R disc not recognized after loading	• Most DVD players can't read CD-R discs, even if they can play normal CDs.
Picture quality alternates between light and dark	• This is caused by Macrovision copy-protection scheme if you copy DVD video to VCR or if you hook up DVD to TV by way of VCR.

288 Strengthen FM Radio Reception

If you're familiar with fixing your TV's reception, you'll be a natural with an FM radio. FM reception is affected by the same things that affect television signal reception—the quality of your antenna, the strength of the signal you're trying to receive, and any obstacles between your antenna and the transmitter.

Steps

1 If you don't have an antenna connected to your FM receiver, purchase a simple dipole antenna—a simple T-shape flexible wire—and connect it to the FM antenna inputs on the receiver. Because FM signals are directional, you'll want to experiment with the positioning of the wire to find the best reception of the station you're trying to receive.

2 If you're still not getting a good signal, try an indoor amplified antenna, which you'll find at an electronics store. Don't buy one unless you get a guarantee that you can return it for full credit if it doesn't solve your reception problems.

3 If your signal is weak because you live a long way from the transmitter, install an outside antenna and mount it as high as is practical. If you're primarily interested in getting signals from one station or from a group of stations in one direction, get a directional antenna and point it toward the transmitters.

4 If you're using a portable FM radio where the only antenna is the power cord, stretch the cord as straight as possible and experiment with positioning again.

5 Temporarily switch to monaural mode to improve a weak signal on an FM receiver.

Tips

Some cable companies offer FM reception as an option. It's also possible to buy an antenna that will work for both television and FM reception if you don't have cable.

Many FM stations now make their programming available over the Internet—a cool way to receive stations that might not even be in the same state as you.

289 Strengthen AM Radio Reception

Although the golden age of AM radio is long past, it's still popular for news, talk shows and sports broadcasts. Noisy reception, though, is a common problem. Several simple techniques can ensure that you're pulling in the best signal possible.

Steps

1 Check to see whether your radio has an input for an AM antenna. If it does, you can attach a length of wire—measuring at least 1 foot (30 cm)—to see if that improves reception. Experiment with moving the wire around.

2 If you've got a portable radio with only a built-in antenna, try turning the radio around to find a position where reception improves. By the way, the telescoping antenna that comes with portable AM-FM radios has no effect on AM reception.

What You'll Need

● At least 1 foot (30 cm) of wire

Tip

AM reception is usually better at night because AM radio signals bounce off the ionosphere.

3 If the radio plugs into the wall with a nonpolarized plug (where both prongs are the same size), try reversing the plug in the outlet. Moving the plug to another outlet might help, too.

4 If possible, position an indoor radio or its antenna near a window. AM reception is affected by walls of brick, metal or concrete, not to mention aluminum siding.

5 Other potential sources of interference are electrical devices in your house—anything from a fluorescent light to a TV. Try positioning the radio away from these things or switch them off while you enjoy the ballgame.

290 Fix a Remote Control

A couch potato without a remote control is like a king or queen without a scepter, but what do you do if the scepter is broken? Don't let your favorite spud lie helplessly on the sofa. Many remote-control problems can be fixed easily.

Steps

1 Open the remote and confirm that the batteries are there.

2 Assuming the batteries are present and not caked in acid (a bad thing), double-check that they are inserted correctly. Someone could have dropped your remote and hastily scooped up the batteries, then surreptitiously reinstalled them the wrong way.

3 While you're checking the battery installation, make sure that the contacts for the batteries aren't corroded or bent. You can clean them with a pencil eraser followed by a nail file. If necessary, gently bend them back to their correct position.

4 Try a fresh pair of batteries. Be sure to put them in the right way.

5 If your remote is a universal model that can be programmed to control multiple devices, consult the manual (or look on the maker's Web site) to find out how to reinitialize it. Maybe it has forgotten its codes.

6 Check to see if the problem is with the TV or another component that you're trying to control. Try unplugging it for a minute and plugging it back in. Some VCRs have a "parental" mode that locks a remote and/or "timer" modes that shut down a remote until the mode is turned off.

7 Test to see if the remote is getting interference from other electrical devices in the room. To do this, turn off absolutely everything except the device you're trying to control.

What You'll Need

- Pencil eraser
- Nail file
- New batteries

Tips

Remote controls are so attractive to dogs that they might as well be bone shaped. If Spot ruins yours, consider replacing it with a programmable model.

Can't find the code for your programmable remote? Try www.xdiv.com/remotes/ for a list of codes for lots of different manufacturers.

291 Fix Audiocassettes

Audiocassettes have enjoyed a nearly 40-year run as a popular medium for storing music and other sounds. But cassette tape and cassettes are fragile. A broken tape or case can be repaired, though you'll need a little fortitude and ingenuity.

Steps

Replacing a broken case

1 Purchase a new cassette that has a shell held together with small screws. Alternatively, you can buy a cassette shell from an electronics store.

2 Carefully take out the screws from the new cassette and lift the top off.

3 If your broken cassette case was held together by screws, do the same thing with that case. If it's glued together, very carefully separate the two halves by prying them apart with a screwdriver and working it around the edges of the case seams (see A).

4 Remove the tape reels from the new cassette after taking careful notice of how the tape is threaded.

5 Carefully transfer the reels of tape from the damaged cassette box to the new one, making sure that you thread the old tape the same way that the new tape was threaded.

6 Replace the top of the new cassette shell and screw it together after checking to make sure the tape reel didn't get pinched.

Fixing a broken tape

1 Purchase a cassette-tape splicing kit from an electronics store. The only way to fix a broken or damaged tape is by splicing it.

2 If the tape is still intact but one section is stretched or damaged, use a pencil to carefully pull the damaged section of tape from the case.

What You'll Need

- New cassette tape or replacement shell
- Small screwdriver
- Cassette-tape splicing kit and razorblade
- Pencil

Tips

Cassette tapes won't last forever, even if they are carefully stored. Ten years is asking a lot of most tapes.

Recordings that you want to preserve longer should be copied to new tapes or, even better, to CD-R media.

Warning

Any repaired cassette is liable to break again, so make a copy of the material you've got stored on it as soon as possible.

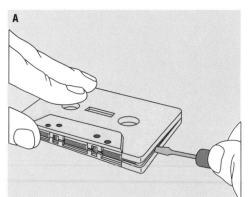

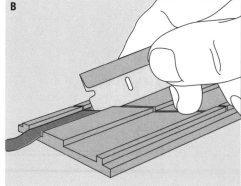

3 If the tape has snapped, open the cassette case to get access to the broken ends of tape. If your original cassette box is held together with screws, you'll be able to reuse it. Otherwise, follow steps 1 through 4 under "Replacing a broken case," opposite page.

4 Follow the instructions that came with your tape-splicing kit to remove the damaged ends of tape and splice the tape back together (see B).

5 Rethread the tape and replace the case top if you removed it. If you had to break apart a glued case, follow steps 5 and 6 under "Replacing a broken case" for transferring the tape to a new case.

292 Fix a VCR Cable Connection

VCRs are famous for the blinking digital clocks that no one ever gets around to setting. An even more basic function that stymies otherwise well-educated people is how to connect the recorder and the TV to a cable hookup so that it works the way it should.

Steps

1 If you haven't hooked up the cable to the TV before, try that out now. Today most TVs are cable ready—meaning you can connect the coaxial cable to an input on the back of the TV. Once you know how to hook up the cable to the TV, you know how to hook up the cable to the VCR.

2 If your TV isn't cable ready, you'll need an RF adapter, which you'll connect to the TV's antenna terminals.

3 Disconnect the coaxial cable from the TV coaxial input and connect it to the VCR coaxial input.

4 Connect the VCR to the TV. The simplest way to do this is to connect a coaxial cable between the VCR coaxial output and the TV's coaxial input (or RF adapter in step 2, above).

5 If your TV has separate audio and video input jacks, you can connect those to audio and video output jacks on the VCR. If you do this, you have the option of not connecting a coaxial cable between the VCR and the TV, but your TV will then work only in video or monitor mode, meaning you'll have to change channels by using the VCR channel selector.

Tip

If you don't have a stereo TV but do have a stereo VCR, you can let the VCR function as the tuner and connect its stereo-sound output to any stereo-system input except the one for a phone. That way, you can listen to programs in stereo while watching them on your monaural TV.

293 Troubleshoot a Cassette Deck

Real repair work on a cassette deck is beyond most of us, but some simple maintenance techniques are within grasp to fix common cassette-deck problems. If you're unsure about a symptom or uncomfortable performing a fix yourself, a trip to the shop may be in order.

PROBLEM	SOLUTIONS
Intermittent or no sound, weak volume, poor sound quality	• Check all cable connections to make sure they're secure. • Change the cable connecting the cassette deck to your receiver. • Clean tape heads with isopropyl alcohol and cotton swabs. Oxide particles can flake off of tapes and collect here. • Clean the contacts on the player and receiver with electronics-grade contact cleaner. • Make sure the cassette output cables are going to the receiver's "tape," "cassette" or "aux" input. The "mon" (monitor) input will produce a low volume.
Wow and flutter (variable pitch that makes it sound like tape is slowing down and speeding up)	• Clean capstan and pinch rollers (the parts that spin around to move the tape) with isopropyl alcohol and cotton swabs. • Inspect any belts (usually thick black rubber bands) that you can see inside the deck for wear. Replace broken, brittle or stretched belts.
Loss of high frequencies	• Make sure the bias settings are correct for the type of tape you're using (I, II or IV) and that the noise-reduction settings used in playback are the same as those used during recording. • Check to see if tape heads need to be realigned or replaced.
Incomplete erasing of tapes	• Demagnetize tape heads with a cassette-deck demagnetizer (available at electronics stores) • Check if the erase head needs to be replaced.
Poor sound with tapes made on other cassette decks	• Try adjusting the bias. On some high-end decks, this can be set by the user.
Muffled or garbled sound, especially with tapes made on other decks	• Angle of the tape head gap, or azimuth, may need to be realigned by a technician. However, doing this will make tapes you've already recorded with the bad alignment sound wrong.
Tapes getting eaten	• The capstan is turning but the take-up reel is not, causing loose tape to bunch up and get jammed. Look for a worn or broken belt or a broken gear that might need replacing.

294 Replace Broken Rabbit Ears

If you're using a rabbit-ear antenna unit for your TV, then you probably spend a lot of time adjusting it to pick up different stations. If you (or someone much clumsier than you) breaks off one of the antennas, though, you can avoid a life of snow-filled screens by installing a replacement. If your antenna is only bent rather than broken, installing a replacement won't improve your reception.

What You'll Need

- Screwdriver
- Replacement antenna

Tip

Because they're so easy to adjust for directionality, in some areas rabbit ears may actually get better reception than fixed antennas.

Steps

1 Make sure your TV is turned off and unplug it from the wall.

2 If you can, draw back or retract the rabbit ears, and disconnect the antenna unit from the TV.

3 Remove the broken antenna from the antenna unit.

4 Bringing the broken antenna and unit with you, go to an electronics store to obtain a replacement that will fit into the antenna unit.

5 Screw the replacement antenna into the antenna unit, and reattach the antenna unit to the TV.

6 Extend the antennas and plug the TV back into the wall.

295 Fix a Jammed Slide Projector

Your friends may let slip a surreptitious sigh of relief when you're forced to interrupt your 150-slide presentation of the family trip to Walt Disney World. But that jammed slide can ruin your carousel projector as well as your show if you don't remove it properly.

Tip

The more slides a carousel holds, the more likely it is to jam, because the slots are closer together. You might want to split a big show between two 80-slide carousels rather than one 140-slide carousel.

Steps

1 Turn off the slide projector and let it cool for a few minutes. This might be a good time to refresh everyone's drinks.

2 Remove the slide tray. This will require loosening a latch or inserting a quarter into a slot in the center of the tray and turning it.

3 With the lock ring in place, turn the tray upside down. Rotate the metal plate on the bottom of the carousel until it clicks into place.

4 Carefully remove the jammed slide from the projector. You may need to press the Forward button.

5 Place the tray back in the projector and, if it's undamaged, return the slide to its slot.

6 Press the button that advances the carousel and spin the tray to where you left off.

296 Get Better Speaker Sound

No matter how much money you pour into your stereo or home-entertainment center, it's never going to sound any better than the speakers you have connected to it. If your speakers don't sound great, it doesn't necessarily mean you need more expensive ones. You may be able to coax better sound just by moving them around.

Steps

1 Decide where in the room you will do most of your listening. For a home-entertainment center, this would probably be your favorite recliner. This position should be about halfway between the speakers and the back wall.

2 If you have only two speakers or a pair of tweeters (the smaller, high-frequency speakers), position each one at ear level and as close to the same distance from your main listening position as possible. Aim them at the recliner.

3 Position the speakers so that the distance between them isn't any greater than the distance between the speakers and your main listening position. Also, place them symmetrically so that they each have the same relationship to surrounding walls.

4 Place your subwoofer (usually a big heavy box) on the floor in a spot where it won't be the same distance from different walls. Because walls tend to emphasize certain bass frequencies, you want to avoid having multiple walls emphasizing the same frequency. Because we can't determine from which direction low-frequency sounds come, it is not necessary to center the subwoofer to the main listening position.

5 Use your ears, the most sophisticated audio-evaluation equipment available, to make your final judgment. Select a piece of music that you're familiar with to evaluate the effectiveness of your speakers' positioning. A recording of solo piano music works well simply because most people have heard what a real piano sounds like.

6 While listening to your test music, experiment with slight changes in speaker positioning until you're satisfied that you're hearing the most natural sound.

7 Don't forget your speaker wires. Although you don't necessarily have to buy audiophile cables for your speakers, a heavier-gauge wire is a good investment because it has less resistance and thus a purer signal. And if the ends of your speaker wire are oxidized (corroded), trim them off and strip them to expose enough fresh wire to reconnect them at least once a year.

Tip

You can buy various kits to improve speaker sound, but make sure you don't do anything to your speakers that you can't undo if you find no improvement—or if the kit makes things worse.

297 Troubleshoot a Digital Camcorder

Digital camcorders offer great picture quality, excellent sound, compactness and lots of features. Combine one with a computer for digital editing and output to DVD, and you could end up the talk of the next Sundance Film Festival. Although these cameras don't have many (if any) parts you can repair yourself, it's still possible to troubleshoot some common problems yourself.

PROBLEM	SOLUTIONS
Colors appear off or look different when you view video on TV or monitor	• Learn how to do a white balance for your camera to compensate for artificial light when you're taping. • If your camera has a color-bar feature, include color bars at the start of each video. Then you can compensate for color idiosyncrasies by adjusting the TV or monitor.
A tape won't eject	• Try turning off the camera and then turning it on with the eject button pressed down. • Remove all power (including lithium batteries) and leave the camera off for 30 seconds. Then reinstall the batteries and turn the camera on with the eject button held down.
FireWire connection to computer keeps getting dropped	• Check with manufacturer to make sure you have the latest driver and firmware updates for your camera and computer. • Always turn the camera's power on before making a FireWire connection. • Disconnect the FireWire cable before turning the camera off. • Use the camera's AC adapter when making FireWire connections. • Try a different FireWire cable and try connecting the camera to a different computer. FireWire cables and ports sometimes fail.
Camcorder won't power up when you turn it on	• Remove all power (including lithium batteries) for 30 seconds. Reinstall batteries, connect AC adapter and see if camera will reset. If not, it probably needs service.
Camcorder won't focus	• Check to see if there's an auto/manual focus switch.
Audio and video are degraded	• Try a fresh tape. Although digital-video tapes should be good for several hundred plays under good conditions, they can wear out. • Clean the camera heads with the manufacturer's head-cleaning kit.
Audio records on only one stereo track	• Check to see if you're using a monaural microphone. If you are, you can buy a mono-to-stereo adapter plug for it.
Warning	Never try to disassemble a digital camcorder yourself, especially for a stuck tape.

298 Troubleshoot a Digital Camera

Digital cameras have brought more fun to photography than anything since the first Polaroid, but there's a little more to making them work than point and click. Short of dropping the camera into a lake, though, most of the problems you'll encounter have simple fixes.

PROBLEM	SOLUTIONS
Image quality is poor	● Check lens to make sure it's clean (see 278 Remove Fingerprints From a Camera Lens).
	● Learn how to focus or prefocus your model of camera.
	● Avoid using digital zoom feature.
	● Check the manual to see what resolutions your camera supports and make sure you know which one is selected. Higher resolutions give better pictures but take up more digital space.
	● If using flash, make sure you're close enough to the subject.
	● Sharpen photos on computer after downloading (see 274 Get Top-Notch Scans).
Camera won't turn on	● Check batteries.
	● Connect camera to an AC adapter.
	● Remove all batteries, disconnect AC adapter, wait a minute, reinsert batteries and reconnect adapter. Turn on camera.
Camera got wet	● Turn off camera if it's on. Remove all batteries and media. Let it dry completely for at least 24 hours before reinserting batteries.
Camera burns through batteries	● Minimize your use of the camera's built-in LCD (assuming it has one) if it has a viewfinder you can use instead. The LCD is the biggest power drain on your camera.
	● Use only heavy-duty batteries (look for ones that say they're suited to digital cameras). Ordinary alkalines won't cut it. Look into upgrading to rechargeable NiMH batteries.
	● If you have or can get an AC adapter for your camera, always use it when downloading photos directly to your computer.
	● If your camera uses PC Cards or SmartMedia cards, get a card reader that will connect to your computer. This will save battery life and improve data-transfer speed.
	● If problem occurs during very cold conditions, warm the batteries in your pocket or hand just before inserting them into the camera and shooting.
Camera won't recognize media	● Make sure media is inserted correctly (this isn't always obvious with SmartMedia, for instance). Make sure media hasn't been write-protected.

PROBLEM	SOLUTIONS
Camera won't connect with computer	• Always use an AC adapter when downloading directly to a computer. • Check with the camera manufacturer (try its Web site) to make sure you have the latest version of the necessary software drivers. • If your camera connects via a serial (COM) port, check for serial-port conflicts. • If you're using a FireWire cable to connect to the computer, turn the computer on, turn the camera on and then connect the cable between the two. Don't turn off the camera while the cable is still attached.
Flash doesn't work	• Check that batteries are fresh. • Check that camera hasn't been set for no-flash mode. • Give the flash time to charge before pressing shutter.
Can't find the pictures you took	• Look for playback or review mode on camera to view pictures on your camera. Use arrow buttons to scroll through pictures. • Make sure battery is attached properly and camera is powered, to confirm pictures were actually taken.
Camera won't take pictures	• Check that camera is not in playback or review mode. • Make sure memory card is in camera and that card is properly formatted. • Memory may be full. Offload images to computer or delete them. • Check batteries. Replace if necessary. • Check flash. It may be recharging.
Screen keeps turning off	• Check message display for explanation such as focus or lighting. • Battery is low; replace or recharge. Some cameras have a power-save mode that shuts down • LCD screen when battery is low. In some models, you may be able to take nonflash pictures with low battery. • Battery may be too cold. Warm it to room temperature.

299 Troubleshoot a CD Player

Although they are high-precision optical devices, most compact disc players provide trouble-free operation for years if they aren't abused. When something does go wrong, it's often an easy fix.

PROBLEM	SOLUTIONS
Intermittent or no sound, weak volume, poor sound quality	• Check all cable connections to make sure they're secure. • Replace the cable connecting the CD unit to your receiver. • Clean the contacts on the player and receiver with electronics-grade contact cleaner.
Discs skipping	• Make sure CDs are clean and unscratched. • Clean the laser lens.
Discs not recognized after loading	• Make sure discs are loaded the right way. Most, but not all, players load discs with the printed label on top. • If player has a transportation lock (usually a screw on the bottom of the unit), make sure it is not engaged. • Clean the laser lens.
Problems with door opening or closing	• Make sure the drawer-loading belt is still tight and elastic. If not, it can be replaced with a belt obtained from an electronic-parts supplier. The replacement should be of equal or slightly greater thickness and should fit snugly but not so tightly that it strains the motor. • Check for broken or loose gears and have them replaced. • Check for obvious sources of contamination such as pet hair or foreign objects that are preventing smooth operation of moving parts. Small children have a habit of inserting items into CD players. • Use electronics-grade contact cleaner to clean the door-position contacts.
Disc number not displaying	• Make sure disc was not inserted upside down. • Check to see if disc is warped, scratched or damaged. Insert new disc to see if disc is causing the problem. • There may be moisture on laser pickup. Allow machine to remain on for 20 to 30 minutes before you attempt to reuse it.
Remote control doesn't work	• Check batteries on remote. Replace if necessary. • Sunlight or fluorescent light may be interfering with remote control sensor on CD player. Reposition CD player or fluorescent light.
Warning	• Disconnect the CD player from its power source before opening the case. • Never look directly into the lens of a CD laser while the unit is turned on.

300 Replace a Headphone Plug

A good set of headphones can last a lifetime, but it's unlikely that the plug at the end of the headphone cord will. If you can solder a wire, though, there's no reason you can't replace it. If you don't know how to solder, you can buy a replacement plug that uses screw-on terminals, although this will be less secure over the long run.

Steps

1 Use wire cutters/strippers to snip the old headphone plug off the cord. Purchase an exact replacement headphone plug at an electronics store.

2 Twist off the shell of the replacement plug and slide it and any insulating sleeve onto the headphone cord.

3 Using the wire cutters/strippers, remove 1½ inches (4 cm) of the outer insulation from the headphone cord. You should find three wires: two insulated wires and one uninsulated wire, which is the ground.

4 Strip ½ inch (12 mm) of insulation from each of the insulated wires (see A).

5 Solder or screw the uninsulated ground wire to the plug terminal that is farthest from the plug tip (see B).

6 Solder the insulated wires to the other plug terminals. If you don't know which terminal on the plug is the right channel and which is the left, you can use a continuity tester (available at electronics or hardware stores) to find out, testing it first on the tip of the headphone jack, which is always the left channel.

7 Squeeze the plug clips together with a pair of pliers to secure the cord.

8 Slide the shell over the plug and screw the plug in place.

What You'll Need

- Wire cutters/strippers
- Replacement plug
- Screwdriver
- Soldering iron and solder (available at hardware stores)
- Continuity tester
- Pliers

Tip

The wires for Sony headphone cords are insulated with a lacquer coating, which you'll need to remove before soldering them to the new plug. The easiest way to do this is to gently scrape it off with a pocketknife.

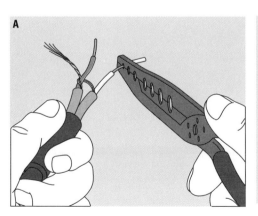

A

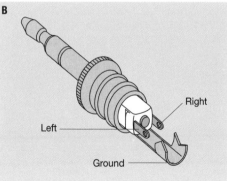

B

Right
Left
Ground

NORING • FIX BAD HABITS • REPAIR A BROKEN EYEGLASS FRAME • REPOSITION A SLIPPED CONTACT LENS • FIX A RUN IN STOCKINGS • JO
REAKOUT • REPAIR A TORN FINGERNAIL • FIX CHIPPED NAIL POLISH • FIX A STUCK ZIPPER • FIND A LOST CONTACT LENS • ELIMINATE BAD
EY THAT STICKS • STOP TELEMARKETERS AND JUNK MAIL • GET SUPERGLUE OFF YOUR SKIN • EXTRACT A SPLINTER • SOOTHE A SUNBUR
HANGOVER • STOP HICCUPS • MEND A BROKEN HEART • MEND A FAMILY FEUD • TREAT A SMALL CUT OR SCRAPE • FIX HAIR DISASTERS •
TTER SEATS • FIX A BILLING MISTAKE • FIX A BAD GRADE • FIX BAD CREDIT • RECOVER FROM JET LAG • RESUSCITATE AN UNCONSCIOUS
PRONOUNS • FIX A RUN-ON SENTENCE • FIX MISUSE OF THE WORD GOOD • FIX YOUR DOG OR CAT • CORRECT BAD BEHAVIOR IN DOGS
SSING BUTTON • REMOVE LINT FROM CLOTHING • FIX A DRAWSTRING ON SWEATPANTS • REPAIR A HEM • REPAIR LEATHER GOODS • MEN
UNDER YOUR CASHMERE • FIX A SWEATER THAT HAS SHRUNK • FIX A SWEATER THAT HAS STRETCHED • FIX A HOLE IN A POCKET • FIX A
LING FROM CLOTHING • FIX A FRAYED BUTTONHOLE • REMOVE DARK SCUFFS FROM SHOES • TREAT STAINS ON LEATHER • PROTECT SUI
JIET SQUEAKY HINGES • TROUBLESHOOT LOCK PROBLEMS • TIGHTEN A LOOSE DOORKNOB • TIGHTEN A LOOSE DOOR HINGE • FIX A BIN
EPLACE CRACKED TILE • TROUBLESHOOT MOLD ON INTERIOR WALLS • REPLACE CRACKED TILE GROUT IN A TUB OR SHOWER • FIX A DRA
LINDS • TROUBLESHOOT WINDOW SHADE PROBLEMS • FIX BROKEN GLASS IN A WINDOW • REPAIR A WINDOW SCREEN • REPAIR ALUMINU
AMAGED PLASTER • REPAIR WALL COVERINGS • TOUCH UP PAINTED WALLS • TROUBLESHOOT INTERIOR-PAINT PROBLEMS • SOLVE A LEAK
ARDWOOD FLOOR • RESTORE A DULL, WORN WOOD FLOOR • TOUCH UP WOOD-FLOOR FINISHES • REPAIR DAMAGED SHEET-VINYL FLOOR
USE • CHILDPROOF YOUR HOME • PREVENT ICE DAMS • CURE A FAULTY FIREPLACE DRAW • START A FIRE IN A COLD CHIMNEY • FIX A W
AL A GARAGE FLOOR • REFINISH A GARAGE OR BASEMENT FLOOR • CONTROL ROOF LEAKS • REDIRECT RAINWATER FROM A DOWNSPOU
AMAGED ASPHALT SHINGLE • PATCH A FLAT OR LOW-PITCHED ROOF • REPAIR ROOF FLASHING • TROUBLESHOOT EXTERIOR-PAINT PROBL
OW WATER PRESSURE • FIX LEAKING PIPES • STOP A TOILET FROM RUNNING • FIX A LEAKY TOILET TANK • FIX A STOPPED-UP TOILET • STC
LOGGED SINK OR TUB • REPAIR A TUB-AND-SHOWER VALVE • REPAIR CHIPPED FIXTURES • QUIET NOISY PIPES • DEFROST YOUR PIPES • D
ONSUMPTION • REPLACE A RECEPTACLE • FIX AN ELECTRICAL PLUG • REPLACE A LIGHT FIXTURE • INSTALL A NEW DIMMER • FIX A LAMP
OORBELL • FIX A WOBBLY OVERHEAD FAN • ADJUST WATER-HEATER TEMPERATURE • RELIGHT A WATER-HEATER PILOT LIGHT • TROUBLES
E MAKER • GET RID OF MICROWAVE SMELLS • FIX A REFRIGERATOR THAT COOLS POORLY • FIX A GAS OVEN THAT HEATS POORLY • CLEAN
SHWASHER PROBLEMS • CORRECT AN OVERFLOWING DISHWASHER • FIX A LEAKY DISHWASHER • FIX A DISHWASHER THAT FILLS SLOWLY
WASHING MACHINE THAT FILLS SLOWLY • FIX A WASHING MACHINE THAT "WALKS" ACROSS THE FLOOR • FIX A CLOTHES DRYER THAT DRI
X YOUR VACUUM CLEANER • REPLACE VACUUM CLEANER BRUSHES • TROUBLESHOOT A PORTABLE AIR CONDITIONER • FIX A WINDOW A
ROCESSOR • FIX A TOASTER • DIAGNOSE MICROWAVE OVEN PROBLEMS • TROUBLESHOOT A GAS GRILL • FIX A TRASH COMPACTOR • REF
ART • TROUBLESHOOT A CRASHING COMPUTER • CLEAN UP LAPTOP SPILLS • FIX BAD SECTORS ON A HARD DISK • QUIT A FROZEN PC A
FECTED COMPUTER • IMPROVE YOUR COMPUTER'S MEMORY • GET RID OF E-MAIL SPAM • CHANGE A LASER PRINTER CARTRIDGE • FIX A
GURE OUT WHY A PRINTER WON'T PRINT • FIX SPELLING AND GRAMMAR ERRORS • RECALL AN E-MAIL IN MICROSOFT OUTLOOK • DIAGNO
LES • TROUBLESHOOT A PALM OS PDA • RESET A PALM OS PDA • REMOVE FINGERPRINTS FROM A CAMERA LENS • TROUBLESHOOT A CD
ALVAGE A VIDEOCASSETTE • TROUBLESHOOT A DVD PLAYER • STRENGTHEN FM RADIO RECEPTION • STRENGTHEN AM RADIO RECEPTION
JAMMED SLIDE PROJECTOR • GET BETTER SPEAKER SOUND • TROUBLESHOOT A DIGITAL CAMCORDER • TROUBLESHOOT A DIGITAL CAM
GHTBULB • FIX A BROKEN WINEGLASS STEM • FIX BLEMISHED WOOD FURNITURE • REPAIR GOUGES IN FURNITURE • RESTORE FURNITURE
AMOUFLAGE A DOG-SCRATCHED DOOR • REPAIR A SPLIT CARPET SEAM • RID CARPETS OF PET ODORS • REINFORCE A SAGGING SHELF •
OINTS OF CHAIRS AND TABLES • REUPHOLSTER A DROP-IN CHAIR SEAT • REVIVE A CANE SEAT • REINFORCE A WEAK BED FRAME • FIX UP
OTTERY • REPAIR CHIPPED OR CRACKED CHINA • UNCLUTTER YOUR HOME • CLEAN CRAYON FROM A WALL • GET WAX OFF A TABLECLOT
AINS • REMOVE CHEWING GUM FROM CARPETING • REMOVE BLEACH SPOTS FROM CARPETING • REMOVE PET STAINS • ELIMINATE WINE
AINS FROM TILE GROUT • REMOVE MILDEW FROM WALLS AND CEILINGS • DISINFECT A TOILET BOWL • REMOVE FIREPLACE GRIME • GET
LEAN OIL SPOTS FROM A GARAGE OR DRIVEWAY • REMOVE STAINS FROM BRICK • WASH AN OUTDOOR GRILL • FIX A FALLEN SOUFFLÉ • F
ESCUE OVERPROOFED YEAST DOUGH • FIX YOUR KID LUNCH • GET RID OF TAP-WATER MINERAL DEPOSITS • CALIBRATE A MEAT THERMO
AUCE • RESCUE A BROKEN SAUCE • REMOVE FAT FROM SOUPS AND SAUCES • FIX LUMPY GRAVY • SUBSTITUTE MISSING INGREDIENTS • F
URNED RICE • REMOVE COOKING ODORS • FINISH UNDERCOOKED MEAT • SALVAGE AN UNDERCOOKED TURKEY • FIX AN OVERSEASONE
ALE BREAD • SMOOTH SEIZED CHOCOLATE • SOFTEN HARDENED SUGARS OR COOKIES • FIX BREAKFAST FOR YOUR SWEETHEART • MEN
GGING TOOLS • RESTORE A BROKEN FLOWERPOT • SHARPEN PRUNING CLIPPERS • REMOVE RUST FROM TOOLS • REVIVE WILTING CUT F
ET RID OF RAMPANT BRAMBLES • TROUBLESHOOT BROWN SPOTS ON A LAWN • CONTROL MAJOR GARDEN PESTS • RID YOUR GARDEN O
ONPERFORMING COMPOST PILE • FIX BAD SOIL • SHORE UP A RAISED GARDEN BED • REMOVE A DEAD OR DISEASED TREE LIMB • TROUB
RAINAGE • TROUBLESHOOT ROSE DISEASES • IDENTIFY AND CORRECT SOIL DEFICIENCIES IN ROSES • TROUBLESHOOT ROSE PESTS • OV
AMAGED DECK BOARDS • REPAIR DECK RAILINGS • STRENGTHEN DECK JOISTS • FIX A RUSTY IRON RAILING • REPAIR A GATE • REPAIR A
RACKED OR DAMAGED CONCRETE • IMPROVE THE LOOK OF REPAIRED CONCRETE • REPAIR AN ASPHALT DRIVEWAY • REVIVE WOODEN O
ARDEN PONDS • CLEAN SWIMMING POOL WATER • TROUBLESHOOT HOT TUBS AND SPAS • REPLACE BRICKS IN WALKWAYS AND PATIOS •
AR WITH JUMPER CABLES • SHUT OFF A CAR ALARM THAT WON'T QUIT • FREE A CAR STUCK ON ICE OR SNOW • DE-ICE YOUR WINDSHIEL
URN-SIGNAL COVER • FIX A CAR FUSE • FIX DASHBOARD LIGHTS THAT WON'T LIGHT • REMOVE CAR SMELLS • CHECK TIRE PRESSURE • IN
PROPERLY INSTALLED CHILD CAR SEAT • TROUBLESHOOT LEAKING OIL • CHECK AND ADD POWER-STEERING FLUID • CHECK AND ADD C
ROKEN EXHAUST PIPE • CHECK AND ADD ENGINE OIL • CHECK AND ADD BRAKE FLUID • CHECK AND ADD FLUID TO YOUR AUTOMATIC TF
ROUBLESHOOT A WINDSHIELD-WASHER PUMP • REPAIR MINOR DENTS • CHANGE A HUBCAP • FIX AN IGNITION KEY THAT WON'T TURN • C

MORY • FIX AN ELECTRIC CAN OPENER THAT DROPS THE CAN • TROUBLESHOOT A CELL PHONE • KEEP MIRRORS FROM FOGGING • ZAP A
EEP A SHAVING NICK FROM BLEEDING • GET RID OF SPLIT ENDS • UNTANGLE HAIR SNARLS • FIX FRIZZY HAIR • FIX BLEEDING LIPSTICK •
CKY SOCIAL SITUATION • FIX A BAD REPUTATION • CLEAN LIPSTICK FROM A COLLAR • FIX A BAD RELATIONSHIP • SALVAGE A BAD DATE •
EEDING NOSE • BEAT THE MONDAY MORNING BLUES • GET OUT OF A FIX • EXTRACT A BROKEN KEY • RETRIEVE KEYS LOCKED INSIDE A C
TOP SOMEONE FROM CHOKING • STOP AN ANT INVASION • STABILIZE A CHRISTMAS TREE • RESCUE AN ITEM FROM THE DRAIN • FIX IMPR
KUNK ODOR FROM YOUR DOG • GET A CAT OUT OF A TREE • CORRECT BAD BEHAVIOR IN CATS • TREAT A CAT FOR MATTED FUR • REPLA
EAM • TREAT MILDEW DAMAGE • GET STATIC OUT OF YOUR LAUNDRY • DEAL WITH A CLOTHES-MOTH INFESTATION • FIX A SEPARATED ZIPI
JR SOCK • TREAT MIXED-WASH ACCIDENTS • TAKE WRINKLES OUT OF CLOTHING • FIX A HOLE IN JEANS • REPAIR A SNAG IN A SWEATER •
TAINS • WASH SNEAKERS • PICK UP A DROPPED STITCH IN KNITTING • RESTRING BEADS • FRESHEN SMELLY SHOES • FIX A SAGGING CLO
• FIX A RUBBING DOOR • FIX A DRAFTY DOOR • TUNE UP SLIDING DOORS • FIX A SHOWER DOOR • SEAL WALL JOINTS AROUND A TUB OI
V • REPAIR A FAULTY WINDOW CRANK • REPAIR VERTICAL BLINDS • REPAIR VENETIAN BLINDS OR MINIBLINDS • REPAIR WOOD OR PLASTIC
REEN WINDOWS • INSTALL NEW SASH CORDS IN WINDOWS • FIX A TIGHT OR LOOSE WINDOW SASH • REPAIR MINOR DRYWALL DAMAGE •
BLEM • REPLACE A DAMAGED CEILING TILE • REPLACE A WOOD FLOORBOARD • QUIET SQUEAKING FLOORS • REPAIR A WATER-DAMAGED
R A VINYL-TILE FLOOR • SILENCE SQUEAKY _____ STER • REPLACE CAULKING ON THE OUTSIDE OF Y
IG STOVE • REPAIR AND PREVENT WOOD RC_____TCH A GUTTER LEAK • TROUBLESHOOT A WET BAS
GGING GUTTER • UNCLOG GUTTERS AND D_____ • REPAIR A CRACKED OR SPLIT WOOD SHINGLE •
RAGE-DOOR TENSION • TROUBLESHOOT A_____RITES • LOOSEN A RUSTY NUT OR BOLT • TROUBLE
JK SWEATING • FIX FLUSHING PROBLEMS •_____FAUCET • FIX A STOPPER THAT DOESN'T SEAL • CI
MP PUMP PROBLEMS • TROUBLESHOOT ELE_____USE • SWAP A FAULTY LIGHT SWITCH • REDUCE EI
HOOT FLUORESCENT LIGHTING • FIX A LOW_____E THERMOSTAT • TROUBLESHOOT HOLIDAY LIGHT
TING SYSTEM • REFRESH A SMELLY REFRIGE_____EMS • FIX A LEAKING REFRIGERATOR • REPAIR A C
TIONING GAS BURNER • REPAIR A RANGE H_____FIX AN ELECTRIC OVEN THAT HEATS POORLY • DIA
YOUR APPLIANCES • CONTROL GARBAGE _____E DISPOSAL • DIAGNOSE WASHING MACHINE PRC
FIX A HAIR DRYER • TROUBLESHOOT A CLC_____AT SPUTTERS • FIX AN IRON THAT LEAVES SPOTS C
ER • FIX A DEHUMIDIFIER • REPAIR A CONS_____DER • HANDLE A MIXER THAT OVERHEATS • REPAIR
G MACHINE • TROUBLESHOOT SMOKE ALAR_____DARD SPILLS • TROUBLESHOOT A COMPUTER THA
REMOVE A WINDOWS PROGRAM • SPEED U_____OUSE • REPLACE YOUR PC'S BATTERY • CLEAN A
T FAILS ITS SELF-TEST • CORRECT MONITOF_____PAPER JAM • TROUBLESHOOT A RECURRING PRINT
NE MODEM PROBLEMS • TROUBLESHOOT A_____REEN GLARE • GET TOP-NOTCH SCANS • RECOVEF
STORE A CD • REPAIR A WARPED CD • CLE_____ • EXTRACT A JAMMED VIDEOTAPE • ADJUST VCR
TE CONTROL • FIX AUDIOCASSETTES • FIX_____OT A CASSETTE DECK • REPLACE BROKEN RABBIT
LESHOOT A CD PLAYER • REPLACE A HEAD_____RASS • SHINE SILVER SAFELY • REMOVE A BROKEN
PLACE A BROKEN TOWEL ROD • REMOVE ST_____FOR NATURAL DISASTERS • FIX A FRAYED CARPE
BORING BATHROOM • REPLACE A SHOWER_____NACE FILTER • REPAIR A BROKEN SLIDING DRAWEF
D CHAIR • FIX A WOBBLY WOOD CHAIR • SF_____OR CRACKED PORCELAIN • REPAIR CHIPPED OR CF
WAX FROM CARPETING • GET RID OF CEILIN_____MOVE MYSTERY STAINS FROM CLOTHING • REMOV
A RUG OR TABLECLOTH • REMOVE BURN N_____NITURE • STRIP WAX BUILDUP FROM FLOORS • RE
ORANT STAINS • ELIMINATE CIGARETTE ODOR • RESTORE SHINE TO YOUR JEWELRY • WASH DIRTY WINDOWS • REMOVE GRIME FROM MIF

Furniture & Housewares

JMBLED CAKE • FIX A PERFECT CUP OF TEA • PATCH A TORN PIE CRUST • KEEP A PIE CRUST FROM GETTING SOGGY • FIX DOUGH THAT W
DULL KNIFE • REMOVE RUST FROM A CAST-IRON PAN • REPAIR LAMINATE COUNTERTOPS • REMOVE STAINS FROM A STONE COUNTERTO
R CHOLESTEROL • TREAT BURNED POTS AND PANS • RESCUE A BURNED CAKE OR PIE • PUT OUT A KITCHEN FIRE • REMOVE THE BITTERN
N UNDERSEASONED DISH • REMOVE OVEN SPILLS • CLEAN UP OIL SPILLS • FIX A DRINK FOR ANY OCCASION • DISENTANGLE PASTA • RE
CUTTING BOARD • KEEP A MIXING BOWL STEADY • FIX GARDEN TOOL HANDLES • REPAIR A LEAKY HOSE NOZZLE • MEND A LEAKY HOSE
ARPEN A POWER MOWER BLADE • SHARPEN PUSH MOWER BLADES • REPAIR BALD SPOTS ON GRASS • RID YOUR GRASS OF DOG URINE
OUBLESHOOT HERBS • TROUBLESHOOT HOUSEPLANTS • OVERCOME SHADE PROBLEMS • RID SOIL OF PESTS AND DISEASES • REVIVE A
ES AND SHRUBS • REPAIR A LEAKING IRRIGATION SYSTEM • UNCLOG A SPRINKLER SYSTEM • CLEAN A CLOGGED DRIP SYSTEM • FIX POC
GUS DISEASES IN ROSES • REPAIR DECK STEPS • RENOVATE A WEATHERED DECK • TIGHTEN LOOSE DECKING • REMOVE DECK STAINS • I
E • LEVEL AND SMOOTH A GRAVEL PATH • FIX A POTHOLE IN A DIRT OR GRAVEL DRIVEWAY • REPLACE PATIO STONES, TILES AND PAVERS •
NITURE • RESTORE WEATHERED METAL FURNITURE • REPAIR CHAIR STRAPS AND WEBBING • REVIVE RUSTED IRON FURNITURE • TROUBLE
LED CAR • SHUT OFF A JAMMED HORN • CHANGE YOUR CAR'S BATTERY • TROUBLESHOOT A CAR THAT WON'T START • FIX A FLAT TIRE •
NED-OUT SIGNAL BULB • FIX A BURNED-OUT HEADLIGHT • ADJUST HEADLIGHTS • FIX A STUCK BRAKE LIGHT • REPLACE A BROKEN TAILL
TIRES • FIX A STUCK CONVERTIBLE TOP • DIAGNOSE A LEAK INSIDE YOUR CAR • REPLACE YOUR AIR FILTER • HANDLE A FAULTY REPAIR •
OL AN OVERHEATED ENGINE • REPLACE A LEAKING RADIATOR HOSE • CHANGE YOUR WIPER BLADES • ADD WINDSHIELD-WASHER FLUID
• TROUBLESHOOT YOUR BRAKES • ADD BRAKE FLUID TO THE CLUTCH MASTER CYLINDER • TROUBLESHOOT DASHBOARD WARNING LIGI
SPARK-PLUG WIRES • DIAGNOSE CAR SMELLS • CLEAN THE OUTSIDE OF YOUR CAR • RESTORE YOUR CAR'S SHINE • WASH THE INTERIO

301 Rejuvenate Tarnished Brass

Chances are your kitchen pantry holds the solution to your tarnished brass. Send blemished brass items for an antioxidizing bath in Tabasco sauce, Worcestershire sauce or ketchup. If you don't have these ingredients, try vinegar or lemon juice, both of which have the acidity to remove oxidation (tarnish) on brass items with a simple soak or good rub. It's an inexpensive recipe for success.

Steps

1 Place the brass item in a pot, pan or plastic container.

2 Cover the item with Tabasco sauce, Worcestershire sauce or ketchup.

3 Let it sit for at least 2 hours.

4 Scrub with mild dishwashing liquid and a soft fingernail brush under cool running water.

5 Dry with a smooth cloth to prevent scratching.

6 To retard future tarnish, rub with a cloth moistened with olive oil.

7 To keep brass house numbers shining longer, apply several coats of paste car wax to protect the finish.

What You'll Need

- Pot, pan or plastic container
- Tabasco sauce, Worcestershire sauce or ketchup
- Mild dishwashing liquid
- Soft fingernail brush
- Soft cloth
- Olive oil
- Paste car wax

Warning

Very old brass items, especially if cracking or peeling, should be professionally cleaned and repaired.

302 Shine Silver Safely

Restore silver or silver plate back to its formerly lustrous self with little more than a quick trip to the bathroom. It takes just minutes to brush away tarnish buildup with ordinary toothpaste. You can apply the same technique using commercial silver polish. However, toothpaste is handier, cheaper and less toxic.

Steps

1 Place a clean cotton sock on your polishing hand.

2 Dampen the sock slightly under cool running water.

3 Squeeze a pearl-size drop of toothpaste on your fingertip area.

4 Apply the toothpaste to the silver using up-and-down rather than circular strokes until the tarnish is gone.

5 Use a twisted bit of rag to get between silverware tines and other tight spaces.

6 Rinse the silver well.

7 Polish it dry with the clean side of the sock.

8 Store silver in an airtight plastic bag or in a chest lined with tarnish-resistant flannel.

What You'll Need

- Cotton sock
- Toothpaste
- Rag
- Airtight plastic bag
- Tarnish-resistant flannel

Warning

Don't put rubber bands around silver or it will tarnish.

303 Remove a Broken Lightbulb

Right when you're trying to remove an old light bulb, it breaks on you, leaving a base stuck inside the socket. Here's how to remove it quickly and safely.

Steps

1 Turn off power to the bulb and unplug the lamp.

2 Put on protective gloves.

3 Grip the metal lip of the bulb with needle-nose pliers.

4 Gently unscrew the bulb base, turning it the same way you would an unbroken bulb. Watch your fingers while turning the bulb base. Sheered glass remnants may still be inside.

5 Remove the bulb base from the socket.

6 Be sure to vacuum up any broken glass from the floor.

What You'll Need

- Protective gloves
- Needle-nose pliers
- Vacuum

Warning

Be sure the power is turned off before placing pliers inside the bulb base.

304 Fix a Broken Wineglass Stem

The party was good—so good, in fact, that a laughing guest sent his wineglass tumbling into two pieces. Resist the urge to follow suit by hurling the glass into the recycling bin; you can actually put it back together. Though you may see the blemish on close inspection, you'll keep your matching set intact.

Steps

1 Place the mouth of the wineglass on a flat surface.

2 Squeeze a small amount of clear adhesive or superglue around the fragmented stem.

3 Holding the broken stem base in one hand and securing the mouth of the wineglass with the other hand, gently press the base piece onto the breakage area, taking care to line up the fragmented edges as closely as possible.

4 Release the hand that's holding the mouth of the wineglass, then gingerly wipe the glued area clean of excess adhesive using a damp rag (paper-towel or dry-rag fibers may stick to the glass).

5 Hold the wineglass in place for 30 seconds.

6 Let it dry overnight before using.

What You'll Need

- Clear adhesive or superglue
- Rag

Tips

Be careful not to get adhesive on fingers or surfaces— it's extremely difficult to remove. See 41 Get Superglue Off Your Skin.

Feel free to place that repaired wineglass in the dishwasher. The adhesive bond will withstand heat up to 400°F (200°C).

305 Fix Blemished Wood Furniture

If a guest dripped soda on your expensive wood table, or roughhousing kids left their mark on your cherished wood chair, don't head to the nearest furniture store for replacements. These everyday spots and scratches are minor irritations that can easily be removed.

Steps

1 Clean the spotted or scratched area with a rag dabbed with mineral spirits (low-odor paint thinner available at paint stores) to remove dust, dirt and debris.

2 Pour furniture oil such as Danish oil on very fine steel wool until saturated.

3 Going with the grain, gently rub the steel wool on the scratched or spotted area. Keep the steel wool well oiled. To prevent surface damage, always scrub gently and carefully when using steel wool on wood.

4 Continue gently scrubbing until the blight is removed, taking care not to mar the wood underneath the finish.

5 Dust away fine powder with a tack cloth or rag.

6 Apply stain, paint or other finish as needed.

What You'll Need

- Rags
- Mineral spirits
- Furniture oil
- Very fine steel wool
- Tack cloth
- Stain, paint or other finish
- Paintbrush

Warning

Mineral spirits are flammable, so take care when you're using, and dilute the rag with water before disposing.

Always apply stain, paint or other finish in a well-ventilated area.

306 Repair Gouges in Furniture

So the movers banged your favorite painted chair on the way to your kitchen, and the housewarming party's tonight. Better get busy. You can have it ready for tonight without breaking a sweat.

Steps

1 Place the chair on a plastic tarp.

2 Apply wood filler or wood paste in gouges or pitted area with a spatula-like tool. Swipe the spatula across the area to remove excess paste. Don't overfill the gouge area, or it'll take you that much longer to sand it flush with the chair. Don't underfill it, either, or you'll leave a pit.

3 Let it dry.

4 Start sanding the filler or paste area using coarse (80-grit) sandpaper until the repair area is nearly flush with the surrounding area. After sanding, run your hand around the area in circles to make sure the surface is level.

5 Finish smoothing with fine (220-grit) sandpaper.

6 Wipe away dust and residue with a tack cloth or rag.

7 Apply a primer to the sanded area. Let dry, then paint to finish.

What You'll Need

- Plastic tarp
- Wood filler or wood paste
- Spatula-like tool
- 80- and 220-grit sandpaper
- Tack cloth or rag
- Primer
- Touch-up paint
- Paintbrush

Warning

Be careful not to get wood paste on clothes or hands; it is very difficult to remove.

307 Restore Furniture Finish

Hot oatmeal or tea can steam the finish off your kitchen or coffee table faster than you can say "Cream, please." Get rid of milky rings and a lackluster finish with a few steps.

Steps

For light to moderate damage

1 Place a plastic tarp or an old sheet beneath the furniture item.

2 Sand the discolored area(s) with very fine steel wool until smooth.

3 Clean off surface dust particles using a tack cloth.

4 Apply stain or paint (matching your furniture color) with a paintbrush.

5 Let it dry.

6 Repeat stain or paint applications until the color matches.

7 Apply polyurethane finish if needed.

For heavy damage

1 Lay tarp or other surface cover on the floor of a well-ventilated room or area. Place the furniture piece in the center.

2 Wearing a respiratory mask, spray furniture stain stripper over the entire area to be stripped.

3 Let it penetrate for 15 minutes (or follow the time directed on the spray can).

4 Scrape off softened finish using a metal or plastic scraper, taking care to remove only the finish and none of the wood.

5 Using medium-coarse steel wool (dipped in water if needed for ease of use), clean away any leftover finish.

6 Wipe clean and dry with a tack cloth.

7 Apply stain or paint (matching your furniture color) with a paintbrush.

8 Let it dry.

9 Repeat stain or paint applications until the color matches.

10 Apply polyurethane finish if needed.

What You'll Need

- Plastic tarp or old sheet
- Very fine steel wool
- Tack cloth
- Stain or paint
- Paintbrush
- Polyurethane finish
- Respiratory mask
- Furniture stain stripper
- Metal or plastic scraper
- Medium-coarse steel wool

Tips

Apply light coats and let the furniture dry thoroughly between coats.

If the entire piece needs refinishing, it may be easier to strip the finish down to bare wood using a furniture-stripping solution.

308 Replace a Broken Towel Rod

If the weight of your son's soggy beach towel snapped a towel rod in two, you don't need to buy a whole new unit. Instead, you can simply replace the rod. You can even ask the culprit to help—or to do it himself.

Steps

1 Loosen the setscrews—the slotted screw to one side of each bracket—with a small flathead screwdriver (the kind that comes with an eyeglass-repair kit or a computer-repair kit).

2 Gently remove the unit from the wall.

3 Remove and discard the broken rod.

4 Place the new rod into the brackets.

5 Place the unit back on the wall hardware.

6 Hold the unit in place while tightening the setscrews.

What You'll Need

- Small flathead screwdriver
- Replacement rod

Tip

To keep the tiny setscrews from disappearing, don't unscrew them all the way. Remove the unit with the setscrews loosened but still in place.

309 Remove Stuck Shelf Paper

Good idea, getting rid of the old shelf paper that harks back to Granny's era. It's just too bad half of it wants to stay put for another half-century. Don't give in—all you need is a putty knife, sandpaper and some patience.

Steps

1 Peel off as much of the stuck paper as you can.

2 Carefully scrape the remainder with a putty knife, holding it at an angle so you avoid gouging the wood.

3 When you've scraped up all you can, rub medium-coarse (120-grit) sandpaper over the remaining gunk.

4 Continue until all traces of the paper are removed.

5 Using a damp rag or a paper towel, wipe up the paper shreds and glue gunk. If some of the glue proves to be tenacious, use hot soapy water and a plastic scrubber.

6 Allow the shelf to dry thoroughly before you refinish it or apply new covering.

What You'll Need

- Putty knife
- 120-grit sandpaper
- Rag or paper towel
- Soap
- Plastic scrubber

Tip

Try to remove as much as you can with the putty knife before sanding the paper. Sanding can be more time-consuming and labor-intensive.

310 Prepare Your House for Natural Disasters

You're pretty sure that a fire, flood, earthquake, tornado, hurricane or other catastrophe will never happen to you. But you've got a nagging feeling that you should do something to secure your home in case of an unlikely disaster. These quick home-protection fixes will help you sleep better at night.

Steps

For earthquakes

1 Fasten lamps, china and other small valuables to shelves or surfaces with puttylike anchoring or museum wax (available at hardware and home supply stores). This also works for crystal and ceramic objects if they're not too heavy.

2 Install latches on cabinet doors (to keep contents inside).

3 Use bolts or L-brackets to secure bookcases, china cabinets and other tall furniture to wall studs.

4 Secure your water heater to a wall stud with a water-heater strap.

For fires

1 Install fire extinguishers in the kitchen and any other rooms where a fire might ignite. The best fire extinguisher is an easy-to-handle 2-lb. (1-kg) or 5-lb. (2.5-kg) model. (See also 379 Put Out a Kitchen Fire.)

2 Place smoke detectors in hallways, bedrooms, the laundry room, the furnace room and anywhere else a fire could ignite.

3 Use a fireplace screen to keep embers inside.

4 Have a spark arrestor installed in your chimney.

For floods, wind and rain

1 Install weather-stripping on and around doors and windows to prevent water from seeping into your home. See 114 Fix a Drafty Door and 121 Fix a Drafty Window.

2 Install storm shutters or create your own using precut sheets of ¾-inch (2-cm) plywood cut to fit snugly in each window.

3 Install storm doors.

4 Consider replacing an older garage door with a hurricane-rated garage door.

What You'll Need

- Anchoring or museum wax
- Cabinet latches
- Bolts or L-brackets
- Water-heater strap
- Fire extinguishers
- Smoke detectors
- Fireplace screen
- Spark arrestor
- Weather-stripping
- Storm shutters or precut sheets of ¾-inch (2-cm) plywood
- Storm doors
- Hurricane-rated garage door

Tip

If you don't have a wall stud to screw into, secure furniture by using a toggle bolt (also known as a Molly bolt).

311 Fix a Frayed Carpet

Annoyed at the sight of tattered edges on your living room carpet? Rest easy. Much like loose sweater threads, your carpet's fuzzy frays can be trimmed so they're unnoticeable. And frayed edges abutting tile, wood or other surfaces can easily be concealed with a carpet bar.

Steps

1 Using a sharp pair of scissors, trim any fuzzy carpet fibers down to the height of the rest of your carpet.

2 To install a carpet bar, measure the width of the passageway with a tape measure.

3 Cut the carpet bar to fit the measurement using a hacksaw (if the bar is metal) or a wood saw. A hacksaw can leave sharp edges on a carpet bar. If necessary, smooth the carpet bar's cut edge using a metal file.

4 Place the carpet bar so it covers the area where the frayed carpet meets the other surface.

5 Use a hammer or screwdriver to attach the carpet bar to the floor. Make sure nails or screws are flush with the carpet bar when you're done.

What You'll Need

- Scissors
- Tape measure
- Carpet bar
- Hacksaw or wood saw
- Metal file
- Hammer or screwdriver

Tip

If the subfloor is concrete, you'll need to predrill holes with a masonry bit for the nails or screws that hold the carpet bar in place.

312 Camouflage a Dog-Scratched Door

Has Scooter redefined the term *doggy door* in your home? Then take a look at this camouflage fix for pet scratches on wood doors. It won't look exactly like new, but it'll be doggone close.

Steps

1 Lay a plastic sheet or an old towel under the door and on the surrounding floor area.

2 Holding the door with one hand, lightly sand away the scratches with the other hand. For deep scratches, start with medium-coarse (120-grit) sandpaper and work your way to fine (220-grit) sandpaper. For light scratches, just use fine (220-grit) sandpaper.

3 Apply a light coat of matching door stain or paint using a paintbrush, taking care to blend the newly finished area with the existing surface color. Apply sparingly to avoid paint or stain drips.

4 Wait 30 minutes or until the door is no longer tacky to the touch.

5 Reapply the stain or paint. Keep the door open until fully dry.

6 If you stained the door, apply a clear finish to protect it.

What You'll Need

- Plastic sheet or old towel
- 120- and 220-grit sandpaper
- Matching stain or paint
- Paintbrush

Tip

Bring home a color chart from a home-improvement store to match the paint or stain color before buying it.

Warning

Always apply paint or stain in a well-ventilated area.

313 Repair a Split Carpet Seam

Heavy foot traffic, improper installation or poor quality—whatever the cause of your split carpet seam, the repair calls for minimal skills and tools. You can have those curled-up edges tacked down in no time— without the cost of a service call.

Steps

1 Measure the length of the split seam.

2 Cut carpet tape (available at hardware and home supply stores) to fit.

3 Pull back one edge of the carpet. Using a pencil, draw a line on the floor along the edge where the other part of the carpet meets the floor (see A). This will determine the center point where you'll place the tape.

4 Pull back both edges of the carpet to make room for the tape.

5 Remove the tack paper from both sides of the carpet tape.

6 Center the tape over the pencil line, then lay the tape on the floor (see B). Get help for this one if you can; it's easier to apply the tape if someone holds up one of the carpet edges for you.

7 Slowly roll down the carpet on the tape, making sure the carpet's edges meet.

8 Walk on the taped area or place a heavy object over it.

What You'll Need

- Tape measure
- Carpet tape
- Scissors
- Pencil
- Heavy object

Tips

Try not to get carpet tape on your fingers, hands and clothing. It can be tough to remove.

Be sure to keep the tape flat once you've peeled off the tack paper; if it sticks together, you'll be cutting a new piece.

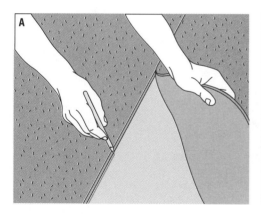

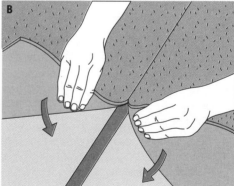

314 Rid Carpets of Pet Odors

Do visiting friends know you have a dog—before Fido bounces into the room? Just because you have a pet doesn't mean your carpet has to smell like him.

Steps

1 Always clean up pet messes as quickly and thoroughly as possible.

2 Identify the odiferous areas of your carpet. If you're not sure where they are, darken the room and turn on a black-light bulb to highlight any dried accident spots.

3 Deep-clean the problem areas using a water-extraction carpet-cleaning machine or a carpet-shampoo machine and cool water only—no chemicals or cleaners. (To rent or buy one of these machines, look under "Carpet & Rug Cleaners' Equipment and Supplies" or a similar heading in the yellow pages.)

4 Sprinkle an enzyme-containing pet-odor–neutralizing powder (available at pet stores or your vet's office) on the affected areas. Pet-odor–neutralizing powders contain live bacteria and enzymes that digest odor-causing protein and bacteria, permanently removing it from the deepest fibers in your carpet. These products also contain a mild cleanser that can help remove discoloration. Alternatively, you can use borax powder or baking soda, but they are less effective in eliminating stubborn odors.

5 Let sit for 8 hours.

6 Vacuum the treated areas. Let sit for 24 hours.

7 If odor remains after you have treated the carpet with an enzyme odor neutralizer, repeat the treatment as needed to eliminate lingering odors.

8 Understand that in severe cases where the soiling has occurred for an extended period of time, you may need to replace the carpet padding.

9 If your pet continues to eliminate in inappropriate areas, treat the underlying cause. Does your pet have easy access to the outdoors or to a litter box? Is your cat demonstrating an aversion to her kitty litter? Is your furry friend suffering from separation anxiety, loneliness or stress? See 74 Correct Bad Behavior in Dogs and 77 Correct Bad Behavior in Cats for more information.

What You'll Need

- Black-light bulb
- Water-extraction carpet-cleaning machine or carpet-shampoo machine
- Pet-odor–neutralizing powder with enzymes
- Vacuum

Tip

For pet stains on your carpet, see 340 Remove Pet Stains.

Warning

Avoid using household cleaners, ammonia and vinegar on urine stains. The strong smell may draw your pet back to the spot to cover the strong stuff with his own scent.

Steam-cleaning urine-stained carpeting can set stains and odors by bonding the protein into the fibers.

315 Reinforce a Sagging Shelf

Is the weight of all those soccer trophies making your daughter's prize shelf droop like a loser? Don't blow the whistle on it just yet. You can have that sagging shelf looking like a winner again.

Steps

1 Measure the existing brackets on the shelf, then go to the hardware store and buy a matching bracket.

2 Hold a shelf-support bracket at the center point, and use a pencil to mark on the wall where the screw holes will go (see A). Remove the bracket.

3 Check the box the anchors came in for the diameter of the holes.

4 Using a hand drill, drill holes at the pencil marks slightly smaller than your plastic wall anchors.

5 Place the anchors in the holes.

6 Tap the anchors lightly with a hammer until flush with the wall (see B).

7 While holding the bracket firmly against the wall, make sure the holes in the bracket line up exactly with the wall anchors.

8 Using a screwdriver or a drill, insert the screws into the anchors until they are flush with the bracket.

9 If the shelf still sags, add additional brackets midway between the new bracket and the existing ones.

What You'll Need

- Tape measure
- Shelf-support bracket and screws
- Pencil
- Hand drill
- Plastic wall anchors
- Hammer
- Screwdriver

Tips

If you have wood walls, skip the wall anchors and screw the bracket directly into the wood.

If the shelf has a severe sag, screw a strip of hardwood to its front edge to reinforce it.

Wall anchors are designed to hold weights of only 20 lbs. (9 kg) or less.

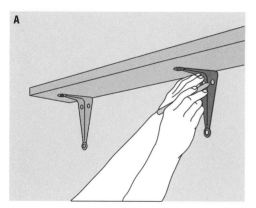

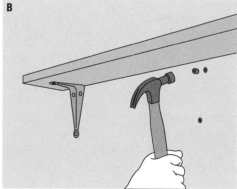

316 Brighten a Boring Bathroom

Nothing makes a bathroom appear smaller and drearier than a mis-placed focal point, lack of eye-catching containers, and contents spilling from every surface. Lighten and brighten a boring bathroom by streamlining what you can and getting creative with what's left. You can make this utilitarian room downright cozy.

Steps

1 Strip the commode of its furry cover to keep it from becoming the room's focal point. Why dress up the one fixture to which you want to call the least attention?

2 Remove that little throw rug to give the illusion of more space.

3 Corral personal hygiene items in interesting jars, baskets or dec-orative boxes—even colorful coffee mugs.

4 If space is at a premium, mount a small coated-wire grid rack on the wall and hang personal appliances (such as a hair dryer and curling iron) from it with S-hooks.

5 Add a wooden chest or a few stacking wicker or rattan boxes to provide character and storage space.

6 Add a freestanding over-the-commode shelf or cabinet and fill it with extra linens or toiletries.

7 Place a folding screen between the sink and toilet to add style and privacy.

8 If the bathroom is windowless, add wall mirrors.

9 Choose cheery colors for bath and hand towels.

10 Paint walls in a color other than white. Use light colors to make a small powder room appear larger.

11 Paint or stain the cabinets in a complementary color.

12 Paint exposed pipes the same color as the walls, or paint on a faux finish in complementary colors.

13 Install new handles and knobs in a bright color, silver or matte white.

14 Fill a glass bowl with seashells or other neighborhood treasures and place it next to your sink for a natural style.

What You'll Need

- Jars, baskets, decorative boxes, colorful mugs
- Coated-wire grid rack
- S-hooks
- Wooden chest or stacking wicker or rattan boxes
- Freestanding shelf or cabinet
- Folding screen
- Wall mirrors
- Colorful towels
- Paint
- Stain
- Paintbrush
- New handles and knobs
- Glass bowl

Tips

To make a room seem larger, decorate with lighter colors such as pale gold, butter and cream.

See 326 Spruce Up Your Decor for more decorating tips.

317 Replace a Shower-Door Sweep

If your floor gets a shower when you take one, chances are your shower-door sweep—the rubberlike strip that lines the bottom of the door—needs to be replaced. A worn strip lets water seep beneath the door and onto your floor. Left unchecked, that leaky little strip could leave you drowning in some serious water damage.

Steps

1 Open the shower door from the outside.

2 Grab the edge of the sweep and pull it toward the outside of the door until the strip is removed from its track (see A). In some cases, you may need to unscrew the sweep from the track.

3 Bring the old shower-door sweep to a hardware or home supply store to purchase a new one that matches its height. Sizes vary slightly.

4 Using the old sweep as a pattern, cut the new sweep to the same length with scissors (see B).

5 Install the new shower sweep. If a sweep that's supposed to fit in a track sticks going in, lightly coat the edge of the sweep with petroleum jelly.

6 If the new sweep doesn't stop the leak, consider recaulking around the shower door area (see 116 Fix a Shower Door) or checking the grout around the shower.

What You'll Need

- New shower-door sweep
- Screwdriver
- Scissors
- Petroleum jelly

Tip

Keep a bathmat in front of the shower entrance to protect the floor from excess moisture and to reduce the chances of someone slipping after a shower.

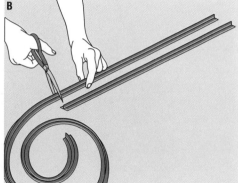

318 Clean or Replace a Furnace Filter

Has it been more than a month since you ventured into your furnace's filter area? Then it's probably time to clean or replace this dust and dirt catcher to prevent you from sneezing your way into winter mornings. A clean filter maximizes your furnace's efficiency and longevity—and minimizes your energy bills.

Steps

1 If the floor or area near the furnace is a dust-bunny breeding area, vacuum or sweep prior to replacing the filter.

2 Locate the service panel, usually on the furnace's lower front or side.

3 Turn off the furnace, then gently pop open or pull down the panel door with your hands; tools usually aren't needed.

4 Locate the filter—a framed-mesh rectangular screen inserted either horizontally or vertically near the intake-outtake blower.

5 Slide the filter screen out (see A).

6 Check for brown, dusty buildup on the mesh screen (or a screen you're unable to see through).

7 If you have a reusable plastic-frame or metal-frame filter, use a hose to rinse away the dust particles on the screen in the backyard or driveway (see B). Let it dry, then return it to the furnace.

8 If you have a disposable cardboard-frame filter, write down the size, then throw it away. Buy a new furnace filter of the same size (available at hardware and home supply stores).

What You'll Need

- Vacuum or broom
- Garden hose
- New furnace filter

Tips

If someone in your home has allergies, you may want to consider an allergenic reduction filter.

To keep the air in your home healthy, replace your furnace filter monthly during chilly months and at least once a season.

Warning

Be sure you turn off the furnace before opening the front panel.

Do not use the furnace until a clean filter is installed.

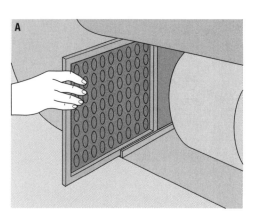

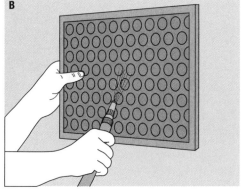

319 Repair a Broken Sliding Drawer

If your silverware drawer has lost its luster and is starting to shimmy when you pull it open, it's probably in need of a new drawer guide. This little notched plastic piece keeps your drawer on track. You can pick up a replacement at your local hardware store.

Steps

1 Remove the drawer's contents.

2 Pull the drawer gently by the handle until it comes all the way off the track (see A). You may need to lift the drawer above the track or press a release lever to release the drawer.

3 Turn the drawer over and locate the drawer guide. Look for a small semicircular or square plastic piece located at the drawer's rear center.

4 Examine the condition of the drawer guide. If the guide is in good condition but merely loose, tighten the screws and replace the drawer. If the guide is held into place with metal staples, replace the staples with small screws, which are sturdier. If the guide needs to be replaced, proceed to step 5.

5 Unscrew the old drawer guide and buy an exact replacement.

6 Position the new drawer guide in place, matching the existing screw holes in the wood or particleboard drawer with the new guide's holes.

7 Tighten all the screws to secure the guide firmly in place (see B). Don't tighten the screws excessively—you could crack the drawer.

8 Gently slide the drawer back onto the drawer track.

9 If a wooden strip on the bottom of the drawer guides the sliding drawer instead of a steel track, tighten the screws that hold the strip in place. You can buy a replacement strip for the drawer at the hardware store if the old one is worn out.

What You'll Need

- New plastic drawer guide
- Screwdriver
- Small screws

Tips

Take care to gently remove the old plastic guide so as not to damage the drawer.

Lightweight plastic guides like these are only meant to support a few pounds. For heavy drawers, consider installing roller guides on each side of the drawer.

See 2 Fix a Drawer That Sticks for more drawer fixes.

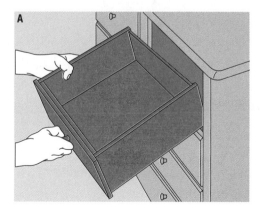

A

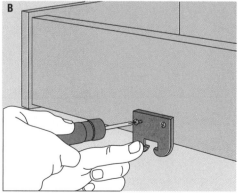

B

320 Reglue Joints of Chairs and Tables

If your kitchen chair doesn't have a leg to stand on, or your dining room table appears more rickety by the meal, it's time for a quick fix. Furniture glue and sandpaper are about all you need to secure loose or missing joints.

Steps

1 Turn the chair or table upside down on a soft surface.

2 Pull out the wobbly leg or arm—whatever joint has lost its grip.

3 Sand the top of the wobbly joint with fine (220-grit) sandpaper until all the old glue is removed.

4 Lightly sand the inside of the joint, using the fine sandpaper.

5 Wipe away the wood dust with a tack cloth or rag.

6 Squeeze a bit of furniture or wood glue such as Dap Swell & Lock around the inside of the hole (see A).

7 Place the furniture leg or arm in the hole. Turn the leg or arm once in the joint to spread the glue evenly.

8 Wipe away excess glue with a damp rag.

9 If needed, tape the leg or arm in position with low-adhesive painter's tape (see B). This tape (available at paint and hardware stores) won't leave any residue on your furniture.

10 Check the chair or table regularly to make sure the leg or arm hasn't moved from its proper position. Remove the tape within 8 hours.

11 Allow the furniture to dry for 24 to 48 hours before using.

What You'll Need

- 220-grit sandpaper
- Tack cloth or rags
- Furniture or wood glue
- Low-adhesive painter's tape

Tip

Be sure to use swelling glue. It expands in the joint to provide pressure against the joint and thus keeps it in place.

Warning

Carpenter's glue can stick strongly to fingers. Wipe off any excess glue immediately.

Lightly sand the parts. If you remove any wood, the parts will fit loosely and the glue won't hold.

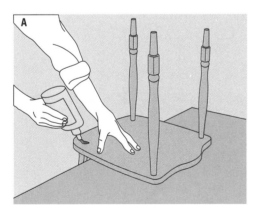

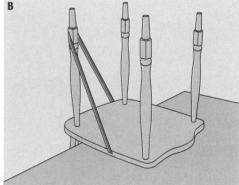

321 **Reupholster a Drop-In Chair Seat**

If Fluffy got feisty with your favorite upholstered chair, you don't have to stash the tattered remains out of sight or relegate the chair to a scratching-post function. It's easy to re-cover a drop-in seat if you have some leftover upholstery fabric.

Steps

1 Unscrew the chair seat from the chair.

2 Using a hammer claw or a small pry bar, remove the tacks or staples that are holding the upholstery to the seat frame.

3 Using the old covering as a guide, cut a new seat cover roughly to size with upholstery scissors or sharp fabric scissors.

4 Cut new batting (padding) using the same guide.

5 Apply spray adhesive (available at hardware and home supply stores) to the seat base.

6 Press the batting to the adhesive on the chair base (see A).

7 Center the fabric over the batting.

8 Turn over the batting and chair base, now one unit.

9 Pull the fabric taut, taking care to center or balance striped or patterned upholstery over the seat base. Then cut the fabric, leaving an overlap for nailing to the seat.

10 Using a tack hammer, tap in upholstery tacks (available at fabric and home supply stores) every few inches (about 8 cm) along each side of the underside of the newly made seat cushion (see B).

11 Turn the cushion back over and screw it back into the chair.

What You'll Need

- Screwdriver
- Hammer claw or small pry bar
- Upholstery scissors or sharp fabric scissors
- 1 yard (90 cm) upholstery fabric
- 1 yard (90 cm) batting
- Spray adhesive
- Upholstery tacks
- Tack hammer

Tip

Be careful not to split wood when tapping in tacks.

Warning

Apply spray adhesive in a well-ventilated area.

322 Revive a Cane Seat

Made from the bark of the rattan tree, cane becomes brittle, cracked and eventually breaks if allowed to dry out. The solution to the parching problem? A stiff drink—for the chair. Give that thirsty cane a shot or two of boiled linseed oil and you'll have a supple, solid seat.

Steps

Repairing cracks

1 Brush boiled linseed oil onto the entire seat with a paintbrush.

2 Allow the oil to absorb. The sheen will dull slightly as the dry reed absorbs the oil. (This is a fast process that will take anywhere from several seconds to several minutes.)

3 Once an area looks dull again, add more boiled linseed oil until no more is being absorbed, then wipe off the excess oil with paper towels or a rag. Remove excess oil from the seat's cracks and crevices using a dry paintbrush.

4 Let it dry for 24 hours.

5 If needed, apply a new coat of paint or a clear coat of finish.

Replacing a split strand

1 Place wet rags or towels atop the split strand(s) in the seat to soften it for removal.

2 Allow the moisture to penetrate for 30 minutes, then remove the entire strand by pulling it out of the weave. If the strand is stapled or tacked on, cut it off as close to the surface as possible.

3 Soak a new cane coil (available at hardware and home supply stores) in water for 30 minutes to 1 hour to soften.

4 Insert the new cane strand into the seat where the old strand was removed. Twist the strand's ends together to anchor the strand for weaving.

What You'll Need

- Boiled linseed oil
- Paintbrushes
- Paper towels or rags
- Paint or finish
- Towels
- Coil of replacement cane

Tip

To extend the life of cane furniture, apply boiled linseed oil whenever a surface appears dull or brittle.

Warning

Do not boil linseed oil at home—it's highly flammable. Purchase boiled linseed oil at a hardware or home supply store.

Be sure to safely dispose of rags or paper towels used for wiping up linseed oil—away from heat or flame. For extra safety, dilute the used rags or paper towels with water prior to disposal.

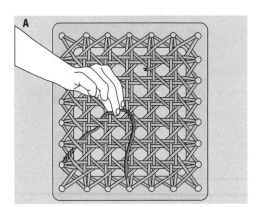

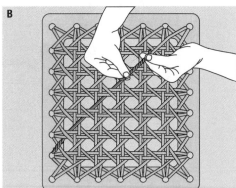

5 Weave the new strand into the seat holes using an up, over and under motion (see A). Keep the cane very damp while weaving to keep it pliable.

6 Finish weaving with the strand under the chair.

7 Twist the strand's ends together (see B). Allow the seat to dry and tighten before using.

323 **Reinforce a Weak Bed Frame**

If your daughter's top-bunk mattress seems to be heading south, it's time to bring in reinforcements. Whether yours is a twin or king, shoring up a sagging mattress is practically child's play. You simply reinforce the frame with a few well-cut wood pieces.

Steps

1 Remove the mattress and lean it against a wall or lay it flat. If possible, get someone to help you move the mattress.

2 Measure the inner width of the frame from side to side with a tape measure.

3 Using a pencil, mark the inner width of the frame on a 1-by-4.

4 Using a carpenter's handsaw, carefully saw the 1-by-4 at the pencil line (see A).

5 Repeat steps 3 and 4 on another 1-by-4.

6 Lay each board on the inner rim of the bed frame, placing each 2 to 2½ feet (60 to 75 cm) from the center (see B).

7 Replace the mattress, taking care not to dislodge the wood slats from their positions.

What You'll Need

- Tape measure
- Pencil
- Two 1-by-4 wood pieces, 6 or 8 feet (1.8 or 2.4 m) long
- Carpenter's handsaw

Tip

Most beds need just two reinforcements. However, a king-size bed may warrant three.

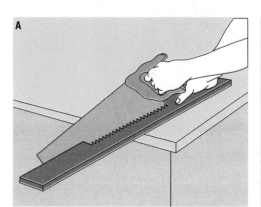

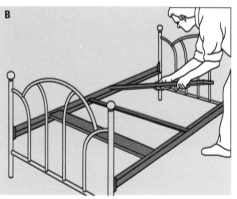

324 Fix Up an Old Wood Chair

That steal from the Saturday flea market may not look like such a find come Sunday—unless you know some tricks for reviving old furniture. Here's how to give that tired old chair a fresh look without breaking into your retirement account.

Steps

1 Place the chair outside or in a garage on a drop cloth or tarp.

2 Sand away years of old paint starting with medium-coarse (120-grit) sandpaper and finishing with fine (220-grit) sandpaper (see A).

3 Fill in nicks and crannies with wood-filler paste using a plastic putty knife. Smooth the surface with the putty knife.

4 Let it dry overnight.

5 Sand patched areas with fine (220-grit) sandpaper.

6 Wipe down the entire chair with a tack cloth to remove dust particles.

7 Apply primer to the entire chair using a paintbrush.

8 Let it dry.

9 Paint the chair (see B). Have fun choosing a color, whether it's a soft pastel for a baby's room, fire-engine red for a child's room or French blue for the kitchen. For an antique look, choose creamy off-white. If you'll be placing your chair outside, be sure to choose an exterior paint.

10 If desired, tie on a seat cushion in a complementary color.

What You'll Need

- Drop cloth or tarp
- 120- and 220-grit sand-paper
- Wood-filler paste
- Plastic putty knife
- Tack cloth
- Primer
- Paintbrush
- Paint
- Seat cushion with ties

Warning

Always apply paint and primer in a well-ventilated area.

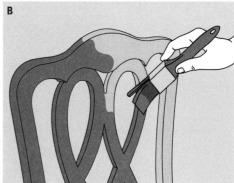

325 Fix a Wobbly Wood Chair

The wear and tear of everyday life can make even the sturdiest chair unsteady. But don't get mad, get even—get your chair's legs even, that is. Simply sand away the unevenness, and it's almost as good as new. See 3 Fix a Wobbly Table for more ideas.

Steps

1 Place the offending chair upside down on top of a plastic tarp or drop cloth.

2 Carefully measure the length of each leg to determine the wobble maker and its length (see A).

3 On the other three legs, make a pencil mark at the same length as the wobbly one.

4 Gently sand each of the longer three legs until you reach the pencil mark, starting with coarse (80-grit) sandpaper and ending with fine (220-grit) sandpaper (see B). It's best to sand outdoors to keep the fine wood dust particles from permeating your home.

Other fixes

1 If the chair has metal, cork or plastic glides, check the legs to make sure one is not missing. If a glide is missing, buy a replacement one at a hardware store. Glides are small disks used to protect floors from furniture.

2 If one chair leg is ¼ inch (6 mm) shorter than the other three, consider placing a glide on the shorter leg to make up the difference instead of sanding down the other three legs.

3 Examine the chair joints—loose ones will cause the chair to wobble. Reinforce a loose joint with wood glue (see 320 Reglue Joints of Chairs and Tables).

What You'll Need

- Plastic tarp or drop cloth
- Tape measure
- Pencil
- 80- to 220-grit sandpaper
- Replacement glides
- Wood glue

Tip

If the chair is painted or stained, plan to have matching paint on hand for a touch-up once you've finished the job.

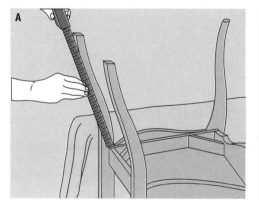

A

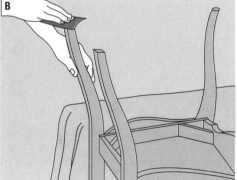

B

326 Spruce Up Your Decor

Who says you need to spend big bucks and entire weekends in design center stores to update your home's decor? A tired-looking home may benefit from a simple dash of color here and a bit of pizzazz there. No major renovation required.

ROOM	QUICK DECORATING FIXES
Lovelier living room	• Place attractive wicker or rattan baskets beneath glass coffee table for added storage with panache. Fill with magazines or folded blankets.
	• Place large, dramatic potted plant in bland corner for added warmth.
	• Rehang prints and paintings in asymmetrical groupings rather than rows for more dramatic effect.
	• Position furniture at angle or floating away from wall, not flush against it, to create depth and softness.
	• Add cozy, colorful throw blanket.
	• Finish with sparkle by placing polished brass or gilded picture frame atop shelf or table.
More dramatic dining room	• Update dining room chairs with slipcovers in eye-catching colors.
	• Drape table in bright seasonal-colored linens even when you're not entertaining.
	• Place flowers in vase for table centerpiece. Buy fresh if possible, or purchase inexpensive silk red roses for winter, purple lilies for spring, yellow daisies for summer and leaves for fall.
	• Display antique or heritage plates on the wall using plate hangers, available at hardware stores.
	• Install a decorative shelf to display a favorite collection, such as colored glassware or milk-white vases.
	• If unsightly electrical cords from ceiling light fixtures are visible, wrap them in white or off-white silk or satin. Wrap small silk flowers around the fabric, using the wire stems to secure the fabric in place. For safety's sake, make sure none of the fabric comes in direct contact with exposed electrical wires.
Cozier kitchen	• Arrange cooking utensils in decorative ceramic vase rather than plastic holder.
	• Stash sponges and scrubbers in small painted pot instead of haphazardly around sink.
	• Hang bright dish towels from refrigerator or oven handle to add splash of color.
	• Fill basket or bowl with seasonal delights: gourds in autumn, chestnuts in winter, lemons in spring, limes in summer. Display atop breakfast table or windowsill.
	• Replace humdrum cabinet and drawer pulls with chrome or brass hardware or colorful plastic fittings.
	• Paint or stain cabinets the color of your favorite vegetable.

ROOM	QUICK DECORATING FIXES
More beautiful bedroom	• Change color of bed linens from dark to light or light to dark. • Add brightly colored pillows to bed or chairs. • Drape richly patterned shawl over single-color bedspread for refreshing, romantic touch. • Replace old bedside lamps with an unusual pair from antique shop or flea market. • Tease your senses by adding scented candles in decorative candle holders. The candles will remove any musty odors and give the room a cozy feel. • Do away with miniblinds, or at the very least camouflage them with diaphanous curtains or drapes. • Stash the pile of books on your nightstand in a storage bin that slides neatly under the bed. Hide your bedside reading bin with a decorative bed skirt.
More enticing entrance	• Make guests feel welcomed with fresh bouquet of flowers in entranceway. • Cover small bulletin board with fabric and crisscrossed ribbon and frame it. Hang it near the door for reminder notes in the morning. • Hang stylish mirror near the entrance so that it reflects sunlight inside. Plus, you'll be able to check your hair or makeup before you leave the house. • Scour antique shops for sturdy, charming coat rack.
Make a small room look bigger	• Paint walls a light color, such as yellow, pink or cream. • Banish clutter from every corner; space begets the illusion of space. • Place furniture, starting with sofa, on corner diagonal. This unusual placement takes focus off room size and places it on furnishings.
Make a big room look cozier	• Paint walls in deep, rich colors like terra-cotta, forest green or blue to add depth and coziness. • Set up secondary area to make the room feel cozier and do double duty: Add desk and chair to window corner, or create family game area with small table and a few chairs. • Bring down the focus from high ceilings by placing bottom edge of lowest print or painting 6 to 8 inches (15 to 20 cm) above top of furniture and work up the wall from there. • For balance, hang petite groupings behind dainty table or chair, or large single picture behind your ample sofa.

327 Repair Chipped or Cracked Porcelain

About to throw out that lovely porcelain vase because of its chips and cracks? Not so fast. Many porcelain problems can easily be repaired at home with an epoxy glue or porcelain enamel to match the piece.

Steps

1 If the porcelain is wet, dry the surface thoroughly with a hair dryer or tack cloth.

2 Following the package's directions, mix the two parts of epoxy glue (it comes in a kit with two tubes) in the tray that's included or in a disposable cup. Then follow these steps, as appropriate:

For chips

1 Apply the epoxy glue to the back of the chipped piece using a toothpick or a cotton swab.

2 Place the piece in its original position, taking care to line up the broken edges.

3 Hold the piece in place for 30 to 60 seconds.

For cracks

1 Apply porcelain enamel over the cracked area with a small brush, a toothpick or an eye-shadow applicator (minus the sponge) until the crack is filled. You can buy porcelain enamel kits at art supply stores.

2 Smooth the surface with an ice-pop stick.

3 Let it dry for 24 hours.

4 One coat of enamel will leave an uneven finish, so you'll want to apply several coats.

For more serious damage

1 If the item is broken into two or more pieces, set it in a large basin or box filled with dry rice or beans after applying epoxy glue. The rice or beans will hold the item in place while it dries.

2 If the porcelain is priceless, hire a professional ceramic restorer to repair it. Ask for a reference at an antiques shop or search the yellow pages or Internet under "ceramic" or "antique" repair and restoration.

3 If your porcelain treasure is beyond repair, consider giving it new life as a mosaic. Use your treasured porcelain pieces to mosaic a picture frame, a mirror or an outdoor tile. Visit an art supply store to purchase mosaic supplies.

What You'll Need

- Hair dryer or tack cloth
- Epoxy glue
- Disposable cup
- Toothpick or cotton swab
- Small brush or eye-shadow applicator
- Porcelain enamel kit
- Ice-pop stick
- Large basin or box
- Rice or beans

Tip

Keep epoxy glue and enamel away from fingers or any surface you don't want it to stick to.

328 **Repair Chipped or Cracked Pottery**

If your favorite pottery dish is chipped or broken, you can have it ready for your next party in no time with a bit of special glue.

Steps

For chips

1 Apply polyvinyl acetate (PVA) adhesive to the back of the chip. (PVA is available at hardware, home supply and art supply stores. Use clear PVA to make the repair less visible.)

2 Place the chip in its original position and hold it for 30 to 60 seconds.

3 Scrape away excess adhesive with a razor blade or X-Acto knife.

4 Let it dry overnight before using.

For cracks

1 Apply PVA adhesive to the cracked edges using a small brush (see A). Use just enough adhesive to cover the broken edges.

2 Applying light pressure, quickly press both pieces together for 30 to 60 seconds.

3 Scrape away excess adhesive with a razor blade or X-Acto knife.

4 Set the pottery down on a flat surface to dry overnight. If the item is broken into two or more pieces, set it in a large container filled with dry rice or beans (see B). The rice or beans will hold the item in place while it dries.

For more serious breakage

1 If the pottery is an antique or of great sentimental value, hire a professional ceramic restorer to do the repair. Ask for a reference at an antiques shop or search the yellow pages or Internet under "ceramic" or "antique" repair and restoration.

What You'll Need

- Polyvinyl acetate (PVA) adhesive
- Small brush
- Razor blade or X-Acto knife
- Large container
- Rice or beans

Tips

Use tweezers to hold small pieces in place.

PVA, also known as white glue, is ideal for fixing pottery because you must adjust the broken pieces precisely before the glue sets. Epoxy and instant glues dry too fast for this type of fix.

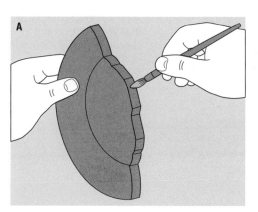

A

B

329 Repair Chipped or Cracked China

China—a smooth, glassy form of baked clay—is among the most beautiful tableware materials ever created. You don't have to break the bank to fix a cracked teacup or a chipped water pitcher.

Steps

For chips

1 Roll equal quantities of milliput, which comes in a kit with two tubes, into a ball until the two colors have fused. You can buy milliput, a type of modeling putty, at art supply stores.

2 Apply the milliput to the chip with a toothpick, then return the chip to its original position.

3 If needed, place masking tape taut across the repaired area to hold in place.

4 Allow the chip to set for 6 hours, then remove any masking tape.

5 Sand gently with fine (220-grit) sandpaper until the milliput is flush with the surface. Take care not to damage the china's glaze or decoration.

6 Touch up with acrylic paint as needed.

7 Brush on a clear glaze, available at art supply stores, if you wish to achieve a glossy finish.

For cracks

1 Put the cracked piece of china in an oven at very low heat—150° to 200°F (65° to 95°C).

2 Mix epoxy glue (which comes in a kit with two tubes) in the tray that comes with the epoxy glue or in a disposable cup.

3 Dip a glue stick, matchstick or toothpick into paint powder that matches the china color. Mix until the color looks right.

4 Take the cracked item out of the oven using oven mitts, then place on a plastic or wood cutting board. The heat of the oven will cause the crack to widen ever so slightly.

5 Fill the crack with the tinted glue mixture, using the small stick. Let dry overnight. The crack will condense as the china cools.

6 Chip away hardened glue with a razor blade or an X-Acto knife.

For more serious breakage

1 If the china is an antique or of great sentimental value, hire a professional ceramic restorer to do the repair. Ask for a reference at an antiques shop or search the yellow pages or Internet under "china" or "antique" repair and restoration.

2 Contact a china replacement company if an irreparably broken piece of china is part of a set.

What You'll Need

- Milliput
- Toothpick
- Masking tape
- 220-grit sandpaper
- Acrylic paint for touch-up
- Paintbrush
- Clear glaze
- Epoxy glue
- Disposable cup
- Glue stick or matchstick
- Paint powder
- Oven mitts
- Plastic or wood cutting board
- Razor blade or X-Acto knife

Tips

Look for paint powder (available at home supply and art supply stores) that is recommended for china.

If you send your china to a ceramic restorer to have it fixed, package each piece separately in bubble wrap or tissue. Many restorers have a backlog and the repair work is time-consuming, so it may take weeks or months for your repair to be completed.

Restored china will never be as strong as the original piece. Use it as infrequently as possible.

330 Unclutter Your Home

Need a bigger house? You probably just need to corral the contents inside the home you have. Start by getting rid of what you can—anything broken beyond repair, items no longer used, clothes that haven't seen daylight in a couple of years—then create a place for what's left. Put these rules for streamlining your home into play today. Your abode will feel positively palatial.

Steps

1 Get rid of what you can. Relieve crammed closets of clothes that haven't been worn in two years or more. Empty drawers, shelves and cabinets of old, unused or broken items. Donate, recycle, toss.

2 Identify items you don't use yet can't bear to part with. Send them to storage in the garage or attic.

3 Find a home for what's left. Everything should have a place, but not every place should have a thing. Leave some open space on cabinets and countertops. Wall-to-wall stuff makes any room look cramped.

4 Look high and low for more storage space. Beneath the stairs, under beds, over doors—these are great places to stash rarely needed items.

5 Create more space. Add shelves in the living room; install a shower caddy in the bath. Whenever you see an opportunity to maximize space, grab it.

6 Give a reprieve to that knickknack-attacked living room. Group small decorative items or collections on tabletops or shelves instead of spreading them haphazardly about the room.

7 Consider stacking or consolidating bigger items such as the TV and the CD player. Create an entertainment, art or reading center by putting such items together.

8 Choose double-duty furnishings. When furniture shopping, select pieces with built-in storage, such as a bed with drawers or a coffee table with baskets underneath.

9 Institute the In-and-Out Rule: For each item you bring home, toss, recycle or give away one item.

10 Create an emergency clutter holder in high-traffic areas such as the kitchen or entryway to keep mail, paperwork and small essentials from cluttering countertops and passageways. Empty the holder regularly.

11 Return misplaced items to their proper location before retiring each evening. It's the secret to a clutter-free household.

What You'll Need

- Trash bags
- Storage boxes or bins

Tips

Don't expect to declutter your home in an afternoon. Start with small tasks like pruning your bathroom drawer of old cosmetics and outdated medicines.

No time to stash stuff? Use a decorative folding screen to camouflage items you don't know what to do with—the vacuum cleaner, extra books, the kids' toys—before the guests arrive.

Warning

This could become a way of life. Proceed cautiously.

ORING • FIX BAD HABITS • REPAIR A BROKEN EYEGLASS FRAME • REPOSITION A SLIPPED CONTACT LENS • FIX A RUN IN STOCKINGS • JO
EAKOUT • REPAIR A TORN FINGERNAIL • FIX CHIPPED NAIL POLISH • FIX A STUCK ZIPPER • FIND A LOST CONTACT LENS • ELIMINATE BAD
Y THAT STICKS • STOP TELEMARKETERS AND JUNK MAIL • GET SUPERGLUE OFF YOUR SKIN • EXTRACT A SPLINTER • SOOTHE A SUNBURN
HANGOVER • STOP HICCUPS • MEND A BROKEN HEART • MEND A FAMILY FEUD • TREAT A SMALL CUT OR SCRAPE • FIX HAIR DISASTERS •
TTER SEATS • FIX A BILLING MISTAKE • FIX A BAD GRADE • FIX BAD CREDIT • RECOVER FROM JET LAG • RESUSCITATE AN UNCONSCIOUS
PRONOUNS • FIX A RUN-ON SENTENCE • FIX MISUSE OF THE WORD GOOD • FIX YOUR DOG OR CAT • CORRECT BAD BEHAVIOR IN DOGS •
SSING BUTTON • REMOVE LINT FROM CLOTHING • FIX A DRAWSTRING ON SWEATPANTS • REPAIR A HEM • REPAIR LEATHER GOODS • MEND
UNDER YOUR CASHMERE • FIX A SWEATER THAT HAS SHRUNK • FIX A SWEATER THAT HAS STRETCHED • FIX A HOLE IN A POCKET • FIX A H
LING FROM CLOTHING • FIX A FRAYED BUTTONHOLE • REMOVE DARK SCUFFS FROM SHOES • TREAT STAINS ON LEATHER • PROTECT SUE
IET SQUEAKY HINGES • TROUBLESHOOT LOCK PROBLEMS • TIGHTEN A LOOSE DOORKNOB • TIGHTEN A LOOSE DOOR HINGE • FIX A BIN
PLACE CRACKED TILE • TROUBLESHOOT MOLD ON INTERIOR WALLS • REPLACE CRACKED TILE GROUT IN A TUB OR SHOWER • FIX A DRA
NDS • TROUBLESHOOT WINDOW SHADE PROBLEMS • FIX BROKEN GLASS IN A WINDOW • REPAIR A WINDOW SCREEN • REPAIR ALUMINUM
MAGED PLASTER • REPAIR WALL COVERINGS • TOUCH UP PAINTED WALLS • TROUBLESHOOT INTERIOR-PAINT PROBLEMS • SOLVE A LEAD
RDWOOD FLOOR • RESTORE A DULL, WORN WOOD FLOOR • TOUCH UP WOOD-FLOOR FINISHES • REPAIR DAMAGED SHEET-VINYL FLOORI
USE • CHILDPROOF YOUR HOME • PREVENT ICE DAMS • CURE A FAULTY FIREPLACE DRAW • START A FIRE IN A COLD CHIMNEY • FIX A WO
AL A GARAGE FLOOR • REFINISH A GARAGE OR BASEMENT FLOOR • CONTROL ROOF LEAKS • REDIRECT RAINWATER FROM A DOWNSPOU
MAGED ASPHALT SHINGLE • PATCH A FLAT OR LOW-PITCHED ROOF • REPAIR ROOF FLASHING • TROUBLESHOOT EXTERIOR-PAINT PROBLE
W WATER PRESSURE • FIX LEAKING PIPES • STOP A TOILET FROM RUNNING • FIX A LEAKY TOILET TANK • FIX A STOPPED-UP TOILET • STOP
OGGED SINK OR TUB • REPAIR A TUB-AND-SHOWER VALVE • REPAIR CHIPPED FIXTURES • QUIET NOISY PIPES • DEFROST YOUR PIPES • DI
NSUMPTION • REPLACE A RECEPTACLE • FIX AN ELECTRICAL PLUG • REPLACE A LIGHT FIXTURE • INSTALL A NEW DIMMER • FIX A LAMP •
ORBELL • FIX A WOBBLY OVERHEAD FAN • ADJUST WATER-HEATER TEMPERATURE • RELIGHT A WATER-HEATER PILOT LIGHT • TROUBLESH
E MAKER • GET RID OF MICROWAVE SMELLS • FIX A REFRIGERATOR THAT COOLS POORLY • FIX A GAS OVEN THAT HEATS POORLY • CLEAN
SHWASHER PROBLEMS • CORRECT AN OVERFLOWING DISHWASHER • FIX A LEAKY DISHWASHER • FIX A DISHWASHER THAT FILLS SLOWLY
WASHING MACHINE THAT FILLS SLOWLY • FIX A WASHING MACHINE THAT "WALKS" ACROSS THE FLOOR • FIX A CLOTHES DRYER THAT DRIE
YOUR VACUUM CLEANER • REPLACE VACUUM CLEANER BRUSHES • TROUBLESHOOT A PORTABLE AIR CONDITIONER • FIX A WINDOW AIR
OCESSOR • FIX A TOASTER • DIAGNOSE MICROWAVE OVEN PROBLEMS • TROUBLESHOOT A GAS GRILL • FIX A TRASH COMPACTOR • REPA
ART • TROUBLESHOOT A CRASHING COMPUTER • CLEAN UP LAPTOP SPILLS • FIX BAD SECTORS ON A HARD DISK • QUIT A FROZEN PC AF
FECTED COMPUTER • IMPROVE YOUR COMPUTER'S MEMORY • GET RID OF E-MAIL SPAM • CHANGE A LASER PRINTER CARTRIDGE • FIX A F
GURE OUT WHY A PRINTER WON'T PRINT • FIX SPELLING AND GRAMMAR ERRORS • RECALL AN E-MAIL IN MICROSOFT OUTLOOK • DIAGNO
ES • TROUBLESHOOT A PALM OS PDA • RESET A PALM OS PDA • REMOVE FINGERPRINTS FROM A CAMERA LENS • TROUBLESHOOT A CD-
LVAGE A VIDEOCASSETTE • TROUBLESHOOT A DVD PLAYER • STRENGTHEN FM RADIO RECEPTION • STRENGTHEN AM RADIO RECEPTION •
AMMED SLIDE PROJECTOR • GET BETTER SPEAKER SOUND • TROUBLESHOOT A DIGITAL CAMCORDER • TROUBLESHOOT A DIGITAL CAME
HTBULB • FIX A BROKEN WINEGLASS STEM • FIX BLEMISHED WOOD FURNITURE • REPAIR GOUGES IN FURNITURE • RESTORE FURNITURE
MOUFLAGE A DOG-SCRATCHED DOOR • REPAIR A SPLIT CARPET SEAM • RID CARPETS OF PET ODORS • REINFORCE A SAGGING SHELF •
NTS OF CHAIRS AND TABLES • REUPHOLSTER A DROP-IN CHAIR SEAT • REVIVE A CANE SEAT • REINFORCE A WEAK BED FRAME • FIX UP A
TTERY • REPAIR CHIPPED OR CRACKED CHINA • UNCLUTTER YOUR HOME • CLEAN CRAYON FROM A WALL • GET WAX OFF A TABLECLOTH
AINS • REMOVE CHEWING GUM FROM CARPETING • REMOVE BLEACH SPOTS FROM CARPETING • REMOVE PET STAINS • ELIMINATE WINE S
AINS FROM TILE GROUT • REMOVE MILDEW FROM WALLS AND CEILINGS • DISINFECT A TOILET BOWL • REMOVE FIREPLACE GRIME • GET
EAN OIL SPOTS FROM A GARAGE OR DRIVEWAY • REMOVE STAINS FROM BRICK • WASH AN OUTDOOR GRILL • FIX A FALLEN SOUFFLÉ • RE
SCUE OVERPROOFED YEAST DOUGH • FIX YOUR KID LUNCH • GET RID OF TAP-WATER MINERAL DEPOSITS • CALIBRATE A MEAT THERMOM
UCE • RESCUE A BROKEN SAUCE • REMOVE FAT FROM SOUPS AND SAUCES • FIX LUMPY GRAVY • SUBSTITUTE MISSING INGREDIENTS • R
RNED RICE • REMOVE COOKING ODORS • FINISH UNDERCOOKED MEAT • SALVAGE AN UNDERCOOKED TURKEY • FIX AN OVERSEASONED
ALE BREAD • SMOOTH SEIZED CHOCOLATE • SOFTEN HARDENED SUGARS OR COOKIES • FIX BREAKFAST FOR YOUR SWEETHEART • MENL
GGING TOOLS • RESTORE A BROKEN FLOWERPOT • SHARPEN PRUNING CLIPPERS • REMOVE RUST FROM TOOLS • REVIVE WILTING CUT FL
T RID OF RAMPANT BRAMBLES • TROUBLESHOOT BROWN SPOTS ON A LAWN • CONTROL MAJOR GARDEN PESTS • RID YOUR GARDEN OF
NPERFORMING COMPOST PILE • FIX BAD SOIL • SHORE UP A RAISED GARDEN BED • REMOVE A DEAD OR DISEASED TREE LIMB • TROUBL
AINAGE • TROUBLESHOOT ROSE DISEASES • IDENTIFY AND CORRECT SOIL DEFICIENCIES IN ROSES • TROUBLESHOOT ROSE PESTS • OVE
MAGED DECK BOARDS • REPAIR DECK RAILINGS • STRENGTHEN DECK JOISTS • FIX A RUSTY IRON RAILING • REPAIR A GATE • REPAIR A F
ACKED OR DAMAGED CONCRETE • IMPROVE THE LOOK OF REPAIRED CONCRETE • REPAIR AN ASPHALT DRIVEWAY • REVIVE WOODEN OU
RDEN PONDS • CLEAN SWIMMING POOL WATER • TROUBLESHOOT HOT TUBS AND SPAS • REPLACE BRICKS IN WALKWAYS AND PATIOS • S
R WITH JUMPER CABLES • SHUT OFF A CAR ALARM THAT WON'T QUIT • FREE A CAR STUCK ON ICE OR SNOW • DE-ICE YOUR WINDSHIELD
RN-SIGNAL COVER • FIX A CAR FUSE • FIX DASHBOARD LIGHTS THAT WON'T LIGHT • REMOVE CAR SMELLS • CHECK TIRE PRESSURE • INF
PROPERLY INSTALLED CHILD CAR SEAT • TROUBLESHOOT LEAKING OIL • CHECK AND ADD POWER-STEERING FLUID • CHECK AND ADD CO
OKEN EXHAUST PIPE • CHECK AND ADD ENGINE OIL • CHECK AND ADD BRAKE FLUID • CHECK AND ADD FLUID TO YOUR AUTOMATIC TRA
OUBLESHOOT A WINDSHIELD-WASHER PUMP • REPAIR MINOR DENTS • CHANGE A HUBCAP • FIX AN IGNITION KEY THAT WON'T TURN • CH

Cleaning

331 Clean Crayon From a Wall

What is it about toddlers and crayons and walls? Instead of sharing those colorful thoughts of yours with the doodling toddler, do something really off-the-wall: Get little Sam or Susie to help you make the colorful wax disappear.

Steps

1 Gently scrape away the wax with a plastic spoon or spatula.

2 Sprinkle baking soda on a damp white cloth.

3 Give the cloth to one of your tots and have him rub the marks off.

4 Dampen a sponge for the other one and have her rinse clean the residue.

5 Really stubborn marks may require Mom or Dad to spray on a very grown-up product: WD-40 or other multipurpose lubricating oil.

6 Wipe the wall clean with a damp towel.

What You'll Need

- Plastic spoon or spatula
- Baking soda
- White cloth
- Sponge
- Multipurpose lubricating oil
- Towel

Tips

Buy washable crayons.

Pencil marks can be removed with an artist's gum eraser (available at most art supply stores).

332 Get Wax Off a Tablecloth

If the warm glow of dinner candles has left you with a cold, hardened tablecloth stain the next morning, don't let it spoil the mood. Here's an easy way to remove caked-on wax and have that tablecloth ready for another romantic meal by tonight.

Steps

1 Scoop up excess wax with a spatula or a spoon.

2 Lay the tablecloth on an ironing board, and place a plain paper sack over the wax stain. Apply a warm (not hot) iron to the paper. Replace the wax-saturated paper bag as needed. Continue until wax is no longer transferring to the paper.

3 Treat colored candle stains with a prewash stain remover, or apply detergent directly on the spot prior to washing. (Remember to pretest spot removers and stain removers in an inconspicuous area prior to treating stains.)

4 Launder the tablecloth with detergent in the hottest water that's safe for the fabric. Wax-based stains must be melted to be removed from the fabric fibers.

5 Make sure the stain is completely removed before placing your tablecloth in the dryer. If you're unsure, wash, wash again.

What You'll Need

- Spatula or spoon
- Iron
- Plain brown paper bags
- Prewash stain remover
- Laundry detergent

Warning

Don't use a hot iron—it can burn the paper and fabric.

Always read the fabric care label.

333 Remove Wax From Carpeting

Few things are as relaxing as dining by candlelight. And few things are more irksome than finding drippings on your carpet the next morning. Don't stress. You can fix this pesky problem fast.

Steps

1 Put ice cubes in a plastic bag and cover the wax until it hardens.

2 Gently scrape the excess using a spatula or a spoon.

3 Set your iron on low heat. Place a brown paper bag without any writing or designs (the ink may transfer to the carpet) over the stain. Press the iron on the bag for no longer than a couple of seconds. Keep iron heat low so carpet fibers don't get scorched.

4 Repeat and replace the bag as necessary until the wax no longer transfers to the paper when heated.

5 Blot with dry-cleaning fluid until color is no longer being removed. (Use cleaning solvents sparingly to prevent damage to carpet backing.)

6 Blot with a solution of ¼ tsp. dishwashing liquid and 1 cup (8 fl oz/250 ml) warm water to remove all traces of cleaning fluid. Rinse and blot dry.

What You'll Need

- Ice cubes
- Plastic bag
- Spatula or spoon
- Iron
- Plain brown paper bags
- Dry-cleaning fluid
- Dishwashing liquid

Warning

Resist the urge to substitute gasoline, lighter fluid or carbon tetrachloride for dry-cleaning fluid. These fire and breathing hazards aren't meant for indoor carpets.

334 Get Rid of Ceiling Stains

Now that you've repaired the leak that caused it, how do rid your ceiling of that lingering brown water stain? Head to your local home supply or hardware store and pick up a can of pigmented stain blocker to brush on before you apply that new coat of paint. It's the secret to making ceiling stains—and odors—disappear.

Steps

1 Make sure the leak is fixed before removing a ceiling stain. Lay a drop cloth or a plastic sheet below the stained area of the ceiling to protect your carpeting or floor from drips. Standing on a stepladder, wipe the stained ceiling surface clean with a damp rag.

2 Apply a pigmented stain blocker such as Kilz or Bullseye on the stained area using a paint roller (for center stains) or a paintbrush (for corner stains). Paint 6 to 12 inches (15 to 30 cm) beyond the stain's edges.

3 Let the ceiling dry for 1 to 24 hours (follow the manufacturer's directions).

4 Apply a coat of ceiling paint. Let dry. Repeat if necessary.

What You'll Need

- Drop cloth or plastic sheet
- Stepladder
- Damp rag
- Pigmented stain blocker
- Paint roller or paintbrush
- Paint tray
- Ceiling paint

Tip

For details on getting rid of mildew, see 346 Remove Mildew From Walls and Ceilings.

335 Remove Clothing Stains

Drips, drops, smudges and smears—no matter what the stain du jour, quick action can keep it from becoming a permanent blemish on your wardrobe. With the exception of delicate fabrics such as leather and silk, this means rinsing or blotting the excess, then laundering as usual. No sink or towel handy when a clothing catastrophe strikes? No problem. The remedies below work even on set-in stains.

STAIN	SOLUTION
Gooey grease Gravy, butter, salad dressing, olive oil, vegetable oils	1 Scrape off excess solids with butter knife. 2 Place stain facedown on plain white paper towel. Replace paper towels as needed. 3 Squeeze small amount of dishwashing liquid on underside of stain to break up grease. 4 Wait at least 1 minute for detergent to break up grease. 5 Pretreat stain again with detergent. 6 Launder garment in warmest water safe for fabric.
Tough tannins Fruit juice, wine, tomato sauce, soft drinks, coffee, ketchup	1 First, even if you can't launder immediately, blot stain with cold water or rinse under cold water. 2 Then, for red wine or grape juice spills, sprinkle with salt to absorb excess liquid, then soak in cold water. Spritz tomato-sauce smears with club soda to counteract the tomato's acidity and loosen up the stain before pretreating. 3 Launder in warmest water safe for fabric, using color-safe bleach.
Problem proteins Dairy products, eggs, grass, blood, urine	1 Soak garment in warm water with an enzyme-containing laundry detergent for 30 minutes (longer if the stain is dry). For a fresh blood stain, soak garment in cold water. (Hot water sets blood.) 2 Launder as usual.
Chewing gum	1 Rub problem area with ice to harden the gum, then use dull knife to scrape off gum. 2 Saturate what remains with prewash stain remover. 3 Rinse and launder as usual.

STAIN	SOLUTION
Ink	1 Hold fabric's stained area tight over mouth of jar or glass. Pour rubbing alcohol very slowly through stained area. The mark will fade as liquid drips into container. 2 Rinse thoroughly and launder as usual.
Mustard	1 Treat garment with prewash stain remover. 2 Launder with chlorine bleach if safe for fabric; if not, use color-safe bleach.
Nail polish	1 Blot nail-polish remover (acetone) on stain. 2 Mix 1 tsp. mild, pH-balanced laundry detergent with 1 cup (8 fl oz/250 ml) lukewarm water. Blot mixture on garment, then sponge with clean water. 3 Launder as usual.
Chocolate and candy	1 Rub a little dishwashing liquid into stained area. 2 Use liquid chlorine bleach or color-safe bleach for laundering.
Makeup	1 Dampen stained area. Rub enzyme-containing laundry detergent directly on discolored area. 2 Launder in hottest water safe for garment.
Deodorant stains	• See 349 Get Rid of Deodorant Stains.
Warning	• Always read and follow the fabric care label. • Test your stain solution on an inconspicuous area of the fabric. • Don't combine ammonia and bleach: Deadly fumes may result.

336 Remove Mystery Stains From Clothing

What's that dark spot on your daughter's jeans? Is it a smudge from her chocolaty hands? A greasy stain from playing in the garage? Sometimes even the best stain detective is clueless about the origins of a fabric stain, spill or smudge. Good thing you don't need a Sherlock Holmes to remove that mystery stain.

What You'll Need

- Sponge
- Zippered nylon mesh bag
- Prewash stain remover
- Laundry detergent
- Dry-cleaning fluid
- Color-safe bleach
- Enzyme-containing laundry detergent
- Mild liquid laundry detergent

Steps

General rules

1 Rinse or soak unknown stains in cold water before laundering or applying a stain remover. Some stains, such as blood, coffee and wine, can set in warm water.

2 Sponge a stain, don't rub it. Rubbing only spreads the stain and may damage the fabric.

3 Read and follow label directions before applying stain treatments. If it says no bleach, even color-safe bleach is a no-no.

4 Protect delicates by washing them in a zippered nylon mesh bag.

5 Check that a stain is completely gone before drying the garment. Heat can set stains.

Small spots and fresh stains

1 Sponge directly on the stain a prewash stain remover, a liquid laundry detergent, or a paste made from powder laundry detergent and a little water. Or dab with dry-cleaning fluid. Let the garment sit for several minutes or leave it overnight.

2 Launder in the hottest water safe for the fabric, using detergent and color-safe bleach. For bleach amounts, follow instructions on the bottle. Repeat if needed.

3 Tumble dry at the setting safe for your fabric.

Large spots and old stains

1 Soak the garment overnight in the warmest water safe for the fabric in a washing machine or sink with ½ cup (4 fl oz/125 ml) to 1 cup (8 fl oz/250 ml) enzyme-containing laundry detergent (adjust amount according to size of garment).

2 Launder as usual, using an enzyme detergent, color-safe bleach and the warmest water that is safe for the fabric. Repeat if needed.

3 Tumble dry.

Delicate fabrics such as lingerie, silk and lace

1 Rub mild liquid laundry detergent directly on the stain. Let the clothing sit for several minutes.

2 Toss the garment in the washing machine or sink, fill with cold water and add mild detergent. Soak overnight.

3 Wash using the delicate or hand-wash cycle on your machine. Repeat as needed.

4 Lay flat to dry.

Unwashables; clothes labeled "dry clean" or "dry clean only"

1 Take your stained garment to the dry cleaner if the label contains the word *only* or if you cannot live without the item. Otherwise, go to step 2.

2 Sponge on dry-cleaning fluid, then allow the garment to dry.

3 Repeat as necessary.

Drying tricks

Now that you've cleared up the mystery, here's how to dry your formerly stained garment the right way. (These techniques work equally well on most of your other laundered, stain-free fabrics, too.)

1 Check wet garments for lingering blights to prevent stains from setting in fabric via dryer heat.

2 To prevent broken and loosened fibers, separate lint shedders (fuzzy sweatshirts, chenille robes, flannels and towels) from lint grabbers (knits, corduroys and synthetics).

3 Dry like items (such as towels and cottons) together, and dry lingerie and permanent press separately, to prevent fabric damage from friction.

4 Loosely shake clothes before tossing them into the dryer to prevent wrinkles and shorten drying time.

5 Zip zippers, button buttons, and hook eye-hooks to prevent snags and fabric tears.

6 Empty pockets of paper, money and tissues to reduce lint.

7 Add fabric softener to make clothes fluffier.

8 Wipe lint from the filter to reduce wear and tear on the machine.

Tips

Resist the urge to wash in cold water. Many fabrics respond best to warm or hot water, and the enzymes in your detergent are activated by higher temperatures, resulting in cleaner clothes.

See also 335 Remove Clothing Stains.

337 Remove Carpet Stains

Ketchup drips. Chocolate drops. Wine spills. If the party's at your place, expect a festive, colorful carpet after your last guest has gone home. If you act fast, you'll keep common carpet visitors from taking up permanent residence in your home. First things first: Blot (don't soak) or spoon up the excess, then try the remedies below. Use a plastic bucket or old plastic container to create the solutions described.

STAIN	SOLUTION—Blot (don't soak) excess, then:
Gooey grease Gravy, butter, salad dressing, olive oil, vegetable oils, mystery spills	1 Sprinkle cornmeal or baking soda on greasy spills to absorb excess. Leave overnight. Vacuum when dry. 2 Blot on small amount of dry-cleaning fluid. 3 Blot with detergent solution of 1 tsp. dishwashing liquid and 1 cup (8 fl oz/250 ml) warm water. Work from outside of stain toward center. Let sit 5 minutes. 4 Sponge with warm water until detergent disappears. Cover with plain white paper towels to absorb liquid overnight. 5 Vacuum or brush when dry to restore texture.
Tough tannins Fruit juice, wine, soft drinks, coffee, ketchup, tomato sauce	1 Blot on detergent solution of ½ tsp. mild liquid laundry detergent and 1 cup (8 fl oz/250 ml) lukewarm water. Or, for red wine and grape juice stains, sponge with club soda or white wine. 2 Sponge on ammonia solution of 2 tbsp. ammonia and 1 cup (8 fl oz/250 ml) warm water. 3 Blot on detergent solution again. 4 Rinse and blot dry. Cover with plain white paper towels. Let sit overnight. 5 Vacuum or brush when dry.
Problem proteins Dairy products, eggs, grass, blood, urine	1 Dab with detergent solution of 1 tsp. dishwashing liquid and 1 cup (8 fl oz/250 ml) lukewarm water. For blood stains, use cold water. If stain is gone, you can stop here. 2 If stain is still visible, blot with a solution of 2 tbsp. ammonia and ½ cup (4 fl oz/125 ml) water. Then sponge with clean water. 3 Blot on solution of 1 cup (8 fl oz/250 ml) white vinegar and 2 cups (16 fl oz/500 ml) warm water. 4 Sponge with clean water. Blot dry. Cover with plain white paper towels. Let sit overnight. 5 Vacuum or brush when dry.
Ink	1 Sponge with small amount of dry-cleaning fluid. 2 Blot on detergent solution (see "Gooey grease," step 3). 3 Sponge-rinse until residue is removed. Blot dry.

For other carpet or rug stains, see 333 Remove Wax From Carpeting, 338 Remove Chewing Gum From Carpeting, 339 Remove Bleach Spots From Carpeting, 340 Remove Pet Stains and 342 Remove Burn Marks on Rugs.

STAIN	SOLUTION—Blot (don't soak) excess, then:
Makeup	1 Blot with dry-cleaning fluid. 2 Blot with powder enzyme laundry detergent and water following directions on box. Rinse. 3 Apply solution of 2 tbsp. ammonia and ½ cup (4 fl oz/125 ml) water. Rinse. 4 Blot on solution of 1 cup (8 fl oz/250 ml) white vinegar and 2 cups (16 fl oz/500 ml) warm water. Rinse. 5 Allow to air-dry, then vacuum.
Mustard	1 Apply small amount of detergent solution (see "Gooey grease," step 3). Blot and rinse several times. 2 Apply vinegar solution (see step 4, above) and rinse. 3 If stain remains, mix solution of powder enzyme laundry detergent and water following directions on box. Cover stain with a cloth drenched in the solution for at least 30 minutes. 4 Rinse and blot dry.
Nail polish	1 Apply small amount of nonacetate nail-polish remover to white cloth. Work gently into stain, working from edge to center. 2 Let sit 5 minutes. Blot several times. 3 Rinse thoroughly. Blot dry, then vacuum.
Chocolate and candy	1 Sponge lightly with cool water; blot. 2 Apply laundry detergent solution (see "Tough tannins," step 1) with brush or towel. Repeat until no stain is transferring to towel. Rinse. 3 Blot on ammonia solution (see "Tough tannins," step 2). Sponge-rinse. 4 Blot dry, then vacuum.
Warning	• Always remove dirty excess and pretest stain solution on an inconspicuous area of the carpet or rug before cleaning. • Resist scrubbing or saturating carpet: Fiber damage and stain setting may result.

338 Remove Chewing Gum From Carpeting

It's a sticky dilemma: What do you do when the Double Bubble lands on your living room carpet? While your natural reaction might be to blow up at the gum chewer in the family, be sweet instead and follow these tips. You'll be out of this mess in no time.

Steps

1 Scrape away as much of the gum as you can using a spatula or spoon (to protect carpet fibers).

2 Vacuum or brush away loose pieces.

3 Rub the remaining gum with a plastic bag filled with ice until the gum is frozen.

4 Chip away the frozen gum fragments using a spatula or spoon.

5 Dissolve any final traces of the stuff by dabbing with a small amount of dry-cleaning fluid. Blot.

6 Blot on a detergent solution of ¼ tsp. mild dishwashing liquid and 1 cup (8 fl oz/250 ml) warm water.

7 Rinse thoroughly.

What You'll Need

- Spatula or spoon
- Vacuum or brush
- Plastic bag
- Ice
- Dry-cleaning fluid
- Mild dishwashing liquid

Tips

You can try this remedy to remove gum from clothes or shoes, too.

Some citrus-based products, such as Orange-Sol or De-Solv-It, break down the stickiness of gum so that it is easier to remove.

339 Remove Bleach Spots From Carpeting

Spills happen during the daily laundry dash, especially when kids get into the washing machine action. And bleach, that must-have for truly white whites, makes for a fierce stain. You can, however, banish such blights from your carpet if you act quickly.

Steps

1 Wear rubber or latex gloves. Blot the excess bleach with a white absorbent cloth or paper towel.

2 Blot-rinse with water.

3 Gently blot detergent solution of ¼ tsp. mild dishwashing liquid and 1 cup (8 fl oz/250 ml) warm water onto the stain, using a clean cloth or paper towel. Work from the stain's outside edge to the center.

4 Let the detergent sit for at least 5 minutes.

5 Repeat blotting with a clean white cloth until no more of the bleach transfers to the cloth and the bleach smell is nearly gone.

6 Rinse thoroughly with cold water.

What You'll Need

- Rubber or latex gloves
- White absorbent cloths or paper towels
- Mild dishwashing liquid

Tips

If the stain is old and has discolored the carpet, contact a carpet professional.

Keep a spray water bottle and white rags or a roll of plain white paper towels on hand in your laundry room for future spills.

340 Remove Pet Stains

If housetraining your puppy is going a bit slow or your cat keeps missing the litter box, you don't always have to live with their pungent reminders. These unpleasant stains can be removed, especially if you catch them when they're still fresh.

Steps

Urine on carpet and upholstery

1 Soak up excess moisture with a white rag or paper towels.

2 Blot on a solution of ¼ tsp. mild liquid laundry detergent and 1 cup (8 fl oz/250 ml) warm water. Repeat until there is no more stain transferring to a towel or rag.

3 Blot with a solution of 2 tbsp. ammonia and 1 cup (8 fl oz/250 ml) water. Rinse with warm water. Repeat. Blot dry.

4 Blot the area with a solution of 1 cup (8 fl oz/250 ml) white vinegar and 2 cups (16 fl oz/500 ml) water. Rinse.

5 Cover with several layers of paper towels weighed down with a heavy, nonfading object. Continue changing paper towels until the carpet is dry.

6 If you can't remove the stain, consider recovering the furniture item or replacing the carpet. (For details on how to replace a section of carpeting, see 342 Remove Burn Marks on Rugs.) This might also be a good time to invest in a dog trainer.

Feces on carpet and upholstery

1 Gently scoop up excess with a spoon or spatula.

2 Blot with an ammonia solution (see step 3, above). Let it soak in for several minutes.

3 Blot, then repeat until the stain is removed. Rinse with cold water. Blot dry.

4 To remove lingering carpet odors, sprinkle baking soda on the spot. Let it sit overnight, then vacuum.

What You'll Need

- White rags and/or paper towels
- Mild liquid laundry detergent
- Ammonia
- White vinegar
- Heavy, nonfading object
- Spoon or spatula
- Baking soda
- Vacuum
- Nose clips

Tips

Enzyme-based products, such as Bio-Aid or Nature's Miracle, available at your veterinarian or a pet store, are also effective.

See 314 Rid Carpets of Pet Odors for ways to combat lingering odors.

341 Eliminate Wine Stains From a Rug or Tablecloth

A good time was had by all, but now you're seeing red over a carpet spotted with Beaujolais Nouveau or a tablecloth spilled with vintage merlot. Relax. You can have your carpet and table linens looking fresh by the next uncorking.

Steps

Carpet

1 Move fast! To keep red wine stains from setting in carpets or linens, quick blotting or rinsing with cold water is key. On a wet stain, dab the carpet or tablecloth with a dry, white absorbent cloth to remove the excess liquid. If it's the next morning or the stain has dried, skip to step 2.

2 Apply a small amount of detergent solution—¼ tsp. dishwashing liquid and 1 cup (8 fl oz/250 ml) lukewarm water—to a white cloth and gently blot, working from the edges of the spill to the center to prevent spreading. Let it sit for several minutes.

3 Repeat as needed until the stain is removed.

4 Rinse with cold water. Dab with a clean rag until dry.

Tablecloth

1 On a new, wet stain, sprinkle coarse salt to absorb liquid from the fabric. Then blot with cold water or rinse under cold water to remove excess sugars and prevent oxidation.

2 For an older, dry stain, rub a bit of liquid laundry detergent into the stained area. Launder in the hottest water safe for the fabric with laundry detergent and color-safe bleach.

3 Repeat as needed until the stain is gone.

What You'll Need

- White absorbent cloths
- Dishwashing liquid
- Coarse salt
- Liquid laundry detergent
- Color-safe bleach

Tips

If at first you don't succeed, blot, blot (or wash, wash) again. It often takes several times for the remedy to do the trick.

To remove wine stains from clothing, see 335 Remove Clothing Stains.

342 **Remove Burn Marks on Rugs**

If a cigarette or candle burn on your carpet has you steaming, here's a solution that will cool you off. While there's no way to make your carpet look brand-new, you can remove and replace the singed fibers so that you're the only one who'll know the marks were there.

Steps

1 Gently rub the burned area with lightweight sandpaper or steel wool to remove the melted fibers.

2 Brush or vacuum the burned area to remove any ashes or loose singed fiber. If the burn marks are gone, you can stop here. If you can still see the burn, you'll need to remove and replace that area of carpeting (steps 3 through 8).

3 Carefully cut out the damaged area with a carpet knife or a utility knife (see A), extending your cut at least 2 inches (5 cm) beyond the burn edges. Make sure you cut only the carpet backing—not your floor beneath.

4 Place the cutout on a piece of paper. Trace with a pencil and cut out the pattern.

5 Place your template on a carpet remnant. Or you can use carpet from an inconspicuous area, such as the back of a closet. Cut and remove the replacement carpet patch.

6 Using a glue gun, cover the back side of the replacement carpet with carpet glue and set the piece in place. Rim the edges with glue to prevent the patch from being dislodged during routine cleaning or use.

7 Blend and seal the seams by rolling over the patched area with a carpet tractor (see B).

8 Allow the carpet to dry thoroughly before foot traffic resumes.

What You'll Need

- Lightweight sandpaper or steel wool
- Stiff brush or vacuum
- Carpet knife or utility knife
- Paper
- Pencil
- Scissors
- Replacement carpet patch
- Carpet glue
- Glue gun
- Carpet tractor (roller)

Tips

You can find carpet glue and a carpet tractor at most hardware or home supply stores.

If the burns don't go all the way down to the carpet backing or you're leery about cutting and pasting, you can trim the fibers from the burn hole and glue in replacement fibers. Clip new fibers from a fresh patch of carpet and glue them in place using tweezers. This works only for small burned areas.

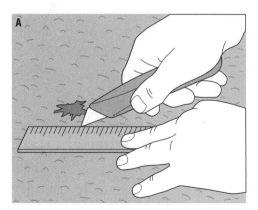

343 Clean Stains From Furniture

Big-ticket items like furniture and upholstery should be dusted and vacuumed regularly. It's the only way to keep in check the airborne cooking oils and dust that inevitably settle on these pieces. But what's the solution to little Jack's chocolate snack that ended up sweetening the ottoman? Or Grandma's makeup smudges on the sofa? Busting these and other stains is a piece of cake.

STAIN	SOLUTION—Blot (don't soak) excess, then:
Gooey grease Gravy, butter, salad dressing, olive oil, vegetable oils, mystery spills	1 Blot on small amount of rubbing alcohol or dry-cleaning fluid. Repeat until there is no more transfer of stain to white cloth or plain white paper towel. If stain is gone, stop here. If not, proceed with steps 2 through 5. 2 Blot with solution of 1 tsp. dishwashing liquid or laundry detergent and 1 cup (8 fl oz/250 ml) warm water. Work from outside side of stain toward center. 3 Rinse with damp sponge to remove detergent. Blot dry. 4 Rinse with solution of ½ cup (4 fl oz/125 ml) vinegar and ½ cup (4 fl oz/125 ml) water. Blot dry. 5 Brush when fully dry to restore texture.
Makeup	1 Blot small amount of rubbing alcohol or dry-cleaning fluid onto the stain using a plain white paper towel. Blot dry immediately. 2 Repeat until stain disappears. Blot with solution of 1 tsp. liquid dishwashing detergent and 1 cup (8 fl oz/250 ml) warm water. 3 Repeat until stain is no longer visible. Blot stubborn makeup mishaps with a solution of ½ cup (4 fl oz/125 ml) vinegar and ½ cup (4 fl oz/125 ml) warm water. Rinse and air-dry. Brush fabric when fully dry.
Ink	1 Blot fabric with rubbing alcohol or dry-cleaning fluid; blot dry immediately. Repeat until ink is invisible. 2 Rinse with solution of ½ cup (4 fl oz/125 ml) white vinegar and ½ cup (4 fl oz/125 ml) water. Blot dry.
Problem proteins Dairy products, eggs, grass, blood, urine	1 Dampen fabric with warm water. Let soak 1 minute. (Use cold water for blood.) Blot dry immediately. If stain is gone, stop here. If not, try one or more of the solutions below. 2 Blot milk and other dairy spills with small amount of dry-cleaning fluid and blot dry. Repeat until no stain transfers to paper towel. 3 Blot a persistent protein stain with solution of 1 tsp. dishwashing liquid and 1 cup (8 fl oz/250 ml) warm water. Blot, then repeat. Rinse with vinegar solution of 1 cup (8 fl oz/250 ml) white vinegar and 1 cup (8 fl oz/250 ml) warm water. Blot dry. Brush fabric when fully dry.

STAIN	SOLUTION—Blot (don't soak) excess, then:
Tough tannins Fruit juice, wine, soft drinks, coffee, ketchup, tomato sauce	1 Wet fabric slightly, then let soak 1 minute. Blot with paper towel. Repeat until no stain is evident on towel, then blot dry. If stain is gone, stop here. If not, try steps 2 and 3. 2 On stubborn stains, rub in detergent solution of 1 tsp. dishwashing liquid and 1 cup (8 fl oz/250 ml) warm water. Repeat until no stain transfers to towel. 3 For red wine and grape juice stains, sponge with club soda or tonic water; blot with paper towel. Sponge on ammonia solution of 2 tbsp. ammonia and 1 cup (8 fl oz/250 ml) warm water. Rinse and blot dry. Apply a 3 percent solution of hydrogen peroxide on stubborn stains. Allow to sit 24 hours. Blot and air-dry 48 hours before use. Brush fabric when fully dry.
Mustard	1 Wet fabric with a little water. Soak 1 minute; blot with paper towel. Repeat until mustard is gone. 2 Blot persistent stains with solution of 1 tsp. dishwashing liquid and 1 cup (8 fl oz/250 ml) warm water. Rinse with water; then rinse with solution of ½ cup (4 fl oz/125 ml) white vinegar and ½ cup (4 fl oz/125 ml) warm water. Blot dry.
Nail polish	1 Apply a small amount of nonacetate nail-polish remover and blot immediately. Repeat until stain is gone. 2 Blot stubborn polish stains with a solution of 1 tsp. dishwashing liquid and 1 cup (8 fl oz/250 ml) warm water. Repeat as needed. Rinse with water.
Chocolate and candy	1 Wet stain with small amount of rubbing alcohol or dry-cleaning fluid; immediately blot dry. Repeat until stain disappears. 2 Bust stubborn chocolate or candy stains with solution of 1 tsp. dishwashing liquid and 1 cup (8 fl oz/250 ml) warm water. Rinse with water; rinse again with solution of ½ cup (4 fl oz/125 ml) white vinegar and ½ cup (4 fl oz/125 ml) warm water.
Warning	• Always remove stain excess, and pretest cleaning solution on an inconspicuous area of the upholstery or furniture. • Resist scrubbing or saturating spills; fiber damage and stain setting may result.

344 Strip Wax Buildup From Floors

If your kitchen floor looks yellowed or grimy or has spots of sticky, built-up wax, it's time to strip it down. Here's how to do it yourself.

Steps

1   Purchase a wax stripper that is appropriate for your floor. Visit a janitorial supply store to get the most effective wax stripper. To make your job easier, select a stripper that does not require rinsing. For best results, use a wax stripper that is the same brand as the floor wax you typically use.

2   Consider renting an electric floor scrubber and a wet-dry vacuum to reduce the elbow grease required. Look in the yellow pages under "Equipment Rentals." The floor scrubber scrubs away wax, and the wet-dry vacuum will suck up the stripper and wax residue afterward.

3   Gather your supplies. You'll need: rubber gloves, wax stripper, a cotton mop, several scrub pads, toothbrush, putty knife, floor squeegee (or a window squeegee), a plastic dustpan, rags and three buckets. (You won't need the squeegee, dustpan and rags if you use a wet-dry vacuum.)

4   Remove any furniture, area rugs or pet food bowls from the area. Sweep or vacuum away any dust, crumbs or loose dirt.

5   Test the stripper on a part of the floor that is not readily visible before you get started. Some older linoleum floors cannot withstand stripping.

6   Determine your plan of attack. You'll want to start in the corner that is farthest from an exit and work your way toward the exit. If you are doing this by hand, plan to strip 2-by-4-foot (60-by-120-cm) sections of the floor. If you are using a floor scrubber, you can strip larger sections.

7   Fill one bucket with the wax stripper. Dilute it according to the manufacturer's instructions. Put all of your scrubbers, scrapers and tools in another bucket. Bring all three buckets to the corner of the room that you plan to use as your starting point.

What You'll Need

- Wax stripper
- Electric floor scrubber
- Wet-dry vacuum
- Rubber gloves
- Cotton mop
- Scrub pads
- Toothbrush
- Putty knife
- Squeegee
- Plastic dustpan
- Rags
- Three buckets
- Broom or vacuum
- Fan
- Floor wax
- Floor sealant

Tips

Use a scrub pad with a long handle (like a mop) to save your back from unnecessary crouching and bending.

If you need to walk on an area that has stripper on it, make a footpath of rags to avoid getting stripper on your shoes, socks or feet.

8   Use the mop to cover two 2-by-4-foot (60-by-120-cm) sections of the floor with the wax stripper. Apply enough stripper to coat the area thoroughly but not so much that it floods the area and soaks between seams or cracks. Apply stripper more liberally in areas with a lot of buildup.

9   Allow the stripper to soak according to instructions, then use the scrub pads (or a floor scrubber) to scrape away the wax buildup in one of the sections while you leave the other section to soak.

10 Use the toothbrush to scrub nooks and crannies and the putty knife to scrape away gobs or multiple wax layers in corners.

11 Use the squeegee to scoop the wax residue and stripper into the dustpan. Soak up excess liquid with rags or the mop. Dump all of this into the third bucket. (Or simply suck the residue up with a wet-dry vacuum if you have one.)

12 Apply stripper to a third 2-by-4-foot (60-by-120-cm) section before you begin scrubbing the second section, so the stripper can soak in and do its work while you scrub the second section.

13 Alternate sections like this until you complete the floor. Make sure to strip the baseboards if they need it. Always apply stripper to the second-to-next section so that the stripper can soak into the wax while you scrub the other section.

14 If you encounter a section where you can't scrub away all of the buildup, remove what you can and then reapply the stripper. Allow it to soak in while you work on another section and then rescrub it.

15 Mop the floor if you used a stripper that requires rinsing.

16 Allow the floor to dry thoroughly. Place a fan near the floor to accelerate the drying process if necessary.

17 Wax the floor and seal it as soon as the floor is dry to provide a protective coat. Apply wax sparingly to avoid future wax buildups.

Before you go to the effort of stripping a floor, consider whether you want to replace the floor entirely. Now might be a good time to do so.

To remove wax buildup from a hardwood floor, use products that are specifically designed for wood floors. Never use water to strip or wash a wood floor. Consult a hardwood floor professional if in doubt.

345 Remove Stains From Tile Grout

You know the story. Your otherwise lovely bathroom has gruesome stains or greenish black mold and fungus growing between the tiles. With some elbow grease, you can stamp out those unsightly stains.

Steps

1 Before cleaning, wipe away any excess wet buildup with a white terry-cloth towel or paper towels. If your grout is crumbling, consider replacing it. (See 120 Replace Cracked Tile Grout in a Tub or Shower.)

2 While cleaning (steps 3 through 6), be sure to wear rubber or latex gloves and safety goggles, and throw open the windows to avoid exposure to the harsh chemical fumes of bleach-containing solutions.

3 Spray on a commercial grout cleaner or a heavy-duty all-purpose cleaning solution with bleach. Wait for several minutes.

4 Scrub the grout with a stiff scrub brush or a grout brush, then rinse thoroughly.

5 Blast mold, mildew or stubborn stains with a bleach-containing cleanser, or make your own using ¼ cup (2 fl oz/60 ml) chlorine bleach and 1 qt. (32 fl oz/1 l) warm water. Let the disinfectant sit at least 10 minutes to thoroughly kill the mold and mildew.

6 Scrub the grout with a stiff brush or a grout brush, rinse, then dry with a white towel or paper towels.

7 Now that the grout's sparkling clean, keep it that way. Apply one to three coats of commercial grout sealer with a small brush or paintbrush. (Commercial grout cleaner, grout brushes and grout sealer are available at home supply centers and janitorial supply stores.)

8 Reapply annually to make certain the only thing scary in your home is the Halloween decor.

What You'll Need

- White terry-cloth towels or paper towels
- Rubber or latex gloves
- Safety goggles
- Commercial grout cleaner or all-purpose cleaner with bleach
- Stiff scrub brush or grout brush
- Chlorine bleach or bleach-containing cleanser
- Commercial grout sealer
- Small brush or paintbrush

Tips

Regular cleanings with a bleach-based cleanser keep mold, mildew and stains in check.

Make sure you seal the grout after cleaning.

Warning

Never mix bleach with an ammonia-based product such as glass cleaner.

346 Remove Mildew From Walls and Ceilings

Seeing fuzzy black or green spots on a bathroom wall or kitchen ceiling? Chances are it's mildew—the common name for the various spores that are both a health hazard and a homeowner's nightmare. Once inside walls and ceilings, mildew is tough to remove. Send these nasty interlopers packing quickly.

Steps

Walls

1 Wear rubber or latex gloves. Spray the wall with a solution of ½ cup (4 fl oz/125 ml) chlorine bleach, ⅓ cup (3 fl oz/80 ml) powder laundry detergent and 1 gallon (4 l) hot water, working from the base of the wall up. (Or you can use a commercial mildewcide, though it's much more expensive than mixing your own.)

2 Gently scrub away surface mildew using a plastic scrubber sponge.

3 Using the scrubber sponge, rinse thoroughly with fresh water.

4 Once dry, consider applying a coat of paint containing an anti-mildew agent so you don't have to do this again any time soon.

Ceilings

1 Wear rubber or latex gloves. Dip a scrubber sponge in a bucket filled with a solution of ½ cup (4 fl oz/125 ml) chlorine bleach, ⅓ cup (3 fl oz/80 ml) powder laundry detergent and 1 gallon (4 l) hot water. (Or you can use a commercial mildewcide, but it's much more expensive than mixing your own.) Squeeze out the excess.

2 Standing on a stepladder, carefully scrub the affected areas.

3 Fill the bucket with fresh water. Using the scrubber sponge, rinse thoroughly.

4 Once dry, consider applying an anti-mildew paint.

What You'll Need

- Rubber or latex gloves
- Plastic spray bottle
- Chlorine bleach
- Powder laundry detergent
- Plastic scrubber sponge
- Anti-mildew paint
- Bucket
- Stepladder

Tips

Keep cleaning solution from dripping onto carpeting or floors.

Prevent mildew by using exhaust fans when cooking and showering.

Throw open windows often to decrease humidity.

See 119 Troubleshoot Mold on Interior Walls for more ways to prevent mildew.

Warning

Always wear rubber gloves when cleaning with bleach.

Make sure the room is well ventilated to avoid inhaling hazardous bleach fumes.

347 Disinfect a Toilet Bowl

If you're flush with reasons not to deal with your toilet, have a seat and relax. Today's disinfecting cleaners make this tedious task a breeze. These steps even work on a toilet that's been neglected for a while, and you can make them a part of your weekly routine.

Steps

1 Wear rubber or latex gloves to protect your hands.

2 Spray a disinfecting toilet-bowl cleaner around the inside of the bowl and under the rim.

3 Or clean with chlorine bleach alone; it both whitens and disinfects. To avoid creating hazardous fumes, do not combine bleach with bowl cleaner or any other product. Pour ¼ cup (2 fl oz/60 ml) bleach in the toilet bowl.

4 Let either product sit for at least 10 minutes to kill germs, bacteria and viruses. While the disinfectant is doing its job in the bowl, you can begin cleaning the seat and lid (see step 7).

5 Swish the cleaner around the bowl, under the rim and as far into the trap as possible using a long-handled toilet brush.

6 Flush.

7 Spray a nonabrasive disinfectant on the seat, lid and outside of the bowl. (Plastic toilet seats can be scratched.)

8 Let sit for at least 10 minutes, then rinse thoroughly.

9 Dry with paper towels (they're the simplest—no rinsing needed and no chance of spreading germs). Don't forget to dry hinge areas and bumpers.

10 Lift the seat and spray with the disinfecting cleaner or chlorine bleach.

11 Rinse thoroughly.

12 Dry with paper towels.

13 Place an in-tank (continuous) cleaner inside the bowl to maintain bowl freshness daily.

What You'll Need

- Rubber or latex gloves
- Disinfecting toilet-bowl cleaner or chlorine bleach
- Long-handled toilet brush
- Nonabrasive disinfectant
- Paper towels
- In-tank cleaner

Tip

If time is short, grab a box of the new pop-up disinfecting wipes, and swab the toilet deck. Toss.

Warning

Don't ever combine bleach with any cleaner; it creates toxic fumes.

Always open the windows when using cleaning products, especially in smaller spaces like a bathroom.

348 Remove Fireplace Grime

Few things are cozier than a roaring fire in the hearth. To make sure your brick or stone fireplace is ready for hot action at a moment's notice, surface-clean it in early fall, before the chill sets in, and in late spring, to buff away a season's worth of soot and creosote buildup.

Steps

1 Wait at least 24 hours after your last fire. Wearing safety goggles and a dust mask, clean up the fireplace with a broom or duster and dustpan, and place the ashes in a lidded metal container.

2 Brush the flue (the pipe that runs between the fireplace and chimney) with a short chimney brush, flue brush or stiff-bristle brush to remove creosote buildup.

3 Scrub the outside of the damper (the metal gate between the firebox and chimney) with a stiff-bristle brush to loosen creosote, soot and ash buildup. Open and close the damper several times to ensure it operates freely.

4 Brush the firebox and hearth floor with a wire brush to remove creosote buildup.

5 Create a cleaner by mixing a 4-oz. (125-g) shaved bar of naphtha soap in 1 qt. (32 fl oz/1 l) hot water in a plastic bucket until the soap is dissolved. Cool, then thoroughly mix in ½ lb. (250 g) powdered pumice and ½ cup (4 fl oz/125 ml) ammonia. Apply the naphtha cleaner to the firebox and hearth floor with a small brush or paintbrush. Since drips or runs onto unclean surfaces may leave marks, start at the bottom and work up. Let it sit for 1 hour.

6 Scrub with a scrub brush and warm water. Rinse clean. (Not all black or brown residue can be removed from porous brick.)

7 Scrape heavy buildup from glass fireplace doors with a razor blade. Finish with a spritz of window cleaner, then buff dry with a towel or dust-free rag.

8 Dust or vacuum the fireplace mantel and screen using a vacuum with the small brush attachment.

What You'll Need

- Safety goggles
- Dust mask
- Broom or duster
- Dustpan
- Lidded metal container
- Chimney brush, flue brush or stiff-bristle brush
- Wire brush
- Plastic bucket
- Naphtha soap
- Powdered pumice
- Ammonia
- Small brush or paintbrush
- Scrub brush
- Razor blade
- Window cleaner
- Towel or dust-free rag
- Vacuum with small brush attachment

Warning

Check for loose bricks or mortar and cracks before each fireplace season.

Always wear safety goggles and a dust mask when cleaning soot and ashes.

349 Get Rid of Deodorant Stains

Did that bargain antiperspirant leave you with embarrassing white streaks on your button-down shirt or unsightly wet marks on your favorite blouse? No worries—you can usually remove these blights without too much effort.

Steps

1 Act as soon as possible to minimize chemical staining. Sponge white vinegar on the underarm stains to loosen the buildup of the deodorant's aluminum chloride or zinc salts, which discolor and weaken fabric over time.

2 Soak stubborn stains overnight in an enzyme-containing laundry detergent.

3 Launder with your usual detergent and color-safe bleach in the warmest water safe for your garment.

What You'll Need

- Sponge
- White vinegar
- Laundry detergent with enzymes
- Color-safe bleach

Tip

Let your deodorant dry before dressing.

350 Eliminate Cigarette Odor

Few odors are more odious, especially to non- and reformed smokers, than lingering cigarette smoke. Whether your goal is to get healthy or to get a loved one off your back, it's easy to keep your home from smelling like the local roadhouse. Just throw open your windows and try out one or more of these easy tricks.

Steps

1 Set small bowls of vinegar, pine-scented cleaner or activated charcoal around the room. If your home has young children or pets, place the bowls well out of reach. Close off the room overnight.

2 Spritz your favorite perfume or cologne on a cold light bulb. When the light is turned on, the warmed scent will fill the room.

3 Place small items (such as gloves, a wool hat or a small pillow) in a zippered plastic bag with a couple of fabric-softener sheets. Leave overnight.

4 Fill ashtrays with cat litter to extinguish cigarettes and capture the odor.

5 Sprinkle baking soda liberally on carpets, rugs and upholstery around the room. Let it sit overnight. Vacuum.

6 Soak a rag or a dish towel in vinegar, wring out the excess and wave it around the room for a minute or two.

What You'll Need

- Several small bowls
- Vinegar, pine-scented cleaner or activated charcoal
- Perfume or cologne
- Light bulb
- Zippered plastic bag
- Fabric-softener sheets
- Ashtrays
- Cat litter
- Baking soda
- Vacuum
- Rag or dish towel

Tip

Launder washable items, including curtains, pillows and slipcovers, for best odor removal.

351 Restore Shine to Your Jewelry

Few things sparkle like spanking-new gold, silver, platinum, and precious or semiprecious stones. After even a few days' wear, though, they can dull from lotions, body oil and everyday dust and dirt. Regular cleaning can keep your baubles looking fresh-from-the-jeweler brilliant all the time.

Steps

Silver

1 With an old soft-bristle toothbrush, rub the piece with toothpaste. Let it sit for 30 minutes.

2 Wash in a bowl of sudsy warm water with a few squirts of dishwashing liquid. Rinse.

3 Polish dry with chamois or other smooth cloth that's free of lint.

Gold, platinum and diamonds

1 Remove greasy film by rubbing with or soaking in rubbing alcohol or vodka.

2 Drop two fizzing tablets (such as Alka-Seltzer or denture cleaner) into a glass of water. Immerse the jewelry for 2 minutes, then remove it. Or soak for several minutes in a bowl of sudsy warm water with a few squirts of dishwashing liquid.

3 Scrub gently with a soft-bristle toothbrush.

4 Rinse thoroughly.

5 Polish dry with a smooth, lint-free cloth or chamois.

Pearls and other soft or porous gems such as emeralds, opals and tanzanite

1 Remove traces of cosmetics and dirt with a tissue.

2 Dip in a sudsy bowl of mild soap (such as Dove) and warm water. Quickly remove.

3 Gently remove buildup with a soft-bristle toothbrush or cotton swab. Rinse.

4 Polish dry with chamois or other soft, lint-free cloth.

What You'll Need

- Toothpaste
- Soft-bristle toothbrush
- Bowl
- Dishwashing liquid
- Chamois or other soft, lint-free cloth
- Rubbing alcohol or vodka
- Fizzing tablets
- Glass for soaking
- Tissue
- Mild soap
- Cotton swab

Tips

Keep your jewelry in a fabric-lined case, or wrap each piece individually in soft tissue paper.

Have a jeweler check yearly for loose prongs, worn mountings and general wear and tear.

Warning

Keep jewelry away from chlorine and harsh chemicals, which can erode the finish and polish of gems.

Never use boiling water to clean jewelry.

352 Wash Dirty Windows

Somebody has to do windows, right? If that someone in your house is you, we've got the tips and techniques to make you—and your windows, naturally—shine.

Steps

1 Before washing interior windows, put a beach towel along the sill to keep the floor or wall from getting wet.

2 Spray a commercial glass cleaner lightly on a clean, lint-free rag. Or mix your own cleaner of ¼ cup (2 fl oz/60 ml) vinegar in 3 cups (24 fl oz/750 ml) warm water.

3 For extremely dirty windows, mix 1 tbsp. ammonia and 3 tbsp. rubbing alcohol or vinegar in 1 qt. (32 fl oz/1 l) warm water.

4 Gently wipe the rag across the window, using horizontal strokes to prevent dripping.

5 Grab your squeegee. Wipe the rubber strip with a cleaning cloth to get started. Holding the squeegee firmly, press it downward. Start each stroke in a dry spot.

6 Keep the squeegee blade dry by wiping it on the cleaning cloth after each stroke.

7 Use old sheets or towels that haven't been washed with fabric softener to dry the windows. For extra sparkle, polish the glass when it's nearly dry with a piece of newspaper or rub a clean blackboard eraser over it.

8 Using a small brush attachment, vacuum the window frame and sills.

9 Dampen a cleaning cloth with diluted rubbing alcohol. Rub along the sill to remove spots and smudges.

10 For exterior windows, start by spraying with a garden hose to loosen or remove grime and debris; then follow the steps above. Second-story and higher windows are best handled by professional window cleaners.

What You'll Need

- Beach towel
- Commercial glass cleaner or vinegar
- Lint-free rags
- Ammonia
- Rubbing alcohol
- Professional-quality squeegee
- Cleaning cloths
- Old sheets or towels
- Newspaper or clean blackboard eraser
- Vacuum with small brush attachment
- Garden hose

Tip

Clean windows on a cloudy day, in the morning or in the late afternoon. Direct sunlight causes streaks.

353 Remove Grime From Miniblinds

Mini. Micro mini. Macro. Vertical. No matter which variation of blinds you have, all have one thing in common: They're magnets for dust, animal dander, kitchen grease and soot. Clean them at least once a year—more often if they're in the kitchen. It's an easy way to brighten up your home.

Steps

1 Tilt blind slats closed.

2 Rub a damp fabric-softener sheet across each slat to remove static and dust, and to leave a fresh scent on the blinds and in the room.

3 Slip inexpensive cotton gloves (or a clean old tube sock) on each hand. Dip one hand into warm, soapy water made from a few squirts of dishwashing liquid. Holding each slat between your thumb and fingers, run the soapy hand along the length of each slat, cleaning both sides as you go.

4 Dip and rinse your hand as needed.

5 Wipe the slats dry with your hand in a dry glove or sock.

6 For seriously dirty miniblinds, follow steps 6 through 10. First, take down the blinds and submerge them in a bathtub filled with warm, soapy water (use dishwashing liquid).

7 Let the blinds sit in the water in the bathtub overnight.

8 Scrub each slat with a plastic scrubber sponge to dislodge the grime.

9 Rinse or soak the blinds in plain water, then take them outside to air-dry on an old lint-free sheet or blanket.

10 Rehang the blinds when they're dry.

11 To keep your miniblinds clean longer, vacuum them weekly with a small brush attachment. Regularly sponge-clean your kitchen miniblinds to remove airborne cooking oils.

What You'll Need

- Fabric-softener sheets
- Cotton gloves or clean old tube socks
- Dishwashing liquid
- Plastic scrubber sponge
- Old lint-free sheet or blanket
- Vacuum with small brush attachment

Warning

Before you take down your blinds, make note of how they're hung.

354 Clean Oil Spots From a Garage or Driveway

A big oil spot in the middle of your driveway can make the most meticulously maintained home look dingy. Whether a leak from your car or someone else's created that mark on your concrete driveway, garage floor or sidewalk, it can all be lightened enough as to be barely visible.

Try the first suggestion, then work your way down the list as necessary. Whatever you do, don't procrastinate. Bare concrete floors are porous and permanently stain if oil, grease and dirt are not removed quickly. End each remedy by hosing down and air-drying the treated area.

Steps

1 Pour cola on the oily or dry stained areas, and leave the cola on overnight. Squirt a generous amount of dishwashing liquid into a bucket until you have a good lather. Rinse with the soapy water, then with a garden hose.

2 Sprinkle baking soda or an absorbent powder such as cornmeal or sawdust on the oily spots. If the stain is dry, wet it first to make a scouring paste. Scrub with a stiff brush or push broom.

3 Sprinkle automatic dishwasher detergent on the oily concrete. Leave it for several minutes, then pour boiling water on the stained area. Scrub with a stiff brush or push broom, then rinse.

4 Try a commercial concrete cleaner such as Garage and Driveway Cleaner by Red Devil Co. or a grease solvent such as Benzine. Follow the manufacturer's instructions.

5 Sprinkle trisodium phosphate (TSP) on the oily concrete. If the stain is dry, wet it first. Let it stand for 30 minutes. Scrub using a stiff broom. TSP is a dangerous product; if you must use it, wear rubber or latex gloves, safety goggles and protective clothing. Also, never wash a TSP product down storm drains.

6 As a last resort, combat tough spills with muriatic acid and a pressure washer. Apply the acid following the manufacturer's directions, and let it soak for several seconds. Follow with a pressure washer set at 2,500 to 3,000 lbs. per square inch (psi), or 176 to 211 kg per square cm. Like TSP, muriatic acid is a dangerous product; likewise, if you must use it, wear rubber or latex gloves, safety goggles and protective clothing, and never wash such a product down storm drains.

7 After trying any of the strategies above, sprinkle baking soda over the cleaned area to neutralize the solution you've used.

What You'll Need

- Cola
- Plastic bucket
- Dishwashing liquid
- Garden hose
- Baking soda, cornmeal or sawdust
- Stiff brush or push broom
- Automatic dishwasher detergent
- Commercial concrete cleaner or grease solvent
- TSP
- Rubber or latex gloves
- Safety goggles
- Muriatic acid (available at a hardware or janitorial supply store)
- Pressure washer (to rent one, look under "Pressure Washing Equipment" in the yellow pages)

Tips

Place cardboard under an oil drop or lawn mower to catch stains before they happen.

Seal concrete to prevent staining. See 158 Seal a Garage Floor.

Get that leaky car fixed!

Warning

Grease solvents are flammable, so make sure you have excellent ventilation and avoid spark and flame.

355 Remove Stains From Brick

Floors, walls and fireplaces made of brick are lovely to look at—until a grease, oil or soot stain spoils them, that is. Then this strong-looking, kiln-fired material can look old and just plain dirty. Bring brick's beauty back with these smart cleaning strategies.

Steps

Soot

1 Create a cleaner by mixing a 4-oz. (125-g) shaved bar of naphtha soap in 1 qt. (32 fl oz/1 l) hot water in a plastic bucket until the soap is dissolved. Cool, then thoroughly mix in ½ lb. (250 g) powdered pumice and ½ cup (4 fl oz/125 ml) ammonia. Apply the naphtha solution with a small brush or paintbrush. Leave it for 1 hour.

2 Rub off with a stiff-bristle brush.

3 Rinse thoroughly.

4 Sponge on a solution of a few squirts of dishwashing liquid in a bucket of warm water.

5 Rinse clean with warm water.

Grease or oil

1 Mix 2 tbsp. dishwashing liquid, a dash of table salt and enough water to make the solution smooth.

2 Rub the solution into the grimy brick surface using a cloth or rag. Let it stand for 10 minutes.

3 Scrub off the grime with a stiff-bristle brush.

4 Rinse clean with warm water.

Stubborn stains

1 Using a stiff-bristle brush, scrub the surface with a cleaning solution of ½ cup (4 fl oz/125 ml) trisodium phosphate (TSP) mixed in 1 gallon (4 l) hot water in a plastic bucket. TSP is a dangerous product; when you use it, wear rubber or latex gloves, safety goggles and protective clothing.

2 Rinse with warm water.

3 Repeat if needed, adding up to another ½ cup (4 fl oz/125 ml) TSP to the cleaning solution.

4 Rinse clean with warm water.

What You'll Need

- Plastic bucket
- Naphtha soap
- Powdered pumice
- Ammonia
- Small brush or paintbrush
- Stiff-bristle brush
- Dishwashing liquid
- Table salt
- Cloth or rag
- TSP
- Rubber or latex gloves
- Safety goggles

Tips

Always try the weaker solution first. If that doesn't cut through the grease, grime or soot, move up to a stronger solution.

Brick or stone is easier to clean if it's sealed with a finish containing tung oil.

A commercial brick cleaner may be used for cleaning.

For cleaning a brick fireplace, see 348 Remove Fireplace Grime.

Warning

Wear rubber gloves and safety goggles when using strong cleaners.

356 Wash an Outdoor Grill

After you remove food from a barbecue, cover the grill and allow it to stay heated for 15 to 20 minutes longer. This process will burn away a lot of the residual grease and grime between uses. A couple of times a year, though, you'll want to give the grill a thorough cleaning *before* you fire it up.

Steps

Charcoal grill

1 Use a stiff wire brush to scrape away any loose debris from the grill and grates, then remove the grill and grates.

2 Scoop out any ash at the bottom of the barbecue with a large spoon or cup.

3 Clean the inside and outside of the barbecue with baking soda (or another abrasive cleaner) and a little water using a metal scouring pad. If your barbecue has a painted, a nonstick or an aluminum surface, use dishwashing liquid, water and a plastic scrubber (not abrasive cleaners and metal scrubbers).

4 Place the grill and grates in a large plastic bag and cover them thoroughly with oven cleaner. Allow them to sit for several hours or overnight. If the grill and grates are aluminum, soak them in dishwashing liquid and water instead.

5 Remove the grill and grates from the plastic bag and place them atop several layers of newspaper.

6 Use a metal scouring pad or stiff brush to scrub them clean. If the grill or grates are aluminum or nonstick, use a plastic scrubber, not a metal one.

7 Hose off the grill and grates to remove any remnants of the oven cleaner. Use the hose to clean out the barbecue itself as well.

8 Allow everything to dry thoroughly, then replace the grill and grates.

9 Coat the grill with vegetable oil to prevent rusting and future buildup.

What You'll Need

Charcoal Grill:
- Stiff wire brush
- Large spoon or cup
- Baking soda or abrasive cleaner
- Metal scouring pad or plastic scrubber
- Dishwashing liquid
- Large plastic bag
- Oven cleaner
- Newspaper
- Garden hose
- Vegetable oil

Gas Grill:
- Paper clip or toothpick
- Dishwashing liquid
- Rag, sponge or plastic scrubber
- Brass wire brush
- Tape
- Garden hose
- Vegetable oil
- Linseed oil

Gas grill

1 Examine the flexible hose. If it is cracked or damaged, replace it with a new one.

2 Consult your owner's manual for basic maintenance tips (see also 245 Troubleshoot a Gas Grill). This will include checking the metal tubes under each burner. Spiders and other creepy crawlies like to nests in these tubes, which causes blockage and possibly even a fire. Use a paper clip or toothpick to clear these holes if necessary.

3 Remember that many gas grills are made of aluminum products, so you'll want to avoid abrasive cleaners, including oven cleaner, and metal brushes or scouring pads.

4 Soak the grill and any removable parts in dishwashing liquid and hot water. Scrub away buildup with a rag, sponge or plastic scrubber.

5 Remove the porcelain grills and flavorizer bars and run them through the dishwasher. Or scrub them with a brass wire brush.

6 Replace the lava rocks every year with new ones or boil them in soapy water to remove built-up grime.

7 Tape over any gas openings and then clean the inside of the barbecue with hot, soapy water and a rag, sponge or plastic scrubber.

8 Clean the outside of the barbecue with hot, soapy water and a rag or sponge.

9 Hose out the barbecue. Allow it to dry thoroughly before you replace all of the parts.

10 After everything is dry, rub the grill with vegetable oil and any wooden parts with linseed oil.

11 If you have a quick disconnect, make sure it is securely fastened before you use the grill.

Tips

Before you fire up the grill, spray it with nonstick cooking spray or wipe it with vegetable oil to make clean-up easier.

If a grill is still warm, not hot, rub a balled-up piece of aluminum foil against it to remove any debris, just like you would a stiff brush.

Some barbecue aficionados prefer to leave carbon buildup on the grill because they believe it adds flavor to barbecued meats and vegetables.

OOKED PICTURE • UNPLUG A STUCK AEROSOL CAN • GIVE BARBIE A MAKEOVER • DEAL WITH A STUCK WINE CORK • REPAIR A BOOK B
ORING • FIX BAD HABITS • REPAIR A BROKEN EYEGLASS FRAME • REPOSITION A SLIPPED CONTACT LENS • FIX A RUN IN STOCKINGS • JC
REAKOUT • REPAIR A TORN FINGERNAIL • FIX CHIPPED NAIL POLISH • FIX A STUCK ZIPPER • FIND A LOST CONTACT LENS • ELIMINATE BAD
Y THAT STICKS • STOP TELEMARKETERS AND JUNK MAIL • GET SUPERGLUE OFF YOUR SKIN • EXTRACT A SPLINTER • SOOTHE A SUNBURI
HANGOVER • STOP HICCUPS • MEND A BROKEN HEART • MEND A FAMILY FEUD • TREAT A SMALL CUT OR SCRAPE • FIX HAIR DISASTERS •
TTER SEATS • FIX A BILLING MISTAKE • FIX A BAD GRADE • FIX BAD CREDIT • RECOVER FROM JET LAG • RESUSCITATE AN UNCONSCIOUS
F PRONOUNS • FIX A RUN-ON SENTENCE • FIX MISUSE OF THE WORD GOOD • FIX YOUR DOG OR CAT • CORRECT BAD BEHAVIOR IN DOGS
SSING BUTTON • REMOVE LINT FROM CLOTHING • FIX A DRAWSTRING ON SWEATPANTS • REPAIR A HEM • REPAIR LEATHER GOODS • MEN
UNDER YOUR CASHMERE • FIX A SWEATER THAT HAS SHRUNK • FIX A SWEATER THAT HAS STRETCHED • FIX A HOLE IN A POCKET • FIX A
LLING FROM CLOTHING • FIX A FRAYED BUTTONHOLE • REMOVE DARK SCUFFS FROM SHOES • TREAT STAINS ON LEATHER • PROTECT SUE
JIET SQUEAKY HINGES • TROUBLESHOOT LOCK PROBLEMS • TIGHTEN A LOOSE DOORKNOB • TIGHTEN A LOOSE DOOR HINGE • FIX A BIN
EPLACE CRACKED TILE • TROUBLESHOOT MOLD ON INTERIOR WALLS • REPLACE CRACKED TILE GROUT IN A TUB OR SHOWER • FIX A DRA
INDS • TROUBLESHOOT WINDOW SHADE PROBLEMS • FIX BROKEN GLASS IN A WINDOW • REPAIR A WINDOW SCREEN • REPAIR ALUMINU
AMAGED PLASTER • REPAIR WALL COVERINGS • TOUCH UP PAINTED WALLS • TROUBLESHOOT INTERIOR-PAINT PROBLEMS • SOLVE A LEAD
ARDWOOD FLOOR • RESTORE A DULL, WORN WOOD FLOOR • TOUCH UP WOOD-FLOOR FINISHES • REPAIR DAMAGED SHEET-VINYL FLOOR
OUSE • CHILDPROOF YOUR HOME • PREVENT ICE DAMS • CURE A FAULTY FIREPLACE DRAW • START A FIRE IN A COLD CHIMNEY • FIX A W
AL A GARAGE FLOOR • REFINISH A GARAGE OR BASEMENT FLOOR • CONTROL ROOF LEAKS • REDIRECT RAINWATER FROM A DOWNSPOL
AMAGED ASPHALT SHINGLE • PATCH A FLAT OR LOW-PITCHED ROOF • REPAIR ROOF FLASHING • TROUBLESHOOT EXTERIOR-PAINT PROBL
OW WATER PRESSURE • FIX LEAKING PIPES • STOP A TOILET FROM RUNNING • FIX A LEAKY TOILET TANK • FIX A STOPPED-UP TOILET • STO
LOGGED SINK OR TUB • REPAIR A TUB-AND-SHOWER VALVE • REPAIR CHIPPED FIXTURES • QUIET NOISY PIPES • DEFROST YOUR PIPES • D
ONSUMPTION • REPLACE A RECEPTACLE • FIX AN ELECTRICAL PLUG • REPLACE A LIGHT FIXTURE • INSTALL A NEW DIMMER • FIX A LAMP •
OORBELL • FIX A WOBBLY OVERHEAD FAN • ADJUST WATER-HEATER TEMPERATURE • RELIGHT A WATER-HEATER PILOT LIGHT • TROUBLESI
E MAKER • GET RID OF MICROWAVE SMELLS • FIX A REFRIGERATOR THAT COOLS POORLY • FIX A GAS OVEN THAT HEATS POORLY • CLEAN
SHWASHER PROBLEMS • CORRECT AN OVERFLOWING DISHWASHER • FIX A LEAKY DISHWASHER • FIX A DISHWASHER THAT FILLS SLOWLY
WASHING MACHINE THAT FILLS SLOWLY • FIX A WASHING MACHINE THAT "WALKS" ACROSS THE FLOOR • FIX A CLOTHES DRYER THAT DRI
K YOUR VACUUM CLEANER • REPLACE VACUUM CLEANER BRUSHES • TROUBLESHOOT A PORTABLE AIR CONDITIONER • FIX A WINDOW AI
ROCESSOR • FIX A TOASTER • DIAGNOSE MICROWAVE OVEN PROBLEMS • TROUBLESHOOT A GAS GRILL • FIX A TRASH COMPACTOR • REF
ART • TROUBLESHOOT A CRASHING COMPUTER • CLEAN UP LAPTOP SPILLS • FIX BAD SECTORS ON A HARD DISK • QUIT A FROZEN PC AI
FECTED COMPUTER • IMPROVE YOUR COMPUTER'S MEMORY • GET RID OF E-MAIL SPAM • CHANGE A LASER PRINTER CARTRIDGE • FIX A
GURE OUT WHY A PRINTER WON'T PRINT • FIX SPELLING AND GRAMMAR ERRORS • RECALL AN E-MAIL IN MICROSOFT OUTLOOK • DIAGNO
LES • TROUBLESHOOT A PALM OS PDA • RESET A PALM OS PDA • REMOVE FINGERPRINTS FROM A CAMERA LENS • TROUBLESHOOT A CD-
ALVAGE A VIDEOCASSETTE • TROUBLESHOOT A DVD PLAYER • STRENGTHEN FM RADIO RECEPTION • STRENGTHEN AM RADIO RECEPTION
JAMMED SLIDE PROJECTOR • GET BETTER SPEAKER SOUND • TROUBLESHOOT A DIGITAL CAMCORDER • TROUBLESHOOT A DIGITAL CAM
GHTBULB • FIX A BROKEN WINEGLASS STEM • FIX BLEMISHED WOOD FURNITURE • REPAIR GOUGES IN FURNITURE • RESTORE FURNITURE
AMOUFLAGE A DOG-SCRATCHED DOOR • REPAIR A SPLIT CARPET SEAM • RID CARPETS OF PET ODORS • REINFORCE A SAGGING SHELF •
OINTS OF CHAIRS AND TABLES • REUPHOLSTER A DROP-IN CHAIR SEAT • REVIVE A CANE SEAT • REINFORCE A WEAK BED FRAME • FIX UP
OTTERY • REPAIR CHIPPED OR CRACKED CHINA • UNCLUTTER YOUR HOME • CLEAN CRAYON FROM A WALL • GET WAX OFF A TABLECLOT
AINS • REMOVE CHEWING GUM FROM CARPETING • REMOVE BLEACH SPOTS FROM CARPETING • REMOVE PET STAINS • ELIMINATE WINE
AINS FROM TILE GROUT • REMOVE MILDEW FROM WALLS AND CEILINGS • DISINFECT A TOILET BOWL • REMOVE FIREPLACE GRIME • GET
LEAN OIL SPOTS FROM A GARAGE OR DRIVEWAY • REMOVE STAINS FROM BRICK • WASH AN OUTDOOR GRILL • FIX A FALLEN SOUFFLÉ • R
ESCUE OVERPROOFED YEAST DOUGH • FIX YOUR KID LUNCH • GET RID OF TAP-WATER MINERAL DEPOSITS • CALIBRATE A MEAT THERMOM
AUCE • RESCUE A BROKEN SAUCE • REMOVE FAT FROM SOUPS AND SAUCES • FIX LUMPY GRAVY • SUBSTITUTE MISSING INGREDIENTS • F
JRNED RICE • REMOVE COOKING ODORS • FINISH UNDERCOOKED MEAT • SALVAGE AN UNDERCOOKED TURKEY • FIX AN OVERSEASONED
ALE BREAD • SMOOTH SEIZED CHOCOLATE • SOFTEN HARDENED SUGARS OR COOKIES • FIX BREAKFAST FOR YOUR SWEETHEART • MEN
GGING TOOLS • RESTORE A BROKEN FLOWERPOT • SHARPEN PRUNING CLIPPERS • REMOVE RUST FROM TOOLS • REVIVE WILTING CUT FI
ET RID OF RAMPANT BRAMBLES • TROUBLESHOOT BROWN SPOTS ON A LAWN • CONTROL MAJOR GARDEN PESTS • RID YOUR GARDEN O
ONPERFORMING COMPOST PILE • FIX BAD SOIL • SHORE UP A RAISED GARDEN BED • REMOVE A DEAD OR DISEASED TREE LIMB • TROUB
RAINAGE • TROUBLESHOOT ROSE DISEASES • IDENTIFY AND CORRECT SOIL DEFICIENCIES IN ROSES • TROUBLESHOOT ROSE PESTS • OV
AMAGED DECK BOARDS • REPAIR DECK RAILINGS • STRENGTHEN DECK JOISTS • FIX A RUSTY IRON RAILING • REPAIR A GATE • REPAIR A
RACKED OR DAMAGED CONCRETE • IMPROVE THE LOOK OF REPAIRED CONCRETE • REPAIR AN ASPHALT DRIVEWAY • REVIVE WOODEN OU
ARDEN PONDS • CLEAN SWIMMING POOL WATER • TROUBLESHOOT HOT TUBS AND SPAS • REPLACE BRICKS IN WALKWAYS AND PATIOS •
AR WITH JUMPER CABLES • SHUT OFF A CAR ALARM THAT WON'T QUIT • FREE A CAR STUCK ON ICE OR SNOW • DE-ICE YOUR WINDSHIEL
JRN-SIGNAL COVER • FIX A CAR FUSE • FIX DASHBOARD LIGHTS THAT WON'T LIGHT • REMOVE CAR SMELLS • CHECK TIRE PRESSURE • IN
PROPERLY INSTALLED CHILD CAR SEAT • TROUBLESHOOT LEAKING OIL • CHECK AND ADD POWER-STEERING FLUID • CHECK AND ADD C
ROKEN EXHAUST PIPE • CHECK AND ADD ENGINE OIL • CHECK AND ADD BRAKE FLUID • CHECK AND ADD FLUID TO YOUR AUTOMATIC TR
ROUBLESHOOT A WINDSHIELD WASHER PUMP • REPAIR MINOR DENTS • CHANGE A HUBCAP • FIX AN IGNITION KEY THAT WON'T TURN •

Cooking

357 Fix a Fallen Soufflé

One cook's fallen soufflé is another chef's Decadent Delight. Although there's no way to pump the air back in, a deflated soufflé tastes just as delicious. Its denser texture mimics a rich cake or quiche perfectly.

Steps

1 Dust a sweet soufflé with confectioners' sugar or cocoa powder. Serve with the sauce from the recipe or top it with a big scoop of ice cream.

2 To create a more deeply disguised dessert, top the soufflé with whipped cream, fresh fruit or sliced almonds.

3 To rescue a savory soufflé, sprinkle with grated cheese and broil until it's melted and golden. Call it a frittata or a crustless quiche.

4 Make a sandwich: Cut the savory soufflé into thick slices. Spread focaccia or soft rolls with prepared pesto or tapenade. Layer the soufflé between the bread with tomato slices, lettuce or roasted red peppers.

What You'll Need

- Confectioners' sugar or cocoa powder
- Dessert sauce or ice cream
- Whipped cream, fresh fruit or sliced almonds
- Grated cheese
- Focaccia or soft rolls
- Pesto or tapenade
- Tomato slices, lettuce or roasted red peppers

358 Rescue a Crumbled Cake

Don't let a minor disaster spoil the party. Whether you flipped a cake layer out of its pan or knocked your frosted masterpiece to the floor, here are a few ways to salvage your dessert.

Steps

1 If a baked layer broke cleanly, use extra frosting to glue the pieces together. Place a cardboard round covered completely with foil or plastic wrap under the layers for support while you reassemble them.

2 Tear some soft bread and use the pieces to fill large gaps. Patch smaller holes and dents with frosting. Continue decorating as planned.

3 If the cake cracks or breaks after it's frosted, ease the pieces together by pressing the sides in with a flat spatula. Smooth frosting over the cake.

4 Use fresh fruit, edible flowers or decorative frosting flourishes to hide imperfections.

5 For a cake that falls apart completely, make a classic trifle: In a pretty glass serving bowl, create layers of crumbled, liqueur-soaked cake, whipped cream, and berries or shaved chocolate. Refrigerate until serving time.

What You'll Need

- Frosting
- Cardboard round
- Foil or plastic wrap
- Soft bread
- Flat spatula
- Fresh fruit
- Fresh edible flowers
- Glass serving bowl
- Liqueur
- Whipped cream
- Berries or shaved chocolate

Tip

Always make extra frosting. It's easy to scale up, and you never know when you'll need a little more for fancy swirls or last-minute touch-ups.

359 Fix a Perfect Cup of Tea

Drinking tea is as much a ritual of contemplation and conversation as it is a delicious way to warm the body and refresh the mind. Tea aficionados are passionate about the details: What kind of clay went into the teapot, what time of year were the tea leaves picked, what exact temperature is the water? Others simply enjoy a reassuring pot when an old friend stops by. Whatever your preference, try these ideas to bring out the best flavors in your tea.

Steps

1 Start with cold water, which retains more oxygen for fuller flavor. If your tap water is hard, use filtered or bottled water.

2 Preheat your teapot: While the water is heating, fill your teapot with hot tap water, let it warm, then drain it completely.

3 Measure into the teapot 1 tsp. of loose tea for every cup you plan to pour. Some tea drinkers, especially those who take milk with their tea, add an extra spoon for the pot. If you're using a mesh tea ball, don't fill it more than halfway, to allow for complete expansion of the tea leaves.

4 For black teas, bring the water to a full boil. Remove the teakettle from the heat as soon as the water begins to boil. Boiling all the oxygen out of the water will flatten the tea's flavor.

5 For more delicate green teas, remove the teakettle from the heat before the water begins boiling, at 165° to 170°F (74° to 77°C). Or you can add 1 part cold water to 4 parts boiling water to cool it to the ideal temperature range.

6 Before steeping, pour a small amount of the hot water over the tea leaves, to allow them to bloom, or open up, and release some of their bitter tannins. Drain immediately.

7 Fill the pot with the boiling water. Keep the spout of the kettle close to the teapot, so the water does not cool as you pour it in. Cover the teapot and leave the tea to brew. In general, black teas are best brewed for 4 to 5 minutes; green teas should brew for no more than 3 minutes.

8 When the tea is ready, pour and serve all the tea. Avoid keeping leaves in contact with the hot water: Overbrewed tea tends to taste bitter.

9 To keep the tea warm through several cups, transfer the tea to an insulated pot or cover your regular teapot with a tea cozy. Don't apply additional heat to keep the tea warm, as this will quickly degrade its flavor.

10 A good-quality tea can be infused three to five times. Just add more boiling water. Let it steep for less time with each brew.

What You'll Need

- Teapot
- Loose tea
- Teaspoon or mesh tea ball
- Teakettle
- Insulated pot or tea cozy

Tips

Select a pot with a brew basket for quick and easy removal of tea leaves.

Since the leaves in tea bags tend to be cut into smaller pieces and thus infuse more quickly, brew tea bags for only 30 seconds to 1 minute.

These steps can be followed for perfect individual cups of tea as well. Use a cup with its own brew basket, high-quality tea bags or, for loose teas, a mesh tea ball.

Store teas in an airtight container away from heat, moisture and light. Tea leaves will keep for up to three months.

360 Patch a Torn Pie Crust

If you're daunted by the idea of rolling out pie dough, take heart in knowing that any tears or holes that appear are easily fixed. And remember, all those irregularities make a home-baked pie the rustic, comforting treat everyone loves.

Steps

1 Check for tears and holes before and after putting the crust in the pie pan.

2 For tears, overlap the edges and press them together.

3 For holes, patch with a piece of surplus dough from another area. Use cold water as glue, if needed. Continue rolling.

4 To fix the crust after it's in the pie pan, use egg wash (one egg beaten with 1 tbsp. water) and press the dough together firmly.

5 If there's a large hole in the bottom crust and you've run out of dough, use a slice of white bread. Pat the bread flat with your palm, tear out a patch without crust, and spread the bread patch with butter on both sides. Patch the hole using egg wash. This will prevent the filling from leaking between the crust and the pan.

What You'll Need

- Egg
- Slice of white bread
- Butter

Tip

Roll out pie dough between two layers of wax paper or plastic wrap. Keep one layer on while transferring the crust to the pie pan.

361 Keep a Pie Crust From Getting Soggy

A moist filling can ruin the most beautiful pastry crust. Fortunately, there are some secrets to preventing soggy messes. Try one or several of these solutions for a crispier, flakier pie.

Steps

1 Brush the bottom and sides of the unbaked crust with melted jelly before filling it.

2 Sprinkle bread, cookie crumbs or cake crumbs on the bottom crust before filling the pie with fruit. The crumbs will soak up some of the juices during baking.

3 Brush the pie crust with beaten egg white. Bake for a few minutes or, if you have a prebaked pie shell, cook completely. The shiny "lacquer" will help the bottom crust resist moisture from the filling.

4 Coat the inside of an already baked crust with a thin layer of melted chocolate. Let the chocolate harden completely before pouring in the fruit or cream filling. Use white chocolate if you'd like a pale color.

5 Cut vent holes in the top crust to let steam escape during baking.

What You'll Need

- Melted jelly
- Bread, cookie crumbs or cake crumbs
- Egg white
- Melted chocolate

Tip

Use a Pyrex or ceramic pie plate, and place the oven rack in the lower third of your oven.

362 Fix Dough That Won't Rise

Cool air or old yeast will keep your bread dough from rising properly. If a bit of heat doesn't revive the yeast, you can mix a little more yeast into the dough.

Steps

1 Create a warmer place for the dough: Fill a large pan with boiling water and place it in the oven on the lowest rack, or heat a mug of water for 2 minutes in a microwave.

2 Place the dough (in its bowl) in the oven or microwave along with the hot water. Leave it to rise.

3 If the dough still doesn't rise, add more yeast. Mix yeast from a new package with ¼ cup (2 fl oz/60 ml) warm water and ½ tsp. sugar. Let it sit for 10 minutes until foam forms, to be sure the yeast is active.

4 Knead the yeast mixture into the dough.

5 Leave the dough in a warm place to rise.

What You'll Need

- Live yeast
- Sugar

Tip

If you have no more yeast, turn the dough into tasty crackers or breadsticks: Knead with grated cheese, roll thin, sprinkle with salt and black pepper, cut into squares or thin strips, then bake at 325°F (165°C) for 10 minutes or until golden brown.

363 Rescue Overproofed Yeast Dough

Warm weather, high altitudes or absent-mindedness can lead to over-proofed dough, with overworked yeast stretching the flour's structure to an unstable puffiness. If you've caught the dough in time, the yeast may still have some life left for a remedial rising.

Steps

1 If this is the first rise, punch down the dough and let it rise again.

2 Continue with the shaping, second rise and baking as usual.

3 If the dough has overproofed after being shaped, then punch it down, reknead and reshape.

4 Before baking, let the dough rise again for a shorter amount of time than the recipe specifies. The dough will not rise as high this time, and the final texture will be affected: The crumbs will be finer, and the bread will be denser but should taste fine.

Tips

Don't bake bread that has overproofed after being shaped; its weakened structure will collapse in the oven.

Follow your own recipe for rising times; they vary widely depending on the type of bread or cake.

364 Fix Your Kid Lunch

Making sure that children eat healthful meals can be one of the biggest challenges for parents. But if you're creative, flexible and organized, you can make lunches that your child will enjoy eating.

Steps

Thinking ahead

1 Involve your child in the shopping and preparation. Choosing containers, selecting bread and helping to pack the lunch all encourage a child to feel invested in the process.

2 Prepare as much as possible the night before. Freeze juice boxes, refrigerate sandwiches, cut vegetables or portion out pasta. This will also allow your child to help out more easily.

3 Prepare ingredients in bulk. Keep enough cut fruit for several days and put in plastic containers. Slice meats and cheeses for the week, and place a week's worth of individual portions between pieces of wax paper.

Making lunch fun

1 Vary ingredients. Instead of just regular bread slices, make sandwiches with shaped rolls, pita bread, English muffins, raisin bread, crackers or bagels.

2 Incorporate unusual shapes or colors. Make wheel-shaped pasta or green noodles. Cut turkey and ham slices with cookie cutters.

3 Make the meal hands-on or interesting to eat. Include a little container of dip for vegetables, or crunchy stir-ins for yogurt.

4 Include funny cartoons, silly photos, riddles or stickers. Write supportive notes reminding your child that he will do fine on the spelling test or that you'll be cheering her on at the basketball game. Collect fun inserts and write notes in advance, then tuck them away. Keep in mind, though, that older children are easily embarrassed among their peers.

5 Alternate lunch containers or decorate a batch of paper bags in advance as a weekend art project.

Taking precautions

1 Wash fruits and vegetables before packing them.

2 Use an insulated container for hot foods. Preheat it with boiling water, fill with piping-hot food and tell your child not to open it until lunchtime.

3 Invest in reusable insulated lunch bags. Keep two or three gel packs in the freezer, so you'll always have one ready. Refrigerate foods overnight.

What You'll Need

- Interesting, healthy ingredients
- Plastic food containers
- Wax paper
- Various eating utensils
- Lunchbox or paper bags
- Insulated container
- Reusable insulated lunch bags
- Cooler gel packs
- Fun inserts

Tips

To slip vegetables into your child's diet, steam and purée them until smooth. Freeze them in an ice cube tray, then stir the cubes into pasta sauces, soups or even mac and cheese (sweet potatoes disappear in the cheese sauce).

Children need at least two servings each of fruit, milk and protein every day. They also need three servings of vegetables and six servings of cereal or grains daily. Here's what constitutes one serving in each food group, respectively: one small apple, 1 cup (8 fl oz/250 ml) of milk, 2 oz. (55 g) cooked lean meat, ½ cup (2 oz/55 g) of raw or cooked carrots, one slice of bread.

365 Get Rid of Tap-Water Mineral Deposits

If the water coming out of your tap contains too much calcium or magnesium, you'll find white deposits, known as lime scales, on your kitchen appliances and fixtures. A common kitchen ingredient is just as effective as a special cleanser—without the harsh chemicals.

Steps

1 Combine 1 part distilled vinegar and 1 part water.

2 Run a pot of the mixture through your coffeemaker to flush out lime deposits, pouring and heating it as if you were making coffee. Follow with plain water.

3 Fill your teakettle with the diluted vinegar and simmer for 10 minutes. Leave for 1 hour and then rinse well.

4 To remove the foggy, white film on drinking glasses, soak them for 10 to 15 minutes in the vinegar mixture.

5 To clean faucets, soak a paper towel with undiluted vinegar. Wrap the faucet well and leave it for 1 hour, moistening the towel with more vinegar if needed. Remove the towel and wipe the faucet clean. Scrub hard deposits with an old toothbrush.

6 If you have laminate or wood surfaces in your kitchen, you can clean them with the vinegar-water solution. Be careful—marble, slate and granite can be damaged by stray drops of an acidic solution.

What You'll Need

- Distilled vinegar
- Paper towel
- Old toothbrush

Tip

Use a rinsing agent in your dishwasher to extend its life and prevent lime buildup.

366 Calibrate a Meat Thermometer

The usual hard knocks of kitchen work can make an analog instant-read thermometer inaccurate over time. Make sure your trusty thermometer is showing you the right temperature.

Steps

1 Bring a small pot of water to a boil.

2 Fill a short glass with water and plenty of ice.

3 Remove the thermometer from its plastic guard and place it in the boiling water.

4 If it doesn't read 212°F (100°C), turn the nut behind the face with needle-nose pliers. Only tiny adjustments are required; recheck as needed.

5 Place the thermometer in the ice water.

6 If it doesn't read 32°F (0°C), adjust the nut. Once it is properly calibrated, the thermometer will read the correct temperatures of both boiling and iced water.

What You'll Need

- Small pot
- Short glass
- Ice
- Needle-nose pliers

Tip

Avoid dropping or hitting your thermometer against hard surfaces.

367 Fix a Dull Knife

Your expensive chef's knife isn't worth much with a dull blade. Sharpening a knife yourself will create a better edge.

Steps

Sharpening your knife

1 Place a medium-grit flat sharpening stone on a table. Lay a damp rag beneath the stone to prevent it from slipping. Position the stone either parallel or perpendicular to the table's edge.

2 If your stone is natural, apply a thin layer of mineral oil to it. If your stone is diamond-coated, sprinkle water on it.

3 Hold the blade at a 20-degree angle to the stone's surface. Place the heel (the part closest to the handle) at one end of the stone. Apply pressure on the top of the blade with the fingers of your other hand. Draw the blade slowly over the stone's surface, sweeping in an arc and pulling the blade entirely from heel to tip through one stroke (see illustrations). Press evenly on the blade throughout the stroke. Press more heavily for a duller knife.

4 Repeat five or six times on each side of the blade. Sweep in one direction only. Alternate sides and flip the blade after each stroke. If needed, wipe the stone clean and apply new oil or water.

5 Repeat steps 1 through 4 with a fine-grit flat stone.

Steeling your knife

1 Use a standard honing steel—a metal rod coated with fine grit and magnetized—to finish the blade's edge and smooth out irregularities. Hold the steel vertically, with its tip pointing straight down and resting on a table's surface. Keep your thumb behind the handle guard.

2 Hold the knife at a 20-degree angle against the steel. Make light, even strokes along the blade's entire length. Alternate sides of the blade for an even edge, stroking five or six times on each side.

What You'll Need

- Medium-grit flat sharpening stone
- Clean rags
- Mineral oil
- Fine-grit flat sharpening stone
- Standard honing steel

Tips

Depending on how much you use it, a knife requires sharpening only once or twice a year. Steel it frequently to maintain its sharp edge.

Stainless-steel knives are too hard to be sharpened, while serrated knives require professional equipment.

368 Remove Rust From a Cast-Iron Pan

Whether you'd like to restore your family's favorite skillet or fix up a garage sale find, removing surface rust from a durable, dependable cast-iron pan is a breeze. As long as the rust isn't too serious—no deeper than ⅛ inch (3 mm)—you should be able to return the pan to cooking shape. After removing all the rust, be sure to season the pan before using or storing it.

Steps

Removing rust

1 Depending on the pan's size, pour 2 to 4 tbsp. salt into the middle of the pan. Add an equal amount of vegetable oil.

2 Scrub the pan vigorously with a folded paper towel, concentrating on the rusted spots but covering all surfaces with the oil and salt mixture. Add more salt or oil as needed.

3 For more serious rust spots, scrub with fine steel wool.

4 Wash the pan with dishwashing liquid and rinse well with hot water. Dry completely.

Seasoning the pan

1 A well-seasoned cast-iron pan will resist rust and create a virtually nonstick surface for cooking. To season it, brush vegetable oil lightly over all its surfaces.

2 Heat the pan in an oven at 250°F (120°C) for 1 hour, recoating it with more oil after 30 minutes.

3 Wipe the pan well with paper towels, and let it cool completely before using it.

4 To preserve this natural, protective coating, do not use soap when cleaning a seasoned pan. Instead, scrub it with salt and oil, rinse it with hot water, then dry it completely over low heat before storing it.

What You'll Need

- Salt
- Vegetable oil
- Paper towels
- Fine steel wool
- Dishwashing liquid

Tips

For quick removal of rust spots, use a hand drill with a wire brush attachment. Take care not to scrape away too much metal; hollows in the pan will lead to uneven cooking and food scorching.

Spun-steel and carbon-steel woks benefit from the same care as cast-iron pans.

369 Repair Laminate Countertops

With time, your countertops will show the effects of water, heat, and daily wear and tear. Minor damage to laminate is inexpensive to fix. For more serious damage, it's best to replace the countertops entirely.

Steps

For peeling laminate

1 For small areas of bubbling, reactivate the adhesive by heating the laminate. Use a hair dryer or an iron on low heat, taking care not to scorch the surface. Weigh down the repair area with heavy books or cans (see illustrations).

2 For large areas of peeling, use a small knife to scrape away old adhesive from the support surface and the back of the laminate.

3 Heat the edging gently, if needed, and press it back into shape.

4 Spread contact cement on both the support surface and the underside of the laminate. Use toothpicks or wood strips to prop up the laminate until the adhesive is almost dry.

5 Press the laminate down firmly, easing out air pockets with a rolling pin. Weight the surface evenly with heavy objects. Use masking tape to hold the edging in place.

6 Let the countertop dry for 24 hours.

For chipped laminate

1 For minor gouges and chips, buy laminate repair paste to match the color of your counter. If needed, blend several colors.

2 Clean the damaged area with rubbing alcohol.

3 Fill the chips with the laminate paste. Smooth it flat with a putty knife. Let it dry completely, leaving it undisturbed for 24 hours.

For stained or scratched laminate

1 Remove stains with distilled vinegar, rubbing alcohol or bleach. For minor scratches, polish the counter with lemon oil or car wax.

What You'll Need

- Hair dryer or iron
- Heavy books or cans
- Small knife
- Contact cement
- Toothpicks or wood strips
- Masking tape
- Rolling pin
- Masking tape
- Laminate repair paste
- Rubbing alcohol
- Putty knife
- Distilled vinegar or bleach
- Lemon oil or car wax

Tips

Replace large areas of damage with tile or a cutting board: With a router, carefully cut away the damaged area. Lay down decorative tiles or butcher block, being sure to seal the edges well.

You can buy contact cement at hardware stores.

Laminate repair paste is sold at hardware stores and countertop suppliers.

370 **Remove Stains From a Stone Countertop**

Hard as they are, granite and marble are porous stones that can easily soak up oils and liquids. Spills that aren't quickly cleaned leave unsightly stains on an otherwise beautiful surface. Applying a simple poultice—a cloth dampened with an absorbing compound—will lift a stain without damaging the stone.

Steps

1 To create a poultice, fold or stack plain white paper towels to make a thick pad of eight layers. It should be slightly wider than the stain.

2 Wear rubber gloves and make sure there's good ventilation in the kitchen.

3 To remove oil-based stains such as those from salad dressing, cream, peanut butter or hand lotion, first clean the area well with ammonia and a clean rag. Soak the paper-towel pad thoroughly with acetone. Oil stains are usually rounded in shape, have darker centers and penetrate more deeply.

4 To remove organic stains such as those from wine, ink, tobacco, coffee, paper or flowers, soak the paper-towel pad with hydrogen peroxide. These stains tend to be irregularly shaped, often following the form of the object causing the discoloring.

5 Cover the stain with the soaked pad. Tap out bubbles and press firmly to ensure full contact with the stone's surface.

6 Cover the pad with a piece of plastic wrap and tape its edges to the counter with masking tape.

7 Leave the treated surface undisturbed for 2 to 48 hours, depending on the age and depth of the stain.

8 Remove the plastic wrap carefully and leave the paper towel until it dries completely.

9 Discard the paper-towel pad. Wipe down the area with a clean, damp rag.

10 Repeat with a newly soaked pad if needed. The stain may require three to four applications to lift completely.

11 If the stain resists several applications of the poultice, contact a local business that specializes in fabricating or cleaning stone countertops to get advice on the type of stone in your counter.

What You'll Need

- Plain white paper towels
- Rubber gloves
- Ammonia
- Clean rags
- Acetone
- Hydrogen peroxide, professional strength
- Plastic wrap
- Masking tape

Tips

You can purchase acetone at hardware stores.

Obtain clear, professional-strength hydrogen peroxide (20 to 30 percent volume) from a beauty supply store. The form available at drugstores (3.5 percent) isn't strong enough.

Clean up any spills immediately. Acidic foods, such as fruit juices, will etch the stone's surface and require repolishing.

If you're in doubt about the material in your countertops, test your cleaning solution on an extra piece or in an inconspicuous area.

371 Fix a Sauce

A sauce with the right body and texture clings lightly to food. Too thin and it spreads across the whole plate. Too thick and it forms unsightly clumps. A classic test for a sauce is to see if it coats the back of a spoon smoothly and evenly. If the texture is less than perfect, here are some ways to fine-tune your sauce or gravy.

PROBLEM	SOLUTION	HOW TO DO IT
Sauce is too thin	Reduction	Simmer 10 to 30 minutes to thicken by evaporation. Not recommended for strongly flavored sauces, as they will become more concentrated.
	Cornstarch	For every cup (8 fl oz/250 ml) of sauce, dissolve 1 tbsp. cornstarch in ¼ cup (2 fl oz/60 ml) cold water; stir into sauce. Simmer 5 minutes. Do not continue cooking, as extended heat will break down starches.
	Beurre manié	With fingertips or fork, work together equal amounts of softened butter and all-purpose flour until smooth. Whisk small pieces gradually into sauce and simmer 5 minutes.
	Liaison	Beat together two egg yolks and ¼ cup (2 fl oz/60 ml) heavy cream in small bowl. Slowly mix in small amount of sauce's hot liquid. While stirring sauce off the stove, drizzle in egg yolk mixture. Warm the sauce over gentle heat. Do not simmer again or eggs will curdle.
	Tomato purée	Stir prepared tomato purée into sauce, 1 tbsp. at a time.
	Vegetable purée	Cook vegetables such as carrots, spinach, squash, potatoes, onions or garlic until soft. Purée in blender. Strain, if desired, and stir into sauces.
	Instant potato flakes	Stir in 1 tbsp. flakes for every cup (8 fl oz/250 ml) of sauce. Add more flakes as needed. Simmer 5 minutes.
	Rice	Simmer the sauce with a few spoonfuls of cooked rice for 10 minutes. Purée in blender until smooth.
	Nuts	Add nut butter or very finely ground nuts to desired consistency.
	Crumbs	Stir in 1 tbsp. dry or 2 tbsp. fresh bread crumbs. Simmer 10 minutes.
	Yogurt	Off the heat, whisk in a small amount of yogurt. Warm the sauce gently and serve it as soon as possible.

PROBLEM	SOLUTION	HOW TO DO IT
Sauce is too thick	Stock	Stir in stock or water gradually to desired consistency. Return to a simmer.
	Wine	Add white wine to light-colored sauces and red wine to dark sauces. Simmer 5 to 10 minutes to bring flavors together. Fortified wines like brandy or sherry add extra depth. To evaporate alcohol or to concentrate flavors, reduce the wine in a separate pan before adding.
	Cider	Sauces for pork or game benefit from the fruity quality of cider. Use like wine (see above).
	Cream	Stir in light or heavy cream or substitute milk. Warm gently over low heat. The color of the sauce will lighten. Acidic ingredients in the sauce, such as vinegar or lemon juice, can lead to curdling. If heated too long, cream sauces can break down (see 372 Rescue a Broken Sauce).
	Fruit juice	Brighten flavors while thinning the sauce. Acidic fruit juices, such as citric or pineapple, can cause cream- or egg-based sauces to curdle.
Sauce is lumpy or curdled	Strainer	Pour sauce through fine-mesh strainer or cheesecloth into another pan. Do not press lumps through. Warm gently.
	Blender	Transfer sauce to blender or food processor, taking care with hot liquids. Purée until smooth. Add a little more liquid if needed. Strain and warm gently.
	Disguise	Stir in chopped garnishes such as olives, lemon zest, pine nuts, sautéed mushrooms, capers, tomatoes, raisins or tiny pieces of carrots and celery. Sprinkle with fresh herbs.

372 Rescue a Broken Sauce

A sauce based on eggs can be temperamental, breaking down from a thick, creamy mixture to a thin liquid with grainy curds in the blink of an eye. Mayonnaise and hollandaise are both emulsions of egg yolks, but when they separate—unlike Humpty Dumpty—you *can* put them back together again.

Steps

Saving a cold emulsion

1 Stop adding oil as soon as you see the mixture loosen and turn grainy. Adding oil too quickly to an egg yolk or forcing more oil than it can hold will break an emulsion such as mayonnaise.

2 In a separate bowl, whisk together a fresh egg yolk and 1 tbsp. lemon juice.

3 While whisking constantly, drizzle the broken mixture very slowly into the new yolk. If you're using a blender, transfer the mixture back into the blender jar.

4 Continue whisking or blending in more oil slowly until you obtain the desired consistency. Unrefined oils such as extra-virgin olive oil tend to separate easily, so use pure olive oil or another refined oil to make a more stable mixture.

Saving a warm emulsion

1 Prepare warm egg-based mixtures like hollandaise or béarnaise sauce in a double boiler over hot (barely simmering but not boiling) water to help prevent breaking and curdling. Whisk in melted butter slowly. Take care not to add more than the yolks can hold.

2 A thin line of oiliness around the edge of the sauce is an early warning that the sauce may separate. At this point, you can try saving it before it actually breaks. Immediately remove it from the heat. Slowly whisk in 1 tbsp. cold water or cream.

3 Once the sauce breaks completely, you'll need to add a fresh egg yolk to rebind the liquids. In another bowl, whisk together 1 egg yolk and 1 tbsp. cold water or cream.

4 While whisking constantly, very slowly drizzle the broken, still-warm sauce into the new egg mixture.

5 Return the sauce to the double boiler. Whisk constantly until it thickens to the desired consistency.

Tips

When making mayonnaise, use whole eggs or whisk in 2 tbsp. lemon juice or water with each cup (8 fl oz/250 ml) of oil to ensure the emulsion has enough liquid to suspend the oil.

Using a blender instead of whisking by hand will create a more stable mayonnaise, as the motorized blades force the oil into finer droplets.

373 Remove Fat From Soups and Sauces

For a healthier meal, remove as much fat as you can during cooking and before serving. Try these techniques.

Steps

1 During cooking, place the pot slightly to one side of the burner. The off-centered bubbling will encourage fat to accumulate on one side of the pot for easier removal.

2 With a large spoon, skim fat off soups and sauces as they simmer.

3 To remove the last spots of fat floating on the surface, drag a clean paper towel across the top. It will soak up most of the remaining oil.

4 When refrigerated, fat rises through liquids and solidifies in a layer at the top. For foods that have been refrigerated, remove virtually all of the fat by breaking it up into large pieces and lifting it away with a spoon.

What You'll Need

- Large spoon
- Paper towels

374 Fix Lumpy Gravy

No matter how many times you make pan gravy, lumps have a way of appearing—usually when you least want them. Don't throw the gravy out. Instead, try one of these quick fixes. You can still put Thanksgiving dinner on the table in time.

Steps

1 Break up larger lumps by whisking the gravy vigorously in a figure-eight motion.

2 Pour the gravy through a mesh strainer. Avoid pressing flour lumps through the mesh.

3 For small, stubborn lumps, purée the gravy in a blender or food processor. To prevent burning yourself, make sure the lid of the blender jar is closed securely before puréeing hot gravy.

4 If you need to thicken the gravy, stir in additional flour or cornstarch that's been dissolved in cold liquid.

What You'll Need

- Whisk
- Mesh strainer
- Blender or food processor
- Flour or cornstarch

Tip

To prevent lumps, blend flour well with oil or butter, or dissolve it completely in a small amount of cold broth or water before adding it to hot liquid.

375 Substitute Missing Ingredients

All cooks have found themselves short of a crucial ingredient at one time or another. Most foods are easily substituted with little problem. Be prepared, though, for unexpected results when substituting ingredients in baked recipes, as they depend on precise measures and complex chemical reactions.

WHAT'S MISSING	POSSIBLE SUBSTITUTES
1 cup (8 oz/250 g) butter	• 1 cup (8 oz/250 g) margarine • ⅞ cup (7 fl oz/210 ml) vegetable oil • ⅞ cup (7 oz/220 g) vegetable shortening • ¾ cup (6 fl oz/180 ml) strained chicken or bacon fat
1 cup (8 oz/250 g) butter, in baking cakes and quick breads	• ½ cup (5 oz/155 g) applesauce plus ½ cup (4 fl oz/125 ml) vegetable oil • ¾ cup (6 oz/185 g) yogurt plus ¼ cup (2 fl oz/60 ml) vegetable oil
1 oz. (30 g) semisweet chocolate	• ½ oz. (15 g) unsweetened chocolate plus 1 tbsp. sugar
1 oz. (30 g) unsweetened chocolate	• 3 tbsp. cocoa plus 1 tbsp. butter or oil • 3 tbsp. carob plus 2 tbsp. water
1 cup (8 fl oz/250 ml) fresh or canned coconut milk	• ¼ cup (2 fl oz/60 ml) canned cream of coconut plus ¾ cup (6 fl oz/180 ml) warm water or nonfat milk
1 whole egg, in baking	• ¼ cup (2½ oz/75 g) applesauce or mashed banana plus 2 tsp. oil
2 egg yolks, in sauces and custards	• 1 whole egg
1 cup (4 oz/125 g) unsifted cake flour	• 1 cup (5 oz/155 g) minus 2 tbsp. unsifted all-purpose flour
1 cup (5 oz/155 g) unsifted self-rising flour	• 1 cup (5 oz/155 g) unsifted all-purpose flour plus 1½ tsp. baking powder and a pinch of salt
1 cup (4 oz/125 g) sifted all-purpose flour	• 1 cup (5 oz/155 g) minus 2 tbsp. unsifted all-purpose flour

WHAT'S MISSING	POSSIBLE SUBSTITUTES
1 cup (5 oz/155 g) unsifted all-purpose flour	• 1 cup (5 oz/155 g) minus 2 tbsp. unsifted whole-wheat flour • 1 cup (5 oz/155 g) plus 2 tbsp. unsifted cake flour
1 clove fresh garlic	• ½ tsp. garlic paste • ⅛ tsp. garlic powder
1 tsp. double-acting baking powder	• ¼ tsp. baking soda plus ½ tsp. cream of tartar • ¼ tsp. baking soda plus ½ cup (4 fl oz/125 ml) buttermilk or yogurt (reduce liquid in recipe by ½ cup)
1 tsp. fresh lemon juice	• ½ tsp. vinegar
1 tsp. grated lemon peel	• ½ tsp. lemon extract
1 cup (8 fl oz/250 ml) whole milk	• 1 cup (8 fl oz/250 ml) nonfat milk or water plus 1 tbsp. melted butter • ½ cup (4 fl oz/125 ml) evaporated milk plus ½ cup water • 1 cup (8 fl oz/250 ml) buttermilk plus ½ tsp. baking soda • 1 cup (8 fl oz/250 ml) soy or almond milk
1 cup (8 fl oz/250 ml) buttermilk	• 1 cup (8 fl oz/250 ml) milk plus 1 tbsp. lemon juice or white vinegar; let sit 5 minutes
1 cup (8 fl oz/250 ml) light cream	• ⅞ cup (7 fl oz/210 ml) milk plus 3 tbsp. melted butter
1 cup (8 fl oz/250 ml) half-and-half	• ⅞ cup (7 fl oz/210 ml) milk plus 1½ tbsp. melted butter • ½ cup (4 fl oz/125 ml) light cream and ½ cup milk
1 cup (8 fl oz/250 ml) heavy or whipping cream	• ¾ cup (6 fl oz/180 ml) whole milk plus ⅓ cup (3 fl oz/80 ml) melted butter

(continued on next page)

WHAT'S MISSING	POSSIBLE SUBSTITUTES
1 cup (8 oz/250 g) sour cream	• 1 cup (8 oz/250 g) yogurt • ⅞ cup (7 oz/220 g) yogurt or buttermilk plus ⅓ cup (3 oz/90 g) butter • 1 cup (8 fl oz/250 ml) evaporated whole milk plus 1 tbsp. lemon juice
1 tbsp. prepared mustard	• 1 tsp. powdered mustard plus a dash of vinegar
1 cup (8 oz/250 g) granulated sugar	• 1¾ cup (7 oz/220 g) unsifted confectioners' sugar • ⅞ cup (7 fl oz/210 ml) honey • 1 cup (7 oz/220 g) packed light-brown sugar plus ¼ tsp. baking soda • 1 cup (8 fl oz/250 ml) molasses plus 1 tsp. baking soda • 1 cup (8 fl oz/250 ml) maple syrup plus ¼ cup (2 fl oz/60 ml) corn syrup
1 cup (8 fl oz/250 ml) light corn syrup or honey	• 1¼ cups (10 oz/315 g) granulated sugar plus ¼ cup (2 fl oz/60 ml) more of liquid in recipe
1 cup (7 oz/220 g) baker's or superfine sugar	• 1 cup (8 oz/250 g) granulated sugar, processed 30 seconds in food processor
1 tbsp. cornstarch	• 2 tbsp. all-purpose flour
1 tbsp. tapioca	• 1½ tbsp. all-purpose flour
1 tbsp. arrowroot	• 2 tbsp. all-purpose flour
1 cup (8 fl oz/250 ml) tomato juice	• ½ cup (4 fl oz/125 ml) tomato sauce plus ½ cup water
1 cup (8 fl oz/250 ml) tomato sauce	• ¼ cup (2 oz/60 g) tomato paste plus ⅔ cup (5 fl oz/160 ml) water
1 cup (8 oz/250 g) yogurt	• 1 cup (8 fl oz/250 ml) buttermilk • 1 cup (8 fl oz/250 ml) milk plus 1 tbsp. lemon juice

376 Reduce Your Cholesterol

Everyone knows that high blood cholesterol leads to blocked arteries and heart disease. But many people aren't aware that their blood cholesterol levels have shot up, since there are often no obvious symptoms. Unpleasantly surprised by your most recent blood-test results? Better take these steps to heart.

Steps

Eat more healthfully

1 Decrease your fat intake to 30 percent of daily calories. (A lower fat level would best be recommended by a physician.)

2 Lower the amount of saturated fat you consume. Saturated fats will drive up your cholesterol more than any other food. They're found in foods derived from animal sources and certain tropical plants—for example, marbling and untrimmed fat in meat, chicken skin, butter, dairy products and coconut oil.

3 In place of saturated fats and trans fats (see Tips), substitute small amounts of polyunsaturated fats and, in particular, monounsaturated fats such as olive, canola and nut oils.

4 Lower the amount of cholesterol in your diet to less than 300 mg per day. Cholesterol is found in foods with animal origins, such as meat, poultry, fish, shellfish, egg yolks, cheese, ice cream and whole milk. When eating meat, decrease your serving size. Switch to skim milk and avoid processed meat products.

5 Eat plenty of fruits, vegetables and whole grains, foods that tend to be low in fat and dense in nutrients.

Exercise regularly

1 Exercise for 30 minutes at least four times a week. Even two 15-minute or three 10-minute exercise breaks are beneficial.

2 Incorporate physical activity into your daily life. Take the stairs. Get off the bus early or park farther from entrances than usual.

3 Establish a program of regular, vigorous exercise. Finding an exercise buddy will inspire you to reach your goals.

Lose weight

1 Shedding even a small amount of weight helps lower your cholesterol level. Lose the weight through slow, long-term diet changes and regular exercise, not by a crash diet.

2 Avoid prepared low-fat and nonfat foods that are high in sugar. You need to lower your overall calorie intake as well as your fat calories, and many of those products are high in calories.

3 You may want to look for a structured program that offers support and professional expertise, one that will help you understand and change behavioral patterns.

Tips

For adults over 20 years old, the ideal blood cholesterol level is less than 200 mg/dl, while levels over 200 mg/dl are considered elevated.

There are two kinds of blood cholesterol: low-density lipoproteins (LDL), which will clog your arteries, and high-density lipoproteins (HDL), which help your body clean out blood cholesterol.

Physical activity helps strengthen your heart and can increase the ratio of HDL to LDL.

To identify fats, remember that most saturated fats are solid at room temperature. Monounsaturated fats tend to be liquid at room temperature but harden when chilled.

Limit your intake of trans fats, or trans-fatty acids, which lower HDL and raise LDL. Trans fats are found in commercial baked goods such as cookies and crackers and in fast food.

Warning

Schedule regular physical exams and consult with your physician before adopting any new diet or exercise program.

377 Treat Burned Pots and Pans

The risotto is nearly done, then the phone rings and the next thing you know, you've got a mess to clean. Scorched foods can leave stubborn spots in pots and pans that no amount of elbow grease can remove. But just a few essentials in your pantry will help restore your pans to practically new.

Steps

1 Wash away as much of the food as possible, using cold water for eggs, chocolate and starch-based foods.

2 Fill the pot with water. Add 1 to 2 tsp. dishwashing liquid and bring to a boil. Simmer for 10 minutes, then cover the pot, turn off the heat and leave the pot to soak for 30 minutes.

3 With a wooden spoon, scrape away as much of the burned food as possible. Rinse well.

4 If burned areas still remain, cover them completely with a generous amount of baking soda. Drizzle in just enough water to create a thick paste, smearing the paste up the sides of the pot if needed. Set aside for at least 4 hours, preferably overnight.

5 Without rinsing the pot, add 3 parts water to 1 part distilled vinegar to cover the burned food by at least 2 inches (5 cm). Boil for 10 minutes and then leave overnight.

6 Repeat steps 2 through 5 as needed.

What You'll Need

- Dishwashing liquid
- Wooden spoon
- Baking soda
- Distilled vinegar

Tips

Avoid using steel wool or abrasive cleansers on polished metal. They can create scratches that will allow food to stick and burn even more easily.

Leaving baking soda on aluminum pans for longer than 1 hour can cause pitting, or dark spots where the alkaline compounds react with the aluminum surface.

378 Rescue a Burned Cake or Pie

Don't despair—there are endless ways to dress up a not-quite-perfect dessert. A little ice cream, a little creativity and *voilà,* your guests will never know what a disaster you averted.

Steps

1 Use a fine-holed grater to scrape away minor burns. Trim larger burned areas with a small serrated knife.

3 Disguise the top with frosting, cocoa powder, confectioners' sugar, fruit or toasted nuts.

4 If the top or bottom of the cake or pie is burned completely, then carefully cut away the entire layer with a serrated knife.

5 Cut the remaining cake or pie crust into decorative shapes, then layer the cake or crust pieces with fruit and ice cream in a large, clear bowl or individual wine glasses.

6 If the pie crust is irretrievably burned, use the hot pie filling as a topping over ice cream or heat it with a little liqueur and serve it as a compote with cookies.

What You'll Need

- Fine-holed grater
- Serrated knife
- Frosting, cocoa powder, confectioners' sugar, fruit or toasted nuts
- Large bowl or wine glasses
- Fruit and ice cream
- Liqueur and cookies

379 Put Out a Kitchen Fire

Fires have a greater chance of starting in your kitchen than anywhere else in your home. There are three kinds of fires; handling each one the right way will help keep the flames from spreading. For the best overall protection, purchase a multipurpose, dry-chemical extinguisher rated for Class A, B and C fires. Hang it in your kitchen, in an easily accessible place away from the stove.

Steps

1 If your clothes are burning, immediately drop to the ground and roll back and forth quickly.

2 If the fire is large or spreading fast, evacuate the residence immediately, then call emergency to report the fire.

3 For fires on wood, paper and cloth, use water or a Class A fire extinguisher to douse the flames. Place small objects in the sink to help contain the fire.

4 If fat or grease in a pan starts burning, quickly slide a lid over the pan to cover it completely and cut off the oxygen supply. Turn off the heat.

5 For small grease fires, throw baking soda over the flames or use a Class B fire extinguisher.

6 For electrical fires, throw baking soda over the flames or use a Class C fire extinguisher.

7 If you have a fire in your oven, close the oven door and turn off the heat to smother the flames.

8 In general, try to put out a fire if it's small. But if the flames begin spreading, do not remain in the kitchen.

9 To prevent future fires, always keep your stove, oven and hood clean, and avoid overloading outlets or circuits with too many appliances.

What You'll Need

- ABC-rated fire extinguisher
- Pan lid
- Baking soda

Tip

To use a fire extinguisher, pull the pin to release the lock, aim the nozzle at the back of the fire and sweep from side to side while squeezing the handle.

Warning

Never use water on a grease fire or an electrical fire. The grease will splatter, making the fire spread even more. Water on an electrical fire can cause serious shocks.

Don't turn on your stove's exhaust fan if there's a fire. This could spread the flames into the walls of the house.

380 Remove the Bitterness in Burned Rice

Even though it's just the bottom layer that's blackened, the smoky smell and bitter flavor of burned rice permeate all the way to the top grains. Salvage overcooked rice with this quick trick.

Steps

1 Transfer the unburned rice carefully from the cooking pot to another lidded bowl or pot.

2 Wipe two or three onions with a clean, damp cloth.

3 Remove the papery outer peels from the onions.

4 Spread the onion peels completely over the surface of the unburned rice.

5 Cover the pot or bowl tightly and let it sit for 15 minutes. The onion peels will absorb the bitterness.

6 Discard the onion peels and serve the rice.

What You'll Need

- Large, lidded bowl or pot
- Two or three onions
- Clean cloth

Tip

While transferring the rice, take care not to scrape the scorched layer away from the bottom or sides of the cooking pot.

381 Remove Cooking Odors

Whether you're frying fish or burning bacon, the smell of your cooking may linger longer than you'd like. Here's an easy way to clear the air without compromising your food.

Steps

Removing odors from the air

1 Combine 2 cups (16 fl oz/500 ml) water, 1 cup (8 fl oz/250 ml) vinegar and 1 tsp. whole cloves in a shallow, wide pan.

2 Simmer uncovered for 10 to 15 minutes.

3 Repeat later if needed.

Removing odors from your hands

1 For garlic, rub your fingers against a stainless-steel spoon or spatula under cold running water.

2 For fishy smells, wash your hands with lemon juice.

What You'll Need

- Vinegar
- Whole cloves
- Shallow, wide pan
- Stainless-steel utensil
- Lemon juice

Tip

If desired, add fresh citrus peels or ½ tsp. pure vanilla extract to the simmering mix.

382 Finish Undercooked Meat

If your dinner guests are ready before your roast is, a quick change of plans is in order. You'll have to cut the meat in the kitchen, and thus take some of the glamour out of serving. But everyone will enjoy dinner sooner rather than later.

Steps

1 Cut the meat into several pieces. If the meat is mostly done, two or three pieces are enough.

2 If the meat is significantly raw, carve the whole roast into thin slices. Cut rib roasts between each bone.

3 Arrange the slices in a shallow baking pan or on an ovenproof platter. Drizzle with sauce or stock, then cover with foil.

4 Turn the oven to 400°F (200°C) and continue cooking to desired doneness, from 5 to 15 minutes for thinner slices and 15 to 30 minutes for thicker pieces. Keep a close watch to prevent over-cooking.

What You'll Need

- Carving knife
- Shallow baking pan or ovenproof platter
- Sauce or stock
- Foil

Tip

Cuts meant for long cooking, such as beef stew chunks or lamb shanks, will be very tough if cooked too quickly. It's best to save these for another meal.

383 Salvage an Undercooked Turkey

The potatoes are mashed, the dressing's done, your guests are seated and hungry—but you're faced with a turkey that's stubbornly pink. It's time for some turkey triage.

Steps

1 Smile, pour some more wine and take the turkey back to the kitchen.

2 Turn the oven to 400°F (200°C). Oil a jelly-roll pan or a shallow baking dish.

3 Carve the turkey as you would for serving at the table. Take extra care, as the uncooked turkey meat can be more difficult to cut.

4 Set aside any pieces that are already done, and cover them with foil to keep them warm.

5 Arrange the uncooked pieces in a single layer in the oiled pan, overlapping them slightly if needed. Drizzle a small amount of stock or water over the turkey pieces during reheating to keep them moist.

6 Drape foil loosely over the pan and cook the turkey until it's no longer pink. This should take only a few minutes, so keep a close watch to prevent overcooking.

What You'll Need

- Oil
- Jelly-roll pan or shallow baking dish
- Carving knife
- Foil
- Stock

Warning

Because color is not a dependable indicator of doneness in meat and poul-try, be sure to use a food thermometer to check that the turkey has reached 180°F (80°C), especially in the thighs.

Cooking

384 Fix an Overseasoned Dish

Ask professional chefs what the secret to good cooking is and they'll
say, "Taste, taste, taste." Once you understand the special relationship
between salty, sweet and sour flavors, you'll be able to fine-tune the
taste of any dish until it's perfect. Try these steps on any dish that can
use some salt, sugar or lemon juice mixed in or sprinkled over it.

Steps

1   Think of salt, sugar and acid as the trinity that holds up all other
    flavors. When these three are out of balance, the other flavors in
    a dish can also fail to come together.

2   To fix a sauce or soup that has too much salt, for example, add
    a dash of sugar and a squeeze of lemon juice.

3   If a sauce or soup is too sweet for you, add salt and lemon juice.

4   If a sauce or soup is too sour, then adjust the flavor with a bit of
    salt and sugar.

5   Adjust seasonings gradually, and stir well after each addition.

What You'll Need

- Salt
- Sugar
- Lemon juice

Tip

Depending on the dish, you
can use wine or vinegar in
place of lemon juice.

385 Fix an Underseasoned Dish

Sometimes a soup or sauce just needs a little something. Stocking your
pantry with a few basic ingredients allows you to add flavor to any dish
that tastes flat. Try these strategies to spice things up.

Steps

1   Add salt to intensify all other flavors.

2   Add lemon juice or a tiny amount of vinegar to brighten the taste
    of a dish.

3   Stir in full-flavored ingredients, such as tomato paste, prepared
    pesto, anchovy paste, soy sauce, roasted garlic purée, cayenne
    pepper, mustard, grated ginger, wine, liqueur, balsamic vinegar
    or fruit juice. Layer two or three ingredients to create depth and
    complexity.

4   Reduce a sauce or soup by simmering it to concentrate its
    flavors.

5   Sprinkle finished dishes with fresh herbs or grated cheese.

What You'll Need

- Salt
- Lemon juice or vinegar
- Assorted flavorings
- Fresh herbs or grated
  cheese

Tip

Experiment with a small
amount in a bowl before
adjusting the flavors of the
whole dish.

386 Remove Oven Spills

Spillovers from fruit pies and casseroles are more than smoky, unsightly messes. They can cause oven fires, so be sure to clean up these spills thoroughly as soon as they happen.

Steps

1 Cover spills thickly with salt as soon as they drop on the oven floor, while the spots are still hot and soft. Continue cooking.

2 When the oven cools, the spills will solidify and lift away easily. Scrape them gently with a wooden spoon or spatula. Sweep away the crumbs with a brush.

3 Use a small pumice stone to clean old, scorched food spots easily without being exposed to harsh chemicals or dangerous fumes. When you rub the burned food with the pumice stone, it will leave a sandy residue that is easily brushed away.

4 Wipe the oven clean with a soapy cloth or sponge.

What You'll Need

- Salt
- Wooden spoon or spatula
- Brush
- Small pumice stone
- Dishwashing liquid
- Cloth or sponge

Tip

Look for natural pumice stones in drugstores and beauty supply shops.

387 Clean Up Oil Spills

A puddle of oil on your kitchen floor can grow bigger and even more slippery when mixed with soap and water. There's a much better way to clean up oily accidents. This remedy also works for broken eggs.

Steps

1 Sprinkle the puddle with a very generous amount of salt. (If you run out of salt, pour flour on the spill and mix before sweeping.)

2 Let it soak for a few minutes.

3 Sweep up the salt.

4 Clean the remaining film of oil with a few drops of dishwashing liquid and damp paper towels.

What You'll Need

- Salt
- Flour
- Broom
- Dustpan
- Dishwashing liquid
- Paper towels

At your next party, welcome your guests with festive drinks to set the mood. Whether you're looking for sophisticated classics or retro fun, mixed drinks and cocktails are easy to prepare. And many

OCCASION	DRINK	MIX IT UP
Cocktail Hour	Martini	Shake or stir 2½ oz. (75 ml) gin and ½ oz. (15 ml) dry vermouth with ice. Strain and garnish with a lemon twist or olive.
	Cosmopolitan	Shake 1¼ oz. (40 ml) vodka, ¼ oz. (10 ml) lime juice, ¼ oz. (10 ml) triple sec and ¼ oz. (10 ml) cranberry juice with ice. Strain and garnish with a lime wedge.
	Manhattan	Stir 1½ oz. (45 ml) whiskey, ¾ oz. (20 ml) sweet vermouth and optional dash of bitters with ice. Strain and garnish with a cherry.
	Whiskey Sour	Shake together 2 oz. (60 ml) whiskey, juice of ½ lemon and ½ tsp. powdered sugar. Strain and garnish with a lemon slice.
Beach Party	Margarita	Rub rim of glass with lime peel and dip in coarse salt. Shake 1½ oz. (45 ml) tequila, 1 oz. (30 ml) lime juice and ½ oz. (15 ml) triple sec with ice. Strain into a glass.
	Daiquiri	Shake 1½ oz. (45 ml) light rum, 1 tsp. powdered sugar and juice of 1 lime with ice. Strain.
	Piña Colada	Blend together 3 oz. (90 ml) light rum, 2 oz. (60 ml) coconut milk, ¼ cup (2 oz/60 g) crushed pineapple and 2 cups (10 oz/275 g) ice. Serve with a straw.
	Tequila Sunrise	Stir together 2 oz. (60 ml) tequila and 4 oz. (120 ml) orange juice. Stir in ice, then slowly drizzle in grenadine.
	Sangria	Stir ¼ cup (2 oz/60 g) sugar and 8 oz. (240 ml) water in a pitcher until dissolved. Add 1 bottle red wine, thin slices of orange and lime, and ice. Stir. Add 6 oz. (180 ml) sparkling water if desired.
Elegant Aperitifs	Kir Royale	Pour 6 oz. (180 ml) champagne in a flute. Add ½ oz. (15 ml) crème de cassis.
	Negroni	Stir ¾ oz. (20 ml) Campari, ¾ oz. (20 ml) gin and ¾ oz. (20 ml) sweet vermouth with ice. Strain.
	Dubonnet	Pour 1¼ oz. (40 ml) Dubonnet, 1¼ oz. (40 ml) gin and dash of bitters over ice. Garnish with a twist.

drinks are quite forgiving: Alcohol amounts can be adjusted for personal preference or, with practice, eyeballed for quick mixing.

OCCASION	DRINK	MIX IT UP
Weekend Brunch	Bloody Mary	Stir together 1½ oz. (45 ml) vodka, 3 oz. (90 ml) tomato juice, ½ tsp. lemon juice, ½ tsp. Worcestershire sauce, 2 drops hot pepper sauce (such as Tabasco), and pinch of salt and pepper. Add ice and garnish with a celery stick.
	Mimosa	Fill flutes halfway with chilled orange juice, then top with chilled champagne.
	Strawberry Sunrise	Pour 2 oz. (60 ml) strawberry schnapps and ½ oz. (15 ml) grenadine over ice into a glass. Top with orange juice. Garnish with a fresh strawberry.
	Pineapple Cooler	Stir together 2 oz. (60 ml) pineapple juice, 2 oz. (60 ml) white wine and ½ tsp. powdered sugar. Stir in ice and 2 oz. (60 ml) club soda. Garnish with orange and lemon slices.
Winter Wonderland	Whiskey Toddy	Fill a cup with 6 to 8 oz. (180 to 240 ml) boiling water. Stir in 2 oz. (60 ml) whiskey and ½ tsp. sugar. Garnish with a lemon slice.
	Irish Coffee	Stir together 6 oz. (180 ml) hot coffee, 1½ oz. (45 ml) whiskey and ½ tsp. sugar in cup. Top with whipped cream.
	Hot Buttered Rum	Fill a cup two-thirds full with boiling water. Stir in 2 oz. (60 ml) dark rum, 1 tbsp. butter and 1 tsp. brown sugar. Sprinkle with nutmeg or garnish with a cinnamon stick.
Teetotaler's Specials	Cranberry Cooler	Stir together 2 oz. (60 ml) cranberry juice and 1 tbsp. lime juice in a glass. Add ice and top with club soda. Garnish with a mint sprig.
	Orange and Tonic	Pour 6 oz. (180 ml) orange juice and 4 oz. (120 ml) tonic water over ice. Garnish with a lime slice.
	Raspberry Cooler	Stir together juice of 1 lemon, 2 tbsp. powdered sugar and 2 tbsp. raspberry syrup in a glass. Add ice and top with club soda. Garnish with lemon and orange slices.
Warning		Serve alcohol responsibly. Offer food with your drinks and provide nonalcoholic alternatives. Always be aware of how much your guests are drinking. Call a cab for those who have consumed too much.

389 Disentangle Pasta

Pasta can clump together in one big mess if left too long before
serving. Returning the pasta to hot water may soften it beyond the
desirable point of al dente (firm "to the tooth"), but it's the fastest
way to untangle pasta.

Steps

1 Bring a large pot of water to a boil. Remove it from the heat.

2 Add the clumped pasta to the hot water, then loosen it gently
with a large wooden spoon.

3 Drain. If you're not serving the pasta immediately, rinse it with
cold water to stop the cooking and toss it with oil.

4 For lasagna noodles, oil a cookie sheet. After separating the
noodles, arrange them flat on the sheet, using plastic wrap
between layers if needed. Set aside until you're ready to
assemble the lasagna.

What You'll Need

- Large pot
- Large wooden spoon
- Oil
- Cookie sheet
- Plastic wrap

Tip

If you're in a rush, try running warm tap water over
the pasta while working it
apart with your fingers.

390 Refresh Stale Bread

Leftover bread doesn't have to be made into bread crumbs. Yesterday's
muffins, bagels or walnut-cranberry semolina loaf can all be revived
easily. Bread that is rock hard, though, cannot be saved by this method.

Steps

1 Preheat oven to 325°F (165°C).

2 Place the stale bread in a clean paper bag. Fold or twist the
bag's opening to close.

3 Dampen the bag lightly and evenly with cold water. The surface
of the bread may become a little wet, but avoid soaking the
bread's interior.

4 Heat the entire bag in the oven until the bread is softened and
warmed through. Sprinkle with more water if the bag dries before
the bread is ready. Allow about 5 minutes for rolls or slices and
at least 20 minutes for large loaves.

5 Be sure to remove the bag from the oven before it scorches
or before you increase the temperature.

What You'll Need

- Paper bag

Tip

This is also a good way to
defrost and heat frozen
breads in one step. Lower
the oven temperature to
275°F (135°C) for baked
goods taken directly from
the freezer.

391 Smooth Seized Chocolate

If chocolate comes into contact with even the tiniest amount of water while melting, it will suddenly "seize," or turn hard and grainy. A single drop of water or a whiff of steam can trigger particles in cocoa butter to solidify into a dull mass. Ironically, adding more liquid will help smooth the chocolate back to its former satiny texture.

Steps

1 Remove the pan from the heat.

2 For every ounce (30 g) of chocolate, add 1 tbsp. of one of the following ingredients, depending on the recipe you are making: warm water, melted butter, vegetable oil, or hot milk or cream.

3 Stir or whisk until smooth. Slowly add more liquid if needed.

4 Chocolate recovered from seizing should be incorporated with other ingredients to make sauces, frostings or batters. It is not suitable for using alone, such as for coating candy or creating decorative curls (it won't have the same shine or delicate texture).

What You'll Need

- Spoon or whisk
- Butter, vegetable oil, milk or cream

Tip

Before you start melting chocolate, add 2 tsp. liquid for every ounce (30 g) of chocolate to prevent seizing. For best results, use one of the liquids in the recipe.

392 Soften Hardened Sugars or Cookies

Brown sugar, honey, syrup and even cookies have a habit of hardening despite storage in airtight containers. Here are some tricks to soften them up.

Steps

1 Place brown sugar in an airtight container with one or two slices of bread. Leave overnight.

2 Microwave brown sugar or honey in an open container. Cover with a damp paper towel and turn on high. Turn or stir well every 30 seconds until the sugar or honey has softened.

3 Place the container of crystallized honey or syrup in a small pan of simmering water. Heat until smooth.

4 Seal hard cookies in an airtight container with apple wedges or bread slices. Set aside for one or two days.

What You'll Need

- Airtight container(s)
- Bread
- Microwave
- Paper towel
- Small pan
- Apple

Tip

Sugars may harden again, but the softening process can be repeated as many times as needed.

393 Fix Breakfast for Your Sweetheart

Waking up to breakfast in bed is a wonderful surprise gift. Don't wait for February 14 or Mother's Day. Turn any lazy weekend morning into a decadent pleasure. You can run to a bakery to gather pastries, but there's nothing like a homemade treat to show just how special someone is to you.

Steps

1 If you have a complex or time-consuming recipe, start preparing breakfast the previous night.

2 Set your alarm, allowing at least 30 minutes before serving time. A watch alarm can be set under your pillow for a discreet wake-up call.

3 Close the bedroom door to filter noises from the kitchen. Leave the door slightly ajar so you can open it more easily later.

4 Place one large, colorful blossom or a few small flowers in a bud vase or a jar of water. Keep the arrangement short to save space and prevent tipping.

5 Place a pretty place mat or cloth napkin on a large tray. You can also cover a cookie sheet with a clean kitchen towel.

6 Set a plate, a small glass, a cup or a mug, a napkin and silverware on the tray. Place the flowers and a newspaper, magazine, small gift or greeting card to the side. Open the newspaper to a favorite section, such as the comics or the daily crossword puzzle.

7 Finish preparing breakfast. Brew coffee or heat water for tea. Keep the kitchen clean. Be forewarned: Leaving a dirty mess will cancel out any and all points gained by cooking.

8 Remove the plate from the tray and arrange the food on it. Fill the glass with juice and the cup with coffee or tea. Leave at least 1 inch (3 cm) of headspace to prevent splashing while you walk.

9 Walk carefully to the bedroom. Quietly place the tray near the bed or on the opposite side of the bed.

10 Wake up the person slowly with the aroma from the coffee cup or a dab of maple syrup on the lips. Or simply declare (in a soft voice) the appropriate happy greetings for the day. Give your loved one time to wake up completely before bringing over the breakfast tray.

11 Carry the tray so that the plate will be in the right serving position when you set down the tray. If you don't have a tray with legs, place a small pillow or a folded blanket on the person's lap.

12 Bask in the happiness and gratitude that you deserve.

What You'll Need

- Ingredients for breakfast
- Alarm clock or watch
- Flower(s)
- Bud vase or jar
- Large tray
- Place mat, cloth napkin or kitchen towel
- Place setting for one
- Newspaper, magazine, small gift or greeting card
- Coffee or tea
- Juice
- Small pillow or folded blanket
- Time to clean up

Tips

Choose recipes with alluring aromas, like cinnamon, chocolate or almonds, for maximum wake-up-with-a-smile effect.

Prepare food that is easily eaten with one hand; cutting with a knife can be messy when eating on a tray.

Many breakfast recipes can be started a day in advance. Soak bread in French toast mix, prepare pancake batter, combine the wet ingredients for muffins (leaving dry ingredients in another bowl) or roll out scone dough; refrigerate.

Join the lucky person in a romantic breakfast for two: Use one place setting, serve enough food for two on the plate, then feed your loved one for a special touch.

394 Mend a Wooden Cutting Board

As soon as you notice cracks, fill them to prevent further splitting and to keep food residue out of your wooden cutting board. Epoxy will stand up to frequent washing and resist the oils and acids in food.

Steps

1 Clear out the crack with a straightened paper clip or a stiff wire.

2 Clean the board and let it dry completely.

3 Fill the crack with clear or wood epoxy, mounding it up a little higher than the board's surface.

4 When the epoxy is cured, rub away excess with fine steel wool.

5 Rub your cutting board regularly with mineral oil to prevent drying. Do not use vegetable oil, which will turn rancid.

What You'll Need

- Paper clip or stiff wire
- Clear or wood epoxy
- Fine steel wool
- Mineral oil

395 Keep a Mixing Bowl Steady

Without a helper, it's impossible to hold a big bowl still while you're whisking egg whites with one hand and adding sugar with the other. When two hands aren't enough, ingenuity has to kick in. Use this handy trick the next time you're blending ingredients.

Steps

1 Wet a kitchen towel until it's evenly damp.

2 Twist it diagonally, rolling it tightly across two opposite corners.

3 Form a circle with the towel at the center of your work surface and overlap the ends in a loose knot.

4 Place the ring on your work surface and rest the bowl's base on the ring, pressing it firmly into the towel base. The bowl will stay steady as you continue mixing or blending.

What You'll Need

- Kitchen towel

Tip

Rubber pads made for opening jars, a square of carpet nonskid padding or some wet paper towels can provide additional traction.

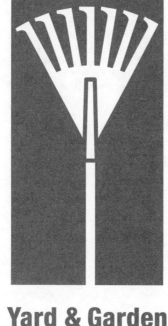

Yard & Garden

396 Fix Garden Tool Handles

Just because the handle has cracked doesn't mean you have to bid good-bye to your favorite rake, hoe or shovel. Substituting a new wooden handle for the old one is easy—and much less expensive than replacing a good tool.

Steps

1 Take the broken tool to a hardware store or garden center and buy a replacement handle.

2 Clamp the tool blade in a bench vise.

3 Wriggle the handle out of the hasp or, if necessary, split the wood using an electric drill and pick out the pieces.

4 If the handle is fastened to the hasp by a rivet, file off the head. Then drive it through, using a hammer and punch.

5 For a wedged-in shovel handle, insert a punch through the hole at the bottom of the hasp and pound with a hammer.

6 Insert the new handle. (If necessary, file away some of the wood to make it fit.) Then, holding the tool by the working end, tap the handle on the ground until it slides into the hasp.

7 Drill through the rivet hole (if there is one) and into the new handle. Insert a galvanized wood screw that is slightly shorter than the diameter of the hasp.

What You'll Need

- Replacement wooden handle
- Bench vise
- Electric drill
- Smooth file
- Hammer
- Punch
- Wood rasp
- Galvanized wood screw
- Screwdriver

Tip

Resist the temptation to repair a broken handle. The result will be weak, and protruding screws, bolts or nails can injure your hands.

397 Repair a Leaky Hose Nozzle

Well-made brass hose nozzles will last for years, but even the best of them can spring a leak now and then. Nearly always, leaks are due to a defective washer.

Steps

1 Disassemble the nozzle and pull out the nozzle insert. At the outer end you will see one or more rubber O-ring washers.

2 Remove the washer, using an awl, ice pick or screwdriver.

3 Slide a new washer onto the shaft.

4 If the leak is occurring at the hose connection, pull out the washer at the base of the nozzle and replace it.

5 A plastic nozzle may be damaged beyond repair. If that's the case—or if the leak is at the base of the nozzle but in the hose itself—buy and insert new end fittings following the steps in 398 Mend a Leaky Hose, opposite page.

What You'll Need

- Awl, ice pick or screwdriver
- Rubber washers, either hose-replacement or regular plumbing type
- Replacement hose-end fittings

Tip

At the end of each watering season, pull out the hose-nozzle insert and coat it with petroleum jelly to prevent corrosion.

398 **Mend a Leaky Hose**

On the scale of life's downturns, a leaking hose is a minor annoyance, but it can seem like a big one when you're in a hurry to get the car washed or the garden watered.

Steps

Making a temporary repair

1 Clean and dry the outside of the hose. If the temperature is above 80°F (27°C) outside, take the hose into the garage or another cool place.

2 Wrap the damaged area with plastic tape. (You can buy special hose-repair tape, but ordinary electrical tape works just as well.) Make tight spirals, overlapping the tape by about a third of its width on each turn. Press firmly, but avoid pulling the tape: If you stretch it, it won't hold well.

3 Extend the tape about 2 inches (5 cm) on either side of the damaged area.

Making a permanent repair

1 Using an ultrasharp knife, remove the damaged section from the hose. Make the cut as straight as possible. If the edges are ragged or the cut angled, the new connection may leak.

2 Take the piece to a hardware store or garden center to find replacement couplings of the right size and type. Most repair fittings will work with either rubber or vinyl hoses, but some will work only with one or the other. Some brands are designed to fit a number of different hose diameters; others come only in single sizes.

3 Attach the male and female couplings to the cut ends, following the directions on the package. Depending on the type of couplings you use, they'll have screw-on fasteners or circular clamps to ensure a snug fit.

4 If the fittings don't slide in easily, soften the hose in hot water, or lubricate it with soap or vegetable oil.

What You'll Need

- Plastic tape
- Sharp knife
- Straightedge
- Hose replacement coupling kit
- Soap or vegetable oil

Tips

Kinking is a prime cause of leaks and damaged connections. To avoid problems, store your hose on a drum-like reel, either wheeled or wall-mounted.

When you pause in watering, turn off the faucet; don't rely on the nozzle's shut-off valve. Water pressure that builds up in the hose can cause leaks.

399 Fix Dull Digging Tools

If working your garden's soil is getting harder and taking longer, it's time for a sharpening session. Spades, shovels, trowels and hoes all work better—and make your job easier—when their cutting edges are clean and sharp. The sharpening process is similar for all these tools.

Steps

1 Find a file of a type and size that you find comfortable to work with. A medium- or bastard-cut mill file about 8 inches (20 cm) long is a popular choice and easy to find at your neighborhood hardware store.

2 Make sure the tool is clean and free of rust (see 402 Remove Rust From Tools). Loose dirt will come off with a rubber kitchen spatula. For more stubborn soil, use a wire brush, nylon pot scrubber or a good blast from the hose.

3 Clamp the tool firmly in a bench vise at a slight angle, with the blade—the metal "business end"—pointing toward the floor. The inside surface should be facing up. (This is the side of a shovel that holds the soil, or the side of a hoe that faces you as you pull it through the soil.)

4 Hold the file firmly with both hands, at the same angle as the tool's original bevel. On most shovels, spades and hoes, this is anywhere from 40 degrees to 75 degrees.

5 Push the file away from your body, using smooth, long strokes (see A). When the edge is shiny and smooth, check the bevel by holding the file in line with the new edge. Don't worry if it doesn't match the original angle exactly, but make it as close as you can.

What You'll Need

- Medium mill file
- Rubber spatula, wire brush, nylon pot scrubber or garden hose
- Bench vise
- Lightweight oil
- Fine-grit grinding stone
- Steel wool
- Absorbent rags

Tips

Avoid using a metal trowel to scrape dirt from a shovel. You could damage both tools.

To maintain wooden tool handles, sand them once a year, then rub them with boiled linseed oil, using a soft cloth.

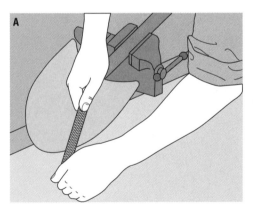

6 Turn the tool over so the back faces up. The blade will have a rough, feathery edge called a burr. Remove it by dribbling light-weight oil onto the blade, then rubbing the burr with a small, fine-grit grinding stone (see B). A lightweight machine oil such as WD-40 will work; so will mineral or vegetable oil.

7 Finally, go over the entire blade with steel wool dipped in the same oil. If you plan to use the tool soon, wipe off the excess. For winter storage, though, leave the blade with a heavy coat to guard against rust.

400 Restore a Broken Flowerpot

What do you do with a cracked flowerpot? Well, you could smash it into shards and use the pieces as drainage aids in other containers—or you could repair it so it's good as new (maybe better, if you like a well-used look in your garden).

Steps

1 If the clay has cracked but not broken all the way through, wrap rust-proof wire around the pot, just under the rim, and twist the ends together.

2 For a broken pot, brush all the soil from the broken pieces, and make sure the edges are clean and dry.

3 Apply a waterproof two-part epoxy resin according to the manu-facturer's directions. (Use one that's formulated to work on terra-cotta, or whatever material your pot is made of.)

4 Press the pieces together and wipe away any excess epoxy.

5 Wrap twine around the pot. Then tighten the pressure by stuffing rags or newspaper between the pot and the twine.

6 Let the epoxy dry thoroughly before adding soil and plants. (Check the directions for exact timing.) When the epoxy has dried, remove the twine.

Warning

Oil-coated rags pose a fire hazard. Spread them out on the ground to dry completely before disposing of them.

What You'll Need

- Rust-proof wire
- Waterproof two-part epoxy resin
- Rags
- Twine
- Newspaper

Tip

All terra-cotta pots need pro-tection from freezing temper-atures, and repaired ones are especially vulnerable. Move them to a sheltered location for the winter.

401 Sharpen Pruning Clippers

Sharp blades make your pruning chores go faster and easier; and the neat, clean cuts they deliver keep your plants healthier.

Steps

1 Note which type of shears you've got. Anvil-type pruners (see A) have a single sharp blade that hits squarely against a blunt anvil. Bypass shears (see B) have two sharp blades that move past one another with a scissors-type action.

2 With an anvil pruner, you'll sharpen the single blade on both sides. With a bypass pruner, you'll sharpen only the outside surface of each blade (thus allowing them to cut cleanly as they slide past each other).

3 For easiest sharpening, use a screwdriver or wrench to disassemble the shears. Clamp the blade in a bench vise. Line up the parts in the order in which you remove them so you can put them back together easily when you're finished.

4 Clean the blades. Remove caked-on soil or other debris with soapy water and a stiff brush. To clean off sap or evergreen pitch, wipe the blades with a rag dipped in kerosene, mineral oil or (believe it or not) mayonnaise.

5 With the blade facing you, place a medium-fine flat file along the slant of the edge. As you sharpen, try to maintain the original angle of the edge. Push the file away from you. (The file will be moving from the edge of the blade toward the back.) As you finish each stroke, lift the file and begin again. Avoid pulling the file toward you.

6 When the edge is even and shiny, flip the blade over. If you see a burr, file it off. Coat the blade with a lightweight oil such as WD-40 or mineral oil.

7 Test the shears on a branch of the size they were designed to handle. If the cut isn't neat, clean and easy, continue sharpening the shears.

What You'll Need

- Screwdriver or wrench
- Bench vise
- Stiff brush
- Soap
- Kerosene, mineral oil or mayonnaise
- Rags
- Medium-fine flat file
- Lightweight oil

Tips

After each use, clean your shears, give them a thin coat of oil and store them where they'll be safe from bumps and dings.

Sharpening a pruning saw is a job that's best left to a pro. With some models, replacing the blade is another option.

Warning

Oil-coated rags pose a fire hazard. Spread them out on the ground to dry completely before disposing of them.

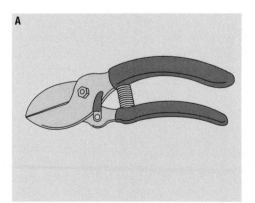

A

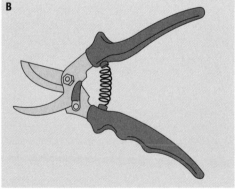

B

402 Remove Rust From Tools

Whether you've just found a treasure in the rough at a tag sale, or your own shovel or hoe has gotten a tad rusty, it's a snap to make tools as shiny as new.

Steps

1 Clamp the tool in a bench vise with the blade pointing down.

2 Coat the blade with kerosene or penetrating oil.

3 Brush downward, using steel wool, emery paper or a wire brush. (Depending on how rusty the blade is, you may need all three.)

4 Wipe away the rust residue with a soft brush or cloth. Then wash the blade in warm, soapy water and dry it thoroughly.

5 Sharpen and oil the blade according to the directions in 399 Sharpen Digging Tools.

6 Prevent rust by cleaning your tools thoroughly after every use and coating them lightly with a lightweight oil such as WD-40 or mineral oil.

What You'll Need

- Bench vise
- Kerosene or penetrating oil
- Steel wool, emery paper or wire brush
- Soft brush or cloth
- Soap
- Lightweight oil

403 Revive Wilting Cut Flowers

Is that drop-dead-gorgeous bouquet beginning to droop? Before you toss those flowers into the compost bin, try this treatment. If they're not too far gone, you can give them a new lease on life.

Steps

1 Fill a clean container with warm water (110°F/43°C) and add a floral preservative.

2 Hold each stem under lukewarm running water. Using a sharp knife or shears, cut the stem at a 45-degree angle, about ½ inch (12 mm) from the bottom, while the stem is under the running water.

3 Remove any leaves that would be underwater in the vase.

4 Immediately set the stem into the container of warm water.

5 Place the recut flowers in a cool spot (but no cooler than 35°F/2°C) for an hour or two.

6 Move them to a place that's out of direct sunlight and away from both cold drafts and heat sources. Keep the flowers well away from unwrapped fruits and vegetables—they produce ethylene, which will shorten the life of the flowers.

7 Add water, with preservative, as the level goes down, and change the water every two to three days.

What You'll Need

- Vase or similar container
- Floral preservative
- Sharp knife or shears

Tip

To make your own preservative, mix 1 part nondiet lemon-lime soda with 3 parts water; for each quart (32 fl oz/1 l) of water, add ¼ tsp. household bleach.

404 Sharpen a Power Mower Blade

A dull mower blade doesn't cut grass blades—it tears them, leaving the grass vulnerable to disease or damage from the sun. How often the mower blade needs sharpening depends on the size of your lawn and how often you mow, but plan on doing the job at least every four to six weeks.

Steps

1 Drain the gas and disconnect the spark plug wire in your power mower so the motor doesn't turn over while you're working.

2 Tilt the mower on its side, and wedge a block of wood between the blade and the mower deck to keep the blade from turning. You can also buy a device called a Blade Buster that locks the blade in place while you work on the mower.

3 Use a scraper or putty knife to clean any built-up debris from the underside of the mower deck.

4 Using an adjustable wrench, remove the bolt from the center of the blade.

5 Pull off the blade and clamp it in a bench vise.

6 Check the blade edges for small nicks, and remove them using a flat medium file.

7 Sharpen the blade by moving the file toward the cutting edge with smooth, even strokes. Follow the original bevel of the blade as closely as you can.

8 Make the same number of strokes on each edge. If you take more metal off one side than the other, the blade will be out of balance. An out-of-balance blade cuts unevenly; it also makes the mower vibrate, which can cause serious damage to the engine.

9 Test the balance by resting the blade on a dowel or the handle of a screwdriver. If one side points up, sharpen the other until the blade lies flat. (Or use a blade balancer, available at garden centers and hardware stores.)

What You'll Need

- Screwdriver
- Block of wood
- Scraper or putty knife
- Adjustable wrench
- Bench vise
- Flat medium file
- Dowel or blade balancer

Tip

Rather than fuss with a blade that's badly nicked or very dull, it's better to have it professionally sharpened— or simply to replace it.

Warning

Never touch the blades of any power mower until the spark plug is completely disconnected. Just a few drops of gas in the tank could be enough to make the mower's engine kick over when you move the blade.

405 Sharpen Push Mower Blades

One of the beauties of a push lawn mower is that it sharpens itself to some extent: As you push the mower, the revolving blades scrape over the cutter bar, and the action tends to make both blades keener, not duller. Every year or two, though, a sharpening job is in order. You could take the machine to a pro, or use this backlapping technique.

Steps

1 Prop up the lawn mower so you can turn the reel by twirling the wheels.

2 Check the blades for nicks and burrs. If you find any, remove them by holding a file flat against the blade and pushing away from the edge.

3 Examine the cutting bar. It should just meet the blades along their entire length. (To make sure it's in the right spot, grasp a wheel and turn it forward; you should hear a whispery sound as the blades pass the bar.)

4 If the bar is out of alignment, adjust it using the screws on the ends of the bar. (There are two at each end; when you look at them, it will be obvious which one will move the bar closer to the blades.)

5 Using your fingers or a soft paintbrush, cover the blades with a thin, even coat of automotive valve-grinding compound (available at auto-parts stores).

6 Grasp a wheel and turn it slowly backward so that the grinding compound is squeezed between the blades and the cutting bar, thereby sharpening both cutting edges as they pass each other. Be sure that each blade touches the bar as you rotate the wheel.

7 Make about a dozen turns, applying more grinding compound when necessary.

8 Examine the blade edges. If they look sharp, wash off all the valve compound with soapy water and rinse thoroughly.

9 Test for sharpness. Insert a sheet of newspaper between the blades and the cutting bar, and rotate the reel forward. (You may need to try a few times to get the paper in the right position.) When the blades cut the paper as easily and as cleanly as a sharp pair of scissors would, you're ready to roll.

What You'll Need

- Flat file
- Screwdriver
- Soft paintbrush
- Automotive valve-grinding compound
- Soap
- Newspaper

Tips

After each use, hose the mower clean and wipe it dry. Then wipe all the metal parts with a thin film of WD-40 or mineral oil.

If you've got a new push mower, check your owner's manual for any specific sharpening guidelines.

Warning

Sharpen blades only by hand. The heat generated by a power grinder or an electric drill with a grinding wheel attached can destroy the temper of the metal.

406 Repair Bald Spots on Grass

No matter what caused your lawn to turn spotty or partially bald, fixing the damage is simple. First, buy seed, sod or plugs of the same variety as your current grass (or a close match). Then proceed as follows.

Steps

1 Remove weeds, dead grass, and other detritus from the injured area (see A).

2 In cases where dog urine, fertilizer burn, or a spilled substance such as gasoline caused the damage, flush the soil with water before you plant. Cultivate the soil to a depth of 6 to 8 inches (15 to 20 cm).

3 Spread about a ½-inch (12-mm) layer of compost on the surface and work it in well.

4 If you're using grass seed, sprinkle the seed over the area. Then tamp it lightly with the back of a spade or hoe so that the seed just makes contact with the soil.

5 Top the seeded spot with straw or other mulch, and water lightly. The soil surface should be kept moist, but not wet, until the seedlings are growing strongly. Then revert to your normal watering schedule.

6 If you're using sod, cut a piece that fits the cultivated area and set it into place. Then tamp the sod firmly to ensure good contact with the soil below. Keep the sod moist to the depth of the grass roots until the blades show active growth.

7 To replant with plugs, use a bulb planter to make holes 4 to 6 inches (10 to 15 cm) apart in staggered rows. Then set in the plugs. As with sod, keep the site well watered until you see active growth.

8 Whichever planting method you've used, lay a wooden board across the repaired spot to make sure the new grass is level with the rest of the lawn (see B).

What You'll Need

- Shovel or trowel
- Compost
- Grass seed, sod or plugs
- Spade or hoe
- Straw or other mulch
- Bulb planter
- Wooden board

Tips

Seed is inexpensive and easy to keep on hand for patching. Sod gives instant results but costs more. With grasses such as St. Augustine or hybrid Bermuda that spread by runners, you must use sod or plugs.

Repair cool-season lawns in early fall. In warm regions, do the job in late spring.

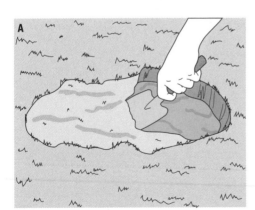

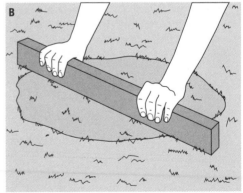

407 Rid Your Grass of Dog Urine Spots

When nature calls, dogs do what they must, where they must (after all, a pristine green lawn is a human invention, far beyond the comprehension of the canine brain). The brown spots caused by urine are simply the result of too much of a good thing—namely, an over-concentration of nitrogen, which burns the grass.

Steps

1 Consider the kind of maintenance your lawn gets. The soil beneath a highly fertilized lawn already contains large concentrations of nitrogen—and a little more, courtesy of a dog doing his duty, is enough to push the grass over the edge. (Female-dog urine is not more potent than that of males. It causes more trouble simply because females tend to urinate all at once in one spot.)

2 Turn on the hose and flood the spot if the deed has just been done. Even within a few days, a thorough flushing should head off any damage, and before long the grass will grow back as good as new.

3 In cases where the damage has been in place for a while, dig out the damaged turf and flush the soil with plenty of water to dilute the excess nitrogen.

4 Reseed or resod the spot.

What You'll Need

- Garden hose
- Shovel or trowel
- Grass seed or sod

Tip

Urine damage has nothing to do with acid, so canine dietary supplements that alter the urine's pH have no effect on the "burn" spots.

408 Get Rid of Rampant Brambles

Once a patch of wild blackberries gets going, there's almost no stopping it—and blackberries' close cousins, domestic raspberries and rugosa roses, are just as pushy. Before you reach for an herbicide, try this method. It does take time and patience—but if you want to avoid toxic chemicals, the results are worth it.

Steps

1 Begin at the front of the patch and start cutting. (The smaller the pieces, the easier they are to dispose of.)

2 Put the cuttings into the trash as you go. (Left on the ground or in the compost pile, at least some of them will take root.)

3 When you've cut back to the stump of a plant, slice around it with a hoe or sharp spade.

4 Reach under the stump and cut it off, taking care to cut each little root where it meets the stem. When the roots are no longer attached to the base of the plant, they'll rot.

What You'll Need

- Pruning shears
- Thick gloves
- Protective clothing
- Trash bags
- Hoe or sharp spade

Warning

Berry and rugosa thorns are wicked. Wear thick gloves, heavy long trousers and a long-sleeved shirt or jacket.

409 Troubleshoot Brown Spots on a Lawn

Dog urine isn't the only source of brown spots in a lawn. Even on the best-kept turf, patches can appear for no reason at all—or so it seems. In most cases, the only cure is to dig out and replace the grass, but knowing what caused the problem will help you keep the new crop healthy.

PROBLEM	POSSIBLE CAUSE	SOLUTION
Buried debris	Objects lingering just under the soil surface, such as bricks, lumber or rocks (even lost toys), leave too little room for good root penetration. When roots can't explore for water, they—and then grass blades—dry out.	Poke around with a thin metal rod or dig with a trowel. If you find an obstacle, remove it.
Compacted soil	When feet beat a trail across a lawn, they make soil particles pack together so that roots can't grow as they need to. Areas blessed with heavy clay soil are especially prone to compaction.	Reroute traffic or go with the flow and install a footpath. If the entire lawn suffers from compaction, use a core aerator in spring, fall or both.
Dull mower blades	A dull blade shreds grass tips, making them dry out quickly.	Sharpen blades after every three to six mowings (depending on the size of your lawn).
Heat reflectors	Large windows, light-colored walls and paved surfaces can reflect the sun's heat onto nearby grass, quickly drying blades to a crisp.	Water sun-baked areas more frequently and deeply.
Human inattention	A power mower that's left running will kill the turf beneath it. So will gasoline, oil and fertilizer spills, or even objects left lying on grass while the sun beats down.	Be careful!
Overfeeding	Too much high-nitrogen fertilizer can burn grass blades.	Find out how much nitrogen your grass variety needs and stay within that limit. The amount can range anywhere from ½ to 1 lb. (250 to 500 g) per year for buffalo grass, to 4 to 6 lbs. (2 to 3 kg) per year for St. Augustine grass.

PROBLEM	POSSIBLE CAUSE	SOLUTION
Overwatering	Giving grass more water than it needs can leach away essential nutrients. It also leaves weakened grass vulnerable to pests and diseases.	Water only when the grass needs it. Grasses differ in their water requirements, but most varieties thrive on 1 to 2 inches (2.5 to 5 cm) a week, whether from rain or your sprinklers.
Scalping	When a mower runs over high spots in a lawn, it cuts the grass too closely, leaving too little cover to protect soil from the sun. The soil dries out and grass blades follow.	Raise the blade before you mow in high spots.
Sloping ground	Water can run off a hillside before it has a chance to sink in.	Aerate so water can penetrate soil. Wearing golf spikes or aerating sandles (available from garden supply stores), walk across the slope to puncture holes in the soil. Or replace grass with a ground cover that thrives in drier conditions.
Thatch	If your grass feels spongy when you step on it, chances are this is your brown-spot culprit. A layer of dead grass blades and stems builds up on the soil surface, blocking the flow of water and nutrients.	Remove thin layers with a de-thatching rake (available at garden centers). If the buildup is 1 inch (2.5 cm) or more thick, rent a powered de-thatcher. To prevent future outbreaks, top-dress lawn once or twice a year with ¼ inch (6 mm) of compost, go easy on fertilizers and avoid frequent, shallow watering.
Tree roots	When trees and grass compete for the same water supply, trees usually win.	Replace grass with an attractive organic mulch or a ground cover that thrives in dry soil.

410 Control Major Garden Pests

A creature that's nonexistent or harmless in one place can be a major nuisance in another. The following culprits, though, seem to cause big trouble everywhere. Here are some environment-friendly ways to reduce their damage.

PEST	WHAT TO DO
Rabbits	• Get a ferret (a first-class rabbit-chaser) or beg some ferret droppings from a pet shop or ferret-owning friend, and scatter the droppings around your plants. • Plant repellent species in and around the rabbits' targets. Good choices include Mexican marigolds, dusty miller, garlic and onions. • Fill 1-gallon (4-l) glass bottles with water and set them among your plants. Sunlight bouncing off the glass will startle the bunnies and send them fleeing. • Fill cloth pouches with cat, dog or human hair and scatter them among your plants.
Deer	• Your only guaranteed protection is a solid fence that's at least 8 feet (2.5 m) high. • To discourage deer, hang or spread any of these around the garden: human or dog hair, blood meal, baby powder, bars of deodorant soap, dirty laundry or shoes, evidence of natural predators (call a zoo and ask if they'll give you hair, urine or feces of a lion, tiger or cougar). • Spray susceptible plants with a commercial product such as Hinder, an organic formula made from fatty acid soaps. • Protect young trees by wrapping the trunks with hardware cloth or a plastic spiral tree protector (available at garden centers). • Replace the deer's favorite food with plants they don't like. For a complete list, consult a book on deer control, but try any of these for starters: Annuals: snapdragon, sweet alyssum, stock, nasturtium, nicotiana, wax begonias, zinnia. Perennials: yarrow, monkshood, foxglove, lavender, coneflower, peonies, iris. Trees and shrubs: bottlebrush buckeye, shadblow, red osier dogwood, spruce, pine, northern red oak, rugosa rose, American holly, Sawara false cypress, Japanese pieris. • Surround your garden with a triple-deep hedge of arborvitaes, which deer love. They'll flock to it and forgo your other plants.
Slugs	• Water in the morning instead of evening; the soil will dry by nightfall, depriving the slugs of needed moisture when they come out to feed. Studies have shown this method to be as effective as classic trap-and-destroy techniques—reducing slug damage by up to 80 percent. • Provide habitat for predators such as toads, birds, turtles and salamanders. • Erect minifences of copper stripping around your planting beds. Just make sure you get all the slugs out of the area before you put up the fences; otherwise, you'll trap the pests inside.

PEST	WHAT TO DO
Moles	● Remove their food supply, grubs, by inoculating your lawn with milky spore disease (available at garden centers). ● Walk over the tunnels to flatten them; this often encourages the moles to go elsewhere. ● Find a tunnel that seems to be a main route and poke holes in it with a stick. Then pour in a castor oil–based repellent such as MoleMed. Or make your own by combining 1 cup (8 fl oz/250 ml) water, 3 fl oz (80 ml) castor oil and 4 tbsp. dishwashing liquid. Then add 2 tbsp. of this mixture to 1 gallon (4 l) water.
Cutworms	● Mix moistened bran with molasses and BTK (*Bacillus thuringiensis* var. *kurstaki*), available from garden centers and catalogs. Sprinkle the mixture over the soil about a week before you plant. You won't kill off all the cutworms this way, but you will reduce the population. ● Install a protective collar (1 inch/2.5 cm aboveground, 1 inch/2.5 cm below) around each seedling or transplant. Good collar makings include aluminum foil, paper-towel rolls and juice-concentrate cans. ● Encourage predators, especially toads and birds. ● Plant dill, alyssum, yarrow or cosmos to encourage parasitic wasps, which prey on cutworm larvae.
Groundhogs, aka woodchucks	● Get a dog. Jack Russell terriers are famed groundhog hunters, but any canine, large or small, will send the rodents packing. ● Borrow the scent of someone else's dog: Give a friend's pooch some old towels or blanket scraps to lie on, then scatter them around the garden. Replace the bedding often to keep the aroma fresh and scary. ● Empty the contents of your cat's litter box into the tunnel entrance. You may need to repeat the process several times, but eventually the groundhog will get discouraged and move out. Then fill up the entrance and exit holes with rocks to keep out newcomers. ● Erect a welded-wire fence that extends 4 feet (120 cm) aboveground and 2 feet (60 cm) below. Bend the top foot (30 cm) of wire outward to form a baffle.

411 Rid Your Garden of Pests

In nature, there is no such thing as a "pest." All the plant-munching critters in your garden—from the tiniest aphid to the biggest buck deer—are simply going about the business of survival. Normally, natural predators ensure that nobody gets the upper hand. Sometimes, though, the balance gets out of whack, and you need to take action.

Steps

1 Invest in a comprehensive pest- and disease-control manual, and learn how to recognize the "enemy." Many destructive insects look almost identical to beneficial ones, and often what appears to be insect damage is actually a symptom of disease or cultural problems.

2 Compare notes with gardening neighbors; pest problems (and solutions) vary greatly from one part of the country to another.

3 Go cold turkey on pesticides. Along with the pests, they kill off beneficial insects and other pest predators. Often this step alone is enough to solve the problem. If you—or your garden's former owners—have been using pesticides for some time, be patient: It could take a few weeks for the balance to right itself.

4 Use chemical fertilizers sparingly if at all. They provide instant nutrition for plants, but they can destroy important organisms in the soil, including beneficial bacteria and soil-dwelling predators.

5 Improve the health of your soil—and thereby your plants—by adding large helpings of organic matter, especially compost and well-cured manure. (Healthy plants can fend off pests better than sickly ones can.)

6 Diversify your plantings. Most pests (insects and larger critters alike) have definite food preferences. If your garden consists of just a few kinds of plants, it's a prime target for whatever culprits fancy that vegetation. By growing a mixed bag of species and varieties, you lessen the appeal for unwelcome diners.

7 Provide habitats for predators (see Tips). A single toad, frog, bird or bat consumes hundreds of insects a day.

8 In the case of an all-out insect invasion, fight fire with fire. Collect a trowelful of the damage-causing pests, and liquefy them in a blender with 1 cup (8 fl oz/250 ml) water. Strain and dilute with 1 gallon (4 l) water, and pour the juice into a spray bottle. Then take aim and let 'em have it. There are numerous theories as to why this odd-sounding recipe works, but it has proved effective on nearly all insect pests, including beetles, squash and stink bugs, cutworms, armyworms—even slugs (see Warning).

Tips

To get most insects off your plants, dislodge them with a strong spray of water, or handpick and destroy them.

Toads need shallow water (a low basin sunk into the ground works fine) and shelter such as ground covers, rock piles or a store-bought "toad abode." Frogs prefer small ponds or water gardens. Bat houses are available from garden centers and catalogs.

Warning

Do not use bug juice (see step 8) on mosquitoes, fleas or other blood-sucking insects that transmit disease.

412 Troubleshoot Herbs

By and large, herbs are some of the easiest-going plants a gardener could ask for. In fact, they're so trouble-free that many people forget that these plants actually can have problems now and then.

SYMPTOMS	CAUSE	SOLUTIONS
Stunted growth; sooty black stuff on stems or leaves; leaves yellow-spotted, curling or turning brown	Whiteflies	Dislodge the flies with a spray of water. Trap them on commercial sticky-traps, or make your own by coating yellow-painted boards with honey or Tangle Foot (a commercial sticky substance available at garden centers and from catalogs). Encourage green lacewings and chalcid wasps with plants such as sunflower, scented geraniums, yarrow and angelica. In case of severe infestations, dig up plants and destroy them.
Plants turning yellow or showing signs of powdery mildew, rust or root rot (see 425 Trouble-shoot Rose Diseases)	Overwatering; poor drainage	If rot has set in, pull up the plants and destroy them. In the earlier stages, cut off affected plant parts and ease off on the water. For most herbs, keep soil dry to a depth of 1 to 1½ inches (2.5 to 4 cm). Improve drainage, or grow your herbs in raised beds or containers.
Stunted or deformed leaves; clear, sticky substance on leaves or stems	Aphids	Dislodge them with a strong stream of water. Spray with this mixture: Combine four to six cloves of garlic, crushed, and 1 tbsp. vegetable oil in 1 qt. (32 fl oz/1 l) water. Let the solution sit for several hours, then strain out the solids. For severe infestations, spray with a variation of bug juice (see 411 Rid Your Garden of Pests). Because tiny aphids are all but impossible to handpick, load your blender with infested leaves. For long-term protection, encourage predators such as ladybugs and green lacewings.
Chewed flowers or leaves (especially on chervil, dill, parsley, fennel or angelica—all members of the carrot family)	Caterpillars (most likely green with black stripes)	Probably nothing. These herbs are host plants for larvae of black swallowtail butterflies. In most cases, they do only minor cosmetic damage (and the presence of the adults will reward your patience). If they're decimating your crop, handpick them and transfer them to a patch of Queen Anne's lace. (Or grow a "lure" crop of carrot-family herbs just for them.)

413 Troubleshoot Houseplants

Are your houseplants looking less than shipshape? Don't toss them overboard. Once you zero in on the problem, chances are you can have them growing well again in no time.

SYMPTOMS	CAUSE	SOLUTIONS
Tiny white or brown shells on leaves, stems or both	Scale	Remove the insects, using a strong water spray, tweezers, a toothpick, or a cotton swab dipped in alcohol. (Take care not to get alcohol on the plant itself; you could injure the tissue.) Wash the plant with a solution of 2 tsp. dish-washing soap (not detergent) to 1 gallon (4 l) water.
Sticky honeydew on leaves; waxy white insects on the undersides	Mealybugs	Follow the procedures above.
Plants lose vigor; roots and soil particles covered with white, waxy powder (most often on cacti and other succulents, African violets, ferns and fuchsias)	Root mealybugs	Wash the roots thoroughly and repot the plant in fresh soil and a clean pot. In severe cases, discard the plant; sterilize the pot before you use it again.
Barely visible dots moving slowly on the undersides of leaves; fine webbing sometimes visible when you hold the plant up to light	Spider mites	Spray the plant with water to dislodge the mites. Wash the plant with soapy water (see "Scale," above).
Clouds of tiny white flies around the plant; sometimes sticky honey-dew on upper leaf surfaces	Whiteflies	Spray the plant with water to dislodge mites. Wash the plant thoroughly with soapy water and a soft brush.
Reduced growth; leaves small and yellow	Nitrogen deficiency	Apply a high-nitrogen fertilizer; consult a houseplant book for specific guidelines.
Wilting foliage and sometimes stems; leaves yellow and falling; roots peeling or disintegrating	Overwatering or poor drainage	Cut back on water. Replant in a better-draining potting mix, and make sure the pot has drainage holes.
Poor growth; wilting leaves	Too little water	Water more frequently; consult a houseplant book for your plant's specific requirements. Improve the moisture retention of the soil by adding compost or commercial water-retention granules.

414 Overcome Shade Problems

Whether you've just acquired a house with a yard that's shadier than you'd like, or nearby construction is stealing your sunshine, don't despair. You *can* have a lush, colorful garden. First, though, you need to know how much shade you've got, when you've got it and where it's coming from.

Steps

Analyze your shade

1 Make a sketch of your yard and its immediate surroundings. Include established planting areas and all sources of shade, such as trees, fences and the walls of your house.

2 Note factors that could change your light level in the near future— for instance, a diseased tree that's destined for removal or a house going up next door.

3 Spend a day tracking the sun's path across your property from dawn till dusk. On your sketch, note the time the sun enters and leaves each planting area. Repeat this procedure in each of the next three seasons.

4 Examine your four seasonal drawings. They'll tell what kind of shade you have in which parts of your yard and at what times of the year.

5 Learn the standard classifications: dense shade (cast by walls or low, thick evergreen branches), dappled shade (the sun is blocked, as by large-leaved trees like maples, but light still enters the site), bright light (common on the north sides of houses, where no direct sun reaches the ground but nothing blocks the sky), filtered light (sun shining through small-leaved trees such as birches) and partial shade, aka partial sun (direct sun for 2 to 5 hours a day).

Let in more light

1 Look at your drawings to see where you want more light and which shade sources you can change.

2 Prune or remove shade-casting trees or shrubs.

3 Replace solid fences with lattice panels.

4 Paint walls or fences white to reflect more sun onto nearby plantings.

5 Before you plant, remember: The effect of sunlight on plants varies depending on the time of day, the season and the region. For instance, plants that need full sun in the North usually prefer partial sun in the South.

What You'll Need

- Sketch pad or graph paper
- Pen or pencil
- Pruning shears or saw
- Lattice panels
- White paint and paintbrush
- Books on shade gardening

Tips

Few plants will survive in dense shade, but in all of the other light levels your choices are many.

Check local events calendars for upcoming garden tours. Plants that thrive in your neighbors' gardens are likely to perform well in yours, too.

Invest in a comprehensive book on shade gardening. Other sources of knowledge and inspiration: shade-plant specialty catalogs and the shade section of your local garden center.

415 Rid Soil of Pests and Diseases

Soil-borne diseases can spell disaster for plants. In many cases, you can control disease organisms by mulching, rotating crops and stocking the soil with large helpings of organic matter. But when you're dealing with soil that's badly infected—especially if disease-bearing nematodes are at work—you need to wipe the slate clean. Solarizing is the way to go.

Steps

1 Understand how solarizing works: It raises the soil temperature to around 150°F (65°C), a lethal level for garden culprits like fungi, nematodes and Colorado potato beetles.

2 To generate the necessary heat, treat your soil in the warmest, sunniest time of the year—July and August in most regions.

3 Dig or pull up all plants, and till the soil to a depth of 12 inches (30 cm). Remove rocks, twigs and other debris.

4 Rake the surface until it's smooth, and shape it into whatever rows, beds or hills in which you intend to plant. (You'll want to disturb the soil as little as possible after it's been treated.)

5 Water until the soil feels moist but not soggy, to a depth of 2 feet (60 cm). If you have very well drained soil, lay a soaker hose across the site (you may need to provide additional water during the treatment period).

6 Cover the plot with a sheet of 3- to 6-mil clear plastic, and pile soil or stones around the perimeter to seal the edges. If you're working with a raised bed, make sure the plastic drapes down over the sides. Leave some slack in the cover so it can puff up, rather than burst or blow away, as the heat intensifies.

7 Install a second layer of plastic if your climate is cool, cloudy or humid. First, place wooden blocks, large stones or aluminum cans every 4 to 6 feet (120 to 180 cm) across the first cover. Lay down the second sheet so that it floats on top of the first, moving the supports around if necessary. Then seal the edges with soil or stones.

8 If you laid down a soaker hose in step 5, pick up a corner of the plastic after a couple of weeks and feel the soil. If it's dried out, run the hose to replenish moisture, then replace the plastic.

9 In the Southwest, leave the plastic in place for a total of three to four weeks; elsewhere wait six to nine weeks. Then remove the plastic; the soil is ready for planting.

What You'll Need

- Shovel or rototiller
- Rake
- Garden hose
- Soaker hose
- 3- to 6-mil clear plastic
- Soil or stones
- Wooden blocks, stones or aluminum cans

Tips

If you don't want to put your whole garden out of action at the height of summer, solarize one section at time, beginning with the most problem-ridden.

If summer thunderstorms occur frequently in your area, try solarizing before or after the height of the stormy period; you'll stand a better chance of clear skies and intense sunlight.

To boost the heat in cool climates, before you cover your plot, apply a 2-inch (5-cm) layer of fresh manure and mix it in well.

Warning

Cultivate solarized ground as little as possible. If you till any deeper than 6 inches (15 cm), you'll bring up untreated soil.

416 Revive a Nonperforming Compost Pile

When it comes to organic matter, compost is la crème de la crème. Making a big batch of the stuff is fairly simple: The key is striking the right balance of 3 parts dry, high-carbon (aka brown) material to 1 part succulent, high-nitrogen (aka green) material. Still, even when you've got the numbers just so, things can go awry.

PROBLEM	SOLUTIONS
Animals are raiding pile	• Grind up fruits and vegetables in a blender before you add them to pile, or bury them in center. • Avoid all meats, fats and oils.
Some pieces are not breaking down	• Take them out, chop them up and put them back in. • Generate heat by adding more "green" material, such as manure, fresh grass clippings, alfalfa meal or seaweed.
Nothing's breaking down	• If pile is dry, add water until center is evenly moist. • In dry climates, cover pile with a tarpaulin to hold in moisture, and check frequently. • If pile is moist, add "greens" and turn pile.
It smells like ammonia and feels moist but not soggy	• Add more "brown" material, such as straw, shredded paper, leaves or sawdust, and turn pile.
It smells bad and feels soggy	• Add "browns" and turn pile. • In wet climates, cover pile with a tarpaulin to keep off rain.
Small pile doesn't heat up, or heats up only in the center; feels moist	• Enlarge pile. It needs to be at least 3 feet (1 m) square to generate necessary heat.
Large pile doesn't heat up; feels moist	• Add "greens" and turn pile.
New pile heats up but cools off before most of the material has decomposed	• Turn pile with a garden fork until all material is thoroughly mixed together.
A matted layer on top doesn't break down	• Turn pile, breaking up matted material and mixing it in thoroughly.
Seedlings are growing on top	• Pull them up. If they're flowers or vegetables, transplant them. If they're weeds that have set seed, destroy them; otherwise, chop them up and mix them into pile. • Add more "greens" to generate heat and kill any remaining seeds.

417 Fix Bad Soil

No matter how poor your soil is, you can have rich, fertile planting beds with no digging and no tilling.

Steps

1 Mark off your site in late summer or early fall, using stakes and string, a rope or a garden hose as guidelines. Leave the turf in place. Trample any tall weeds, but you needn't cut them.

2 Lay a 1-inch (2.5-cm) layer of newspapers over the site, over-lapping the edges as you go. Wet them down thoroughly. Spread 1 to 2 inches (2.5 to 5 cm) of peat moss over the paper.

3 Cover the peat with 4 to 6 inches (10 to 15 cm) of organic matter such as compost, well-cured manure, leaves, dried grass clip-pings, seaweed, shredded paper—or any combination thereof. Avoid oils, fats and animal protein.

4 Add alternate layers of peat moss and organic matter until the bed has reached 12 to 24 inches (30 to 60 cm) high.

5 Water until the material is saturated. By spring, your heap will have decomposed into 6 to 8 inches (15 to 20 cm) of rich soil.

6 Sow your seeds or set in your plants, and mulch with compost, peat moss or dried grass clippings. As the plants grow, continue to mulch with the compost, peat moss or clippings. As the news-paper disintegrates and the organic matter decomposes, the layer of loose, rich soil will extend deeper into the ground (thanks to earthworms, bacteria and other soil-dwelling organisms).

What You'll Need

- Stakes and string, or long rope
- Newspaper
- Garden hose
- Peat moss
- Organic matter

Tips

The key ingredient in the no-dig recipe is the bottom layer of newspaper. It draws earthworms, which decom-pose the soil.

Avoid tilling your beds, espe-cially if you have clay soil. Tilling can actually damage soil structure and, if done repeatedly, can cause hard-pan to form.

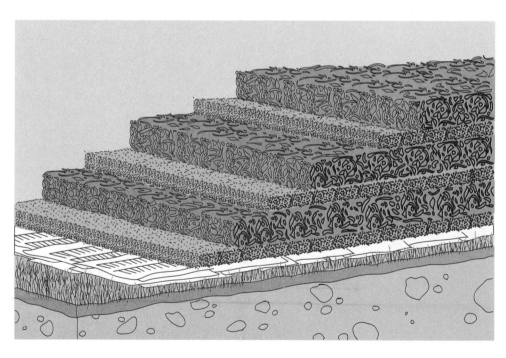

418 Shore Up a Raised Garden Bed

Here are some fairly easy fixes to make sure you'll have sturdy, straight beds for seasons to come.

Steps

Adding corner supports

1 If any nails have begun to pull loose, hammer them back in to close any gaps between the ends and sides of the bed.

2 Measure and cut four lengths of 2-by-2 lumber, each 10 inches (25 cm) longer than the height of your raised bed. Make the cut on one end straight across, and on the other at a 45-degree angle (use a protractor to draw the angle, or cut the wood in a miter box).

3 Apply wood preservative to the supports if necessary.

4 Dig away some of the soil from inside each corner of the bed. Push a support into each corner, with the pointed end down, until the flat end is flush with the top of the bed.

5 Drive two 3-inch (7.5-cm) galvanized screws through one side of the bed close to the corner, and one screw through the adjoining side of the bed close to the same corner (see A). All three screws go into the same corner brace. Fill in around the supports with soil.

Adding a center brace

1 Measure the bed to see if the sides are the same distance apart in the middle as at the ends. If necessary, pull the sides closer with a long clamp or have someone help you push them closer.

2 Cut a length of 2-by-2 lumber as long as this distance. Apply any preservative or stain.

3 Place the 2-by-2 brace flush with the top of the bed. Drive a 3-inch (7.5-cm) galvanized screw through each side of the bed into the ends of the brace (see B).

What You'll Need

- Hammer
- Measuring tape
- 2-by-2 lumber
- Protractor or miter box
- Electric or hand saw
- Wood preservative or stain
- Paintbrush
- Trowel or shovel
- 3-inch (7.5-cm) galvanized screws
- Screwdriver or electric drill with screwdriver bit
- Clamp

Tip

Pressure-treated lumber is durable, but it contains chemicals that may leach into the soil. If you are growing edibles such as vegetables, and not just flowers, it's a good idea to make your supports (and your raised beds, in fact) from an untreated rot-resistant wood like cedar.

419 Remove a Dead or Diseased Tree Limb

Dead, diseased and injured branches affect more than a tree's appearance. They can fall and injure people or property, or spread diseases to other plants in the garden. If the limb is high off the ground or so large that you'd need power equipment to prune it, call a professional arborist. Otherwise, get out your pruning saw and proceed as follows. You can remove diseased or damaged limbs at any time without harming the tree, but the wound will heal fastest if you prune before spring growth begins.

Steps

1 Find the branch collar—the slight swelling where the limb meets the trunk. When you remove the limb, you want to leave this doughnut-shaped mass intact; it contains living trunk tissue and serves as the tree's natural defense against pests and diseases.

2 Choose the right tool. For a limb up to about 2 inches (5 cm) in diameter, or one that's growing close to another, a narrow, curved pruning saw works best. To cut a larger branch, use a straight pruning saw that has teeth on both sides of the blade.

3 Reduce the weight of the limb (thereby preventing it from tearing bark from the trunk as it falls). This process involves two cuts. First, cut up from the underside of the branch, 12 to 18 inches (30 to 45 cm) from the branch collar, about two-thirds of the way through (or until you feel the saw blade start to bind) (see A).

4 Make the second cut from the top, directly above or just a little out from the first one. Cut straight down until the limb falls (see A).

5 Take off the remaining stub by cutting downward at a 45- to 60-degree angle, just beyond the branch collar (see B).

6 If the removed limb was diseased, swab your saw blade with household bleach, then rinse and wipe it dry before you store it or use it on another tree.

What You'll Need

- Pruning saw
- Bleach
- Rag

Tip

Be sure to remove all branch stubs. They serve as entryways for disease organisms.

Warning

Conventional wisdom used to advocate coating a pruning wound with tree paint. New research has found that this step is useless. If you've made your cuts properly, the tree will heal by itself. If you haven't, nothing will help.

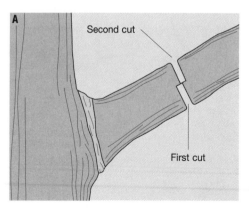

A — Second cut / First cut

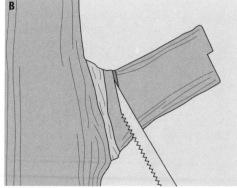

B

420 Troubleshoot Trees and Shrubs

Tree and shrub ailments can be hard to diagnose. Unless you can spot an obvious culprit, such as tent caterpillars, it is usually best to call in a pro. First, though, run through this list.

SYMPTOMS	CAUSE	SOLUTIONS
Newest leaves develop yellow areas between veins (especially common in acid lovers such as azaleas, rhododendrons, hydrangeas, camellias)	Overly alkaline soil	• Test soil pH and correct it to 6.0 to 6.8 if possible. • Use a fertilizer formulated to the particular kind of plant. • Use a high-acid mulch, such as pine needles.
Branches dying; leaves mottled, silvery colored or speckled white or tan	Road salt, air or ground pollution	• Feed and water plant thoroughly. • Avoid using salt for ice removal. • Discontinue all herbicides. • Or remove plant and replace it with a more resistant variety.
Bark turns dark brown, cracks, splits open and dies; canker (cauliflowerlike growths) on the damaged bark	Sunscald	• Remove cankers with a sharp knife, and treat cuts with a solution of 1 part chlorine bleach to 10 parts water. • Fertilize to encourage new growth (check guidelines for the variety in a comprehensive tree book or the label that came with your plant). • Protect plant from sun or move it to a shadier spot.
Wilted, scorched or dropping leaves	Too little water reaching the roots	• Water slowly and thoroughly from trunk to drip line. • Mulch with compost or well-cured manure.
Top branches dying; leaves turning brown or wilting; general decline in vigor and appearance	Poor drainage	• If possible, move plant to a site with better drainage. • Otherwise, improve drainage. See 424 Fix Poor Soil Drainage or consult a landscape contractor.
Plant growth slow and spindly; older, lower leaves turn yellow and may drop	Nitrogen deficiency	• Dig compost into the soil, along with a high-nitrogen amendment such as well-cured manure, fish meal or dried blood. • Avoid wood-chip mulch, which can deplete nitrogen.

421 Repair a Leaking Irrigation System

If an earthquake or an errant shovel bursts your irrigation pipes, you know it instantly. But smaller leaks can go undetected for months—until you realize that your water bill has skyrocketed, or you've got a patch of soggy ground that won't dry out.

Steps

Finding a leak aboveground

1 Bear in mind that aboveground leaks are likely only in drip, or micro-irrigation, systems.

2 Remove any mulch or ground cover that covers the supply pipe.

3 Turn on the water and check for spraying or bubbling.

Finding a leak below ground

1 Remember that an underground leak can occur with either a micro-irrigation system or a high-pressure sprinkler system.

2 Cap all the spray heads in the system.

3 Turn on the water and wait for puddles to appear on the surface of the soil.

4 Avoid digging in search of the leak—at best, you could unearth much of the system and have to spend time reburying the pipes; at worst, you could cut into a pipe and cause extensive damage. Instead, call in a professional who can use special equipment to trace the leak.

5 When you've located the source of the leak, dig a trench that's deep enough and wide enough so that you can work with the pipes easily.

Repairing a small leak

1 Note the site of the leak. If the problem is a faulty seal in the pipe joints, simply tighten the clamps where the seepage is occurring. If the leak is in the pipe itself, proceed with the following steps.

What You'll Need

- Shovel
- Adjustable wrench or gripping pliers
- Hacksaw or plastic-pipe cutters
- Repair (aka dresser) coupling
- Replacement pipe and fittings
- PVC primer and solvent cement
- Stainless-steel hose clamp
- Screwdriver

Tips

Before you even start tracking the source of the leak, check your sprinkler system's operating manual for any special instructions.

Before reburying either PVC or poly pipe, flush the system thoroughly and check for any signs of seepage.

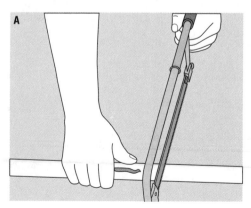

A

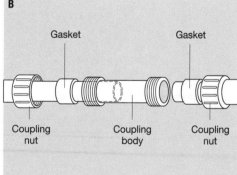

B

Gasket   Gasket

Coupling nut   Coupling body   Coupling nut

2 Mend a leak in the pipe with a repair coupling (also called a dresser coupling). It consists of a coupling body, two rubber gaskets and two coupling nuts.

3 Turn off the water and cut through the pipe at the leak, using a hacksaw or plastic-pipe cutters (see A).

4 Separate the cut ends far enough that you can slip the coupling components onto the pipe ends. Slide a coupling nut onto each piece of pipe, then follow with a gasket. Slip the coupling body over one cut end, then insert the other end into the body. Slide a coupling nut and gasket onto each end of the body, and tighten the nuts (see B).

5 Flush the system thoroughly and check for any sign of seeping before reburying the pipe.

Repairing a major leak

1 In the case of a major leak, or when connections have been pulled apart by earth tremors or frost heaving, you need to insert an additional length of pipe. First, turn off the water.

2 Cut out the damaged section of pipe, using a hacksaw or plastic-pipe cutters.

3 To mend PVC pipe, first clean the area to be cemented and dry it thoroughly. Then apply PVC primer and solvent cement according to the directions on the cement can (see C).

4 Slide a replacement fitting onto each end of the replacement pipe. Then insert it between the two cut ends, slipping an end into each replacement fitting (see D). Let the bond set for the length of time recommended on the can (usually 12 to 24 hours).

5 To mend a polyethylene (aka poly) pipe, slip a stainless-steel hose clamp over the pipe and insert the fitting. If the fitting won't slide in easily, soak the end of the pipe in warm water. Move the clamp into place over the ridged section of the fitting, then tighten it with a screwdriver.

C

D
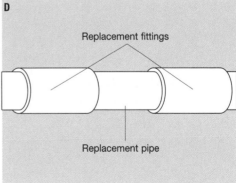

Replacement fittings

Replacement pipe

422 Unclog a Sprinkler System

Dirt and debris can build up in all parts of a sprinkler system—pipes, risers and nozzles. If the water spewing from your sprinklers isn't as strong as it should be, it's time for a cleaning.

Steps

1 Turn off the system and remove all the nozzles and heads.

2 Turn on the water and let it run until a solid, clean stream flows from each head opening. Then turn the water off.

3 Dismantle each nozzle according to the directions in your owner's manual.

4 Hold the nozzle under a faucet or hose to blast out debris. Open small, clogged holes using a piece of wire or a paper clip.

5 Rinse out the filter basket or screen.

6 Reassemble and replace the heads and nozzles. Then turn on the water. If the system still seems sluggish—and your indoor water pressure is normal—the problem could be a leak in the line (see 421 Repair a Leaking Irrigation System).

What You'll Need

- Garden hose
- Wire or paper clip

Tip

To dismantle some nozzles, you'll need a screwdriver or a special key that came with your system; other types you can take apart by hand.

423 Clean a Clogged Drip System

When your drippers stop dripping, your garden can dry to a crisp in no time. If your system is clogged, clear it out with this method.

Steps

1 To clear a single clog, turn on the water and hold your finger over the dripper outlet for several seconds. The resulting back flush should get rid of any debris.

2 If a number of drippers are stopped up, remove the end closure from each tubing line and flush it until the water runs clear. Then put the closures back in place.

3 Clean the filter. If it's an in-line filter, remove the cylindrical filter screen and rinse it with running water. Use a toothbrush or bottle brush to remove any accumulated particles.

4 Most permanent drip systems have a self-cleaning Y-filter. For moderate clogging and routine cleaning, simply turn on the flush outlet, or "dump valve." If the system is badly clogged, unscrew the valve cover and wash the filter screen.

5 Check the system again. If it's still not working properly, chances are there's a break in the line. (See 421 Repair a Leaking Irrigation System; the repair process is the same.)

What You'll Need

- Wrench or screwdriver
- Toothbrush or bottle brush

Tips

To prevent debris buildup, flush your drip lines and clean the filter once a month during the operating season.

In areas with hard water, lines and filters need more frequent attention. Check a week after cleaning to see how fast deposits are building up.

424 Fix Poor Soil Drainage

Poor drainage is the leading cause of death for garden plants. Adding organic matter will improve poorly draining soils. If you've tried that, though, and your site still retains water for hours after a short, heavy rain, further action is called for. A shallow trench and drainage pipe could solve the problem.

Steps

1 Find a spot below the level of the garden where the water can drain away safely. A storm drain, dry well or drainage ditch is an ideal choice.

2 Measure the distance from the lowest point in the problem site to the drainage area. Then buy enough perforated 4-inch (10-cm)-diameter pipe to cover that distance. (Either black ADS or white PVC pipe will work fine.)

3 Dig a trench 18 inches (45 cm) deep and 12 inches (30 cm) wide, sloping downhill between the two points. Try for a drop of about 1 inch (2.5 cm) for every 10 feet (3 m) of ground.

4 Test the slope by driving a stake into the soil at each end of the trench. Run a string between the two stakes, and use a spirit level to measure the drop between them (see A).

5 When the slope is at the correct angle, line the trench with about 3 inches (7.5 cm) of gravel or crushed stone.

6 Lay the pipe on the stone (see B), and make sure any joints are fastened tightly.

7 Cover the pipe with agricultural fabric to prevent soil from clogging the perforations (tuck the cloth under the pipe at its uphill opening).

8 Add 6 more inches (15 cm) of stone over the pipe.

9 Replace the soil in the trench.

What You'll Need

- Tape measure
- Perforated pipe (black ADS or white PVC)
- Shovel
- Wooden stakes
- String
- Spirit level
- Gravel or crushed stone
- Agricultural fabric

Tips

If your drainage problem is severe, you may need professional help. Before you try any do-it-yourself steps, consult a landscape contractor.

On a large site, consider simply going with the flow. Many gorgeous plants, including cardinal flower, Japanese iris and astilbe, thrive in moist soil.

Another alternative to expensive, time-consuming drainage correction is to grow your plants in containers.

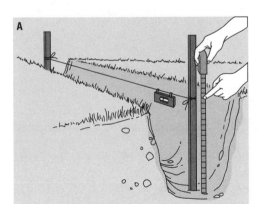

A

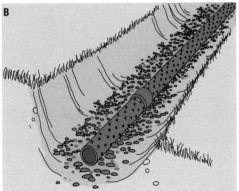

B

425 Troubleshoot Rose Diseases

Roses have earned a reputation as the temperamental divas of the plant world. It's true that the romantic rascals attract their share of illnesses—but these are easier to conquer than you might think.

SYMPTOMS	CAUSE	SOLUTIONS
Some buds open only partially or not at all. Outer petals turn pale brown, dry and papery. In wet weather, bud develops gray mold, then rots and drops off	Balling (fungus)	Remove affected buds before mold develops to prevent dieback. See 428 Overcome Fungus Diseases in Roses.
Purple-black spots on leaves; later, yellow halos develop. Leaves drop prematurely	Blackspot (fungus)	See 428 Overcome Fungus Diseases in Roses.
Discolored buds that fail to open. Flowers rot from inside; outer petals turn brown and moldy	Botrytis blight (fungus)	See 428 Overcome Fungus Diseases in Roses.
Discolored areas on canes. Canes die back or fail to produce new growth. In damp weather, gray mold forms on infected areas. Usually occurs only on plants that have been under stress	Canker and dieback (fungus)	See 428 Overcome Fungus Diseases in Roses.
Cauliflowerlike growths on roots, canes or bud union	Crown gall (soil-borne bacteria)	Cut out small galls and swab the cuts with a solution of 1 part chlorine bleach to 10 parts water. Remove infected plants. Remove and replace soil in the root zone before replanting.
Whitish powder on leaves and buds. Yellow, distorted or falling leaves	Powdery mildew (fungus)	See 428 Overcome Fungus Diseases in Roses.
Dark brown masses appear under leaves. Leaves become twisted and die. Young twigs may be affected	Rust (fungus)	See 428 Overcome Fungus Diseases in Roses.
Leaves streaked, mottled or spotted in light green or yellow. Distorted leaves. Stunted plant growth. Broomlike clusters forming a knot or swelling	Viruses such as rose mosaic, rose rosette, rose leaf curl and rose ring pattern	If symptoms are severe, dig up and destroy the plant. Call the supplier and ask for a replacement—viruses are nearly always spread by using infected material when grafting buds.

426 Identify and Correct Soil Deficiencies in Roses

Often what appears to be a disease may be a symptom of a nutritional deficiency. If you suspect dietary problems in your roses, send a soil sample to your Cooperative Extension Service or a private testing laboratory and request a pH and nutrient analysis. (The horticulture department at your state university should be able to put you in touch with both public and private labs.) When the results come back, they'll include instructions for incorporating whatever amendments your soil needs.

DEFICIENCY	SYMPTOMS
Nitrogen	• Thin stems and leaves smaller than normal. • New growth reduced. • Foliage turns yellow, dries to light brown and drops.
Phosphorus	• Slow growth. • Dark green foliage that turns purplish or sometimes yellow between the veins.
Potassium	• Lower leaves gradually turn yellow from the edges toward the center. • Margins turn brown and curl under, and leaves drop.
Iron	• Iron deficiency most often occurs in soil that's either too acid or too alkaline to suit roses. (Their ideal pH range is between 5.5 and 7.0.) Chlorosis (yellowing) of younger leaves in areas between veins; veins retain normal green color.
Magnesium	• Older leaves develop chlorosis and often become puckered or curled.
Organic matter	• Soil that is deficient in organic matter can neither hold nutrients nor allow them to be absorbed by plants' roots. The result could be any or all of the symptoms described above.

427 Troubleshoot Rose Pests

So you've got bugs chewing on your prize roses? Well, here's something the folks at the nursery probably didn't tell you: Rose pests rarely cause permanent damage. Furthermore, most of them have natural predators that usually keep bad-guy populations in check if you don't use pesticides.

SYMPTOMS	CAUSE	SOLUTIONS
Distorted, curled and sticky foliage	Aphids	Dislodge pests with a strong stream of water. Spray with insecticidal soap. Encourage their prime predators, ladybugs, by planting a variety of flowers.
A hole in the end of a cut cane	Cane borers	Cut off and destroy infested canes. Apply white glue or petroleum jelly to cuts.
Holes in flowers and buds; skeletonized leaves	Japanese beetles	Handpick the adults. Plant garlic or chives among the roses. Apply milky spore to the lawn to kill grubs.
Clean oval, round or scalloped holes in leaves	Leaf-cutter bees	Remove damaged leaves if you want. Otherwise, do nothing—leaf-cutter bees cause only minor cosmetic damage, and they're valuable pollinators of many garden plants.
Young shoots and flower buds turn black and die	Rose midges	Remove and destroy affected plant parts. Spray with insecticidal soap. Act quickly—an unchecked infestation can end flowering from late spring through early fall. (It will not hurt the plants' health, however.)
In early stages, small holes in leaves; later, skeletonized foliage	Bristly rose slug	Blast them off with water, or handpick and destroy them. In severe cases, spray the undersides of leaves with insecticidal soap.
Deformed buds that fail to open; petals of open flowers marked with brown spots; young leaves distorted and yellow-flecked	Thrips	Blast them off with water. Remove and destroy affected plant parts. Encourage (or buy) predatory mites (available from catalogs). Spray with insecticidal soap. Remove nearby weeds and grass to eliminate alternate hosts.

428 Overcome Fungus Diseases in Roses

The vast majority of rose diseases are caused by fungi. Regardless of which nasty fungus is attacking your roses, the treatment is pretty much the same: Cut off the affected parts of the plant and destroy them. To avoid spreading the disease, dip your shears in rubbing alcohol or peroxide after every cut. Then, to get the plants back on their feet, follow this routine.

Steps

1 Water the soil, not the plant. Moisture that clings to leaves, stems and flowers is an open invitation to fungi.

2 Keep the beds clean. Pick up and destroy plant litter as soon as you see it, especially at the base of the plant, where fungal spores thrive.

3 Cut off odd-looking leaves or canes the minute you see them. Then burn them as soon as you can or toss them out with the weekly trash. Don't add them to the compost pile, or you'll be asking for more trouble.

4 Prune with a vengeance. Each year, cut out all diseased or damaged canes, and any canes more than three years old. (Vigorous, new wood is far less vulnerable to diseases—and to pests.) Aim for a structure that lets air circulate to all parts of the plant, especially to the bud union, where new canes develop.

5 Be careful when you're working or playing around rose bushes. Nicked or broken canes are open doors to fungi.

6 Feed the plants heavily in early spring and again just after each big flowering. Roses thrive especially well on large quantities of well-cured manure.

7 Spray once a week with this fungicide developed at Cornell University: In 1 gallon (4 l) water, mix 3 tsp. baking soda and 1 tsp. nondetergent dishwashing liquid (such as Ivory) or 1 tsp. canola oil—not both.

8 Reduce fungal woes by planting disease-resistant varieties. You'll find them identified as such in garden catalogs, especially those that specialize in roses. (Bear in mind, though, that no rose—or any other plant—is guaranteed to be completely trouble-free.)

9 Keep in mind that fungi thrive in damp, humid weather. Roses growing in Seattle or Atlanta will always be more prone to problems than those in Tucson or Palm Springs.

What You'll Need

- Pruning shears
- Alcohol or peroxide
- Well-cured manure or commercial organic rose food
- Baking soda
- Nondetergent dishwashing liquid or canola oil

Tip

With organic treatments, such as the Cornell fungicide (see step 7), the key to success is consistency. You need to spray every week without fail.

429 Repair Deck Steps

Deck stairs come in two basic types. In one, the stringers—the two diagonal side supports—are cut in a sawtooth shape to provide flat surfaces to support the treads you walk on. In the other, the treads (the boards you step on) are enclosed within the stringers and are held up by wooden or metal cleats. The following procedure concentrates on the sawtooth variety, but most of the information applies to both kinds of steps.

Steps

Replacing a tread

1 Remove the old tread by prying it up, one end at a time, with a hammer and pry bar.

2 Cut a replacement tread of the same thickness, width and length.

3 Install the new tread by hammering two nails into each stringer or cleat. If each step is made of two boards, make sure you leave a ⅜-inch (1-cm) space between them for drainage.

4 Apply stain or preservative to match the rest of the steps.

Repairing a stringer

1 Carefully remove the treads above the damaged part of the stringer. Make a straight horizontal cut with a handsaw, then a vertical cut (see A), to remove the rotted top of the stringer.

2 Measure and cut a replacement piece; glue it in place, then nail it on top of the stringer (see B).

3 Apply preservative if necessary; replace treads as described in step 3 above.

What You'll Need

- Hammer
- Pry bar
- Tape measure
- Replacement lumber
- Electric saw or handsaw
- Galvanized nails
- Stain or preservative
- Glue
- Flat board
- 2-by-4 scrap wood
- Pencil
- Sledgehammer
- Patio block
- Shovel
- Gravel
- Level

Tips

To prevent treads and stringers from splitting, predrill holes before hammering in nails.

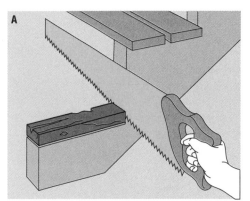

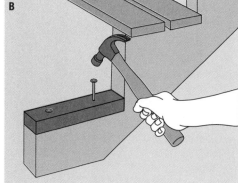

Bracing a stringer

1 Place a 12-inch (30-cm) length of flat board underneath the part of the stringer that needs extra support.

2 Place a 2-by-4 piece of wood vertically on top of the flat board. Draw a pencil line on it at the place where it meets the bottom of the stringer.

3 Cut the 2-by-4 along that line; nail through the bottom of the flat board into the square end of the 2-by-4 to make a brace.

4 Put the brace under the stringer; hit the side of it with a hammer until it is firmly lodged against the stringer (see C).

5 Drive a nail at an angle up through the brace into the bottom of the stringer (see D).

Reinforcing a stair footing

1 Remove the bottom treads of the stairs (see "Replacing a tread," opposite page).

2 Install a temporary brace tall enough to hold up the stringer several inches (about 7 cm) above the ground.

3 Remove any damaged concrete or patio block foundation with a sledgehammer or pry bar.

4 Purchase a patio block 16 to 18 inches (40 to 45 cm) square. Dig a hole slightly larger than the block and about 5 inches (13 cm) deep where the footing will go. Fill the hole with gravel and tamp it down, leaving enough room to fit in the patio block.

5 Slide the patio block under the stringer. Remove the brace so that the stringer rests firmly on it. Check for level and add or remove gravel as needed. Replace the bottom tread of the steps.

For the replacement treads to match the older steps, you may need to round over the front edge with a sander or router.

Another way to reinforce a damaged stringer is to install another stringer next to it, similar to the sister joist described in 435 Strengthen Deck Joists.

If you find you need to replace an entire stringer, use the old one as a pattern for cutting out a new one.

You can also make a footing out of concrete poured into a wooden form. This takes more time and effort, but the footing will be more permanent and stable.

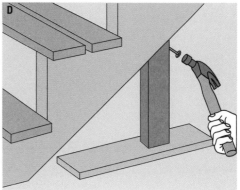

430 Renovate a Weathered Deck

Within a year or two, the sun's ultraviolet radiation makes the wood on most decks turn some degree of gray. This color change affects only a very thin top layer of the wood, so it doesn't compromise your deck's strength and durability. If you want to brighten up your deck's appearance, though, here are some things you can do.

Steps

1 Clean your deck thoroughly, following the steps outlined in 432 Remove Deck Stains. Regular cleaning alone will do a lot to keep up your deck's looks.

2 Check your deck boards for rot, splintering, long cracks, cupping and twisting. Replace any decking that has serious structural problems (see 433 Replace Damaged Deck Boards).

3 Sand the deck if needed to smooth rough spots or remove old stain. Use a belt sander for spot sanding or a floor sander for an entire deck. Make sure all nail heads are below the surface or the sandpaper will catch and tear. Begin sanding across the wood's grain, then diagonally, and finish by going with the grain.

4 To brighten a newly cleaned deck, make a mixture of 4 oz. (125 g) oxalic acid crystals per gallon (4 l) of warm water, or buy a commercial deck brightener.

5 Apply the brightener to the deck with a sponge, mop, nylon brush or garden sprayer. Be sure to wear rubber gloves and safety goggles; you should also cover any nearby plants that might be affected by the acid.

6 To increase your deck's resistance to water and to stabilize its color, you have a few choices. The first is a clear sealer. Apply according to the manufacturer's instructions; you'll need to reapply every one to two years.

7 A second option: Apply a semitransparent stain. This will allow most of the wood's beauty to show through; it will need to be reapplied every two to four years.

8 Another choice is to apply a solid stain. This will cover up much of the wood's natural appearance, but if your deck has some unattractive or slightly mismatched replacement boards, it will give a more consistent appearance.

What You'll Need

- Belt or floor sander
- Oxalic acid crystals or commercial deck brightener
- Rubber gloves and safety goggles
- Plastic drop cloths
- Dust mask
- Sponge, mop, nylon brush or garden sprayer
- Deck sealer or stain

Tips

If you actually like a weathered look so much that you want to accelerate the graying process, mix up a solution of one 16-oz. (500 g) box of baking soda, 1 gallon (4 l) water and a little dish detergent. Mop it on the deck, let it sit for 15 minutes, rinse and repeat.

A regular paint finish is usually a poor choice for a deck. Deck boards expand and contract in different seasons and weather; this is likely to cause cracks in the paint on their surface.

Warning

Always wear a dust mask when sanding pressure-treated wood.

431 Tighten Loose Decking

When a board or two on your deck gives a little bounce or creak every time you step on it—and especially when you find you're always stepping over a board to avoid this—it's time to batten it down. Over time, decking nails may lose some of their grip or boards may become twisted. Either way, you should be able to fix it easily if the boards are in good shape overall.

Steps

1 Look along the length of the loose board from its end, and then from a low angle across the deck, to see if the board contains any high or low spots. This will tell you where some fasteners may have pulled out slightly or if one side of the board has twisted up.

2 If you find a low spot, you can raise it by hammering a shim between the underside of the decking and the joist below it (see A).

3 To fix boards that have pulled up, use an electric drill with a screwdriver bit to drive in a galvanized screw at an angle through one side of the board into the joist that is below its loosest section (see B). Start with the higher side of the board, if there is one, as it may have twisted up.

4 Drive another screw at an opposite angle into the other side of the board at the same joist. This should lock the board into place.

5 If the length of the board is still not completely secure, drive a pair of screws through it into each of the other joists below.

6 Check to make sure you haven't created any low spots, and use a shim to raise up any significant ones. You may need to back out the screws first, then level the spot and drive them back in.

What You'll Need

- Hammer
- Small wooden shim
- Electric drill with screw-driver bit
- Galvanized decking screws

Tips

If there is creaking and movement throughout your deck and not just on a board or two, check to see if the joists and supports underneath the decking are loose.

When a board is seriously cracked along much of its length, it is difficult for any fasteners to hold down the entire board securely. Putting in a new board (see 433 Replace Damaged Deck Boards) is probably your best solution.

To prevent decking from splitting, always predrill holes before you nail or install screws.

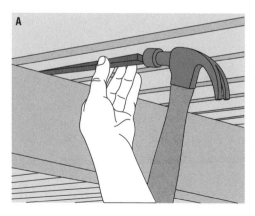
A

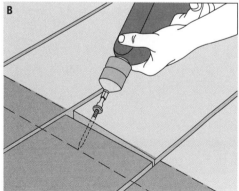
B

432 Remove Deck Stains

The instructions below should help you to thoroughly and evenly clean your deck and remove any stains. Try these solutions in the order shown and only move on to more serious measures if needed.

Steps

1 Sweep the deck with a stiff broom. Dislodge old dirt, leaves and debris from cracks and corners with a putty knife. Make sure there is some space between the decking boards and the corners so that water can run through.

2 Wash down the deck thoroughly with a garden hose.

3 If there are no visible stains on your deck, clean it with a stiff broom and a mixture of household cleaner and warm water.

4 For a thorough cleaning job, rent a pressure washer. Wear goggles while using it, as it provides a very powerful stream. Start in the middle of the deck and work outward, keeping the sprayer's head about 4 to 6 inches (10 to 15 cm) from the deck's surface.

5 If you need to use a bleach solution or a strong commercial deck cleaner to remove stains, cover any nearby plants or shrubs with plastic drop cloths to avoid discoloration or unwanted chemicals.

6 Make a solution of 1 cup (8 fl oz/250 ml) bleach per gallon (4 l) of warm water in a plastic bucket, or use a commercial deck cleaner and follow the directions for application. Whatever you use, wear rubber gloves. Also wear safety goggles if you are using bleach or if you are bending down to clean parts of the deck by hand. Use a stiff broom (you may want to purchase a smaller broom that is made just for decks) to scrub the cleaner into the deck.

7 For any stubborn stains that remain visible, clean thoroughly by hand with a scrub brush and the cleaning solution.

8 Hose off the cleaning solution and any remaining dirt thoroughly with plain water.

9 If stains remain, reapply deck cleaner by hand.

10 To treat mildew, apply a solution of 1 part water to 2 parts bleach. Be sure to rinse it off thoroughly after a few minutes.

What You'll Need

- Stiff-bristle broom
- Putty knife
- Garden hose or pressure washer
- Household cleaner
- Safety goggles
- Plastic drop cloths
- Bleach or commercial deck cleaner
- Plastic bucket
- Rubber gloves
- Stiff broom or deck-cleaning broom
- Scrub brush

Tips

If you want to clean a stain from only one spot, be sure not to use too strong a chemical or bleach solution —you may end up replacing a small, somewhat noticeable dark spot with a large, really noticeable lighter area.

You can discourage stains and lodged-in debris by hosing down your deck with a strong spray every few weeks.

433 Replace Damaged Deck Boards

If you have only a few cracked or rotted sections on your deck, replacing a board or a section of one could be the answer. Just make sure to use the same type of decking and the same stain or preservative as was originally used, so that your guests won't know for sure what you've done other than make your deck look a little newer and nicer.

Steps

Replacing one section of a board

1 Use a jigsaw or keyhole saw to cut through the decking directly next to the two joists on either end of the bad section (see A). You may need to drill a hole in the board first to be able to start the saw blade.

2 Cut a 2-by-4 cleat to fit in the space next to the joist (see B). Start one or two galvanized nails into the cleat before putting it in place, and then attach it flush to the top of the joist.

3 Cut a length of decking to fill the space. Attach it to the cleats with galvanized nails or decking screws. For nails, use a nail set to put their heads below the surface.

4 If the new board is not flush with the deck surface, sand down any high spots. Apply the same stain or preservative you used on the rest of the deck.

Replacing entire boards

1 Remove any damaged boards by prying up slowly from the end with a pry bar or, if necessary, by cutting the board in pieces as in step 1, above.

2 Measure and cut a board to the length you need. If the decking will overhang an end joist, cut the boards a few inches long, then use a saw to trim the new boards flush with the adjoining decking after installation. Attach each board as in step 3, above, and apply stain or preservative to match the rest of the deck.

What You'll Need

- Jigsaw or keyhole saw
- Drill with ½-inch (12-mm) wood bit
- 2-by-4 scraps
- 3-inch (7.5-cm) galvanized nails or screws
- Hammer
- Replacement deck board(s)
- Nail set
- Belt sander
- Deck stain or preservative
- Pry bar
- Tape measure

Tip

If a deck board has no structural problems such as cracks or rot but simply has an impossible-to-get-out stain or some gouges in the wood, you may be able to carefully remove the board (you'll probably need the pry bar), flip it over and reattach.

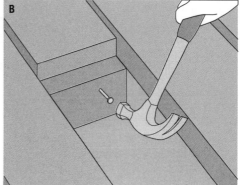

434 Repair Deck Railings

A railing gives a deck a nice feeling of enclosure and makes it safer as well. In fact, most building codes require you to put a railing around any deck 30 inches (76 cm) or more above the ground. But a railing can't do its job if it has broken or missing balusters, or wobbly handrails or posts. Deck parts are fairly standard, so there's a good chance you'll be able to find premade pieces at your lumberyard that will make the repairs below as easy as possible.

Steps

Replacing a baluster

1 Remove the damaged baluster by backing out its screws using an electric drill with a screwdriver bit. If it's nailed on, hammer near the top of the baluster on the opposite side of the nails to loosen them, then pry off the baluster with a hammer or pry bar. (Note: In some deck railings, the balusters are attached to a rail on top and to the end joist of the deck on bottom.)

2 Cut a replacement baluster to the length of the old baluster. The ends should be cut at a 45-degree angle; use a power miter saw or a saw and a miter box.

3 Hold the new baluster in position against the rails, centered between the balusters on either side. The angled cuts on the ends will be facing outward.

4 With a ⅛-inch (3-mm) drill bit, make a pilot hole through the baluster at each end, drilling through the flat front about ½ inch (12 mm) from the angled ends, and into the rails.

5 Drive a 2½-inch (6-cm) galvanized screw into each pilot hole to attach the baluster to the rails (see A).

6 Apply wood preservative or finish if necessary.

Reinforcing a handrail

1 Cut a pressure-treated 2-by-4 scrap so that its length is the same as the width of the railing post. Use a power miter saw or a saw and a miter box.

2 Place the scrap inside the corner formed by the handrail and the railing post.

3 Using an electric drill with a screwdriver bit, drive two 3-inch (7.5-cm) galvanized screws through the block and into the post.

4 Drive one 2½-inch (6-cm) screw down through the handrail and into the block, being careful not to run into the first two screws.

5 If possible, drive one 2½-inch (6-cm) screw through the side rail or the side of the top rail into the end of the block.

What You'll Need

- Electric drill with screwdriver bit
- Hammer
- Pry bar
- 2-by-2 lumber (or premade balusters)
- Power miter saw or miter box and saw
- ⅛-inch (3-mm) drill bit
- 2½-inch (6-cm) galvanized deck screws
- Wood preservative or finish
- Scrap of pressure-treated 2-by-4 lumber
- 3-inch (7.5-cm) galvanized deck screws
- Socket wrench
- 4-by-4 lumber (or premade deck railing post)
- Handsaw
- Drill bit for pilot holes
- 5-inch (13-cm) lag screws with washers

Tips

While you're repairing the railing, consider installing some premade decorative post caps. They're available at lumberyards in a variety of designs.

Sometimes balusters on a fairly new deck become loose or cracked due to shifts caused by the deck's settling in the ground.

Apply an extra coat of preservative to the ends of any pieces you've cut on an angle.

Replacing a post

1 Detach the handrail and any long side rails from the post. Back out any screws holding them to the post; to remove nails, hold a wood scrap underneath the handrail or inside the rail, and hammer on the block until the nails release enough to be pried off.

2 Remove the old post from the base of the deck. This will require either removing nails as above or removing lag screws from the side of the post with a socket wrench.

3 Using the old post as a template, draw lines on a length of 4-by-4 lumber to replicate its length and shape.

4 Cut along the lines on the 4-by-4 with a handsaw, and cut out a notch in the bottom so that it will fit over the base of the deck and align with the remainder of the railing. Use a saw and a miter box (or a power miter saw) to make an angled cut at the bottom of the post.

5 Apply wood preservative to the inside surfaces of the notch.

6 Put the new post in place so that the handrail and side rails meet it at the proper places.

7 Drill two pilot holes through the bottom part of the post into the base of the deck.

8 Install two 5-inch (13-cm) lag screws with washers into the pilot holes; tighten firmly (see B).

9 Reattach the handrail and side rails to the new post, using 2½-inch (6-cm) screws.

10 Apply wood preservative or stain to any new parts as needed.

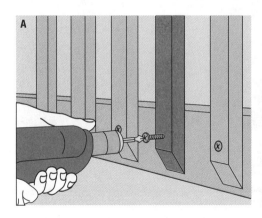

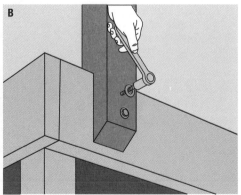

435 Strengthen Deck Joists

Are you getting the shakes each time you step out on your deck? Firming up the joists under the decking may solve your problem. But first make sure you don't have any rotted or loose beams.

Steps

Adding a sister joist

1 Measure and cut another joist the same size as any joists that are split, broken or otherwise damaged. Clamp the new sister joist alongside the older joist. Drive 3-inch (7.5-cm) galvanized screws through the sister joist to attach it; remove the clamps. Drive two screws through the end joist into each end of the new joist. Drive one deck screw through each piece of decking and into the new joist.

Adding bridges to your joists

1 Measure the width of the spaces between the joists. Add ⅛ inch (3 mm) to that measurement and mark the total length onto a board of the same thickness and width as your joists. Cut the board at your mark to make bridges for every 6 to 8 feet (1.8 to 2.4 m) of joists.

2 Tap a bridge into place between the joists, and drive two nails or screws through the joists into each end of the bridge (see illustration). Install the other bridges, each offset from the previous one by several inches (about 7 cm) so you have room to drive in the nails or screws.

What You'll Need

- Tape measure
- Boards of the same size and wood as current joists
- Electric saw or handsaw
- Clamps
- Galvanized screws or nails
- Electric drill with screwdriver bit
- Hammer

Tip

For low decks with no space to work below them, you'll have to remove the decking to add sister joists or bridges.

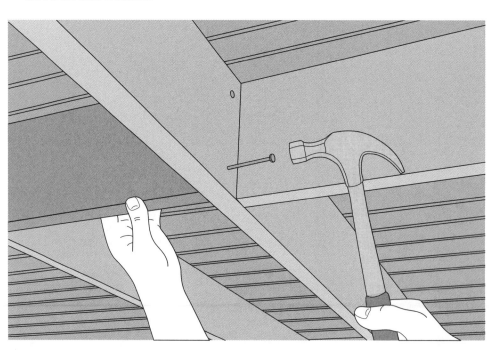

436 Fix a Rusty Iron Railing

An iron railing makes an elegant statement and will last a lifetime if you halt the progress of rust, which usually starts where the posts contact concrete or wherever paint has chipped. Apply a rust neutralizer, touch up chipped paint immediately, and repaint the bottom part of the posts every year and the entire railing every six to eight years. Here's how to do it all.

Steps

Fixing a loose post

1 Drill or chisel out the concrete, leaving about ½ inch (12 mm) of space around the posts. If the railing is loose enough, remove it to make this task easier, and make any other repairs while it's off.

2 Position and brace both sides of the railing so it's plumb and level. Fill the holes with a fast-setting cement grout. Level and smooth the grout around the post with a mason's trowel. Clean the post with a wet sponge before any grout dries on it.

Controlling rust

1 Cover the area under the railing with a drop cloth to protect nearby surfaces from stains, avoid contaminating the soil and reduce cleanup time.

2 Remove any loose rust with a scraper and wire brush. Sand or grind the rusty surfaces to smooth them out. The goal is to make them look neat when painted, not to remove all the rust. Use a wire brush or a wire wheel on an electric drill, or hand-sand with emery cloth, as seems appropriate.

3 To halt the corrosion process, chemically neutralize the rust. Brush on a rust neutralizer according to the product directions.

Priming and painting

1 Remove any loose paint. For a better bond, degloss the surface with emery cloth. Emery cloth won't tear like sandpaper on hard-to-sand areas.

2 Scrub with a solution of laundry detergent and water to remove all dust and grime.

3 Apply two coats of rust-inhibiting (direct-to-metal) primer and a paint topcoat. If you're using spray paint, hold the spray nozzle 8 to 12 inches (20 to 30 cm) from your work and keep the can moving. To avoid drips, paint *out of,* not into, interior corners, and check just-painted areas frequently. If you lay on the paint with a roller or an airless sprayer, immediately follow up with a brush to work it into the surface.

What You'll Need

- Drill or chisel
- Cement grout
- Mason's trowel
- Sponge
- Drop cloth
- Wire brush
- Scraper
- Drill with wire wheel
- Sanding discs
- Emery cloth
- Rust neutralizer such as Rust Reformer (Rust-Oleum) or Neutra Rust (NYBCO)
- Laundry detergent
- Rust-inhibiting primer
- Touch-up paint and paint-brush
- Paint roller or airless sprayer

Tips

Use a paint conditioner such as Penetrol to better seal the surface. Mix it into the primer or brush it on.

When spraying, it's better to apply several light coats than a single heavy one.

Warning

Wear goggles and clothing that covers your skin. If your railing was installed prior to 1978, see 137 Solve a Lead-Paint Problem for special precautions you need to take.

437 Repair a Gate

A wooden gate takes a lot of punishment from all that opening and closing—and even more abuse once your kids find out how much fun it is to hang on and go for a ride on it. If your gate sags, or it won't open or close easily, first check the gatepost with a carpenter's level to make sure it is plumb and sturdy, and then fix it with the techniques below if necessary. Without a strong supporting post, any repairs to the gate itself will just be a temporary solution.

What You'll Need

- Carpenter's level
- Shovel
- Long, narrow stones
- 2-by-4 scrap lumber
- Hammer
- Screwdriver
- Wood putty
- Galvanized or stainless-steel screws
- Electric drill with bit
- Turnbuckle tension rod kit
- Plane
- Paint or stain

Steps

Straightening a gatepost

1 Dig away the soil from the side toward which the post is leaning to create a hole about 18 inches (45 cm) deep and 10 inches (25 cm) around.

2 Loosely pack some long, narrow stones into the hole; stop a few inches (about 7 cm) below ground level.

3 Position the post so it is perfectly vertical (check this with a carpenter's level).

4 Cut a piece of 2-by-4 scrap lumber to make a 2-foot-long (60-cm-long) wedge, cutting the angle along its length. Place the long, flat (not angled) side of the wedge against the post.

5 Hammer down the top of the wedge (see A) until it is flush with the ground level and the stones are locked in place.

6 Shovel soil on top of the rocks; tamp down.

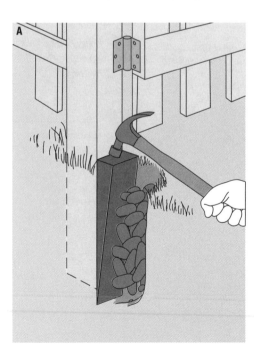

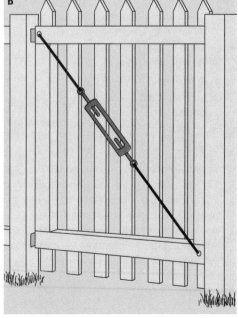

Pulling up a sagging gate

1 Reinstall any gate-hinge screws that are coming out of the post. To do this, first remove the screws holding the bottom hinge to the post, then remove the top hinge screws. Remove the gate.

2 Fill the holes with wood putty; let it harden.

3 Replace the top hinge first, then replace the bottom hinge. Use screws that are as long as possible without coming out the other side of the post.

4 If there is enough room, add a new third hinge in the middle for extra support.

5 With a level, check to see if the gate is now level across the top and plumb at the end.

6 If the gate sags at all, install a turnbuckle tension rod assembly to opposite corners of the gate frame (see B). Make sure the high side of the cable is installed on the side of the gate with the hinges.

7 Tighten the turnbuckle until the gate is level and clears the ground properly.

Making a gate close smoothly

1 Check with a level to make sure the side of the gate with the latch and the post next to it are both plumb. Straighten the post or the gate as above if needed.

2 If the gate sticks closed in wet weather due to wood expansion, plane off ¼ inch (6 mm). Paint or stain the newly exposed wood.

3 If the latch falls short of its catch in dry weather due to wood contraction, remove the latch and reposition it so that it easily reaches the catch.

Tips

If the wood at the base of a gatepost has rotted so much that you can push a screwdriver into it more than ½ inch (12 mm) all the way around, you'll need to replace the whole post. Another option is to support it with a new sister post (see 438 Repair a Picket Fence).

Another way to support the gate itself: Square the gate, then screw a long wooden brace diagonally to two opposite corners. Wooden braces are attached in an opposite direction from the turnbuckle assembly shown here: The lower end of the brace goes on the side of the gate nearest the post.

A turnbuckle tension rod can also be used to straighten and support any gate or fence post.

438 Repair a Picket Fence

A classic picket fence adds beauty to any front yard or garden. Unfortunately, it can also add more maintenance headaches than most other types of fencing. Paint or stain your fence regularly (at least every other year), and you'll minimize the number of times you'll have to repair an occasional picket, rail or post as described below.

Steps

Replacing a picket

1 Loosen the old picket by hammering on it on the side opposite the nails.

2 Complete the removal of the picket with the hammer and a pry bar. Use the claw end of the hammer to remove any nails that remained in the rail.

3 Cut a picket to the length of the one you're replacing. If you don't have a premade picket in the same style, trace the outline of the top of the old picket onto a new board that's the same thickness and width of the old picket. Then cut along the lines with an electric jigsaw.

4 Attach the new picket by driving two galvanized nails through it into each rail.

5 Apply paint or stain to match the rest of your fence.

Reinforcing a rail

1 Chip away any rotted wood near the end of the rail.

2 Cut a 2-by-4 to make a wooden block that is as long as the fence post is wide, usually about 3½ inches (9 cm).

3 Nail the block to the post, just below the rail (see A), using two galvanized nails.

4 Nail the rail to the wooden block.

5 Apply paint or stain to the end of the rail and to the new block.

What You'll Need

- Hammer
- Pry bar
- Replacement picket or board
- Saw
- Electric jigsaw
- Galvanized nails
- Paint or stain
- Paintbrush
- 2-by-4
- Shovel
- Sledgehammer
- Gravel or small stones
- Tape measure
- 4-by-4 piece of pressure-treated lumber
- Electric drill
- Two lag bolts with nuts and washers
- Wrench
- Carpenter's level
- Concrete
- Trowel

Tips

Keep soil from building up around the bottom of pickets (a regular raking will do it), and they'll be much less likely to have rot and water damage.

Installing a "sister" post

The following is a good way to repair a post that has become rotten underground without having to remove the entire post—and possibly a whole section of fence with it.

1 Cut through the post about 2 inches (5 cm) above the ground.

2 Dig around the base of the post. If the post is encased in concrete, use a hammer or sledgehammer to break up the concrete.

3 Remove the underground section of the post.

4 Dig around the edges of the hole to make it straight-sided, about 1 foot (30 cm) wide, with a center that is 2 to 3 inches (5 to 7 cm) from the side of the old post.

5 Pour a 4-inch (10-cm) layer of gravel or small stones into the bottom of the hole.

6 Measure the depth of the new hole.

7 Cut a 4-by-4 piece of pressure-treated lumber so it's twice as long as the hole is deep. Cut the top end of the new post at a 45-degree angle, so water will run off it after installation.

8 Place the sister post in the hole, with its longest side facing the old post.

9 Drill two ½-inch (12-mm) holes about 1 foot (30 cm) apart through both the new post and the old. Insert a lag bolt through each hole, and fasten a nut and washer to the other end (see B).

10 Use a level to make sure the original post is plumb.

11 Mix and pour enough concrete to fill the hole to a few inches above ground level. With a trowel, smooth the concrete so that it slopes slightly down away from the post.

Looking for some wood in just the right thickness to make new pickets? Pry a few boards off an old wooden pallet with a hammer and pry bar.

Any damage to wood in a post that is well above ground might be the work of termites or carpenter ants; in that case you probably should replace the entire post.

Warning

Older fences may be covered with some layers of lead paint, which was in common use until the mid-1970s. If your fence dates from before then, and it has a lot of old, peeling paint, check with a professional before doing any significant paint removal or sanding.

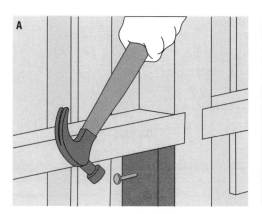

A

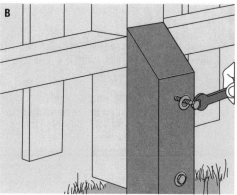

B

439 Level and Smooth a Gravel Path

Over time, a neat, smooth gravel path can become bumpy and clogged with dirt and weeds. A good path requires a solid base—either of tamped-down sand or coarse gravel—that is covered by landscape fabric with a layer of fine gravel on top. Here's how to spruce up that top layer, and to make a few other repairs as well.

Steps

1 Rake away the top 4 to 5 inches (10 to 13 cm) of gravel from the path until you reach either landscape fabric, a layer of sand or a layer of coarser gravel.

2 Tamp down the surface. You can make your own wooden tamping tool from a small square of ¾-inch (2-cm) plywood nailed to the bottom end of a 4-foot-long (120-cm) 2-by-4.

3 Install a layer of landscape fabric if there is none. This must be permeable enough to let water drain through it but not so open that it allows any weeds to grow upward.

4 Check the path's edging. If the stone, brick or landscape timbers are broken or misaligned, repair or replace them.

5 If the path has no edging, install plastic landscape edging on each side. The edging should be installed so that the top of it is ½ inch (12 mm) above the level of the ground on either side of the path.

6 Take any debris out of the gravel you removed by raking back and forth through it or turning it over with a shovel.

7 Shovel the cleaned gravel back into the path and smooth it with the rake.

8 Add new screened fine gravel as needed to reach within 1½ to 2 inches (4 to 5 cm) of the top of the edging; rake the path level.

9 Water the path with a garden hose; let the water drain through, then tamp again.

10 Spread a ½- to 1-inch (12-mm to 2.5-cm) layer of fine crushed stone on top of the path until it is 1 inch (2.5 cm) below the top of the path's edging.

11 Cut a 2-by-4 to be as long as the width of the path between the edgings. Use the board as a screed and pull it along the surface of the fine stone to smooth the path.

What You'll Need

- Metal rake
- Tamping tool
- Landscape fabric
- Plastic landscape edging
- Shovel
- Screened fine gravel
- Garden hose
- Fine crushed stone
- 2-by-4 lumber
- Saw

Tips

When you move the gravel completely off the path, put it either in a wheelbarrow or on a large plywood square so that it won't damage the rest of your lawn or garden.

There are several other terms, besides those given here, that people sometimes use for the same grades of stone and gravel. If you're not sure what to get, tell the folks at the stone yard what project you're working on and ask their advice.

440 Fix a Pothole in a Dirt or Gravel Driveway

When entering your own driveway is like running a slalom course, it's time to fix that pothole. Water trapped below the surface can cause potholes, so it is important to improve the underground drainage before finishing off the top surface.

Steps

1 Rake or shovel out any loose stones, gravel or soil from the bottom of the pothole.

2 If the sides of the pothole are loose, cut them straight down with a shovel to create firm edges to the hole.

3 Fill the hole with coarse gravel to about 3 inches (7 cm) below the level of the driveway (see A).

4 Tamp down the gravel. You can make your own wooden tamping tool from a small square of ¾-inch (2-cm) plywood nailed to the bottom end of a 4-foot-long (120-cm) 2-by-4.

5 For a dirt driveway: Shovel soil into the hole until it is mounded a few inches (about 7 cm) above the surface.

6 Water the soil, and tamp it down as firmly as you can.

7 If necessary, add enough soil to raise it a little above the driveway surface again, and tamp it down again.

8 For a gravel driveway: Fill the last 3 inches (7 cm) with gravel that matches the driveway. Mound it just above the surface.

9 Rake the new gravel to blend with the rest of the driveway (see B).

10 For either type of driveway: Run a wheel of your car over the spot a few times to compact it down.

What You'll Need

- Metal rake
- Shovel
- Coarse gravel
- Soil
- Tamping tool
- Gravel

Tips

For proper drainage, a driveway should have a slight crown in the middle—at least 1 inch (2.5 cm) of height for each 4 feet (120 cm) of width—or else it should mildly slope all the way across in the same direction that water tends to drain.

The pieces of crushed stone on a driveway should be pointed and with clear, not rounded, edges in order to pack together tightly.

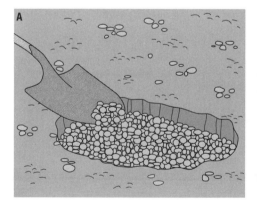

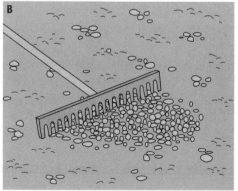

441 Replace Patio Stones, Tiles and Pavers

First, let's sort out a few terms: Any piece used to pave a patio or walkway can be called a *paver,* though sometimes the word is used specifically for small concrete or (more traditionally) granite paving blocks. As for *stones,* we're talking here mostly about flagstones, which are about 2 inches (5 cm) thick and irregular in shape. *Tiles* come in square or other geometric shapes, and they're usually thinner than flagstones or pavers. Whatever type of surface you have—and whatever you call it—how you repair it will be most determined by whether it is set in mortar or is simply resting on a sand base.

Steps

Repairing a surface set in sand

1 Wearing work gloves, remove damaged or displaced pavers with an old screwdriver or a pry bar.

2 Spray water on the exposed sand base.

3 Tamp down the sand with a tamping tool.

4 Add a thin layer of fine sand, water lightly and tamp again until the sand layer is very slightly above the bottoms of the other pavers.

5 Beginning in a corner of the open space, install one of the pavers. Tap on top of the paver with a rubber mallet until it is flush with the adjoining pavers, and check it with a level. Pick up the paver, and add or remove sand below for any necessary adjustments; replace the paver.

6 With the mallet, gently tap the sides of the paver so that it is snug against all adjoining pavers.

7 Install remaining pavers in the same way.

8 Sprinkle fine sand over the repaired area and sweep the sand into the cracks. Rinse the entire surface.

Repairing a surface set in mortar

1 Remove damaged paving stones, using a pry bar or a cold chisel and a mason's hammer, if necessary.

2 Chisel off the remaining mortar from the exposed base and from the edges of adjoining pavers.

3 Lay down the new pavers in place as a dry run to make sure they fit properly, then set them aside. If you're using flagstones, cut any pieces to fit as necessary (see "Cutting flagstones to fit a space," opposite page).

4 Put dry premixed mortar (or a mixture of 1 part cement and 3 parts sand) in a mortar box or wheelbarrow. Mix in water a little at a time until the mortar is the consistency of mud.

What You'll Need

- Work gloves
- Flathead screwdriver or pry bar
- Garden hose
- Tamping tool
- Fine sand
- Replacement pavers, tiles or flagstones
- Rubber mallet
- Carpenter's level
- Broom
- Cold chisel
- Mason's hammer
- Mortar mix, or cement and sand
- Mortar box or wheelbarrow
- Mason's trowel
- 2-by-4 scrap
- Pointing trowel
- Stiff nylon brush
- Chalk
- Safety goggles
- Bolster chisel

Tips

To protect your hands, always wear work gloves when handling stones or working with concrete and mortar.

On a patio, consider leaving unpaved a space 2 to 3 feet (60 to 90 cm) across and planting a shrub or small tree there.

5 Wet the surface you'll be working on. Don't work on more than 4 to 6 square feet (1.2 to 1.8 square m) at a time, and start working in a corner if you can.

6 With a mason's trowel, lay down a 1-inch (2.5-cm) layer of mortar where the new pavers will go.

7 Use a short 2-by-4 wood scrap to smooth the mortar until it is level.

8 Place the paving units in the mortar, checking frequently to make sure they are level and flush with adjoining pavers. If a paver is a little too high or is raised on one side, tap it lightly with a rubber mallet (see A); if it's too low, pick it up and add some mortar before replacing it.

9 When all the pavers are placed, fill the joints between them with another batch of the same mortar mix, using a small pointing trowel (see B). You can leave this mortar flush with the tops of the pavers, or use the trowel to recess it slightly.

10 After 3 to 4 hours, brush off any excess mortar using a stiff nylon brush.

Cutting flagstones to fit a space

1 Draw a chalk line across the part of the stone that needs to be removed. Flip over the stone and continue drawing the line on the other side.

2 Place the stone on a surface that is firm but not too hard, such as a lawn or a bed of sand.

3 Wearing safety goggles, tap along the line with a bolster chisel and a mason's hammer. Tap back and forth along the line several times.

4 Flip the stone over and do the same on the line on the other side.

5 Turn the stone over again, and hit on the line with gradually increasing force until a strong blow breaks off the piece.

Remember to lift heavy objects—whether a stone or a sack of concrete—by bending your knees and lifting carefully, and not by bending your back and risking injury.

Wearing steel-toed work boots is always a good idea if you'll be moving a lot of stones. At least be sure to avoid wearing sneakers—or open-toed sandals!

Warning

When you're cutting or trimming stones, always be sure to wear safety goggles.

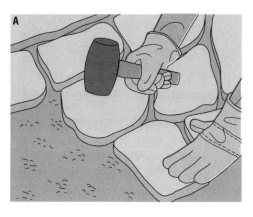

A

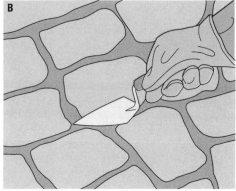

B

442 Fix Cracked or Damaged Concrete

Timely concrete repairs may prevent water intrusion and extensive damage, enhance the appearance of surfaces, and correct potential safety hazards. Concrete patches are hard to disguise, but see 443 Improve the Look of Repaired Concrete for a solution.

Steps

Preparing the surface

1 Whether you're repairing a walkway, patio, driveway, basement or other surface, remove cracked and loose materials with a stone chisel and/or wire brush.

2 Use a grinder with an abrasive masonry wheel to widen hairline cracks for filling.

3 Clean the surface with a hose and nozzle, or a pressure washer.

4 Use a shop vacuum to clean out cracks and holes.

5 Dampen the surfaces with a hose or spray bottle, and brush off any standing water.

Filling a small crack with pourable grout

1 Cut the tip off the grout container to create a hole a little smaller than the width of the crack. Pour in the grout to fill the crack.

2 For deep cracks, pour in the grout one layer at a time and allow complete drying between layers.

Filling a large crack

1 For cracks wider than about ½ inch (12 mm), use a mason's hammer and chisel to cut the crack so it is wider below the surface than at the surface, a process called undercutting. Undercutting prevents the patching material from being forced out in response to temperature changes.

2 Mix vinyl concrete patcher with water as directed. Press the material into the crack with a mason's trowel in layers no more than ¼ inch (6 mm) thick. Allow each layer to dry completely before applying the next.

3 Using a steel trowel, wood float (a wood block with a handle), broom or brush, finish and texture the surface to match the surrounding area. A steel trowel gives the smoothest surface; hold it flat and use a swirling motion.

Repairing a broken step

1 Apply a concrete bonding adhesive to surfaces you'll be covering with new material. Use an old paintbrush to work the milky liquid into the surface. This extra precaution is worth taking, considering what could happen if the patch were to fail and break off

What You'll Need

- Stone chisel
- Wire brush
- Grinder with abrasive masonry wheel
- Hose and nozzle, or pressure washer
- Shop vacuum
- Spray bottle
- Pourable grout
- Mason's hammer and chisel
- Vinyl concrete patcher
- Mason's trowel
- Steel trowel, wood float, brush or broom
- Concrete bonding adhesive
- Old paintbrush
- Masking tape
- Mixing container
- Fortified concrete mix, or standard sand or concrete mix
- Latex primer or additive
- Lumber for wooden form
- Drywall screws and screwdriver
- Wooden braces, bricks or concrete blocks
- Stiff brush
- Edging tool
- Plastic cover

Tips

If you plan to use a resurfacer after making the repair, don't bother filling small cracks with vinyl patcher. You can use the resurfacer itself to do so.

For fast repair of a small but deep crack in concrete that isn't structurally important, fill the crack to within ¼ inch (6 mm) of the surface before you apply pourable crack filler.

underfoot. The primer or adhesive will stain adjacent surfaces, so mask them with tape.

2 Wash the brush immediately after use with soap and water, or discard it.

3 Mix an already fortified concrete mix (typically a nonsagging formula designed specifically for this type of repair) with precisely the amount of water indicated by the manufacturer. If you'll be applying the materials in layers, mix only what you can use in each layer. Or use a latex primer or additive in lieu of water if you choose a standard sand or concrete mix. Measure quantities carefully. Otherwise, concrete can fail.

4 For shallow or small repairs, use a mason's trowel to apply the patch mortar. Press firmly to work the initial layer into the surface for a good bond.

5 Allow each layer to dry completely before applying the next one.

6 For large repairs, screw together a wooden form and hold it in place with wooden braces, bricks, concrete blocks or similar heavy objects. Then apply the fortified concrete in layers as directed by the manufacturer until the form is filled (see A). Again, work in the initial material well to eliminate all voids.

7 When the patch is firm but not yet dry, remove the form by taking out the screws and carefully lifting off the pieces.

8 Finish or texture the repair to match, and feather it into the surrounding area with a wood float or stiff brush (see B). Use an edging tool in a back-and-forth sanding motion to round over the corners, if that's how the existing nosing on the tread is finished.

9 Cover the repair with plastic to retard evaporation and slow curing, which helps prevent cracking. Keep the surface damp for the next two or three days by misting it with water and keeping it covered.

Use screws instead of nails to assemble the form so you can remove it more easily without disturbing the fresh concrete.

Warning

A large or growing crack in a foundation wall indicates a structural problem that requires professional evaluation and repair.

Silica dust, portland cement, muriatic acid, and the other tools and materials used to repair concrete can be dangerous. Read labels and wear proper protection, such as goggles, a dust mask and work gloves.

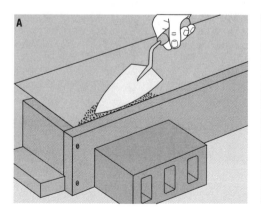

443 Improve the Look of Repaired Concrete

The newly available brush-on resurfacers restore a like-new appearance to walks, drives and patios. Often they're the only way to disguise a repaired concrete surface, such as porch steps.

Steps

1 Make any required repairs to large cracks, broken corners, steps or similar concrete damage (see 442 Fix Cracked or Damaged Concrete).

2 Cut back any grass or plants along a walk or driveway you're resurfacing, and press foam backer rods into expansion joints so you won't end up filling them with resurfacer.

3 Pretreat stains, which can interfere with bonding, using muriatic acid. Dilute the acid in a plastic pail or spray bottle by adding 1 part of 20 percent acid to 4 parts water (see Warning). Carefully apply the acid solution to the affected areas using a brush or spray bottle. Allow it to work for a few minutes, then hose it off.

4 Wash surfaces from the center outward. Use a hose and nozzle or (better) a pressure washer, which you can rent.

5 Use a shop vacuum to clear loose material out of cracks. Don't blow it out or you'll contaminate the surfaces you just cleaned.

6 After you've gathered your tools, soak the surface with water and brush off any standing water.

7 Mix the resurfacer with water as directed, using a ½-inch (12-mm) drill with a paddle mixer.

8 Level depressions and fill small cracks. Allow these repairs to dry before coating the entire surface.

9 On horizontal surfaces, apply resurfacer with a trowel on small areas, such as stair treads, or with a wide squeegee on large areas, such as walks. For vertical surfaces, such as stair risers, mix the material with slightly more water and apply it with a plaster brush. Have containers of water available so you can quickly rinse off trowels and brooms between uses. Work in manageable sections. Proper application techniques take some practice, and the material sets up quickly (in about 20 minutes).

10 Finish and texture the material as you apply it. For a smooth surface, use a steel trowel in a circular pattern. For a slightly rougher texture, use a wood float, which you can make by putting a handle on a block of wood that has slightly rounded corners. For the very rough finish typical of sidewalks, draw a stiff broom or brush across the surface.

What You'll Need

- Foam backer rods
- Muriatic acid
- Plastic pail and brush, or spray bottle
- Hose and nozzle
- Pressure washer
- Shop vacuum
- Brush
- Concrete resurfacer
- Mixing container
- ½-inch (12-mm) drill
- Paddle mixer
- Steel trowel
- Wide squeegee
- Plaster brush
- Wood float
- Stiff broom or brush

Tip

Use liquid-concrete colorant as directed to color the resurfacer.

Warning

Muriatic acid is highly corrosive. Read the warning label carefully. Wear goggles and rubber gloves, and *never add the water to the acid.* It will spatter like water added to hot fat.

Wear work gloves, knee pads and other protective clothing as needed.

444 Repair an Asphalt Driveway

Sealing a driveway doesn't significantly prolong its life, but promptly filling cracks and holes and cleaning up oil spills do. Although you would typically handle fixes in the summer when you apply sealer, winter is the best time to fill cracks—and when it comes to most driveway repairs, there's no time like the present.

Steps

Cleaning the driveway

1 Use an ice chipper, a lawn-edging tool or a spade to scrape grass or weeds off the driveway and out of cracks.

2 Remove any loose asphalt from damaged or cracked areas with a blast of water from a garden hose or with compressed air.

3 Brush off all debris with a broom.

4 Scrub the driveway with diluted driveway cleaner to remove all dirt and oil film. Repeat as necessary to remove oil stains, and apply an oil-spot primer on any remaining stains.

5 Hose the driveway with as much pressure as possible. Start on the uphill and rinse toward the sides.

6 Use a shop vacuum to remove all loose debris from cracks. These must be very clean and dry before filling.

7 Let the driveway dry thoroughly before moving to the next step.

Making repairs

1 For cracks ⅛ to ½ inch (3 to 12 mm) wide, use rubberized asphalt-emulsion crack filler, applied with a caulking gun or poured. Avoid getting the filler on the surface. Smooth it with a putty knife.

2 For a very wide crack or pothole, shovel in packaged cold-patch blacktop, leveling large areas with an iron rake. Compact the material with a rented tamper or the end of a 4-by-4. Add more material until the hole is slightly overfilled. Cover it with scrap plywood and drive over it.

Filling and sealing

1 Mist the driveway with water. Then pour a ribbon of acrylic driveway sealer or filler 1 foot (30 cm) wide across the driveway. Spread the strip to a width of 3 to 4 feet (about 1 m) with a brush or squeegee applicator.

2 Remove all excess sealer, using the brush or squeegee and pulling toward you. Work your way down the driveway.

What You'll Need

- Ice chipper, lawn-edging tool or spade
- Air compressor or garden hose with nozzle
- Broom
- Driveway cleaner
- Oil-spot primer
- Stiff broom
- Shop vacuum
- Rubberized asphalt-emulsion crack filler
- Caulking gun
- Putty knife
- Cold-patch blacktop
- Shovel or trowel
- Iron rake
- Tamper or 4-by-4
- Scrap plywood
- Acrylic driveway sealer or filler
- Brush or squeegee applicator

Tips

Undercut the edges of a pothole with a cold chisel and mason's hammer.

For cracks more than ½ inch (12 mm) wide, stuff in a non-porous foam backer rod until the crack is only as deep as it is wide.

Warning

Wear eye protection such as goggles when cleaning, chiseling or hosing the driveway.

445 Revive Wooden Outdoor Furniture

If you have an old picnic table or some Adirondack chairs with peeling paint and chipped or splintered wood, it's not that hard to make them look (almost) as good as new. Furniture refinishing of this sort is much closer to carpentry and house painting than it is to restoring an antique sideboard. That's fine, though, because without much effort you'll be able to cover up any minor imperfections and have a good-looking result.

Steps

Patching damaged wood

1 Scrub the splintered, chipped or dented area with a stiff wire brush to remove any loose paint or wood chips.

2 Apply a waterproof glue to any splintered pieces and clamp them until the glue dries.

3 With a putty knife, spread a paste wood filler over the damaged area, covering it completely.

4 Smooth down the wood filler until it is flush with the wood surface. Let dry overnight.

5 Sand the patch gently with 220-grit sandpaper, feathering out the edges to make the patch less visible.

6 Wipe off the sanding residue with a damp cloth.

Repainting outdoor furniture

1 Remove any peeling paint with a stiff wire brush.

2 Sand the item with 120-grit sandpaper, along the grain.

3 Switch to 180-grit paper, and sand again until the item is fairly smooth, especially along the edges between the painted and unpainted areas.

4 Paint any bare wood with a primer; let dry.

5 If the wood has a number of knotholes or dark blemishes that you want hidden, paint them with a stain-killing primer. Let dry.

6 Paint the entire piece with an exterior paint—even the hard-to-see places underneath, which will need the paint for protection, if not appearance. Let dry.

7 Apply a second coat; let dry.

What You'll Need

- Stiff wire brush
- Waterproof glue
- Clamp
- Putty knife
- Paste wood filler
- 120-, 180- and 220-grit sandpaper
- Cloth
- Paintbrushes
- Wood primer
- Stain-killing primer
- Exterior paint

Tips

When painting a bulky piece of furniture such as a picnic table, prop it up on one end first, to expose its underside and other parts you might not notice.

Either latex or oil-based primers will work here, but latex paint is much easier to clean up. Latex paint has also improved in quality and adhesion in recent years, and it is used by most painters for most jobs.

Paint the end grain of the wood twice while applying each coat (painting it first and then again at the end will make this easy to remember). This ensures that the paint completely covers the grain.

446 Restore Weathered Metal Furniture

Some types of metal furniture look best painted, while others are better left all natural. For lightweight aluminum furniture, such as the webbed folding chair described in 447 Repair Chair Straps and Webbing, here's how to revitalize the metal and bring out its shine. For the sturdier metal furniture often found in patio sets, you can take years off its appearance with a brand-new paint job.

Steps

Shining up aluminum furniture

1 Use a stiff wire brush to remove any loose rust.

2 Wearing rubber gloves, scrub around the frame with a nonabrasive scouring pad dipped in kerosene or a commercial aluminum brightener. Take care to keep the liquid off straps and webbing, as it could stain them.

3 Rinse the frame with warm water, and dry well with a cloth rag.

4 To help prevent corrosion and add shine, you can wipe on a very light coat of car wax with a cloth rag.

Repainting metal furniture

1 Scrub off any loose paint or rust with a stiff wire brush.

2 Abrade the entire surface of the piece with 180-grit aluminum-oxide sandpaper. This will provide a better surface for the paint to stick to.

3 Cover the area under the piece with a drop cloth. If you're planning to use a spray paint, make sure that all nearby areas — particularly walls and plantings — are also covered.

4 Apply a metal primer, either the brush-on or spray variety; let dry.

5 Brush or spray on the new enamel paint; let dry. If you are making a drastic change in color, or if it is recommended on the label, apply a second coat.

What You'll Need

- Stiff wire brush
- Rubber gloves
- Nonabrasive scouring pad
- Kerosene or commercial aluminum brightener
- Cloth rags
- Car wax
- 180-grit aluminum-oxide sandpaper
- Drop cloths
- Metal primer
- Paintbrush
- Enamel paint

Tips

Be sure to get an enamel paint designed for using on metal that offers protection against rust.

Have a paintbrush on hand even if you're using spray paint. Some spots may need to be smoothed out or have excess paint removed.

447 **Repair Chair Straps and Webbing**

Spending a little time each fall performing some maintenance and repair—along with a good cleaning—will keep your chairs looking good for years to come.

Steps

Installing a vinyl chair strap

1 Turn the chair upside down. If the damaged straps are held on by metal screws, remove the screws; for plastic rivets, pop them off with a flathead screwdriver. For fasteners inside a slot in the frame, cut the strap with a utility knife very close to where it goes into the slot. The fastener should then fall loose.

2 With a measuring tape (or a length of twine you can measure later), measure the length of the strap you'll need. The tape or twine will need to go over the hole or slot in the frame, around the frame, over to the other side, and then around the frame again to cover the opposite hole or slot. Pull as tight as you can when measuring.

3 Cut a length of strap 1 inch (2.5 cm) shorter than your measurement. This will ensure that you stretch the strap as tightly as possible when installing it.

4 With an awl or the point of a screw, make a hole about ¼ inch (6 mm) from each end of the strap.

5 Attach one end of the strap with a sheet-metal screw (see A). If you are using plastic rivets, you'll need to drive them in with a rubber mallet or very gently with a hammer. Loop the other end of the strap around the other side of the frame, pull tightly and attach in the same manner. Replace any other straps as necessary.

Replacing nylon webbing

1 With a screwdriver, remove the screws or metal clips holding the webbing. If only one or two straps are torn and the rest look good, you may want to replace only them. If the chair has a

What You'll Need

- Screwdriver
- Utility knife
- Measuring tape or twine
- Roll of vinyl strapping
- Scissors
- Awl
- ½-inch (12-mm) sheet-metal screws
- Plastic rivets or metal clips (depending on the type of chair)
- Rubber mallet or hammer
- Web repair kit or roll of nylon webbing

Tips

To clean a vinyl-strap chair, use an ammonia-based cleaner and a sponge. For a web chair, an ordinary household cleaner and a scrub brush will work best.

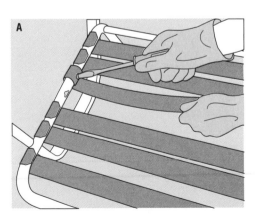

A

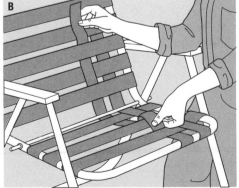

B

drooping seat or many frayed straps, you'll need to remove all the webbing.

2 Using the method described in step 2, opposite page, measure the distance from the slots or holes for each of the horizontal straps. Remember, the chair back and seat may not be the same width, so take measurements for each.

3 Unroll a length of nylon webbing. If you are attaching the horizontal straps with screws, add 2 inches (5 cm) to each measurement, and cut the roll into strips of that length with scissors. If you are using clips, add 1½ inches (4 cm).

4 For chairs with screws, fold down the corners at one end of the strap to form a point (you'll be able to see from the old webbing how this is done). Make a hole with an awl or screw about ½ inch (12 mm) from the tip of the point. Screw in one end of the strap, pull it around tightly, and screw in the other end.

5 If you're using clips, fold ¾ inch (2 cm) of strap around the clip and insert it in the slot (again, you should be able to see from the old webbing how to do this).

6 After all the horizontal webbing is done, install the vertical webbing using the same methods as above. You'll need to weave the vertical straps in and out of the horizontal webbing (see B). Make sure the vertical straps all run behind the bar that is the pivot between the back and the seat.

To really stretch the nylon strap across the seat, soften it by soaking it in very hot water for 10 minutes, then take it out (use rubber gloves for this) and quickly install it. Be sure to punch the holes in the strap ends first.

The best time to clean the chair's frame is while the straps are off. For an unpainted metal chair, apply an aluminum brightener with a nonabrasive scouring pad to perk it up.

448 Revive Rusted Iron Furniture

Whether it's cast or wrought, iron ranks among the most popular materials for outdoor furniture. It does have one major flaw, though: If you're not careful, it can rust. With this method, you can make your furniture look like new again.

Steps

1 Rub the rusted sections with kerosene, and scour with fine-grade steel wool until you reach bare metal. For persistent spots, reapply the kerosene and leave it on long enough to loosen the rust.

2 Sand the edges of the bare spots to make a smooth transition between them and the surrounding painted sections.

3 Rinse the piece to remove all dust, and wipe it with an absorbent towel. Let the piece sit until it's thoroughly dry.

4 Spray with a rust-inhibiting primer, according to the product's instructions. Follow with a rust-resistant spray paint.

5 Allow the paint to dry for a day or two. Then, using a soft cloth, rub the piece of furniture with car wax.

What You'll Need

- Kerosene
- Fine-grade steel wool (No. 000 or 0000)
- Fine-grit sandpaper
- Absorbent towel
- Rust-inhibiting primer
- Rust-resistant spray paint
- Soft cloth
- Car wax

Tip

Once a year, wipe down iron with white vinegar (no need to rinse) and follow with a coat of car wax.

It's not that easy to have a garden pond with clear water, healthy plants and thriving fish all summer long. After all, a pond with all those elements is not just a decorative ornament—it's your own little backyard ecosystem. Your pond residents are engaged in a fierce struggle for nutrients and oxygen.

PROBLEM	POSSIBLE CAUSES	SOLUTIONS
Excessive algae	Too little competition	Introduce other plants to keep algae from gobbling up all the oxygen and nutrients.
	Too much sunlight	Algae thrives on sunlight that reaches underwater; add floating plants like water lilies to help shade the bottom.
	Too many nutrients	Don't use regular potting soil or fertilizers for pond plants; they leach excessive nutrients into the water. Instead, use soil especially made for aquatic gardens and slow-release aquatic plant food.
Cloudy, brown water	Pump and filter not working efficiently	Regularly clean the pond filter (as often as weekly in summer). For a foam filter, remove it, wash with water and liquid detergent, squeeze it out and replace; for a cartridge filter, hose it down with a strong stream. Several times a season, clean inside filter pipes with a small brush.
	Too much algae	Follow steps for "Excessive algae," above.
Leaves and plant debris in pond	Dead leaves from nearby trees	Skim pond surface regularly with a net on a long pole. If you have several trees very close to the pond, catch leaves in fall by stretching garden netting all the way across pond surface and anchoring it on both sides.
	Dead leaves from pond plants	Frequently examine pond plants and remove any yellowing or dying leaves.
Floating plants appear unhealthy	Plants have outgrown container	When a plant such as a water lily has excessive leaf growth, with leaves rising above the water surface, it probably isn't getting enough nutrients from its container to promote blooming. Remove the plant from the container, divide it, and put half of it in a second container elsewhere in the pond.

Sometimes the less attractive inhabitants—such as the amazingly persistent algae—may gain the upper hand at the expense of your elegant water lilies and beautiful koi. Follow the instructions below, and you'll be able to put things back in balance.

PROBLEM	POSSIBLE CAUSES	SOLUTIONS
Unhealthy or dying pond fish	Lack of oxygen	Add more submerged oxygenating plants like duckweed and eel grass. Reducing amount of algae will also help.
	Overpopulation	A general rule is to have 1 to 2 inches (2.5 to 5 cm) of fish length for each square foot (929 square cm) of pond. For example, in a 60-square-foot (5.5-square-m) pond, 15 fish 4 inches (10 cm) long is acceptable, and 30 fish is an absolute maximum.
	Too much chlorine or chloramine in the water	Both of these are deadly to fish. A pool store will have kits to test for these chemicals, and also commercial treatments to reduce them to a safe level.
Plants or fish frozen under ice	Winter	Move fish and container plants that are not winter-hardy to a sheltered place. To provide oxygen and air circulation for the remaining fish and plants, leave a large plastic ball on the surface all winter; its motion will keep a section of the pond unfrozen. You can also create an air-space between ice and water by knocking a small hole in the ice and siphoning out some water.
Dense, matted underwater plants	Excessive growth of submerged plants	Once or twice a season, thin out submerged plants; divide them if necessary.
Low water level	Evaporation, particularly in hot weather	Check water daily in summer; top off with a hose as needed.
	Leak in pond liner or fiberglass form	Repair tears in a pond liner with a patch made from a scrap of liner attached by epoxy. Fix cracks in a rigid pond form with a fiberglass-repair kit. Your only chance to find submerged leaks is when you empty the pond—which should happen only once every few years—so be sure to check the entire pond thoroughly at that time.

450 Clean Swimming Pool Water

Let's face it—the only thing essential about a swimming pool is that the water be fresh and clean. Let's face something else, too: Achieving this can involve more chemistry than you may have seen since junior year in high school—if then. Don't worry, though. Here are all the important concepts and terms you need to know to keep your pool clean. Just be sure to follow all manufacturer's directions on the package of a chemical *carefully*.

Steps

Balancing the water

Note: The three factors mentioned here—pH, total alkalinity and calcium hardness—all affect one another, so it will take some trial and error to get all three in the proper range at once. Also note that before you add any chemical—especially an acid—to the water, you need to first turn on the pool's filter.

1 Use a water-testing kit to measure the calcium hardness (how "hard" or "soft" the water is). The proper calcium hardness is between 200 and 400 parts per million (ppm).

2 Following package directions, add calcium carbonate dihydrate to raise calcium hardness; add sodium hexametaphosphate to lower it. Carefully pour the chemical mixture into the pool at various spots a foot or two (about half a meter) away from the sides of the pool.

3 Measure the water's total alkalinity. This figure should be in the range of 80 to 150 ppm; 100 to 120 ppm is best.

4 Adjust the total alkalinity by adding sodium bicarbonate (baking soda) to raise it or sodium bisulfate (dry acid) to lower it.

5 With a pH tester, measure the water's pH. The proper pH for a pool is in the range of 7.2 to 7.6.

6 To lower the pH, add sodium bisulfate or liquid muriatic acid. To raise it, add soda ash (sodium carbonate).

7 Add more chemicals as needed until the water is in balance.

What You'll Need

- Pool-water testing kit
- Calcium carbonate dihydrate
- Sodium hexametaphosphate
- Sodium bicarbonate (baking soda)
- Sodium bisulfate (dry acid)
- pH tester
- Liquid muriatic acid
- Soda ash (sodium carbonate)
- Rubber gloves
- Safety goggles
- Chlorine granules
- Leaf net
- Broom
- Garden hose with high-pressure nozzle

Tips

Don't add harsh chemicals to the water through the pool skimmer, as that could damage the equipment.

Take water samples for testing from at least a foot (30 cm) below the surface for a truer reading.

Treating water with chlorine

1 Scoop chlorine granules into water in a nonmetal container, following package directions. Always wear goggles and rubber gloves when handling chlorine, and always put the chlorine into the water—don't pour the water over the chlorine.

2 Stir for about 30 seconds, and leave for 30 minutes to settle.

3 Turn on the filter. Reaching as far into the middle of the pool as possible (perhaps by standing on a diving board), pour the chlorine into the pool. Discard any sediment left in the container.

4 Add chlorine three to four times a week for a pool in heavy use.

5 Occasionally—no more than once a week—you may need to superchlorinate (also called shock) the pool to burn any built-up bacteria, algae and ammonia. Following chlorine package directions, make a solution for superchlorination (it will be three to five times as strong as normal chlorine).

6 Add the chlorine solution to the pool after sundown, if possible, as the sun's rays break down chlorine.

7 Before allowing anyone to go in the pool, test the residual chlorine level to make sure it has gone back down below 3.0 ppm. This will take at least several hours.

Chlorine also comes in a more expensive but convenient liquid form, and in tablets and sticks that you place in dispensers to slowly dissolve.

Keeping the water dirt- and debris-free

1 Remove any leaves from the pool with a leaf net each time you go swimming.

2 Empty and rinse off the strainer basket of the skimmer once or twice a week, and as often as daily during falling-leaf season.

3 Keep the deck clean by regularly sweeping and then rinsing it with a garden hose.

4 Use a cover over your pool as often as possible.

5 Thoroughly clean your pool filter at least monthly. Clean a sand filter by backwashing: Reverse the flow of water through the filter for 2 to 3 minutes until the wastewater is clear.

6 For a cartridge filter, remove the filter cartridge and wash it with a hose with a high-pressure nozzle. Replace the cartridge.

451 Troubleshoot Hot Tubs and Spas

You'd think that a hot tub or spa, being so much smaller than a swimming pool, would be much easier to maintain. But a hot tub requires special care for a couple of reasons: With its higher water temperatures (around 100° to 104°F/38° to 40°C) and lesser water volume, any problems with water quality can grow and spread very quickly. Fortunately, after putting in a little extra effort to properly maintain your tub, you can reward yourself with a nice warm soak.

PROBLEM	SOLUTIONS
Cloudy water	• Make sure filter is working properly. Filter basket should be emptied every week, and filter should run at least 2 hours a day (more often with heavy use). • A pH of over 7.6 can cause cloudiness. Treat water so that pH falls within recommended range of 7.2 to 7.6. • Eventually, residue builds up in water. Every two to four months, empty tub completely. Clean sides with a nonabrasive cleanser and sponge, rinse and wipe with household disinfectant. Refill tub. (Make sure a wooden tub is not left empty for more than two days. The pressure of the water's weight keeps the joints between boards tightly closed.)
Water irritates eyes and skin	• The pH may be too low or too high; treat water to adjust it. • Water may have too much chlorine (free chlorine should measure from 1.0 to 3.0 parts per million [ppm]). Once a week, shock (or superchlorinate) water by adding a much greater amount of chlorine than usual. Follow package directions very closely, and don't go into spa again until chlorine level has gone back down.
Leaks in a wooden tub	• If leaks are coming from between staves, tighten bands around tub. If tub still leaks, plug leak with silicone caulk.
Scale	• To avoid these rough calcium deposits, keep pH in the proper range and treat water so that its calcium hardness is between 150 and 400 ppm.
Algae	• Drain and clean spa as described in "Cloudy water," above. To keep algae off, chlorinate regularly, and keep tub covered when not in use.
Stains and colored water	• These usually indicate metals, such as copper, in water. You should be able to find products for removing metals at a pool store or water-care company.

452 Replace Bricks in Walkways and Patios

Each spring, as the ground heaves with each freezing and thaw, some of the bricks on a patio or walkway can become damaged or simply pushed out of place. Whether the bricks are set in sand or in mortar, it's a relatively simple task to replace or reinstall a few of them to maintain an attractive, level surface.

Steps

Replacing unmortared bricks

1 Remove the bricks you're replacing or reinstalling with an old flat-head screwdriver. Spray water on the exposed sand base.

2 Tamp down the sand with a metal or wooden tamping tool; for a small area such as one or two bricks, you can use the end of a 2-by-4 scrap.

3 If necessary, add a layer of fine sand (available at home supply stores) so that it rises just barely above the bottom of the bricks that are still in place. Gently use the 2-by-4 scrap to smooth the new sand until it is level.

4 Place the bricks on the sand one at a time. If a brick is too high, remove some sand from below; if it's too low, add a small amount of sand. Frequently check to make sure the bricks are level.

5 When all the bricks are in, scatter a ½-inch (12-mm) layer of fine sand over the area. Sweep it back and forth until the cracks between the bricks are filled with sand.

6 With a gentle spray, wash off the remaining sand from the bricks.

Replacing bricks set in mortar

1 Remove the bricks to be replaced or reset; use a cold chisel and a mason's hammer to break up the mortar around the edges if necessary. Chip or brush off mortar from the surrounding bricks that are still in place.

2 Mix the mortar: Place premixed mortar (or a mixture of 1 part cement and 3 parts sand) in a mortar box or wheelbarrow. Add water a little at a time, and mix with a mason's trowel until it is the consistency of mud.

3 Use a trowel to put down a ½- to 1-inch (1.25- to 2.5-cm) layer of mortar as a base. Level the mortar with the 2-by-4 scrap.

4 With a small pointing trowel, spread a ¾-inch (2-cm) layer of mortar on the sides of a brick. Push it onto the base and tightly against the adjoining bricks. When all the bricks are in, use the pointing trowel to grout the mortar between the bricks.

5 Let the mortar dry, then brush away any excess mortar on top of the bricks.

What You'll Need

- Flathead screwdriver
- Garden hose and nozzle
- Metal or wooden tamping tool
- 2-by-4 scrap
- Fine sand
- Level
- Bricks
- Broom
- Cold chisel
- Mason's hammer
- Mortar mix, or cement and sand
- Mortar box or wheelbarrow
- Mason's trowel
- Pointing trowel

Tips

Make sure you buy solid bricks. The bricks with three round holes through them are for building walls, not walkways.

When you're checking the brick surface for levelness, check it side to side and front to back.

Lay down a square of plywood next to the area you're working on; you'll be able to kneel more comfortably, and you won't be as likely to accidentally displace the rest of the bricks.

UCKED PICTURE • UNPLUG A STUCK AEROSOL CAN • GIVE BARBIE A MAKEOVER • DEAL WITH A STUCK WINE CORK • REPAIR A DOOR •
ORING • FIX BAD HABITS • REPAIR A BROKEN EYEGLASS FRAME • REPOSITION A SLIPPED CONTACT LENS • FIX A RUN IN STOCKINGS • JO
EAKOUT • REPAIR A TORN FINGERNAIL • FIX CHIPPED NAIL POLISH • FIX A STUCK ZIPPER • FIND A LOST CONTACT LENS • ELIMINATE BAD
Y THAT STICKS • STOP TELEMARKETERS AND JUNK MAIL • GET SUPERGLUE OFF YOUR SKIN • EXTRACT A SPLINTER • SOOTHE A SUNBURN
HANGOVER • STOP HICCUPS • MEND A BROKEN HEART • MEND A FAMILY FEUD • TREAT A SMALL CUT OR SCRAPE • FIX HAIR DISASTERS •
TTER SEATS • FIX A BILLING MISTAKE • FIX A BAD GRADE • FIX BAD CREDIT • RECOVER FROM JET LAG • RESUSCITATE AN UNCONSCIOUS
PRONOUNS • FIX A RUN-ON SENTENCE • FIX MISUSE OF THE WORD GOOD • FIX YOUR DOG OR CAT • CORRECT BAD BEHAVIOR IN DOGS
SSING BUTTON • REMOVE LINT FROM CLOTHING • FIX A DRAWSTRING ON SWEATPANTS • REPAIR A HEM • REPAIR LEATHER GOODS • MEN
UNDER YOUR CASHMERE • FIX A SWEATER THAT HAS SHRUNK • FIX A SWEATER THAT HAS STRETCHED • FIX A HOLE IN A POCKET • FIX A H
LING FROM CLOTHING • FIX A FRAYED BUTTONHOLE • REMOVE DARK SCUFFS FROM SHOES • TREAT STAINS ON LEATHER • PROTECT SUE
IET SQUEAKY HINGES • TROUBLESHOOT LOCK PROBLEMS • TIGHTEN A LOOSE DOORKNOB • TIGHTEN A LOOSE DOOR HINGE • FIX A BIN
PLACE CRACKED TILE • TROUBLESHOOT MOLD ON INTERIOR WALLS • REPLACE CRACKED TILE GROUT IN A TUB OR SHOWER • FIX A DRA
NDS • TROUBLESHOOT WINDOW SHADE PROBLEMS • FIX BROKEN GLASS IN A WINDOW • REPAIR A WINDOW SCREEN • REPAIR ALUMINUM
MAGED PLASTER • REPAIR WALL COVERINGS • TOUCH UP PAINTED WALLS • TROUBLESHOOT INTERIOR-PAINT PROBLEMS • SOLVE A LEAD
RDWOOD FLOOR • RESTORE A DULL, WORN WOOD FLOOR • TOUCH UP WOOD-FLOOR FINISHES • REPAIR DAMAGED SHEET-VINYL FLOORI
USE • CHILDPROOF YOUR HOME • PREVENT ICE DAMS • CURE A FAULTY FIREPLACE DRAW • START A FIRE IN A COLD CHIMNEY • FIX A WO
AL A GARAGE FLOOR • REFINISH A GARAGE OR BASEMENT FLOOR • CONTROL ROOF LEAKS • REDIRECT RAINWATER FROM A DOWNSPOU
MAGED ASPHALT SHINGLE • PATCH A FLAT OR LOW-PITCHED ROOF • REPAIR ROOF FLASHING • TROUBLESHOOT EXTERIOR-PAINT PROBLE
W WATER PRESSURE • FIX LEAKING PIPES • STOP A TOILET FROM RUNNING • FIX A LEAKY TOILET TANK • FIX A STOPPED-UP TOILET • STO
OGGED SINK OR TUB • REPAIR A TUB-AND-SHOWER VALVE • REPAIR CHIPPED FIXTURES • QUIET NOISY PIPES • DEFROST YOUR PIPES • DI
ONSUMPTION • REPLACE A RECEPTACLE • FIX AN ELECTRICAL PLUG • REPLACE A LIGHT FIXTURE • INSTALL A NEW DIMMER • FIX A LAMP •
OORBELL • FIX A WOBBLY OVERHEAD FAN • ADJUST WATER-HEATER TEMPERATURE • RELIGHT A WATER-HEATER PILOT LIGHT • TROUBLESH
E MAKER • GET RID OF MICROWAVE SMELLS • FIX A REFRIGERATOR THAT COOLS POORLY • FIX A GAS OVEN THAT HEATS POORLY • CLEAN
SHWASHER PROBLEMS • CORRECT AN OVERFLOWING DISHWASHER • FIX A LEAKY DISHWASHER • FIX A DISHWASHER THAT FILLS SLOWLY
WASHING MACHINE THAT FILLS SLOWLY • FIX A WASHING MACHINE THAT "WALKS" ACROSS THE FLOOR • FIX A CLOTHES DRYER THAT DRIE
K YOUR VACUUM CLEANER • REPLACE VACUUM CLEANER BRUSHES • TROUBLESHOOT A PORTABLE AIR CONDITIONER • FIX A WINDOW AIR
OCESSOR • FIX A TOASTER • DIAGNOSE MICROWAVE OVEN PROBLEMS • TROUBLESHOOT A GAS GRILL • FIX A TRASH COMPACTOR • REPA
ART • TROUBLESHOOT A CRASHING COMPUTER • CLEAN UP LAPTOP SPILLS • FIX BAD SECTORS ON A HARD DISK • QUIT A FROZEN PC AF
FECTED COMPUTER • IMPROVE YOUR COMPUTER'S MEMORY • GET RID OF E-MAIL SPAM • CHANGE A LASER PRINTER CARTRIDGE • FIX A F
GURE OUT WHY A PRINTER WON'T PRINT • FIX SPELLING AND GRAMMAR ERRORS • RECALL AN E-MAIL IN MICROSOFT OUTLOOK • DIAGNO
LES • TROUBLESHOOT A PALM OS PDA • RESET A PALM OS PDA • REMOVE FINGERPRINTS FROM A CAMERA LENS • TROUBLESHOOT A CD-
LVAGE A VIDEOCASSETTE • TROUBLESHOOT A DVD PLAYER • STRENGTHEN FM RADIO RECEPTION • STRENGTHEN AM RADIO RECEPTION •
JAMMED SLIDE PROJECTOR • GET BETTER SPEAKER SOUND • TROUBLESHOOT A DIGITAL CAMCORDER • TROUBLESHOOT A DIGITAL CAME
GHTBULB • FIX A BROKEN WINEGLASS STEM • FIX BLEMISHED WOOD FURNITURE • REPAIR GOUGES IN FURNITURE • RESTORE FURNITURE
AMOUFLAGE A DOG-SCRATCHED DOOR • REPAIR A SPLIT CARPET SEAM • RID CARPETS OF PET ODORS • REINFORCE A SAGGING SHELF •
INTS OF CHAIRS AND TABLES • REUPHOLSTER A DROP-IN CHAIR SEAT • REVIVE A CANE SEAT • REINFORCE A WEAK BED FRAME • FIX UP A
OTTERY • REPAIR CHIPPED OR CRACKED CHINA • UNCLUTTER YOUR HOME • CLEAN CRAYON FROM A WALL • GET WAX OFF A TABLECLOTH
AINS • REMOVE CHEWING GUM FROM CARPETING • REMOVE BLEACH SPOTS FROM CARPETING • REMOVE PET STAINS • ELIMINATE WINE S
AINS FROM TILE GROUT • REMOVE MILDEW FROM WALLS AND CEILINGS • DISINFECT A TOILET BOWL • REMOVE FIREPLACE GRIME • GET F
LEAN OIL SPOTS FROM A GARAGE OR DRIVEWAY • REMOVE STAINS FROM BRICK • WASH AN OUTDOOR GRILL • FIX A FALLEN SOUFFLÉ • RE
SCUE OVERPROOFED YEAST DOUGH • FIX YOUR KID LUNCH • GET RID OF TAP-WATER MINERAL DEPOSITS • CALIBRATE A MEAT THERMOM
UCE • RESCUE A BROKEN SAUCE • REMOVE FAT FROM SOUPS AND SAUCES • FIX LUMPY GRAVY • SUBSTITUTE MISSING INGREDIENTS • R
URNED RICE • REMOVE COOKING ODORS • FINISH UNDERCOOKED MEAT • SALVAGE AN UNDERCOOKED TURKEY • FIX AN OVERSEASONED
ALE BREAD • SMOOTH SEIZED CHOCOLATE • SOFTEN HARDENED SUGARS OR COOKIES • FIX BREAKFAST FOR YOUR SWEETHEART • MEND
GGING TOOLS • RESTORE A BROKEN FLOWERPOT • SHARPEN PRUNING CLIPPERS • REMOVE RUST FROM TOOLS • REVIVE WILTING CUT FL
ET RID OF RAMPANT BRAMBLES • TROUBLESHOOT BROWN SPOTS ON A LAWN • CONTROL MAJOR GARDEN PESTS • RID YOUR GARDEN OF
ONPERFORMING COMPOST PILE • FIX BAD SOIL • SHORE UP A RAISED GARDEN BED • REMOVE A DEAD OR DISEASED TREE LIMB • TROUBL
RAINAGE • TROUBLESHOOT ROSE DISEASES • IDENTIFY AND CORRECT SOIL DEFICIENCIES IN ROSES • TROUBLESHOOT ROSE PESTS • OVE
AMAGED DECK BOARDS • REPAIR DECK RAILINGS • STRENGTHEN DECK JOISTS • FIX A RUSTY IRON RAILING • REPAIR A GATE • REPAIR A F
RACKED OR DAMAGED CONCRETE • IMPROVE THE LOOK OF REPAIRED CONCRETE • REPAIR AN ASPHALT DRIVEWAY • REVIVE WOODEN OU
ARDEN PONDS • CLEAN SWIMMING POOL WATER • TROUBLESHOOT HOT TUBS AND SPAS • REPLACE BRICKS IN WALKWAYS AND PATIOS • S
AR WITH JUMPER CABLES • SHUT OFF A CAR ALARM THAT WON'T QUIT • FREE A CAR STUCK ON ICE OR SNOW • DE-ICE YOUR WINDSHIEL
URN-SIGNAL COVER • FIX A CAR FUSE • FIX DASHBOARD LIGHTS THAT WON'T LIGHT • REMOVE CAR SMELLS • CHECK TIRE PRESSURE • INF
PROPERLY INSTALLED CHILD CAR SEAT • TROUBLESHOOT LEAKING OIL • CHECK AND ADD POWER-STEERING FLUID • CHECK AND ADD CO
ROKEN EXHAUST PIPE • CHECK AND ADD ENGINE OIL • CHECK AND ADD BRAKE FLUID • CHECK AND ADD FLUID TO YOUR AUTOMATIC TRA
OUBLESHOOT A WINDSHIELD WASHER PUMP • REPAIR MINOR DENTS • CHANGE A HUBCAP • FIX AN IGNITION KEY THAT WON'T TURN •

Cars

453 Start a Stalled Car

If your car won't start due to a dead or low battery or a broken starter, you can push-start it in just a few minutes. Try the following methods to get it rolling again.

Steps

1 Determine if your car has a dead battery or a bad starter. If the engine cranks (makes a *rr-rr-rr* sound), your problem lies elsewhere. If the engine is silent or you only hear clicks when you turn the key, then your battery or starter is probably bad, and a push-start may be just what you need.

2 If your car isn't on a hill, ask a couple of friends or passersby for help.

3 Turn the key to the On position.

4 Release the parking brake.

5 Push down on the clutch pedal and put the transmission in second gear.

6 Keeping the clutch pedal depressed, either shout to your friends to start pushing or let the car roll downhill.

7 When the car is rolling as fast as a person running, slowly release the clutch pedal while giving the engine a little gas with the accelerator pedal. The engine should start.

What You'll Need

- A downhill slope or several people to give you a push

Tip

This method works only with a car that has a manual transmission (a clutch).

Warning

The car may jump forward when you release the clutch. Make sure there are no people or obstructions in front of the car.

454 Shut Off a Jammed Horn

Although horns do not commonly get stuck on, knowing what to do in this situation will not only save your battery but also keep the neighbors happy. Try these steps in the order suggested.

Steps

1 Push on the horn button a few times—this may dislodge a stuck connection inside the steering wheel. If the horn doesn't stop, try this again while turning the steering wheel back and forth.

2 Find the fuse box. It is usually located below the steering wheel to the left. Some cars have several fuse boxes inside the engine compartment.

3 Locate the fuse with the horn label. There should be a fuse diagram on the lid of the fuse box.

4 Pull the horn fuse with the fuse puller (you may find one in the fuse box) or a pair of needle-nose pliers. In a pinch, you often can remove a fuse with your fingers.

5 If all else fails, disconnecting the battery's negative terminal will silence the horn, but it will also prevent your car from starting.

What You'll Need

- Fuse puller or needle-nose pliers

Tip

Pulling the fuse is only a temporary fix. Make an appointment with your mechanic to find the cause of the problem.

455 Change Your Car's Battery

Most batteries come equipped with a 60-month warranty. Keep track of your battery's life and replace it before it leaves you stranded.

Steps

1 With the engine off, pop the hood and find the battery (see illustration). Detach the negative battery cable from the battery. First loosen the nut with a combination wrench and then twist and pull up on the end of the cable with your hand. You may need to pry up the cable end with a screwdriver if it sticks.

2 Detach the positive battery cable from the battery using the same method.

3 Using a combination wrench or a socket and ratchet, remove the battery hold-down clamp.

4 Take the battery out of the battery tray. Batteries are heavy, so grab from the bottom using both hands.

5 Use water and a wire brush to clean any corrosion from the battery tray and the hold-down clamp.

6 Clean the battery cable connectors with a wire brush. To remove heavy corrosion from the connectors, use battery-cleaning solution (available at any auto-parts store).

7 Place the new battery in the battery hold-down tray and secure the battery with the hold-down clamp. Attach and tighten the positive battery cable. Attach and tighten the negative battery cable. Spray both terminal ends with anti-corrosion solution (optional). Check that all cable connectors are tight. If you can move them at all, your car may not start.

What You'll Need

- New battery
- Combination wrench
- Screwdriver
- Socket and ratchet
- Wire brush
- Battery-cleaning solution
- Anti-corrosion solution

Warning

Battery acid is extremely corrosive. Don't let it splash out. Take care not to spill any on your hands, body or clothing, or on car paint.

The old battery cannot go into the regular trash. Take it to a facility that accepts hazardous material for recycling. You can also return the used battery to the auto-parts store where you bought the new one.

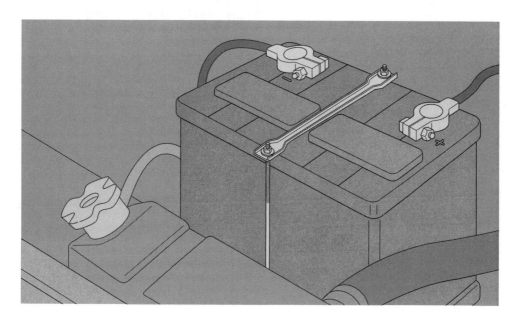

456 Troubleshoot a Car That Won't Start

When your car won't start, you can easily check quite a few things before calling a tow truck. Use this simple chart to diagnose what might be wrong and what you can do to get back on the road again.

PROBLEM	SOLUTION
Engine won't crank	Generally caused by either a dead battery or a bad starter, although you should check steps 1 through 5 to make sure it's not an operator error.
	1 If car is automatic, check that transmission is in park and your foot is on brake.
	2 If car is stick shift, check that clutch pedal is fully depressed. Check neutral safety switch behind clutch pedal (small button that prevents engine from starting when transmission is in gear). If clutch pedal doesn't fully engage neutral safety switch, engine will not crank.
	3 Check that driver's seat belt is fastened (some cars will not start with seat belt unlatched).
	4 Make sure you've properly inserted key. Turn it to On position and give steering wheel quarter turn in either direction.
	5 Make sure alarm system is not activated, preventing car from starting (see owner's manual for car alarm).
	6 Check for dead battery. Test wipers, radio, headlights and heater fan. If all work normally, battery is probably charged and you may have bad starter. If they don't work, move on to next step.
	7 Check connection at battery and at starter (see steps 8 and 9). If battery connections are good and all accessories work, consider jump-starting car (see 458 Start a Car With Jumper Cables).
	8 Open hood and check battery connections at terminals. If either connector is loose enough to move, problem may be bad connection. Jiggle or tighten cable end. Corrosion at battery terminal will also prevent car from starting. Clean terminal with wire brush or water and rag and tighten battery cable connectors.
	9 Check connection at starter. Follow battery cable from positive battery terminal to starter. Make sure connection isn't loose. Lightly tap outside of starter with hammer. Sometimes this will free stuck components inside so car can start.
	10 Consider push-starting car (manual transmission only) if battery or starter is at fault (see 453 Start a Stalled Car).
	11 Call tow truck.

PROBLEM	SOLUTION
Engine cranks slowly	Only one thing causes this condition: a battery that is not fully charged.
	1 Open hood and check battery connections. If there is any movement at positive or negative battery terminal, car may not start. Jiggle or tighten cable connector. Corrosion at battery terminal will also prevent car from starting. Clean battery cable ends and battery terminal with wire brush or water and rag and tighten battery cable ends.
	2 Check battery-acid level (only possible with some types of batteries). Use screwdriver to pop open small caps on top of battery. Add water until level reaches top of plastic split inside each battery cell (distilled recommended, but tap water will work).
	3 Jump-start or push-start car.
	4 Call tow truck.
Engine cranks but car won't start	There are hundreds of possible reasons your car cranks but doesn't start. Here are a few quick items to check before calling a tow truck.
	1 Turn key to On position and check gas gauge to make sure car's not out of gas.
	2 Open hood and look for disconnected spark-plug wires or vacuum lines.
	3 Check fuse box for blown fuses (see 467 Fix a Faulty Car Fuse).
	4 Call tow truck.
Engine runs but car won't go	A problem with the transmission or the wheels puts your car in this state.
	1 Release parking brake.
	2 Make sure transmission is properly in gear. Put it into park and then back into gear.
	3 Check ground outside car for objects blocking wheels.
	4 On manual transmission cars, open hood and check fluid level in clutch master cylinder (see 489 Add Brake Fluid to the Clutch Master Cylinder).
	5 Check level of automatic-transmission fluid (see 487 Check and Add Fluid to Your Automatic Transmission).
	6 Call tow truck.

457 Fix a Flat Tire

Most drivers face a flat at least a few times in their lives. Although it can be daunting the first time you attempt it, changing a flat tire is not difficult. Almost anyone can do it in under 15 minutes—less time than it usually takes for a tow truck to arrive.

Steps

1 Turn the flashers on and slowly and safely pull off the road. Find a spot that is visible but also away from traffic. Avoid soft shoulders and inclines. Put the hood up to indicate to other motorists that you are in mechanical distress, or set a few flares out on the road at 10-foot (3-m) intervals.

2 Apply the hand brake and put the transmission in park or in gear so the car won't roll.

3 Open the trunk and take out a spare tire, leverage pipe, jack, lug-nut wrench and (if it's dark out) flashlight (see illustration). The leverage pipe is simply a piece of hollow pipe that can help you loosen a lug nut previously tightened with an air ratchet; you can buy this at a hardware or plumbing supply store.

4 Chock the other wheels with a large rock or a log to prevent the car from rolling.

5 Remove the hubcap (if necessary) with a screwdriver. Many newer cars have hubcaps that don't require removal for access to the lug nuts.

What You'll Need

- Spare tire (with air in it)
- Leverage pipe
- Jack
- Lug-nut wrench
- Flashlight
- Chock
- Screwdriver
- Lug-nut key (for locking lug nuts only)
- Rag

Tips

Check the air pressure in your spare tire every month. Many drivers forget about the spare tire tucked away in the trunk and let it go flat.

Practice changing a tire in your driveway. Figure out how your jack works so you'll be less stressed when the real thing occurs.

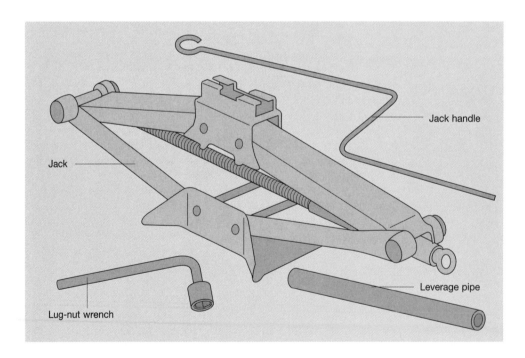

Jack handle

Jack

Leverage pipe

Lug-nut wrench

6 Use the lug-nut wrench to loosen the lug nuts on the flat tire (but do not remove them). To loosen a bolt or nut, turn counterclockwise. Remember: lefty-loosy, righty-tighty. If it doesn't come off easily, place the leverage pipe over the end of the lug-nut wrench and pull up rather than push down to avoid back injury. If one lug on each wheel looks different from the rest and the lug-nut wrench doesn't fit it, then you have locking lug nuts (to prevent wheel theft). Check the glove compartment for a special key that fits on this lug nut and makes removal with the lug-nut wrench possible.

7 When all the nuts are loose, jack up the car, making sure the jack is vertical and well planted on the hard surface of the road (do not jack up a car on sand or dirt). You'll find diagrams indicating where to place the jack either in the car owner's manual or on a sticker affixed to the jack. Most cars have a small slot near each tire for the jack. Jack up the car slightly more than needed to remove the flat tire; the spare will be larger because it is full of air.

8 Remove the lug nuts. Put them in your pocket or someplace else where they won't get lost.

9 Take the flat tire off and put it in the trunk.

10 Put the spare on. If you are unsure which way the wheel goes on, look for the air-pressure valve—it always faces out.

11 Tighten the lug nuts by turning clockwise (see A). Use a crisscross or star pattern so the wheel doesn't go on cockeyed (see B).

12 Lower the car and remove the jack.

13 Tighten the lug nuts again using the leverage pipe. Make them as tight as you can.

14 Pop on the hubcap (if applicable).

15 Put everything away neatly so it's ready for next time.

16 Remove the chock, then drive to a tire shop. Most shops can fix flats while you wait, and it's usually inexpensive.

Warning

Jacks for changing tires are meant for that purpose only. Do not crawl under a car you've jacked up with a tire-changing jack.

Many smaller cars come equipped with a temporary spare, a smaller and thinner tire not intended for driving long distances at highway speeds. This will be indicated on the side of the tire. A small spare requires more air than a regular tire does.

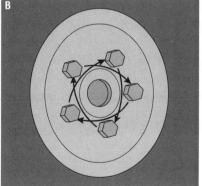

458 Start a Car With Jumper Cables

If your car won't start because the battery is low or dead, a jump-start will get you back on the road in a matter of minutes. This is an easy procedure that anyone with a pair of jumper cables can accomplish.

Steps

1 Determine that a dead battery is the reason your car is not starting. If the engine cranks when you turn the key, the problem is not the battery and jump-starting won't help. If the windshield wipers, lights and heater blower all work, the battery is probably fine and you may have a bad starter. A jump-start won't help if you have a bad starter. If you hear no sound at all when you turn the key or if the engine cranks very slowly and the accessories do not work, then you have a dead or low battery and it's time to break out the jumper cables. You'll need a flashlight if it's dark outside.

2 Find someone with a running car that can give yours a jump.

3 Open the hoods on both cars and determine where the batteries are. Park the booster car (the one that's running) so that the batteries are adjacent.

4 Turn off the booster car.

What You'll Need

- Flashlight
- Booster car
- Jumper cables
- Rag

Tips

Always store a set of jumper cables in the trunk of your car.

Holding up jumper cables indicates clearly to passing motorists that you need a jump—but stay safely out of the road when you do so.

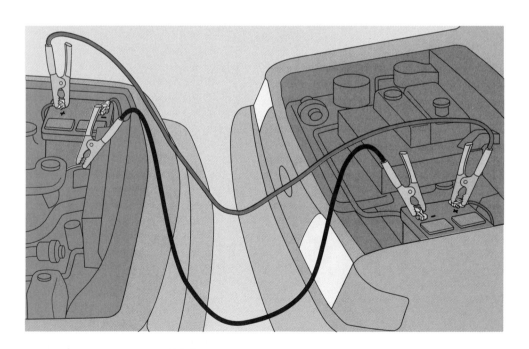

5 Attach the red jumper cable's end to the positive terminal on the dead battery. Use a rag to wipe the battery clean if you can't see the Pos or plus (+) sign on the battery. The positive terminal is always slightly larger than the negative one.

6 Attach the other end of the red cable to the booster battery's positive terminal.

7 Attach the black jumper cable's end to the booster battery's negative terminal.

8 Attach the other end of the black jumper cable to a ground on the dead car's engine; any solid metal part works fine. You may see a small spark when you attach the last end. This is normal.

9 Turn on the booster car and rev the engine.

10 Turn on the dead car. If it doesn't start, you may have a poor connection at any of the four cable ends. Jiggle each cable end and try starting the car again.

11 Once the car starts, disconnect the cables in reverse order of attachment: negative, negative, positive, positive.

12 Keep the engine running on the jumped car for at least 20 minutes or longer so the alternator has sufficient time to recharge your battery.

When buying jumper cables, choose a set that is at least 8 feet (2.5 m) long; this makes it easier to connect the two cars.

Warning

Do not reverse the polarity. Make sure the cables are attached as described, to avoid damaging your car's electrical equipment or causing the battery to explode.

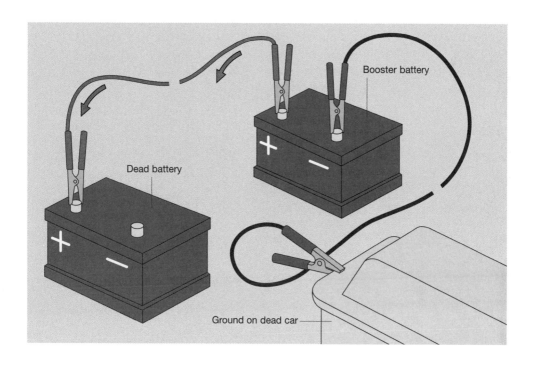

Booster battery

Dead battery

Ground on dead car

459 Shut Off a Car Alarm That Won't Quit

It's annoying when a neighbor's car alarm won't quit and embarrassing when your own is the culprit. Knowing how your particular alarm works will save you (and others) from ringing ears. Read through the owner's manual *before* you have a problem. When the alarm is blaring, your wits may desert you.

Steps

1 Check for user error. Consult the owner's manual for directions on how to turn the car alarm on and off.

2 Put the key in the ignition and try to start the car. On many systems this will shut off the alarm.

3 Find the alarm's fuse. It may be in the fuse box, usually located below the steering wheel to the left. Many cars also have other fuse boxes (sometimes three or even more) inside the engine compartment. If it's an aftermarket alarm (installed after the car left the factory), you'll find the fuse under the hood, usually on a wire connected to the positive battery terminal.

4 Locate the fuse that has the alarm label. You should find a fuse diagram on the lid of the fuse box. An aftermarket alarm won't have any label. Don't worry; removing the wrong fuse won't cause any damage. If you pull out a fuse and the alarm stays on, put that fuse back in and try another.

5 Pull the alarm fuse with the fuse puller (sometimes found in the fuse box) or a pair of needle-nose pliers. Sometimes you can remove a fuse using your fingers.

6 As a last resort, disconnecting the battery's negative terminal will stop the alarm, but it will also keep your car from starting.

What You'll Need

- Fuse puller or needle-nose pliers

Tip

Shut-off procedures for different car-alarm systems vary. Check the owner's manual for specifics.

460 Free a Car Stuck on Ice or Snow

Drivers living in snowy regions quickly become pros at maneuvering cars through deep snow. The rest of us may need a little help freeing a car that gets stuck in snow. Try these maneuvers one at a time.

Steps

1 Put the transmission into four-wheel drive (if your car has it).

2 Shift into the lowest gear available.

3 If the car won't go forward, put it into reverse and try backing up.

4 Turn the steering wheel slightly and try driving in a different direction.

5 Grab your shovel and remove as much snow as you can from in front of all the wheels.

6 Determine which wheel(s) are slipping by having a friend look at the wheels while you step on the accelerator. Place sand, salt, dirt, cat litter or a piece of old carpet in front of the slipping wheel(s).

7 Ask friends or passersby to push while you slowly depress the gas pedal. Make sure nobody is standing in front of the car. Be careful—accelerating too much makes the tires spin and heats up the snow underneath, turning it into ice.

8 Be prepared to steer and brake after your wheels gain traction.

What You'll Need

- Shovel
- Sand, salt, dirt, cat litter or piece of carpet
- Several people to help push

Warning

Establish clear signals between the people pushing the car and the driver to avoid dangerous misunderstandings. You don't want to accidently hit someone.

461 De-ice Your Windshield

A windshield coated with ice and snow shouldn't set you back more than a few minutes when you need to hit the road.

Steps

1 Turn on the car. Put the defroster on the hottest setting and turn on the air conditioner (many modern cars automatically engage the air conditioner when you turn on the defroster).

2 Set the defroster fan to low.

3 Brush snow off the windshield.

4 Spray de-icing solution on the windshield. (You can make your own de-icing solution—a mixture of half water and half vinegar.)

5 Scrape the ice off the outside of the windshield using an ice scraper or, in a pinch, a credit card.

What You'll Need

- Ice scraper or a credit card
- De-icing solution

Warning

Pouring hot water on an icy windshield can crack the glass.

462 Fix a Burned-Out Signal Bulb

Avoid a fix-it ticket or a trip to the auto-repair shop by doing this simple repair yourself. It is often no more difficult than changing a lightbulb at home.

Steps

1 Determine whether you access the bulb from the outside (by removing the plastic light cover) or from inside the trunk or under the hood.

2 If the bulb is accessed from the outside, remove the screws that secure the light cover. Usually this will only require a Phillips screwdriver. On some cars, you may need a socket and ratchet.

3 If the bulb is accessed from inside the trunk or under the hood, there will probably be a plastic protective cover. Twist the knob or tab on the cover to loosen it.

4 Remove the burned-out bulb by pushing it in and turning counter-clockwise.

5 Take the bulb to an auto-parts store to get the right replacement.

6 Clean the inside of the bulb socket if it is dirty with a wire brush, or a small piece of sandpaper, and a rag.

7 Screw in the new bulb by pushing it in and turning clockwise.

8 Test the bulb (turn on the device) before replacing the light cover.

9 Replace the light cover and tighten the screws.

What You'll Need

- New bulb
- Phillips screwdriver or socket and ratchet
- Wire brush or sandpaper
- Rag

463 Fix a Burned-Out Headlight

This is an easy fix with a relatively low frustration quotient. If only one headlight is burned out, resist the urge to replace both headlights at the same time. You don't want them to burn out simultaneously in the future.

Steps

1 Turn on the lights and determine which headlight is burned out.

2 Figure out what kind of headlight your car uses. Some cars have a replaceable halogen bulb inside the headlight. On other cars, you need to replace the entire headlight.

3 Buy the headlight or bulb you need at an auto-parts store. The salespeople can help you find the right headlight or bulb for your car. The procedure differs depending on what type of headlight you're installing.

Install a new halogen bulb

1 Open the hood and find the wires that go into the back of the headlight.

2 Twist the black plastic ring at the back of the headlight to release the bulb.

3 Pull out the bulb and unplug it.

4 Carefully take the new bulb out of the box without touching the glass part with your fingers (see Warning). Plug it in and place the bulb back into the headlight.

5 Twist the plastic ring back on and test the new headlight.

Replace an entire headlight

1 Unscrew the tiny screws that secure the thin metal frame holding down the headlight. Do not turn the ones that have little springs behind them (see Warning). You may not need to take out all the screws to remove the headlight; sometimes you can leave the frame hanging by one screw.

2 Put the screws in your pocket.

3 Pull out the headlight and unplug it.

4 Plug in the new headlight.

5 Turn on the headlights to make sure the new light works.

6 Put the metal frame back on and screw it down. A magnetized screwdriver will will make it easier to hold the screws in place.

What You'll Need

- New headlight or halogen bulb
- Screwdriver

Warning

Do not touch the glass on a new halogen bulb. The oil from your fingers will cause the bulb to fail prematurely.

Don't turn the adjusting screws when replacing the headlight or you will have to readjust it. The adjusting screws have little springs behind them. The screws that hold the headlight in place are smaller and have no springs behind them.

464 Adjust Headlights

Although mechanics use a highly accurate headlamp adjuster to ensure that both headlights are pointing in exactly the right direction, in a pinch a screwdriver will fix misdirected beams enough so you can safely drive in the dark.

Steps

1 Park your car on level ground with the headlights about 10 to 15 feet (3 to 4.5 m) from a wall or garage door.

2 Find the adjusting screws for the headlights. They will probably be inset adjacent to the headlight. You'll find a horizontal and a vertical adjusting screw, with small springs behind them. Some cars come equipped with a small level (like a carpenter's level) attached to the top of the headlight under the hood to help you get the correct adjustment.

3 Turn the headlights on.

4 Notice where the light shines, using the wall or garage door as your gauge. Check for uneven or cross-eyed light beams.

5 Turn the adjusting screws with a Phillips screwdriver while looking at the wall. Turn slowly and continue to check the wall (see illustration) until the light beams are even and tilted slightly downward (so your car's headlights won't blind oncoming traffic).

6 Test-drive in the dark and repeat steps 1 through 5 as necessary.

What You'll Need

- Phillips screwdriver
- Level ground near a wall or garage door

Tip

Turn the adjusting screws slowly and review the beam's location frequently to avoid adjusting the headlights in the wrong direction.

465 Fix a Stuck Brake Light

You know what to do when your neighbor reminds you that you left the headlights on, but what if the brake light is stuck on? Try these steps in the order shown.

Steps

1 Check the brake-pedal switch. This small button behind the brake pedal is activated when you press down on the brake pedal and makes the brake light go on. Press the switch by hand to see if it's stuck. If it is, pressing it may force the stuck part.

2 Find the fuse for the brake light and pull it out. Remember to put it back in before driving again (see 467 Fix a Faulty Car Fuse).

3 Find the brake lightbulbs and remove them. Remember to put them back in before driving again.

4 Disconnect the negative battery cable. You will have to reconnect it again to start and drive your car.

5 Make an appointment with your mechanic to have the problem diagnosed and repaired.

Warning

Driving with inoperative brake lights can cause an accident. These fixes are temporary—all they do is keep your battery from going dead when you park. Make an appointment with your mechanic to find the cause of the problem.

466 Replace a Broken Taillight or Turn-Signal Cover

Parallel parking and city living mean that taillights and turn-signal covers get damaged or cracked with some regularity. There's no reason to spend time and money at the shop when you can easily replace these plastic covers. The following steps work for standard covers, but in some new cars the cover is part of an assembly and you'll have to replace the whole thing.

Steps

1 Purchase a new light cover at your auto dealer or an auto-salvage yard. Call ahead to ensure they have it in stock. Remember to specify your car's make and model and exactly which light cover you are purchasing (front or rear, left or right).

2 Remove the screws that secure the broken or cracked light cover. Usually this requires just a Phillips screwdriver and can be done quite easily. On some cars, you may need a socket and ratchet. Take care not to misplace the screws.

3 Insert the new light cover and tighten the screws.

What You'll Need

- New taillight or turn-signal cover
- Phillips screwdriver or socket and ratchet

Tip

To avoid getting a fix-it ticket, you can temporarily fix a broken light cover with red or orange tape made specifically for this purpose and sold at auto-parts stores.

467 Fix a Faulty Car Fuse

Fuses protect your car from electrical short circuits and power over-
loads that can damage equipment or start a fire. Often, a fuse will blow
due to a momentary overload, and replacing the bad fuse as directed
below will fix the problem (a car's horn or interior lights may cease to
work, for example). If a fuse blows repeatedly, it indicates an electrical
problem that will require a trip to your mechanic.

Steps

1 Find the fuse box (see A). It is usually located under the dashboard to the left of the steering wheel, at about knee level. Many
cars have additional fuse boxes in the engine compartment.
Check your owner's manual or call the dealer for the exact
location(s).

2 Open the fuse box cover and locate the blown fuse. There are
two ways to find the bad fuse: Look for a fuse with a melted
center strip (see B, which shows two types of broken fuses).
Or, if you know which device isn't working—for example, the
radio—look for the fuse that handles that device. The fuse panel
may have labels for each device, or the information may be in
your owner's manual.

3 Remove the bad fuse with a fuse puller (a small pair of plastic
tweezers that should come with the fuse box). Or use a pair of
needle-nose pliers.

4 Check the number on the bottom or side of the bad fuse. This
indicates the amperage.

5 Buy a new fuse with the same amperage and push it into the slot
in the fuse box with your fingers.

What You'll Need

- Fuse puller or needle-
  nose pliers
- New fuse (same amper-
  age and type as the one
  you are replacing)

Tip

You can purchase fuses at
an auto-parts store. Buy an
assortment of different-
amperage fuses to keep in
your glove compartment.

Warning

Never replace a fuse with
one of bigger amperage.
This could damage the
device the fuse is meant
to protect.

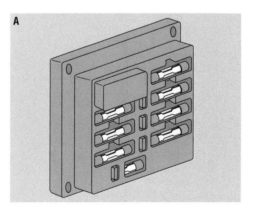

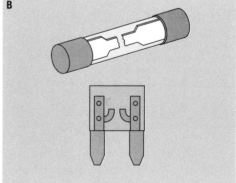

468 Fix Dashboard Lights That Won't Light

If all the lights on your dashboard seem to be out, the problem could be a bad fuse or even something like a turned-off switch.

Steps

1 Locate the knob or dial that controls the brightness of the dashboard lights. If the control is not immediately evident, check your owner's manual.

2 Make sure the brightness control is turned on. If it is and the lights aren't working, the problem may be a bad fuse.

3 Check the fuse that controls the dashboard lights (see 467 Fix a Faulty Car Fuse, opposite page). Replace the fuse if necessary.

4 Call your mechanic if neither of these steps fixes your problem.

Tip

If just one part of the instrument panel is not lighting up, then you have either a burned-out bulb or a wiring problem, neither of which you can easily fix at home.

469 Remove Car Smells

You can remove even the worst smells with the right product. The sooner you clean the area, the easier it is to remove lingering odors.

Steps

1 Find the cause of the smell. If it's a solid, remove it from the car.

2 Use paper towels to blot any liquid stains gently.

3 Clean the soiled area with a heavy-duty auto-upholstery cleaner, available at an auto-parts store. There are two types, one for the floor mats and one for the seats.

4 Apply bacteria/enzyme digester to the affected area with a sponge or rag. This product kills odors by destroying bacteria. You can purchase it at a cleaning supply or household-goods store.

5 Open the windows to let the spot air-dry.

6 Consider burning a stick of incense in your car. Car fresheners often have a strong artificial scent.

7 For persistent smells you can't get rid of, make an appointment to get the inside of your car professionally detailed.

What You'll Need

- Paper towels
- Auto-upholstery cleaner
- Bacteria/enzyme digester
- Sponge or rag
- Incense

Tips

Keep the windows rolled up tightly when your car is parked to prevent rain from coming in. Wetness creates a musty smell.

See also 496 Diagnose Car Smells.

470 Check Tire Pressure

Check all of your car's tires once a month or whenever they look low. Low tire pressure can lower your gas mileage, make your car handle poorly and even lead to blowouts.

What You'll Need

- Tire-pressure gauge

Tip

The spare tire may require more air than the others if it is a smaller, temporary spare. Look on its sidewall for the tire-pressure specifications.

Steps

1 You can't tell whether a tire has the correct air pressure just by looking at it. Always use a tire-pressure gauge. You can buy a good-quality tire-pressure gauge at your local auto-parts store. If you don't have one, the pressurized-air machines at many gas stations and garages have gauges, although they might not always be accurate or functioning.

2 Find the air-pressure specifications for your car's tires. You'll usually find them on a sticker located on the driver's side doorjamb. Or the sticker may be in the glove box or trunk. Don't look at the tire's sidewall for the air-pressure specifications, as it lists the maximum pressure for the tire.

3 Unscrew the plastic cap on the air valve. Put it in your pocket so you don't lose it.

4 Press the tire-pressure gauge against the valve and hold it down firmly (see illustration). If you hear a hissing noise, you are letting air out. Press down harder.

5 Read the measurement on the gauge.

6 Add air as needed (see 471 Inflate Your Tires, opposite page), but don't overfill the tire.

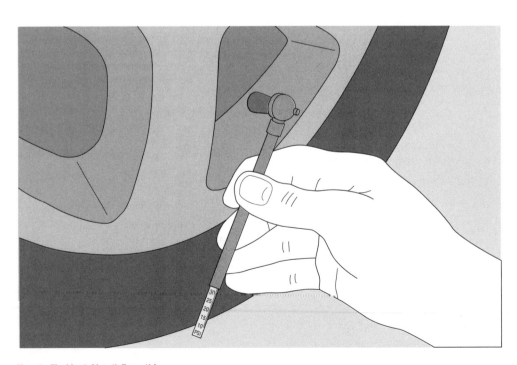

471 Inflate Your Tires

Full-service gas stations are a thing of the past. It's up to you to check and add air to your tires monthly. You cannot tell whether your tires need air by looking at them or even by kicking them. Keep a good-quality tire-pressure gauge in your car's glove box (a nice electronic one costs only about $20). Don't forget to check your spare tire and add air as necessary.

Steps

1 Go to a gas station or garage that has pressurized air with a gauge.

2 Park your car so you can reach all four tires with the air hose.

3 Find the air-pressure specifications for your car's tires. Look for a sticker located on the driver's side doorjamb or in the glove box or trunk.

4 Unscrew the plastic cap on the air valve. Put it in your pocket so you don't lose it.

5 Check the air pressure using either your own tire-pressure gauge or the one on the gas station air pump. Press the gauge against the valve and hold it down firmly. If you hear a hissing noise, you are letting air out. Press down harder.

6 Add air as necessary. Press the air pump hose on the valve while squeezing the lever on the end of the hose.

7 Check the air pressure with your gauge, or use the one on the air pump hose.

8 Let some air out of the tires if you accidentally overfill them. Press down on the small needle in the center of the valve to let air out. Most tire-pressure gauges have a small knob for this purpose, but a fingernail or a pen will do the trick.

What You'll Need

- Gas station or garage with pressurized air
- Tire-pressure gauge

Tip

If a tire needs air every time you check, ask a tire shop to inspect it for a slow leak.

Warning

Don't look at the tire's sidewall for air-pressure specifications, as it lists the maximum pressure for the tire.

Always use a tire-pressure gauge to get the right air pressure; you don't want to over- or underinflate your tires.

472 Fix a Stuck Convertible Top

If your convertible's top suddenly won't budge, you may not need to interrupt your day with an emergency trip to the auto-repair shop. Often the hood will not go up or down for simple reasons that you can check yourself. Try the following before calling your mechanic.

Steps

1 Check all the latches that hold the top open or closed. You'll feel sheepish but happy if this is the cause of the problem.

2 If the hood won't close, make sure the lid for the boot (hood hide-away or cubby) is open. If it's not, open it.

3 Check for a blown fuse (see 467 Fix a Faulty Car Fuse).

Tip

Some cars have manual tops—only steps 1 and 2 apply to these.

473 Diagnose a Leak Inside Your Car

There's really no such thing as an insignificant leak. Leaks always get bigger over time. Paying attention to damp spots or small puddles inside your car can save you money in the long run. Visit your mechanic after determining what kind of leak your car has. Wetness inside your car can come from a few different sources.

LOCATION	POSSIBLE SOURCE
Under driver's feet	Brake-fluid leak. Slippery, clear liquid indicates leak from either brake master cylinder or clutch master cylinder. Check fluid levels to find out which reservoir is low and leaking. See 486 Check and Add Brake Fluid and 489 Add Brake Fluid to the Clutch Master Cylinder.
Under passenger's feet	Coolant leak. Sticky, green, sweet-smelling fluid indicates leak in cooling system. Either heater core or heater hose is leaking.
Exhaust smell inside car	Leak in exhaust system, broken tailpipe, or worn or improperly seated rubber seal around hatchback.
Water inside car when it rains	Close doors and windows tightly on dry day. Ask someone to hose down car while you sit inside and look for signs of water entering. It may take a while, but it's the best way to find rain leak.
Water under dashboard when it doesn't rain	Check air conditioner duct. Water can collect in duct and drip into car if drain tube for air conditioner is plugged with debris.

474 Replace Your Air Filter

Changing the air filter should be part of any major tune-up, but if you drive on dirt roads or in other dusty conditions, you will need to replace it more frequently. On most cars, this is a fairly simple procedure.

Steps

1 Pop the hood and find the air-filter housing. It will be either square (on fuel-injected engines) or round (on older carbureted engines) and about 12 inches (30 cm) in diameter.

2 Use a Phillips screwdriver to remove the screws or clamps that hold on the top of the housing.

3 Take out the old air filter (see illustration) and clean any dirt and debris from the housing with a clean rag.

4 Put the new air filter in.

5 Screw or clamp the lid of the air-filter housing back on.

What You'll Need

- New air filter
- Rag
- Phillips screwdriver

475 Handle a Faulty Repair

Even worse than a big repair bill is a bad repair. Before jumping down your mechanic's throat, take a deep breath and envision the best possible scenario: that he or she simply made a mistake and that the shop will fix it at no additional cost to you. When it comes to receiving good customer service, a little politeness goes a long way.

Steps

1 Return to the shop as soon as you realize something is wrong.

2 Bring along a friend who knows a lot about cars.

3 Ask to speak to the service manager and the mechanic who worked on your car.

4 Explain the nature of the problem in as much detail as possible.

5 Take notes and ask as many questions as necessary so you understand the situation.

6 Go on a test drive with the mechanic and point out the problem.

7 Be firm but pleasant: Let them know that you will leave the car until they fix it.

8 If the first mechanic can't locate the problem, ask to go on a test drive or look at your car with a different mechanic at the same shop.

9 Consider the possibility that the problem may not be related to the recent fix (if that's what the mechanic suggests) and go to another shop for a second opinion.

10 Call the office of your state attorney general and ask for the name and number of the agency that regulates auto-repair businesses in your state. You may be able to get a mediator to sort out a repair or bill dispute.

What You'll Need

- Receipt or work order
- A dose of courage
- Courtesy

Tips

Find a reputable garage *before* your car breaks down.

Test-drive your car before paying, to make sure it was fixed right.

Do not have major work done on your car before leaving town on a long trip.

Keep all receipts and work orders in a safe place.

476 Fix an Improperly Installed Child Car Seat

Studies show that over one-half of all child car seats are improperly installed in the United States. Your local police or fire station most likely has a trained inspector who will check your car seat for free. Although installing a car seat may seem like a simple thing, many factors figure into a good fit, and not all car seats fit well in all car models. Use the following steps as a guideline, but make an appointment to get your car seat inspected by a trained professional.

Steps

1 Buy a car seat or booster seat appropriate for your child's current weight and age. Do not buy a used car seat. It may not have been designed for today's more stringent specifications.

2 Call the manufacturer or visit its Web site to make sure your car seat has not had any safety recalls.

3 Read the owner's manual and instruction book that came with your car seat. Many manufacturers list a toll-free number you can call for help installing your seat.

4 Place the car seat in the proper place and direction. Infants must always be placed in rear-facing car seats until they are at least 1 year old and 20 lbs. (9 kg). Babies younger than 1 year old and more than 20 lbs. (9 kg) should ride in a rear-facing seat approved for heavier babies until at least 1 year old. Children more than 40 lbs. (18 kg) should always ride in a booster seat until at least 8 years old. The middle of the backseat is the safest place for a car seat or booster seat.

5 Thread the seat belt through the designated slots and snap the seat belt together. Tighten the seat belt before and during this process.

6 Push the car seat firmly against the seat.

7 Ask a friend to lean down on or sit on the car seat while you tighten the belt as tight as possible.

8 Use the locking clip that came with the car seat if you have an over-the-shoulder seat belt or the kind that locks up only when jerked hard. The locking clip secures the shoulder belt to the lap belt.

9 If the seat belt is connected to the door frame, you may need a tether, which you can have installed at a car dealership.

10 Make sure the car seat cannot move more than 1 inch (2.5 cm) in any direction. If it does, push it against the back of the seat and lean down on it while tightening and refastening the seat belt.

11 Have a car-seat inspector check your installation.

Tips

For a list of facilities in your area that inspect car seats, call the Safe Kids Coalition at (888) 832-3219, or call your local fire or police department.

Most states have laws requiring children to ride in a booster seat once they are too big for their car seat. Age and weight requirements vary from state to state. Visit www.safekids.org to find out about laws and regulations in your state.

There is a very effective product called Mighty Tite. It's a seat belt tightener that uses a simple ratcheting system to tighten and secure the seat belt holding the child car seat.

Warning

Never put a child car seat in the front seat.

Do not use a car seat that has been in an accident.

477 Troubleshoot Leaking Oil

Contrary to popular belief, cars do not use up engine oil. If your car is consistently low on oil, you either have an oil leak or an engine that's burning oil. You can detect the latter condition by blue smoke coming out of the tailpipe. Cars that burn a lot of oil are candidates for engine rebuilding. Although you may not be able to fix an oil leak, you can help diagnose it, saving your mechanic's time (and your money).

Steps

1 Open the hood and look for obvious signs of wetness. Oil leaks usually come from a gasket: a piece of material, usually rubber, cork or silicone, that creates a seal between two metal parts. Look for places where different parts of the engine are bolted together.

2 Inspect underneath the car with a flashlight for signs of wetness. Oil here could be from a leak under the engine, or it could be collecting from a leak higher up. Wipe the suspect areas clean with a rag so you can inspect them closely and pinpoint the leak's source.

3 Consider getting the engine professionally steam-cleaned at an auto-repair shop if oil has leaked everywhere. This will make it easier for you or your mechanic to locate the leak.

4 Place a large piece of cardboard on the ground under the engine. Make marks on the cardboard to indicate its location in relation to the tires and the car's front and rear. Leave it in place overnight. Use rocks to hold it down if you park outside. (Some oil leaks occur only when the engine is running, but the cardboard method described here will still help locate these kind of leaks, because the oil will drip down.)

5 Check the cardboard in the morning to determine the amount of leakage and where it's dripping from.

6 You may find other types of leaks. Motor oil out of the bottle is the color of honey. Oil that has been in the engine for a little while is dark brown or even black. Coolant is green and smells sweet. Brake fluid is very light brown (almost clear) and very slippery. Automatic-transmission fluid and power-steering fluid are usually red.

What You'll Need

- Flashlight
- Rags
- Large piece of cardboard

Tips

Repair leaks as they occur. It is more difficult to diagnose a leak when everything is wet and seeping than on an otherwise dry and clean engine.

If you have a leak, be extra vigilant about checking all fluids regularly.

Warning

Stop driving immediately if the oil light on the dashboard comes on. Running an engine without enough oil will lead to very expensive repairs.

478 Check and Add Power-Steering Fluid

Check the power-steering fluid when you check the other fluids under the hood. You don't want to let a leak go undetected. Small leaks usually turn into large ones over time.

Steps

1 Open the hood and find the reservoir for the power-steering fluid. It will probably be labeled on the cap. If not, look near the belts for a pulley-driven pump with a plastic or metal reservoir on top.

2 Open the cap. It may unscrew or pop off.

3 Check the fluid level (see illustration). If the reservoir is made of clear plastic, look for full and low indicator lines on the outside. The cap will have a small dipstick attached if the reservoir isn't see-through. Wipe the dipstick clean with a rag and put the cap back on. Remove the cap and check the level on the dipstick. Your car may have both full hot and full cold indicators, as the fluid level will vary depending on whether the engine is cold or hot.

4 Add power-steering fluid as needed, using a funnel to avoid spilling. If the engine is hot, fill to the hot line. If the engine is cold, fill to the cold line.

5 Put the reservoir cap back on.

What You'll Need

- Power-steering fluid
- Rag
- Funnel

Tip

If you can use only one hand to parallel-park, then you have power steering.

Warning

Running out of power-steering fluid will damage the pump. Replacing a cracked power-steering hose or loose clamp is cheap compared with the cost of replacing the pump.

Check the label on the fluid to make sure it's the correct type for your car.

479 Check and Add Coolant

Coolant doesn't get used up during a car's normal operation. If the coolant level is consistently low, your car has a coolant leak. Your mechanic can pressure-check the cooling system to find any leaks. A small hole in a radiator hose or a loose clamp could end up costing hundreds or even thousands of dollars if the coolant leaks out and the engine overheats.

Steps

1 Find the coolant reservoir. Follow the hose that comes from the top of the radiator cap—it will lead to the coolant reservoir. It is usually a clear plastic tank with full and low indicators on the outside (see illustration).

2 Open the cap and add coolant to the coolant reservoir, using a funnel to avoid spilling. Coolant is a mixture of half antifreeze and half water. In a pinch it is OK to add only water or only antifreeze. (On some cars, it is difficult to see the full line on the coolant reservoir. Bounce the car up and down while looking to see how full the reservoir is.)

3 Put the cap back on the coolant reservoir.

4 Add coolant to the radiator as well if the reservoir was completely empty. Make sure the engine is completely cool before opening the radiator cap.

5 Some older cars don't have a coolant reservoir; in that case, add the coolant directly to the radiator.

What You'll Need

- Coolant
- Funnel
- Rag

Warning

Never open a radiator cap on a hot engine. The radiator is pressurized and the coolant could spurt out and scald you.

Some German cars have pressurized coolant reservoirs. Wait for the engine to cool down before opening the cap to add coolant.

Do not leave coolant out where children or pets can get to it. It has a sweet smell but is very toxic.

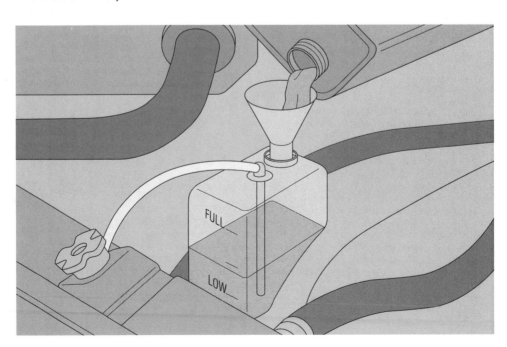

480 Cool an Overheated Engine

Engine overheating is a symptom of another problem—usually low coolant level caused by a leak, a thermostat that's stuck closed, an inoperative cooling fan or a clogged radiator. The most important thing is to turn off the car before the overheating does any damage.

Steps

1 Put on your turn signals and/or flashers to indicate you are pulling off the road.

2 Turn both the heater setting and the heater blower to high to divert heat from the engine. This may help, but only if the problem is a broken fan or fan belt (it's always worth a try).

3 Pull over and find a safe place to park on the side of the road.

4 Turn off the engine.

5 Open the hood.

6 Check the coolant level by looking at the coolant reservoir, a plastic tank. (Do not open the radiator cap when the engine is hot. The radiator is under pressure, and hot coolant could seriously burn you.) On some German cars the plastic coolant tank is pressurized—wait for the engine to cool before opening the tank to add coolant. This may take up to 20 minutes.

7 Use a funnel to add coolant to the reservoir if the level is below the low line. Always wait for the engine to cool down before opening the radiator cap. When everything is full, visit your mechanic right away to find and repair the leak.

8 If a low coolant level is not the problem, you have a more complicated cooling system problem and should call a tow truck.

9 If this is the case, wait for the engine to cool down, then drive to a phone or a garage. Check the temperature gauge as you drive to make sure it isn't going into the red. If the gauge starts to rise again, pull over, turn off the engine, and wait for it to cool again.

What You'll Need

- Coolant
- Funnel
- Rag
- Patience

Tips

Regular maintenance reduces the possibility of overheating. Change the coolant every autumn, periodically check the belts and hoses, and bring your car to a mechanic to check for leaks if the coolant level is consistently low.

Coolant is a mixture of ½ antifreeze and ½ water, but in a pinch it's OK to add just one or the other.

Warning

Never let the needle on your dashboard's temperature gauge go into the red. Don't wait for the next exit if you see the needle approaching the red zone; pull over and turn off the engine before you blow a head gasket.

481 Replace a Leaking Radiator Hose

Replacing a leaking radiator hose can be easy and quite painless on most cars. Check that both ends of the leaking hose are easily accessed before attempting this repair, because on some cars the hoses are tightly tucked away and this job might be better left to a professional.

Steps

1 Turn off the engine as soon as you suspect a leak, to prevent the engine from overheating.

2 Determine which radiator hose is leaking and exactly where the leak is coming from by looking for wetness.

3 Purchase a gallon (4 l) of antifreeze and the correct replacement radiator hose from your local auto-parts store or dealer. (Radiator hoses are not interchangeable. They come in specific sizes and shapes for your particular car model.)

4 Wait for the engine to cool down, at least 20 minutes, before beginning any work on the cooling system.

5 Place a large pan or wide bucket on the ground under the hose to catch the coolant.

6 Use a screwdriver to loosen the hose clamps at both ends of the hose you are replacing.

7 Remove the radiator hose by twisting and pulling where it connects to the radiator and engine. If the hose won't budge, use a utility knife to cut it off the fittings.

8 Remove the hose clamps from the old radiator hose and slide them onto the new hose.

9 Put the new radiator hose on. Spray the inside of the hose ends with WD-40 if the hose is hard to get on. Tighten the hose clamps.

10 Refill the radiator and the coolant reservoir with a 50-50 mixture of water and antifreeze.

11 "Burp the cooling system" by running the engine with the radiator cap off until the engine warms up. Keep the engine running until both the upper and lower radiator hoses feel warm (this indicates that the thermostat is open and the coolant is flowing through the entire system). Burping the cooling system allows any air bubbles to escape. Add coolant to the radiator as needed.

12 Look for leaks. Inspect around the hose clamps for dampness. Tighten the hose clamps if there is any wetness.

13 Put the radiator cap back on.

14 Check the coolant level after driving, to ensure there are no leaks.

What You'll Need

- New radiator hose
- Antifreeze
- Large pan or wide bucket
- Flathead screwdriver
- Utility knife
- WD-40 silicone spray
- Funnel

Tips

If the leak is coming from around the clamp holding on the hose end, tighten the clamp with a screwdriver. This may be all you need to do if a loose clamp is causing the leak.

In a pinch, you can add either plain water or pure antifreeze if that's all you have, but your cooling system normally uses a mixture of ½ antifreeze and ½ water.

Warning

Never open the radiator cap or loosen a radiator hose clamp when the engine is warm or hot. The coolant could spray out and burn you.

Dispose of used coolant properly. Bring it to a repair shop or parts store for recycling. Do not pour it down the sink or into the gutter.

482 Change Your Wiper Blades

Though it seems easy at first glance, replacing worn windshield-wiper blades can be an exercise in frustration if you've never done it before. The package usually comes with elaborately folded directions in five languages and enough clips and attachments to make you tear out your hair. But once you have mastered how the attachments on your particular wipers work, replacing them is a breeze.

What You'll Need

- New pair of wiper blades
- Small screwdriver

Steps

1 Purchase the correct replacement windshield-wiper blades for your car at an auto-parts store. Buy the entire blade, not just the rubber blade insert.

2 Open the package and find the attachment that matches the one on the wiper blade on your car. Read through the directions to see how to connect the attachment to the blade.

3 Pull the wiper arm up so it is no longer resting on the windshield.

4 Remove the old wiper blade from the wiper arm (see A). This typically involves pushing on a tab and pulling the wiper blade off or lifting a tab with a small screwdriver.

5 Insert the attachment onto the new blade or onto the wiper arm (see B). On some cars, it may be easier to put the attachment on the wiper blade first; on other models, it is easier to first put the attachment onto the wiper arm. Listen for a click.

6 Tug on the wiper blade to make sure it is securely attached and won't fly off later.

7 Gently lower the wiper arm onto the windshield.

Tips

In preparation for winter, replace your windshield-wiper blades every fall.

If you have trouble accessing the wiper blades, turn on the wipers, then switch off the ignition when the blades are vertical on the windshield.

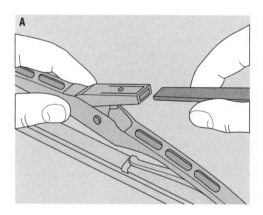

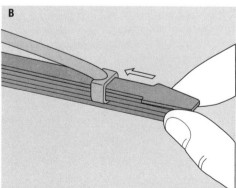

483 Add Windshield-Washer Fluid

A dirty windshield can block your view and potentially lead to an accident. To keep your windshield clean, make sure your car always has a full supply of windshield-washer fluid.

Steps

1 Open the hood and find the windshield-washer fluid reservoir. Look for a large, clear plastic container that may be labeled with words or a symbol on the cap showing two spurts of water.

2 Check the fluid level. You can fill this reservoir all the way to the top.

3 Add windshield-washer fluid using a funnel. Fill the reservoir completely.

4 Put the cap back on the reservoir.

What You'll Need

- Windshield-washer fluid
- Water (if fluid is concentrated)
- Funnel

Tip

Buy concentrated windshield-washer fluid. It comes in a small bottle and won't take up as much space in your trunk as premixed.

484 Fix a Broken Exhaust Pipe

You don't want to drive with a rusted-through exhaust pipe dragging noisily on the road. Before you get to the muffler shop, here's what to do with an exhaust pipe that is about to fall off.

Steps

1 Wait for the engine to cool down so the exhaust pipe is cool enough to touch. Place your hand near the pipe to gauge how hot it is before actually touching it, or wrap a thick rag around your hand.

2 If part of the pipe is about to fall off, remove the hanging part by bending and twisting it until it breaks free. You needn't reattach it, since you must have it replaced or welded on at a muffler shop anyway.

3 If you can't break off the hanging pipe, untwist a wire coat hanger or use some mechanic's wire (available at an auto-parts store). Wrap one end around the hanging pipe and fasten the other end to the underside of the car. Do not wrap the wire around the drive shaft or anywhere where it risks becoming tangled with the drive shaft. Wrap it around a stationary part underneath the car.

4 Make an appointment at the muffler shop.

What You'll Need

- Rag
- Wire coat hanger or mechanic's wire

Tip

Fix-it tape for exhaust systems can only cover up a hole or a crack in an exhaust pipe. It will not hold a broken pipe together.

485 Check and Add Engine Oil

Motor oil is the lifeblood of your car's engine. The oil lubricates, cleans and cools the engine. Running out of oil can ruin your engine and lead to very expensive repairs. Check your oil at least once a month. Engine oil does not get used up. If your engine repeatedly needs oil, either you have a leak or the engine is burning oil—both conditions your mechanic needs to check out and repair.

Steps

1 Turn off the engine and open the hood.

2 Locate the oil dipstick. If you are not sure where it is, check your car owner's manual or ask your mechanic.

3 Pull out the dipstick, noting where you pulled it from (see A).

4 Wipe the dipstick clean with a rag and look at the indicator at the bottom of the dipstick.

5 Push the dipstick back into the hole, making sure to push it back in all the way.

6 Pull out the dipstick again and see where the oil has left a residue in relation to the indicators (see B).

7 If the oil level on the dipstick reads "low" or "add," add oil through the oil-filler hole located at the top of the engine. Add ¼ qt. (250 ml) at a time to avoid overfilling and use a funnel to avoid spilling.

8 Recheck the oil level, following steps 3 through 6.

What You'll Need

- 1 or 2 qts. (1 or 2 l) motor oil
- Rag
- Funnel

Tip

Carry 1 or 2 qts. (1 or 2 l) of engine oil in your trunk for emergencies.

Warning

Stop driving and turn off the engine immediately if the oil light on your dashboard comes on.

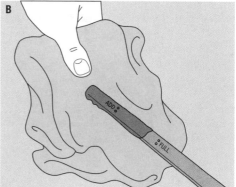

486 Check and Add Brake Fluid

Check the brake fluid when you check the other fluids in your car (once a month) or if the brake light on the dashboard goes on. Low brake fluid level may indicate a leak in your brake's hydraulic system —a situation that requires immediate attention.

Steps

1 Open the hood and locate the brake master cylinder. It will almost always be close to the back of the engine compartment on the driver's side. The cap may be labeled.

2 Clean the top of the cap with a rag to prevent dirt from entering the reservoir when you open it.

3 Open the reservoir cap (see illustration). It may screw off or just pull off.

4 Check the fluid level. You will see full- and low-level indicators on the side of the reservoir or inside the opening.

5 Add brake fluid up to the full line if needed. Use a funnel to avoid spills.

6 Put the cap back on and close the hood.

What You'll Need

- Brake fluid
- Rag
- Funnel

Warning

Brake fluid is very corrosive. Take care not to spill any on your hands, clothes or car paint.

Check your car owner's manual regarding what grade of brake fluid your car requires (DOT 3 or 4).

487 Check and Add Fluid to Your Automatic Transmission

Check the automatic-transmission fluid (ATF) when you check the other fluids in your car. Small leaks usually turn into large ones over time, and fixing a leak is cheap compared with the cost of repairing or replacing your transmission.

Steps

1 Look in your car owner's manual to determine whether the engine should be on or off when checking the ATF. On most cars, the engine must be fully warmed up and running. On some, however, the engine should be warm but turned off.

2 Open the hood and locate the ATF dipstick at the back of the engine, on the opposite side of the belts. The top of the dipstick may be labeled.

3 Pull out the dipstick and wipe it clean with a rag.

4 Put the dipstick back in the hole. Make sure you push it all the way back in.

5 Pull out the dipstick and check the fluid level. All ATF dipsticks have lines indicating full and low levels.

6 Pour the ATF into the dipstick hole if the level is low. Use a long, thin funnel and add ¼ qt. (250 ml) at a time if the level is not at the full line. Check the fluid level each time to avoid overfilling.

7 Push the dipstick back into the hole and close the hood.

8 Service your transmission every 24,000 miles (40,000 km) or every two years, whichever comes first. A transmission service includes replacing the filter, draining and replacing the ATF, and replacing the transmission-pan gasket. This service is not part of a regular tune-up; you must specifically ask for it.

What You'll Need

- Rag
- ATF
- Long, thin funnel

Warning

The transmission will be damaged if you run out of ATF.

Only use the type of transmission fluid specified in your owner's manual.

488 Troubleshoot Your Brakes

The best prevention is regular maintenance. Have your car's brakes checked at least once a year, more if you drive frequently in city traffic or live in a hilly area. If you wait until you hear grinding noises coming from the brakes, you'll be spending extra money on your next brake job. Here are some things to check if you suspect brake problems.

Steps

1 Make sure you're not driving with the parking brake on.

2 Get the brakes checked if you hear a high-pitched squeak that goes away when you step on the brakes. This noise comes from a brake-pad sensor—a soft piece of metal that scrapes against the brake rotor when the brake pads need replacing.

3 Check the brake-fluid level (see 486 Check and Add Brake Fluid).

4 Bring your car to a mechanic for a brake check if the brake master cylinder is consistently low on brake fluid. If you need to add brake fluid more than once every few months, there is probably a leak in the brake system.

5 If the pedal slowly sinks down to the floor when you brake, you may have a bad brake master cylinder.

6 If the pedal feels soft and mushy but gets harder when you pump up and down, have your mechanic bleed the brake lines to remove any air pockets in them and check for a faulty brake master cylinder.

7 If the brakes pulsate when you step on them, your car may have warped rotors, which can affect stopping ability. Have your mechanic check them.

8 If the brake pedal sinks to the floor or gets soft when you're using the brakes on a long, steep downhill grade, the problem could be brake fade. This occurs when the brake fluid gets so hot that it boils. Your mechanic may not find anything wrong with your brakes because the problem disappears after the brake fluid cools down.

Warning

You should not drive for more than a short distance if the brake light has come on. Check the brake fluid and make an appointment to have the brakes checked.

489 Add Brake Fluid to the Clutch Master Cylinder

Cars with manual transmissions use either a clutch cable or a hydraulic system. If your car has a hydraulic clutch, you must check and add brake fluid to the clutch master cylinder when you check all the other fluids. See your car owner's manual to find out what grade of brake fluid your car requires (DOT 3 or 4).

Steps

1 Find the clutch master cylinder's reservoir. It looks like the brake master cylinder's reservoir, but it's smaller and usually closer to the driver's side fender.

2 Clean the top of the reservoir with a rag so debris won't fall in when you open the cap.

3 Remove the cap and check the level (see illustration). The cap may screw off counterclockwise or may pop off. There may be low and full indicators. If not, the full level should reach the top of the reservoir.

4 Add brake fluid if the reservoir is low, using a funnel to avoid any spills.

5 Replace the cap.

6 If the fluid was low, recheck it weekly for a few weeks to make sure your car doesn't have a leak.

What You'll Need

- Rag
- Brake fluid
- Funnel

Tip

A faulty clutch master cylinder may leak brake fluid inside your car. If you notice a clear, slippery substance behind the clutch pedal, you probably have a leak.

Warning

Brake fluid is corrosive. Take care not to spill any on your hands, clothes or car paint.

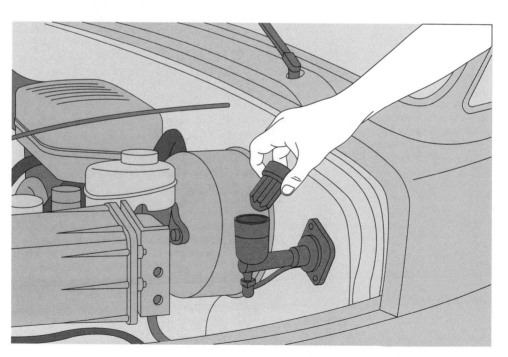

A red light on the dashboard can mean you should stop driving right away, or you may have a little time before you have to bring your car into the shop. Know what's what so you don't get stuck.

LIGHT	SOLUTIONS
Check Engine light	• Car's computer senses engine problem. Difference in performance may not be noticeable, but make appointment to have car diagnosed. • OK to drive. • If problem is serious, computer may switch to limp-home (low-power) mode and you won't have option of waiting to bring car into shop.
Oil light	• Either engine is very low on oil or there is no oil pressure. • Pull over and turn off engine immediately. • Check oil level and add oil if low. Turn engine back on to see if light has gone off. If oil light is still on, bad oil pump (no oil pressure) is likely. • Call tow truck.
Battery charge light	• Alternator is not charging. • OK to drive, but turn off any unneeded electrical devices (radio, heater, defroster) and avoid starting engine more than necessary. • Bring car into shop soon to avoid getting stranded. When alternator is not charging, battery loses charge and car stops working.
Brake light	• Make sure you are not driving with hand brake on. • Check brake-fluid level. Top off brake fluid if low and make appointment to check brakes. • Driving with brake light can be dangerous; deal with this soon. Call tow truck or drive carefully and slowly to shop.
ABS (antilock brake system) light	• Indicates either low brake-fluid level, stuck brake caliper or faulty ABS. • Check brake fluid and make appointment to get brakes checked. • Call tow truck or drive carefully and slowly to shop.
Emissions lights (O_2 sensor, EGR, check emissions)	• Depending on car model, these lights may indicate problem with emissions sensor or may light up at certain mileage, usually 60,000 miles (100,000 km). Get sensors checked. • OK to drive. If problem exists, car might get poor gas mileage.
Air bag light	• Get air bags checked. Problem could prevent them from activating in accident. • OK to drive, but not safe in accident.

491 Troubleshoot a Windshield-Washer Pump

Follow these steps to determine why your windshield-washer fluid is not flowing freely, and soon you'll be driving with clean windows again. The problem may be something simple like a disconnected hose, or dirt in the spray nozzle.

Steps

1 Turn on the windshield washer with the engine off and the key in the On position.

2 Listen for a humming sound to determine whether the windshield-washer motor is operative. Open the hood and ask a friend to listen while you turn on the windshield washer. If you don't hear any sound, check the fuses.

3 Replace the fuse if it is blown (see 467 Fix a Faulty Car Fuse). If the fuse is not blown and the motor is silent, have your mechanic replace the windshield-washer motor. If you hear the motor humming, proceed to step 4.

4 Check the reservoir and add windshield-washer fluid if its level is low or empty. You can fill the reservoir right up to the top—usually it doesn't have any full or empty indicators. Use a funnel to avoid spills.

5 Check that the water is not frozen in the reservoir. This will only happen in cold weather if you filled the reservoir with plain water instead of windshield-washer fluid.

6 Make sure the small rubber hose that plugs into the windshield-washer reservoir is attached.

7 Follow the hose to the rear of the hood. Check for crimped, torn or broken lines. The line from the reservoir splits into two lines at the hood. If damaged, remove the line by pulling at the base where it attaches. Bring it to an auto-parts store and purchase a hose of identical width and length. Install it and check for leaks.

8 Clear any leaves or debris away from the area around the washer-fluid nozzles on top of the hood.

9 Clear the washer-fluid nozzle's passage with a needle or a pin.

10 Unhook the washer lines at the reservoir and at the hood, then force compressed air through the lines to dislodge anything stuck in them.

What You'll Need

- Windshield-washer fluid
- Funnel
- Replacement hose
- Needle or pin
- Compressed air and air nozzle

492 Repair Minor Dents

This is an afternoon project for those with access to the right tools. There are dent-pulling kits available that use suction cups or hot glue, avoiding the need to drill a hole into the dent. If you want your car to look like new, though, consider a trip to the auto-body shop.

Steps

1 Borrow a dent-pulling tool (looks and acts like a slide hammer), a dolly (a tool designed especially for flattening and shaping metal) and a metalworking hammer.

2 Find the center of the dent and drill a hole in it using a ⅛-inch (3-mm) drill bit (see A). (Or, using the hot glue gun that comes with some kits, glue the plastic adapter to the center of the dent.)

3 Thread the dent-pulling tool into the hole you just drilled (see B) (or attach the dent-pulling tool to the plastic circle you just glued on). Pull on the dent-pulling tool to flatten or pop out the dent.

4 Hammer the front of the dent with the metalworking hammer while holding the dolly against the back of the dent. You may need to get underneath the car or open the hood or the trunk to reach the back of the dent.

5 Using a medium surface-conditioning disk on your drill, grind all the paint down to bare metal extending at least 1 inch (2.5 cm) around the dent. Fill the entire area with body filler.

6 Let the filler dry, then sand with sandpaper wrapped around a block of wood. Start with 36-grit sandpaper and work your way down to 120-grit.

7 Prime the area with spray primer for cars. Apply six coats, letting primer dry between coats.

8 Sand the primer with 600-grit wet-and-dry sandpaper to remove any scratches. Touch up the area with matching car paint. Re-sand and repeat if paint is not smooth.

What You'll Need

- Drill
- ⅛-inch (3-mm) drill bit
- Dent-pulling tool
- Dolly
- Metalworking hammer
- Medium surface-conditioning disk for drill
- Body filler such as Bondo
- Sandpaper
- Block of wood
- Spray primer for cars
- Touch-up car paint

Tips

Replacing the entire dented body panel (or hood or trunk) may be easier than fixing a large dent. Call a few salvage yards for price and availability.

If the dent is on a door, you will need to remove the inside door panel.

Warning

This method of pulling out a dent will work only on dents that have no creases. To repair dents with wrinkles, go to an auto-body shop.

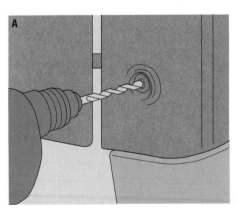

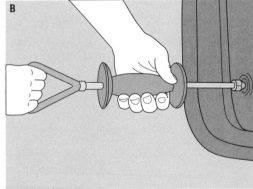

493 Change a Hubcap

Parallel parking too close to the curb not only is bad for your tires but can also damage or dislodge hubcaps. Fortunately, a hubcap is one of the easier things to replace on a car.

Steps

1 If a hubcap is missing, look at the other wheels to see how the hubcaps are attached to the car. Some screw on and off, some pop on and off, and others are held on by the wheel lug nuts, which you must remove before putting the hubcap on or taking it off.

2 If your car has the screw-on type, remove the screw that holds the hubcap on. It may be under a small plastic cover that you can pry off gently with a screwdriver. (If the hold-down screw is missing, remove a screw from another wheel and match it up at an auto-parts store or a hardware store.) Place the new hubcap on the wheel and reattach the hold-down screw.

3 If your car has the push-on type, remove the hubcap by prying around the rim with a screwdriver. Push on the new hubcap and gently tap around the rim until it stays on by itself. Then use a rubber mallet or the bottom of a sneaker to hammer it until snug (a regular hammer will dent the hubcap).

4 If your hubcaps have lug nuts, see 457 Fix a Flat Tire.

What You'll Need

- New hubcap
- Screwdriver
- Rubber mallet or sneaker

Tip

Hubcaps, especially the push-on kind, sometimes cause wheels to squeak when driving. Remove the hubcap and test-drive the car to diagnose whether this is the source of the squeak. Reinstalling or reseating the hubcap may fix this problem.

494 Fix an Ignition Key That Won't Turn

This common situation arises when the steering-lock mechanism binds, usually because the wheels are jammed against the curb.

Steps

1 Make sure the transmission is in park (for cars with automatic transmissions).

2 Set the parking brake to prevent the car from rolling farther against the curb.

3 Pull hard on the steering wheel while turning it in both directions. If this doesn't free the wheel, move on to step 4.

4 Release the parking brake and put the transmission in neutral. Let up on the foot pedal just enough to rock the car slightly.

5 Turn the steering wheel again. The key should turn now.

Tip

To prevent the steering wheel from locking up, always set your parking brake, especially on hills.

495 Change Your Spark-Plug Wires

A bad spark-plug wire can keep your car from running well or starting at all. You should replace the spark-plug wires every 30,000 miles (50,000 km), although a tune-up won't necessarily include this service. Unless you have asked for them to be replaced, your car's spark-plug wires may be quite old.

Steps

1 Purchase a set of spark-plug wires at an auto-parts store. It is also possible to buy a single wire if only one needs replacing.

2 Look under the hood to find the spark-plug wires.

3 Pull off one spark-plug wire at a time by grasping it at the base of the wire. Use a spark-plug wire puller or just your fingers.

4 Match it up by length with a new plug wire. Each spark-plug wire is a specific length, so make sure to replace the wire with one of exactly the same length.

5 Attach the new wire to the spark plug on one end and to the distributor cap on the other end. Listen for a small click or pop as you connect the wire.

6 Repeat steps 3 through 5 for all the other plug wires.

7 Replace the coil wire (if your car has one). This is the wire that goes from the middle of the distributor cap to the coil. Use the same method as for replacing the other plug wires.

What You'll Need

- Spark-plug wire(s)
- Spark-plug wire puller

Tip

Spend the extra money for a good-quality set of spark-plug wires. Cheap ones are not worth the effort of installation; they will fail early, creating performance problems.

Warning

Do not disconnect the spark-plug wires all at once. Take them off and replace them one at a time so you don't mix up their order.

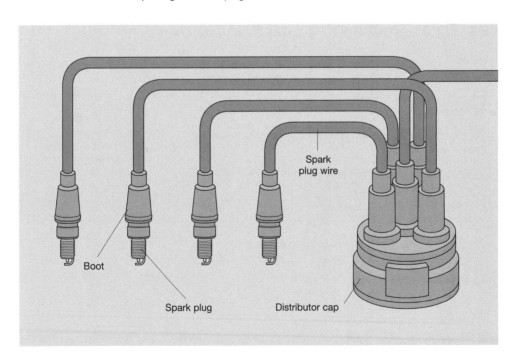

Spark plug wire

Boot

Spark plug

Distributor cap

496 Diagnose Car Smells

Some automotive problems are accompanied by a distinct odor. Use this chart to diagnose the source of any odd smells in your car.

SMELL	PROBLEM	SOLUTION
Exhaust	Indicates either leak in exhaust system (hole in tailpipe, muffler, exhaust pipe, exhaust manifold) or worn seal on hatchback or rear door.	Take care of situation immediately; carbon monoxide not only causes headaches but can be deadly. Bring car to mechanic or muffler shop right away.
Raw gas	Indicates leak in fuel-delivery system (fuel lines, fuel filter, gas tank). Potentially dangerous; leaking fuel can cause car fire.	Check that you haven't left gas cap off. If not, make appointment with mechanic.
Rotten eggs	Indicates plugged catalytic converter or very rich air-fuel mixture (can cause poor gas mileage).	Call mechanic.
Burning plastic	Plastic bag left in road may stick to part of hot exhaust beneath your car.	Check under car with flashlight. Difficult to get rid of. You can wait for bag to burn off or crawl under car with scraper and remove bag.
Burning rubber	May indicate melting rubber hose resting on hot exhaust manifold, or belt shredded by jammed pulley.	Turn engine off and inspect all rubber hoses and belts under hood. Replace damaged items.
Burning coolant	Blown head gasket results in coolant mixing and burning with gasoline. Thick, sweet smell and whitish smoke from tailpipe.	Bring car to mechanic to check tailpipe emissions for possible blown head gasket.
Leaking oil	Oil leak at top of engine (typically from valve-cover gasket) can spill onto exhaust manifold and burn, causing foul smell and occasionally light smoke.	Find leak. Check oil frequently. Take car to mechanic to fix leak.

497 Clean the Outside of Your Car

With a little time and the right clothes (dress to get wet), washing your car can actually be quite relaxing—even meditative.

Steps

1 Roll up the windows tightly and shut all the doors.

2 Rinse the car with a hose. Start with the roof and continue down to the tires.

3 Fill a bucket with warm water and car detergent. (Although many people use mild dishwashing liquid to wash their car, it's best to buy automotive car soap designed to protect your paint job.)

4 Wash the car with a sudsy sponge or rag. Start with the roof and work your way down. Wash the windows and tires, too. Use a step stool if you have difficulty reaching the roof of your car.

5 Rinse off all the soap with a hose.

6 Dry the entire car with a clean, dry chamois cloth or towel.

7 Clean the windows with paper towels or newspaper and window cleaner.

8 Apply vinyl protectant with a clean rag to any vinyl parts such as the bumper and trim.

9 Use metal or chrome cleaner on the wheel rims.

What You'll Need

- Garden hose
- Bucket
- Car detergent
- Sponge or rags
- Step stool
- Chamois cloth or towel
- Paper towels or news-paper
- Window cleaner
- Vinyl protectant
- Metal or chrome cleaner

Tips

Wash your car in the shade to avoid streaking.

Old cloth diapers make excellent rags for cleaning and drying.

498 Restore Your Car's Shine

Pick a nice shady place and crank up the tunes. Before you know it your car will be as shiny as new.

Steps

1 Purchase a nonabrasive car wax at the auto-parts store.

2 Choose a shady place to wash and wax your car. Otherwise, the sun will roast the wax onto your car and could damage your paint job.

3 Wash and dry your car (see 497 Clean the Outside of Your Car).

4 Apply the wax to the car using a damp sponge. Make small cir-cles with your sponge when applying the wax. Use care around seams and creases to avoid getting wax in the cracks. You can remove any built-up wax with a soft toothbrush.

5 Wipe off the wax with a terry-cloth towel after you have applied it to the entire car. Start with the section where you first applied the wax.

6 Buff the entire car with cheesecloth or an old cloth diaper to make it shine.

What You'll Need

- Car wax
- Sponge
- Soft toothbrush
- Terry-cloth towel
- Cheesecloth or cloth diaper

Warning

Letting car wax sit on your car for more than 2 hours makes it extremely difficult to remove and polish.

499 Wash the Interior of Your Car

All it takes is some time and a little elbow grease to make the inside of your car look as though you've had it cleaned by the pros.

Steps

1 Clear out all trash and large items from the inside of the car. Clean under the seats and check for large objects before vacuuming. Empty the ashtray.

2 Pull out the floor mats and shake thoroughly.

3 Remove the seat covers (if applicable) and wash them according to the directions. If you don't have a manual for the seat covers, call the store where you purchased them (or the car dealer, if you had them installed there) and ask for cleaning directions. You can wash some seat covers in the washing machine, but always check the directions first, because different materials require different care.

4 Vacuum the seats, floor and floor mats.

5 Clean any stains on the floor mats using a scrub brush and carpet cleaner.

6 Clean stains or spots on fabric seat cushions with a stain remover or carpet cleaner.

7 Open the car windows to allow the seats and carpets to air-dry.

8 Leave the floor mats outside in the sun to dry.

9 Clean the inside and outside of the windows using paper towels or newspapers and window cleaner.

10 Clean the dashboard, doors and other vinyl areas with a clean rag and a vinyl protectant.

11 Put the seat covers and floor mats back in the car after everything dries.

What You'll Need

- Vacuum
- Scrub brush
- Carpet cleaner
- Stain remover
- Paper towels or newspapers
- Window cleaner
- Rag
- Vinyl protectant

Warning

Do not clean leather seats with carpet shampoo. It is too harsh and will take the color out of leather. Use a cleaner specially designed for leather car seats, available at an auto-parts store.

DRING • FIX BAD HABITS • REPAIR A BROKEN EYEGLASS FRAME • REPOSITION A SLIPPED CONTACT LENS • FIX A RUN IN STOCKINGS • JO
EAKOUT • REPAIR A TORN FINGERNAIL • FIX CHIPPED NAIL POLISH • FIX A STUCK ZIPPER • FIND A LOST CONTACT LENS • ELIMINATE BAD
Y THAT STICKS • STOP TELEMARKETERS AND JUNK MAIL • GET SUPERGLUE OFF YOUR SKIN • EXTRACT A SPLINTER • SOOTHE A SUNBURN
ANGOVER • STOP HICCUPS • MEND A BROKEN HEART • MEND A FAMILY FEUD • TREAT A SMALL CUT OR SCRAPE • FIX HAIR DISASTERS •
TER SEATS • FIX A BILLING MISTAKE • FIX A BAD GRADE • FIX BAD CREDIT • RECOVER FROM JET LAG • RESUSCITATE AN UNCONSCIOUS
PRONOUNS • FIX A RUN-ON SENTENCE • FIX MISUSE OF THE WORD GOOD • FIX YOUR DOG OR CAT • CORRECT BAD BEHAVIOR IN DOGS
SING BUTTON • REMOVE LINT FROM CLOTHING • FIX A DRAWSTRING ON SWEATPANTS • REPAIR A HEM • REPAIR LEATHER GOODS • MEND
UNDER YOUR CASHMERE • FIX A SWEATER THAT HAS SHRUNK • FIX A SWEATER THAT HAS STRETCHED • FIX A HOLE IN A POCKET • FIX A H
LING FROM CLOTHING • FIX A FRAYED BUTTONHOLE • REMOVE DARK SCUFFS FROM SHOES • TREAT STAINS ON LEATHER • PROTECT SUE
ET SQUEAKY HINGES • TROUBLESHOOT LOCK PROBLEMS • TIGHTEN A LOOSE DOORKNOB • TIGHTEN A LOOSE DOOR HINGE • FIX A BIN
PLACE CRACKED TILE • TROUBLESHOOT MOLD ON INTERIOR WALLS • REPLACE CRACKED TILE GROUT IN A TUB OR SHOWER • FIX A DRA
NDS • TROUBLESHOOT WINDOW SHADE PROBLEMS • FIX BROKEN GLASS IN A WINDOW • REPAIR A WINDOW SCREEN • REPAIR ALUMINUM
MAGED PLASTER • REPAIR WALL COVERINGS • TOUCH UP PAINTED WALLS • TROUBLESHOOT INTERIOR-PAINT PROBLEMS • SOLVE A LEAD
RDWOOD FLOOR • RESTORE A DULL, WORN WOOD FLOOR • TOUCH UP WOOD-FLOOR FINISHES • REPAIR DAMAGED SHEET-VINYL FLOORI
USE • CHILDPROOF YOUR HOME • PREVENT ICE DAMS • CURE A FAULTY FIREPLACE DRAW • START A FIRE IN A COLD CHIMNEY • FIX A WO
AL A GARAGE FLOOR • REFINISH A GARAGE OR BASEMENT FLOOR • CONTROL ROOF LEAKS • REDIRECT RAINWATER FROM A DOWNSPOU
MAGED ASPHALT SHINGLE • PATCH A FLAT OR LOW-PITCHED ROOF • REPAIR ROOF FLASHING • TROUBLESHOOT EXTERIOR-PAINT PROBLE
W WATER PRESSURE • FIX LEAKING PIPES • STOP A TOILET FROM RUNNING • FIX A LEAKY TOILET TANK • FIX A STOPPED-UP TOILET • STO
OGGED SINK OR TUB • REPAIR A TUB-AND-SHOWER VALVE • REPAIR CHIPPED FIXTURES • QUIET NOISY PIPES • DEFROST YOUR PIPES • DI
NSUMPTION • REPLACE A RECEPTACLE • FIX AN ELECTRICAL PLUG • REPLACE A LIGHT FIXTURE • INSTALL A NEW DIMMER • FIX A LAMP •
ORBELL • FIX A WOBBLY OVERHEAD FAN • ADJUST WATER-HEATER TEMPERATURE • RELIGHT A WATER-HEATER PILOT LIGHT • TROUBLESH
E MAKER • GET RID OF MICROWAVE SMELLS • FIX A REFRIGERATOR THAT COOLS POORLY • FIX A GAS OVEN THAT HEATS POORLY • CLEAN
HWASHER PROBLEMS • CORRECT AN OVERFLOWING DISHWASHER • FIX A LEAKY DISHWASHER • FIX A DISHWASHER THAT FILLS SLOWLY
WASHING MACHINE THAT FILLS SLOWLY • FIX A WASHING MACHINE THAT "WALKS" ACROSS THE FLOOR • FIX A CLOTHES DRYER THAT DRIE
YOUR VACUUM CLEANER • REPLACE VACUUM CLEANER BRUSHES • TROUBLESHOOT A PORTABLE AIR CONDITIONER • FIX A WINDOW AIR
OCESSOR • FIX A TOASTER • DIAGNOSE MICROWAVE OVEN PROBLEMS • TROUBLESHOOT A GAS GRILL • FIX A TRASH COMPACTOR • REPA
ART • TROUBLESHOOT A CRASHING COMPUTER • CLEAN UP LAPTOP SPILLS • FIX BAD SECTORS ON A HARD DISK • QUIT A FROZEN PC AP
ECTED COMPUTER • IMPROVE YOUR COMPUTER'S MEMORY • GET RID OF E-MAIL SPAM • CHANGE A LASER PRINTER CARTRIDGE • FIX A F
URE OUT WHY A PRINTER WON'T PRINT • FIX SPELLING AND GRAMMAR ERRORS • RECALL AN E-MAIL IN MICROSOFT OUTLOOK • DIAGNO
ES • TROUBLESHOOT A PALM OS PDA • RESET A PALM OS PDA • REMOVE FINGERPRINTS FROM A CAMERA LENS • TROUBLESHOOT A CD-
LVAGE A VIDEOCASSETTE • TROUBLESHOOT A DVD PLAYER • STRENGTHEN FM RADIO RECEPTION • STRENGTHEN AM RADIO RECEPTION •
AMMED SLIDE PROJECTOR • GET BETTER SPEAKER SOUND • TROUBLESHOOT A DIGITAL CAMCORDER • TROUBLESHOOT A DIGITAL CAME
HTBULB • FIX A BROKEN WINEGLASS STEM • FIX BLEMISHED WOOD FURNITURE • REPAIR GOUGES IN FURNITURE • RESTORE FURNITURE
MOUFLAGE A DOG-SCRATCHED DOOR • REPAIR A SPLIT CARPET SEAM • RID CARPETS OF PET ODORS • REINFORCE A SAGGING SHELF • F
NTS OF CHAIRS AND TABLES • REUPHOLSTER A DROP-IN CHAIR SEAT • REVIVE A CANE SEAT • REINFORCE A WEAK BED FRAME • FIX UP A
TTERY • REPAIR CHIPPED OR CRACKED CHINA • UNCLUTTER YOUR HOME • CLEAN CRAYON FROM A WALL • GET WAX OFF A TABLECLOTH
AINS • REMOVE CHEWING GUM FROM CARPETING • REMOVE BLEACH SPOTS FROM CARPETING • REMOVE PET STAINS • ELIMINATE WINE S
AINS FROM TILE GROUT • REMOVE MILDEW FROM WALLS AND CEILINGS • DISINFECT A TOILET BOWL • REMOVE FIREPLACE GRIME • GET F
EAN OIL SPOTS FROM A GARAGE OR DRIVEWAY • REMOVE STAINS FROM BRICK • WASH AN OUTDOOR GRILL • FIX A FALLEN SOUFFLÉ • RE
SCUE OVERPROOFED YEAST DOUGH • FIX YOUR KID LUNCH • GET RID OF TAP-WATER MINERAL DEPOSITS • CALIBRATE A MEAT THERMOM
UCE • RESCUE A BROKEN SAUCE • REMOVE FAT FROM SOUPS AND SAUCES • FIX LUMPY GRAVY • SUBSTITUTE MISSING INGREDIENTS • R
RNED RICE • REMOVE COOKING ODORS • FINISH UNDERCOOKED MEAT • SALVAGE AN UNDERCOOKED TURKEY • FIX AN OVERSEASONED
ALE BREAD • SMOOTH SEIZED CHOCOLATE • SOFTEN HARDENED SUGARS OR COOKIES • FIX BREAKFAST FOR YOUR SWEETHEART • MEND
GGING TOOLS • RESTORE A BROKEN FLOWERPOT • SHARPEN PRUNING CLIPPERS • REMOVE RUST FROM TOOLS • REVIVE WILTING CUT FL
T RID OF RAMPANT BRAMBLES • TROUBLESHOOT BROWN SPOTS ON A LAWN • CONTROL MAJOR GARDEN PESTS • RID YOUR GARDEN OF
ONPERFORMING COMPOST PILE • FIX BAD SOIL • SHORE UP A RAISED GARDEN BED • REMOVE A DEAD OR DISEASED TREE LIMB • TROUBL
AINAGE • TROUBLESHOOT ROSE DISEASES • IDENTIFY AND CORRECT SOIL DEFICIENCIES IN ROSES • TROUBLESHOOT ROSE PESTS • OVE
MAGED DECK BOARDS • REPAIR DECK RAILINGS • STRENGTHEN DECK JOISTS • FIX A RUSTY IRON RAILING • REPAIR A GATE • REPAIR A P
RACKED OR DAMAGED CONCRETE • IMPROVE THE LOOK OF REPAIRED CONCRETE • REPAIR AN ASPHALT DRIVEWAY • REVIVE WOODEN OU
ARDEN PONDS • CLEAN SWIMMING POOL WATER • TROUBLESHOOT HOT TUBS AND SPAS • REPLACE BRICKS IN WALKWAYS AND PATIOS • S
R WITH JUMPER CABLES • SHUT OFF A CAR ALARM THAT WON'T QUIT • FREE A CAR STUCK ON ICE OR SNOW • DE-ICE YOUR WINDSHIELD
RN-SIGNAL COVER • FIX A CAR FUSE • FIX DASHBOARD LIGHTS THAT WON'T LIGHT • REMOVE CAR SMELLS • CHECK TIRE PRESSURE • INF
PROPERLY INSTALLED CHILD CAR SEAT • TROUBLESHOOT LEAKING OIL • CHECK AND ADD POWER-STEERING FLUID • CHECK AND ADD CO
ROKEN EXHAUST PIPE • CHECK AND ADD ENGINE OIL • CHECK AND ADD BRAKE FLUID • CHECK AND ADD FLUID TO YOUR AUTOMATIC TRA
OUBLESHOOT A WINDSHIELD-WASHER PUMP • REPAIR MINOR DENTS • CHANGE A HUBCAP • FIX AN IGNITION KEY THAT WON'T TURN • CH

Sports & Recreation

500 Fix Your Basketball Free Throw

When the game is on the line and everyone is watching, you better be prepared to hit your free throws. Being effective from the foul line is all about practice. Study the steps below, then start practicing. Hint: It may help to pretend that the only thing between you and an NCAA championship is one last free throw with no time left.

What You'll Need

- Basketball
- Basketball hoop

Steps

1 Stand with your feet square to the basket. The foot that corresponds to your shooting hand should be slightly ahead of the other. For example, if you're right-handed, your right foot should be ahead of your left foot.

2 Place the ball in your shooting hand with your fingers spread wide and pointing up. Effective shooting depends on using one hand only. As you prepare to shoot, rest your nonshooting hand lightly against the ball to balance it. Do not move this hand when you shoot the ball.

3 Place the elbow of your shooting arm directly below your hand, not off to one side.

4 Bend your shooting arm slightly, but do not bring the ball all the way back to your shoulder. The angle of your elbow bend should be greater than 90 degrees.

5 Bend both knees as you prepare to shoot. Send the ball in a high arc toward the basket. Aim for a spot on the backboard just over the rim. Your knees and your shooting arm should reach full extension at the same time. Do not jump off the ground as you shoot.

6 Follow through with your arm motion. Push the ball off your hand so that it spins backward as it travels toward the basket. This backspin will give the ball a soft bounce as it comes off the backboard.

7 Your goal is to achieve the exact same shot every time.

501 Regrip a Golf Club

A golf club grip is designed to give your club a precise, sure feel. As a grip ages, it hardens and becomes smooth. A new grip will restore your club's performance. Many people send their clubs to a shop for regripping. But you can do the job yourself and take pride in personalizing your equipment.

Steps

1 Remove the club's grip, with a knife if need be. Remove any tape that remains on the shaft, and clean any tape residue using grip solvent and a piece of cloth.

2 Wrap double-sided tape around the shaft, from the end to the point where the grip will stop (see A).

3 Fill the little hole at the end of the new grip with a golf tee. Pour solvent into the open end of the grip. Cover the open end with your thumb and shake it to distribute the solvent.

4 Pour the solvent onto the taped area of the shaft, and slide the new grip onto the club (see B). Remove the golf tee from the end.

5 Make sure the grip is properly aligned. Let the grip dry for 6 to 10 hours.

What You'll Need

- Knife
- Grip solvent
- Rag
- Double-sided tape
- New grip(s)
- Golf tee

Tip

Grip solvent is available at golf shops.

Warning

This fix is best performed in a garage; grip solvent can damage floors and rugs.

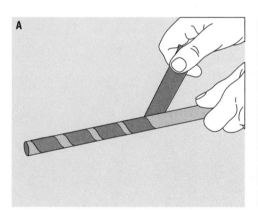

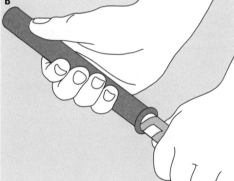

502 Fix Your Golf Swing

Do people take cover when you come to the tee? Did your last set of golf balls head for the Bermuda Triangle? It's time to visit the driving range and work on your swing.

Steps

1 Grip the club with your left hand so that your thumb lies along the shaft (see A). The line between your thumb and index finger should point toward your right eye. Wrap your right hand over your left so that your left thumb fits into the cup of the right palm. (Steps 1 through 5 apply to right-handed golfers. If you're a left-handed golfer, reverse the instructions referring to right and left, thus creating a mirror image of what's described.)

2 Fine-tune your stance by pointing your knees in slightly. Point your right foot straight ahead. Point your left foot slightly to the left.

3 Bring your elbows and arms as close together as possible. When you're in your stance, your right elbow should point directly at your right hip, and your left elbow directly at your left hip.

4 Imagine a flat plane extending from your shoulders to the ball (see B). Throughout your backswing, your hands should move parallel to this plane. Begin your backswing with your hands, followed immediately by your arms and shoulders.

5 Begin your downswing by rotating your hips back toward the ball. Any swing that does not begin with the hips will lack power. Your left wrist bone should be pointing at the ball when the club makes contact.

What You'll Need

- Five-iron
- Bucket of golf balls

Tip

For a five-iron, your feet should be shoulder width apart. Longer clubs require a wider stance. Shorter clubs require a narrower stance.

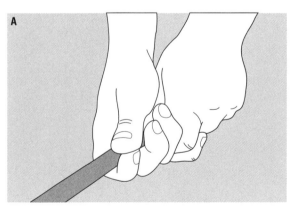

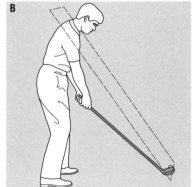

503 Fix Common Golf Problems

After you have practiced your golf swing (see opposite page), you can move on to fixing specific problems. Here are golf's most common trouble spots and what you can do about them.

Steps

Poor putting

1 Stand comfortably, with your feet closer than shoulder width apart. Grip the club lightly.

2 Stand with your eyes directly over the ball. Your eyes should be parallel to the direction of the putt.

3 Control the putter with your dominant hand. Maintain the same speed on your backstroke as on your forward stroke.

Slicing and hooking the ball

1 Review step 4 (opposite page) to be sure you understand the swing plane.

2 The goal is to hold the club so that the shaft is parallel to the target line when you're at the top of your swing. If the club points to the left at the top of your swing, the result is a slice. If the club points to the right, the result is a hook.

Poor chip shots

1 Use a narrower stance than you do with short irons. Point both feet slightly toward the target.

2 Position your hands so that they are slightly ahead of the ball at the start of your swing.

3 Swing through the ball and resist the urge to decelerate the club before impact.

What You'll Need

- Golf balls
- Set of golf clubs

504 Fix Your Snowboard Turn

Some people think snowboarding was invented by orthopedic surgeons looking for a steady stream of customers. But it doesn't have to be that difficult. Just be sure to practice on a relatively warm day (above 30°F/1°C) in order to avoid icy conditions. Use the instructions below to solve the most common problem—the outside turn.

Steps

1 Take a run down the hill to get warmed up. When you're comfortable and have found a gentle slope, you're ready to work on your outside turn. An outside turn is when you make the transition from facing the hill to having your back to the hill.

2 Prepare to turn by bending your knees and shifting your weight onto your forward foot. Angle the board down the hill and into the turn.

3 Maintain your weight on your forward foot and roll your weight onto the heel of this foot. Bring your rear foot through the turn smoothly and quickly. Your speed will increase as you begin the turn. This speed will be controlled by keeping your weight forward, pressuring your forward heel and bringing your rear foot through the turn.

What You'll Need

- Snowboard
- Gentle slope

Tips

If you are nervous about trying this move, have a friend who is not on a board stand in front of you and hold you while you practice the turn.

If you have been making progress with this turn but your feet feel loose or your board feels unstable, have a qualified shop or instructor look at your bindings.

505 Fix a Slow Skateboard

Skateboards have a tough life. They get dirty, wet and neglected but are expected to roll forever without complaint. It's no wonder they get cranky once in a while and toss you into the gutter. If your old board feels slow, try the following.

Steps

1 Using an adjustable wrench, remove the nut holding each wheel in place. In the center of each wheel are the wheel bearings, one on each side. Using a screwdriver, remove both bearings from each wheel. Simply put the tip of the screwdriver into the center of the bearing and pop it free.

2 Using a rag, wipe off any dirt from each bearing. Drop the bearings into a cup of paint thinner. Leave them in the thinner for an hour. Remove the bearings and let them dry thoroughly. Spin each bearing to remove any paint thinner from the inside.

3 Place all the bearings in a cup of motor oil and leave them overnight. Remove them from the oil and wipe them dry. Replace them in the wheels and reinstall the wheels on the board. Be sure that each wheel spins freely and that the wheel nuts are not overly tight.

What You'll Need

- Adjustable wrench
- Screwdriver
- Rags
- Plastic cups
- Paint thinner
- Motor oil

Warning

Paint thinner fumes are toxic. Be sure to work in a well-ventilated area.

506 Improve Your Running Form

You get too tired, or you get hurt. How can something as apparently simple as running be so tricky to master? Take a few lessons from Fluffy. Cats stretch regularly, have excellent balance and excel at relaxation. These same principles apply to running. Remember, cheetahs are the only animals on earth that can reach speeds of 70 miles (110 km) per hour.

Steps

1 See a physician before you begin a new exercise program. Take a treadmill stress test to ensure that your cardiovascular system can handle the rigors of running.

2 Stretch. Spend about 10 minutes before and after the run stretching your hamstrings, quadriceps, calves, ankles, glutes, back and shoulders. Hold each stretch for 15 to 30 seconds. Stretching increases flexibility, reduces risk of injuries, and improves form and fitness.

3 Adopt a balanced running posture. Keep your back straight and your face looking straight ahead a few yards (meters). If you need to turn your head, use your neck to avoid unnecessary twisting of your back and hips.

4 Keep your shoulders, arms and hands relaxed while you run. Let your arms swing freely at your sides, bent at a 90-degree angle. Keep your fingers loosely curled, not in a fist.

5 Strive for a smooth heel-to-toe encounter with the ground. Land softly on your heel or midfoot; your foot should be straight below your hip when it comes in contact with the ground. Push off from the ball of your foot when your foot leaves the ground. Make sure your feet are straight, not pigeon-toed or pointed outward.

6 Breathe deeply and rhythmically through your nose and mouth to ensure your muscles are getting plenty of oxygen.

7 Start at a slow pace when you begin a run to allow your body to warm up.

8 Run at a comfortable, steady pace with even strides. Keep your pace slow enough so that you are able to carry on a conversation. If you experience pain, fatigue or heavy breathing, slow down the pace and/or take a brief stretching break.

9 Walk or jog slowly for 5 minutes at the end of your run to cool down, allowing your heart to return to its normal rate. And remember to stretch afterward.

Tips

Improper stretching causes injuries. Stay properly aligned as you stretch and move slowly and smoothly; avoid bouncing or sudden jerks. Muscles shouldn't hurt when you stretch. If they do, you probably are overextending the stretch.

Pull yourself up straight and tall while you run to discourage slouching or leaning. Take care not to overarch your back.

Check yourself while you run to make sure your shoulders haven't tightened up inadvertently. If they have, pull them down to release tension and relax. Stop to do some shoulder stretches if necessary.

Your arms help you keep your balance. If you feel off-kilter, make sure your arms aren't crossing in front of you or swinging too far back. They should move along your sides in rhythm with your leg movement.

You can buy insoles for your running shoes to correct feet that turn inward or outward. Consult a store that specializes in running gear.

507 Shape Up Your Physique

There are hundreds of companies selling machines and devices that promise to magically transform you into a vision of fitness and beauty. The fact is, simple activities and exercises provide all the fitness and toning you need, at little or no cost. Follow the chart below to work on specific areas.

AREA OF BODY	SOLUTIONS
Abdominal muscles	**Exercises:** Crunches are very effective at toning the abdominal muscles. Do one set of 20 every morning before you get dressed: Lie on the floor with your knees bent. Lock your hands behind your head, and bring your elbows and knees together by flexing your abdominal muscles. Aim your elbows and chest toward the ceiling; lift shoulder blades 2 inches (5 cm) off floor. Avoid fully extending your legs, as this can place too much strain on your lower back. **Activities:** Great ab workouts include rowing, tennis and yoga. These activities work the entire set of abdominal muscles, promoting overall strength. (They're also much more fun than sit-ups and crunches.)
Bicep muscles (front of arm)	**Exercises:** Men secretly like to worry about their biceps. Fortunately, these are very easy to improve. Any small hand weight of 10 to 15 lbs. (4.5 to 7 kg) can be used while you're in front of the TV or at your desk. While sitting, brace your elbow against your hip bone and bring the weight to your shoulder. Do several sets of 10 repetitions. You should see results in just a few days. **Activities:** Rock climbing will work the biceps, with the added advantage of simultaneously building forearm strength. As any parent knows, lifting a toddler throughout the day provides a good bicep workout, too.
Tricep muscles (back of arm)	**Exercises:** Cure flabby arms by working the triceps. Use a light weight at first, up to about 5 lbs. (2.5 kg). Holding the weight in one hand, extend your arm straight over your head. Keeping your elbow still and shoulder down, lower the weight. Do several reps before switching to the other hand. **Activities:** Lots of sports will work the triceps. Cross-country skiing is probably the best and also provides important cardiovascular benefits. Swimming and rowing are also good choices. Start slowly. These muscles can get very sore.
Quadricep muscles (front of thigh)	**Exercises:** Stand with your feet shoulder width apart. Keeping your upper body straight, flex your knees so that your hips lower straight down toward your heels. Keep your weight back on your heels. Continue dropping your hips as low as you can comfortably go. Do not sink all the way to the floor, as this stresses the knees. Return to standing position. Repeat 20 times. **Activities:** The best activity for your quads is bicycling. A stationary bike works fine, but a real bike is much more fun. Pedal easily and go for distance instead of speed. Skiing also provides a fantastic quadriceps workout.

Keep in mind that spot-reducing is a myth. You won't just lose fat around your stomach, for example, you will lose it everywhere, even if you only work your abdominal muscles. However, you *can* tone muscles in a specific area, and the additional strength will combat flabbiness.

AREA OF BODY	SOLUTIONS
Hamstring muscles (back of thigh)	**Exercises:** These are the largest muscles in the body, and it is important to keep them strong and loose. Sporting-goods stores and physical therapists carry large elastic bands such as Therabands, designed to provide resistance workouts similar to weight lifting. Purchase one of these bands and tie the ends together in a knot. Secure the band underneath a heavy piece of furniture. Sit in a chair placed 2 feet (60 cm) beyond the end of the band. Loop the band behind your ankle and pull against it by bringing your foot back to the chair. Release slowly. Repeat 20 times with each leg. **Activities:** Almost any activity will work your hamstrings. Walking and jogging are probably the easiest. Again, go for distance rather than speed to get the best workout.
Stretching	A vital part of any workout schedule is stretching. Loose muscles are more resistant to injury and will allow you a greater range of comfortable motion. Incorporate stretching into your daily activities, and pretty soon it will become second nature.
Hamstring stretch	Sit on the floor with your legs apart or together. Bend forward slowly from the waist. Keep your knees straight. Reach your fingers toward your feet. Don't bounce your body. Hold for 30 seconds, then slowly return to sitting. Don't worry if you can't reach your feet. Take it slowly.
Calf muscle stretch	Stand with your toes on the edge of a stair or curb. Lower your heels toward the ground until you can feel your calf muscles gently stretch. Hold for 30 seconds, then rest. Repeat several times. This is an important stretch because tight calf muscles can contribute to shin problems.
Abdominal stretch	Stand with your feet widely spread. Reach both arms straight over your head. Bend slowly to the left until you can feel the muscles along your right side stretching. Do not rotate your hips or shoulders. Slowly return to the starting point, then bend to the right. Repeat 10 times.
Quadriceps stretch	Brace your left arm against a wall or table. Raise your right foot toward your back and grab it with your right hand, keeping your knees together. Relax your right leg muscles as you gently pull up and back on your foot. Hold for 30 seconds, then repeat for the other foot. Repeat three times.

508 Repair a Damaged Surfboard

The waves may be soft and fluffy, but between you and the ocean is a beach full of rocks. Drop your board on something hard, and you're likely to damage the fiberglass coating. If you don't fix it, the board can become waterlogged and weak. You don't have to go to a surf shop for the repair materials. Hardware stores and auto-parts stores carry everything you need.

Steps

1 Dry the board and allow any absorbed water to evaporate.

2 Cut away any loose bits of fiberglass with a sharp knife. If the fiberglass is cracked but in place, do not remove it.

3 Using a pair of scissors, cut a piece of fiberglass cloth so that it is slightly larger than the area to be repaired.

4 Mix fiberglass resin and hardener in a paper cup according to the manufacturer's directions. Stir well with a small wood strip such as an ice-pop stick.

5 Coat the repair area with the resin mixture. Place the cloth over the repair area and saturate it with the mix. When dry, this cloth will form the new skin of the board. Smooth with a wood strip to remove any air bubbles caught under the cloth.

6 Watch for the resin mixture to become firm. Be prepared with the knife to trim any excess cloth or mixture before the resin is fully hardened.

7 Smooth the repair with sandpaper once the mixture has hardened completely. Start with 100-grit paper to remove the roughest sections, then use the 220-grit and finally finish with the 400-grit. If the finish is not smooth enough, consider using 600-grit sandpaper.

8 Go surf.

What You'll Need

- Sharp knife
- Scissors
- Fiberglass cloth
- Fiberglass resin and hardener
- Paper cup
- Small wood strips
- 100-, 220-, 400- and 600-grit sandpaper
- Killer waves

Tips

Surfboards usually have a foam core with a fiberglass coating. Holes in the foam core can be filled with fiberglass.

Fiberglass hardens best in warm conditions with low humidity.

Warning

Fiberglass is toxic and can be a skin irritant, so work outdoors and avoid breathing fumes or dust.

509 Get Rid of Swimmer's Ear

Has your daily backstroke left bacteria swimming in your ear? Swimmer's ear, a bacterial or fungal infection of the outer ear canal, causes painful, swollen or itchy ears or redness in the ear area. Other symptoms include mild hearing loss or a milky discharge.

Steps

1 Use over-the-counter antiseptic ear drops or apply a drop or two of isopropyl alcohol with a medicine dropper in the ear canal. Shake your head to swish about the drops and then tilt the head to allow the canal to drain out. The ear drops or alcohol dry up excess water and help kill bacteria.

2 Ease the pain with a heating pad or hot water bottle.

3 Visit a doctor for a proper diagnosis, especially if the lymph glands are swollen, if the ear is swollen shut or extremely painful, or if a fever accompanies the infection. A doctor may prescribe antibiotics (drops or oral), corticosteroid ear drops to reduce swelling, or medication to reduce pain.

4 Avoid swimming or submersion in water for at least 10 days after treatment to allow the ear to fully dry out and heal.

5 To prevent swimmer's ear, wear a swimming cap. After a swim, shake and tilt your head to remove water from the ears. If water remains, use a hair dryer on a low setting or antiseptic ear drops (or alcohol) to dry out the ears.

What You'll Need

- Antiseptic ear drops or isopropyl alcohol
- Medicine dropper
- Heating pad or hot water bottle
- Swimming cap
- Hair dryer

Warning

Swimming in nonchlorinated water increases the risk of swimmer's ear.

Never stick an object, including cotton swabs, into your ear canal.

510 Defog a Diving Mask

While there are a few high-tech solutions to this problem, most people rely on this preventive technique that has been around for decades.

Steps

1 Dip your mask in the water to rinse it out. Empty as much of the water from the mask as possible.

2 Spit into the inside of the mask.

3 With your fingers, rub the spit over the inside surface of the lens. Dip the mask again briefly, then empty it as much as possible.

4 Avoid exhaling into the mask as you put it on. Your breath can fog the lens.

What You'll Need

- Diving mask

Tip

If spitting in your mask doesn't appeal to you, you can buy an anti-fogging solution at most dive shops.

511 Repair a Ripped Wetsuit

A ripped wetsuit is a bit like alcohol-free wine—not useless but definitely lacking. With the proper equipment, however, it's easy to fix most wetsuit rips.

Steps

1 Large rips, or rips along seams, need to be sewn closed. Use strong thread or dental floss and a heavy sewing needle. Hold the two sides of the rip together and use a spiraling stitch to sew them together.

2 Coat both sides of the newly sewn rip with neoprene cement to make it watertight. Neoprene cement can be purchased at surf and dive shops.

3 Small cuts and rips can be sealed using only neoprene cement. Hold the rip together and coat with cement. Apply to both sides. Let dry for 10 minutes and apply a second coat.

What You'll Need

- Strong thread or dental floss
- Heavy sewing needle
- Neoprene cement

Tip

Avoid rips by removing your wetsuit slowly and carefully.

512 Fix Your Bump Shot in Volleyball

Most people have trouble developing a consistent bump shot in volley-ball. This shot, the most basic in the game, can be used to pass, set or hit the ball over the net.

Steps

1 Extend your arms straight out in front of you, perpendicular to the floor with your palms up. Lay one hand in the palm of the other and then roll your thumbs together so that you can see your two thumbnails facing up and next to each other. This creates a loose and comfortable grip for your bump shot. Now flex your arms so that you create a flat platform between your wristbones and elbows, keeping your arms straight.

2 Extend your elbows until they are locked. Your arms and shoulders should move as one unit. Keep your feet shoulder width apart, knees bent with weight on your toes, and stay low. You want to contact the ball at waist level, always trying to be directly behind the ball and in line with your target. Practice pivoting at the waist, not the shoulders. As you pivot to the side, raise your hands to keep the platform level.

3 Have a friend serve the ball over the net. Get into position early so that you are stable and directly behind the ball when it arrives. Keep your arms steady at contact and keep watching the ball until it hits your arms. Do not swing at the ball but rather gently push your shoulders and arms forward toward the target as the ball comes in contact with your arms. Practice proper positioning and form, not power.

What You'll Need

- Volleyball
- Volleyball court
- Partner

Tip

Keep one foot slightly in front of the other and transfer your weight from back to front as you contact the ball. This will give you more power and better directional control.

513 Fix Your Softball Swing

Hitting a round ball with a round bat is never easy. That's why top players spend so much time practicing their hitting. Practice with a friend so you can take turns pitching and batting.

Steps

1 Hold the bat near the end with your hands close together. Stand back from home plate so that the tip of the bat just reaches to the far edge of the plate. Place your feet shoulder width apart and perpendicular to the pitcher's mound. Do not rest the bat on your shoulder.

2 Keep your eye on the ball. Begin watching the ball before it leaves the pitcher's hand.

3 Hold your back elbow out and away from your body. Begin your swing by rotating your hips toward the ball. Follow with your shoulders and arms. Keep the bat level with the ground. As you swing, transfer weight from your back foot to your front foot.

4 Higher bat speeds produce stronger hits. Rotate the tip of the bat into the ball by bending your wrists forward as you swing.

What You'll Need

- Bat
- Softball
- Pitcher

Tip

Concentrate on developing a smooth, precise swing. When your swing is consistent, then you can work on developing extra power.

514 Fix Your Curveball

Does your curveball refuse to break? Is it straight as an arrow? Fixing this pitch requires practice and the mastery of a few fundamentals. The first step is to develop a consistent fastball—all of your other pitches should derive from it. The following method for perfecting your curveball is based on your existing fastball.

Steps

1 Warm up by delivering several moderate fastballs. Concentrate on smoothness and accuracy. For a curveball, grip the ball so that your first two fingers run along the seams of the ball.

2 Begin your delivery as you would for a fastball. Keep your shoulder and elbow high to maintain power and accuracy.

3 Release the ball at the same point you would for a fastball, but bring your throwing arm vigorously down and into your body upon release. Coaches like to compare this arm motion to pulling down a window shade, as compared to the relatively straight arm motion of the fastball.

4 Drag your back leg significantly more for a curveball than you do for a fastball. Combined with the arm-release motion, dragging your leg has the effect of cutting the delivery short. The goal here is to create topspin on the ball, producing a downward and sideways curve.

What You'll Need

- Baseball
- Partner

515 Fix Your Soccer Shot

Soccer is a simple game. To win, you kick the ball into the opponent's net while kicking it away from your own net. But, like many apparently simple things, perfecting the subtle skills required to effectively kick a soccer ball can take years. Practice the following penalty shot drill and it will help your overall game.

Steps

1 Place a soccer ball on the penalty line, in front of the goal. Your objective is to hit a strong, accurate shot into the net. Take three big steps back from the ball. Take one step to the side. A right-footed kicker should step to the left. A left-footed kicker should step to the right.

2 Approach the ball by taking your first step with your kicking foot. On your third step, your nonkicking foot should be even with the ball and about 6 inches (15 cm) to the side. The toes of this foot should point at your intended target. Keep both knees bent and your arms wide for balance. Repeat steps 1 and 2 until these actions become automatic.

3 Bring your kicking foot smoothly forward and strike the middle of the ball with the inside edge of your foot. Your knee should be directly over the ball when your foot strikes it. Swing your leg and foot through the ball so that your foot ends up pointing at the target. Lock your ankle in place when striking the ball to get the best power. Your shot should skim the ground and bury itself in the back of the net.

4 When you have mastered steps 1 through 3, you can modify your shot for more power. Strike the middle of the ball with the top of your foot by pointing your toe down and holding your ankle locked in this position as you swing through the ball. Again, follow through so that your foot points toward the target. As you get better at this shot, your planted foot should move slightly back and farther to the side of the ball.

5 Develop additional power by initiating the kick with your hips and accelerating your foot with your knee. Accuracy is more important than power, so work on this step slowly.

What You'll Need

- Soccer ball
- Soccer goal
- Soccer field

Tip

Modify your shot further by practicing lofted shots and ground shots. Planting your nonshooting foot farther back will give the ball height. Planting your nonshooting foot directly beside the ball will force it along the ground.

516 Fix a Punctured Bicycle Tire

Punctured tires seem to be an inevitable part of bicycling. Experienced cyclists make a habit of carrying the necessary repair materials on their bike at all times. With a little preparation you'll never need to worry about being stranded. Want even more safety and peace of mind on the road? Practice this repair at home.

Steps

1 Remove the wheel from the bicycle and the tire and inner tube from the rim, following the steps in 520 Change a Bicycle Tire, "Removing the old tire."

2 Inspect the inner tube for holes by inflating it with a bicycle-tire pump until you can hear air escaping. Many holes are not visible until the tube is highly pressurized.

3 Locate the hole. Hold the tube close to your cheek and feel for escaping air if necessary (see A). Lightly rough up the area around the hole with sandpaper.

4 Apply glue both to the tube and a rubber patch. Wait for the glue to become tacky before applying the patch.

5 Firmly press the patch onto the hole (see B) and allow it to dry for several minutes.

6 Reinstall the tire, inner tube and wheel according to the steps in 520 Change a Bicycle Tire, "Installing the new tire."

7 Replace the patched tube with a new inner tube as soon as possible.

8 If you plan on riding a lot, carry a pump and a patch kit, and even replacement inner tubes, on your bicycle at all times.

What You'll Need

- Set of three tire tools (tire irons)
- Tire pump
- Tire patch kit (rubber patches, glue, sandpaper)
- Replacement inner tube

Tip

There are two types of valves used on bicycle inner tubes: Schrader valves and Presta valves. Schrader valves are identical to the type used on car tires and can be inflated at most gas stations. Presta valves are smaller and lighter and require a special pump.

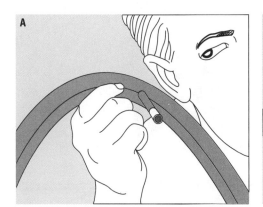

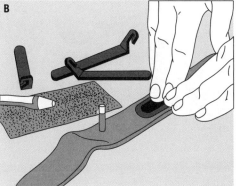

517 Fix a Bike Chain That Has Fallen Off

A bicycle chain is enormously strong and relatively lightweight. But unfortunately, it is not trouble-free and sometimes slips off the sprockets. Oddly enough, this is not necessarily a sign that the bike is in bad shape—sometimes a chain slips off for no apparent reason. But an experienced rider can fix this problem in seconds, and a novice can learn to do it in a few minutes.

A chain that repeatedly jumps off is a sign that something is out of line. Start by checking the rear wheel alignment. The wheel should spin freely and not wobble from side to side. Additional checks, most likely with the help of a bike shop, include making sure the derailleur is properly aligned and none of the sprockets are worn or bent.

Steps

1 Quit pedaling as soon as you realize the chain has slipped out of place. Further pedaling can jam the chain between the sprockets and the frame.

2 Stop the bike and get off.

3 Free the chain if it has jammed. Forget about keeping your fingers clean.

For a chain that has slipped off the front sprockets

1 Lay a section of the chain across the top of any of the front sprockets (see A). You do not need to wrap the chain all the way around the sprocket.

What You'll Need

- A willingness to get your fingers greasy

Warning

A bicycle with only a rear coaster brake (a brake that is activated by the pedals) has no brakes if the chain falls off. Do not ride this type of bike if you suspect there are problems with the chain.

Keep your fingers clear of the sprockets when turning the pedals.

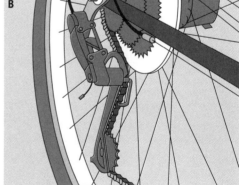

2 Lift the rear tire of the bike slightly off the ground. Slowly rotate the pedals. The chain should fall into place on the sprocket and spin freely.

3 If the chain immediately slips off the front sprockets again, adjust the position of the front shift lever and try again. You will not damage the bike by moving the shift levers while the pedals are stationary.

4 If the chain stays on the sprockets but continually makes a rubbing or clicking noise, adjust the position of the front shift until the noise disappears. If the noise does not disappear, you will need to adjust the derailleur alignment (see 518 Fix a Poorly Shifting Bicycle).

For a chain that has slipped off the rear sprockets

1 If the chain has slipped off the largest rear sprocket, check to see that the rear derailleur is not in danger of jamming in the rear wheel spokes. Lift the rear of the bike and spin the wheel. Look to see if there is clearance between the derailleur and spokes. If there isn't, do not use the largest rear sprocket until you have a chance to adjust the derailleur alignment (see 518 Fix a Poorly Shifting Bicycle). Otherwise, you can ruin the wheel and the derailleur, and possibly crash.

2 Lay the chain across the top of any of the rear sprockets. Don't worry if it crosses over several sprockets at first.

3 Make sure the chain travels through the rear derailleur freely. It should follow both guide wheels in the rear derailleur (see B).

4 Lift the rear tire of the bike slightly off the ground. Slowly rotate the pedals until the chain falls into place. If the chain slips or jams, adjust the position of the rear shift lever and start over.

5 If the chain continues to fall off, avoid setting the shift lever at the extreme positions (very high or very low) until you have a chance to check the derailleur alignment (see 518 Fix a Poorly Shifting Bicycle).

518 Fix a Poorly Shifting Bicycle

This fix is not always easy. It will probably require some practice, but the results and satisfaction will be worth it. Most bicycles these days have 24 or more speeds, achieved by mounting 3 sprockets at the pedals and 8 or more at the rear wheel (3 x 8 = 24 speeds).

Shifting is controlled by levers at the handlebars, connected by cables to the front and rear derailleurs. The derailleurs—devices through which the bike's chain passes—move from side to side to shift the chain from one sprocket to the next.

There are only two factors that affect the derailleur's function: cable tension and derailleur alignment.

Steps

Adjusting cable tension

1 Begin by inspecting each shift lever. These are usually located directly on the handlebars. On older bicycles, they are sometimes attached to the frame, immediately below the handlebars. If there is a screw securing the lever, be sure it's tight and that the lever stays in whatever position it's set in. If you're lucky and deserving, this will fix the problem. Take the bike for a test spin to find out.

2 Find, on the front derailleur, the cable coming from the handlebar. The front derailleur is attached to the frame, just above the front gears. At the derailleur, use an Allen (hex) wrench to undo the nut or bolt that secures the cable (see illustration).

3 Using only your hand, pull the cable taut (pulling with pliers creates too much tension). While holding the cable taut, resecure the cable with the nut or bolt.

4 Repeat steps 2 and 3 for the rear derailleur. The rear derailleur is attached to the frame and hangs just below the rear gears.

5 Shift through all the gears while riding the bike to check your adjustment. If shifting is still not perfect, you'll need to adjust the derailleur alignment (see below).

Adjusting derailleur alignment

1 Have a helper lift the rear wheel of the bicycle slightly off the ground.

2 Kneel beside the bike and turn the pedals slowly by hand. Using the shift lever, adjust the front derailleur so that it rests at about the midpoint of its movement range.

3 If the initial problem is that the chain won't shift onto the largest rear gear, locate the two small side-by-side adjustment screws on the rear derailleur. Turn the left (or upper) adjustment screw

What You'll Need

- Set of Allen (hex) wrenches
- Small Phillips screwdriver
- Helper

Tips

The cables that control shifting and braking on a bicycle can wear out quickly. If you follow the steps here and shifting is still poor, you might need new cables. A bike shop can replace them easily.

Worn-out shift cables might be a sign that your brake cables are bad. Better to find this out now than during a ride.

Allen wrenches usually come in a set containing various-size wrenches attached to a handle.

counterclockwise a quarter turn with a small Phillips screwdriver. If the initial problem is that the chain won't shift onto the smallest rear gear, skip to step 6.

4 Continue turning the pedals and shift through all the rear gears. If the chain will still not go onto the largest rear gear, shift the chain back down to the smallest rear gear. Turn the right (or lower) adjustment screw clockwise as far as possible before the chain begins to click or rattle.

5 Shift through the gears again to test. If necessary, turn the left (or upper) screw counterclockwise another quarter turn.

6 If the initial problem is that the chain won't shift onto the smallest rear gear, begin by turning the right (or lower) adjustment screw counterclockwise a quarter turn. Shift through the gears to test.

7 If the chain still won't go onto the smallest rear gear, shift the chain to the largest rear gear. Turn the left (or upper) adjustment screw clockwise as far as possible before the chain begins to click or rattle. Shift through all the gears to test.

8 Follow steps 1 through 7 for the front derailleur, which operates on exactly the same mechanism as the rear derailleur (you still lift the rear wheel in step 1). There are two side-by-side adjusting screws that control alignment.

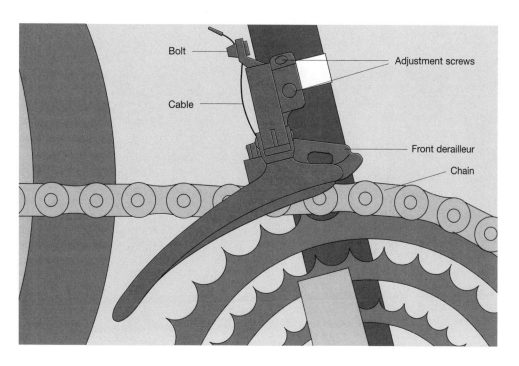

Bolt

Adjustment screws

Cable

Front derailleur

Chain

519 Tighten or Loosen Bicycle Brakes

The latest bicycle brakes are designed to be incredibly powerful and safe. But you still need to take care of them. Brakes have only two problems: They can be too tight or too loose. Brakes that are too tight rub against the wheel and slow you down; brakes that are too loose don't provide enough stopping power. Keep them properly adjusted, and your riding will be easier and safer.

This fix applies only to bikes that utilize a frame-mounted brake to grasp the wheel rim. Bicycles with hydraulic disk brakes should be serviced by a qualified mechanic.

Steps

Fix rubbing brakes

1 Lift the bicycle off the ground and spin each wheel. If the rubbing is very faint, the problem can be fixed using the brake-alignment screw. You'll find this small screw on the brake by the wheel rim.

2 Turn the screw slowly with a small Phillips screwdriver, in either direction, until the brake no longer contacts the rim (see A). Work slowly, and frequently spin the wheel to check for rubbing. A small adjustment should be sufficient.

3 Severe rubbing requires an adjustment of the brake cable. Using an adjustable wrench or an Allen (hex) wrench, loosen the nut holding the brake cable to the brake itself. Allow the cable to loosen slightly and resecure the nut.

What You'll Need

- Small Phillips screwdriver
- Adjustable wrench or set of Allen (hex) wrenches
- Pliers

Tips

If either of the wheels on your bicycle is obviously bent or warped, it may not be possible to prevent the brake from rubbing against the rim. To fix the wheel, bring it to a reputable bike shop.

Allen wrenches usually come in a set containing various-size wrenches attached to a handle.

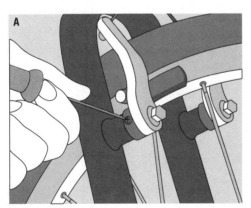

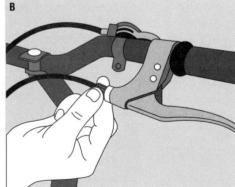

4 Spin the wheel to test for rubbing. Squeeze the brake lever a few times to be sure the new slack in the cable has reached the brake. Loosen the cable further if necessary.

5 Repeat steps 1 through 4 for the other wheel.

Fix slipping brakes

1 Immediately in front of the handlebar brake lever is a screw adjuster, through which the brake cable passes. Turn the adjuster counterclockwise to add tension to the brake cable and thereby increase braking power (see B).

2 Test the brakes for sufficient tension. If you can pull the brake lever all the way back to the handlebar, continue adding tension.

3 If the adjuster doesn't add enough tension, the brake cable must be pulled tighter at the brake. Return the adjuster to the middle of its adjustment range by giving it a few clockwise turns.

4 Follow the brake cable to where it attaches to the brake. Loosen the nut holding the cable to the brake, using either an adjustable wrench or an Allen (hex) wrench (see C).

5 Using a pair of pliers, pull the cable taut (see D). While holding the cable taut, resecure the brake cable by tightening the nut with a wrench.

6 Repeat steps 1 through 5 for the other brake. Ride the bike to test the brakes. If you have added too much tension and the brakes rub slightly, try turning the screw adjuster clockwise. This will remove a bit of tension from the brake cables.

Warning

Bicycles with only a rear, internal-hub brake (coaster brake) should be treated with caution, as this type of brake doesn't provide reliable stopping power.

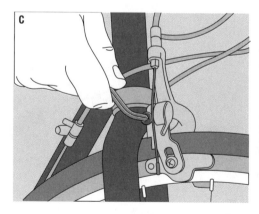

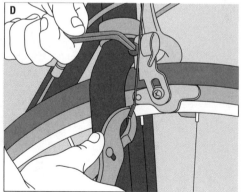

520 Change a Bicycle Tire

Want a fun way to change the character of your bike? Change the tires. A set of smooth tires on your mountain bike, for example, will give a much faster ride on pavement. Tires also wear out, of course, and learning to replace them will save you money. Because tires come in many sizes, take your old tire with you when purchasing a replacement, to make sure you get the size right.

Steps

Removing the old tire

1 Remove the wheel from the bike. Most bikes now have a quick-release lever on each axle. Simply flip one of the levers to loosen the wheel. Once loose, the wheel can be pulled free.

2 Older bikes usually have two axle nuts holding each wheel in place. Use an adjustable wrench to loosen one of the nuts, thus allowing the wheel to come free.

3 Completely deflate the tire.

4 Slide the rounded end of one of the tire tools between the tire and the rim. Working slowly and taking care not to pinch the tube, pry the tire away from the rim by locking the free end of the tire tool into the spokes.

5 Slide a second tire tool between the tire and rim. Work this tool around the rim until the tire pops free (see A).

6 If the tool gets stuck, lock the free end into the spokes and begin working with the third tire tool.

7 Remove the tire and inner tube from the rim.

What You'll Need

- Adjustable wrench
- Replacement tire
- Set of three tire tools (tire irons)
- Tire pump

Tips

There are two types of valves used on bicycle inner tubes: Schrader valves and Presta valves. Schrader valves are identical to the type used on car tires and can be inflated at most gas stations. Presta valves are smaller and lighter and require a special pump.

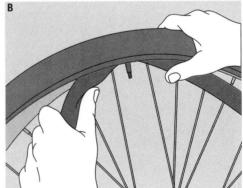

Installing the new tire

1 Take a new tire and slip one edge of it all the way around the rim. It should be possible to do this by hand, although you can use one of the tire tools if necessary.

2 Place the inner tube completely inside the new tire, taking care to line up the inner tube valve with the valve hole in the rim (see B). Push the tube as far into the tire as possible. It might help to inflate the tube very slightly.

3 Using your hands, push as much of the second edge of the tire onto the rim as possible. Continue pushing the tube into the tire as needed.

4 Insert a tire tool between the rim and the portion of the tire that is not yet installed.

5 Slowly lever the tool upward and force the tire over the rim edge. Use a second tool to push the tube into place if necessary.

6 Gently roll the tire into place over the rim edge. Work slowly and avoid snapping the tire into place as this tends to pinch the tube and cause air leaks.

7 Inflate the tire to the recommended pressure written on the side of the tire, and replace the wheel on the bike.

You can't change your tire diameter, but you can consider a change in width. A wider tire can give a more comfortable ride and better traction. A narrower tire offers easier pedaling and better speed.

Keep a spare set of inner tubes on hand. They are fairly cheap, and punctures are common.

521 Replace Mountain Bike Hand Grips

This is an easy fix if you know the secret but very annoying if you don't. If your bike has seen some hard use, or if you plan on changing the handlebars, you'll need to know how to do this.

Steps

1 Remove the old grips. Cut them off with a knife if necessary.

2 If you have replaced the entire handlebar, be sure the shift levers and brake levers are properly in place on the handlebars before installing the new grips.

3 Spray a generous amount of hairspray inside one of the new grips. Slide it into place on the bar.

4 Repeat step 3 for the other grip.

5 Allow the hairspray to dry for several minutes and the new grips will stay in place.

What You'll Need

- Sharp knife
- Hairspray
- Replacement grips

522 Fix a Bicycle Spoke

If you've broken a spoke on your bike, either you're riding hard or your bike is getting old. Either way, you need to fix it fast. Ignore it, and the entire wheel could fall apart. This fix is usually easy unless the broken spoke is next to the rear sprockets. In that case, a bike shop will need to help you remove and reinstall the rear sprockets.

Steps

1 Take the wheel off the bicycle, and remove the tire and inner tube from the rim, following the steps in 520 Change a Bicycle Tire, "Removing the old tire."

2 If there is a plastic band around the rim, underneath the inner tube, remove this as well.

3 Remove both pieces of the broken spoke from the rim. Save the nut, or nipple, from the end of the spoke. Take the broken spoke to a bike shop and buy a replacement that is exactly the same length as the original.

4 Starting at the wheel hub, insert the new spoke into its hole from the proper direction. Study the adjacent spokes and follow the pattern you see.

5 Thread the new spoke through the existing spokes and insert the end of the spoke through the hole in the rim.

6 Screw the nipple into place at the end of the new spoke. Using the spoke wrench, tighten the nipple until the spoke tension is similar to that of the surrounding spokes.

7 Reinstall the tire, inner tube and wheel according to the steps in 520 Change a Bicycle Tire, "Installing the new tire."

What You'll Need

- Adjustable wrench
- Set of three tire tools (tire irons)
- Replacement spoke
- Spoke wrench
- Tire pump

Tips

Save both pieces of the broken spoke. You will need to purchase a replacement that is exactly the same length as the original.

A spoke wrench and tire tools aren't expensive. Once you own a few basic tools, you might be surprised how quickly you can master common repairs.

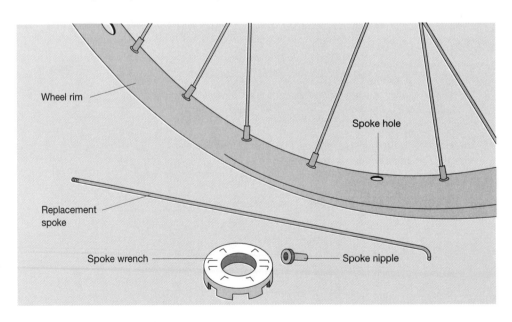

Wheel rim

Spoke hole

Replacement spoke

Spoke wrench

Spoke nipple

523 Fix a Rusty Bicycle Chain

Does your bicycle squeak like violins on the first day at music camp? Do dogs cover their ears when you ride by? It's probably just a rusty chain. This is an easy fix that every bicycle owner should know.

Steps

1 Apply lightweight oil such as WD-40 to the whole length of the chain. Rotate the pedals several times to ensure that the entire chain is oiled.

2 Wait several minutes for the oil to soak in.

3 Wrap a rag around the chain and vigorously wipe the oil, dirt and rust from the chain. Again, rotate the pedals several times.

4 Inspect the chain for links that don't flex freely. If you find one, oil it heavily and scrub off any visible rust with an old toothbrush.

5 Oil the entire chain a final time.

What You'll Need

- Lightweight oil
- Rag
- Old toothbrush

Warning

Take care not to run your fingers into the gears while handling a moving chain.

524 Fix a Hole in a Raft

If you're riding huge swells in the North Atlantic and your life raft calls it a day, you don't need this book, you need a Hollywood miracle. But if you discover a small leak in your inflatable rubber raft while on summer vacation, don't worry. It's easy to fix.

Steps

1 Locate all the holes by inflating the raft and listening for leaks. Mark the holes with a felt-tip pen.

2 Using scissors, cut a piece of patch material so that it extends about 3 inches (7.5 cm) beyond the hole. If there's more than one hole, cut an appropriate-size patch for each one.

3 Using 100-grit sandpaper, rough up the patches and the area around each hole. This is essential for a strong bond.

4 Apply a very thin layer of raft-repair glue onto each patch and each hole area with a small paintbrush. Cutting the paintbrush bristles in half makes it easier to apply and spread a thin layer of glue. Let the glue dry completely. A thin glue layer is very important; a thick layer won't create a strong bond.

5 Apply a second thin coat. Wait 10 minutes, then apply the patch to the hole area.

6 Let the glue dry according to the manufacturer's instructions.

What You'll Need

- Felt-tip pen
- Scissors
- Patch material
- 100-grit sandpaper
- Raft-repair glue
- Small paintbrush

Tips

Raft-repair glue and patch material are available at boating supply stores.

Try to do repairs in temperatures around 70°F (21°C) and out of direct sunlight.

525 Fix a Hole in a Canoe

Dangerous rapids and whitewater aren't the only obstacles for a canoe. Many canoes get damaged on their way to the water, usually by falling off a car top. Small holes and leaky seams can easily be fixed by using a variety of methods that work equally well on wood, plastic or aluminum canoes.

Steps

Field repairs

1 Locate the hole. If it isn't obvious, dry off the canoe bottom, put water in the canoe and watch to see where the water escapes.

2 Small holes can be temporarily patched with duct tape. For the best adhesion, make sure the repair area and the tape are warm.

3 For a leaky seam, try a favorite old-timer's trick: Using a small stick, apply pine pitch along the leak. Pine pitch, the sticky gum found on pine trees, is extremely durable and waterproof.

Permanent repairs

1 Dry the canoe thoroughly.

2 Remove any dents around the damaged area if possible. Dents in plastic or aluminum canoes are sometimes pushed out from the inside.

3 Using a pair of scissors, cut a piece of fiberglass cloth slightly larger than the repair area.

4 Mix fiberglass resin and hardener in a paper cup according to the manufacturer's directions. Stir well with a wood strip such as an ice-pop stick.

5 Coat the repair area with the resin mixture. Place the fiberglass cloth over the repair area. Saturate the cloth with the mixture. Smooth the cloth with a wood strip to remove any air bubbles caught underneath it.

6 Watch for the resin mixture to become firm. Be prepared to trim any excess cloth or mixture with a sharp knife before the repair is fully hardened.

7 Smooth the repair with sandpaper once the mixture has hardened completely. Start with 100-grit paper to remove the roughest sections, then use 220-grit and finally finish with 400-grit.

What You'll Need

Field Repairs:
- Duct tape
- Small stick
- Pine pitch

Permanent Repairs:
- Scissors
- Fiberglass cloth
- Fiberglass resin and hardener
- Paper cup
- Wood strips
- Sharp knife
- 100-, 220- and 400-grit sandpaper

Tip

A high-quality wooden canoe deserves a repair job that preserves its original beauty. Unless you're an expert woodworker, consider hiring a professional.

526 Undo a Stuck Knot

We've all struggled with knots that won't come undone. Determination is the most common tool for this job, but the pros prefer to use a marlin spike. This is a small steel spike, frequently carried by sailors, that can be used to pry open stuck knots. You'll find them at hardware or boating supply stores. Some pocket knives also include a marlin spike.

Steps

1 Create as much slack as possible in the rope surrounding the knot. This will allow you maximum access to the knot.

2 Inspect the knot. Many knots appear completely tight, but in fact have a loose section that can be used to relax the entire knot.

3 Insert a marlin spike or a screwdriver into the loosest part of the knot. Work the tool back and forth and check for loosening.

4 Reinsert the spike into the knot in as many places as possible. Feed loose rope into the knot by pushing it with the spike if necessary. Work carefully with the spike to avoid damaging the rope.

What You'll Need

- Marlin spike or screwdriver

Tip

Some knots, particularly bowlines and figure eights, can be broken by grasping the knot in both hands and bending it as you would a stick that you want to snap in half. With practice, you can feel the knot loosen up.

527 Fix Lumpy Down

To provide warmth, a down jacket or sleeping bag needs to be light and airy. Sometimes down can lose its loft and become lumpy. In order to restore its warmth, try the following methods.

Steps

1 Make sure the item is completely dry. If it's wet, lay it flat where it can dry completely. This alone may be sufficient to restore the down's loft.

2 If the lumps remain, place the item in a clothes dryer along with three clean tennis balls.

3 Turn the heat to the lowest setting. Set the timer for 20 minutes.

4 Remove the item from the dryer. The loft should be fully restored.

5 Down should be stored in a closet with breathing room—jackets on a wide coat hanger, and sleeping bags in a large mesh storage bag—not compressed in a trunk, drawer or stuff sack.

What You'll Need

- Three tennis balls
- Wide hanger
- Large mesh storage bag

Tip

Store your down sleeping bag in a loose sack that doesn't compress the down. Small stuff sacks are suitable only for short storage periods.

528 Fix a Fishing Rod Tip

Fishing is extremely hazardous. Not for you, of course, but for your fishing rod. Overhead tree branches, boat railings and other obstacles can snap the tip off your rod in an instant. Fortunately, most broken tips can be easily replaced, even while you're out in the field.

Steps

1 Inspect the broken tip and practice fitting it back into place—you'll need to achieve the original alignment when you replace the tip.

2 Using a lighter or a match, heat a glue stick until it begins to drip.

3 Place one drop of glue onto the broken end of the rod, making sure you don't get any glue on the fishing line. Fit the rod tip into place.

4 Hold the two pieces in position until the glue hardens. This should take only a few seconds.

5 Check the alignment. If the fishing line moves freely, you're done.

What You'll Need

- Lighter or match
- Hot glue stick

Tips

Hot glue sticks are available at most hardware stores.

If you don't have a glue stick, a temporary fix can be made with duct tape.

529 Untangle a Snarled Fishing Line

Fishing is a bit like golf—so frustrating sometimes that you wonder why you do it. But you wouldn't give it up for the world. That's what you tell yourself, anyway, when you're waist-deep in cold water watching your line do a bird's-nest snarl around the reel. But don't be embarrassed. Even the pros suffer this problem on occasion.

Steps

1 Move to a comfortable spot and put your pole down as soon as you realize there's a problem.

2 Inspect the tangle. It may not be as bad as it looks. Sometimes a seemingly large snarl will disappear with the release of a single loop. Resist the urge to tug on the line.

3 Free any loops that are caught around or in the reel.

4 Look for tight sections of line that are trapping other loops. Pull the trapped loops free.

5 Work slowly to continually loosen the snarl. Flip loose coils out of the way.

6 When the snarl is cleared, inspect the reel for damage. If it is bent, the line may begin to snarl again. A bent reel will probably require professional attention.

7 Consider dipping the reel into the water for cleaning if it has been dropped in the dirt. This may help clear obstructions from the reel mechanism.

What You'll Need

- Patience

Tips

Many pros use the 3-minute rule: If they can't clear a snarl in 3 minutes or less, they will probably cut the line, then retie the leader and fly onto the shortened line.

If you're using two flies on the same line, place the heavier fly at the end of the line.

530 Extract a Fish Hook From Skin

You spent hours getting to a secret spot. Peering around a branch, you see a big one swimming to the surface. Envisioning a perfect cast, you raise your rod. You can already imagine reeling this monster in as the hook sinks into your skin and brings you back to reality. The solution to this problem isn't pretty, but it's better than the alternatives.

Steps

1 Inspect your wound. Fish hooks have a barb, a backward-facing point that prevents them from being pulled free. If the hook isn't embedded up to the barb, you can simply pull it out. If the hook is embedded past the barb (see A), resist the urge to pull on the line. This will be more painful than following the steps below.

2 Cut the line with a knife at any convenient spot to free yourself from the fishing pole. Set your pole and any other gear on the ground.

3 Using wire cutters, clip the head off the hook, leaving part of the shaft visible. The head is the circular part that the line ties to.

4 Push the point of the hook through the skin in a curved path that brings it to the surface in the shortest possible distance (see B). Once the point is visible, the hook can be pulled out in the same direction. This sounds gruesome, but it's the least disruptive way to remove the hook.

What You'll Need

- Knife
- Wire cutters

Tip

Avoid pulling on the line. Any pulling will only set the hook deeper.

Warning

An embedded fish hook is a potential source of infection. Treat the wound with an antiseptic solution as soon as possible.

A deeply embedded hook means a trip to the nearest doctor.

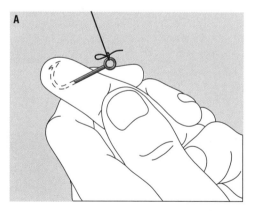

A

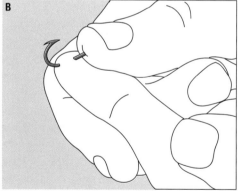

B

531 Deal With a Blister While Hiking

Nothing says "fun's over!" on a hike like a nasty blister. Be prepared to treat blisters by taking along a small first aid kit when you go on longer hikes. Be sure that the kit includes moleskin blister cover and a small pair of scissors.

Steps

1 You can prevent most blisters by planning ahead. Wear a light, synthetic sock next to your skin. Be sure this sock fits snugly and has no bulky seams. Wear a medium-weight wool or wool-blend sock over this.

2 Lace your boots snugly enough to prevent your heel from lifting with each step. Make sure your boots have enough room for your toes to move freely as you walk.

3 Treat potential blisters early, as soon as you feel a painful area or hot spot developing. Stop and remove your boots. If there is no blister, but the area is tender or red, slather on the Body Glide. Then sprinkle liberally with foot powder, and put your socks back on carefully. This combination provides a good friction barrier.

4 Using a small pair of scissors, cut a piece of moleskin that is ½ inch (12 mm) larger than the blister in all directions. Cut a circle out of the middle of the moleskin that is the size of the blister.

5 Place the moleskin over the blister so that the hole in the middle is directly over the blister area. The thickness of the moleskin will prevent the boot from contacting the blister.

6 After a few hours, put on fresh sock liners to minimize moisture.

What You'll Need

- Moleskin blister cover
- Small scissors
- Body Glide lubricant (or petroleum jelly)
- Foot powder

Tip

Moleskin is the common name for a padded blister covering. It can be purchased at drugstores or camping supply stores.

532 Unjam a Sleeping-Bag Zipper

A jammed sleeping-bag zipper can make for a cold night. You can crawl into your friend's bag, or fix it yourself and stop shivering.

Steps

1 Arrange the bag so that you have access to both sides of the zipper. For example, if you're lying in the bag, move the zipper to the top.

2 Cut with a knife any frayed threads that are caught in the zipper and pull them free. Gently test the zipper to see if it moves.

3 Pull any caught material away from the zipper at a right angle. In other words, pull it to the side, not up and down. Test the zipper again.

4 If necessary, pull firmly on the zipper to force it over the caught material. Holding the zipper-pull by the body rather than by the handle piece will provide more power.

What You'll Need

- Knife

Tips

Avoid zipper jams by aligning the two rows of teeth as closely as possible before you begin zipping. The zipper will jam if half the sleeping bag is folded under you.

See 31 Fix a Stuck Zipper for additional zipper help.

533 Fix a Torn Sleeping Bag

On a camping trip, a torn sleeping bag could be a major problem. The longer you wait to fix it, the more insulation you lose. As they say in the Boy Scouts: Be prepared and be cozy!

Steps

1 For a tear less than 2 inches (5 cm) long, the easiest fix in the field is to cover the tear with duct tape (see A). This provides a strong, durable patch that will stay in place. In very cold weather, be sure to warm up the tape first.

2 Larger rips require a needle and thread. The easiest sewing style is to pinch the opposite sides of the tear together and stitch a spiraling thread pattern across the hole (see B). Place the stitches ¼ inch (6 mm) back from the edge of the rip to ensure that they hold.

3 Remove the duct tape at the earliest opportunity, then replace it with an iron-on nylon patch. Stitching can be left in place if it isn't too bulky.

4 Using a pair of scissors, cut the nylon patch so that it extends about 2 inches (5 cm) beyond the edges of the rip.

5 Using the excess pieces of the patch, practice ironing a patch onto a scrap of cloth to determine the minimum heat setting that will work. An iron that is too hot can melt your sleeping bag.

6 Arrange the sleeping bag on an ironing board so that the iron will touch only the patch.

7 Iron the patch into place, moving the iron continuously for about 20 seconds. The bag should now be fully repaired.

What You'll Need

- Duct tape
- Needle and thread
- Iron-on nylon patch
- Scissors
- Iron

Tips

Iron-on nylon patches can be found at camping supply stores.

Duct tape that is left on the sleeping bag eventually leaves a gummy residue that is very difficult to remove.

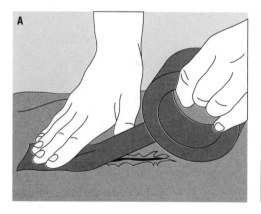

A

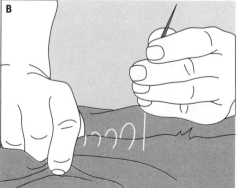

B

534 Fix a Torn Tent

The "close enough" approach to tent repair won't get you very far. Tents are subject to heavy stresses from rough ground, high winds and just normal use. Take a deliberate approach and you won't be sorry. A standard sewing machine should easily handle the work, but if you don't have experience with sewing machines, consider finding someone who does. Seam-sealing glue and heavy-duty nylon cloth are available at camping supply stores.

Steps

1 Clean the torn area with dishwashing liquid and water, then thoroughly dry the tent.

2 Cut two patches of heavy-duty nylon cloth about 2 inches (5 cm) larger than the tear (see A).

3 Coat one side of each patch with seam-sealing glue. Let them dry until the glue becomes tacky.

4 Apply one patch to each side of the torn area. Be careful to keep the tent material under the patch as flat as possible. This will ensure watertightness.

5 Using a sewing machine, zigzag-stitch completely around the edge of the patches. Continue stitching over the patches in a dense zigzag pattern (see B).

6 Apply additional seam-sealing glue to the stitching, both inside and out.

What You'll Need

- Dishwashing liquid
- Heavy-duty nylon cloth
- Scissors
- Seam-sealing glue
- Sewing machine with heavy-duty nylon thread

Warning

Tents intended for mountaineering or extreme weather should be considered survival equipment. Have the manufacturer or a professional assess whether the tent can be repaired.

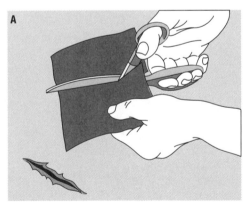

535 Patch Leaking Boots

No matter how much you love those old boots, they won't last forever. But with a little effort, you might get a few more years out of them. Try the following techniques. If they don't work, it might be time for a little shopping.

Steps

1 Inspect your boot for obvious holes. If the stitching is giving out or there are holes in the leather, go to a shoe repair shop for an expert's opinion.

2 Coat leather boots with a thick layer of a wax-based sealant such as SnoSeal. This seals small holes and increases overall water resistance. Be careful with dress shoes, as most sealants alter the leather color.

3 For rubber boots, small holes can be covered with a silicon-based glue such as Shoe Goo. Locate the hole and rough up the area with sandpaper. Place a small dab of the sealant over the hole. Let the boots dry for 24 hours.

What You'll Need

- Wax-based sealant
- Silicon-based glue
- Sandpaper

Tip

If you don't find an obvious hole in a boot, they may need to be resoled. Over time, the stitching around the sole can weaken, allowing water to get in. Consult a shoe repair shop.

536 Replace a Grommet in a Tent

Grommet—not only is it fun to say, it's also an important equipment feature. A grommet is a metal ring placed near the edge of a tent or tarp to provide an attachment point for a rope. With repeated use, it can pull out of the fabric, leaving a hole. To keep the hole from spreading, fix the problem before your next trip to the mountains.

Steps

1 Inspect the torn grommet. If the grommet has simply popped free of the material, you can set a new grommet in the same spot with no additional repairs. If the material has torn, you'll need to set the replacement grommet in a new spot.

2 Remove the grommet, then repair the hole by following the steps in 534 Fix a Torn Tent, opposite page.

3 Place a board or a piece of cardboard under the area where the new grommet will be located. Set the grommet-cutting tool on the target spot and strike it with a hammer to create a hole.

4 Place the grommet back-piece on the board and insert it through the new hole. Place the grommet front-piece on top of the board.

5 Place the grommet-setting tool on top of the new grommet and tap it several times with the hammer to fold the grommet over on itself and form a tight fit.

6 Inspect the grommet and continue using the hammer as needed.

What You'll Need

- Board or cardboard
- Replacement grommets
- Grommet-cutting and -setting tool
- Hammer

Tip

You can buy replacement grommets and a grommet-cutting and -setting tool at hardware and camping supply stores.

537 Replace Washers in a Lantern

Camp lanterns and camp stoves rely on air pressure to feed fuel to the burner. Safety and proper function therefore depend on airtight seals on all the fittings—that's where washers come in. A leak can result in a weak flame or dangerous gas emissions.

Fixing these devices isn't hard, but be prepared to safely deal with spilled fuel. There are usually two rubber washers on a lantern or a stove. One ensures an airtight seal around the gas cap. The other seals the gas valve, which you use to control gas flow to the burner or mantle.

Steps

1 Remove the gas cap.

2 Using the point of a small knife, remove the washer from inside the gas cap (see A).

3 Insert a replacement washer. Use the knife to press the washer firmly into place. Put the gas cap back on.

4 Using an adjustable wrench, remove the nut holding the gas valve in place (see B). Pull the gas valve free from the lantern or stove. Some fuel will leak during this step (see Warning).

5 Using the knife, remove the washer inside the gas-valve nut. Insert the replacement washer and press it into place with the knife point.

6 Put the gas valve back into place and tighten the nut.

7 Pressurize the gas tank with the lantern's pump and listen for leaks. If you hear pressure escaping, check the tightness of the gas cap and the gas-valve nut. If you cannot achieve a seal, check that the new washers are fully pushed into place.

What You'll Need

- Small knife
- Replacement washer(s)
- Adjustable wrench

Warning

Do not work on a lantern or stove that is hot to the touch. Spilled fuel could ignite.

Work in a well-ventilated area, preferably outdoors.

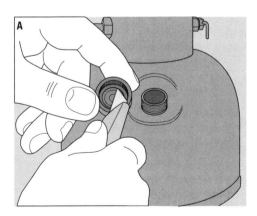

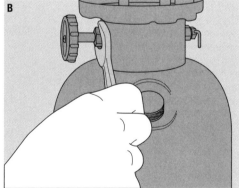

538 Replace a Mantle in a Lantern

With the proper equipment and experience, unplanned challenges are a fun part of camping. Without the right gear, these challenges quickly become big problems. Practice fixing your camp lantern before you head out, and you'll be king of the campfire.

Steps

1 Turn the gas valve completely off.

2 Unscrew the lantern cover. Remove the cover and the glass globe that surrounds the mantle (see A).

3 Remove any remnants of the old mantle.

4 Tie a new mantle into place on the gas outlet pipe using the attached string (see B).

5 Pressurize the gas tank by operating the pump on the side of the tank. Open the pump valve by rotating the handle, cover the hole in the pump handle with your thumb, pump repeatedly, then close the valve.

6 Hold a lighted match or lighter near the mantle. Open the gas valve slightly. The mantle should begin to burn. Replace the glass globe and the cover.

7 Open the gas valve fully when the mantle glows brightly. Close the gas valve completely to shut it off.

8 Pressurize the gas tank regularly for best results.

What You'll Need

- Spare mantle
- Matches or lighter

Tip

Spare mantles are available at camping supply stores and many hardware stores.

Warning

Be sure you're familiar with how your lantern operates. Improper use can cause a fire or an explosion.

Do not use a lantern or stove inside a tent.

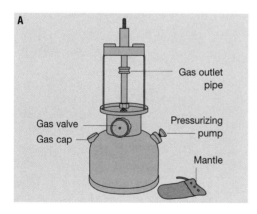

A

Gas outlet pipe

Gas valve

Gas cap

Pressurizing pump

Mantle

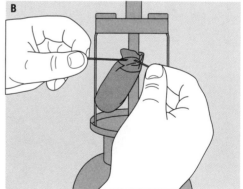

B

539 Fix Slow Skis

Do you think your skis are slow and worn out? Maybe they just need a proper wax job. A waxed ski slides faster and turns more easily than an unwaxed ski. But if your skis have lots of gouges or rusty edges, you're probably better off having a ski shop give them a full tune-up.

Steps

1 Warm your skis by bringing them inside.

2 Place them upside down across two sawhorses or chairs. (A garage or basement with a cement floor is the best place for waxing skis. Dripping wax can damage floors and carpets.)

3 Set an iron on medium-low heat. Melt a block of ski wax against the iron so that the drips land on the ski bottom. Place the drips about 1 inch (2.5 cm) apart, along the entire ski.

4 Run the iron along the ski until a thin layer of wax evenly coats the bottom surface.

5 Let the ski cool completely.

6 Using a plastic ski scraper, remove any rough spots in the wax.

What You'll Need

- Two sawhorses or chairs
- Iron
- Ski wax
- Plastic ski scraper

Tip

Cleaning wax from an iron is very difficult. It's best to have a separate iron for your skis.

540 Retape a Hockey Stick

Properly taping a hockey stick is one of the old rituals of the game. If you want to be taken seriously at the rink, you'd better know how to do it right. Follow these steps and your stick will be faultless. As for your skating skills, that's up to you.

Steps

1 Remove any old tape. Apply a strip of black cloth tape along the bottom edge of the blade, then fold the excess up each side of the blade.

2 Wrap tape around the blade, beginning at the end. After the first wrap, run the tape at a slight angle to create an overlap of about ¼ inch (6 mm).

3 Keep the tape flat across the inside of the curved blade. Press the tape as flat as possible across the outside of the blade.

4 Continue wrapping until the blade begins to angle into the handle.

5 Wrap tape around the handle, beginning about 6 inches (15 cm) below the top and continuing up to the top.

6 Build up a knob of tape at the end about ¼ inch (6 mm) thick to keep your hand from slipping off.

What You'll Need

- Black cloth tape, 1 or 1¼ inches (2.5 or 3 cm) wide

Tip

Black cloth tape is available at sporting-goods stores.

541 Repair a Gouged Ski

You've just run your expensive new skis over a sharp rock. Are they ruined? Not at all. Experienced skiers know this is inevitable. Become skilled at this repair, and you'll be in demand at ski cabins everywhere. This repair is best performed in a garage or basement with a cement floor, because hot P-Tex drippings can damage floors and carpets and cause fires.

Steps

1 Bring the damaged ski inside, where it can get warm. Dry it off. Allow it to warm up to room temperature.

2 Place the ski upside down across two sawhorses or chairs in a garage or basement. The more stable you can make the ski, the better. Try aligning the ski so that the tail end rests against a wall.

3 Inspect the gouge. Remove any embedded rocks or dirt. Using a sharp knife, trim any rough edges off the gouge until a smooth hole remains.

4 Ignite the end of a P-Tex candle. This can be done with a match but is much easier with a lighter. As the candle heats up, molten P-Tex will drip from the end of the candle. Take care not to drip it onto yourself.

5 Take the candle to the ski and drip P-Tex into the gouge. Don't worry about getting drips onto other parts of the ski. They can be easily scraped off later. You can control the drip rate by rotating the candle. For a deep gouge, dab the candle directly against the ski.

6 Continue filling the gouge until the repair material is slightly higher than the original ski base. Blow out the candle.

7 When the repair area is cool enough to touch, use a metal ski scraper to shave down the repair until it's level with the original ski base. Work slowly with the scraper; aggressive scraping can damage the ski bottom.

8 Hold the scraper in both hands and draw it toward you across the repair. Angle the scraper so that you are pulling the blade across the repair. When the repair is nearly level, you can push the blade across the repair.

9 Remove any stray P-Tex drips.

10 Some gouges may not fill completely the first time. Repeat if necessary.

11 Show off your work to your friends around the fire.

What You'll Need

- Two sawhorses or chairs
- Sharp knife
- P-Tex candle
- Match or lighter
- Metal ski scraper

Tips

P-Tex candles can be bought at most ski shops. They come in several colors to match different-color ski bottoms; a clear candle will work on any ski.

A metal ski scraper can also be found at ski shops.

Warning

Work in a well-ventilated area to avoid inhaling toxic fumes.

542 Sharpen Your Poker Skills

Fans of the game insist that poker is the perfect combination of skill and luck. However, you can play for years and find that you still have a lot to learn. Heed the advice below if you seem to be making the same mistakes over and over, or if you are a novice just getting into the game. These steps are geared toward five-card draw, but the general strategy and psychology apply to any version of poker.

Steps

1 Know the ranking and probabilities of possible poker hands (while keeping in mind the psychology of the game—see steps below). The best hand is a straight flush, comprised of five consecutive cards of the same suit. The best possible straight flush, a royal flush, is 10 through ace of any one suit. In descending order, the remaining hands are: four of a kind, full house (three matching cards combined with a pair), flush (cards of all one suit), straight (five consecutive cards), three of a kind, two pair and one pair. There are roughly 2.5 million possible poker hands. The likelihood of a hand containing a pair is about 42 percent. The likelihood of a straight flush is about .0015 percent.

2 Make sure you know the basic rules and terms. After the cards are dealt, the player to the left of the dealer has the option to fold, check or bet. To fold is to retire your hand because you do not think you are capable of winning. Folding results in the loss of any money you have so far put into the pot but prevents you from losing more. To check is to stay in the game but to decline to bet. Betting means that you put additional money in the pot, and anyone wishing to stay in the game must do the same.

3 Prepare for the draw by deciding which cards you want to keep. Experienced players try to avoid drawing more than two cards, because doing so signals that you have a weak hand and limits your ability to bluff.

4 Understand that the game changes as the stakes increase. For example, in a nickel-ante game, bluffing is not likely because no one is likely to be scared away at such low stakes. As bets increase, bluffing becomes a more effective technique.

5 Poker is primarily a game of psychology, not chance. You are playing against other people, not against the cards. Study your opponents for "tells," revealing traits that convey information about their hands. Does a player whistle when bluffing? Tap their feet when agitated? Look for these signals and remember them, while being conscious of any tells that you may be sending.

6 Keep your game competitive by avoiding patterns. Patterns in your play are signals that your opponents will pick up. If, for example, you follow the same betting pattern every time you bluff, opponents will figure this out. Poker is infinitely variable and every hand is unique.

What You'll Need

- One or more poker partners
- Deck of cards
- Poker chips or cash

Warning

Before you play, decide how much money you can afford to lose. When you reach this amount, stop playing.

543 Fix a Poker Game

Some things can be fixed that aren't strictly broken—a poker game, for instance. The following trick is known among professionals as the cold deck. Rent a video of *The Sting,* put on your best poker face and put in the fix. Now, do we need to say it? Don't be a fool. This is a fun gimmick to play on your friends, but don't try it in a real casino. You won't win enough to cover your bail.

Steps

1 Arrange to meet three friends for poker. This trick depends on knowing in advance the number of players who will be present.

2 Buy two identical decks of cards. Leave the first deck unopened. Open the second deck and remove the jokers and any other unnecessary cards.

3 Separate this second deck into stacks of four so that all the aces are together, all the kings are together, and so on. Leave the individual stacks facing up.

4 Visualize yourself as the dealer. Every fourth card from the deck will land in your hand. The idea is to arrange the deck so that every fourth card will come together to form a winning hand.

5 Select a random low card. Place it as the first card in the deck.

6 Continue selecting cards for the second and third spots. Now pick an ace for the fourth spot.

7 Continue stacking cards in the deck, making sure you don't provide any matching cards for the other players. Four aces for yourself might be too obvious. Try a full house with three aces and two queens.

8 Shuffle the remaining cards together and place them on the bottom of the deck. Hide this deck in a pocket.

9 Arrive at the game and bring out the unopened deck. Pass it to another player and begin the game. Until it is your turn to deal, you will be playing with the unaltered deck.

10 As your turn to deal approaches, palm the secret deck in your left hand. Bring the current deck to you with your right hand and drop it into your lap as you bring your left hand onto the table. Practice this move before the game. If you can get your friends to leave the table for a beer, even better.

11 Begin play with the new deck and collect your fortune.

What You'll Need

- Two identical decks of cards
- Three poker partners

Tip

If you get caught at playing this trick, you will look like a cheat. Tip off one friend ahead of time that you will be playing a joke during the game.

Warning

Cheating your friends is not nice. Give them their money back.

544 Sharpen Your Blackjack Technique

Is it you or the cards? Why do you keep going bust? Blackjack appears to be a simple game, but to become a true expert you will need to pay your figurative and literal dues. Fortunately, you can also study and practice at home. The following simple strategy, developed by Michael Shackleford, the Wizard of Odds, will help you deal with most hands while allowing the house an edge of only 0.93 percent under standard Las Vegas rules.

Steps

1 Familiarize yourself with the game. If you're a first-timer, find a table that is friendly to beginners and has a low minimum bet.

2 If your hand (with no aces) totals any number between 12 and 16 and the dealer's exposed card is a 2 through 6, always stay. In blackjack shorthand, this can be summarized as: Stand on hard 12-16 against dealer 2-6. A hand with an ace in it is a "soft" hand because the ace can be counted as either a 1 or an 11. "Hard" therefore refers to a hand with no aces.

3 Always "double down" if you have a total of 10 or 11 against a dealer's exposed card of 2-9. To double down means to double your bet while agreeing to take only one more card. This is a valid tactic only when you are confident you have a strong hand relative to the dealer's hand.

4 Always "split" 8s, 9s and aces. When both cards in your hand are the same, you can elect to split. This is to play each individual card as a separate hand. For example, if you had two 8s, you would split them and take hits on the first 8 until you either went over 21 or decided to stand. Then you would move on to the other card and do the same. This tactic essentially gives you two chances to beat the dealer.

5 Always stay on soft 18 or higher. If your cards, including one ace, total 18 or more, do not take a hit.

6 Always stay on hard 17 or higher. If your cards, with no aces, total 17 or more, do not take a hit.

7 If the situations in steps 2 through 6 do not apply, then take a hit. Never bother to take insurance against a dealer blackjack. Insurance is an option whenever the dealer's exposed card is an ace. As a long-term strategy, insurance does not pay.

8 Summarize these rules in your mind and practice them.

What You'll Need

- Deck of cards
- One or more playing partners

Warning

Before playing, decide on a maximum amount of money that you can afford to lose. If you reach this amount, stop playing.

Avoid the temptation to recoup previous losses with one big bet. Over time, this leads to sloppy play and large losses.

545 Improve Your Pool Game

Skilled pool players have an annoying habit of making the game look easy. The following steps will help you overcome the most common challenge in pool—handling very long shots where the smallest error will result in a wide miss.

What You'll Need

- Pool cue
- Pool table and balls

Steps

1 Develop a consistent, smooth cue shot. Place your forward hand on the table so that it is as stable as possible. The cue stick needs to slide smoothly through this hand.

2 Use your cue stick as a sight by placing the tip of the cue stick in the target pocket. Align the stick across the middle of the ball you intend to sink. The stick now traces a line through the ball to the pocket. Where this line (your stick) crosses the outer edge of the ball is the point where you want to hit it with the cue ball.

3 After you are in position and have lined up the shot, don't look at the target ball, look at the cue ball. Strike the cue ball with your stick slightly below the center line.

4 Keep your shooting arm close to your body and your elbow bent at 90 degrees. The shooting movement should come from your shoulder. Use only enough force to make the shot. Additional power is not necessary and can disrupt your aim.

546 Straighten a Gutter Ball

Professional bowlers prefer to curve their shots so that the ball strikes the pins from the side. However, beginners should start with the straight delivery described here.

What You'll Need

- Bowling ball
- Bowling alley

Steps

1 Stand on the foul line at the start of the lane. Back up four big steps. This is your starting point.

2 With your fingers in the proper holes, lift the ball up to your chest. Look for the arrow marking the center of the lane. Align your shooting arm with this center arrow.

3 Prepare to take a four-step approach to the foul line. Begin your steps with the foot that corresponds to your shooting arm. For example, if you're right-handed, take your first step with your right foot.

4 On your second step, begin bringing the ball down and back. On your third step, the ball should reach full extension behind you. On your fourth step, keep your shoulders square to the lane and bend both knees as you deliver the ball. Release the ball as it passes your forward foot.

547 Change In-Line Skate Wheels

Do your skates no longer take instructions from your legs? Do they wobble and vibrate? It probably means you need to replace the wheels. A new set is easy to install and will make your skates as good as new.

Steps

1 Remove the bolt running through the center of each old wheel. Using an adjustable wrench, grasp the nut on the end of the bolt. Turn the other end of the bolt with an Allen (hex) wrench (see A).

2 Pull the bolt free and remove the wheel. Take care not to lose any plastic spacers that may be beside each wheel.

3 Repeat steps 1 and 2 for the other wheels.

4 Inspect your new wheels for wheel bearings (silver disks in the center of each wheel). If these are included, the new wheels are ready to be installed.

5 If your new wheels do not include wheel bearings, transfer your existing wheel bearings to the new wheels. There are two bearings in each wheel, one on each side (see B). Remove the bearings by popping them free with the end of an Allen (hex) wrench. Again, take care not to lose any spacers that may be held between the bearings.

6 Install the bearings into the new wheels by pushing them into place with your fingers. Be sure to include any spacers.

7 Slide the wheels into place on the skate. Insert a wheel bolt through each wheel. Place a nut on each bolt and tighten with the adjustable wrench and Allen (hex) wrench. Make sure that the wheel bolts are securely tightened but the wheels spin freely. If a wheel does not spin freely, loosen the wheel bolt very slightly. If the wheel bolt is loose and the wheel still fails to spin freely, remove the wheel and check for proper installation of the bearings.

What You'll Need

- Replacement wheels
- Adjustable wrench
- Allen (hex) wrench set

Tips

In-line skate wheels wear out at different rates, depending on how you skate. For example, some people wear out the front wheel on each foot first. To make your wheels last longer, occasionally rotate them from front to back or from foot to foot.

Allen wrenches usually come in a set including various-size wrenches attached to a handle. Different brands of skates require different-size wrenches.

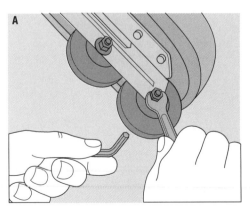

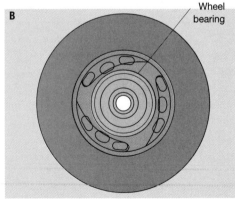

Wheel bearing

548 Fix Your Tennis Serve

An effective serve is the starting point for playing winning tennis. Many players work for years perfecting their serve but find they still need help. The following steps will give you the necessary tools to fix common problems and help develop a powerful, consistent serve.

Steps

1 Stand near the court baseline, about 1 foot (30 cm) behind the line. Don't stand too close to the line or you will be worried about stepping over it, which is a foul.

2 Hold a tennis ball with only the fingertips of your free hand. Turn your hand so that the ball is facing straight up. When practicing, hold only one ball in your hand.

3 Stand with your knees slightly bent. Lift your racquet arm so that your hand is slightly above and slightly behind your head, with the racquet tilted slightly behind you.

4 Smoothly toss the ball into the air in front of you by fully extending your arm. Don't throw the ball too high. It only needs to rise a short distance above the height of your upstretched hand, equal to the distance from your racquet grip to the middle of the strings. Understanding the importance of this initial toss is vital, because all other parts of the serve flow from it. Your goal is to make the throw identical every time.

5 As the ball nears the top of its rise, bring your racquet arm forward while extending your legs. Swing the racquet with your wrist as well as your arm. The racquet should be arcing slightly downward when it contacts the ball.

6 If you're having trouble establishing a rhythmic swing, put down your racquet for a minute and try the following exercise: Stand at the baseline and throw a few balls into the service box. This helps to establish a smooth arm motion. Pick up your racquet and start over.

What You'll Need

- Bucket of tennis balls
- Racquet
- Tennis court

549 Regrip Your Tennis Racket

Whether you're smashing an overhead volley or finessing a drop shot, a racket that feels good in your hand is vital to a solid game and can prevent fatigue. Regripping your racket will keep it feeling new and comfortable.

Steps

1 Decide what type of new grip material you want to use. If you're happy with the diameter of your current grip, select a new grip material that is similar to what you have now.

2 Remove the existing grip material, starting at the end nearest the strings. Simply remove the tape holding the grip material in place and unwind.

3 Remove the tack or staple holding the grip material at the butt of the racket. Save this staple for reuse. There is no need to remove the plastic cap on the butt of the racket.

4 Apply rubber cement or double-sided tape on two opposite sides of the racket grip area. Don't use too much, or you will affect the grip diameter.

5 Inspect the new grip material. One end of the material should already be trimmed to a point. Begin wrapping this end at the butt of the racket. Reinsert the staple to hold this end in place.

6 Pull the material taut as you go. Hold the racket in your right hand and the material in your left. Rotate the racket clockwise.

7 Overlap the material by about ¼ inch (6 mm) so that the racket can't be seen through the material.

8 Holding the end of the material in place with your thumb, trim around the top of the wrapping with a knife so that it is cut off square.

9 Secure the top of the material with electrical tape.

What You'll Need

- Replacement grip wrap
- Rubber cement or double-sided tape
- Knife
- Electrical tape

Tip

In a tennis shop, spend a few minutes experimenting with the rackets on display. You might find ideas about new grip material for your own racket.

550 Relace a Baseball Glove

Is your baseball glove a relic from your youth, purchased back when digital watches were expensive and gas was cheap? If so, it probably needs some new lacing. You could buy a new glove, of course, but repairing your old one is so much more satisfying. With a little care, this glove could be passed on to your kids.

Steps

1 Treat the new rawhide lacing with a leather softener or glove oil before you begin work. This will allow the leather to soften and make it easier to handle.

2 Inspect the lacing and memorize the lacing pattern.

3 Remove one section of the broken lacing (see A). If necessary, use a pair of scissors to cut it free.

4 Tie a simple overhand knot at one end of a long piece of the new rawhide lacing. Pull the knot as tight as possible.

5 Using a leather awl, ice pick or other pointy tool, push the lacing through the first hole in the stitching pattern (see B). Pull the lacing through, up to the knot in its end.

6 Continue threading the lacing through the holes, following the lacing pattern of the original. Pull the lacing as tight as possible without deforming the glove. The lacing will stretch over time, so tightness is essential to a lasting repair.

7 Place another overhand knot in the lacing at the end of the section. Adjust the knot so that it is snug against the glove. Cut off any excess lacing.

8 Continue working on other sections as needed.

What You'll Need

- Leather softener or glove oil
- Scissors
- Rawhide lacing
- Leather awl, ice pick or other pointy tool

Tips

Don't remove all the old lacing on your glove at once, or you will probably forget the lacing pattern. Work section by section.

Rawhide lacing, leather softener and a leather awl can be purchased at hardware stores.

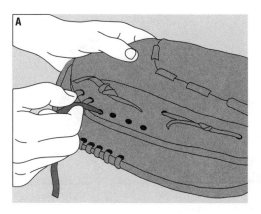

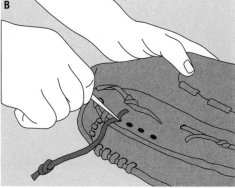

551 Improve Your Photography Techniques

Photography can be extremely rewarding or extremely frustrating, depending on your ability to adjust to constantly changing conditions. The following chart will help you improve both your indoor and outdoor color photography.

LOCATION	PROBLEM	SOLUTIONS
Indoor Photography	If your indoor pictures suffer from any of the following problems, try shooting a roll of 400ASA color film while practicing these solutions.	
	Blurry pictures	If the autofocus function on your camera can be switched on and off, be sure that it is on. Blurry pictures indoors can also result from not using the flash. This forces the shutter to stay open too long, blurring the image. Use the flash when shooting indoors.
	Photos are too dark	You usually need the flash when shooting indoors, even when there seems to be a lot of light. If in doubt, take one picture using the flash and one without, to be sure that at least one image will be good.
	Flash fails to fire	Check battery power. Flashes require a lot of power. For detachable flash units, check that the flash is fully engaged on its mount. Some flashes have their own on-off switch. Be sure it is on. In certain situations, the camera may fail to realize that the flash is needed. On some cameras, there is a setting, usually called Fill Flash, that will cause the flash to fire on every shot. Set the Fill Flash function on.
	People in photos have red eyes	See 16 Get Rid of Red-Eye in Photographs.
	Prints contain glare from flash reflection	Position yourself so that there are no mirrors, windows, shiny walls or TVs behind your subjects. If this is unavoidable, move the camera to the side as much as possible.
	Poorly framed shots	A final step before you click the shutter is to be aware of the frame of the picture. Be sure not to cut off people's heads, for example. If you're wearing gloves, take them off and don't hold anything else in your hands while using the camera. This will help you avoid accidentally blocking the lens.

LOCATION	PROBLEM	SOLUTIONS
Outdoor Photography	If your outdoor pictures need help, load a roll of 100ASA color film and practice the following solutions. These instructions apply to conditions of bright sunlight. If less sunlight is expected, use a slightly higher number film, such as 200ASA.	
	People in photos are squinting	• Have everyone close their eyes and relax for a few seconds before taking the picture. When you're ready with the camera, have them open their eyes fully and smile.
	People in photos are shadowy or too dark	• This usually occurs when the sun is directly in front of the photographer. Be aware of the sun's location and try to take pictures with the sun behind you. If you can't get the sun behind you, arrange the shot so that the sun is as far to one side as possible.
		• If you have to take a picture with the sun in front of you, use the flash to reduce shadows on the front of your subjects.
		• If your camera has a focus lock, first point your camera at a bright spot. Keep your finger partially down on the shutter to lock the focus and exposure. Then move the camera to the shot you want and take the picture.
	Confusing background objects	• When taking pictures, beware of trees, buildings and other objects behind your subjects. In your photos, these can appear to come straight out of the heads of people.
	Boring scenery shots	• It is difficult to capture the beauty of mountain vistas and ocean sunsets with the average camera. Try to include people or activity in the foreground. This will capture a fun event in a beautiful setting rather than another empty scenery shot.
	Boring posed shots	• Who wants one more dull picture of someone standing in front of the Eiffel Tower? Position yourself so that you can frame the desired background while capturing your friends and family behaving candidly.
		• At a large event, such as a parade or wedding, concentrate on framing individuals or small groups rather than snapping shots of the entire gathering.

INDEX

CONTRIBUTORS

Tara Aronson is the author of *Simplify Your Household,* a book of simple solutions for home cleaning, organization and laundry dilemmas. She also writes the *San Francisco Chronicle* column "Coming Clean" and is consumer advocate for the Whirlpool Institute of Fabric Science.

Roy Barnhart is a freelance writer, editor and consultant in the home improvement field. He has written for over a dozen magazines and contributed to or authored numerous home improvement and repair books. Roy brings to this book his experience as a former building and remodeling contractor and a lifelong do-it-yourselfer.

Sharon Beaulaurier is a writer who lives in the San Francisco Bay Area. She learned the ins and outs of fixing things as the managing editor of a how-to Web site, eHow.com. Her stints in television news production and investigative journalism also taught her a handy skill or two.

James Bradbury is a former computer magazine editor who now lives and works in San Francisco, where he writes for a variety of technical and music publications. If he could keep only one consumer electronic, it would be his iPod.

Kevin Ireland was formerly managing editor at both *American Woodworker* magazine and Rodale Woodworking and Do-It-Yourself Books. He is an avid home renovator and is now rebuilding his third house.

Julie Jares spent several years in the dot-com fray as a writer and editor for eHow.com and Sidewalk.com. Currently a freelance writer, her recent projects include *Out to Eat San Francisco* and Lonely Planet's forthcoming guide to Hawaii's Big Island. She is also the San Francisco correspondent for Concierge.com.

Larry Shea is a writer and book editor in Avon, Massachusetts. He has previously worked on the staffs of *Fine Gardening, Home Furniture* and *Ladies' Home Journal* magazines.

Thy Tran is a San Francisco–based food writer and culinary instructor. A graduate of the California Culinary Academy, she has wide experience working in the kitchens of restaurants, caterers and national food magazines.

Ren Volpe is the author of *The Lady Mechanic's Total Car Care for the Clueless.* She worked for 10 years as an auto mechanic and has taught hundreds of women how to fix their cars. Most days she walks to work.

Vicki Webster is the author of numerous books and magazine articles and has also written extensively for electronic media. She is a former editor at Storey Publishing and *Better Homes and Gardens* and *Country Home* magazines.

Derek Wilson lives in the Lake Tahoe area of California, where he divides his time between writing projects and economic consulting. His last book project was *Burritos: Hot on the Trail of the Little Burro.* He says the only thing better than fixing sporting goods is breaking them in the first place.

Sharron Wood finally took advantage of all the tutoring her mother, a professional dressmaker, foisted upon her to write about sewing and clothing repair for this book. She is the author of *Chow San Francisco!* and has contributed to more than 20 travel guides to California and San Francisco.

Weldon Owen wishes to thank the following people for their generous assistance and support in the production of this book: Rex Cauldwell; Rebecca Forée; Marilyn Howard at Creative Freelancers Management Inc.; Kevin Ireland; Sioux Jennett; Donald Kessler; Liberty Pumps; Deirdre McLoughlin, MSPT; Dr. Theresa Musser, DVM; Mike Radtke; Michael Shackleford; John Swartzberg, MD, Clinical Professor of Medicine, University of California, Berkeley and San Francisco; Glenn Ware of Ware's Hardware Store, San Mateo, CA; Wayne Water Systems; and Heidi Wilson Photography.